TREES

for Architecture and Landscape

TREES
for Architecture and Landscape

Second Edition

Robert L. Zion

Photographs by Maude Dorr, Peter Lieberstein, and others

VAN NOSTRAND REINHOLD
I(T)P   A Division of International Thomson Publishing Inc.

New York • Albany • Boston • Detroit • London • Madrid • Melbourne
Mexico City • Paris • San Francisco • Singapore • Tokyo • Toronto

For more information, contact:

Van Nostrand Reinhold
115 Fifth Avenue
New York, NY 10003

Chapman & Hall GmbH
Pappelallee 3
69469 Weinheim
Germany

Chapman & Hall
2-6 Boundary Row
London
SE1 8HN
United Kingdom

International Thomson Publishing Asia
221 Henderson Road #05-10
Henderson Building
Singapore 0315

Thomas Nelson Australia
102 Dodds Street
South Melbourne, 3205
Victoria, Australia

International Thomson Publishing Japan
Hirakawacho Kyowa Building, 3F
2-2-1 Hirakawacho
Chiyoda-ku, 102 Tokyo
Japan

Nelson Canada
1120 Birchmount Road
Scarborough, Ontario
Canada M1K 5G4

International Thomson Editores
Seneca 53
Col. Polanco
11560 Mexico D.F. Mexico

2 3 4 5 6 7 8 9 10 QEBKP 01 00 99 98 97 96

Library of Congress Cataloging-in-Publication Data
Zion, Robert L.
    Trees for architecture and landscape / Robert L. Zion ;
photographs by Maude Dorr, Peter Lieberstein, and others.
        p.   cm.
    Includes index.
    ISBN 0-442-01314-0
    1. Ornamental trees. 2. Landscape architecture.   I. Title.
SB435.Z5   1994
715'.2—dc20
                                            94-31719
                                            CIP

CONTENTS

LIST OF
TREE PORTRAITS

Trees in Color

Blossom

Foliage

Evergreen Trees

PREFACE

The reader will perhaps be interested in some of the difficulties encountered in assembling photographs for the "Tree Portraits" section of this book. It was decided at the outset not to use any photographs of trees showing architectural background since such backgrounds were found to be distracting, particularly to architects. This restriction excluded many fine accessible trees, such as the handsome magnolias outside the Frick Collection in New York City.

From the beginning long delays were encountered in the search for specimen trees growing in the open, silhouetted against the sky. This was considered an essential requirement in order to show the form of the tree in winter, distinctly, without the branching of other trees in the background.

Then, the necessity of using a wide-lense aperture to record maximum detail required an almost total absence of air current to avoid the blurring caused by leaf movement. Many hours of ideal light conditions were lost in waiting for absolute stillness, which sometimes never arrived.

In addition, the optimum position of the sun in relation to the tree, in terms of shadow, also created difficulty when this position proved to be identical for several trees in an area. During the time consumed in setting up camera equipment and waiting for the proper wind and cloud conditions for one tree, the sun had often passed the optimum point for other trees remaining to be photographed. Often, in an area several hundred miles from home base, only one tree could be photographed in an entire day.

I am especially grateful to Maude Dorr and Peter Lieberstein, the two photographers responsible for most of the tree portraits; their task was especially demanding. I owe thanks also to my former secretary, Gail Bullock, for her patience in retyping the many revisions and additions included in this new edition. To my editors, Wendy Lochner, for her many valued suggestions in revising the original text and, Patti Brecht, for her careful editing of the manuscript and calm ushering of the project through production. To Princeton Nurseries for providing me with color photographs. And to Halka Nurseries, Inc. for permitting me to photograph several fine specimens in its nursery in Englishtown, New Jersey.

Time-consuming and frustrating as the work proved to be, it has nevertheless been an extremely satisfying experience to address myself to a need of fellow professionals and laymen interested in trees.

Robert L. Zion
Creamridge, New Jersey

Magnolia soulangeana at the Frick Collection in New York City.

ix

THE PURPOSE OF
THIS BOOK:
HOW TO USE IT

This is a book about trees—trees whose structure, habit, and other characteristics make them especially useful in relation to buildings and outdoor spaces. It is primarily a book of photographic tree definitions, or portraits, intended to facilitate communication between the landscape architect and client—both professional and layman. The accompanying text covers additional matters of concern to the architect or owner, such as the protection and preservation of trees existing on the site, problems involved in planting trees in cities and on rooftops, cost considerations, lists of trees for special uses, and other matters.

As with many familiar objects, mere verbal descriptions of trees cannot convey successfully their basic visual characteristics: their form, structure, leaf texture, etc. Conventional descriptive phrases such as "vase-shaped" and "broad-headed" are meaningless to anyone who has never *seen* the characteristics they describe. However, once seen, these designations are immediately understood.

For the architect, this accurate visual information is essential, for he thinks of a tree in relation to his building—tree height to building height, leaf texture to wall surface, density or sparsity of foliage to building fenestration, spring and autumn coloration to building material, tree form to overall composition, and other relationships. Photographs of purely aesthetic orientation seldom give proper prominence to the qualities of structure, color, texture, and the like that are *typical* of the species and therefore of great importance to the architect or designer. Line drawings often used for this purpose, though charming, are rarely successful in capturing these typical attributes.

It is the author's intention to fill this need by providing an accurate *visual* description of each of the tree species selected—photographs taken with the same attention to form and detail that an architect employs in photographing his building, showing clearly those characteristics that make each tree most suitable to a specific design use. The tree is here considered as an element of design, an ever-changing, living object available to the designer for the embellishment of buildings and enrichment of outdoor spaces.

An emphasis has been placed on seasonal change as an important design factor. Each deciduous tree has been photographed from the *identical* location in both winter and summer, and the photographs have been juxtaposed in order to dramatize the miraculous transformation that most vitally concerns the professional designer and never ceases to amaze even the professional grower. For this purpose, it was considered desirable to select only mature specimens for photographic portraits, thereby illustrating the full natural development potential of the tree. However, these portraits are also supplemented by photographs of the same trees in sizes commonly available in commercial nurseries. These supplementary photographs are included in Part III, Design Data, pages 171–230.

This book is intended to assist the layman in the interpretation of landscape architectural plans and also to serve as a reference, aiding visually in the selection of tree species and varieties that best fulfill the designer's specific requirements of form, height, fall color, blossom, and so forth. For architects and professional renderers who are called on to depict specific trees, it will answer the question: "What does the tree look like?"

Not all available trees have been included here. Some species and varieties in common use have been omitted because it is the author's opinion that the design requirements are more handsomely and hardily met by those that he has selected.

Whenever practicable, the text has been presented in outline form in order to provide information most conveniently. Technical facts not relevant to design have been omitted (number of leaf lobes, alternate or opposite branching, etc.) for these can be found in any standard botany text.

The book is divided into four parts:

Part I, pages 1–104, contains winter and summer portraits of trees of outstanding design merit. These photographs are arranged in alphabetical order based on the common, or English, name of each tree, which appears in the lower left-hand corner together with the Latin name. The portraits are grouped into three sections: deciduous trees (those that annually lose their leaves); the blossom and foliage of a small group of trees in color; and evergreen trees.

Part II, pages 105–170, contains the text, in chapters whose titles clearly indicate their content. It supplies information intended to develop in both the layman and professional—particularly the architect—an understanding of the material that appears on landscape plans and specifications, thereby making possible more intelligent use of the landscape architect's services.

Part III, pages 171–230, contains brief factual outlines of the major characteristics of each tree included in the portrait section, together with suggestions as to its use in landscape design. Accompanying data include the following: height, spread, form, foliage, texture, fall color, blossom, fruit, rate of growth, culture, zone of hardiness, transplanting information, special maintenance requirements.

This section contains photographs of most trees in small sizes readily available in nurseries. Additional photographs are included to illustrate any unusual characteristics of leaf, bark, or structure. A map is included that indicates zones of hardiness. It has been prepared by the Agricultural Research Service, U.S. Department of Agriculture.

Part IV, pages 231–340, contains lists of trees by states, oriented to various design needs. In all lists, an asterisk indicates that the tree so marked appears in the photographic "Tree Portraits" section of this book. Categories included in these lists are as follows:

Trees designated as official state trees
Evergreen trees
Trees classified by height:
  20–35 feet
  35–75 feet
  75 feet or over

Trees classified by form:
  Pyramidal
  Columnar
  Weeping
  Rounded or globe-shaped
  With horizontal branching
Trees classified by color of blossom:
  Yellow
  White
  Pink
  Red
  Blue
Trees classified by color of summer foliage:
  Blue
  Silver to gray
  Red to purple
Trees classified by color of fall foliage:
  Yellow
  Red
  Purple
Trees with interesting bark:
  Gray
  White
  Red
  Reddish brown
  Yellow
  Corky
  Flaking
Trees for the city:
  Trees for wide streets
  Trees for medium streets
  Trees for suburban streets
Soil tolerance:
  Trees tolerating acid soil
  Trees tolerating moist soil
  Trees tolerating dry or poor soil
Pest-resistant trees
Trees for seashore planting
Trees for hedging or barriers

All lists are organized alphabetically by state. Thus, when seeking a tree suitable for use on a city street in New Jersey, one turns to the New Jersey lists to find a selection under the heading "Street Trees." Among the trees listed, one finds the following: Norway Maple, Ginkgo, Littleleaf Linden, Catalpa.

Trees indicated for the northeast section of the country represent the author's personal preferences; trees of other sections represent a composite of the personal choice of leading landscape architects or educators of the region and of a leading nurseryman whose selection is based on demand as reflected in sales.

*To my Mother and Father
who encouraged me to take up
Landscape Architecture*

TREES

for Architecture and Landscape

TREE PORTRAITS

Deciduous Trees, Winter and Summer

Pages 2–77 contain portraits of the following deciduous trees photographed from the identical position in winter and summer:

Trees in Color, 78–82
Evergreen Tree Portraits, 83–104

Common Apple (*Malus pumila*).

American Beech (*Fagus grandifolia*).

European Beech Grove (*Fagus sylvatica*).

European Beech, Cutleaf (*Fagus sylvatica laciniata*).

European Purple Beech (*Fagus sylvatica atropunicea*).

Weeping Beech (*Fagus sylvatica pendula*).

European Weeping Birch (*Betula pendula gracilis*).

Gray Birch (*Betula populifolia*).

Horse-Chestnut (*Aesculus hippocastanum baumanni*).

Amur Cork (*Phellodendron amurense*).

American Elm (*Ulmus americana*).

Ginkgo (Maidenhair Tree) (*Ginkgo biloba*).

Sweet Gum (*Liquidambar styraciflua*).

Katsura Tree (*Cercidiphyllum japonicum*).

European Larch (*Larix decidua*).

Crimean Linden (*Tilia euchlora*).

European Linden (*Tilia europaea*).

Little-leaf Linden (*Tilia cordata*).

Silver Linden (*Tilia tomentosa*).

Black Locust (*Robinia pseudoacacia*).

Honey-Locust (*Gleditsia triacanthos*).

Saucer Magnolia (*Magnolia soulangeana*).

Japanese Maple (*Acer palmatum*).

Red Maple (Swamp Maple) (*Acer rubrum*).

Sugar Maple (*Acer saccharum*).

Columnar English Oak (*Quercus robur fastigiata*).

Pin Oak (*Quercus palustris*).

White Oak (*Quercus alba*).

Japanese Pagoda Tree (Scholar Tree) (*Sophora japonica*).

Bradford Callery Pear (*Pyrus calleryana bradfordi*).

Common Pear (*Pyrus communis*).

Lombardy Poplar (*Populus italica nigra*).

Sorrel Tree (Sourwood, Tree Andromeda) (*Oxydendrum arboreum*).

Sycamore (American Plane Tree) (*Platanus occidentalis*).

Tree of Heaven (*Ailanthus altissima*).

71

Tupelo (Pepperidge, Black Gum, Sour Gum) (*Nyssa sylvatica*).

Weeping Willow (*Salix babylonica*).

American Yellow-wood (*Cladrastis lutea*).

TREES IN COLOR

Hawthorn (*Crataegus*).

Golden Rain (Varnish Tree) (*Koelreuteria paniculata*).

Downy Serviceberry (*Amelanchier canadensis*).

Golden Chain (*Laburnum*).

Flowering Crab Apple (*Malus*).

Flowering Cherry (*Prunus*).

Flowering Dogwood (*Cornus florida*).

Sorrel Tree (Sourwood, Tree Andromeda) (*Oxydendrum arboreum*).

80

Japanese Pagoda Tree (Scholar Tree) (*Sophora japonica*).

Star Magnolia (*Magnolia stellata*).

Saucer Magnolia (*Magnolia soulangeana*).

*Viburnum tomentosum (*var. *mariesi)*.

FOLIAGE

A Japanese Maple blankets the ground with its crimson leaves. (Michael Boys.)

Fallen leaves of the previous year create the soft brown carpet of this beech grove. (Mike Williams.)

Leaves of a cherry create a startling pool of color on the ground. (Michael Boys.)

The spectacular fall foliage of the Sugar Maple.

Evergreen Tree Portraits

Blackwood Acacia (*Acacia melanoxylon*).

Carob Tree (*Ceratonia siliqua*).

Blue Atlas Cedar (*Cedrus atlantica glauca*).

Deodar Cedar (*Cedrus deodara*).

Cedar of Lebanon (*Cedrus libani*).

Monterey Cypress (*Cupressus macrocarpa*).

Longbeak Eucalyptus (Eucalyptus camaldulensis rostrata).

Douglas Fir (*Pseudotsuga menziesii*).

Rusty-leaf Fig (*Ficus rubiginosa australis*).

Canada Hemlock (*Tsuga canadensis*).

Weeping Hemlock (Sargent) (*Tsuga canadensis pendula*).

94

Southern Magnolia (*Magnolia grandiflora*).

California Live Oak (*Quercus agrifolia*).

Southern Live Oak Grove (*Quercus virginiana*).

Common Olive (*Olea europaea*).

Austrian Pine (*Pinus nigra*).

Eastern White Pine (*Pinus strobus*).

Japanese Black Pine (*Pinus thunbergi*).

Monterey Pine (*Pinus radiata*).

Coast Redwood (*Sequoia sempervirens*).

Norway Spruce (*Picea abies*).

PART II

SOME PRACTICAL CONSIDERATIONS

TREES: THE FACTS OF LIFE

Preventive health care of humans requires a fundamental understanding of the functioning of the human body. And so it is with trees. If we are to take adequate measures to protect and cultivate trees, we must have a basic knowledge of their functioning.

Life span varies widely among trees of different types: The Gray Birch is old at 30 or 40; the Sugar Maple lives as long as 500 years; Oaks are known to live for 1500 years; and some giant Sequoias are believed to exceed 4000 years. It is unlikely, however, that any tree has yet died of old age. Death is usually due to drought, malnutrition, insects, fungi, or *abuse by man*. The architect or designer who is aware of the important contribution that trees can make to his building or outdoor space must make himself aware of the arboreal facts of life in order to understand the proper methods of protecting trees existing on a site, as well as the special problems involved in planting trees on rooftops, on city streets, and in other unnatural situations. Much tree damage is inflicted through ignorance of the physiology of trees, and many architects have unwittingly caused the death of the very trees they wished to preserve. As simply as possible, here are the facts.

A tree has been described as a "water system." Water is taken from the soil through the *roots*, passed through the *trunk* to the *leaves* where it is finally evaporated into the air. This entire process is called transpiration.

In the water are minerals that are converted into starches and sugars by means of chlorophyll, a substance contained in the leaves, which utilizes sunlight to create these foods for the tree.

It is immediately clear, then, that the *preservation of the tree involves protection of its three basic components: roots, trunk, and leaves.*

The Roots

The roots of a tree spread radially from the trunk, seldom to a depth of more than 4 feet. A rich, moist soil will foster a shallow root system; a dry soil will encourage the development of a deep root system as a means of obtaining

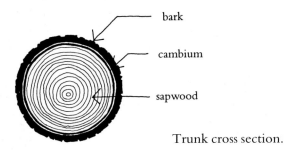

Trunk cross section.

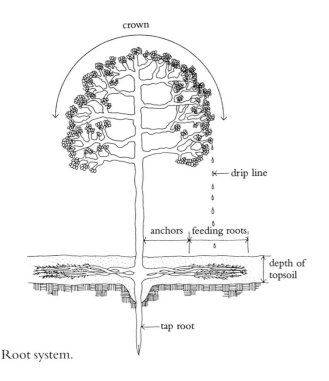

crown

← drip line

anchors ⎸ feeding roots⎹

depth of topsoil

← tap root

Root system.

more moisture. In some instances, a single, long root, called a taproot, will descend to a greater depth.

The heavy roots near the trunk serve principally as anchorage; it is the fibrous roots occurring at the root tips that take up minerals in solution from the soil. These fibrous roots are usually found in greatest profusion at the drip line of the leaf canopy where water, dripping from the tree, is most plentiful. It is not difficult, then, to see that tampering with the water supply at the drip line—either by compacting the soil and preventing absorption of surface water, as might be done by the passage of heavy construction equipment, or by trenching and thus carrying the water off, as might be done in installing new utility lines in the area—can seriously affect a tree.

Although a tree can survive the loss of as much as one-half of its roots, any such extensive damage to the root system must be accompanied by immediate remedial action. The moisture-absorbing ability of the tree has been reduced by such root loss, and therefore, a corresponding amount of the leaf system must be removed to reduce similarly the amount of evaporation and thus keep the process of transpiration in balance. *The amount of water evaporated through the leaves must never exceed the amount taken in by the roots.* If such an imbalance does occur, nature intervenes by reducing the evaporating surface of the tree: Leaves wilt and branches die. Man can anticipate this "die back" by proper pruning or "cutting back" the crown. But these are emergency measures. If we understand the nature of the tree, we can usually avoid the action that induces such a reaction. Sometimes, damage

to the root system cannot be avoided in the process of construction, especially during the installation of underground utility lines. In such cases, it is imperative that this relationship of leaf to root be kept in mind so that proper steps may be taken to prevent permanent damage.

Oxygen also plays a vital part in the functioning of the tree and must be freely available to the root system. It can, therefore, readily be understood why a poor soil, lacking in this component, will not support a healthy tree and, similarly, why paving of the surface immediately above the roots, compacting the soil by the use of heavy equipment, flooding and waterlogging the area, using clay or other nonporous fill, or in some other way curtailing the supply of oxygen to the roots are all likely to cause the death of a tree.

The Trunk

It is the trunk of the tree that carries the minerals absorbed by the roots to the leaves, where they are then converted into food.

Just beneath the bark of the trunk is a thin, pale green layer of tissues called the *cambium,* a "juicy sleeve" that is responsible for the tree's growth. The cambium is clearly the vital tissue of the tree: It produces the sapwood or circulation system that brings raw materials to the leaves and then transports the manufactured food to various parts of the tree and in winter returns it to the trunk for storage; the cambium also produces its own protective covering, the bark, without which the tree would be subject to the drying action of the sun and wind and become prey to insects. It is the internal pressure of the growing cylinder of cambium that causes the bark to crack and forms patterns characteristic of each tree: the mottled Sycamore, the shaggy Hickory, the peeling Birch, etc.

If a cut, only a fraction of an inch deep, girdles the trunk and severs the cambium, thereby cutting off the circulation system, it will kill the tree. However, a vertical cut, no matter how long, will seldom be fatal, for the unsevered portion of the cambium continues to function. Since cambium heals in a lateral direction only, a narrow vertical wound *6-feet long* will heal simultaneously along its entire length in less time than a razorlike *lateral* cut only *6 inches long.* The depth of a wound is of little importance after it has gone beyond the cambium. A nail driven to the center of the trunk is no more damaging than a quarter-inch nick with a pocket knife that has merely pierced the cambium.

Armed with this basic information, there should be little doubt of the importance of keeping the tree trunk free from abrasion by equipment or careless workmen, and from the excessive heat and consequent drying action of fires built too close to the tree. The need can also be seen for immediate treatment of all accidental wounds by the professional tree expert and for the strict enforcement of all protective measures of specifications set forth in the next chapter, "Protection of Existing Trees."

The Leaf

The leaf has been called the lung and stomach of the tree. The leaf traps the sunlight and then by means of chlorophyll manufactures food from the minerals absorbed by the roots. The leaf also contains tiny breathing pores or *lenticels* that evaporate moisture during the manufacturing process and take carbon dioxide from the air, using it, together with sunlight and the minerals absorbed by the roots, in the creation of the starches and sugars that the tree needs for growth. The lenticels thus play a vital part in the process of transpiration outlined earlier. The importance of lenticels makes clear the necessity of protecting the leaf from the heavy smoke of pitch, tar, and other materials often used in building construction, for this smoke will quickly fill the tiny pores and prevent breathing. It also explains the survival difficulties of trees in the polluted atmosphere of our cities.

With an understanding of the process of transpiration and the necessity of preserving a balance between the amount of moisture taken in by the root system and the amount given off in evaporation by the leaf system, the layman can readily understand why a plantsman will often remove every leaf from a tree he has planted out of season. In this way, he has reduced evaporation and lessened the strain on the root system, which invariably suffers some damage in transplanting. Buds for the following year, formed at the base of each leaf, will be forced into service in such an "emergency," but the new set of leaves will develop gradually, and in smaller size, in order to maintain a balance in transpiration.

If this defoliation were not performed artificially by the plantsman, the process would take place naturally; leaves would turn brown and fall off. Often, however, this natural process is not rapid enough; evaporation continues through the dying leaf, thus seriously taxing the root system and possibly exhausting the moisture supply completely, thereby causing the death of the tree.

The reader can now understand that defoliation by caterpillars or other insects, so dreaded by the layman, is not as serious an occurrence as it appears to be. Although few objects present a more hopeless appearance than a leafless tree in summer, a new set of leaves will soon appear. Indeed, such defoliation might in some instances prove to be a blessing, as in time of drought, by bringing evaporation to a virtual halt. A repeated loss of leaf,

however, would eventually weaken the tree by seriously curtailing its manufacture of food.

Basic Requirements of Trees

The basic structure and functioning of the tree have now been outlined above. This system establishes specific requirements for *moisture, soil, light,* and *heat.* Proper use of a tree in design and proper postplanting care must be based on an understanding of these requirements.

Soil

Soil contains minerals, humus (decayed vegetable matter), bacteria, and water that holds minerals and oxygen in solution. Different soils contain these ingredients in different proportions, and various tree species have different soil preferences. Soil on a site must always be analyzed, and it is advisable to consult a landscape architect as to the kind of tree best suited to it.

The symbol "pH" is used to indicate the hydrogen iron concentration in the soil. The pH values in soil range from 3.0–10.0. Values below 7.0 are acid, and values above 7.0 are alkaline. Some tree species prefer an acid soil, others prefer alkaline. The most appropriate planting is that which is best suited to existing local conditions; trees already growing on the site and in surrounding areas should be studied carefully as a guide to the best selection for new plantings. If necessary, however, the composition of soil can be changed by adding missing ingredients in accordance with the following instructions:

To raise soil pH one point, spread ground limestone at the following rates per acre:

Sandy loam soil	1½ tons
Loam soil	2 tons
Clay loam soil	2½ tons

To lower soil pH one point, spread powdered sulfur and aluminum sulfate at the following rates per acre:

Powdered sulfur

Sandy loam soil	300 pounds
Loam soil	430 pounds
Clay loam soil	600 pounds

Aluminum sulfate

Sandy loam soil	2000 pounds
Loam soil	3000 pounds
Clay loam soil	3500 pounds

For a listing of trees with a high tolerance of acid soil, consult the state tree lists on pages 231–339.

Moisture

Perhaps more than any other single factor, the moisture supply affects the form, growth, and structure of a tree. Since the minerals of the soil can be used by the roots only in the form of vapor, it is essential that moisture be deep in the soil, not on the surface, so that it will be absorbed as it rises, laden with mineral particles.

Large trees have been known to evaporate as much as 3000 gallons per day through the leaf system. It is not difficult, then, to understand the importance of assuring an adequate supply of water to a planting. This is especially vital in the case of city street trees or trees planted on rooftops, where in both cases they are cut off from ground water as well as most surface water.

Tree species vary in their water requirements.

For a listing of trees tolerating moist soil, consult the state tree lists on pages 231–339.

Light

Light affects the growth of a tree. Growth is seriously retarded when light conditions are not adequate. Some trees, however, such as Dogwood, Beech, and Hemlock, can grow in shade. Other trees, such as Birch, Pine, Poplar, and Willow, prefer full light. Light conditions and requirements are important aspects in the selection of trees for design.

Heat

The heat requirement of trees determine their hardiness or lack of it in various sections of the country. Heat also influences the amount of evaporation from the leaves and will therefore determine water requirements of the tree.

Appropriate soil, moisture, light, and heat—these four basic needs of the tree—must be available on the site or they must be supplied artificially. Since requirements vary among species, it is imperative that the needs of each tree included in a planting be thoroughly understood and anticipated.

As mentioned in the discussion of soil, the most appropriate plant material for good planting design is that which is native to the area and therefore accustomed to local conditions. If this aspect of planting is disregarded, the effectiveness of the design must rely precariously on the willingness or ability of the owner and his staff to administer proper care. Complete dependence on maintenance by others for the survival of a planting should be avoided, except in such entirely unnatural circumstances as rooftop planting.

With this basic knowledge of the structure and functioning of a tree, both architect and layman will be better equipped to understand and anticipate the landscape architect's recommendations relating to the selection, placement, and care of trees.

PROTECTION OF
EXISTING TREES

Existing tree and new wall: A handsome compromise. (Zion & Breen Associates, Landscape Architects and Site Planners.)

Building sites are often selected because of the presence of mature trees, which represent an irreplaceable design asset. In the interval between the acquisition of the property and the completion of construction of new buildings, these trees must be protected zealously. Their protection is the responsibility of those entrusted with the development of the site.

First, they must be protected from the owner, who may be anxious to start clearing the land of the vegetation he considers valueless—often before an architect is retained. They must also be protected in the early days against the designer himself—against the too hasty decision involving the placement of buildings and access roads, all of which will change many times as he becomes better acquainted with the site and as the design evolves. Finally, they must be protected against injury caused by the actual procedures of grading and site improvement, as well as the hazards of accident and carelessness during construction. This chapter will outline the protective measures necessary to avoid loss of existing trees to these distinctly different hazards.

Immediately following is a recommended approach to the selection and restoration of trees upon acquisition of the site. A second section includes a recommended approach to the protection of trees during construction; for the convenience of the architect and in the interest of brevity, this section will be presented in the form of outline specifications. A third section covers the dollar evaluation of trees for tax and insurance claims in the event of loss.

It should be stressed, however, that since site conditions are divergent and requirements so special among trees of different varieties, the specifications outlined are under no circumstances intended to preclude an on-site inspection by a landscape architect as the first step in the proper development of any site. The information presented here is intended to help architects and laymen anticipate and understand the reasons behind the advice of the professional.

1 An Approach to the Selection and Restoration of Existing Trees

Extreme Caution

No tree should be destroyed or altered until the design of the buildings and circulation system has been made final. The process of design is a gradual one, and the destruction of trees on the basis of an early concept often proves regrettable.

Identification of Species

Trees on the site should be identified as to species and located accurately on a topographic survey. It is essential that the topographic information be accurate and include a spot elevation at the base of each tree marked for preservation. This information is necessary to the designer to make certain that the finished grading in the area will be close to the existing grade, thus ensuring minimum disturbance to the roots of the tree.

The apparent good health of a tree at the time the site is purchased is not sufficient basis for its incorporation into the design. The identification of species tells much about the value of a tree in terms of life expectancy, susceptibility to disease and insect pests, watering and general maintenance requirements, and sensitivity to changes of grade, sunlight, and moisture caused during construction. As examples, we point to the susceptibility of the Elm to the fatal Dutch Elm disease, the short life expectancy of the Lombardy Poplar, and the infestation of the Gray Birch by the birch leaf miner.

Examination

A thorough examination of the physical condition of all specimen trees should be made, covering wounds, pests, disease, or fungus, in order to determine the extent to which each tree can be relied on to contribute to the completed design. An estimate of the age of each tree would be an important part of such an examination.

Evaluation

Based on the identification and examination, an evaluation can now be made in which certain trees will prove to be more valuable than others to the completed design. Such an evaluation should be an important factor in the placement of buildings, circulation patterns, and other construction. It should also be the basis on which certain trees will be "favored" or encouraged to develop their full natural shape, whereas other trees of lesser design value or limited longevity will be sacrificed to the advantage of the tree with a future.

At this point, a word of caution is offered to the designer tempted by the beauty of an existing tree to incorporate it into the design of the building itself, making it the central feature of an interior court or in some other way relying heavily on a single tree or group of trees. DANGER! Tree life, as human life, cannot be predicted with accuracy. Much of the tree is below ground where conditions are constantly changing, particularly in the vicinity of new construction. Subsurface water conditions often vary with time and weather. New diseases and insect pests are always a threat.

Reconditioning

When the design value of existing trees has thus been determined, steps should be taken immediately to insure the continued good health of the trees selected for preservation. In this way, they will be more likely to make the maximum contribution to the completed design in terms of form, branching, and foliage. Such care includes the removal of dead wood, treatment of scars, feeding and pruning when necessary, removal of surrounding trees that are impeding proper growth, and other conservation measures.

Protection of existing trees on a construction site.

2 Protection of Existing Trees from Physical Damage During Construction

The protective measures recommended against accidental injury or carelessness, as well as damage in the process of construction or grading are outlined below. Section (a) is in the form of specifications to the contractor, which will serve as an example:

(a) Protection from damage by equipment, fire, etc.:

    (1) All trees to be preserved on the property and all trees adjacent to the property shall be protected against damage during construction operations by fencing or armoring. The tree protection shall be placed before any excavation or grading is begun and shall be maintained in repair for the duration of the construction work unless otherwise directed. No material shall be stored or construction operation carried on within 40 feet of any tree designated to be saved. Tree protection shall remain until the planting work is started and then be removed. The extent of fencing and armoring shall be determined by the landscape architect at the time he designates trees to be left standing.

    (i) *Individual trees* near heavy construction traffic shall be wrapped with burlap and 2 inch × 4 inch planks shall be wired vertically as armor around trunks and spaced no more than 2 inches apart to a height of 5 feet above ground.

    (ii) All other *trees in groups* near construction traffic shall be protected by fencing in the following manner: Fences shall have posts equivalent to 4 inches × 4 inches set 3 feet in the ground and extending 5 feet above the ground, set at intervals not to exceed 8 feet. Two walers shall be provided, equivalent to 2 inches × 6 inches, and vertical 1 inch × 6 inch boards applied not over 6 inches apart.

    (iii) Trees having low hanging branches liable to damage shall be fenced around the outer perimeter of the spread of their branches. Fences shall be standard 48 inch high snow fence mounted on standard steel posts set not more than 6 feet apart.

(2) The contractor shall install snow fencing held in place by metal posts along the contract limit lines to protect the trees *and forest floor* outside these limits.

(3) Any damage to existing tree crowns or root systems shall be repaired immediately by an approved tree surgeon. Roots exposed and/or damaged during grading operations shall immediately be cut off cleanly and topsoil spread over the exposed root area. If any trees to be saved are severely injured by mechanical equipment, the contractor agrees to pay for each tree 3 to 6 inches in caliber, the sum of 000 dollars, and for each tree 6 inches and over in caliber, the sum of 000 dollars as fixed and agreed liquidated damages. (Actual dollar amounts should vary with location, quantity of existing trees, and other site conditions.)

(4) Fires, for any reason, shall not be made within 50 feet of any trees selected to remain and shall be limited in size and kept under constant surveillance.

(b) Protection of existing trees from grade manipulation.

The reaction of different species to changes in the depth of soil coverage of their roots is too varied to be included in a book addressed primarily to the designer. Professional advice on this subject should be sought at the time the tree is identified. It is necessary here only to point out that certain deep-rooting species such as the Elm are more tolerant of the lowering of the soil level than surface-rooting species such as the Maples, which cannot survive anything but a gradual lowering of the soil at their base over a period of several years. Certain species, on the other hand, such as the Beech, Tulip, and Sugar Maple, react badly to the slightest additional cover of soil, whereas the roots of others, such as the Elm, Poplar, and Willow, can be covered by as much as several feet of soil without unfavorable reaction.

(1) Existing Trees in Area of Cut

Lowering the soil cover around a tree involves the actual removal of roots. If the roots removed are the fibrous ones on which the tree relies for food, and the quantity removed is appreciable, it is not difficult for the layman to understand the problem. It has already been mentioned that some trees root closer to the surface than others; therefore, the problem is more acute in the case of such species.

If we apply information set forth earlier in Chapter 1, it is clear that if roots are removed in the process of lowering the soil cover, a corresponding amount of leaf surface must also be removed to maintain the balance of water absorbed and water evaporated. If the grade can be

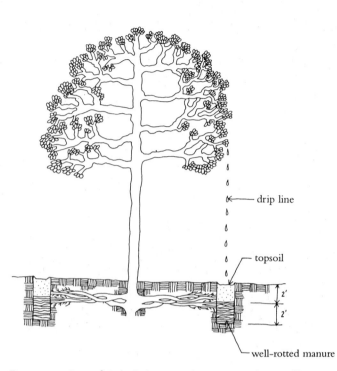

Root pruning of an existing tree in cut to induce a fibrous root system at a lower level.

lowered gradually over a period of several years, and severe pruning accompanies each curtailment of the root system, it is possible to preserve trees that otherwise would not survive. The lowering of grade around a tree must always be done by hand and under strict supervision —never by machine.

It is also possible to induce a tree to increase its fibrous root system at a lower level, but this requires at least one growing season. The tree should be trenched circumferentially to a depth of 4 feet at the drip line. At the bottom of the trench, to a depth of 2 feet, a layer of well-rotted manure should be installed. The trench should then be refilled and thoroughly saturated at 10-day intervals throughout the growing season. This rich supply of food and moisture at a lower level will encourage growth of new feeding roots and will draw them downward to the newly enriched soil. (See diagram.)

In the case of trees to be preserved in areas of cut, it is imperative that all roots be cleanly cut and the tree be thoroughly watered at 10-day intervals throughout the growing season.

(2) Existing Trees in Area of Fill

Increasing the depth of soil covering (fill) is more easily accomplished than lowering the level, since the problem is basically that of making certain that the supply of air and

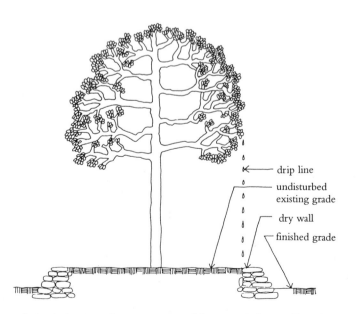

An existing tree in cut protected by a retaining wall.

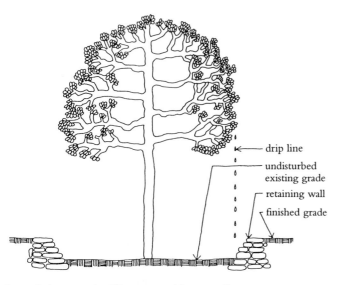

An existing tree in fill protected by a well.

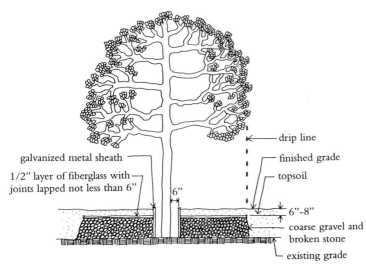

An existing tree in fill protected by coarse gravel.

water to the root system is not substantially curtailed. A well created around the tree to the drip line will retain the natural soil in the area of the feeding fibrous roots, but this is not always possible for reasons of space, cost, or safety; nor is it always desirable aesthetically.

An alternate to this solution is to raise the soil level around the tree. This can be done without ill effect by covering all but the top 6 inches with rough rock fill of the sort that will not key or fit together tightly and will therefore assure an adequate supply of oxygen to the roots. The top 6 or 8 inches of fill may consist of topsoil so that grass can be grown to the base of the tree if so desired. The one caution that should be observed is that moist soil should not be allowed to come into direct contact with the trunk of the tree, for bark is extremely susceptible to

rot. An expandable galvanized metal collar should be placed around the base of the tree to protect it from this hazard.

The following is a general specification covering the preservation of trees existing in an area to be filled: Existing trees that are to remain in areas of fill not over 24 inches in depth shall be preserved as shown in the drawings and in the following manner: The trunks of such trees shall be protected by a cylindrical sheath of galvanized metal placed within 6 inches of the trunk on all sides. Before soil is placed over the root area, a layer of broken stone or coarse gravel shall be set down, to within 6 inches of finished grade. A ½ inch thick fiberglass blanket, with joints lapped not less than 6 inches, shall be spread over the gravel fill to prevent topsoil from clogging interstices of layer, thereby preventing air circulation to roots. The remaining 6–8 inches shall be filled with topsoil. The area to be treated in this manner shall extend to the outer drip line of the branches.

(3) Existing Trees in Pavement

Very often, in the development of a site, large existing trees occur where the ground surface is to be paved. If the pavement requires a concrete setting bed, the tree will

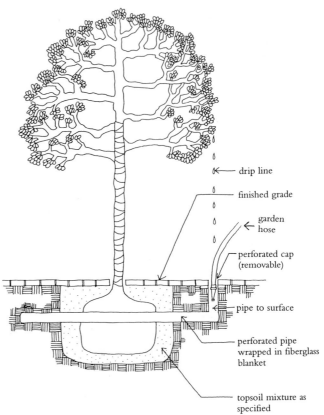

Tree in pavement. (A variation of detail used in Paley Park.)

Pipe system will assure adequate supply of air and moisture to newly planted trees in an area to be completely paved. Paley Park, New York City. (Zion & Breen Associates, Landscape Architects and Site Planners.)

be deprived of much of its supply of surface water and oxygen. The preservation of such trees involves first of all a severe pruning to reduce evaporation. In order to guide water as well as oxygen to the root system, four lateral perforated pipes should be installed at original grade at right angles to each other at the drip line, forming a square. At each corner of the square vertical, pipes to the surface should be introduced by means of elbow pipes. These verticals should be wide enough to receive a garden hose and should be screened at the surface for the safety of pedestrians. The same precautions should be taken when new trees are introduced into paved areas.

(4) Existing Trees and Foundation Footings

Where an existing tree occurs next to a proposed free-standing wall, large roots can be let through the footing by making a suitable wood or cardboard form around the root before the concrete is poured, allowing room for future growth.

Where a tree is found to be close to building wall, a distance of 3 feet, and in some cases even less, is all that need be left between the building and the tree, for with proper pruning a tree can survive the removal of half its root system. Approximately half the foliage should be removed before the roots have been severed. The principal caution in such a situation is that sufficient root anchorage be allowed to remain in order to keep the tree from falling. If this is not possible, proper guying should be installed either to the building itself or neighboring trees.

A garden pavement designed to preserve an existing tree and protect its exposed roots, as an important part of the floorscape.

3   Dollar Evaluation of Trees

In attempting to establish the value of trees for purposes of insurance or tax claims in the event of loss as a result of a storm, accident, willful act, or for insurance claims against a contractor for carelessness or ignoring the specifications regarding the protection of trees on the site as outlined above, a specific dollar value must be attached to the tree, and this valuation must be established by a recognized expert. Sentimental value is not acceptable and replacement value in the case of large old trees is not generally allowed by the Internal Revenue Service.

It must be emphasized that evaluation of this nature is not absolute, and therefore substantiation by a qualified expert becomes extremely important in pressing any claim.

The value of a tree basically is determined by its size, species, physical condition, contribution to the landscape design, and current dollar value.

In the case of large specimen trees purchased for the development of a property, receipts for the tree and its planting costs, as well as photographs showing the tree in place and other photographs after its demise, are all valuable documents in substantiating a claim to the Internal Revenue Service or an insurance company. A statement from a landscape architect familiar with the site or a real estate broker of the area as to how much, in their professional opinions, the property has declined in value because of the loss of the tree would be very helpful. Documents such as these are also the only means of substantiating a claim for the destruction of a large tree preexisting on the site when no receipts documenting the cost of the tree are available. Its contribution to the site, in the opinion of such experts, is essential.

On the Edge of Extinction.   The American Elm, although besieged by Dutch Elm disease and *Phloem necrosis,* will succumb not to disease but to *disuse.* If we are to preserve this most majestic tree for future generations, we must include at least one Elm in every planting design until science provides a solution.

"This Old Tree"
Preservation of a Special Tree

Many properties include one special tree that merits every possible effort to preserve and protect it. The 300-year-old tree shown here thrives happily on the author's property in southern New Jersey. It has been the recipient of almost every known procedure to protect such specimens and for this reason is worth inspecting in detail.

This American Sycamore (*Platanus occidentalis*), known also as a Buttonwood, was planted in 1696 to shield from the summer sun a small half-timber dwelling still existing on the site. Its first 250 years were without major event, although its annual rings,★ evident in some recently removed limbs, indicate frequent years of drought. By 1940, it had reached a height of 100 feet with a spread of 80 feet. Its trunk measured more than 5 feet across—a truly magnificent specimen.

Tree, 300 years old, on author's property.

In 1941, the farmer-owner of the property, noticing that a family of racoons had taken up residence in a small opening in an upper branch, became concerned that this limb overhanging the house might fall and destroy the building. Not aware that the simple and inexpensive procedure of *cabling* would have protected the house, he

---

★See Glossary.

proceeded to remove the central vertical branch (100 feet) as well as a major side branch that extended 80 feet from the trunk.

Cabling

Cabling is a worthwhile precaution in the case of a tree with an especially interesting structure. A stout steel cable is inserted into the limb to be protected, with a bolt or metal plate attached to the outside end of the cable. The other end is attached in a similar manner to the main trunk or a stronger branch at a location from which the cable will supply the greatest support. It is advisable to include a turnbuckle on each cable in order to take up slack as the wire stretches. Cables are identified in the A section of the photograph below.

Pruning

Having made this tragic blunder, the farmer also ignored a primary rule of pruning: When removing lateral branches, even small ones, it is essential first to make a cut only a few

A) Cable installed to support major branch. B) New leader encouraged by proper pruning.

inches deep on the underside of the branch, close to the trunk, before starting to saw from above. This *undercutting* prevents the sawn branch from stripping the bark, including the vital circulation system of the tree (the cambium[†]), as it falls to the ground. An undercut not having been made, the large lateral branch fell to the ground, creating an open wound almost 3 feet wide and 6 feet long (see the A section of the left-hand photograph below).

A second major pruning error was made when the vertical branch, termed the *leader,* was removed. It is a firm principle in removing any vertical branch that the wound be able to shed water. Rain falling on a flat surface, where it does not readily run off, will begin quickly to rot the inner core of the remaining section. The leader of this tree was sawn to form a perfectly flat surface, and rot began to occur early in 1940. By 1964, accelerated by the activity of racoons, squirrels, chipmunks, woodpeckers, and others, the interior of the main trunk had rotted away sufficiently to enable a man to stand within it (see the A section of the right-hand photograph below).

Prevention of Rot

In remedying such a condition, it was considered good horticultural practice, well into this century, to fill such a hollow trunk with concrete, allowing the tree to heal over the filling. This procedure was intended to give stabilization to the trunk, but far from halting the deterioration, it gave to the fungus that causes the rot precisely what it requires to flourish (darkness, dampness, and warmth) and made it impossible ever again to monitor the condition of the interior of the tree.

The accepted procedure today is to leave such rotting areas open, after removing all rotted material, to allow for frequent inspection. The warm air of spring and summer and possibly some direct sunlight will also help to keep the interior dry and discourage the continuation of decay. The author, in pampering this tree, has taken the further precaution of covering all major wounds with sheets of earth-toned canvas that keep out rain and snow, allow for some exchange of air and the admission of light, and facilitate frequent inspections to prevent further deterioration. The canvas covers can be seen in the A section of the left-hand photograph on the next page.

A) Wound caused by failure to undercut in pruning. B) An ill-advised painting of wound surface.

A) Rot caused by improper pruning.

[†]See Glossary.

A) Canvas used to cover cavity to prevent entry of rain and snow.

The wound in 1965, 36 inches wide.

Healing Process (*Callusing*)

The old Buttonwood also illustrates dramatically how tree wounds heal. The right-hand photograph above shows the wound in 1965, measuring 36 inches across. The A section of the photograph to the right, taken in 1992, shows the wound to have decreased by 27 inches in width, clearly illustrating that wounds heal horizontally. The severity of a wound is measured not by its vertical length but its width, which indicates how much of the tree's vertical circulation system, which carries nutrients,★ has been impaired. A razor-thin incision girdling the trunk will kill a tree, having completely cut off all internal circulation, whereas a 3 foot wide vertical slash 10 feet long as illustrated here has severed only 3 feet of the cambium—a relatively small matter for this tree that has a trunk circumference of more than 5 feet.

A) The wound in 1992, 9 inches wide. B) Branches retained to expedite healing.

★See page 107 for an explanation of the internal circulation system.

Hastening Healing

The gradual closing or healing of the wound, termed callusing, can actually be accelerated to some degree by man. One means of doing so has been employed on the old Buttonwood: At the top of each wound, two small branches have been allowed to take hold and thrive although they clearly do not contribute to the beauty of this rugged trunk (see the B section of the bottom right-hand photograph on the page opposite). These two branches, however, and the leaves they bear draw the vital fluids of the circulation system directly to the area of the wound, giving added impetus to the healing process. Eventually, these branches will be removed.

Lightning Protection

The installation of a lightning protection system is a worthwhile precaution for large trees that stand alone in a clearing or close to a structure. Braided copper conductor wires are affixed to all major branches. These are then connected to a wire along the main trunk and "grounded" at the base of the tree.

It is important to inspect an installation at least every 2 years to make certain that the expanding trunk has not healed over any wires. If this condition is not corrected, a lightning strike will destroy the cambium as it races through the system to the ground, possibly causing more damage than if the protection system had not been installed.

The Painting of Wounds

Until very recently, good horticultural practice required that all wounds be treated with a specially prepared antiseptic paint. This now is considered to be a useless procedure that may even impede healing because of the caustic quality of the paint.

The author discovered fortuitously that the use of *any* paint on the *inner* surface of a wound can also endanger the tree. Viewed from within the house, the exposed cavity in the Buttonwood's trunk had a sculptural quality that attracted much attention. In an attempt to heighten this dramatic effect, the exposed inner surface was coated with an application of ordinary black paint (see the B section of the left-hand photograph on page 119). Within 2 years' time, however, decay began to occur at an accelerated rate. It was determined that the paint had acted as a sealant, impeding the drainage of what little moisture had seeped through the canvas covers mentioned above. The paint was removed; the decay ceased.

Forming a New Leader

With all the precautions outlined above taken to ensure the longevity of "this old tree," it is not surprising that an attempt was made—with apparent success—to restore the "leader" or central trunk, the removal of which had severely disfigured this handsome specimen.

From among the many sucker branches that sprang up around the saw wound, the most vertical one was selected for retention, and all others were removed. Later volunteers or suckers were removed each year until after several seasons this small branch began to assume stature. Now, 27 years later, it has a caliber dimension of 12 inches and is swelling at the rate of more than an inch each year (see section B of the right-hand photograph on page 118).

To ensure the future stability of this new leader, a stout log (18 inches) of Black Locust (*Robinina pseudoacacia*) was inserted into the trunk cavity. This wood was selected over other varieties for its lengthy resistance to rot (75 years). The locust log has been bolted to the interior of the trunk at several points and will eventually be totally enclosed within the tree's interior as the original point of rot has been callused over by the new leader.

The author chuckles as he contemplates the confusion and speculation he will have caused a century from now—or two or three—when the old tree finally falls to the ground, a victim of vandalism or "progress," and contemporary botanists and other scientists are summoned to explain how a locust log came to find its way into the maw of a Buttonwood. At least one such expert will pontificate—and perhaps all will agree—that in "those days" (primitive) the Buttonwoods devoured the Black Locusts in a fierce struggle to survive.

ON BUYING TREES

This chapter will touch briefly on the more important points to be considered in the purchase of trees to implement the planting plan. It will provide a checklist or guide for the layman.

How Big?

There are almost no physical or horticultural limitations to the size in which trees can be transplanted successfully. It can be stated generally that if the complete root system can be raised undisturbed in a compact earthball, any tree will survive transplanting, provided it receives proper postplanting care.

With the exception of large trees (14-inch caliber or more) and certain species that transplant less readily in large size, the question of whether to plant large or small trees is principally one of balancing the cost against the importance of an immediate effect, with the added consideration that smaller trees suffer less physical setbacks in the transplanting than larger trees and therefore tend to grow sooner after a move.

The range of sizes in which trees begin to be effective and are easily transplanted and readily available in nurseries is the 2-inch through 4-inch caliber measurement for shade trees and 6-feet through 10-feet height measurement for flowering trees.

Trees larger than 6 inches in caliber are generally in short supply, for most nurseries find it wasteful to devote the necessary space required to retain them and often destroy specimens that remain unsold beyond several years. However, it is encouraging to note that as of the date of this book's publication, several nurseries are beginning to specialize in large trees. The subdivision of large estates in the past has made limited quantities of mature trees available from time to time, but their availability was unpredictable. At present, large trees must often be obtained or "collected" from the wild where changing circumstances have permitted them adequate room for growth.

Where to Buy?

It cannot be repeated too often that previous care and cultivation, as well as the manner in which the tree is dug and handled, are extremely important in terms of future growth. For this reason, it is essential that purchases be made only from nurseries of recognized reputation. As a further safeguard, it is wise to check the references of satisfied clients.

This discussion is an appropriate place to point out the danger of including the planting of a large project in the work of a general contractor. Economically, it makes little sense, for two groups would profit from the transaction since the general contractor usually applies an overriding charge. But more important, the planting of a project should be withheld from the general contractor in order to ensure greater control over the choice of planting contractor, quality of material selected, and digging and planting care. In all cases, the past performance and experience of each bidder must be thoroughly scrutinized.

Guarantee

Guarantees vary among nurseries and landscape contractors in the same locality and from region to region. In general, all plant material should be guaranteed "true to name and variety," and the plantsman should be required to replace all material not in vigorous growing condition at the end of a year from the date of planting. It should also be plainly stated in the guarantee that plants that have lost mature branches and have therefore lost their design value should be replaced, even though they are alive at the end of the guarantee period.

Some contractors offer a 2-year guarantee. This is not as generous a gesture as it appears to be, for if a tree survives the first year of transplanting in vigorous health, it is not likely to fail during the second year. The terms and conditions of other contractors under consideration being equal, however, such a provision should not be ignored.

Replacement is generally made without any charge to the owner. As has been mentioned, practice varies among contractors, which makes it important to check the wording of the guarantee closely before purchase. Some offer to replace the material but make a charge for the digging, or planting, or both; others (usually in very small print) qualify their guarantee relative to the weather, refusing to replace material that fails after a "severe" winter or drought. The vagueness of such a guarantee and the difficulty of arriving at a mutually satisfactory definition of "severe" make this kind of guarantee undesirable. It is also the practice of many contractors not to guarantee trees planted in the city because of the difficult atmospheric conditions. The fairness of this qualification depends largely on the city in question; this should be established clearly beforehand. Plant material to be placed in tubs is also often excluded from the guarantee because of the unnatural growing conditions (limitation of root growth, excessive evaporation due to exposure of the sides of the container to sun, frost damage, etc.).

In all cases, and this is only fair, a guarantee by the plantsman is based on the assumption that proper care will be administered to the tree during the period of the guarantee. In this respect, the landscape architect, in supervising the postplanting care, protects both the owner and plantsman.

A typical specification covering the guarantee is as follows:

(a) The contractor (or nursery) guarantees that all plant material shall be true to name and variety.

(b) The contractor shall guarantee all plant material installed under the contract for a period of 1 year from the date of acceptance. Any material dead, not healthy, dying, or the design value of which, *in the opinion of the landscape architect,* has been destroyed through loss of branches shall be replaced by the contractor at no cost to the owner. The removal of the plant material, the fertilizer and topsoil mixture for the replacement, and all labor shall be at the contractor's expense.

Costs

Costs vary among competitive contractors and from one section of the country to another. Much also depends on the quantities involved, the time of year, and availability.

To obtain a cost figure that will include planting and guarantee, one should triple the cost listed in a wholesale nursery catalogue. When large quantities are involved, and for a very competitive market, it is conceivable that the cost per tree might be reduced to double the wholesale catalogue price.

Except for certain trees in very short supply, there is only a small variation in cost between trees of different species. The principal element of cost is the labor involved in digging, transporting, and planting.

Across the country, there are a small number of nurseries that carry large specimens, as large as 20-inch caliber and higher. As of the date of this publication, one can expect to pay as much as $1,000 per inch of caliber for such specimens delivered to the site, plus a charge of 30–40% for planting.

Measurements

In purchasing or specifying trees, there are certain basic standards with which the designer or owner should be familiar.

Height Measurement

Height measurements are designated in single-foot increments for trees under 6 feet, for example, 5–6 feet. For trees over 6 feet, height is specified in 2-food increments, for example, 8-10 feet.

Caliber Measurement

For trees up to 4 inches in caliber, measurement of the trunk is taken 6 inches above ground level. For larger trees, measurement is taken 12 inches above ground level.

Height Relationship to Caliber

The following list gives the acceptable height range related to the caliber measurement of standard shade trees such as the following:

Norway Maple, Red Maple, Silver Maple, Sugar Maple, White Ash, Green Ash, Ginkgo, Honey-Locust, Thornless Honey-Locust, Tulip Tree, Plane Tree, Poplar, Oaks (Scarlet, Pin, Willow, Red, and Black), Lindens (American, Big-leaf, and Silver), American Elm.

Caliber	Height range
2 –2½ inches	12–14 feet
2½–3 inches	12–14 feet
3 –3½ inches	14–16 feet
3½–4 inches	14–16 feet
4 –5 inches	16–18 feet
5 –6 inches	18 feet and up

For slower growing shade trees such as the following, the height for each caliber measurement should not be less than two-thirds of that indicated in the preceding list:

Horse-Chestnut, Birch, Hackberry, American Yellowwood, Beech (American and European), Kentucky Coffee Tree, Sweet Gum, Black Gum, Hop-Hornbeam, Oaks (White and Swamp-white), Ash, Lindens (Littleleaf, Crimean, European).

Ball Size

The ball should be of sufficient diameter and depth to include the fibrous and feeding root system necessary for the full recovery of the tree after transplanting. Minimum sizes of earth balls are given in the following list covering standard shade trees and smaller trees:

Earth ball diameter for small trees

Height	Minimum diameter of ball
7– 8 feet	20 inches
8– 9 feet	22 inches
9–10 feet	24 inches
10–12 feet	26 inches

Earth ball diameter for larger trees

Caliber measurement	Minimum diameter of ball
2 – 2½ inches	28 inches
2½– 3 inches	32 inches
3 – 3½ inches	38 inches
3½– 4 inches	42 inches
4 – 4½ inches	48 inches
4½– 5 inches	54 inches
5 – 5½ inches	57 inches
6 inches	60 inches
7 inches	70 inches
8 inches	80 inches
9 inches	90 inches
10 inches	104 inches

Earth ball depth in relation to diameter

Diameter of ball	Minimum depth of ball
Under 20 inches	75 % of diameter
Under 20–30 inches	66⅔% of diameter
Under 31–48 inches	60 % of diameter

Earth ball size and weight

Diameter of ball	Depth of ball	Weight of ball
24 inches	16 inches	310 pounds
36 inches	24 inches	1,052 pounds
48 inches	33 inches	2,571 pounds
60 inches	36 inches	4,383 pounds
72 inches	36 inches	6,310 pounds
84 inches	42 inches	10,020 pounds
96 inches	42 inches	13,087 pounds
108 inches	42 inches	16,562 pounds
120 inches	48 inches	23,366 pounds
132 inches	48 inches	28,270 pounds
144 inches	48 inches	33,645 pounds

Bare-Root Trees: Spread of Roots

The following list indicates the desirable spread of roots related to the height of trees being moved bare-root (without earth ball; see the illustration on page 126).

Caliber	Height range	Minimum root spread
2 –2½ inches	12–14 feet	28 inches
2½–3 inches	12–14 feet	32 inches
3 –3½ inches	14–16 feet	38 inches

Collected Trees

"Collected trees" is the term used for trees taken from native stands that have therefore received no horticultural attention. This is of little consequence in the case of small trees, but collected trees 5 inches or more in caliber must have good fibrous root systems in order to survive transplanting successfully. In some species, a root system of this sort can be induced only by periodic pruning of the roots; such pruning is often administered regularly to nursery trees. Collected trees should have a root spread one-third greater than indicated in the list of root spread for bare-root trees.

Certain species such as the Pin Oak, however, have by nature a highly fibrous root system and consequently can be transplanted from the wild with almost as little risk as transplanting nursery-grown trees. Others such as the Sour Gum or Tupelo would prove extremely risky if large sizes were collected without any previous care. For this reason, it is wise to specify that collected plants will not be accepted without express permission. If used, such trees should be selected at least one growing season (preferably two) in advance of transplanting and severely root-pruned in order to induce a fibrous root system. Trees purchased from private estates are considered collected material, but they are likely to have received better care than those collected from the wild and can be considered less of a risk.

Generally, collected trees should be avoided unless size is an overriding factor. The possibility of failure is much higher than with nursery-grown trees and postplanting care must be more thorough. If the physical difficulties and inconvenience of replacement are great, as would be the case with trees for an interior courtyard where material must be transported through the building, or if the maintenance burden must be kept to a minimum, collected trees should be refused; the planting specifications must then be explicit in stating that no collected material will be accepted.

Specimen Trees

"Specimen trees" are those that have departed in some respect from the standard characteristic of the species and developed a character of shape, size, or branch structure that gives them special interest. Ideal light and soil conditions and unlimited room for lateral growth have perhaps encouraged a much fuller form than ordinarily expected in a tree of a given caliber or height measurement. In other cases, a crowded condition in the nursery has forced growth upward in a struggle for light, producing a taller, higher-branching specimen than the ordinary nursery stock. In some instances, an early injury has destroyed the leader (the central vertical branch) and the tree has developed an asymmetrical, tortuous habit. These and other conditions produce unusual trees that are useful for emphasis at important points in the spatial composition; they are designated by the landscape architect as "specimen." Some nurserymen consider such trees undesirable because they take up more growing space than standard plants or they are malformed or atypical; others, however, cultivate such plants for their value to the landscape architect. Specimen trees should always be selected in the field, for the special shape and quality desired can seldom be covered adequately in a written specification. Certain terms, however, are useful in indicating the general direction in which the specimen tree should deviate in its form from the natural growth habit. Such terms include the following:

Bush form: Branching close to the ground
Clumps: Trees with two or more stems originating at the ground
Sheared: Trees pruned to form a heavier than usual branch system
Topiary: Trees clipped to a geometric form

Such other terms as weeping, columnar, pyramidal, and horizontal branching are self-explanatory.

Latin Names

The use of Latin names on the plant list has an important purpose and is not, as is often thought, an affectation intended to make the design plan appear more erudite. It is an extremely useful means of elminating the confusion that develops when different nurseries adopt local names of trees. Tupelo, for example, is known in different localities as Black Gum, Sour Gum, or Pepperidge. The Sorrel is known as Sourwood or Tree Andromeda, etc.

The importance of the Latin name was conclusively proved to the author during his work in 1959 in the former Soviet Republic, where Zion & Breen Associates served as site planners and landscape architects of the American National Exhibition. In spite of all the difficulties encountered in communicating with the Russians on the most basic matters, the selection of trees was made effortless through the use of Latin plant names.

4

ON PLANTING TREES

Moving trees in the eighteenth century.

It is not important for the architect or layman to be familiar with all the details of the planting procedure. A knowledge of the basic reasons behind each step will, however, prove useful in enabling him to recognize the importance of requiring the planting contractor to adhere closely to all specifications, some of which, on the surface, may appear to be unimportant. Brief nontechnical explanations of the major steps follow.

Moving trees in the nineteenth century.

Moving trees in the twentieth century.

1 Proper Equipment

It is naive and unwise to assume that all planting contractors or their foremen have the knowledge or the will to perform their duties in the best interests of the trees being planted. Planting specifications should take nothing for granted, including even the type and quantity of equipment to be made available at the job site:

For all trees except the largest specimens, a *tail-gate elevator* should be required in order to avoid a damaging drop from truck to ground. Trees with earth balls larger than can be accommodated on such elevators should be lowered from the truck by skids and rollers (see photo above) or a crane device.

Mechanized winches for proper positioning of the tree should be used when the truck has easy access to all sections of the site. When this is not the case, a block-and-fall and adequate pivot devices should be available. In this connection, caution should be exercised in granting permission to use existing trees as pivots because of the possibility of damage to the pivot tree.

When maneuverability is not a problem, a crane is the most effective and rapid means of positioning a tree in the ground, as well as of lifting it from the truck with minimum damage to the ball. If a crane is to be used, it is wise to provide the tree with a platform. Without a platform, the straps used to cradle the tree often cut into the earth ball as a result of the weight placed on them.

2 Placement

It is wise to stipulate that the contractor shall have staked the location of each tree as accurately as possible from the planting plan before the trees are delivered. The trees, as they arrive, should be placed on the ground at each stake, with major branches untied to reveal their shape. In this way, the landscape architect will not be required to stand by during the unloading process, spending unnecessary time in supervision, which is often charged on a time basis.

The specimen tree out of the ground bears surprisingly little resemblance to its earlier appearance in the nursery. Changes from the printed plan are therefore inevitable. One is often dolefully warned by the planting contractor that additional movement will weaken the earth ball and thereby reduce the tree's chance of survival. However, mechanized winches, which should be a part of any contractor's equipment, simplify such movement, and there is little such danger if the earth ball has been dug properly and tied securely, covered with burlap, and in the case of all trees with an earth ball over 5 feet in

A tree with a large earth ball lowered from a truck by means of skids and rollers.

diameter, placed on a sturdy wooden platform of adequate size. (See the illustration on page 127.)

For the most effective implementation of a landscape design, it is best to specify that no holes will be predug before the arrival of the tree—and then only after the designer has had an opportunity to reassess the composition. More complaints from the contractor, perhaps, but a more successful design!

3 The Tree Pit

a Dimensions

Dimensions of the tree pit are related to the size of the earth ball. The minimum excavation should be 18–24 inches wider than the lateral dimension of the earth ball and 6 inches deeper than its vertical dimension. For bare-root planting, the minimum lateral dimension of the pit should be 12 inches beyond the spread of the roots in every direction.

It is an erroneous impression of the layman that the bulk of the topsoil should be placed beneath the tree. Six inches is all that is necessary, for the fibrous or feeding roots tend to grow laterally; only the anchor roots and tap roots grow down.

All excavated material should be removed from the site unless permission is expressly granted for on-site disposal.

b Drainage

When the excavation operation is complete, an inspection should be made to ascertain drainage conditions. Provision for adequate drainage is the responsibility of the contractor. However, since damage resulting from improper drainage conditions may not be recognized until after the expiration of the contractor's guarantee, it is a wise precaution to make at least a spot check of pits in doubtful areas by filling them with water and observing the rate of absorption. If drainage is slow, the depth of the pit should be increased by at least 12 inches and an equal amount of coarse gravel placed at the bottom. When drainage is extremely poor and water is found to remain unabsorbed for

15 minutes or longer, the advisability of planting in the area should be severely questioned, and the trees used should be only those that tolerate very moist conditions. (See Part IV.) If the design requires that trees must be placed in these areas, then it is advisable to construct a second pit alongside the first one, extending 3–4 feet below the depth of the original tree pit. This second excavation should be filled with coarse gravel to the level of the bottom of the tree pit and connected with it by a clay pipe or channel 1-foot in diameter, also filled with coarse gravel. This second pit will thus serve as a dry well to carry off excess water from the tree pit.

Boxed.

Balled and burlapped.

Balled, burlapped, and platformed.

c Scarification

A final word of caution concerning excavation for tree plantings is in order. The bottom of the pit should be thoroughly scarified or loosened in order to ensure porosity. This is especially necessary on sites where the use of heavy equipment in the area has compacted the soil. A crowbar or pickax will ordinarily serve the purpose; in extreme cases, a drill may be necessary. The importance of this precaution cannot be overemphasized, for entire plantings have failed when it has been overlooked.

The sides of the pit should also be well scarified to make it easier for newly formed fibrous roots to knit with the surrounding soil. This is especially important if the tree pits are being dug with a mechanical auger since the action of the auger tends to glaze the wall of the pit.

4 Planting

a Backfill

The specifications should be explicit as to the quality and content of the soil to be used in the tree pit. If additives are to be used, the proportions should be included in the specifications; it is important to make certain that they are thoroughly mixed into the soil before it is placed in the pit. An inspection of the backfill is a valuable step too seldom taken.

From time to time, major changes are introduced into horticulture. Practices that have been in use for centuries are sometimes found useless and even harmful. One of the foremost pioneers in the field, Carl Whitcomb, Professor of Horticulture at Oklahoma State University, determined recently to his satisfaction and that of many others that it is unnecessary to introduce additives or amendments (peat moss, lime, manure, etc.) to the soil in the transplanting of a tree. It is Whitcomb's contention that it is necessary only to backfill the tree pit with soil from the site. In a large planting, this practice could save much time and money, but it is the author's opinion that such additives can only help and will not harm the plant. The jury is still out on this major departure. In general, however, Whitcomb's "rules for planting" are sound and should form the basis of any planting specification. For that reason, they are reproduced below:

A) Delivery to site.

(1) Select plants well-adapted to the soil, light level, and microclimate of the site. In this regard, the specifications should clearly state that the tree's orientation in the nursery must be duplicated at the site. To ensure that precaution is taken, the north side of the tree as it stood in the nursery should be clearly marked on the trunk or burlap covering the ball or by tying a ribbon of specified color on a northerly branch.

(2) Transplant only when the plant has ample reserves of stored food.

(3) Make the planting hole as wide as possible, at least 18–24 inches wider than the root ball.

(4) If in doubt, plant slightly shallower rather than slightly deeper.

(5) Remove all containers, cord, and wire from the planting site.

(6) Expose roots to air for an absolute minimum of time.

(7) If the spade has glazed the sides of the hole, break up the compacted soil.

(8) Fill the hole with the same soil removed from the hole. Don't mix amendments with the backfill.

(9) Mulch heavily, 5–7 feet out from the tree, and 3–4 inches deep, but don't suffocate the bark. Use peat or compost.

(10) Fertilize immediately after planting and again the next fall after leaf drop. Use slow-release fertilizer. Apply it only on the soil surface.

B) Ready for hoisting by crane.

C) Properly strapped for hoisting.

D)

E)

F)

G) Transplanted White Pine in place and ready for straightening.

One of the most vital aspects of the planting operation is the manner in which the backfill is placed in the pit. It is essential that the entire surface of all roots be completely covered by soil. Any root surface exposed to air will dry and die; obviously, therefore, every effort must be made to eliminate air pockets, which form readily during the process of backfilling.

The most effective method of compacting the soil and destroying air pockets is by the use of water; flooding the newly placed soil as each 6 inches of depth is added will force air to the surface. The process of tamping soil to eliminate air pockets has been proved less effective, although it is still advocated by some plantsmen.

When the backfilling operation has been completed, it is advisable, as a further precaution, to insert a garden hose, with the nozzle removed, down through the backfill to the bottom of the pit, allowing the water to run with medium force. The rising water will force to the surface any air that might have evaded the water administered during the backfilling. A crowbar can be used to speed the flow of water through the backfill.

b Guying

The purpose of guying or supporting a newly planted tree is to prevent movement of the trunk by wind; any swaying movement of the tree will cause movement of the earth ball, and this, however slight, will pull the growing fibrous roots from their footing in new soil beyond the original earth ball, causing them to dry out and die back.

The layman is often under the impression that guying is done in order to keep the tree from falling and will sometimes elect to omit this step from the planting operation. If guying is omitted, especially in windy locations, new growth is noticeably slow; many times, it does not take place at all because root growth remains almost at a standstill.

Guying should be done immediately after planting to prevent the tree from settling in an improper position. After guying, a thorough watering should be administered to compact the soil around the roots.

For the sake of appearance, galvanized wire is preferred for guying purposes; two strands should be used, twisted for rigidity as well as appearance. Larger trees require a turnbuckle to facilitate tightening the slack in the wire that inevitably occurs after a windy season. In the case of smaller trees, the guy wire can be tightened by hammering the stakes deeper into the ground.

c Staking

Staking is an integral part of the guying process; it is the means of anchoring the guy wires in the soil. There are three basic methods of staking related to the size of the tree and space available. The vertical staking method (see diagram A) is recommended when a tree is placed in a paved area where there is insufficient room to carry wires out at the proper angle. This method is also more desirable in plantings open to the public, where wires become a safety hazard.

The use of ground-level stakes (differentiated from vertical stakes; see diagram B) is recommended for trees under 3 inches in caliber. Above this size, guy wires should be attached to deadmen (logs buried beneath the surface) for better anchorage. See diagram C.

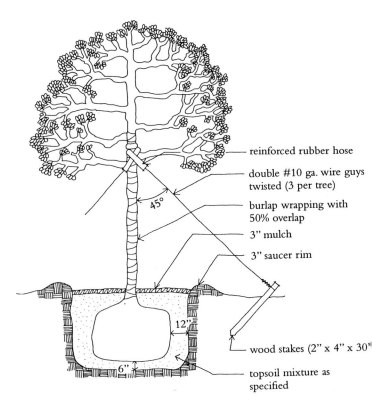

B) Ground-level staking.

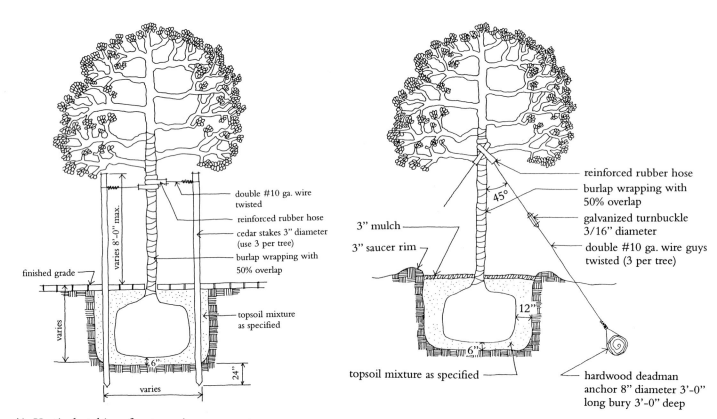

A) Vertical staking for trees in pavement or areas open to the public.

C) Deadmen used to secure a tree.

d Wrapping

After planting, the trunk of the tree should be wrapped to the first major crotch with a high-grade burlap or specially prepared paper. The purpose of this wrapping is to reduce the evaporation of much-needed moisture through the trunk. It is essential that the specifications prohibit wrapping until the trunks have been inspected for possible wounds sustained during the planting, or for infestation of fungus, scale, borers, and such that may have been overlooked during the initial inspection. If any of these are present, proper treatment should be administered before the wrapping takes place. Wrapping should be allowed to remain through the second winter after transplanting.

For purely aesthetic considerations, burlap is the material of choice for wrapping. The papers available for the purpose are not as durable and tend to unravel within a year. It is suggested also that the wrapping material be dark brown in color; lighter shades are jarring in the landscape and emphasize the newness of the planting.

e Pruning

By now, the importance of pruning as a means of keeping the evaporation of water in balance with the intake when a portion of the root system has been destroyed has been well established. For this reason, it is advisable to reduce the branching of newly planted trees by approximately one-third. This cannot be a steadfast rule, for the design value of many trees could be severely diminished by strict adherence to this proportion. However, it should be approached as an optimum, and when it cannot be accomplished, special attention should be given to the watering of the tree to ensure an adequate supply of moisture.

f Mulch

Immediately after the guying has been completed and the first watering applied, a mulch, or blanket, 3 inches in depth, of a moisture-retaining material such as peat moss, wood chips, or vermiculite should be spread over the surface of the ground from the trunk to the outer limits of the excavation. This covering will serve to retain moisture in the area of the root system.

Mulch serves an equally important purpose in the winter. It maintains a more even temperature in the root zone, eliminating periodic freezing and thawing of the soil. It is extremely important, however, that the winter mulch not be applied until after the first heavy frost. If this advice is ignored, or the summer mulch is not removed at the end of the dry season, rodents of all types will make their winter home in the mulch material and feed on the bark of young trees, often completely girdling the trunks and killing them.

g Saucer

After the tree has been mulched, an earth berm, or raised brim approximately 3 inches high, should be created, encircling the tree at the outer limits of the earth ball. The saucer thus formed will facilitate the watering operation by retaining water that would otherwise run off the surface before being absorbed. The saucer is also useful in retaining rainwater. (See diagrams A, B, and C.)

5 When to Plant

a Spring vs. Fall Planting

The question of fall or spring planting will never be resolved to the satisfaction of all plantsmen—nor, for that matter, of all trees. Some trees have a very strong preference for the time of transplanting. These preferences, when they exist, have been noted in the data relating to each recommended tree, in Part III. This is not to say that such trees cannot be transplanted successfully at other times of the year. They will, however, require more careful digging, speedier planting, and more diligent postplanting care when planted "out of season."

A spring planting is most favorable in colder climates; a tree moved early in the spring will be able to replace some of its root loss and partially reestablish itself before hot weather arrives. A tree planted in the fall must withstand the rigors of winter immediately after sustaining the shock of transplanting. Evergreens in the northeast prefer to be transplanted in late August. Birch trees, for their own reasons, prefer very early spring planting, as do Magnolias whose injured roots are subject to a fungus that they appear more able to resist in the spring when their entire system is functioning. Princeton Nurseries, one of the oldest and most prestigious nurseries in the country, lists the following species for which they consider fall planting inadvisable.

Acer rubrum and varieties	*Platanus acerifolia*
Betula varieties	*Prunus*: All Stone Fruits
Carpinus varieties	*Pyrus*: All Pears
Cornus florida and varieties	*Quercus*: All Oaks
Crataegus varieties	*Salix*: Weeping varieties
Halesia	*Styrax japonica*
Koelreuteria	*Tilia tomentosa*
Liquidambar styraciflua	*Zelkova* varieties
Liriodendron tulipifera	

In such matters, it is best to rely on the experience and judgment of local plantsmen.

b Out-of-Season Planting

Although the introduction of antidessicant sprays has facilitated out-of-season planting, it is nevertheless inadvisable to dig any tree when the year's new leafgrowth is still tender. Much of the success of transplanting trees in full leaf is dependent on proper digging. Experience has shown, for example, that a tree in full leaf is better able to survive transplanting when the digging is performed in two stages in which all but the bottom roots are dug in one operation followed by a thorough watering, and the remaining roots severed 7–10 days later. Postplanting care, especially proper watering, is the other vital factor in the successful out-of-season planting of trees.

6 Planting Specifications

It is the author's hope that the foregoing discussion of the planting operation will underscore the importance of enforcing strict adherence to every requirement of the planting specification. The outline specification below covering tree planting can be used as a checklist to ensure inclusion of all major items:

(1) General

    (a) At no time will the planting contractor be allowed to subcontract any portion of his work without approval.

(2) Work Included

    (a) Furnish all labor, materials, and proper and adequate equipment necessary for the completion of planting. This includes, but is not necessarily limited to, the following items of equipment.

    (b) Existing topsoil shall be tested and, if necessary, made to conform to the pH acidity range and percentage of organic matter as listed below. If additional topsoil is required, it shall be tested and made to meet these requirements.

(3) Materials

    (a) Topsoil.

        (i) General description.

        (ii) Acidity range and mechanical analysis.

        (iii) Admixture composition and proportions for deciduous trees.

        (iv) Admixture composition and proportions for evergreen trees.

    (b) Specifications for materials used.

        (i) Plant material: The contractor shall furnish plant material in quantities specified. Plants shall have the habit of growth that is normal for the species and shall be sound, healthy, vigorous, free from insects, plant diseases, and injuries. All plants shall equal or exceed measurements specified in the plant list. Plants shall be measured before pruning, with branches in normal position. Necessary pruning shall be done at the time of planting.

        (ii) Manure (description of type, age, etc.).

        (iii) Lime (description of standards).

        (iv) Commercial fertilizer (description of standards).

        (v) Bone meal (description of standards).

        (vi) Humus (description of standards).

        (vii) Water (description of standards).

        (viii) Peat moss (description of standards).

        (ix) Guying, staking, and wrapping materials (description of wire, gauge, etc.), turnbuckles (size), size and color of hose sheathing for wire, wrapping materials (type and color), wrapping instructions, and stakes (size and wood variety).

(4) Workmanship

    (a) Adequate notice to be given in advance of the delivery of any plant material to the site. Delivery slips to be furnished, covering all plant material transported to the site.

    (b) Establishment of planting schedule to avoid conflicts in the landscape architect's supervision schedule, as well as the general construction schedule for the building.

    (c) Size and preparation of the pit. Description of backfill operation and compacting of soil.

    (d) Outline of care to be administered to material delivered and stored at the site in advance of planting, in order to prevent damage from elements.

    (e) Guying and wrapping instructions as indicated on drawings.

    (f) Protection. Outline of protection to be provided to planted areas against damage and trespassing.

    (g) Maintenance of planting until acceptance (watering, pruning, weeding, settlement correction, etc.).

    (h) Planting dates. Period during which planting will be permitted, varying with local seasons and types of trees.

5

STREET TREES

In earlier days, street trees commanded respect and performed an important function; they shaded our roadways against the summer sun and thereby kept horses from going mad. The latter problem has been solved today by the elimination of the horse, and street trees have become merely a visual amenity. Until recently in this country, this has not always been considered an important function, and street trees—particularly in the city—have gone begging.

Trees for City Streets

The city is a hostile environment for the tree. Almost totally lacking is the natural leaf mulch of the forest floor, the constant enrichment of the soil through the decay of organic matter, the pure air permitting unimpeded transpiration, the mutual protection from wind afforded by other trees, and the spongy absorbent soil retaining moisture. Certain other facts of city life must influence the designer's selection of species to be used as street trees: air pollution, limited moisture, lack of sufficient light, glare and reflection of heat from pavement and building walls, urine scald from an ever-increasing canine population, the use of salt or chemicals to aid in snow removal, compaction, and "tired" or depleted soil.

Tree grates add interest to the walkways of the city.

137

"Elbows" produced by repeated cutting to the same point. These trees are pruned annually by the municipality of a Swiss city.

Air Pollution

In most American cities, the air is poisoned by gases and a heavy content of dust and soot. Soot clogs the breathing pores of tender-leaved deciduous trees, forcing them to abandon the city to a few species that produce tough, leathery leaves. Needled evergreens cannot survive in most of our larger industrial cities because they retain their needles for 2 or more years, and during this period the needles accumulate so much debris that it becomes impossible for them to function. Urban conditions in America have improved in recent years, but watering and pruning care in most cities are far behind.

Limited Moisture Supply

The supply of ground water in most cities has been all but cut off from the street tree by subways, underground utilities, basements, and subbasements. Surface water is limited to the infinitesimal quantity of rain water that manages to seep between paving blocks or to the occa-

sional pail of water provided through the kindness of the proprietor of a nearby store.

Recalling the statistic cited earlier, that a large tree can evaporate more than 1000 gallons of water per day, reflect now on the plight of the trees that line our city streets. The problem has been met intelligently by Europeans, who have always placed more importance than Americans on the amenities of city life. In Europe, the city tree is considered the precious ward of all city dwellers; its care is not entrusted to the nearest property owner, but is zealously protected by the city government. Trees are watered and sprayed regularly by municipal tank trucks and pruned annually by experts employed by the city.

Care

Pruning and *watering* are the two most important measures in the care of the city tree. Because of the restricted water supply, evaporation through the leaves must be kept in balance with the amount of water taken in through the root system. As explained earlier, if this balance is not

Trees have a tendency to lean toward the source of light: Plane Trees on a Manhattan street.

maintained artificially by removal of excess leaf growth (pruning), then the tree will care for itself by curtailing or dying back at the tip of each branch, a condition that can be found in a very high percentage of trees in cities across our nation. In many European cities, when trees reach their optimum size in relation to the available water supply and growing space, they are cut back annually to the same point on each branch. This repeated cutting produces an "elbow" that adds considerable interest to the winter silhouette. (See photo on opposite page.)

Fertilizer should be applied annually in late fall or early spring at the rate of 3 pounds per inch of caliber. A liquid fertilizer is most easily handled. The mix should be 15-15-15 or 10-8-4. These figures represent the proportions of nitrogen, phosphoric acid, and potash. A spray program is also essential to prevent fungus, insect damage, and disease.

Light conditions in some sections of the city make it useless to attempt the planting of *any* tree. In other sections, the low intensity of light and tendency of a tree to lean toward the source of light (phototropism) will cause a severe bending of the trunk over the years. This tendency appears to be stronger in some trees (see Plane Trees, photo opposite) than others (Ginkgo, Linden, Maple) and if, from the design point of view, the upright habit is considered important, these latter trees should be favored.

Glare or reflection of heat from pavement or buildings will cause burning or scorching of the leaves of tender-leaved species. Although this is seldom fatal, it is unsightly. Scorch can be prevented in part by spraying the leaves with an antidesiccant solution when they first appear, but this additional maintenance problem can be avoided by choosing from among the list of leathery-leaved trees recommended for city use (see page 141). If, however, the design requires the inclusion of a tree with some special characteristic, its maintenance requirements must be considered.

Urine scald will always be a problem in areas of large canine population. It is best prevented by the installation of a galvanized metal guard at the base of the tree.

Snow removal by means of chemicals injurious to plant life has become an important cause of failure of city street trees. The use of *sodium nitrate* is recommended in place of the commonly used sodium or calcium chloride, for it has proved equally effective and has the added advantage of providing a source of nitrogen for trees, grass, and other plant material.

Soil of proper consistency is extremely important; it must drain well but have sufficient moisture-retaining qualities to carry the tree through infrequent waterings. A good mixture would be the following: 50% coarse sand, 25% screened topsoil, 15% peat moss, and 10% reed-sedge peat.

Planting

The size of the tree pit depends, of course, on the desired maximum growth of the tree. However, a working minimum should be a 5-foot square excavated to a depth of 4 feet. The incorporation of the tree into the sidewalk design or floorscape varies from city to city, but the most satisfactory solution from the point of view of the tree as well as the floorscape is a metal grate at least 4 feet square (see photo on page 137). Such a grate will permit an accumulation of rain water, but will prevent the compaction of the soil by pedestrian traffic that prevents proper absorption of moisture and oxygen. The introduction of a pattern into the design of such grates can add much interest to the walkways of the city.

Design Considerations

The regular spacing of street trees is an anachronism. It is no longer necessary now that the horse is gone, and fur-

Honey-Locusts in the heart of New York City, planted at 12-foot intervals to create a leafy ceiling for an outdoor room: Paley Park. (Zion & Breen Associates, Landscape Architects and Site Planners.)

Grouped and pruned architectonically, trees can be made to define or enclose a space. (Nancy, France.)

thermore, it involves difficult and expensive replacement to maintain symmetry in the event of the failure of mature trees. Lateral spacings between trees should be varied, and plantings need not necessarily line both sides of the street; alternating from one side to the other can be extremely effective in emphasizing certain buildings, vistas, or special areas of activity.

The varying of species in order to introduce variation in height, form, and texture can also do much to relieve the monotony of the cityscape, as well as to set certain areas apart or create desired emphasis. Smaller species can be used in areas of smaller buildings to reflect a change of scale.

Groupings of trees as in bosks of closely spaced rows of trees (10–12 feet) can create a canopy of green to roof an open space. Grouped and pruned architectonically, they serve as green walls to define a space.

Trees That Tolerate City Conditions

A small group of trees has shown a definite propensity for city life and this group has been quickly befriended by those in charge of planting our city streets. The *Linden* has lent its name to the heavily planted Unter Den Linden in Berlin; the *Horse-Chestnut* of the Champs Elysées is also renowned, although its heavy demand for water cannot be met in the city, causing it to scorch and dry out in August. The *Sycamore* and *Norway Maple* are very tolerant of city conditions, as are the *Sweet Gum* and *Honey-Locust*. The *Ginkgo* appears to be the most durable of the city trees, but it is not without its weak points: Its conformation can often be too exotic, its shade is less dense than others, and the female of the species sheds a foul-smelling fruit. All trees, however, have some disadvantages, and since the choice is limited, the designer cannot be too demanding. The following is a list of urban-hardy species. (*Note:* Species marked with an asterisk are included in the "Tree Portraits" section of this book):

Ash, Green (*Fraxinus pennsylvatica lanceolata*)
★Crab Apple (*Malus*)
Elm, Augustine (*Ulmus Americana* var. "Augustine")
★Ginkgo (Maidenhair Tree) (*Ginkgo biloba*)
★Hawthorn (*Crataegus*)
★Honey-Locust (*Gleditisia triacanthos*)
Hornbeam, European (*Carpinus betulus*)
★Horse-Chestnust (*Aesculus hippocastanum*)
★Linden, Little-leaf (*Tilia cordata*)
★Locust, Fastigiate (*Robinia pseudoacacia* var. *fastigiata*)
Maple, Norway (*Acer platanoides*)
Mulberry, Sterile (*Morus alba tatarica sterile*)
Oak, Red (*Quercus borealis*)
★Pear, Callery (*Pyrus calleryana*)
Persimmon, Common (*Diospyros virginiana*)
Plane Tree, London (*Platanus acerifolia*)
★Poplar (*Populus alba bolleana, populus nigra italica,* and *populus maximowiczi*)
★Scholar Tree (*Sophora japonica*)
★Tree of Heaven (*Ailanthus altissima*)
★Willow, Weeping (*Salix babylonica*)
Zelkova, Japanese (*Zelkova serrata*)

The United States Department of Agriculture favors the following selections of city-tolerant trees for the five major sections of the country:

Northeastern United States

Ginkgo (staminate form), London Plane Tree, Norway Maple (special selections), Red Maple (special selections)

Plains area

American Sycamore, Box-Elder, Bur Oak, Green Ash, Hackberry, Maples (special selections), Russian Mulberry, Siberian Elm

Southeastern United States

Deciduous: Common Crape-Myrtle, Sugarberry, Sweet Gum, Water Oak, Willow Oak
Evergreen: Cabbage Palmetto, Camphor Tree, Laurel Oak, Live Oak, Southern Magnolia

Southern Rocky Mountains

Green Ash, Lanceleaf Poplar, Linden, London Plane Tree, Narrow-leaf Poplar, Northern Catalpa, Norway Maple, Siberian Elm, Velvet Ash, White Ash

North Pacific Coast

Common Hackberry, European Linden

Trees for Suburban Streets

The suburbs do not present difficulties of tree culture to the same degree as the city. Hazards here are principally damage by cars, delivery trucks, and snow removal equipment; conflict with utility lines; and the widening of roads in growing communities. The safeguarding of trees on suburban streets is essentially a problem of design—of proper placement in order to avoid the hazards mentioned.

The ideal placement of the suburban street tree would be within the private properties adjoining the street, approximately 12 feet from the roadway. Trees thus planted should be considered public property and not altered or removed without permission of the community government. Such an arrangement, however, requires cooperation, which is often difficult to obtain. As a reasonable compromise, the street tree should be planted between the sidewalk and private property boundary, rather than between sidewalk and street, as has been the common practice. This arrangement (approximately 8 feet from the roadway) affords protection from vehicles, particularly tall vans and buses that must pull close to the curb. Care of the street trees should not, however, be relegated to the owners of adjacent properties, but must be considered a community responsibility to be performed properly and regularly.

Variation in the spacing of trees on suburban streets should be introduced for the same reasons as in the city. Variation in species can be greater here because more favorable atmospheric conditions permit the inclusion of evergreens, and the reduced scale of buildings permits the effective use of small flowering trees.

Tree and power line, an eternal struggle.

The problem of widening streets is not always solved in favor of the tree, as it has been in this Italian town.

Trees for Highways

Trees for highways and parkways should not be chosen as casually as they have been in the past. With the increase in the speed of automobiles, trees properly selected and placed can do much to increase the safety of the roadway.

Monotony, which induces fatigue, is the enemy of the motorist. The spacing of trees on high-speed roads should therefore avoid regularity in order to avoid monotony. Trees of very definite shape or outline create rhythms that tend to be soporific; these should be dismissed in favor of varied massings of more anonymous types.

The set-back of plantings should also be varied. Proximity to the roadway should be governed by probable future expansion and the requirements of snow removal, as well as the danger resulting from storm damage.

The selection of plant material of unusual nature, such as flowering or fruit trees, should be made judiciously, for it has been found that exotic shapes and colors are distracting and in some cases will cause dangerous driving deceleration to admire or pick blossoms. For this reason, as well as for reasons of tree culture, only native varieties should be used on high-speed roadways.

The use of trees to instruct the motorist is an aspect of design widely overlooked. Curves of the roadway can be emphasized and drivers warned by a curvilinear planting; changes in species or height can attract attention in order to emphasize certain areas; the roadbed can be clearly defined by tree plantings that emphasize narrowness or width; distracting views can be screened, and attractive vistas framed by plantings.

Finally, the selection of species for highway planting must be based on durability and low maintenance costs, for when funds are not forthcoming, it is an unwise design decision to select trees with high moisture requirements that, in order to look well, must be sprayed constantly or otherwise treated to prevent disfiguring infestations of pests or disease.

6

ROOFTOP PLANTING

Trees planted on a rooftop encounter the same survival problems faced by trees planted on our city streets: no supply of ground water, limited room for root growth, no natural replenishments of soil nutrients, plus the added hazards of greater exposure to dehydration from the action of sun and wind.

If we assume that there is sufficient exposure to daylight (prolonged periods of direct sunlight are essential only to produce blossoms on flowering trees), the requirements for the success of rooftop plantings are these: (a) adequate water supply; (b) good drainage; (c) sufficient room for future growth; and (d) periodic feeding.

Size of Tree Pit

Adequate provision for future growth dictates the dimensions of the area to receive the tree. The actual dimensions of the pit will naturally vary with the size and variety of the tree. A depth of 4 feet will accommodate any tree adequately and allow for proper drainage. Some trees can be planted in a depth of 3 feet, but this should be considered a minimum, for a provision of at least 3 inches of gravel must be made for drainage at the bottom of the pit.

As for the lateral dimensions of the pit, these will vary with the size of the tree to be received and the maximum future size considered desirable from the point of view of design. When a tree is to be planted on a rooftop, the designer must decide at the outset the ultimate spread of the crown he desires. Since the extent of the root system is a function of the spread of the crown and generally reaches to the drip line of the branches, it is a simple matter to determine adequate lateral dimensions for the tree pit.

Drainage

After the depth and width of the tree pit or box have been determined, steps must be taken to provide for rapid and thorough drainage.

The floor of the pit must be sloped carefully toward a drain. It is essential to test this slope with water before the soil is installed in order to disclose any defect in workmanship. From 3–5 inches of coarse gravel should be placed over the bottom of the pit to facilitate drainage. A 1-inch blanket of fiberglass between the gravel and soil is recommended in order to keep the soil from mixing with the gravel and eventually clogging the drain.

The drain itself, contrary to the general impression, is best placed in a corner of the pit rather than the center. Perforated clay pipes, full-round or half-round depending on the depth of the gravel bed, are placed so as to conduct water from each of the other three remaining corners to the drain opening. The installation of a vertical clay pipe directly over the drain itself will permit a constant visual check on the functioning of the drain; such a check would naturally be impossible if the drain were situated in the center of the pit directly beneath the earth ball of the tree. A corner location also facilitates probing, should clogging occur, without disturbing the root system or requiring the removal of the tree. It is a wise precaution to perforate this vertical pipe and surround it with 2–6 inches of coarse gravel; then, should damage occur to the pipes at the bottom of the pit through carelessness of plantsmen or defective materials, standing water—always fatal to a tree—will thus be drained off through this vertical pipe.

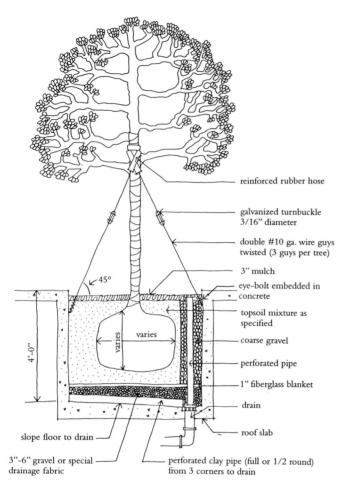

reinforced rubber hose

galvanized turnbuckle
3/16" diameter

double #10 ga. wire guys
twisted (3 guys per tree)

3" mulch

eye-bolt embedded in
concrete

topsoil mixture as
specified

coarse gravel

perforated pipe

1" fiberglass blanket

drain

roof slab

45°

4'-0"

varies

varies

slope floor to drain

3"-6" gravel or special
drainage fabric

perforated clay pipe (full or 1/2 round)
from 3 corners to drain

Rooftop tree pit.

Water Supply

The amount of water necessary to sustain a tree on a rooftop will vary with the variety and size of the tree, as well as the state of its root system.

Other variable factors also determine the necessary quantity of water and frequency of watering. For example, in a raised box considerable amounts of water will be evaporated because of the drying action of the sun on the sides of the box. This is not the case when the planting is flush with the roof surface.

Therefore, the proper quantity of water for each tree can be determined only by close observation by those entrusted with maintenance, observing the tree daily, monitoring such factors as feel of leaf, coloring, and other indications of its state of health.

Automatic devices that water all trees in a planting without regard for differences in individual requirements are dangerous. Trees, like human beings, vary in the amount they can drink and still remain happy. Underground saturating devices can also cause trouble since they tend to make the task of watering too simple, thereby engendering carelessness on the part of those charged with maintenance. Watering below the surface also makes it difficult to perceive an overwatered condition without testing the soil by means of an augur (a probing device) that, if used frequently, can cause injury to the root system. When watering is administered on the surface, standing water that cannot be absorbed is immediately visible and serves as a warning. Manual watering is thus the safest method of transporting moisture to rooftop plantings.

Feeding

Since the quantity of food required and formula preferred vary greatly among different tree species, no blanket recommendation can be made concerning the feeding of trees planted on rooftops, but it is important to understand clearly the need of at least an annual application of plant food (a liquid mix is the most convenient and most readily absorbed). Under normal conditions, soil is constantly being enriched by the decomposition of plant matter and animal and insect life. In the case of rooftop planting, however, existing nutrients in the soil are rapidly depleted and must be replaced artificially. The individual requirements of specific trees should determine the frequency of feeding. The poor color and undersized leaves will quickly show the need for additional feedings.

Antidesiccants

Because plantings on rooftops are usually more exposed to high winds than street-level plantings and because of the intense reflection of the sun's rays from the paved areas of the roof, trees so used can profit from the application of an antidesiccant spray, usually containing a latex base, that slows down the transpiration process, thus reducing the danger of dehydration. Again, the frequency of application depends on the special conditions prevailing in a specific location. As a general practice of preventive care, at least three applications during a year are recommended: one in the late spring as soon as leaves are fully formed, another application to the bare branches after leaves have fallen in the autumn, and once again on a warm day in February. (Latex sprays cannot be effectively applied in temperatures below 40 degrees.)

Further Precautions

Some further technical matters that must considered in rooftop plantings are the following: means of guying; the weight factor as it affects structure; the raised vs. flush tree pit; and finally, selection of the proper tree species.

Large Weeping Cherry being installed on the rooftop of shopping center, Long Island. (Zion & Breen Associates, Landscape Architects and Site Planners.)

Guying is essential to the survival of any newly planted tree, as has been explained in Chapter 4. However, greater exposure to high winds and other rooftop conditions present special problems in guying.

Guying at ground level in unexcavated earth can be done simply with stakes or deadmen, but in a freshly filled rooftop pit, the earth offers no resistance. Hence, it is advisable to incorporate eye-bolts in the walls of the planting box, sufficiently below the surface so that wire can be attached to the tree at one-third of its height at an angle of 45 degrees. Wire must be attached to these eye-bolts before soil has been introduced into the pit.

The importance of the *weight factor* in relation to the roof structure is self-evident. For determining the feasibility of rooftop planting, the weight of the tree can be computed at the rate of 75–100 pounds per inch of caliber.

To determine the weight of an earth ball for tree sizes likely to be considered for such plantings, consult the tables on page 124.

In a rooftop planting, it is advisable to lighten the weight of the soil by admixing lightweight water-retaining elements such as perlite, vermiculite, or peat moss. An acceptable mixture would be 25% topsoil, 25% peat moss, and 50% sand.

The design of the tree pit, whether it is to be *raised* or *flush,* is almost entirely a matter of aesthetics beyond the consideration, already mentioned, that the raised box evaporates more moisture because its side surfaces are exposed and the root system is subject to greater frost damage for the same reason.

In the author's opinion, the raised box or free-standing tub can, if used sparingly, prove effective even though the overuse of this style in large projects has

The raised planting box should be used with caution since its side surfaces expose roots to the heat of the sun and frost damage.

reduced it to a tiresome cliché. In many projects, either sufficient depth for flush planting cannot be obtained or the cost is greater than the owner wishes to undertake. In such cases, the use of raised plant containers may be indicated, but caution is suggested.

The selection of the proper species for use in raised tubs, where they cannot be avoided, is important to the visual success of the design. The eye finds it unsettling to see a tall, wide-spreading tree emerging from a raised container. Such species should be used on rooftops only if they can be planted flush with the floor, simulating natural conditions. Smaller short-stemmed flowering trees such as the Crab Apple and Magnolia are more appropriate for use in raised tubs.

A pleasing alternative to the raised plant tubs on rooftops where it is impossible to obtain planting depth below the roof slab is the gentle mounding or sloping of the soil to a height of 3½ or 4 feet. If the roof area is adequate and such mounding is limited, the effect is more agreeable to the eye, and the weight load is considerably reduced by the elimination of heavy concrete pots (see the photo on opposite page).

In selecting the proper trees for rooftop plantings, such considerations as exposure to sun and wind, extremes of temperature, sun reflection, atmospheric pollution, susceptibility to disease, and special maintenance requirements must all be taken into account. Overlooking any one of these factors will surely cause problems. Replacement of trees on a rooftop can be difficult and costly after a building is in operation. For this reason, too, special care should be taken to see that the digging and planting have been expertly done.

Most Suitable Trees

A list of trees most suitable for use in rooftop plantings follows (those marked with an asterisk are included in the "Tree Portraits" section of this book):

Trees for roof plantings protected from wind

*Birch, Gray (*Betula populifolia*)
*Golden Rain Tree (*Koelreuteria paniculata*)
Maple, Amur (*Acer ginnala*)

Rooftop plantings flush with the floor are visually and horticulturally more satisfactory. Note ventilator to truck tunnel in lower left and guy wires anchored to sides of pit. (Zion & Breen Associates, Landscape Architects and Site Planners.)

*Pagoda Tree (*Sophora japonica*)
  Pine, Scotch (*Pinus sylvestris*)
*Serviceberry, Downy (*Amelanchier canadensis*)
  Willow, Laurel (*Salix pentandra*)

Trees for roof plantings with little protection from wind

*Crab Apple (*Malus floribunda*)
  Elaeagnus, Autumn (*Elaeagnus umbellata*)
*Golden Rain Tree (*Koelreuteria paniculata*)

*Hawthorn, English (*Crataegus oxyacantha*)
*Honey-Locust (*Gleditsia triacanthos*)
  Hornbeam, Columnar European (*Carpinus betulus fatigiata*)
  Olive, Russia (*Elaeagnus angustifolia*)
  Pea Tree, Siberian (*Caragana arborescens*)
  Pine, Bristle Cone (*Pinus aristata*)
  Pine, Blue Japanese White (*Pinus parviflora glauca*)
  Pine, Waterer Scotch (*Pinus sylvestris watereri*)

Planting on a garage roof. A pleasing alternative to individual tree tubs on rooftops where planting depth below the roof slab is not available. (Zion & Breen Associates, Landscape Architects and Site Planners.)

7

SPECIAL EFFECTS

Triple U shape.

Espalier

Espalier is the name given to a process of training a tree to grow in a flat plane, expanding only in two dimensions, width and height, with no breadth. This practice originated in early Rome where plantings were often restricted to interior courtyards. It flourished again in medieval times when personal safety demanded that most gardening be done within castle walls. The espaliered tree has again become useful in contemporary landscape architecture with the revival of the interior court and extensive use of walls as a means of effecting privacy.

The process of training the espaliered tree usually requires from 5–6 years. Although many amateur gardeners have been successful in this work, there are several large-scale suppliers from whom trees can now be obtained with little difficulty. Cost will vary naturally with the size of the tree and intricacy of the form.

The design use of the espaliered tree need not be confined to the embellishment of walls. Free-standing, they can be used as fences, or low barriers, or background screening; in tubs they become sculpture. Espaliered fruit trees have the decided advantage of producing sizable fruit harvests within limited space, and simplifying the chores of spraying and picking fruit. Usually, they are grafted on a dwarfing root stock, which causes an early maturing and fruiting on very young plants.

Those trees that lend themselves most readily to espalier are the Apple, Pear, Southern Magnolia, and Cherry. The Saucer Magnolia, Sourwood, Flowering Plum, and Tamarisk can also be trained in this manner.

The espalier tree can generally be placed against a wall in any location, although, in order to fruit, walls facing south, southeast, and southwest must be used so the tree is provided with at least 5 hours of sun each day. The use of a wall facing south will provide an early ripening fruit and also permit the use of trees that are normally not hardy in the area. (A large Southern Magnolia has been growing for many years against the south wall of a house in Brooklyn. A photograph of it is shown in the Southern Magnolia data section.)

Horizontal T.

Palmette verrier.

U shape.

Belgian fence.

Palmette oblique.

Pleached arbor, Colonial Williamsburg, Virginia.

Espaliers should be planted from 10–12 inches in front of a wall and are usually tied to the wall by horizontal wires (#10 gauge, copper) placed at 12–18-inch intervals and stretched between lagscrews set into the wall. Often, additional support will be provided by lath strips that follow the positions of the arms of the tree. All major shoots are attached to the lath or wire with raffia.

The geometric forms most often found in espalier trees are those illustrated. Pears and Apples lend themselves readily to the cordon and Belgian fence; Peaches, Apricots, and Cherries are best trained as fans. Other trees will usually train best to an informal design.

Other Special Effects

Pleaching

A method of training adjacent trees to interlace so as to create walls or canopies. Shown is a pleached arbor at Colonial Williamsburg, Virginia.

Pollarding

Shaping trees by rigorous pruning to serve design purposes, practical or whimsical. (See below.)

Plane Trees pollarded to enclose a garden pool.

DESIGNING WITH TREES

There are no hard and fast rules of design in any medium—merely a personal approach that, if valid and combined with a mastery of technical aspects, can lead to good design. Presented here is a series of observations comprising the author's personal approach to the use of trees in the landscape design.

The Tree in Design

Landscape architecture is the forming and interrelating of countless compositions in space intended to be walked through, run through, driven through, played in, sat in, and freely used in general. These spaces are enriched by the landscape architect from a palette of design elements, of which the tree is only one, although certainly the most interesting.

Trees can be considered essential to a design, rather than an embellishment, only when they are massed to form the wall of a space. This architectonic use of trees was characteristic of the gardens of Le Notre and his followers in eighteenth century France, where trees were pleached and pollarded to form walls and canopies of green for vast outdoor rooms. (See the pollarded Plane Trees on page 151.)

Skills of the Landscape Architect

Following is a list of the basic skills of those who design outdoor spaces.

A thorough knowledge of arboriculture is an absolute essential to the successful use of trees in landscape design—about this

there can be no compromise. Such knowledge must extend far beyond the identification of genus or species, or familiarity with sources of supply; it must be a knowledge based on experience with every aspect of the tree: its growth habit, soil preference, reaction to transplanting and pruning; its hardiness to climatic extremes, resistance against or susceptibility to diseases or fungi or insect pests; its moisture requirements; its life expectancy; sunlight or shade requirements; tolerance of salt spray; sensitivity to carbon monoxide, or other hazards, natural or of man's making; and finally, a knowledge of the "company it keeps," more technically termed ecology—those plants with which it is at home in nature, which have similar preferences of cultivation, and with which it looks most natural.

Knowledge of the medium in which one works is clearly essential to success in any field. In landscape architecture, it is not a simple matter acquired automatically with a college degree; it can be gained only by working with trees, by having planted and transplanted and cultivated them, by constantly observing them, and mentally recording observations of their reactions. Only with such knowledge can trees be used properly in landscape design. Some nursery experience would provide excellent background for a career in landscape architecture.

A sensual imagination, the ability to project one's self into a design and to understand how it "feels" to walk this way or that in a space which exists at first only on paper. This is perhaps the most important attribute of a creative landscape architect.

A skillful designer must also have *a highly developed visual imagination,* an ability to see each tree in its maturity, to see its changing colors in each season and its changing form over the years. Among designers today, there seems to be an emphasis of the visual over the sensual, and it is in this aspect that the designs of different landscape architects differ most radically. It is the author's opinion that, although the visual aspect must be pleasing, no landscape can claim true success if it is not refreshing to be *in*. This quality of design has become increasingly important today. With the rapid disappearance of open space, it is extravagant merely to create pretty pictures. Outdoor space must perform an important function, especially in our cities. It must refresh the soul.

The author's particular, and perhaps peculiar, approach to design consists of "role playing" in which the designer, in his imagination, plays the part of the users of the place he is designing. For a university campus, he is a parent accompanying a child on a first visit, he is the student himself, he is a professor considering joining the faculty, or a resident of the town in which the school is located. In all these roles, both visual and sensual imagination play a major part in determining what should be included in the place in order to appeal to all those who will be using it. In the design of Paley Park, the first "vest pocket" park in New York City, the author first determined the urgent need for outdoor recreational space for those who spend a large portion of their day in the busiest sections of our cities. Then by playing the role of the executive on his way to work, the office worker on his lunch break, the shopper seeking an opportunity to rest, etc., he determined that to appeal to these divergent personalities, this park would include falling water to drown the unpleasant noises of the city, a grove of closely planted Honey-Locusts to provide a leafy ceiling to the space, movable chairs and tables offering a choice of orientation in sharp contrast to the regimentation of most urban amenities, and vine-covered walls, forming a vertical lawn. Finally, it was the author's observation that unlike Europeans, most Americans experience a feeling of uneasiness, perhaps guilt, when sitting idle during "working hours." In anticipation of this reaction, a shop dispersing light food and drink was included in the design to give a "purpose" to idleness.

Constant But Predictable Change

Trees change constantly in shape, color, and size, but they are not mercurial. All changes can be anticipated by the designer who knows and understands trees. The fall foliage color of each variety is predictable and varies only in intensity from year to year. General conformation varies only in minor degree among different specimens of the same variety. Only a design that anticipates these changes of color and form and capitalizes on them can be truly successful, for such a design elicits the maximum contribution from each tree.

Four-Dimensional Design

This element of change means that for the landscape architect, a design is not completed when his plans have been executed. The completion of a planting is only the beginning of a process in which time in combination with the natural phenomenon of growth carries the design forward. A capable designer will anticipate the rate and ultimate growth to be expected of the trees he has used in his design, and thereby ensures proper spacing in maturity in relation to buildings and to each other. Designers unfamiliar with trees ignore future development, considering only the immediate effect. Their designs have often been acclaimed and photographed by admirers, who return after an interval to see a space disintegrate because trees have been used much like a two-dimensional building material instead of living, growing objects that must be considered in time as well as space.

Appropriate Design

Since landscape architectural design is often created in relation to buildings, it must relate itself closely in quality to the surrounding architecture. It must be *appropriate*: appropriate in choice of plant materials and degree of enrichment, appropriate in color and vitality to the buildings of which it is a part, and appropriate to the use for which it has been designed. The word appropriate is used here much as the word contextural is used by architects to describe the quality of a building that fits comfortably with its neighbors.

Perhaps appropriate design is the landscape architect's greatest challenge, for in accomplishing this, he must often restrain his efforts to the level of the created architecture and the general environment. A landscape development that by its very excellence calls attention to itself can never be an integral part of a composition and cannot therefore be considered successful. Appropriateness can be attained only by a thorough and perceptive study of the architecture that enframes the space, the materials used, the uses to which the structure and spaces are to be put, the people who will be using the space, the design and materials used in neighboring projects in the area, and similar related items.

The concept of appropriateness of design applies also to the selection of tree species. Trees used in a design should be consistent with those existing on the site and in neighboring plantings. Beautiful and wondrous as trees are, they can often be inappropriate in shape, size, or intensity of color for a specific use. Properly selected and placed, they can augment the visual and sensual aspects of a space; inappropriately used, they can destroy the space itself.

Dominant Tree

To insure unity in a planting design, it is wise to select one tree species to be used in greater quantity than any other and to be placed in all principal spaces. Such a dominant tree will, by the repetition of its form, color, and texture, lend unity to the design.

Similar emphasis by repetition of smaller trees, particularly flowering species, is especially useful in effecting recall from one area to another.

Mass Planting

Boldness in designing with trees, as with other forms of design, can seldom fail. When space permits it, the clustering or mass planting of groups of the same variety is one of the most effective uses of trees in landscape design. This is especially true in the use of flowering trees.

Limited Plant List

As in architecture, a restful elegance can be achieved in planting by the simplicity of detail and material. The use of only a few tree species and varieties closely related in texture, form, and color will lend this quality to a design. Such restraint in the use of trees is especially important in close proximity to buildings to avoid distracting from the architecture.

Architectonic Trees

Certain species have a regularity and compactness of form that is retained without pruning. This quality makes such trees useful for formal or geometric spacing, as in an avenue or grove where all trees must be matched. For architectonic plantings of this kind, it is inconsistent to use a tree such as the common Honey-Locust with its lacy foliage and characteristically nonconforming open crown, or the Ginkgo with its irregular, jagged outline. Such plantings call for a density of foliage and branching in order to present a strongly outlined silhouette in winter as well as summer: The Little-leaf Linden is such a tree.

Evergreen Skeleton

A planting design that disintegrates in winter when the defoliation of deciduous trees takes place is a weak design. Evergreens, properly used, can provide a skeleton that gives year-round structure to outdoor space, contributing color and contrast as well. Evergreen trees are also useful in providing recall from one area to another.

Color

Color in the landscape must be massed to be effective. The use of single trees of colorful foliage or blossom creates a restless scene; groups of trees (three or more) of similar color are more effective. Colorful trees also aid in providing recall. A word of caution, however, against too great a variety of unrelated colors and the use of colors that conflict with architecture.

Specimen Tree

The isolated specimen, a tree of unusual size, shape, color, or texture, is an excellent device to emphasize a point in the spatial composition or draw the eye toward or away from some aspect of the architecture. The specimen tree placed in a space of proper proportions should be used as one would use sculpture.

"Dirty" Trees

Every client has some private tree prejudice; there is always some tree considered "dirty." This concept remains an anomaly to the author, for most trees drop their leaves, all flowering trees lose their blossoms, and many trees shed their bark. But these all have the compensating advantages of seasonal change, handsome trunks, etc. It is true that most fast-growing trees have brittle wood that is often broken in storms, littering the ground, but these trees also have the distinct advantage of rapid growth and immediate effect at less cost than other varieties.

Native Trees

It is always wise to plant species native to the site if they fulfill adequately the design requirements, for they have already proved themselves hardy in the soil and climatic conditions of the area. This will mean fewer maintenance problems in terms of winter protection, summer watering, soil enrichment, and other care.

Whenever possible, trees should also be purchased from local sources, since plants introduced from great distances must struggle with the problem of adjustment to climatic differences in addition to the shock of transplanting.

Immediate Effect

Immediate effect is the term given to a planting that, because of the size of the tree used, presents a mature appearance from the outset. Under most circumstances, planting an entire residential project for immediate effect is an error, for the owner then has nothing to look forward to. Even those who are most in a hurry should be given the pleasure of watching some trees mature. In commercial projects, however, where the planting assumes a certain advertising value, immediate effect is often an appropriate approach. And even under the most stringent budgetary limitations, it is always desirable to use a few trees of 4-inch caliber or more at important locations in the design to relieve the "new look" of a project.

Planting for the Future

Planting for the future is seldom done in this country. We have lost the patience necessary to watch small trees mature. For this reason, some of our most handsome but slow-growing species are neglected, yet the Beech groves that we find so enchanting in England today would not exist if this attitude had prevailed there 75 years ago.

College campuses and certainly public buildings with a long life expectancy should be planted with long-lived varieties such as the Beech and White Oak that are very slow to mature. These can be used in combination with faster-growing varieties to provide some immediate effect.

Tree Ecology

The designer is wise to respect certain ecological relationships among trees. Trees associated in nature have a more comfortable appearance when used together; they are usually complementary in color and texture, and have similar cultivation requirements. When they are used together, maintenance is obviously simpler than when trees with different moisture and soil requirements are grouped.

Minimum Maintenance

A planting design that needs, for its continued good appearance, more care than it is likely to receive is a bad design. The choice of trees requiring special pruning, spraying, or watering care should be avoided at all costs unless adequate maintenance is assured or a special design effect is desired that cannot be equaled by any other tree. The data relating to trees shown in the "Tree Portraits" section of this book include special care requirements.

Composing with Trees

Since trees do not have standardization of shape or size as do architectural materials, the planting plan is not the end of the landscape architect's contribution, but rather a starting point for composing with actual trees when they have been delivered to the site. It is inconceivable that any but the most static design can be executed directly from a planting plan without the personal supervision of the designer in the final placement of major trees. The author's own approach to the implementation of the planting plan is as follows:

(1) All trees are inspected in the nursery prior to digging.

(2) Self-locking seals bearing the designer's imprint, as well as a number, are placed on all trees. The numbers of individual trees are then recorded on the plan so that these trees will be delivered to the proper area of the project.

If one side of the tree has a more interesting branch structure, this is noted in some distinctive manner to expedite the proper positioning when the tree arrives at the site. At the same time, the north side of the tree should be indicated by a ribbon or small spot of paint on the trunk. It is felt by many arborists that changing the orientation of the tree creates an additional trauma to the many that are faced by the transplanted tree.

Other considerations being equal, it is wise to maintain this orientation, If, however, the conformation of the tree makes it desirable in terms of the landscape composition to deviate from the original orientation, it is probably a risk worth taking. Often, some measures can be taken to ameliorate the shock to the tree, such as an application of an antidesiccant, a more sturdy wrapping of the trunk, etc.

(3) While the trees are being dug in the nursery, the planting contractor is requested to place stakes on the site for each tree as shown on the drawing. When the trees are delivered to the site, they are placed at these positions and untied in order to show their branch structure. (The branches of larger trees are tightly bound to facilitate transportation.)

Common Name	Latin Name	Bark
*Beech	*Fagus*	Smooth blue-gray with black markings (usually scares of former branches).
*Birch (many varieties)	*Betula*	Varying degrees of white. Paper Birch (*papyrifera*) the most striking.
*Amur Cork	*Phellodendron amurense*	Corklike, deeply ridged. Handsome in maturity only.
*Kousa Dogwood	*Cornus kousa*	Exfoliating. Reveals underbark in tones of reddish brown and gray.
Chinese Elm (Lace-bark Elm)	*Ulmus parvifolia*	Highly attractive; exfoliation reveals underbark in shades of gray, green, and brown.
American Hornbeam	*Carpinus caroliniana*	Gray, sinewy, musclelike.
*Black Locust	*Robinia pseudoacacia*	Deeply fissured, long narrow plates. Almost gothic in appearance.
*Saucer Magnolia	*Magnolia soulangeana*	Smooth gray, much like Beech.
Paperbark Maple	*Acer griseum*	Exfoliating bark revealing red-brown underbark. Very handsome.
Persian Parrotia	*Parrotia persica*	Exfoliating. Reveals underbark in shades of green, gray, and brown.
Lace-bark Pine	*Pinus burgeana*	Exfoliating. Reveals underbark in shades of white and brown.
*Plane Tree	*Platanus*	Exfoliating. Reveals underbark in shades of gray, cream, white, and green.
*Serviceberry (varieties)	*Amelanchier*	Smooth gray with reddish tone. Finely fissured.
American Yellow-wood	*Cladrastis lutea*	Smooth gray, much like Beech.

*An asterisk indicates that a photo of this species appears in this volume.

At this point, the patience of both the contractor and landscape architect are put to the test, for a thorough designer must circulate through the space, viewing the trees from every possible angle, studying their relationships to the architecture as well as each other, making certain that architectural details are not concealed, and that strong points of the building are emphasized and weak points camouflaged. The placement of trees must be studied further from many other points of view: the pedestrian's progression through the space from light to shade, the play of shadow on the ground and building masses, future growth, etc. The landscape composition has no top or bottom or right side or wrong; it must work from every possible approach. Such study requires much time and endless patience. It often involves moving and turning each tree several times.

In order to make such composing on the site possible, all the specimen trees must be available at one time. This should represent no hardship for the contractor since it is merely a matter of scheduling. To be forced to compose around missing trees is much like attempting to paint with important pigments missing from the palette.

Tree Trunk in Design

Many designers see beauty only in the solitary tree branched to the ground and with full crown. They overlook the possibility of composing with the dark, textured verticals of tree trunks. The photographs here illustrate the potential of featuring the beauty of trunks.

Tree trunks: An important vertical and textured element of design.

Tree Bark in Design

Selecting trees for their beauty or interest is usually made on the basis of form, color of foliage, or blossom. Often overlooked are the texture, pattern, and color of the bark.

Most of us have come to admire the bark of the Birch from childhood, associating it with Indian canoes and notes written on its pure white surface. However, the beauty and fascination of tree bark are much more varied than is realized.

The limitless color and texture of bark. (Donald Richardson.)

The plaited bark of a Scotch Pine.

In selecting a specimen tree for any project, the color, texture, and marking of the bark should rank high among the criteria used. Any list of trees possessing interesting bark should include the species listed in the table here.

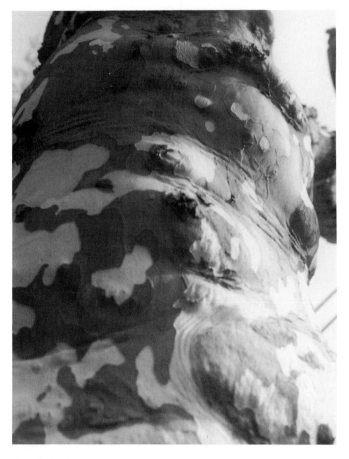

Beech bark.

"Gothic" ridging of Black Locust bark.

Tree Roots in Design

Surface-rooting trees are often avoided because grass cannot be grown with any success within their spread. What is visually overlooked is the beauty inherent in the intricate patterns created on the ground by the roots themselves.

These patterns are most frequently created by the erosion of the soil (usually sand) in the vicinity of the trunk, but they can be induced by planting the tree slightly higher than the existing grade and washing away the surface soil after the tree has taken hold.

Tree roots exposed for their beauty, Kyoto, Japan. (Donald Richardson.)

Short-Lived Species

Short-lived, fast-growing trees are usually shunned by designers, but they can be very useful in implementing a landscape design where an immediate effect is desired when sizable specimens of the tree of choice are unavailable or too costly. In such an instance, it is possible to attain a desired effect more rapidly by selecting a fast-growing although short-lived species of similar conformation to be alternated with the tree of choice. For example, if an allée of columnar trees is desired, the fastigiate variety of the English Oak★ (*Quercus robur fastigiata*) would be an excellent choice. If, however, large specimens of this species are not available, a mature affect can be attained rapidly by alternating small specimens of English Oak with the fast-growing Lombardy Poplar★ that possesses the same fastigiate form, but lives for only 15–20 years in most areas of this country. A 10-foot high

★See photos on pages 52 and 53, 64 and 65.

Lombardy Poplar can reach a height of 20 feet in 3–4 years' time and will have reached 40 or 50 feet when it begins to decline. By this time, the English Oak on either side of the Poplars will have attained stature and begin to fill in the space vacated by their "deceased" neighbors.

"Trees in Waiting" (The Successor Tree)

Many property owners, in anticipation of the eventual demise of an old and favorite tree in decline, insist on planting a young specimen of the same species beside it in

TREES OF OUTSTANDING BLOSSOM DISPLAY

Common Name	Latin Name	Period of Bloom
*Cherry (many varieties)	*Prunus*	Late April, May. White, pink, single and double flowers.
*Flowering Crab Apple (many varieties)	*Malus*	May. White, pink, red, crimson; single and double flowering varieties.
*Flowering Dogwood	*Cornus florida*	April. White and pink.
Kousa Dogwood	*Cornus kousa*	June. White, creamy white.
Dove Tree	*Davidia involucrata*	June. White, creamy white.
Korean Evodia	*Evodia danielli*	June, July. White.
Franklin Tree	*Franklinia alatamaha*	August. White.
*Golden Chain	*Laburnum*	May. Yellow.
*Golden Rain or Varnish Tree	*Koelreuteria paniculata*	July. Yellow.
*Hawthorn (many varieties)	*Crataegus*	May. White, red.
Common Horse-Chestnut	*Aesculus hippocastanum*	May. Pink, white, red.
Japanese Lilac	*Syringa reticulata japonica*	June. White.
*Magnolia (many varieties)		White, pink, purple.
Callery Pear	*Pyrus calleryana*	April. White.
Eastern Redbud	*Cercis canadensis*	April. Purple, white.
*Scholar Tree, Japanese Pagoda Tree	*Sophora japonica* (var. regent)	July, August. Creamy white.
Carolina Silverbell	*Halesia carolina*	April, May. White, pink.
Japanese Snowbell	*Styrax japonicus*	White.
*Sourwood, Sorrel Tree	*Oxydendron arboreum*	June. White.
Korean Stewartia	*Stewartia koreana*	July. White.
American Yellow-wood	*Cladrastis lutea*	May. White.

*An asterisk indicates that a color photo of this species appears in this volume.

an effort to have an immediate successor ready to perpetuate the landscape design when the old tree succumbs.

Such a practice detracts from the majesty of the large specimen, clutters the landscape, and, in the author's opinion, is mildly macabre. Placing such "successors" in a less visible portion of the property, establishing perhaps an on-site nursery of a few young trees in waiting, would be a far better solution and permit the faithful old patriarch—or matriarch if it is a female of the species—to die with dignity.

Monoculture

A large-scale planting of a single species can sometimes place a landscape design in jeopardy. In a single year, 1906, the American Chestnut, perhaps our most handsome native tree, was completely wiped out by what is now known as the Chestnut blight (*Endotheia parasitica*). The city of New Haven, whose world-famous tree-lined streets and beautiful campus of Yale University earned it the appellation "Elm City," lost its visual identity in a few short years after Dutch Elm disease developed in this country.

Such sad lessons should always be kept in mind, but "monoculture" should not be used as a bugaboo to rob a smaller landscape design of the unity and strength inherent in multiple plantings of a single species or variety. Moderation is wise, but some risk—on a small scale—should be taken if the design effect is worthy.

Progression of Bloom

Color of blossom is not the only aspect to be considered in the selection of flowering trees for use in landscape design. Time is also an important factor since species differ widely in their period of bloom, varying only slightly from year to year as the weather varies from the norm.

The most effective use of flowering trees takes into consideration this time factor to effect an intriguing progression of bloom throughout each season. One of the author's favorite groupings of plants is based on the period of bloom of three plants: the Flowering Dogwood (Cornus florida), the Kousa Dogwood (Cornus kousa), and *Viburnum tomentosum mariesi,* a handsome shrub with flowers resembling the Dogwood blossom. Massed together in the landscape, they provide more than 2 consecutive months of similar blossom. The Flowering Dogwood blooms for 3 weeks in mid–May and is followed with slight overlapping by the Viburnum for 2 weeks, which is then followed into early July by the Kousa Dogwood.

For the designer, we list in the accompanying table some of the most useful flowering trees with an indication of their period of bloom, as well as the color of their blossoms.

Fallen Leaves

No one who has ever walked on a carpet of amber leaves beneath a grove of giant Beech or admired a pool of crimson leaves on the intensely green grass of early September—the fallen leaves of the Japanese Maple—can ever forget the beauty of the scene. The photographs on page 82 are intended to recall the moment for those who have been so inspired and to introduce the beauty of fallen leaves to those who think only of the chore of carting them away.

Advertising with Trees

In recent years, as corporate headquarters and commercial establishments have sought more rural sites, landscape architects have been called on not only to create pleasing settings in which to work, but also have more frequently been requested to provide high visibility from major roadways. Most useful in this regard are evergreen and flowering trees which, when planted in large numbers and boldly massed, serve as striking advertisements along major highways. The photographs on the opposite page illustrate this potential in an installation created for the General Foods Corporation beside the New Jersey Turnpike. This simple planting of 80 Bradford Callery Pears stretching over a quarter of a mile has been designed to be appreciated by motorists traveling at high speed during all seasons. The spring blossoms shown here are followed in summer by a dense, lustrous green foliage, a deep wine color in the fall, and a round densely branched mass in winter. It is not possible to pass the planting without admiring it and, in the case of those seeing it for the first time, taking note of the corporation it "represents."

The Tree Palette

The landscape designer's tree palette is a broad one, varying widely from area to area. However, the general attributes that dictate the choice of one species or variety over another should be kept clearly in mind when the design is being conceived. Basically, the palette can be outlined as follows.

Size attained by tree in maturity

Small: under 25 feet
Medium: 30 feet
Large: 40 feet and over

Form of mature tree

Fastigiate: Extremely narrow, tapering to a point (Lombardy Poplar)
Columnar: Very narrow, but not possessing a pointed tip (Sentry Maple)
Spreading: (Sugar Maple)
Open-headed: Loose branch structure, indistinct silhouette (Silk Tree)
Rounded-top: A distinctly rounded profile (White Oak)
Pyramidal: Almost conical outline (Little-Leaf Linden)
Weeping: Pendulous branches (Weeping Willow)

Texture

Coarse: Large leaves, heavy branches (Horse-Chestnut)
Medium: Less opaque and strong in outline (American Elm)
Fine: A feathery appearance, providing light shade (Honey-Locust)

Rate of growth

Slow: Under 1 foot per year under ideal conditions of growth (European Beech)
Medium: 1–2 feet per year (Maples)
Fast: 2 or more feet per year (Lombardy Poplar)

Blossom

Color
Period of bloom

Fruit

Color
Size and profusion

A quarter-mile massing of Bradford Callery Pears along the New Jersey Turnpike: A subtle advertisement of the General Foods Corporation.

Fall foliage

Color

Bark

Special interest

This chapter has been offered not as a definitive guide to the use of trees in the design of outdoor space, but as an outline of the

Fastigiate.

Columnar.

Spreading.

Open-headed.

Rounded-top.

Pyramidal.

Weeping.

Form of mature trees.

author's personal approach to using trees. If one general or all-inclusive counsel is to be set down here for the layman, it is this: It is essential to keep the tree in its proper perspective. It is not the essence of landscape architecture and should be regarded more as an embellishment—as furniture with which an outdoor room can be enhanced. Without denying the beauty and fascination of the tree in the landscape, the layman should be cautioned against confusing the tree with the design itself.

An Unusual Planting Experience

Working in Moscow in 1959, as landscape architect of the American Exhibition, was a challenging and educational experience. Many of the principals of design first learned at the Harvard Graduate School of Design were dramatically emblazoned on my mind for all time!

Site Unseen

In February of 1959, very early in my career, I received from the U.S. State Department, our client, a topographical map annotated in Russian with symbols for trees scattered across the page in what later proved to be a romantic but highly inaccurate pattern. I was told to present a site plan within 2 weeks' time. The map held no indications of tree spacing, caliber, height, or spread. Not very different, really, from the types of plans we are often given by clients in this country except that the contour interval was expressed in meters rather than feet—nothing indicated of conditions on the neighboring properties, no mention of wind direction or velocity—in short, nothing provided that could assist the designer in experiencing the quality of the site, what the eighteenth century landscape architects termed the "genius of the place."

True, topographical maps and site plans that include contour dimensions convey a suggestion of land form, but what lines on paper can begin to convey the "feeling" of a rolling or rugged landscape? And those small circular indications bearing Latin names: How can they begin to suggest the branch structure of an Oak or the full form of a Willow? And certainly no printed plan can convey the coolness of a Birch grove or the smell of moist soil. However, these are all vital aspects of a site and must be considered in the total design. Infinite manipulations of T-square and triangle are no substitute for a full familiarity with the site acquired *first-hand.*

We were forced in New York to present a landscape concept for the American Exhibit in Moscow based on a vague and inaccurate document. The inevitable result, of course, was a design that was inappropriate in every way and had to be totally revised when we reached Russia. My first Russian lesson: *Never, ever* commence a site plan without having studied the site thoroughly *in person* and

on foot. It is my fervent hope that readers of this book, whether designers or owners, will make a similarly firm resolve to demand of the landscape architect or site planner a thorough knowledge of the site garnered from personal observation. Never a site unseen!

Trees from a Deep Freeze

The Soviet system of transplanting trees was extremely efficient and thorough under what would in this country be considered uneconomical planting conditions. Because of a 4-foot-deep frost, the trees were dug by pneumatic drill with a rectangular earth mass (see photo). The location to which the tree was to be transplanted was first attacked by a battering ram dropped from a crane in order to break up the frozen soil, and then finished with a pneumatic drill. Next, a fire was built in the pit, which was then covered with an iron lid, and the fire allowed to burn for 24 hours in order to thaw the surrounding soil. Topsoil (prethawed off the site) was then placed in the pit, and the tree, with frozen earth cube attached, was planted. Out of 100 trees there were no losses.

Early in my career, before global warming, I remember observing, in a Long Island nursery, trees already dug but not covered with burlap or tied with twine. They were standing above ground and were being watered for several consecutive days in the middle of a very cold winter. This was an ingenious means of eliminating the time-consuming balling and burlapping procedure, for when the earth ball was frozen solid, the tree could be dragged across rough ground without fear of damage. The earth ball had been transformed literally into an ice cube.

Arborifilia

So great is the Russian love of trees that we were not permitted to destroy a single one; any tree in the way of an exhibit had to be transplanted or the exhibit moved. This presented a great difficulty since one-third of the site was heavily wooded, and there was not enough money in our budget to move more than 35 large trees. The Russians cooperated admirably by transplanting all other trees for us without charge.

This respect for trees was most impressive. Even the smallest sapling was considered worth saving. The Soviets do not use the ball-burlap-platform method of transplanting. Instead, the tree is dug with a rectangular earth mass and boxed in with lumber on the bottom and four sides (see photo). Particularly impressive was the generous size of the earth mass allotted to each tree (even a sapling of 1½-inch caliber was given a 4-foot-square box). The great weight of these large boxes necessitated the use of cranes in the removal of the tree from the pit and in the planting. This also was beneficial to the tree, for with a crane the tree can be gentled into its new location without disturbing the earth around the roots. These procedures influenced us to risk moving collected Birch trees in mid–July to meet the unreal deadline of the arrival of the Vice President of the United States. The use of cranes for any but the largest specimen trees would have been too costly for us capitalists.

Once the tree was in its new location, the Soviet techniques of planting were much the same as our own, although as mentioned, the Soviets were a good deal more generous in the size and depth of the pit and the quantity of topsoil used. Postplanting care would also strike joy in the heart of any landscape architect! Watering trucks arrived promptly every day. Ingenious spraying devices mounted on the front bumpers of tank trucks kept the leaves and earth balls constantly moist. It was a delight to observe.

"My Finger for a Tree"

Yet another example of the Soviet respect for trees evidenced itself in the instance of a large existing Birch tree close to the main pavilion. The Soviets gave a resounding "niet" to the suggestion that it be removed; Victor Michailovitch Abramov, the Chief Engineer, said that he would sooner cut off his finger than destroy that tree (American civil engineers, please note). A hole was cut in the roof (see photo).

Lemon into Lemonade

Finally, what seemed to be an insurmountable problem was the fact that a good portion of the exhibit site con-

A) **A Typical American Woman (according to Russian visitors to the sculpture garden)!** The La Chaise sculpture loaned by the Museum of Modern Art shown at home in New York City also looks out upon a Birch grove, much smaller. (Architect: Philip Johnson.)

B) **American National Exhibition in Moscow.** Sculpture garden. Mounds of grass form pedestals amid rows of existing Birches. (Zion & Breen Associates, Site Planners and Landscape Architects.)

sisted of a large Birch grove, formerly the falconry of the Czar. All these trees were considered sacrosanct—a strange inconsistency when you recall the rude treatment given the last Czar and his lovely family. What to do? After much thought, a solution arrived: Convert the deep rows of closely spaced Birch trees into a sculpture garden, carpet it with local yellow sand, and create platforms of grass for each piece. A dream!

"A Typical American Woman"

Arborial problem solved, we stumbled next on a very strange snag indeed. What we all considered to be the gem of our sculpture exhibit was La Chaise's beefy nude female figure loaned by the Museum of Modern Art of New York City. On the day of the opening, hordes of excited Russians poured out of the main exhibit hall into the sculpture garden. But as they perceived in the distance

this huge naked female, arms akimbo, they stopped short and turned to avoid a confrontation. We had not been informed that the Russians (in those days, at least) found the naked torso shocking.

Within a week, however, there was a sudden and strange reversal. Larger crowds each day—all heading straight for La Chaise. The explanation? Someone had passed the word that this was the portrait of a typical American woman. As the word spread, the crowds grew. Overweight Russian women (and that included most!) came for a laugh. La Chaise became the star of the show. A scenario worthy of Phineas T. Barnum.

E) Soviet womanpower to the rescue. Many of the hand laborers were women. Here holes are being dug for transplanted trees.

C) Green islands were shaped around existing trees *that could not be moved or cut.* Paths of compacted earth were laid through the rows, lined with steel edging, and covered with yellow sand.

D) Frozen earth ball cut by pneumatic drill in February. Author is at left.

F) Rather than move or damage this Birch tree close to a pavilion, the Soviet engineer insisted on piercing the roof.

Trees at Work

Photographs A through P that follow through page 170 are a brief sampling of the author's landscape architectural designs in which trees have been used to accomplish specific goals, which are described in the captions.

A)
Statue of Liberty. A landscape design for Liberty Island for the 1986 Centenary. Three rows of Little-leaf Lindens 15 feet apart wall the new esplanade to create a formal approach.

B)
Paley Park, 53rd Street, New York City. This small outdoor space (40 feet × 100 feet) is roofed by the branching of tightly spaced Honey-Locusts. The ivy-covered walls serve as "vertical lawns" where grass could not survive the heavy use of this popular park.

C)
Chatham Center, Pittsburgh, Pennsylvania. To create a grove of large trees on a rooftop without the use of cumbersome tubs, a raised terrace with angled sides for softness has been created to accommodate the roots of the Pin Oaks.

D)
IBM World Headquarters, New York City. Bamboo, a most satisfactory indoor tree, deliberately planted to lean heavily over the walkways adds softness and grace to counteract the rigidity of the urban scene.

E)
Residence, Aspen, Colorado. A new Aspen forest planted around a large Colorado house relates the building to the surrounding landscape.

F)
Residence, Fisher's Island, New York. Existing Japanese Black Pines have been preserved in this large lawn transformed into a ship's deck overlooking Long Island Sound.

G)
Residence, East Hampton, Long Island. These mature Japanese Black Pines have been included in a large deck or "wooden lawn" to add shade and verticality to a large multileveled terrace.

H)

Residence, Princeton, New Jersey. Dense, naturalesque plantings of Hemlock and Holly surround a circular swimming pool designed to appear as a garden pool as seen from the house.

I)

Kanawha Plaza, Richmond, Virginia. Callery Pears and Southern Magnolias in naturalesque groupings conceal the fact that this park forms a "green" bridge spanning a major highway.

J)

Co-op City, New York City. The largest sandbox in the world! Japanese Black Pine, probably the most salt-tolerant evergreen tree, was used to provide interest in this large area of ocean sand.

K)
Triangle Park, Lexington, Kentucky. A grove of Callery Pears 20 feet apart create a low-ceilinged room of dense shade in pleasant contrast to the bright open areas of water.

L)
Weybosset Hill Public Open Spaces, Providence, Rhode Island. The Little-leaf Linden, an excellent urban tree, shades a seating area and enriches the pavement with the shadow pattern of its leaves.

M)
Princeton University, Firestone Plaza, Princeton, New Jersey. Sculpture raised to provide seating on the library plaza is surrounded by high-branching Sugar Maples for shade.

N)
International Hotel, Kennedy Airport, New York. Lombardy Poplars planted in large circular groves provide mutual protection on this windy site and create a bold effect in all seasons.

O)
State University of New York, Oswego Campus. Not all budgets can produce trees of sufficient size to create a desired effect. *Patience!*

P)
Institute for Advanced Study, Princeton, New Jersey. Courtyard planting. This grove of mature Weeping European Birch, reflected in the glass walls of the courtyard, was intended as a contemporary "grove of academe." The specimens selected, 7–8 inches in caliber, provide an immediate effect.

All photos on pages 165–170 reflect work of Zion & Breen Associates, Landscape Architects and Site Planners.

DESIGN DATA

The following pages contain factual outlines of the major design attributes of each tree shown in the "Tree Portraits" section, together with some related varieties of design interest. This section shows photographs of most trees in sizes readily available in commercial nurseries; additional photographs illustrate unusual characteristics of leaf, bark, structure, etc. Zones of hardiness referred to are based on information supplied by the U.S. Department of Agriculture, as shown on the map that appears on the next two pages.

Deciduous Trees (pages 174–218)

Apple, Common
Baldcypress
Beech (varieties)
Birch (varieties)
*Cherry, Flowering (varieties)
*Chestnut, Horse-
Cork Tree, Amur
*Crab Apple
*Dogwood (varieties)
Elm, American
Ginkgo (Maidenhair Tree)
*Golden Chain Tree (Laburnum)
*Golden Rain Tree (Varnish Tree)
Gum, Sweet
*Hawthorn (varieties)
Katsura Tree
Larch, European
Linden (varieties)
Locust (varieties)

*Magnolia (varieties)
Maple (varieties)
Oak (varieties)
*Pagoda Tree, Japanese (Scholar Tree)
*Pear, Callery (varieties)
*Pear, Common
Plane Tree, London (varieties)
Poplar, Lombardy
Redwood, Dawn
*Serviceberry, Downy
*Sorrel Tree (Sourwood, Tree Andromeda)
Tree of Heaven, Tupelo (Pepperidge, Black Gum, Sour Gum)
Willow, Weeping (varieties)
Yellow-wood, American

Evergreen Trees (pages 218–230)

Acacia, Blackwood
Carob Tree
Cedar, Blue Atlas (varieties)
Cypress (varieties)
Eucalyptus, Longbeak
Fig, Rusty-leaf
Fir, Douglas

Hemlock, Canada (varieties)
Magnolia, Southern
Oak (varieties)
Olive, Common
Pine (varieties)
Redwood, Coast
Spruce, Norway

Trees marked with an asterisk are pictured in color on pages 79–82.

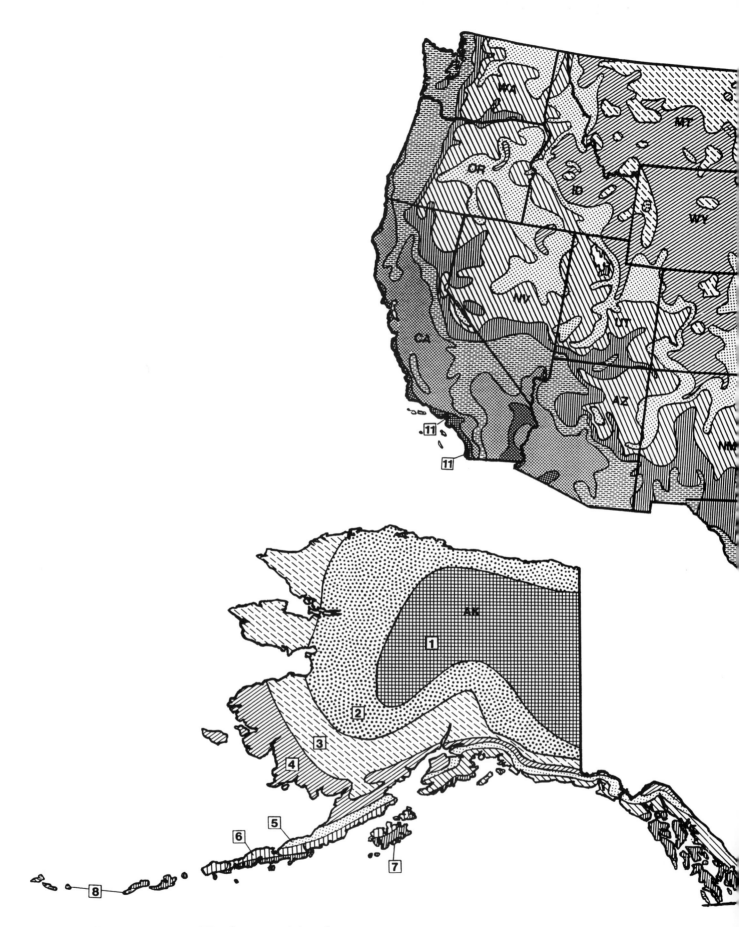

Plant Hardiness Zone Map The above map is based on a
map prepared by the U.S. Agricultural Research Service,
U.S. Department of Agriculture.

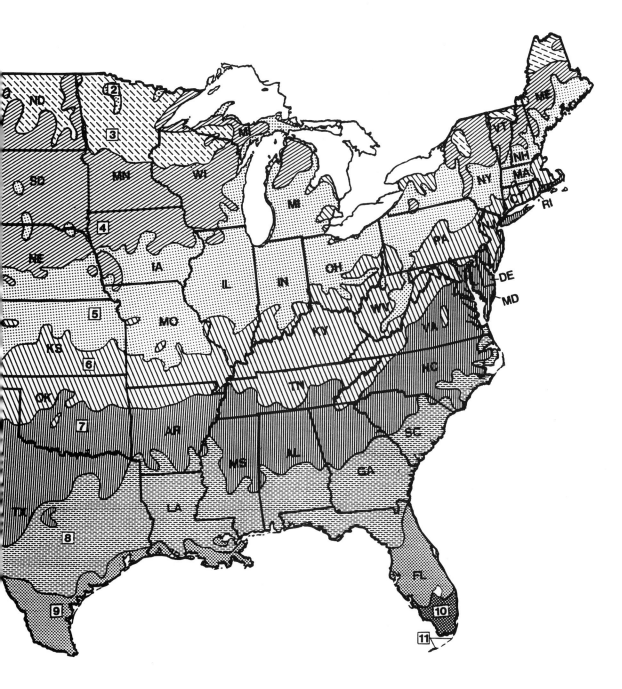

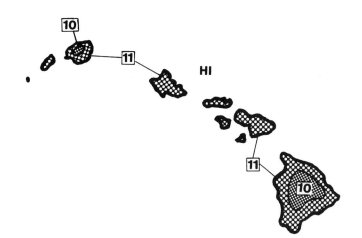

RANGE OF AVERAGE ANNUAL MINIMUM TEMPERATURES FOR EACH ZONE

ZONE 1	BELOW -50° F	
ZONE 2	-50° TO -40°	
ZONE 3	-40° TO -30°	
ZONE 4	-30° TO -20°	
ZONE 5	-20° TO -10°	
ZONE 6	-10° TO 0°	
ZONE 7	0° TO 10°	
ZONE 8	10° TO 20°	
ZONE 9	20° TO 30°	
ZONE 10	30° TO 40°	
ZONE 11	ABOVE 40°	

DECIDUOUS TREES

APPLE, COMMON (*Malus pumila*)

A deciduous tree, generally round in form, with rugged, open branching. By nature and aided by judicious pruning—to which it responds well—the Apple will develop a handsome, sculptural form. This, together with the delicate pink blossom in May and familiar fruit that begins to color in late August, makes the Apple one of the most valuable trees in the designer's palette.

The Apple has much the same sculptural quality as the *Magnolia soulangeana*. Its bark, rugged and dark gray, is not as interesting as the silver-gray Magnolia bark. Its blossom, though considerably smaller and less conspicuous in color, can, in its profusion, however, be equally spectacular. The Apple has the advantage of being hardy considerably farther north than the Magnolia. It has no conspicuous fall color.

Design Use

The Apple can be used as a specimen tree, with branches sweeping the ground, or it can be pruned to serve as a shade tree on lawn or terrace. Its design value can be heightened by periodic thinning of side branches to expose its interesting trunk structure. (See pages 2 and 3.) Placed approximately 20 feet apart, it lends itself well to ordered architectonic plantings, as in an orchard. An excellent tree to line a drive and for planting in proximity to buildings where a small but rugged-looking tree is desired. In some public locations, the ripening fruit may be considered undesirable.

Data

Height: 18–20 feet.
Spread: 20 feet.
Form: Round, open branching, sculptured trunk.
Foliage: Small, leathery leaf.
Texture: Medium.
Blossom: Pink (opening in May) fading to white.
Fruit: Red, yellow, or green (August through September).
Bark: Mottled gray and dark brown.
Fall color: None.
Rate of growth: 1–2 feet per year.

Culture: Sandy loam.
Hardiness zone: 4–8.
Transplanting: Easily moved.
Special maintenance requirements: Pruning for shape, removal of dead wood. Frequent spraying against scale and to obtain edible fruit.
Special characteristics: Fallen apples and attraction of bees considered by some to be a disadvantage. Susceptibility to scale and insect infestation requires constant care.

Desirable Varieties

Cortland Very winter-hardy.

Prima Disease-resistant.

Stayman Winesap Fruit stores well.

Apple Tree nursery specimen: 6–8 feet high, 4-foot spread, 2-inch caliber, 24-inch ball.

BALDCYPRESS (*Taxodium distichum*)

A stately deciduous conifer with fernlike foliage. Thrives in moist, sandy soil. Can reach height of 100 feet in maturity, but generally ranges between 50–75 feet with a spread of 20-30 feet.

Design Use

Its fine-textured but dense foliage and columnar form make this a handsome specimen tree for park or large property. It also has potential as a street tree to line an important roadway. Excellent tree for wet areas. Especially handsome in groves.

Data

Height: 60–70 feet.
Spread: 20–30 feet.
Form: Columnar when young, pyramidal in maturity.
Foliage: Fernlike, deciduous. Yellow-green in spring.
Texture: Fine.
Fall color: Light brown.
Rate of growth: Medium.
Culture: Moist, sandy soil. Prefers acidity.
Hardiness zone: 4–7.
Transplanting: Little difficulty even in large sizes.
Special maintenance requirements: Soil must be kept moist and acid.

Baldcypress nursery specimen: 8–10 feet high, 8-foot spread, 3-inch caliber, 36-inch ball.

BEECH, AMERICAN (*Fagus grandifolia*)

A very impressive tree, difficult to transplant in large size. Trunk light gray. Taller than European Beech. Tends to lose lower branches. Hardiness zone: 4, southern portion.

Design Use

There is no better species growing in America for use as a single tree in isolation or in grove. Its strong, dense form and enormous spread (50–70 feet) and height (80–100 feet) make it an appropriate tree in relation to the most massive building. To develop properly, it must be given at least 40 feet of clearance in all directions.

In grove plantings (spacing 20 feet apart) (see pages 6 and 7), the interior spaces will never see the summer sun; they thus provide cool, fragrant places in which to stroll or rest. Because of the dense shade and closeness to the surface of the Beech's feeder roots, the floor of a Beech grove or forest will be devoid of vegetation, and the accumulation of leaves will provide a soft, moist surface on which to walk.

Its vigorous response to pruning and its characteristic retention of dried leaves through the winter make this an excellent hedge plant and an easy tree to pleach. (See Chapter 6.) Excellent tree for a school campus, park, golf course.

Beech Bark. Public plantings of Beech Trees are always subject to vandalism of this sort. The smooth gray bark scars in a deeper shade, encouraging initialling—and sometimes worse.

Data

Height: 50–75 feet.
Spread: To 70 feet.
Form: Dense, rounded, low branching, open crown, small trunk.

Weeping Beeches form a background for displays in the Sculpture Garden of the Museum of Modern Art, New York.

American Beech nursery specimen: 6–8 feet high, 6-foot spread, 2½–3 inch caliber, 24-inch ball.

Foliage: Deep green.
Texture: Medium and fine (cutleaf variety).
Fall color: Bronze.
Rate of growth: Slow.
Culture: Rich well-drained, moist soil; prefers open sunny site; tolerant of exposure to wind and salt spray.

Hardiness zone: 3–9.
Transplanting: Easily moved in large size because of fibrous root system.
Special characteristics: Majestic proportions. Striking gray bark with strong black scars provides winter interest. Retains dried leaves well into winter. Long-lived (300 years or more). Responds well to pruning (summer or early fall), can be used as hedges. Cannot withstand compaction of soil or even moderate fill around roots because of their closeness to the surface.

BEECH, EUROPEAN (*Fagus sylvatica*)

A strongly rounded, deciduous tree, with very light gray bark, dense foliage, and branches sweeping the ground. In many ways, the most majestic of ornamental trees.

Because of its smooth, tight-fitting, gray bark and large, rounded trunk, the Beech is one of the few deciduous trees that remains as effective after leaf-fall as it is in full leaf. The black scars left by fallen branches add much interest in winter.

The foliage has a bronze color in the fall and a tendency to remain on the lower branches throughout the winter. Fallen leaves retain their bronze coloration on the ground.

Young Beeches can be established as an excellent hedge plant; they respond well to clipping and are among the most effective of deciduous screening plants since they retain many of their leaves in a dried state throughout the winter.

It is almost impossible to grow anything beneath the spread of a Beech Tree because of the dense shade it creates and because its fibrous roots remain close to the surface. An advantage of such a root system, however, is that it makes the Beech easy to move, even in large size.

It is tolerant of some salt spray and, if given rich soil, can be grown close to salt water.

The Weeping Beech, a variety of the European Beech (var. *pendula*), is one of the most spectacular of weeping trees. (See photo above.) There are also varieties with leaves of deep purple (*atropunicea*) and copper (*atropunicea* var. *riversi*) coloring, as well as a cutleaf variety (*laciniata*). The variety *fastigiata* resembles closely the English Columnar Oak (*Quercus robur fastigiata*) illustrated in a portrait on page 53 and in the "Design Data" section on page 203.

Although some feel that the Beech will not thrive in the city because of atmospheric conditions, a group of Weeping Beech have been planted with success in the garden of the Museum of Modern Art in the middle of New York City. It is also true that this tree has been avoided in towns because of its great space requirements.

Possibly the most handsome specimen tree we have in each of its several varieties.

Design Use

Similar to American Beech.

Data

Height: 50–60 feet.
Spread: To 45 feet.
Form: Dense, rounded, or pyramidal, branched to ground.
Foliage: Deep green.
Texture: Medium or fine (cutleaf variety).
Bark: Smooth, gray.
Fall color: Bronze, may remain through winter.
Rate of growth: Slow.
Culture: Siimilar to American Beech. Cannot withstand extreme heat or cold.
Hardiness zone: 4–7.

Transplanting: Easily moved.
Special characteristics: Similar to American Beech.

Other Useful European Beech Varieties

Weeping Beech (*Fagus sylvatica pendula*)

The most spectacular of all weepers (see photo opposite).

Purple Beech (*Fagus sylvatica atropunicea*)

Leaves of deep purple coloring.

Copper Beech (*Fagus sylvatica cuprea*)

Upright or Columnar (*Fagus sylvatica fastigiata*)

Cutleaf or Fern Leaf (*Fagus sylvatica laciniata*)

BIRCH, CANOE (Paper Birch, White Birch)
(*Betula papyrifera*)

A deciduous tree, usually single-stemmed, with outstanding chalky white bark, punctuated by black scars where branches have died. A tall tree, 60–75 feet, high branching, with light, open foliage that turns yellow in fall. As with all Birches, it should be planted in full sun but will thrive in dry or wet soil. It grows at a rapid rate, transplants easily (this should be done in early spring), and is less susceptible than other varieties to the destructive bronze birch borer. Not recommended for use south of New England because of its preference for a cold climate.

Design Use

The principal design attribute of this Birch is its exceptionally white bark that is unequalled by any other tree. It is extremely striking in both winter and summer when silhouetted against a background of evergreen trees—especially against the White Pine with which it often associates itself in nature. Especially effective as a grove. It is not a good choice for unsupervised public plantings because of the temptation to peel the bark. Because it generally has a single stem and is vaguely symmetrical in form, it lends itself somewhat to architectonic planting design.

Data

Height: To 75 feet.
Spread: To 35 feet.

Multistemmed specimens of **Canoe Birch**.

Form: Narrow, high branching.
Foliage: Light, open. Dark green.
Texture: Medium
Fall color: Yellow.
Bark: Whitest of all birches.

Rate of growth: Rapid.

Culture: Moist loam.

Hardiness zone: 2–6.

Transplanting: Easily moved. Should be transplanted in early spring.

Special characteristics: Should not be planted south of New England; does not do well on exposed sites.

Special maintenance requirements: Should be sprayed twice each year to combat leaf miner.

Specimen Canoe Birch against an evergreen background.

Detail of Canoe Birch bark shows typical markings.

Other Useful Birch Varieties

Birch, European Weeping (*Betula pendula gracilis*)

Smaller leaves and pendulus branches with nonpeeling bark almost as white as Canoe Birch makes this an extremely useful tree as a specimen or in a grouping. It has unusual grace and dignity and appears to be quite hardy in the city, perhaps because its narrow leaves do not collect as much soot as the broad-leafed varieties. Subject, as all Birches, to leaf miner requiring two sprays per year. Most susceptible to bronze birch borer, which can be controlled if constantly checked for infestation.

An effective grouping has been thriving in the Sculpture Garden of the Museum of Modern Art in the middle of New York City for almost 30 years. Useful in parks, campuses, cemeteries, as well as smaller residential properties. Excellent in grove planting. Hardiness zone: 2–6.

Birch, Gray (*Betula populifolia*)

A multistemmed tree with bark not as white as the Canoe Birch, but with more prominent scars. Smaller in height (30 feet). Thrives in sandy, dry soil, particularly in burned-over areas. Transplants easily, grows rapidly, and is extremely effective because of its multiplicity of trunks, which enables the designer to create dense groves of almost immediate effect. This is a short-lived tree, however, (20 years) and is highly susceptible to the bronze birch borer, which is extremely difficult to control, and the birch-leaf miner, for which it must be sprayed at least twice each season. Its foliage is open, permitting penetration of sufficient sunlight to support grass below. Its usefulness is in the quick effect it provides the designer and in the winter interest of its white trunk. Excellent in grove planting. The Grey Birch does not lend itself as well as the Canoe Birch to architectonic planting design. Hardiness zone: 3–6.

Pyramidal European Birch (*Betula alba fastigiata*)

A unique, narrow tree, 30–40 feet high. Useful for architectonic plantings and whenever a longer-lasting substitute for Lombardy Poplar is required.

River Birch (*Betula nigra*)

Useful for wet areas, but tolerates dry ones as well. Interesting exfoliation revealing light brown, inner bark. Often multistemmed. Effective in grove planting. Hardiness zone: 4–9.

A grove of **Gray Birch**.

Multistemmed Gray Birch nursery specimen: 7–8 feet high, 3–4 foot spread, 1½-inch caliber, 23-inch ball. In young trees, the bark is dark brown.

CHERRY, FLOWERING (*Prunus*)

Small- to medium-sized tree (20–40 feet) useful in the landscape principally for its blossom that appears in early spring in shades of pink or white. (Shown in color on page 80.)

The native American and European cherries have an inconspicuous blossom and most are of little design use; the Asian varieties, on the other hand, are known for their spectacular display of flowers, the Tidal Basin planting in Washington being perhaps the most familiar to Americans.

There are many varieties of Cherry available on the market. Unfortunately, an overemphasis has been placed on the size of the blossom at the sacrifice of the form of the tree, with the result that many varieties appear discordant in the landscape composition once their blossom has passed. This is especially true of the *Kwanzan* variety that has a rigid upswept form.

In the author's opinion, the Common Sour Cherry used in pies (*Prunus cerasus*) has the most pleasing shape and blossom. It is a small tree (30 feet) with a rounded head and light, open branching. The blossom is white, single, and small (¾–1 inch), far less spectacular but very much more natural than the contrived double-flowering varieties. The Sour Cherry has three distinct advantages: It is the hardiest of the Cherries (zone 3); it can thrive in shaded locations; and its fruit is edible. As with most Cherries, there is no fall color.

The Sargent Cherry (*Prunus sargenti*) is a large tree (75 feet), has single pink blossoms, and is one of the few

Flowering Cherry Tree in bloom. (Shown in color on page 80.)

Cherries exhibiting a vivid red fall foliage color. Too large for small property, the Sargent Cherry makes an excellent shade or specimen tree.

Yoshino Cherry (*Prunus yedoensis*) is the tree planted at Tidal Basin in Washington and is outstanding for the proliferation of its blossom. This variety attains a height of over 40 feet with a spread of 30–40 feet.

All Cherries are subject to borers and scale and attract a host of leaf-eating insects that require annual spraying for control. They are relatively short-lived trees and should not be relied on for more than 20 years. Soil and moisture requirements are ordinary.

Design Use

As with most flowering trees, the Cherry is most effective when planted in masses or drifts against an evergreen background, although single specimens of such species as the Sargent are effective. Most Cherries have a shiny, black bark that has considerable interest in winter.

Data: *Prunus cerasus*

Height: 20–30 feet.
Spread: 15-20 feet.
Form: Round head, light open branching.
Foliage: Light green.
Texture: Medium.
Blossom: White, mid–May.
Fruit: Red or black, early summer.
Fall color: Yellow.
Rate of growth: Medium.
Culture: Good garden soil, moderate moisture, tolerant of shade.
Hardiness zone: 3–8.
Transplanting: Moved easily in small size (under 3-inch caliber).
Insect pests: Many, including aphids, tent caterpillar, borers, scale.

Other Useful Cherry Varieties

Sargent (*Prunus sargenti*)

The hardiest. Spreading, upright form. Single pink flower, dark green foliage.

Kwanzan (*Prunus kwanzan*)

One of the two Japanese Cherries that line the Tidal Basin in Washington, D.C. Double, deep pink flower. Profuse bloomer. Available in two forms—avoid the tree form (rigid upswept branching often used as street tree).

Shirofugen (*Prunus serrulata shirofugen*)

Very vigorous. White double flower.

Autumn Flowering
(*Prunus subhirtella autumnalis*)

Blooms in October as well as early spring. Semidouble flowers. Good open spreading form. Interesting as specimen or planted in drift.

Yoshino (*Prunus yedoensis*)

Japanese Cherry used with Kwanzan in Washington, D.C. Fragrant single flowers, white to pale pink.

CHESTNUT, HORSE- (*Aesculus hippocastanum*)

A deciduous tree, oval in form, with large, leathery leaves held horizontally in clusters. It has a dark, dull bark, strong, ascending limbs that turn down and then up at the tips, heavy, dark twigs and large buds, which all contribute to a rugged appearance and an outstanding winter silhouette. Spikes or candles of flowers (white, pink, or yellow) appear above the leaf clusters in mid–May.

Design Use

A good, dense shade tree, excellent for the long view where the boldness of silhouette provides detail. Blossoms provide interest for 2–3 weeks in mid–May, which contributes much to the popularity of this tree (the Champs Elysée in Paris is lined with Horse-Chestnuts). It is tolerant of city atmospheric conditions, but is extremely sensitive to moisture deficiency, which evidences itself in a disfiguring browning of leaves by mid-August of a dry summer. The disadvantages of using the Horse-Chestnut are principally those of maintenance; in addition to its heavy water requirements, its droppings (flowers, fruit,

Horse-Chestnut
nursery specimen: 6 feet high, 3-foot spread, 2-inch caliber, 24-inch ball.

bud scales, and leaves in midsummer) demand more attention, unfortunately, than the average municipality is prepared to give. Good as a lawn tree; descending roots permit good turf growth in its proximity. Excellent specimen tree for a large property, park, campus, etc.; too massive for small residential planting.

Data

Height: 40–60 feet.
Spread: 30–40 feet.
Form: Oval, with ascending branches turning down and up again at tips. Majestic.
Foliage: Dense, leathery. Large clusters born horizontally.
Texture: Coarse.
Bark: Dark brown.

Blossom: White, pink, red, or yellow, 6–8-inch upright pyramidal clusters.
Fall color: Inconspicuous, with the exception of the Ohio Buckeye (*Aesculus glabra*) that is a small tree, 30 feet in height, with brilliant orange fall color.
Rate of growth: Medium.
Culture: Rich and moist soil; sun.
Hardiness zone: 3 (southern portion) to 7.
Transplanting: Easily moved (fibrous root system).
Special maintenance requirements: Removal of faded flowers and fruit.
Special characteristics: Reacts unfavorably to insufficient moisture. Susceptible to leaf blotch, powdery mildew.
Varieties: Double flowers (*baumanni*); pink flowers (*rubicunda*).

CORK, AMUR *(Phellodendron amurense)*

A deciduous tree of extremely open, irregular branching. Deeply fissured, corky bark, gray-brown in color. Foliage is light, with a tendency to appear only toward the extremities of the branches. Leaves appear late in the spring and drop shortly after turning yellow in the fall. Small, white flowers appear early in June and are followed, in some specimens (sexes are separate), by clusters of black berries; neither is conspicuous. The outstanding characteristics of this tree are its wide, open habit and heavily textured bark, which give it year-round interest.

The Amur Cork is easily transplanted because of its fibrous root system and tolerates city conditions as well as heat and drought (an interesting specimen has been thriving for many years near the steps of St. Bartholomew's Church on Park Avenue in New York).

Design Use

Its interesting branch structure and unusual bark texture make the Amur Cork an ideal specimen when space is not limited. An excellent shade tree; its sparse foliage permits sufficient light to encourage the cultivation of grass in its shadow. Properly used, it should be placed at a good distance from a building, for its spread sometimes exceeds its height.

This would make an interesting street tree for country roads or lanes: Its narrow foliage offers little wind resistance, and its strong wood make it safe for this use. Its tendency to branch low makes it vulnerable when trucks

Distinctive bark texture.

Amur Cork on Park Avenue, New York.

and buses press close to the curb; hence, it is necessary to discourage low branches by early pruning. City-tolerant. A good park tree.

Data

Height: 30–50 feet.
Spread: 30–40 feet.
Form: Open, wide-spreading short trunk, rounded crown of a few large branches with few side branches, strong winter outline.
Foliage: Deep green, sparse, and open; appears late in spring.
Bark: Deeply fissured corky bark in older specimens.
Texture: Medium to fine.
Fall color: Yellow.
Rate of growth: Medium.
Culture: Adapts easily to poor soil conditions, as well as heat and drought.
Hardiness zone: 3, southern portion, to 7.
Transplanting: Transplants easily (fibrous root system).
Special maintenance requirements: Cleanup of fallen fruit.
Special characteristics: Corky bark and wide spreading

branches with a few side branches make interesting winter silhouette. Light foliage permits cultivation of grass in its shadow.

Amur Cork nursery specimen: 12–15 feet high, 8-foot spread, 3–3½ inch caliber, 48-inch ball.

CRAB APPLE, FLOWERING (*Malus rosaceae*)

A small, deciduous tree (15–25 feet) with a variety of forms (round head, pendulous, columnar, weeping), the Crab Apple produces masses of flowers in shades of pink, red, or white, in mid–May, and red or yellow fruits that persist into winter and are attractive to birds. Certain varieties such as the Siberian Crab Apple *(Malus baccata)* are hardy well into Canada and can be found as far south as Florida.

Design Use

An excellent tree for massing of color throughout the design. Some varieties such as the Japanese Flowering Crab *(Malus floribunda)* also have an interesting form that can be emphasized by proper pruning. (Shown in color on page 80.)

One of the hardiest of flowering trees, it has the ability to withstand the air pollution of the city and rigors of life near the ocean, as well as severe cold.

Other Useful Crab Apple Varieties

The Crab Apple is a very durable and colorful tree by virtue of *blossom* as well as its fruit and foliage and has therefore been a tempting subject for plant breeders. The result is an enormous variety of color, shapes, and sizes too

numerous to include in its entirety in a volume such as this. The following list, taken from the catalog of Princeton Nurseries of Allentown, New Jersey, gives a generous selection. Smaller, local nurseries can provide many more.

Crab Apple nursery specimen: 6–8 feet high, 6-foot spread, 2-inch caliber, 24-inch ball.

American Beauty Crab
(*Malus* "American Beauty")

Height: 20–25 feet. Hardiness zone: 4. Exceptionally large, double clear red flowers. Foliage is bronze-red when young, bronze-green at maturity.

Carmine Crab (*Malus atrosanguinea*)

Height: 10–15 feet. Hardiness zone: 4. Single red flowers in abundance. Small red fruits.

Siberian Crab (*Malus baccata*)

Height: 20–25 feet. Hardiness zone: 2. Very hardy. Pure white flowers in profusion. Waxlike yellow or red fruits. A splendid street tree. Disease-resistant.

Bridal Bouquet Crab (*Malus* "Bridal Bouquet")

Height: 18–20 feet. Hardiness zone: 3. A small Crab Apple bearing clouds of very large, double white flowers. It has good disease-resistant foliage and bears very few fruits.

Beverly Crab (*Malus* "Beverly")

Height: 20–25 feet. Hardiness zone: 4. Rounded branching, single blushing pink flowers, good bright red fruit set.

Candied Apple or Weeping Crab
(*Malus* "Candied Apple")

Height 14–16 feet. Hardiness zone: 4. A picturesque weeping Crab Apple with an irregular branching habit. Deep pink flowers, dark green textured foliage with a slight red cast. Good bright red, long-lasting fruit. Disease-resistant.

Eley Flowering Crab (*Malus eleyi*)

Height: 10–15 feet. Hardiness zone: 4. A free-blooming Crab. Reddish foliage, crimson flowers. Vigorous grower.

Japanese Flowering Crab (*Malus floribunda*)

Height: 10–15 feet. Hardiness zone: 4. Single rose-colored flowers. Yellow fruits. The standard variety for landscape planting. Disease-resistant.

Harvest Gold Crab (*Malus* "Harvest Gold")

Height: 22–25 feet. Hardiness zone: 4. Single white flower producing a colorful gold fruit that lasts into December. Vigorous upright branching habit. Disease-resistant.

Hopa Red Flowering Crab (*Malus hopa*)

Height: 12–15 feet. Hardiness zone: 4. Rose-red flowers. Red fruit.

Katherine Crab (*Malus* "Katherine")

Height: 10–14 feet. Hardiness zone: 4. Double pink Crab with masses of 2-inch flowers. Even young plants are covered with flowers.

Pink Perfection Crab (*Malus* "Pink Perfection")

Height: 18–20 feet. Hardiness zone: 4. Large double flowers, red in bud, fading to clear pink when fully open. Thick healthy, green foliage.

Prairie Fire Crab (*Malus* "Prairie Fire")

Height: 22–24 feet. Hardiness zone: 3. A single, red-flowering Crab with good foliage and abundant flowers. The foliage resists disease and the tree bears dark red fruits in the fall that are held on the branches very late into the season.

Radiant Crab (*Malus* "Radiant")

Height: 12–15 feet. Hardiness zone: 4. A vigorous, upright-growing Crab, especially fine for street tree planting. Bears single red flowers and red fruits.

Red Jade Crab (*Malus* "Red Jade")

Height: 10–12 feet. Hardiness zone: 4. A picturesque weeping branching habit with single, white flowers and profuse small red fruit retained well into the winter, which adds considerable interest. Disease-resistant.

Sargent Crab (*Malus sargenti*)

Height: 6–8 feet. Hardiness zone: 5. A really dwarf Crab with masses of white flowers. The bright scarlet fruits persist late into the winter. Disease-resistant.

Scheidecker Crab (*Malus scheideckeri superba*)

Height: 18–20 feet. Hardiness zone: 4. Double red buds changing to pink. Yellow fruits.

Snowcloud Crab (*Malus* "Snowcloud")

Large double flowers, pink in bud, a pure glistening white when fully open. An upright grower with dark green, healthy foliage.

Snowdrift Crab (*Malus* "Snowdrift")

Height: 18–20 feet. Hardiness zone: 4. Large, pure white flowers, pink in bud. Upright-growing habit.

Spring Snow Crab (*Malus* "Spring Snow")

Height: 22–24 feet. Hardiness zone: 3. A vigorous Crab Apple forming a rounded crown at maturity. Bears very abundant white flowers. It is especially useful for street planting because it is almost completely sterile and bears very few fruits.

Tea Crab (*Malus theifera* or *Malus hupehensis*)

Height: 15–20 feet. Hardiness zone: 4. Picturesque, open habit. Each branch covered with pink flowers. Good espalier plant. Disease-resistant.

Strawberry Parfait Crab
(*Malus* "Strawberry Parfait")

Height: 15–20 feet. Hardiness zone: 4. Large fragrant pink flowers with red margins. Very heavy bloomer, with leathery dark green foliage resistant to both mildew and apple scab. The branching habit is open and vase-shaped like that of the Tea Crab.

Van Eseltine Crab (*Malus* "Van Eseltine")

Height: 22–25 feet. Hardiness zone: 4. An upright grower with large, double, rose-pink flowers.

White Cascade Crab (*Malus* "White Cascade")

Height: 10–12 feet. Hardiness zone: 4. Bright pink flower buds opening to pure white cascading flowers. Small yellow fruit. Disease-resistant. A weeping ornamental.

Zumi Crab (*Malus zumi calocarpa*)

Height 12–15 feet. Hardiness zone: 4. Small, handsome bright red fruit and large white flowers. A strong growing type. Abundant glossy red fruits that persist well. Disease-resistant.

DOGWOOD, FLOWERING (*Cornus florida*)

A small, deciduous, flowering tree, with widely spaced, distinctly horizontal branches and upcurved twigs. Hardy in the eastern half of the United States, this native woodland tree prefers semishade but thrives in full sun—where it blooms more profusely—when given *ample moisture*. Flowers appear in mid–May in white and various shades of pink. The natural pale pink is to be preferred to the muddy, overly rich wine color of the hybrid varieties.

The branching of the **Dogwood** is open and strongly horizontal. Multistemmed specimens are generally available.

Berries follow the blossoms and turn scarlet in early fall. The gray-green pointed buds of flowers for the ensuing year remain all winter. Foliage is light green with pointed, curled ends; fall color is a deep red or wine. Trees are single or multistemmed, the latter being the more common outside the nursery and more valuable for design use. Bark is broken into small, quadrangular scales, vertically ridged. A rapid grower in its early years, it seldom exceeds 30 feet. (Shown in color on page 80.) Prefers moist soil and does not thrive on windy, open sites. The "flower" is actually composed of sturdy bracts and therefore lasts longer than the display of other flowering trees (3–4 weeks). It is extremely useful because of its ability to thrive and bloom in dense shade.

If a large existing specimen is to be included prominently in the design, a thorough examination should be made for Dogwood borer, especially in the pink variety, and extreme caution must be observed to prevent any curtailment of the water supply to which the tree has become accustomed.

It is unfortunate that the Dogwood is being widely used as a suburban street tree. The beauty of its branch structure is, in large part, destroyed by training it to a single, high-branching stem. Furthermore, it is subject to damage by trucks and buses because its crown is too low to clear the bodies of the vehicles, which can usually be cleared by a standard street tree.

The transplanting of large specimens (6-inch caliber and up) is not uncommon, but it is inadvisable, for although with reasonable care the tree will probably outlive its guarantee, it will often begin to decline after several years.

This species has recently been stricken with a type of *anthracnose* for which there is, at present, no cure, making it a risky selection unless it is to be thoroughly pampered, on the theory that when trees, like humans, eat properly (fertilizer) and drink properly (plenty of water), infectious diseases can be warded off.

Design Use

The Dogwood is most effectively used in group plantings, spaced at random as in nature, at the edge of a woodland, or deep within it. Because of its small scale, its use as a single, free-standing specimen is limited to smaller residential properties.

Dogwood nursery specimen: 8–10 feet high, 6-foot spread, 2½–3 inch caliber, 30-inch ball.

Data

Height: 15–30 feet.
Spread: 12–20 feet.
Form: Flat crown, widely spaced. Horizontal branching, low branched, upcurved twigs.
Foliage: Light green, curled, pointed tips.
Texture: Medium.
Blossom: White and variations of pink, April to mid–May, 2 weeks' duration.
Fall color: Deep red. Scarlet berries, gray-green flower buds.
Rate of growth: Medium.
Culture: Well-drained, acid soil. Does not tolerate wet soil or standing water.
Hardiness zone: 5-9.
Transplanting: Easily moved in sizes under 5-inch caliber. Move with earth ball. Avoid moving larger specimen, which tends to fail gradually after 2–3 years.
Special maintenance requirements: Constant surveillance against borer: Remove and apply DDT. Ample water supply and partial shade essential.

DOGWOOD, JAPANESE (*Cornus kousa*)

Arguably the most handsome Dogwood flowers, they appear in June, approximately 3 weeks after Flowering Dogwood, and last for more than 4 weeks. When this variety is planted with *Cornus florida* and interplanted with *Viburnum tomentosum* (var. *mariesi*), a tall shrub with blossoms that from a distance cannot be distinguished from Dogwood, almost 2 months of similar flowers can be obtained. Excellent for massing along the edge of woods. Strong horizontal lines silhouette well against building walls. Profuse and very conspicuous fruit that resembles a very large raspberry (1-inch diameter) hangs in clusters August–October, red fall color, exfoliating bark. Variety Summer Stars (Plant Patent 1355) retains flowers late into summer. Resistant to disease problems of the Flowering Dogwood.

Other Useful Dogwood Variety

Cornelian Cherry (*Cornus mas*)

A shrublike deciduous tree with a heavy, oval crown. Heavy branches give some strength to winter outline. Outstanding characteristic is display of small but numerous yellow flowers in very early spring before forsythia. Excellent for use in mass along edge of woodland. It reaches a height of 20–25 feet and spread of 12–15 feet.

Japanese Dogwood nursery specimen: 8–10 feet high, 4-foot spread, 2–2½ inch caliber, 20-inch ball.

ELM, AMERICAN (*Ulmus americana*)

New Hope for Elms

Attacked by two fatal diseases (Dutch Elm disease and *Phloem necrosis*), which have reached into nearly all areas where Elms are grown, the American Elm appeared doomed to imminent extinction. Now the prognosis of research being conducted into the cause and prevention of these diseases, long negative, has become more optimistic.

At this writing, some of the most encouraging news in the battle for the preservation of the Elm is the discovery of an insect parasite, a wasp called Dendrosoter, that feeds on the larvae of the Elm bark beetle. This wasp is now being imported from France and experiments are being conducted in several states. Interesting experiments have also been conducted involving gene mutation. However, until these experiments have been proven successful, it remains unwise to use the Elm as an element of design, but it is recommended that a single Elm be included in every planting. Unless such action is taken, it is possible that the Elm will become extinct through disuse fully as much as through disease.

A Substitute

There is no true substitute for the American Elm. No other tree can equal the stately, high-branching grace that has made it the most popular shade tree in America through the years and therefore endowed it with so many historical associations, particularly in the New England area. From the design point of view, however, the tree that can, in selected specimens, most nearly approximate the characteristic vase or urn shape is the Silver Maple (*Acer saccharinum*). Its use as a substitute for the American Elm should, however, be restricted to the role of specimen tree in open, grassed areas, for its wood is soft and subject to storm damage, as well as boring insects. It has the advantage of being very fast-growing and tolerating dry, poor soil and sooty atmospheric conditions. Most experts and textbooks discourage the use of the Silver Maple, and under no circumstances should it be used as a street tree, where its susceptibility to storm damage makes it a safety hazard. However, when the high-branching beauty of the Elm is sought, the Silver Maple is the closest substitute. (See page 201.)

Elm Substitute. The Silver Maple resembles most closely the form of the American Elm.

GINKGO (Maidenhair Tree) (*Ginkgo biloba*)

A deciduous tree, which in maturity attains an open habit with large, ascending branches projecting plumelike beyond the general foliage line. The strange, fan-shaped, light green leaf that turns yellow in the fall contributes to its exotic aura, as does the stark winter silhouette bristling with spiky buds.

The Ginkgo is very slow to mature and is often ungainly (but oddly attractive) for as long as 20 years. The portraits on pages 24 and 25 illustrate this quality. There are distinct differences in male and female trees that make it worthwhile to determine the sex of trees to be used. The male tends to be a slender tree; the female tends to spread. The female also bears an unpleasant-smelling fruit that presents a slippery hazard when it falls to the ground after ripening—two strong reasons for insisting on male trees for use in areas frequented by the public.

The Ginkgo is reputedly the oldest living species in the world today, with fossil evidence of its existence over 10 million years ago; in all its forms, it has the appearance of some giant, prehistoric fern. Over the years, it has developed an immunity to disease and insect pests and is therefore extremely easy to maintain. It is also apparently impervious to the corrosive effects of soot and other impurities in the atmosphere of our busiest cities and is consequently increasingly used as a city street tree.

The young tree—and in the Ginkgo youth lingers for 20 years or more—has an angular, spiky, almost jagged appearance, undisciplined and strangely exotic. In proximity to a building, it can be extremely disconcerting. As a specimen, a single young Ginkgo invites almost too much attention. The mature Ginkgo, on the other hand, with its wide-spreading, open form, is among the most graceful of shade trees. Its height (80 feet) and spread (40 feet) in maturity limit its successful use to large open spaces.

Because of its immunity to disease and pests and apparent indifference to carbon monoxide, the Ginkgo has great value for city use, particularly in public parks where there is sufficient room for its natural spread. Limited observation also indicates that the inevitable struggle for light in the city does not cause the Ginkgo to lean toward the source of light (a reaction called *phototropism*; see the photo on page 139) as heavily as other species, thus ensuring a more upright posture through the years. In rural or suburban areas with wider rights of way, the Ginkgo makes an excellent street tree, if the unquiet jaggedness of its youth can be born with patience. In Japan, the Ginkgo used as a street tree is pruned annually to a narrow, pyramidal outline. The frequent pruning results in dense foliage. There is a fastigiate variety named Sentry.

Design Use

As an element of design, the young Ginkgo and the mature specimen should be considered separately, for they are very different in appearance.

Spikelike buds stud the bare branches of the **Ginkgo** in winter.

The Ginkgo's unusual fan-shaped leaves grow in thick clusters.

Data

Height: 80 feet.
Spread: 40 feet.
Form: Jagged, spiky outline when young, maturing to open, spreading tree, with large, ascending branches.
Foliage: Fan-shaped, light green.
Texture: Medium.
Fall color: Strong yellow.
Rate of growth: Slow.
Culture: Tolerant of most soils.
Hardiness zone: 4–8.
Transplanting: Easily moved in largest sizes; fibrous root system.
Special characteristics: Female produces obnoxious fruit and tends to have spreading form. Male tends to be slender. No diseases. Thrives in city.
Special maintenance requirements: None.

Ginkgo nursery specimen: 10–12 feet high, 3-foot spread, 2–2½ inch caliber, 24-inch ball.

GOLDEN CHAIN TREE (Laburnum)
(*Laburnum wateri, Laburnum vossi,* or *Laburnum alpinum*)

This small, deciduous, flowering tree is recommended only for its pendulous clusters of bright yellow flowers that appear in late May and remain for approximately 2 weeks.

Design Use

The Golden Chain Tree is an upright tree that tends to lose lower branches; its usefulness in landscape design rests solely on its display of flowers. (Shown in color on page 79.) Ineffective as a single specimen. Plant in groups. Can be pleached with ease. Seeds are extremely poisonous. Should not be planted where children are likely to play.

Data

Height: 15–20 feet.
Spread: 6–8 feet.
Form: Narrow, upright.
Foliage: Light green.
Texture: Medium.
Blossom: Yellow, late May. Pendulous clusters resembling wisteria.
Fall color: None.
Rate of growth: Rapid.

Golden Chain Tree in bloom. (Shown in color on page 79.)

Culture: Moist, well-drained soil, partial shade preferred.
Hardiness zone: 5–7.
Transplanting: Moved easily.
Special maintenance requirements: Shelter from sun to prevent leaf scorch. Some protection suggested against severe cold to prevent splitting of trunk. Short-lived.

GOLDEN RAIN TREE (Varnish Tree)
(*Koelreuteria paniculata*)

A low (30 feet) round-headed tree outstanding for its pyramidal clusters of yellow flowers that appear in early summer and its bladderlike seed pods that follow and turn from pale green to pink to brown as the summer progresses. Its coarse foliage has no fall color, but is a coral red as it first appears in the spring. Widely used in the Ohio valley. Tolerant of most soils. (Shown in color on page 79.)

Design Use

One of the very few yellow-flowering trees. Good in clumps or groves, but usually not sufficiently interesting to be used singly. Suitable for use as street tree on streets lined with buildings of domestic scale.

Data

Height: 30 feet.
Spread: 30–40 feet.
Form: Round-headed, dense, with spreading and ascending branches.
Foliage: Light green (coral red at first).
Texture: Medium.
Blossom: Yellow, early summer.
Fruit: Inflated bladderlike pods, green to pink to brown throughout the summer.
Fall color: Yellow.
Rate of growth: Medium.

Golden Rain Tree in bloom. (Shown in color on page 79.)

Culture: Tolerant of wide range of soils as well as drought and heat; tolerant of city atmosphere.
Hardiness zone: 5–9.
Transplanting: Moved easily; fibrous root system.
Special maintenance requirements: None.

GUM, SWEET (*Liquidambar styraciflua*)

A pyramidal tree of dense foliage, retaining a balanced shape under almost all circumstances. Gray bark, deeply ridged, with a corky appearance on smaller branches.

Varied autumn coloration of deep wine shades, as well as orange and yellow. Star-shaped leaves give this tree distinction, as do the clusters of seed balls or burrs (not unlike small sea urchins) that remain on the tree for a time after the leaves have fallen.

The Sweet Gum prefers rich, wet soil and thrives in areas subject to flooding, but adapts easily to other conditions except severe cold. It should not be planted where temperatures go below zero. It is a rapid grower, generally reaching 60–80 feet. It has few diseases.

Design Use

The Sweet Gum, because of its unvarying symmetry and dense foliage, is an excellent street tree, with the added

Sweet Gum nursery specimen: 8 feet high, 4-foot spread, 2-inch caliber, 24-inch ball.

interest of rich fall coloration. Its one disadvantage in this use is its proliferation of seed balls that litter the pavement in late fall.

It is an excellent tree for the woodland where it can be planted quite closely and contributes to the richness of fall color.

The Sweet Gum is an excellent shade tree, but when conditions permit the use of trees of more interesting habit, this should not be the first choice.

Data

Height: 60–100 feet.
Spread: 30 feet when young to 70 feet in maturity.
Form: Pyramidal, symmetrical, straight trunk extends through tree. In late maturity it attains a wide-spreading form.
Foliage: Deciduous, star-shaped leaf, very dense.
Texture: Medium.
Fall color: Variegated; deep red, wine, orange, yellow.
Bark: Silver gray; deeply furrowed, corky on younger twigs.
Rate of growth: Rapid.
Culture: Rich and wet soil, but adapts easily and can be used as street tree.
Hardiness zone: 5–9.
Transplanting: Difficult to transplant in large size. Best moved in early spring.
Special maintenance requirements: None.

HAWTHORN (*Crataegus*)

A small, deciduous, flowering tree, with a rounded head, densely branched, growing to a height of approximately 25 feet with only a slightly smaller spread. The Hawthorn has some of the horizontality of the Dogwood, which becomes more pronounced in older trees. Its branching is much more profuse than that of the Dogwood and together with its thorns it produces a much more dense form and finer texture. The flowers of the Hawthorn are not as spectacular as those of the Dogwood, but the berries, which vary from scarlet to orange, are retained on some varieties through the winter. This tree is prey to infestations of scale, lace bug, borer, leaf miner, and red spider, and therefore requires frequent attention. Specimens larger than 4-inch caliber are difficult to transplant. (Shown in color on page 79.)

Design Use

The Hawthorn has much the same usefulness in landscape design as the Dogwood. Several characteristics of the Hawthorn make it a useful tree for special purposes. It is very tolerant of salt spray and can be planted quite close to salt water. It responds excellently to clipping and proves an excellent hedge. It has also been used effectively as a headlight barrier on the islands of divided highways. Thrives in the city. Effective in close groups. The horizontality of branching in mature trees makes it useful at the base of large buildings. Finally, the presence of thorns, which makes the tree impractical for certain uses, such as children's playgrounds, renders it all-impervious as a barrier or living fence. When maintenance is not likely to be performed properly and another flowery tree will fill design requirements, the Hawthorn should be avoided.

There are a wide variety of Hawthorns available including a thornless one (*Crusgalli inermis*). If a single choice were to be made, it would be in favor of the Washington Hawthorn (*Crataegus phaenopyrum*), which has a highly glossy foliage, excellent fall color (scarlet to orange), and fruit that remains through the winter. This variety is available in a tree form with a single stem.

Hawthorn. Glossy leaves, profuse branching, and long thorns.

Data

Height: 25 feet.
Spread: 20 feet.
Form: Short trunk, rounded head, densely twigged, thorny wide horizontal branches.
Foliage: Bright green.
Texture: Medium to fine.
Blossom: White (pink to scarlet in some varieties), late May.
Fruit: Orange to scarlet berries (retained into winter).
Fall color: Bronze to red.
Rate of growth: Slow.

Culture: Prefers sun, tolerant of moist soils.

Hardiness zone: 3–7.

Transplanting: Easily moved in sizes under 3 inches in caliber. Older trees are difficult to move. Spring is preferred planting time.

Special maintenance requirements: Several sprays required to keep Hawthorn pest-free. This is usually necessary for trees under close scrutiny.

Other Useful Hawthorn Varieties

Paul's Scarlet (*Crataegus laevigata*)

Double red flowers, very showy but very susceptible to leaf blight.

Crimson Cloud (*Crataegus laevigata*)

Red single flowers, resistant to leaf blight. Tolerant of city conditions.

Hawthorn nursery specimen: 8–10 feet high, 5-foot spread, 2½–3 inch caliber, 30-inch ball.

KATSURA TREE (*Cercidiphyllum japonicum*)

A deciduous tree, generally vertical in appearance (male trees are more narrow than female) with many branches separating from main trunk almost at ground level. It reaches a height of 60 feet and spread of 30–40 feet. The head is small and round, contributing to a fine texture. The foliage has three distinct, seasonal colors, rose in spring, turning to blue-green in summer, and yellow and sometimes scarlet in the fall. Bark is shaggy, forming narrow vertical strips.

Design Use

Its ascendant shape makes the tree useful as a punctuation mark in the landscape with possibilities also for effective massing in groves or architectonic grouping in relation to buildings. Can be used to line a drive or allée. Mature tree makes elegant lawn or park specimen. Fine-textured foliage with three distinct seasonal color changes add to its interest.

Data

Form: Vertical, with wide spread in mature trees.

Height: 40–60 feet.

Spread: 30–40 feet, or greater.

Foliage: Small, round, rose-colored in spring; blue-green in summer.

Texture: Fine.

Fall color: Yellow (apricot); occasionally scarlet or purple.

Rate of growth: Fast.

Culture: Rich, moist soil and open, sunny site. Prefers early spring planting.

Hardiness zone: 4–8.

Special maintenance requirements: None (disease-free).

Katsura Tree nursery specimen: 12–15 feet high, 4-foot spread, 3–3½ inch caliber, 28-inch ball.

LARCH, EUROPEAN (*Larix decidua*)

The Larch is the unusual phenomenon of a needled and cone-bearing tree that loses its "leaves" each winter. A tall, pyramidal tree. In maturity, it develops a slightly irregular head.

The foliage is its most outstanding feature. Its unusually light green color in the spring and pale yellow in the fall are reasons enough for inclusion in the planting design. The fine texture of the needles gives the tree an appearance of delicacy and grace that is maintained in its winter silhouette by the profusion of tiny branchlets. Round, dark buds that regularly punctuate the branches provide considerable interest to the winter appearance. So light is the shadow cast by the foliage that grass can be grown without difficulty beneath even the mature tree.

The Larch is subject to severe attack by a foliage-destroying insect (the large case-bearer) that will rob it of its beauty for an entire season unless it is sprayed at precisely the right time in the development of the insect. Fungus and canker also attack the Larch, but this is not sufficient reason to eliminate it from use; it should merely not be placed in key positions in the planting design, unless proper maintenance is assured.

Prefers moist, well-drained, rich soil, although it adapts readily to sandy conditions. Rate of growth is relatively rapid.

Characteristic burst of needles along the branches of the Larch.

Larch nursery specimen: 6–7 feet high, 3-foot spread, 1½–2 inch caliber, 24-inch ball.

Weeping variety of the European Larch.

Design Use

As a specimen tree for large property, singly or in groups at 25- to 30-foot spacing, the Larch is extremely handsome. Silhouetted against a building, the fineness of its leaf texture and branching provide an excellent contrast. Planted at close intervals (12–15 feet), Larches provide a delightful grove, heavily carpeted by the swift accumulation of fallen needles.

Data

Height: 70–80 feet.
Spread: 30 feet.
Form: Pyramidal, drooping branches.
Foliage: Needles, very light green in spring, deepening in summer.
Texture: Very fine.
Fall color: Yellow.
Rate of growth: Rapid.
Soil preference: Moist, rich, well-drained, but adapts to sandy soil. Full sun.

Hardiness zone: 2–6.
Transplanting: Easily moved.
Special characteristics: Its light foliage permits cultivation of grass in its shadow. Prefers clean, dry atmosphere.
Special maintenance requirements: Spraying (timely) to eliminate case-bearer.

Other Useful Larch Variety

Japanese Larch (*Kaempferi*)

Larger, more graceful than *Larix decidua*.

LINDEN, LITTLE-LEAF (*Tilia cordata*)

A deciduous tree with the unusual—and very useful—design characteristic of consistently maintaining a striking symmetry in its branch structure. The mature Linden often gives the impression of having been freshly pruned, so finely is the length of branches graduated from the broad base that often sweeps the ground to the narrow tip.

A small, dense tree with oval to pyramidal head of ascending branches. Seldom reaches beyond 60 feet in America, although in Europe it reaches 90 feet in maturity. Spread is approximately 40 feet. Leaves are small (1½ –3 inches) and thus present a finer texture than other varieties; leaves are heart-shaped (characteristic of all Lindens) and dark green above with paler underside. This variety maintains a stricter symmetry of branching than all others. It is also the hardiest of all varieties against cold and seems to be the most successful in surviving air pollution. A fibrous root system ensures easy transplanting. Tolerant of most soil conditions, but requires ample moisture. Slowest growth rate of all Lindens. An outstanding strain of this variety is the Greenspire Linden that exhibits an unusually straight trunk even in young trees and a very uniform pattern of branching radially around the trunk.

There are several varieties of Linden that differ quite strongly in design qualities; they will be outlined individually below. All, however, reflect in varying degrees the symmetry already mentioned. Other characteristics include an inconspicuous but highly fragrant flower that appears in June or early July and is attractive to bees; a pale yellow autumn color; an apparent insensitivity to cold (hardy as far north as Manitoba); and a resistance to the corrosive atmosphere of our cities. Lindens also respond particularly well to pruning and can easily be clipped into geometric forms, pollarded, or pleached. A very useful tree.

Design Use

The symmetrical outline of the Linden makes it an excellent tree for architectonic plantings, particularly for groves or blocks where trees are spaced at equal intervals (15–20 feet). Their excellent response to pruning enhances their architectural usefulness, permitting shaping into cubes or pleaching into green walls.

The Linden's dense foliage makes it an incomparable specimen shade tree, with one definite but not overpowering drawback: Unless the tree is sprayed against aphid infestation, a sticky dropping from the leaves, known as honeydew, litters objects beneath its shade—a distinct disadvantage in proximity to car-parking areas. The Linden is also heavily favored by the Japanese beetle that does no permanent damage, but can decimate the foliage.

Apparent ability to withstand adverse atmospheric conditions makes the Linden an excellent tree for city streets. The Lindens of Unter Den Linden are to Berlin what the Horse-Chestnuts of the Champs Elysées are to Paris.

Characteristic swelling of the **Linden's** main trunk where secondary branches originate.

Data

Height: 50–70 feet.
Spread: 25–40 feet.
Form: Oval to pyramidal.
Foliage: Dense, dark green, lighter underside.

Texture: Medium.

Fall color: Pale yellow.

Rate of growth: Slowest of lindens.

Culture: Deep, moist soil, but adapts to sandy soil. Ample moisture required.

Hardiness zone: 3–7.

Transplanting: Easily moved.

Special characteristics: Compact, symmetrical appearance. Easily pruned to architectural forms. Tolerant of severe cold and air pollution.

Special maintenance requirements: Must be sprayed to prevent infestation by aphids and Japanese beetle. Prune to prevent heavy side limbs in young tree.

Other Useful Linden Varieties

Linden, American or Basswood (*Tilia americana*)

Height 100 feet, spread 50 feet, dense wide-spreading with rounded top. Lower branches characteristically droop and then curve upward at ends. Prefers rich moist soil. Medium growth rate. Because of size, not as suitable to city use as other Lindens. A stately tree especially suited to use as lawn specimen in large residential properties and parks.

Linden, Common or European (*Tilia europaea*)

Height 60–80 feet, spread 40 feet, pyramidal as young tree, becomes broader in maturity. Trunk is often strangely curved due to frost-cracking. Tolerant of most soils, but growth is very limited in sandy soil. Medium growth rate. Least tolerant of city atmospheric and moisture conditions.

Linden, Crimean (*Tilia euchlora*)

An excellent fast-growing shade tree with long, glossy, bright green foliage. Very fragrant when in bloom in July.

Linden, Silver (*Tilia tomentosa*)

A broad and tall tree (100 feet), oval in outline, whose foliage conceals an almost vertical branch system. The

Little-leaf Linden nursery specimen: 12–15 feet high, 6-foot spread, 2½–3 inch caliber, 32-inch ball.

winter silhouette is strongly ascendant; the summer outline is earth-bound. The dense foliage is green above and bluish white beneath, covered with fine hairs. This characteristic leaf coloring adds considerable interest to the tree during breezy weather. Good specimen lawn tree. Tolerates heat and drought better than most Lindens; therefore, it is a good city tree.

Linden, Pendant Silver (*Tilia petiolaris*)

A more open branch structure, less regular in outline than other varieties, with branches arching gracefully downward, often sweeping the ground. The leaves are green above and white below as in the Silver Linden and possess the same hairiness or pubescence on the underside, making it also a poor choice for use in the city.

LOCUST, BLACK (*Robinia pseudoacacia*)

A deciduous tree of slender form and tall, straight trunk usually terminating in jagged Japanesque branching. An extremely rugged, deeply ridged, almost gothic bark (see photograph) contrasting sharply with the short, jagged side branches and delicate, feathery foliage. No fall color.

Apparently indifferent to drought or cold and favoring poor, sandy soil, this tree is found in almost every state east of the Rockies. It is one of the latest trees to come into leaf in the spring and bears tiny, white, pea-shaped blossoms in June, which, because of the height of the tree, are usually inconspicuous.

A fast-growing tree, it reaches a height of 60–80 feet.

Design Use

Because of its exotic oriental appearance, handsome, rugged bark, straight trunk, and light foliage, the Locust is an excellent tree for use in groups in lawn areas, since the lightness of the foliage and deep rooting do not impede the growth of grass. The narrowness of the silhouette and straightness of the trunk make it less desirable for use as a single specimen. Its preference for sandy soil and its tolerance of salt spray make this an excellent choice for use near the ocean. Its rugged look is distinctly un-urban. Its tendency to die back at the top revealing dark, jagged branches above the foliage creates an interesting aspect, but does not suit it well to the city, although it apparently withstands soot and smoke.

Susceptible to borers and leaf-eating insects, which can be controlled by chemicals, this tree should be considered only for informal plantings. An excellent tree for areas of poor soil and surface erosion such as highway cuts, steep embankments, etc.

Feathery leaves give the tree an exotic oriental look.

Young **Black Locust Tree:** 8–10 feet high, 5-foot spread, 2-inch caliber. Fast-growing and useful for immediate effect.

Data

Height: 50–70 feet.
Spread: 20 feet.
Form: Slender, tall, straight main trunk, jagged side branching.
Foliage: Delicate, feathery.
Texture: Fine.

Bark detail showing "gothic" ridging.

Fall color: None.
Blossom: White, fragrant, inconspicuous.
Bark: Deeply ridged, gothic pattern, extremely rugged appearance.
Rate of growth: Rapid.
Culture: Sandy, poor soil.
Hardiness zone: 4–8.
Transplanting: Difficult in large sizes.
Special characteristics: Tolerant of salt spray and soot. Subject to twig die-back as well as fungus, which weaken tree and make it vulnerable to wind damage.
Special maintenance requirements: Frequent examination and treatment for borers.

LOCUST, HONEY- (*Gleditsia triacanthos*)

A deciduous tree of feathery foliage and open, irregular crown. Its strongest characteristics are its loose, almost unruly branching habit and its interesting winter silhouette. Hardy from New England south to Alabama and west to Nebraska, it thrives best in Indiana and Illinois. The foliage is composed of as many as 28 tiny leaflets, in pairs along the stem, that appear late in spring and are among the earliest to drop in the fall. Autumn color is a weak yellow. Large, twisted pods (as long as 1 foot) appear in the fall on many trees and remain on the leafless tree well into winter.

The trunk in mature trees is black, which makes the winter silhouette especially stark. The trunks and branches are often covered with long, forked thorns, a vestigial protection against grazing animals.

The Honey-Locust is a medium-sized tree, usually attaining a height of 70 feet. It is a moderately rapid grower, easily transplanted, extremely drought-resistant, sturdy, little troubled by disease or pests—although locust-leaf miner requires spraying. Adapts well to moist soil conditions and is very tolerant of city atmosphere.

Design Use

The characteristic branching habit creates an interesting appearance. This, together with the large seed pods that remain into winter and the clusters of thorns on trunk and branches of some varieties, make it less desirable when the design calls for regularity of form. The fine texture of its foliage also deprives it of a strength of outline and shadow that is required of an architectonic planting. This lightness of foliage, however, and the fact that it comes into leaf late in spring and defoliates early in the fall make it possible to grow other plant material successfully in its shadow, thus making the Honey-Locust an excellent lawn tree. The light shade is especially desirable in the city. For these attributes, the Honey-Locust was chosen for use in Paley Park in New York City where a lacey canopy was sought to roof that small space. (See photo on page 140.)

Its ability to withstand drought as well as the corrosive atmosphere of the city and its relative freedom from disease and pests make it a tempting tree for street planting. However, its "weak" foliage and irregular outline make it less suitable for the avenue than for the park or parkways, where it can be planted in groups. Some of the patented varieties appear to be more regular in outline, and one variety, *inermis,* is devoid of thorns, which present a hazard when the public is involved. The ease with which large specimens can be transplanted makes this a useful tree when an immediate effect is desired, especially in urban areas (several specimens of 10 inches or larger

Honey-Locust nursery specimen: 25 feet high, 12-foot spread, 3½—4 inch caliber, 36-inch ball.

The feathery leaves are more delicate than those of the Black Locust.

caliber have been placed on Fifth Avenue in New York in front of Rockefeller Center). The sturdiness of its wood and resistance to storm damage and its response to pruning are additional qualities that make it a useful city tree. The dark coloring of the trunk makes a striking winter silhouette, endowing even the young specimen with a distinctive outline.

Data

Height: 40–50 feet; can grow to 80 feet.

Spread: 20–30 feet.

Form: Broad-headed, open, irregular outline, coarse winter silhouette.

Foliage: Feathery (many small leaflets), dark green above, yellow-green below.

Texture: Fine.

Fall color: Weak yellow.

Rate of growth: Moderately rapid.

Culture: Very tolerant, prefers moist acid soil, tolerant of drought.

Hardiness zone: 4, southern portion, to 8.

Transplanting: Moved easily in large size.

Special characteristics: Drought-resistant, tolerant of city atmosphere.

Special maintenance requirements: Removal of pods. Spraying for locust mite and mimosa web-worm that cause premature defoliation.

Preferred Varieties (All Thornless)

Shademaster Ascending branches, open irregular outline, too few pods.

Skyline Pyramidal form; deep, dense foliage.

Even when small (4-inch caliber), many specimens begin to display the open form of the mature tree.

Moraine No pods, most resistant to web worm.

Halka Full, rounded head; compact branching system; more numerous pods than other varieties in maturity.

MAGNOLIA, SAUCER (*Magnolia soulangeana*)

A deciduous flowering tree, rounded in form with strong, sculptural branch system. Often multistemmed. Leaf is coarse in texture and large (6–8 inches).

When it is hardy, this Magnolia is one of our most handsome of flowering trees. In its form, it resembles the apple, but it has the added interest of a silver-gray bark and spectacular blossoms (5–6 inch diameter) that open in May before the leaves appear. (Shown in color on page 81.)

Specimens as large as 8–9 inches in caliber can be moved safely if they are dug in the spring, just before flowering. Spring planting is strongly recommended because the roots are fleshy and subject to rot when bruised unless the plant is in active growth and healing can thus be expedited.

Design Use

The Magnolia's principal use is as a specimen tree. Planted alone and treated as sculpture, it is one of the few trees that looks well when raised, as on a pedestal.

In spite of its contorted branching, it is regular in outline, often being as wide as it is tall (20 feet). It therefore lends itself well to symmetrical placement.

Because the leaves are large, it is often necessary to cut away the small side branches from time to time to reveal the handsome structure throughout the summer.

As with all flowering trees, it is most effective if provided with a darker background of building or evergreen plant material.

The Saucer Magnolia has a cultivated, almost "manmade," look and is therefore unusually well suited for plantings closely related to architecture. For the same reason, it appears out of place when planted against a rural background.

There is a great difference in color among the different varieties (see data). The author's strong preference is for the pink and white varieties.

The Magnolia is very tolerant of city conditions. Some very handsome specimens, along with the variety *stellata,* can be found growing at the Frick Museum on Fifth Avenue in New York. It is hardy as far north as Boston (specimen shown in the portrait section of this book is growing at the Arnold Arboretum of Harvard University).

Data

Height: 20–25 feet.

Spread: 20–25 feet.

Form: Round, tortuous branching, low branching.

Foliage: Large (6–8 inches).

Texture: Medium to strong.

Blossom: White to purple (varies with variety) appearing in May (before leaves).

Bark: Silver-gray.

Fruit: Green, resembles closely the stylized "pineapple" of hospitality in Colonial carving. Opens in early fall to reveal bright red seeds.

Fall color: Bronze.

Rate of growth: Medium.

Culture: Rich, moist soil, slightly acid. Cannot tolerate prolonged drought. Must have sun.

Hardiness zone: 5, southern portion, to 9.

Special maintenance requirements: Selective pruning to reveal structure.

Note: The wide variation in color among the varieties of this tree makes it imperative that the desired variety be specified. A list of the more easily obtainable varieties follows:

White: *Amabilis*

Rose-purple outside, pure white inside: *Alexandrina*

Deep rose-purple outside, white inside: *Lennei*

Deep purple outside, off white inside: *Nigra*

Other Deciduous Magnolias

Magnolia, Star (*Magnolia stellata*)

A smaller tree than the Saucer Magnolia, but a reasonable substitute for it. The branching, not quite so strong and sturdy-looking, is more dense and usually retained to the ground, presenting a shrublike appearance.

Its soil preference and other qualities are the same as those for Saucer Magnolia. It has the following special characteristics:

Saucer Magnolia nursery specimen: 10–12 feet high, 8-foot spread, 3-inch caliber, 40-inch ball.

Blossom is much smaller than *Magnolia soulangeana* (4 inches) and has many petals (12–19), giving it a starlike appearance. (Shown in color on page 81.) There is a white and pink variety that lacks fragrance.

Magnolia, Sweet-Bay
(*Magnolia virginiana, magnolia glauca*)

This tree has a small but extremely fragrant blossom that blooms throughout the summer. Handsome foliage of deep green with blue underside. An unusual addition to the planting design when placed in proper relation to prevailing wind to make the most of its fragrance. Prefers moist, rich soil and partial shade.

MAPLE, JAPANESE (*Acer palmatum*)

A deciduous tree, seldom reaching a height of 20 feet, with an extremely exotic branch structure associated with the Japanese landscape.

The general form is low, with a round top composed of twisted, irregular branches. Leaves are either green or red (*atropurpureum*) with even more intense red coloring in the fall. Bark is smooth and gray, making the leafless winter silhouette extremely sculptural.

The Japanese Maple should always be moved with an earth ball and prefers an early spring transplanting.

Design Use

The exotic and exciting form and color of this tree limit its usefulness in the landscape to that of a specimen because of the attention it invites. It is difficult to imagine its use as anything other than a living sculpture. Its placement must be considered with particular reference to scale. The Japanese Maple is a small tree (barely 20 feet) and should not be made to stand either in the open landscape or close juxtaposition to a massive building. Its size and delicacy suggest its use in small, enclosed outdoor spaces where it is a dominant feature without conflict or competition. This is especially true of the variety *dissectum* (Thread-leaf Maple), a small tree (never more than 10 feet) with deeply cut, almost shredded foliage of brilliant red fall color. Unless it is artfully pruned, its handsome structure will be concealed by its delicate but dense foliage.

The tender leaves are subject to scorch; it should therefore not be located where heat reflected from buildings or pavement will cause damage.

The foliage of the **Japanese Maple** is usually delicate in appearance.

Japanese Maple nursery specimen: 6–8 feet high, 5-foot spread, 2½–3 inch caliber, 30-inch ball.

Data

Height: 20 feet maximum.
Spread: 20 feet.
Form: Broad with upright branches with exception of variety *dissectum*.
Foliage: Deep green or red (*atropurpureum*), dense.
Texture: Fine.
Fall color: Brilliant red.
Rate of growth: Slow to medium.
Bark: Smooth and gray.
Culture: Well-drained, rich soil; prefers partial shade; tolerates full sun.
Hardiness zone: 5–8.
Transplanting: Early spring. Ample earth ball, care required. Difficult to tie branches of mature specimen (the major branches should be reinforced with bamboo strips before tying).
Special maintenance requirements: None.

Choice Japanese Maple Varieties

Threadleaf Japanese Maple (*Dissectum*)

4–6 feet. A dwarf and slightly weeping rounded tree with finely cut, feathery foliage; strangely contorted branching habit, pure sculpture. Unique orange fall coloring; gray bark. A most outstanding specimen for a small space.

Atropurpureum

15–18 feet. Rich purple foliage, upright branching. Color most intense when planted in full sun.

Bloodgood

10–12 feet. Strongest red coloring of foliage; retains color longer than most.

MAPLE, NORWAY (*Acer platanoides*)

A broad-headed and dense shade tree, very regular in outline. Fall color (yellow) not as spectacular as that of the Red and Sugar Maples. Feeding roots are very close to the surface, making it impossible to grow acceptable turf within its spread. Texture is coarse. Advantages: Withstands city conditions and is tolerant of salt spray, making it useful near sea coast. Columnar form (*Acer platanoides columnare*).

Data

Height: 40–50 feet.
Spread: 40 feet.
Rate of growth: Moderately rapid.
Hardiness zone: 3–7.
Transplanting: Easily moved.
Special maintenance: No special care.

MAPLE, PAPERBARK (*Acer griseum*)

Small (height to 30 feet, spread 15–30 feet), compact rounded form. Rich brown exfoliating bark is its out-standing feature. Excellent small specimen tree.

MAPLE, RED (Swamp Maple)
(*Acer rubrum*)

A round or oval, densely leafing, deciduous tree of outstanding spring and fall color. The spring color, appearing very early, is composed of many tiny, red flowers that when they fall, retain their color and carpet the ground. The fall color is among the earliest to appear and attains outstanding shades of scarlet, orange, and yellow. In the old tree, the trunk and major branches are dark and furrowed, but young trees and the ends of the branches of the older trees are smooth and light gray, not unlike the Beech. This variation in color adds considerable interest to the tree in winter.

The Red Maple prefers wet soil, but is peculiarly adaptable to all moisture conditions, temperature, and other climatic factors and is found thriving from Quebec and the Dakotas to Texas and Florida. It is a rapid grower (up to 2 feet per year), reaching heights of from 50–70 feet, and is not particularly susceptible to diseases. It resists storm damage and is considered long-lived.

Design Use

Its early spring color and the brilliance of its fall color make the Red Maple an important tree in terms of design. Because of the brightness of its coloration, the tree should be planted in groups in order to avoid spottiness. Great attention should be given to its placement on the site in order to create the best possible composition, recalling color from area to area.

The Red Maple has a good spread (40 feet) and therefore makes an excellent shade tree whereby it is allowed to assume its full development. Planted in groups, however, it does equally well and lends itself particularly to woodland plantings.

Its preference for wet soil (it is called Swamp Maple in many areas of the country) and its tolerance of salt spray make it a useful tree near the shore. It adapts easily, however, to other soil conditions. A good tree to line a street or drive. Excellent shade tree for parking area. Often available in clump form.

The variety *columnare* is upright in habit and can be planted in close juxtaposition to building walls where a tree of greater spread would require constant pruning.

Data

Height: 50–70 feet.
Spread: 40 feet.
Form: Round or oval; high branched (does not usually branch to the ground). Symmetrical, ascending branches.
Foliage: Dense.

The **Red Maple** is often available in multistemmed specimens, usually collected from woodlands.

The younger branches of the Red Maple are smooth light gray in contrast to the dark brown ridged covering of the main trunk.

Red Maple nursery specimen: 12 feet high, 6-foot spread, 2½–3 inch caliber, 3-foot ball.

Texture: Medium.

Spring color: Bright red (small flowers that retain color for 5–7 days after falling).

Fall color: Scarlet, orange, yellow.

Bark: Dark and furrowed on trunk and older branches, becoming smooth and light gray on ends of branches and in young trees.

Rate of growth: Rapid, 2 or more feet per year.

Culture: Rich, wet soil, but adapts well to all soils, sun, or shade.

Hardiness zone: 3–9.

Transplanting: Easily moved in all sizes (fibrous root system).

Special maintenance requirements: None.

Special varieties: Fastigiate form (*columnare*). Globe form (*globosum*): compact, 35-foot height.

Choice Red Maple Varieties

October Glory Spectacular fall color.

Red Sunset Very hardy; excellent color.

Armstrong or Bowhall Fastigiate form.

Northwood Withstands extreme cold.

The fastigiate form of Maple is very useful when space is limited. (*Acer rubrum columnare*.)

MAPLE, SILVER (*Acer saccharinum*)

Selected specimens can be used as design substitutes for the American Elm. This tree often attains a 100-foot height with a 60–70 foot spread. The main trunk tends to divide into several large, ascending branches that form a broad, open crown, recalling the vase shape of the Elm.

A rapid grower, which results inevitably in brittle wood, the Silver Maple should not be planted close to buildings or road sides unless thorough cabling precautions have been taken. It prefers moist, rich soil, sun or partial shade.

Data

Height: 90 feet.

Spread: 65 feet.

Form: Trunk divides into several ascending branches, with drooping, smaller branches.

Foliage: Long leaves, deeply lobed, silver underside.

Texture: Medium.

Fall color: Spectacular display in red and yellow-orange.

Bark: Shaggy, silver-gray.

Rate of growth: Rapid.

Culture: Prefers moist soil, but can adapt to most soil conditions.

Hardiness zone: 3–9.

Transplanting: Easily moved (fibrous root system).

Maintenance requirements: Pruning to retain shape. Spraying to control fungi. Removal of dead wood.

Special characteristics: Good lawn tree because its roots generally descend in search of moisture and thus do not interfere with turf.

MAPLE, SUGAR (*Acer saccharum*)

A deciduous tree, oval in form with upswept branches. Foliage is dense with spectacular fall coloring in shades of yellow and orange. Bark of the mature tree is dark gray and deeply furrowed; the upper bark is smooth light gray.

The Sugar Maple requires well-drained soil and a generous moisture supply; it suffers badly from drought but resists storm damage more successfully than the Norway Maple. It is a long-lived tree, a moderate to slow grower, attaining a height in maturity of approximately 85 feet. It is easily transplanted, having a good fibrous root system, and thrives in every state east of the Great Plains (and Canada) except the southeast (hardy as far as Georgia). A columnar form is available (*Acer saccharum monumentale*; see photograph).

Design Use

Excellent as a specimen shade tree and especially effective in massing for fall color. Traditionally used to line avenues because of its regular shape and dense shade. Dry locations should be avoided and especially locations such as car parks, where large areas of pavement reflect heat and cause leaf scorch and excessive moisture evaporation. The Sugar Maple does not withstand smoke or dust and should not be used in most cities. (Shown in fall color on page 82.)

Excellent specimen shade tree suitable for suburban street, large lawns, parks, etc.

Sugar Maple nursery specimen: 12–15 feet high, 5–6 feet spread, 2–2½ inch caliber, 36-inch ball.

Sentry Maple (*Acer saccharum monumentale*) nursery specimen. A columnar form of the Sugar Maple.

Typically rough bark of the Sugar Maple.

Data

Height: 70–85 feet.
Spread: 40–50 feet.
Form: Oval, ascending branches.
Foliage: Deciduous, dense. Medium to deep green.

Texture: Medium.
Fall color: Brilliant yellow, orange, scarlet.
Bark: Lower bark shaggy or fissured; upper bark smooth, gray.
Rate of growth: Moderate to slow.
Culture: Sandy loam, adjusts to other soils, must drain well.
Hardiness zone: 3–8.
Transplanting: Easily moved (fibrous root system).
Special characteristics: Reacts sharply to insufficient moisture and smoky atmosphere. Requires full sun.

Choice Sugar Maple Varieties

Columnar Form: Sentry Maple
(*Acer saccharum monumentale*)

Bonfire Excellent red fall color, rapid growth.

Green Mountain Dark green foliage, less affected by heat and drought.

MAPLE, SYCAMORE (*Acer pseudoplatanus*)

The most useful design quality of this tree is its ability to withstand strong winds and remain erect. This, coupled with its tolerance of salt spray and salty soil, makes it especially valuable at the shore.

Data

Form: Rounded crown. Very dense.
Height: 40–60 feet.
Spread: 25–40 feet.
No interesting fall coloration.
Hardiness zone: 4–7.
Transplanting: Easily moved.
Special maintenance requirements: No special care.

Other Useful Maple Varieties

Amur Maple (*Acer ginnala*)

Small (to 18 feet), very hardy in cold areas, more tolerant of shade than most Maples. Excellent tree for use in aboveground plant tub. Tolerant of city life. Zones 2–7 (north portion).

Hedge Maple (*Acer campestre*)

Small (30–35 feet), rounded, dense foliage, very tolerant of dry, alkaline soils. Useful as street tree where overhead wires interfere with taller varieties. Zones 4–7.

OAK, ENGLISH (*Quercus robur*)

A rugged, handsome tree, with stout trunk and completely rounded crown of gnarled branches. Difficult to transplant in size and slow growing, this is an outstanding specimen tree for the landscape design of public buildings. Much like the White Oak. Retains large proportion of dried leaves through winter, thus providing year-round screening.

Data

Height: 50–60 feet.
Spread: 80–100 feet.
Hardiness zone: 4–8.

OAK, ENGLISH COLUMNAR (*Quercus robur fastigiata*)

A narrow-growing Oak with small, deep green foliage. Very similar to Fastigiate European Beech. Also resembles Lombardy Poplar. Although it is more compact and rigid and much slower-growing than the Poplar, it is infinitely more hardy.

Design Use

This is a superb tree for lining driveways or narrow roadways. An ideal substitute for the short-lived Lombardy Poplar.

Data

Height: 50–60 feet.
Spread: 10–15 feet.
Form: Columnar.
Foliage: Small leaf, dark green.
Texture: Medium.
Fall color: Negligible.
Rate of growth: Slow.
Culture: Well drained, slightly acid soil; prefers full sun.
Hardiness zone: 4–8.
Transplanting: Moves easily.

Columnar English Oak (*Quercus robur fastigiata*) nursery specimen: 10–12 feet high, 3-foot spread, 2½-inch caliber, 36-inch ball.

Special maintenance requirements: None.
Special characteristics: Trunk usually covered to base with dense ascending branches.

OAK, LIVE (*Quercus virginiana*)

An outstanding majestic evergreen tree for use in zones 7–10. Ideal for large properties such as campus, golf course, etc. Complements large buildings. Used effectively also as street tree.

OAK, PIN (*Quercus palustris*)

A deciduous tree, pyramidal in shape with finely chiseled, deep olive-green foliage, which, together with the very dense but slender branching, creates an unusually delicate texture for a tree of such size (75 feet). It is characteristic of the Pin Oak that upper branches are upright, the middle ones horizontal and lower ones drooping. When these lower branches are removed or die and drop off for lack of sunlight, the branches above gradually assume a pendulous character. There are no massive branches, but an extreme twigginess that contributes to the dense appearance and fine-textured winter silhouette. The Pin Oak favors moist soil and is often found growing in flood areas: it does not like alkaline soil. The bark is finely ridged in older sections of the trunk and smooth gray on branches. Autumn color is scarlet. The Pin Oak has an unusually fibrous root system that simplifies the moving of very large specimens. It thrives from New England south to Virginia and west to Missouri and Arkansas.

The Pin Oak is easily transplanted in large size: newly planted specimens, 14 inches in caliber, planted at New York World's Fair, 1964. (Zion & Breen Associates.)

Pin Oak nursery specimen: 15–20 feet high, 5-foot spread, 3-inch caliber, 30-inch ball.

The limbs of the Pin Oak are not massive, but they are very numerous and twiggy.

Design Use

An outstanding specimen tree that when given sufficient room will sweep the ground with its drooping lower branches. The almost rigid symmetry of its pyramidal form and fineness of the texture of its foliage and branching make it a useful tree for a more formal planting design. It is extremely effective for lining roadways, except for the fact that the lower branches must be removed periodically to retain sufficient clearance for automobiles. It is tolerant of urban conditions, but for unknown reasons (possibly atmospheric conditions or lack of moisture) tends to become flat-topped and somewhat stunted in the city. Because of the success with which large specimens can be moved, the Pin Oak is useful when an immediate effect is desired.

Data

Height: 75 feet.
Spread: 40 feet.
Form: Pyramidal, densely branched, strong straight tapering stem extending to very top (origin of name "pin").

Foliage: Dense.
Texture: Fine.
Fall color: Scarlet.
Rate of growth: Medium to fast.
Culture: Moist, rich soil preferred. Adjusts to other soils.
Hardiness zone: 4–8.
Transplanting: Fibrous root system makes moving extremely easy in any size.
Special maintenance requirements: Lower branches must be removed periodically when used as a street tree. Susceptible to chlorosis evidenced by a yellowing of leaves and poor growth. Can be corrected by administering capsules of ferric ammonium citrate into soil.

OAK, RED (*Quercus borealis* or *Quercus rubra*)

Round-topped, high branching, oval tree. Grows faster than any other Oak. Excellent for use on streets or in grassed areas. Tolerant of city conditions. Brilliant red fall color. It transplants more easily than most Oaks, prefers acid, well-drained soil.

Red Oak (*Quercus borealis*).

OAK, VALLEY (*Quercus lobata*)

Deciduous tree with round-topped broad crown and spreading branches, ending in long, drooping branchlets, which often sweep the ground. It attains a height of 100 feet with a greater spread. Foliage is dark green, with a lighter underside. It thrives in the hot, interior valleys of California, in deep soil, and withstands some frost.

Design Use

A specimen tree even in nature where individual trees almost invariably stand well apart from each other. The Valley Oak has not been cultivated successfully outside of California, but in the hot, interior valleys, away from the cool fogs of the coast, it is an excellent specimen for parks and other public areas where it has room to grow.

Valley Oak
(*Quercus lobata*).
Carmel Valley,
California.

Data

Height: 60–100 feet.
Spread: 60–150 feet.
Foliage: Deciduous, upper surface dark green, lower light green.
Texture: Medium.
Bark: Bark of old trees very thick (5–6 inches). Light gray in color.

Rate of growth: Slow to medium.
Culture: Requires deep soil and warmth.
Hardiness zone: 9. Valleys of western and central California up to 2000 feet.
Transplanting: Difficult (tap root).
Special maintenance requirements: None.

OAK, WHITE (*Quercus alba*)

A massive, deciduous tree, rounded in shape, with a short, stout trunk and far-reaching almost horizontal branches, which become interestingly contorted with age. It is symmetrical in shape; its broad, rounded crown thickly covered with lustrous, deep green, regularly indented leaves.

The fall color of the White Oak is deep rose to purple. It retains its leaves well into winter and is very late to foliate in the spring. Its bark is whitish gray with deep perpendicular ridges.

The rate of growth is approximately 1 foot per year, and although it attains an impressive height (80–100 feet), it takes at least a generation for it to reach mature form. Prefers dry, gravelly, or sandy soil and is hardy from Maine to Minnesota, south to northern Florida, and west to Texas. Difficult to transplant in large size because of tap root.

Design Use

The White Oak serves best as a specimen tree left to itself with ample room to attain a spread of 50–80 feet. Because it is slow to mature (50 years) and very long-lived (800 years), it is more suitable for plantings of an institutional character, where an immediate effect is not essential. Its handsome, symmetrical structure, rugged winter silhouette, wine-red fall color and lustrous, deep green foliage make the White Oak one of the best specimen shade trees, but it is too often shunned by designers because of its slow growth. It was a tree most favored by farmers to shade grazing cattle and is frequently found today standing in the middle of a field of an older farm preserved by sentimental farmers for its beauty long after cattle are no longer the principal crop.

White Oak (*Quercus alba*). Far-reaching almost horizontal branches make it one of the best shade trees.

Data

Height: 80–100 feet.
Spread: 50–80 feet.
Form: Rounded, wide-spreading, horizontal branches. Short, stout trunk.
Foliage: Deciduous, lustrous, deep green; dead leaves remain into winter.
Texture: Coarse.
Bark: Beige-gray, deeply ridged and somewhat shaggy.
Rate of growth: Slow.
Culture: Prefers dry, gravelly, or sandy soil.
Hardiness zone: 3–9.
Transplanting: Difficult to move in large size.
Special maintenance requirements: None.

OAK, WILLOW (*Quercus phellos*)

A deciduous tree, pyramidal in smaller size (to 10-inch caliber), becoming broad and open in maturity. Densely branched and twiggy with foliage of extremely fine texture, similar in size and shape to that of the Willow leaf. This

Oak is not unlike the Pin Oak in its texture, slender branching, and twigginess. It prefers moist soil, as does the Pin Oak, and is equally easy to transplant in size. It is not hardy, however, north of New York, and trees in the

New York area have occasionally suffered from winter weather. It thrives on the eastern seaboard and in the Gulf states. A fast-growing tree (2 feet per year), it attains a height of 50 feet. Its deep, rich green foliage turns a mild yellow in the fall. It has no pests of importance.

Design Use

Much the same as the Pin Oak, the Willow Oak is suitable as a specimen shade tree and street tree. Its foliage is unusual and lower branches do not become pendulous; for these reasons, it is preferred to the Pin Oak when both are hardy. It is an extremely wide-spreading tree in maturity and should not be planted when space is limited.

Data

Height: 50–75 feet.
Spread: 40 feet.
Form: Rounded top, slender branches, finely twigged.
Foliage: Willowlike; dense, deep green.
Texture: Fine.
Fall color: Mild yellow.
Rate of growth: Rapid (2 feet per year).
Culture: Moist loam; adjusts to other conditions.
Hardiness zone: 6, southern portion, to 8.
Transplanting: Moved easily. (Shallow, fibrous root system.)
   Should not be planted in fall.
Special characteristics: No pests of importance.
Special maintenance requirements: None.

Other Useful Oak Varieties

Oak, Scarlet (*Quercus coccinea*)

A narrow tree with rounded crown, brilliant scarlet fall color, rapid growth, and an excellent shade tree. Not as easy to transplant as the Red Oak.
Height: 70 feet.
Spread: 40 feet.

Oak, Shingle (*Quercus imbrecaria*)

A majestic specimen tree, sturdy from Pennsylvania to Georgia (zone 5) and throughout the central states to Nebraska. Less difficult to transplant than many oaks. Attractive shiny laurellike leaves.
Height: 60–75 feet.
Spread: 40–60 feet.

Leaves of the **Willow Oak** resemble those of the Willow.

Willow Oak (*Quercus phellos*) nursery specimen: 12–15 feet high, 6-foot spread, ½–3 inch caliber, 32-inch ball.

PAGODA TREE, JAPANESE (Scholar Tree)
(*Sophora japonica*)

A deciduous tree, growing to a height of 50–70 feet, with a spread of approximately 50 feet. Round-headed, on a short trunk, mature trees tend to become open-branched. The tree is tolerant of pruning that is necessary if it is to be kept compact and round-headed.

Foliage is bright green and made up of many small leaflets, resembling that of the Black Locust. The flower is creamy white and pealike, borne in upright panicles or clusters in August. These are followed by yellow pods that often remain through the winter.

The Pagoda Tree has a fibrous root system and therefore is easily transplanted. It thrives in poor, dry soils and tolerates heat and drought, as well as the atmospheric conditions of the city. (Shown in color on page 81.) This tree is often referred to as Scholar Tree.

Design Use

An excellent city street tree because of its minimal cultural requirements. Its late summer blossom and attractive pods are all in its favor for city use as well as for a specimen shade tree for which it was used around Buddhist temples in Japan (hence its name).

Data

Height: 70 feet.
Spread: 50 feet.
Form: Round head on short trunk, compact in youth, spreading in maturity.
Foliage: Deciduous, dark green, much like Black Locust.
Texture: Fine.

Pagoda Tree nursery specimen: 8–10 feet high, 6-foot spread, 3–3½ inch caliber, 28-inch ball.

Fall color: Yellow.
Blossom: Creamy white, large pyramidal clusters born upright. August.
Fruit: Yellowish pods immediately following flowers and often remaining through winter.
Rate of growth: Rapid.
Culture: Prefers a light soil but thrives on dry, poor soil. Withstands cold climates.
Hardiness zone: 4–8.
Transplanting: Moved easily.
Special maintenance requirement: Pruning of young plants necessary to keep dense, rounded head.

PEAR, CALLERY (*Pyrus calleryana*)

The Callery Pear has gained popularity because of its apparent imperviousness to the air pollution of the city and resistance to fireblight. For this reason, it is at present being recommended highly as a city street tree.

The glossy green foliage and compact crown of younger specimens (3–8 inch caliber) resemble closely those of the Linden. The profuse white blossoms in late May are much in its favor.

The Callery Pear is considered sterile, its blossoms produce only an insignificant berrylike fruit.

Its fall color varies widely from a very deep red—almost a burgundy—to orange.

The tree is densely branched, which gives it a presence even without foliage. Planted in staggered rows at 18–20 feet spacings, it becomes an effective year-round screen (see photo on page 60). In summary, a handsome and very useful tree. Unfortunately, at this writing it is being overused.

Data

Height: 25–35 feet.
Spread: 20–25 feet.
Form: Pyramidal in younger trees. Broadens in maturity.
Foliage: Deep green, highly glossy.
Texture: Medium.
Fall color: Very effective but with wide variation. Deep red to yellow-orange.
Rate of growth: Rapid in early years.

Blossom: White. Extremely profuse.
Culture: Tolerates most soils. Appears to thrive in difficult city conditions.
Hardiness zones: 4–8.

Transplanting: Difficult to plant in leaf. Strong preference for late winter or spring transplanting although some plantsmen claim to have no difficulty out of season.

Other Useful Callery Pear Varieties

Aristocrat

Maintains central leader. Flowers slightly less spectacular than the Bradford. Less subject to snow damage.

Bradford

The most handsome but subject to splitting under weight of heavy, wet snow. Another Callery Pear should be used where such weather conditions are common.

Chanticleer

Narrower than the Bradford. More upright. Good as a street tree and preferable—because of narrowness—when damage by bus or truck is possible.

Bradford Callery Pear nursery specimen: 8–10 feet high, 6–8 feet spread, 2–2½ inch caliber.

Redspire

Narrow, more oval than pyramidal. Flower clusters larger than the Bradford.

Whitehouse

More pyramidal in maturity than Bradford. Good for narrow streets. Fast grower.

PEAR, COMMON (*Pyrus communis*)

A narrow, deciduous, fruiting tree with leathery foliage and white blossoms that appear in late spring.

Design Use

Its narrowness and limited height (20–25 feet) make it especially suited in scale to the small outdoor space, such as a dining terrace where the spread of most species would overpower. Because the branches ascend at an acute angle and are held close to the trunk, little of the useful floor area is taken up by the tree, which makes it especially valuable in such spaces. The Pear is most readily trained as an espalier (see Chapter 6).

Data

Height: 20–25 feet.
Spread: 12–15 feet.
Form: Distinctly narrow and compact. Usually high branching.
Foliage: Dark green, leathery and glossy.
Texture: Medium.
Blossom: White, late May.
Fall color: Dull deep red to brown.
Rate of growth: Medium.
Culture: Adjusts to most soils.

Hardiness zone: 4–8.
Transplanting: Especially difficult in large size. No difficulty encountered in normal nursery sizes.
Special maintenance requirements: Subject to scale, which can be controlled by spraying, and fireblight, a disease that has been less common in recent years but causes leaves to turn black very suddenly.

Pear Tree nursery specimen: 6–8 feet high, 2–3 feet spread, 2-inch caliber, 24-inch ball.

PLANE TREE, LONDON (*Platanus acerifolia*)

A deciduous, wide-spreading tree, generally oval in form, open in habit, with straight trunk and exfoliating or peeling bark. The most interesting aspect of this tree is the mottled appearance of its bark. Its leaves are large and have little fall color; its structure when unrestrained becomes rangy.

The real importance of the Plane Tree is its hardiness in the city and at the shore, two areas where the plant palette is extremely limited.

Some consider this a "dirty" tree because it sheds its bark annually. Others consider this a small price to pay for the attractive underbark that is revealed.

Design Use

The London Plane Tree, because of its resistance to soot and drought and other hazards of city life, has for years been among the first choices for use as a city street tree.

Its vigorous response to pruning has led designers to choose it for pollarding and pleaching (see Chapter 6). Its rapid rate of growth also makes it desirable for city use when an immediate effect is important.

It is the most tolerant of city conditions and the most resistant to twig blight (anthracnose) that afflicts the species. The leaf of this variety is large and similar to the Maple; its seed balls form in clusters of two or more. The underbark exposed by peeling is cream color. The Bloodgood strain of this tree (*Plantanus acerifolia bloodgood*) is a superior selection, withstanding difficult site conditions and exhibiting the greatest resistance to anthracnose.

Data

Height: 80–100 feet.
Spread: 50–75 feet.
Form: Wide-spreading; open, generally rounded.
Bark: Upper bark (tan color) flakes off, revealing patches of inner bark.
Foliage: Large leaves, 4–8 inches across.
Texture: Coarse.
Fall color: None.
Rate of growth: Very rapid.
Culture: Sandy loam; adjusts to poor soil.
Hardiness zone: 5 (southern portion) to 8.
Transplanting: Easily moved in large size.
Special characteristics: Interesting peeling bark; tolerant of city atmosphere, as well as salt spray.
Special maintenance requirements: Spray twice annually for anthracnose; treat canker stain; remove infected parts. Removal of flaking bark is not an important maintenance problem.

Sycamore nursery specimen (*Platanus acerifolia*): 18–20 feet high, 6-foot spread, 3½-inch caliber, 32-inch ball.

Young Sycamore Tree 25 feet high, 5–6 inch caliber. Specimens of this size are immediately effective in a landscape design.

Other Useful Plane Tree Varieties

Oriental Plane Tree (*Platanus orientalis*)

Grows to much greater size and therefore becomes less useful than the London Plane Tree in the city, where its spread must be limited, except, perhaps, for the grand avenue. The underbark of the Oriental Plane Tree is greenish white. Seed balls form in clusters of three or more.

American Plane Tree or Sycamore
(*Platanus occidentalis*)

A giant among trees attaining a height of as much as 170 feet along stream banks and near ponds. Its underbark is

Typical flaking bark of this species.

creamy white. It makes a handsome specimen shade tree, but is the most susceptible of all Plane Trees to anthracnose (bud blight).

POPLAR, LOMBARDY (*Populus italica nigra*)

A deciduous tree, unique in its slender, columnar form. Often reaches a height of 100 feet. Experts will advise against the use of this tree for a variety of reasons—all valid—but there is no other species that can equal its slim grace.

The Lombardy Poplar is subject to a trunk canker that will cause most trees to die within 30 years—usually much earlier. Its roots are so voracious in their search for water that they often pry open sewer lines. As is the case with all fast-growing trees, the wood is brittle and liable to break in heavy winds. Finally, it is a short-lived tree, generally succumbing to its ailments within 15–20 years.

All true. Yet, again, there is no true substitute for the design qualities of this tree. And when these qualities are strongly desired, the tree should not be eliminated but rather used in such a manner that its failure cannot destroy the design. It should not, therefore, be used as a focal point, but for secondary effect, where the dying of several tops or breaking of branches will not be a major loss. In other words, the Lombardy Poplar should never be planted as a single specimen; it should always be planted in clusters where the failure of one or several will not matter, and where they can be quickly replaced with younger specimens. It also follows that this tree should not be used in any design that demands symmetry. Even when an allée or long avenue is contemplated—for which this tree has no equal—several rows 5–8 feet apart should be used in order to avoid the inevitable missing-tooth appearance caused by failures in a single-row planting.

As for its destructive roots, these can be kept from sewer lines by flushing 1 pound of copper sulfate crystals into the system four times each year, after which no other wastage should be flushed through the pipes for several hours. The wandering root system can also be kept some-

what in check by plentiful watering and the introduction into the soil of moisture-retaining agents, such as peat moss, in the area where it is desired to confine the root system.

The Lombardy Poplar is extremely fast-growing (3 feet per year is not unusual in young plants). It can also be transplanted bare-root in 15–20 foot heights, providing an immediate effect at little cost. It thrives in the atmospheric conditions of the city, but requires a thoroughly moist soil; responds vigorously to pruning and can be treated as a super-hedge by clipping the tops to a uniform height.

A design should not be deprived of the beauty of this tree or any other short-lived tree merely on the basis of longevity. Rather, it should be planted together with a hardy species that most closely approaches its beauty (in this case, the Fastigiate English Oak). An immediate effect can be obtained with Poplars in the largest size; the Oaks can be planted in smaller sizes calculated to mature by the time the Poplars begin to fail. This combined planting of different species similar in appearance should be used in all cases where an immediate effect is desired, but a slow-growing tree is preferred.

Design Use

In masses or drifts, the movement of these trees in the slightest breeze is an unusually pleasing sight. The great advantage of this mass use of the Lombardy Poplar, as has been pointed out, is that such asymmetric plantings are in no way damaged by the failure or wind destruction of single specimens. Spacing in these plantings can vary from 3–10 feet. Lombardies have been planted in this manner at the International Hotel at Kennedy International Airport in New York (Zion & Breen Associates, Landscape Architects and Site Planners). (See photo on page 169.)

The Lombardy Poplar thrives in city locations where replacements can easily be made in the event of failure; it is highly recommended because the rapid growth and great height of this tree can provide green against tall buildings with an effectiveness that cannot be equalled in the same period of time by other species. Furthermore, its narrowness makes this Poplar especially suited to the limited planting areas available in a crowded city. It should not, however, be used as a street tree, but rather in land now available through set-backs, as well as interior courts.

In the private city garden, the Lombardy Poplar can be used as a hedge planting, 3–5 feet apart.

The easy swaying of the Poplar in the wind is one of its most attractive attributes.

Substitutes

The Simon Poplar (*Populus simoni* var. *fastigiata*) is probably the closest substitute for the Lombardy Poplar. The Bolleana Poplar (*Populus alba* var. *pyramidalis*) would be a second choice, Both varieties are more long-lived, but *neither* has the grace of the Lombardy. *Quercus robur* variety *fastigiata* is recommended as the best long-lived substitute.

Data

Height: 50–100 feet.
Spread: 10–15 feet.
Form: Narrow, vertical.
Foliage: Dense.
Texture: Medium.
Fall color: Strong yellow.
Rate of growth: Very rapid.
Culture: Rich, moist soil; can adjust to gravelly loam when sufficient moisture is available.
Hardiness zone: 4.
Transplanting: Easily moved in all sizes. Bare-root planting of trees 15–20 feet in height in not uncommon.
Special maintenance requirements: Removal of dead branches, spraying for removal of scale.
Special characteristics: Short-lived. It succumbs to canker for which there is no known cure as early as 12–15 years after planting. Trunk usually completely covered to base with tightly ascending branches, providing excel-

An effective linear planting of **Lombardy Poplars**.

Lombardy Poplar nursery specimen: 12 feet high, 1-foot spread, 1-inch caliber, 3-gallon can in place of earth ball.

lent screening. Can destroy sewage or drainage pipes unless proper precaution is taken (see Chapter 4). Short-lived; subject to trunk canker, causing tops to die.

REDWOOD, DAWN   (*Metasequoia glyptostroboides*)

Deciduous conifer. A rapid grower reaching a height of 70–100 feet with a spread of 25 feet. Some specimens known to have grown to 120 feet. Until recently, this tree was known only as a fossil, but was discovered growing wild in China in 1941.

Design Use

Similar in appearance and usefulness to the Baldcypress. Similar fernlike foliage but developing a broader, rounder crown in maturity. Excellent specimen for larger properties such as parks and golf courses. Good choice for lining a monumental approach road. Extremely fast-growing. Tolerant of urban pollution.

Data

Height: 70–100 feet.

Spread: 25 feet.

Form: Single trunk, pyramidal when young, developing broader, rounder crown with age. Feathery appearance.

Foliage: Fernlike. Bright green.

Texture: Fine.

Fall color: Reddish brown.

Rate of growth: Very rapid.

Culture: Thrives in moist, well-drained soil, slightly acid. Prefers open, sunny location.

Hardiness zone: 4–8.

Transplanting: Easily moved.

Special maintenance requirements: None. Needs little or no pruning. Retains pyramidal shape.

Dawn Redwood specimen.

SERVICEBERRY, DOWNY (Shadbush)
(*Amelanchier canadensis*)

A small white-flowering tree with an open, rounded crown, native to woodland. Its early white flowers, preceding Dogwood and Cherry, make it an especially useful woodland tree. The light gray bark and slender trunk are very delicate in appearance, as is the apricot-orange fall foliage. It is a good tree for mass planting for spring and fall color, and to attract birds. Excellent for planting along the edge and through the interior of existing woodlands. (Shown in color on page 79.) Salt-tolerant; hardy near the shore.

Data

Form: Small, rounded, open crown; slender branches; light, delicate silhouette.

Height: 20–30 feet.

Spread: 12–15 feet.

Blossom: White, early spring.

Foliage: Small leaf, medium to fine texture.

Fall color: Subdued orange.

Bark: Light gray.

Culture: Rich, moist soil preferred, but will adapt to other soils. Requires generous moisture. Prefers shady site.

Hardiness zone: 3–7.

Transplanting: Easily done with young plants (8–12 feet high).

Special maintenance requirements: None.

Amelanchier laevis, variously called Shadblow, Shadbush, or Allegheny Serviceberry, is a narrower tree and more irregular in outline.

The Serviceberry has a strong horizontal branching habit.

Downy Serviceberry nursery specimen: 6–8 feet high, 4-foot spread, 1½–2 inch caliber, 22-inch ball.

SORREL TREE (Sourwood, Tree Andromeda)
(*Oxydendrum arboreum*)

A deciduous tree, generally small (20–25 feet) although it sometimes reaches a height of 70 feet. Often multistemmed, it is oval in form with spreading, drooping branches. Its most outstanding characteristics are its blossom and fall color. The flowers, which appear in mid–July, are small, creamy-white, and resemble closely the blossom of the lily-of-the-valley. Clusters of several sprigs of blossoms hang from the tips of the branches. The fruit that develops from these flowers remains on the tree far into the winter as dried capsules and creates a feathery appearance.

Foliage is leathery and lustrous. Fall color is deep maroon, occasionally approaching crimson in certain weather conditions.

Design Use

The Sorrel Tree should be considered a flowering tree and used as such in a planting design. It is best used in groups or clusters, although a single, large, mature specimen can certainly stand by itself. It is not a particularly fast grower, and nurseries seldom carry specimens larger than 3 or 4 inches in caliber (15–20 feet high). Large specimens (7–8 inch caliber, 25–30 feet high) are occasionally available and not especially difficult to transplant. (Shown in color on page 80.)

This tree has something of the natural woodsy appearance of the Dogwood and can be used well in relation to existing woods, particularly as a fall color accent. Related to Dogwood, Rhododendron, Laurel, and Pieris (heath family), it is an excellent choice for grouping with these plants. It is a good substitute for the Dogwood. The deep red fall coloring presents something of a problem when used in relation to building materials of a reddish hue.

The late period of bloom (mid–July through August) is an important design factor, suggesting its selection for areas in active use during this season.

Full sun is required for maximum blossom, but the Sorrel Tree is tolerant of shade and adjusts well to most soil conditions and the rigors of city life. An excellent but underused tree.

Data

Height: Most commonly under 30 feet (occasionally reaches 70 feet).
Spread: 15–20 feet.
Form: Slender, oval with irregular top in mature trees.
Foliage: Glossy and leathery, deep green.
Texture: Medium.

The flower, which appears in mid–July. (Shown in color on page 79.)

Sorrel Tree nursery specimen: 8–10 feet high, 4-foot spread, 2–2½ inch caliber, 24-inch ball.

Fall color: Deep red.
Flower: Creamy white, resembles the lily-of-the-valley, appears in clusters, components of which curve upward.
Fruit: Cream-colored seed capsules remain late into winter.
Rate of growth: Slow.
Culture: Moist, well-drained loam, slightly acid; adjusts to almost all conditions, sun or shade.
Hardiness zone: 5–9.
Transplanting: Easily moved (fibrous root system).
Special characteristics: Interesting blossom in mid-July. Fruit (dry capsules) remains into winter. Tolerant of city conditions.
Special maintenance requirements: None.

TREE OF HEAVEN
(The "Tree That Grows in Brooklyn")
(*Ailanthus altissima*)

The hardiest tree we have for undesirable planting and atmospheric conditions! Its form varies widely with its situation. When grown in the open sun, it can attain a wide-spreading, rounded form. It is most usually seen—especially in the city—as a single-stemmed, high-branching tree. It reaches a height of 50 feet and spread of 30 feet.

Design Use

Although infrequently used, the *Ailanthus* has design potential especially in the city where it appears to thrive in the most sooty and dusty atmosphere and impoverished soil conditions. It is often seen piercing the concrete of sidewalks or streets, with no apparent source of air or surface water. Another area in which the *Ailanthus* fills a design gap is at the shore, where it is extremely tolerant of salt spray and sandy soil.

The winter silhouette is very stark, which is a serious drawback, and it is the last of the trees to foliate in spring. However, its foliage, composed of many leaflets, creates an interesting texture and an almost tropical, palmlike appearance. This can be accentuated in specimen trees by removing all but the terminal swirl of leaves on each branch.

Another interesting effect of an exotic or tropical nature can be attained by planting several single-stemmed saplings or whips in one pit, creating "instant thickets." When these trees have been stripped of side branches, the effect is much like that of bamboo.

Fall color is negligible, but the fruit that appears in late summer can be extremely showy (orange-red or yellow-green) if the tree is grown in open sun.

The *Ailanthus* is short-lived (25–30 years), which limits its usefulness in some circumstances. This is compensated for to some extent by its extremely rapid growth.

Data

Height: 50 feet.
Spread: 30 feet.

Tree of Heaven. At home in the asphalt jungle.

Form: Varies from single stem with narrow spread to rounded crown with several large spreading branches.
Foliage: Medium to fine texture (small leaflets). Deep green.
Fall color: Orange if tree is in open, sunny location; otherwise, negligible.
Fruit: Late summer, 8-inch panicles, bright orange-red to yellow-green.
Rate of growth: Very rapid (often 5 feet per year).
Culture: Tolerant of almost any soil.
Hardiness zone: 4–8.
Transplanting: Bare-root whips (saplings) are most dependable.
Special maintenance requirements: Control of suckers. Pruning for design effect.
Special characteristics: Excellent for city and shore plantings. Resistant to soot and salt spray. Very stark winter silhouette.

TUPELO (Pepperidge, Black Gum, Sour Gum) (*Nyssa sylvatica*)

A deciduous tree of varied habit, tending to be pyramidal or conical when young. Older specimens develop a characteristic jaggedness of outline. Foliage of the Tupelo is outstanding. In summer, it is highly glossy, deep green, leathery, and dense; in autumn, the scarlet and orange coloration is probably the most brilliant of all our trees.

Use of this tree in planting design is unfortunately limited by two of its characteristics: First, it is a difficult tree to transplant in size, having a deep tap root and lacking a fibrous root system. Trees over 5 inches in caliber are generally considered risky, although many larger trees have successfully been moved after thorough root-pruning and feeding to encourage a more fibrous root system. When an immediate effect of some stature is desired, this tree is thus limited in its usefulness. Nurseries seldom have dependable specimens available in sizes larger than 5 inches in caliber, and the species is not a notably rapid grower.

The other characteristic of the Tupelo that limits its design use is its apparent need for a wet location with rich soil. Although many specimens may be observed growing far from an apparent source of water, particularly on Long Island, it is quite probable that the deep tap root has approached the water table or some underground spring.

The Tupelo produces an inconspicuous black fruit and is therefore attractive to birds. It is little troubled by insects or disease.

Design Use

If the proper conditions of soil and moisture are available and an immediate effect is not required, there are few trees that can equal the Tupelo as a specimen tree in an open area (it matures to approximately 60 feet in height, with a spread of 30 feet). Its glossy, green foliage and brilliant autumn color, as well as its irregular, open form and particularly fine network of branchlets, give it year-round interest.

As a young tree, it is pyramidal in form and often branches to the ground. These lower branches are generally lost as the tree matures.

In establishing or redeveloping a woodland, this is an outstanding tree to be massed in low, moist lands.

Tupelo nursery specimen: 6 feet high, 3-foot spread, 1½–2 inch caliber, 24-inch ball.

Data

Height: 40–60 feet.
Spread: 20–30 feet.
Form: Pyramidal, densely branched when young, maturing to open crown, irregular in outline, branches contorted, generally horizontal.
Foliage: Deep green glossy, leathery, dense.
Texture: Medium.
Fall color: Outstanding coloration; intense scarlet and orange.
Rate of growth: Medium.
Culture: Rich, acid and moist soil.
Hardiness zone: 4–9.
Transplanting: Difficult in large sizes (long, descending tap root with few fibrous roots).
Special maintenance requirements: None.

WILLOW, WEEPING (*Salix babylonica*)

A deciduous tree with a unique, immensely rounded form on a short, stout trunk. Forty feet high in maturity, it often also attains a spread of 40 feet, with its long pendulous branches touching the ground. Its leaves are small (2–4 inches) and born on long, flexible stems that move easily in the slightest breeze.

The Willow is usually the first tree to foliate in the spring and the last to lose leaves in the autumn. Its twigs begin to turn green as early as February in the northeast.

It is an extraordinarily rapid grower and for this reason its wood tends to be weak and especially subject to storm damage. Its roots are voracious water-seekers and may cause damage to water and sewer installation if planted within range (50 feet).

The Willow transplants easily and thrives in a sunny location when given an adequate moisture supply.

Design Use

When planted in groups of three or more, the billowy outline of the foliage mass provides an unequalled design effect. It is the use of single specimens at a pond or grave that has become a cliché and doubtless led to the decline of the Willow's popularity.

Its extremely rapid growth and the ease with which it can be transplanted in large size make it especially valuable when an immediate effect is desired.

Because its foliage appears so early in spring and remains until late fall and its twigs begin to color in February, the Willow affords year-round interest.

Interesting design effects can be obtained by lining walks or roadways with the Babylon Willow, creating a dark tunnel of green, lengthening the apparent distance. Planting the Willow at different levels as on a mound will also intensify the "billowiness" of the foliage outline.

Properly used, the Weeping Willow has no substitute. However, it is well to be aware of its several weak points: Its roots are destructive of sewer and water lines; its leaves yellow and fall after a prolonged dry spell, earning it a reputation of being untidy; its wood is weak and subject to storm damage; its great foliage mass offers strong wind resistance, which makes it the first to fall in a summer wind storm (planting in groves affords some self-protection).

Data

Height: 30–40 feet.
Spread: 30–40 feet.
Form: Rounded; weeping branches trailing to ground.
Foliage: Light green, long, narrow.
Texture: Fine.
Fall color: Yellow.
Rate of growth: Very rapid.
Culture: Moist soil, open, sunny location.
Hardiness zone: 5–8.
Transplanting: Moved easily.
Special characteristics: Leaves fall readily in dry weather; branches break easily in storms and must be pruned often; destroys sewer pipes.

Other Useful Willow Varieties

Niobe Weeping Willow

Has yellow branches and is slightly more hardy, but it is not as "weepy" as the *babylonica*, which is preferred by the author.

Laurel Willow (*Salix pentandra*)

Has deep green, lustrous leaves, much like those of the Mountain Laurel. Highly susceptible to leaf diseases, causing early leaf-fall.

Black Willow (*Salix nigra*)

Is by nature multistemmed and its trunks create enormous interest. This species is difficult to obtain in nurseries and usually collected from the woods. It thrives along streams and in marshy areas.

Weeping Willow nursery specimen: 6–8 feet high, 6-foot spread, 1½–2 inch caliber, 5-gallon can in place of earth ball.

By nature, the **Black Willow** is multistemmed.

The striking beauty of the trunks in a Black Willow grove.

YELLOW-WOOD, AMERICAN (*Cladrastis lutea*)

A deciduous tree, broad-headed, with open branching revealing a handsome, light gray bark similar to that of the Beech. It attains a height of 40–50 feet and spread of as much as 40 feet.

The Yellow-wood produces a wisterialike, drooping white blossom in late spring, which is concealed to a great extent by dense light green foliage.

Design Use

A graceful specimen tree with the added interest of its gray bark, soft winter silhouette, and spring flower. Effective when planted singly, or in groups. An excellent shade tree.

The smooth gray bark of the **Yellow-wood** closely resembles that of the Beech.

Spray formation of the leaves adds to the pleasing grace of the Yellow-wood.

American Yellow-wood nursery specimen: 10–12 feet high, 7-foot spread, 2½ -inch caliber, 30-inch ball.

Data

Height: 40–50 feet.
Spread: 40–50 feet.
Form: Oval, broad head, open structure.
Foliage: Delicate, bright green.
Texture: Medium.
Fall color: Bright yellow.
Rate of growth: Medium.
Blossom: White, late spring. Flowers profusely in alternate years.
Bark: Smooth, light gray, similar to that of Beech.
Culture: Prefers moist, rich soil.
Hardiness zone: 4 (southern portion) through 8.

Transplanting: Difficult in trees larger than 6 inches in caliber because of far-spreading, shallow roots.
Special maintenance requirements: Summer pruning preferred; trees bleed profusely when pruned in winter or spring.

EVERGREEN TREES

ACACIA, BLACKWOOD (*Acacia melanoxylon*)

An evergreen tree of pyramidal form and medium height (30–40 feet). Its divided foliage, almost fernlike, together with its rapid growth when planted in good soil, have made it a popular tree. Of easy culture when provided with ample water and good drainage. Its use as a street tree has been waning because of its tendency to seek water, reaching under sidewalks toward irrigated lawns and resulting in broken pavements.

Design Use

The Blackwood Acadia, because of its medium height, dense, dark, gray-green appearance, is an excellent tree for background plantings. Its rapid rate of growth makes it useful when an immediate effect is desired.

Data

Height: 30–40 feet.
Spread: 20–30 feet.
Form: Pyramidal. Straight trunk extends through the tree.
Foliage: Evergreen, dense and dark gray-green. Finely divided.
Texture: Fine.
Blossom: Yellow, January to March.
Bark: Medium dark gray, lightly furrowed.
Rate of growth: Very rapid.

Blackwood Acacia.

Culture: Requires ample water and good drainage. Will not tolerate temperatures of less than 18 degrees.
Hardiness zone: 10.
Transplanting: No difficulty encountered if balled or canned; very difficult to transplant otherwise.
Special maintenance requirements: None.

CAROB TREE (*Ceratonia siliqua*)

Evergreen tree of rounded form and dense, glossy, evergreen foliage. The Carob or St. John's Bread Tree thrives only in warm, dry climates.

Design Use

The Carob, because of its solid, compact habit, freedom from disease, and outstanding ability to thrive in dry soil, is an excellent street tree, especially suitable for use in public open spaces where its shade is needed. Avoid the variety *Bolser*, which produces an unusual profusion of pods.

Data

Height: 30–40 feet.
Spread: 30–40 feet.
Form: Rounded and compact.
Foliage: Dark, evergreen, glossy.
Texture: Medium.
Rate of growth: Slow.
Culture: Dry, sandy soil.
Hardiness zone: 10.
Transplanting: Difficult to transplant unless balled or boxed or from cans.
Special maintenance requirements: None.

CEDAR, BLUE ATLAS (*Cedrus atlantica glauca*)

An evergreen tree, growing to a height of 120 feet with a spread of 80–100 feet, pyramidal in form, with downy needlelike foliage of an unusual, light blue color. The open horizontal branches from which the side branchlets grow downward produce an exotic and highly textured appearance.

The fruit of the Cedar is a cone that requires two years to mature and during this period adds interest to the tree since it is borne on the upper side of the branches and is highly visible.

The Cedar of Lebanon is very similar in appearance, but does not have a blue-colored variety. Its needles are more coarse.

Design Use

The Blue Atlas Cedar makes a starkly interesting—almost grotesque—specimen for a large open space. Although it is fairly rapid in growth, the young tree is rather tightly pyramidal and of little interest. Large specimens, which are at present hard to come by, are strongly recommended.

Because of its unusual color and very jagged outline, this tree may be too rich for any but the most severe architectural facade.

If the blue foliage is not considered desirable, an appropriate substitute would be the green form (*Cedrus atlantica*) or the Cedar of Lebanon that also has green foliage but of a firmer nature.

The blue of this Cedar stands out handsomely against the darker evergreen background.

Data

Height: 40–60 feet (can reach 120 feet).
Spread: 30–40 feet.
Form: Pyramidal, with open, horizontal branching. Jagged in outline.
Foliage: Needlelike, very light blue, downy.
Texture: Fine.
Fruit: Cones require two years to mature, borne on upper side of branches.
Rate of growth: Medium.
Culture: Requires good soil.
Hardiness zone: 6–9.
Transplanting: Somewhat difficult in the large size.
Special maintenance requirements: None.

Blue Atlas Cedar nursery specimen: 8–10 feet high, 4-foot spread, 2½–3 inch caliber, 30-inch ball.

CEDAR, DEODAR (*Cedrus deodara*)

Evergreen tree of pyramidal form and great height (150 feet), with extremely graceful, pendulous branches (50-foot spread). Blue coloration.

Design Use

Because of its striking shape and habit, the Deodar Cedar should be allowed the maximum of space in which to develop its characteristic form. An extremely majestic and graceful specimen tree.

Data

Height: 60–70 feet (can reach 100 feet).
Spread: 40 feet.
Form: Pyramidal when young; broad and flat-topped in maturity.
Foliage: Dark bluish green, dense.

Texture: Fine.
Fruit: Large cones (4 inches long) almost continuously in evidence on upper side of branches.
Rate of growth: Slow to medium.
Culture: Prefers heavier, well-drained soils. Avoid wet ground.
Hardiness zone: 6–9.
Transplanting: No difficulty if balled or planted from cans.
Special maintenance requirements: None.

Other Useful Cedar Variety

Cedar of Lebanon (*Cedrus libani*)

One of our most picturesque trees in its mature form. Closely resembles the Atlantic Cedar. Needles are firmer. Other characteristics and requirements are identical.

CYPRESS, LEYLAND (*Cupressocyparis leylandii*)

Design Use

An excellent tree as specimen or for screening purposes. In its hardiness zones, it serves as well for this latter purpose as the White, Austrian, and Japanese Black Pines do farther north. Very tolerant of heavy pruning; makes excellent hedge.

Data

Height: 50–70 feet (can reach 100 feet).
Spread: 12–15 feet.

Form: Somewhat columnar.
Foliage: Feathery.
Texture: Fine.
Fruit: Cones.
Rate of growth: Rapid.
Transplanting: Best planted from containers. Roots are wide-spreading, making this tree difficult to ball and burlap.
Culture: Tolerant of almost all soil types, as well as salt spray.
Hardiness zone: 6–10.

CYPRESS, MONTEREY (*Cupressus macrocarpa*)

Perhaps the rarest, certainly the most unusual tree of North America, this rugged tree subsists under almost any condition of soil or exposure, even to being lashed by salt spray. Loosely pyramidal. Short, horizontal branches above and wide-spreading limbs below, originating from a short, heavy trunk. Its native habitat, along the 17 Mile Drive of the Pacific Coast, finds it confined to two groves, one at Cypress Point north of Carmel, and the other at Point Lobos State Park, south of Carmel, California.

Design Use

This tree makes a solid windbreak. The fact that it subsists under almost any condition of soil or exposure, when planted along the coast, makes it of value in those areas of fog and wind. It will not thrive out of reach of damp sea winds.

Data

Height: 40 feet, occasionally to 60 feet.
Spread: 30–40 feet.
Foliage: Dense and dark, bright green when young.
Texture: Medium.
Rate of growth: Slow, after a medium start.
Culture: Sandy soils, rocky. Survives under almost any condition of exposure or soil.
Hardiness zone: 7.
Transplanting: Difficult except from cans or boxes.
Special maintenance requirements: None.

The rugged nature of the **Monterey Cypress** is dramatically demonstrated here.

EUCALYPTUS, LONGBEAK
(*Eucalyptus camaldulensis rostrata*)

A large, handsome evergreen tree of symmetrical form, attaining as much as 200 feet in height. It withstands high temperature, as well as considerable frost. One of the most drought-resistant of trees, it endures even the intense heat of the southern Colorado desert. Grows in inundated land, withstands alkali.

Design Use

An excellent evergreen specimen shade tree when ample space is available to accommodate its height and spread. A good park tree and especially useful in areas of intense heat and drought and heavy concentration of alkali.

Longbeak Eucalyptus.

Data

Height: 60–100 feet.
Spread: 30–50 feet.
Foliage: Evergreen; narrow, dark green leaves.
Texture: Medium.
Bark: Reddish twigs and gray bark that usually flakes off in patches.

Rate of growth: Slow in height, rapid in spread.
Culture: Adjusts to any soil condition; endures intense heat and considerable frost.
Hardiness zone: 9.
Transplanting: Difficult, unless taken out of hard soil.
Special maintenance requirements: None.

FIG, RUSTY-LEAF (*Ficus rubiginosa australis*)

An evergreen tree with large, spreading, deep green leathery foliage, with rusty underside. This tree is superior to other rubber trees available because of its relatively compact habit.

Design Use

The principal design interest of this tree is its foliage, which resembles that of the Southern Magnolia in its size and rusty underside. Its limited height, relative to other rubber trees, makes it suitable for use when space is limited. Its bushy habit, rounded form, and dense foliage give it strength to anchor a large building.

Rusty-leaf Fig.

Data

Height: 30–50 feet.
Spread: 30–50 feet.
Foliage: Dark green, leathery, rusty underside; leaves similar in size to the Southern Magnolia (approximately 5 inches).
Texture: Course.
Bark: Medium gray-brown.
Rate of growth: Fast to medium.

Hardiness zone: 9.
Transplanting: Moderately difficult because of heavy root system.
Special maintenance requirements: None.

FIR, DOUGLAS (*Pseudotsuga menziesii* or *taxifolia*)

An evergreen tree, attaining a height of 200 feet with a spread of only 20 feet, pyramidal in form, with needlelike foliage. Dense in appearance while young, it develops open branching in maturity.

The Douglas Fir is characterized by a deep tap root, but can be transplanted without difficulty when properly root-pruned to encourage a fibrous root system. It requires full sun and good, moist soil; it is easily injured by wind. Its appearance is greatly enhanced by its cones, which hang in clusters.

Design Use

An excellent single specimen or massed when soil and sun conditions are acceptable.

The Douglas Fir is very tolerant of pruning and can be used as a tall hedge.

Data

Height: 70–80 feet (can reach 200 feet).
Spread: 15–20 feet.
Form: Pyramidal, dense in youth, open branching in maturity. Lower branches drooping, upper branches ascending.
Foliage: Evergreen, needlelike. Blue-green.
Texture: Medium.
Fruit: Cones that hang in clusters.
Rate of growth: Fastest of evergreens.

Douglas Fir nursery specimen: 15 feet high, 6-foot spread, 3–3½ inch caliber, 42-inch ball.

Culture: Requires moist soil. Injured by high winds.
Hardiness zone: 4–6.
Transplanting: Easily moved when root-pruned to discourage formation of deep tap root.
Special maintenance requirements: None.

HEMLOCK, CANADA (*Tsuga canadensis*)

An evergreen with needlelike foliage and generally pyramidal form, reaching a height, in maturity, of 90 feet with a spread of 30 feet or more.

The deep green foliage is especially fine in texture and dense and under proper growing conditions is retained to the ground. It responds very well to pruning and clipping.

The Hemlock thrives only in deep, moist loam and will tolerate shade. Rate of growth is moderately rapid after establishment. It is currently being threatened by the Woolly Adelgio and Hemlock Scale, both of which can be controlled by chemical spray. Local agricultural extension services can advise as to prevalence and appropriate spray.

Design Use

The dense foliage of the Hemlock makes it excellent for screening or as background for other specimen or flowering trees. In maturity, it also makes an excellent specimen for the large open space, but it is very slow in attaining its open mature form.

As a year-round screening plant, the Hemlock is unexcelled since it generally retains its foliage to the

Typical feathery formation of **Hemlock** branches.

ground and will thrive in light shade, which few other evergreens will do. It is thus very useful for adding winter color and height, as well as screening in a wooded area.

The Hemlock also serves very well as a hedge since it responds excellently to clipping and can be kept indefinitely as low as 3 feet or at any desired height.

The Hemlock looks best when planted in masses, for individual young trees have an uninteresting outline. It has a natural "forest" look and appears out of place in sophisticated planting designs. It fares poorly in the atmospheric conditions of the city.

Data

Height: 90 feet.
Spread: 30 feet.
Form: Pyramidal, with slightly drooping branches.
Foliage: Evergreen, needlelike, deep green, dense.
Texture: Very fine.
Rate of growth: Medium to rapid.
Culture: Moist, rich, acid soil. The best evergreen for light shade.
Hardiness zone: 3–8.
Transplanting: Little difficulty with ample earth ball, in sizes up to 15 feet in height.
Special maintenance requirements: Soil must be kept generally moist. Affected by intense heat and strong wind.

Other Useful Hemlock Varieties

Carolina Hemlock (*Tsuga caroliniana*)

Even more dense of foliage, but is not hardy as far north.

Canada Hemlock nursery specimen: 10–12 feet high, 6-foot spread, 3-inch caliber, 42-inch ball.

Weeping (Sargent) Hemlock
(*Tsuga canadensis pendula*)

A weeping form of the Canada Hemlock. It is extremely exotic in appearance, forming a billowy mound several times broader than it is high. In the author's opinion, this tree is too opaque and without structure to sustain interest.

MAGNOLIA, SOUTHERN (*Magnolia grandiflora*)

A tall, pyramidal evergreen tree with extremely large (5–8 inches long) lustrous green leaves with a deep rust-brown underside and large (8 inches in diameter) white flowers that appear in late May and into the summer.

It is almost invariably a single-stemmed tree, growing as tall as 100 feet with a spread of 50 feet. It is native from the Carolinas south through Florida and west to Texas and thrives on both coasts in hardiness zone 7. It is hardy only to the extreme southern section of New Jersey, although it has been grown in sheltered areas as far north as Brooklyn, where a large specimen now exists (see photo on opposite page).

As with other Magnolias, the southern variety prefers rich, deeply acid soil and will not tolerate the alkaline soil or climate of our north central states. It demands a well-drained site, leading many plantsmen to place a layer of coarse stones at the base of the pit to improve drainage. Its

fleshy roots are particularly slow to heal and subject to rot. It is therefore wise to plant this tree with a large earth ball in the spring when healing and regeneration are most likely to be rapid.

Design Use

The size of the tree and coarseness of its foliage, together with its single trunk and pyramidal form, indicate its use as a specimen tree in the foreground of large buildings, or in open space on a large property. Its large, deep green, glossy foliage with a brown underside and immense blossoms make it a striking specimen. Its ability to withstand urban atmospheric conditions makes it an excellent choice for city plantings. It is very successfully used in Washington, D.C.

Data

Height: 60–90 feet.
Spread: 30–50 feet.
Form: Pyramidal, single trunk.
Foliage: Evergreen. Large, deep green, rust-brown underside. 5–10 inches long.
Texture: Coarse.
Blossom: Large white blossoms (8 inches in diameter) in late May and into summer.
Rate of growth: Medium.
Culture: Prefers rich, acid, garden soil and will not tolerate alkaline soil.
Hardiness zone: 7–9.
Transplanting: Bare root inadvisable. Large specimens can be moved if transplanting is done in early spring and with a generous earth ball.
Special maintenance requirements: Almost pest-free.

Although not normally hardy above Washington D.C., this **Southern Magnolia** is thriving on the south side of a house in Brooklyn, New York.

OAK, CALIFORNIA LIVE (*Quercus agrifolia*)

An evergreen tree with deep green foliage. Round-headed, with irregular, wide-spreading branches, it thrives on the seacoast and prefers well drained, gravelly soil. Difficult to transplant in size because of tap root.

Design Use

The great spread and irregular shape of this tree make it an excellent specimen for large, open spaces. Too large for a street tree. Excellent for use near the shore where it thrives and is helpful in retaining steep banks of loose soil because of its deep root system.

Data

Height: 60–80 feet.
Spread: 40–60 feet.
Form: Round-headed, with irregular, wide-spreading branches.
Foliage: Evergreen. Dense, small, rounded leaves, dull green above.
Texture: Medium.
Bark: Rough, black or dark gray.
Rate of growth: Slow to medium.
Culture: Well-drained soil, preferable open or gravelly.
Hardiness zone: 6. Coastal ranges of California, from sea level up to 4500 feet.
Transplanting: Difficult to transplant in large size (tap root).
Special maintenance requirements: Avoid too much water in summer to prevent mildew on the growing tips.

OAK, SOUTHERN LIVE (*Quercus virginiana*)

An evergreen tree of fine-textured, glossy foliage, growing to a height of 60 feet with a spread greater than its height. One of the most impressive trees of North America, its enormous horizontal branches are invariably festooned with blue-gray streamers of Spanish "moss." Near its limits of hardiness (Northern Virginia), the Southern Live Oak drops its leaves in winter.

Design Use

The Southern Live Oak is an excellent shade tree and can be used as a street tree when pruned regularly. However, its great spread limits its usefulness to the unrestricted site and wide boulevard. Excellent tree for campus, golf course, or large private property. When space permits, an excellent tree at the base of tall buildings.

Data

Height: 40–80 feet.
Spread: 60–80 feet.
Form: Rounded, wide spreading.
Foliage: Evergreen (deciduous in northern sections of Virginia). Lustrous deep green.

Texture: Medium.
Rate of growth: Medium.
Culture: Withstands arid soil. Very adaptable, prefers moist, open, sunny location.

Hardiness zone: 7–10.
Transplanting: Transplanted successfully in all sizes when severely pruned.
Special maintenance requirements: None.

OLIVE, COMMON (*Olea europaea*)

Small- to medium-sized evergreen having broad compact rounded crown to a height of 25 feet, with an exceptionally handsome and distinctive grey-green foliage. Older trees have gnarled, twisted trunks and branches. This characteristic beauty of the Olive is lost when it is planted where it will receive water regularly. Grows best in meager soils in arid regions.

Design Use

The Olive makes an excellent specimen tree for public and private projects, requiring a minimum of care. Grey-green foliage, rugged trunk and branching, and ability to withstand drought make it an excellent choice for use in southern California. Hardy to 10 degrees. Frequently transplanted in mature size, it is the most widely used tree in California when a mature evergreen of strong character is required for immediate effect. Its one disadvantage is that of ripening olives that drop on pavements and leave a dark, oily stain when stepped on.

Data

Height: 18–25 feet.
Spread: 12–15 feet.
Form: Round-topped, open structure.
Foliage: Small, evergreen willowlike leaves, dull green above, silvery and white on the underside.
Texture: Fine.
Bark: Gray when young, twisted, furrowed branches in later years.
Rate of growth: Slow to medium.
Culture: Tolerates all soils if deep and well-drained; must be kept dry.
Hardiness zone: 9–10.
Transplanting: Easily moved even as a mature tree.
Special maintenance requirements: None.

PINE, AUSTRIAN (*Pinus nigra*)

A rugged-looking, very dense evergreen tree, generally pyramidal in shape, with straight trunk and regularly spaced branches, slightly downswept. Coarse, dark green needles.

In the young tree, branches are closely spaced, which in healthy specimens almost completely conceals the structure. As the tree matures, the spacing between branches becomes greater and the top tends to broaden. Bark in the mature specimen is heavy, shingled, and dark gray in color, contributing to the impression of ruggedness.

Retains its lower branches longer than many pines and is, therefore, valuable as a screening tree.

Moderately tolerant of salt spray and sandy soil, this Pine can be used with success near the shore. As with all Pines, it prefers full sun.

In recent years, the Austrian Pine has fallen victim to *diplodia*, a fungus for which there is as yet no known cure, thus making this Pine of questionable landscape value for the present.

Austrian Pine nursery specimen: 8–10 feet high, 6-foot spread, 3–3½ inch caliber, 36-inch ball.

Design Use

The Austrian Pine serves well as both a specimen tree in maturity, standing alone, and a screening tree placed 12–15 feet apart on centers in staggered rows. The fact that it tends to retain its lower branches increases its effectiveness as a screen or wind break. Hardier in the city than most Pines.

If a Pine with a less restrained and more irregular outline is desired, hardy in similar soil and in proximity to the ocean, the Japanese Black Pine would be a better choice.

Data

Height: 60–80 feet; mature appearance at 30 feet.
Spread: 40 feet (a 30-foot tree would have a 12–15 foot spread).

Form: Compact, pyramidal, symmetrical tree in youth, branched to the ground, maturing to a broad, flat-topped tree with a short trunk and wide spacing between branches.
Foliage: Dark evergreen needles.
Texture: Coarse.
Bark: Deep gray-brown, heavily shingled.
Rate of growth: Rapid.
Culture: Does well in acid as well as lime soil, loam, clay or sand.
Hardiness zone: 4–7.
Transplanting: Must be moved with an earth ball. Large specimens should be root-pruned before moving as this Pine tends to form a tap root with few fibrous roots. Most safely moved in late August in the northeast.
Special characteristics: Tolerant of salt spray. Coarse needles. Avoid use of this tree in areas where the fungus *diplodia* has appeared.

PINE, EASTERN WHITE (*Pinus strobus*)

An open, horizontally branched, evergreen tree, possibly the handsomest of our Pines. Branches in mature specimens stand at right angles to the trunk. Bark is greenish on young trees and becomes thick, dark, and ridged in mature trees. Fine, light green needles are held on the upper surface of the branches.

In young trees, branches are closer together, presenting a compact appearance. Branches below 6 feet are often lost in trees 20 feet or more when not in full sun; therefore, White Pine cannot be relied on for screening purposes unless underplanted with broad-leaved evergreens.

When the leader or terminal shoot has been removed or destroyed, the top branches continue to grow at an angle, giving the tree an interesting, wind-swept appearance.

Thrives in poor, sandy soil or rich loam, but not near the seashore (scorches in salt wind). Prefers full sun. Transplants easily in a large size.

In maturity, branches are horizontal and the needles are carried in flat formation on the upper surface.

Design Use

Excellent background for smaller flowering trees, such as Birch or Dogwood. A good tree for parks and parkways. When used for screening, the White Pine should be underplanted with broad-leaved evergreens that will gradually assume the screening function as the tree loses its lower branches. Mature specimens have unusually handsome horizontal branching.

Data

Height: 60–80 feet.
Spread: 20–40 feet.
Form: Open, horizontal branching in maturity; dense, pyramidal when young.

Needles of the **White Pine** are extremely fine in texture.

Foliage: Light evergreen needles, very soft in appearance, appear on upper surface of branches.

Texture: Fine.

Rate of growth: Rapid.

Culture: Loam or sandy soil, well-drained.

Hardiness zone: 3 (southern portion) to 8.

Transplanting: Easily moved in large sizes (10–14 inch caliber), especially when root-pruned and moved in late August in the northeast.

Special maintenance requirements: Remove and burn dead shoots that shelter pine weevil. Water heavily for 2 years after transplanting.

Note: White pine weevil destroys leader shoots, but makes for an interesting-looking tree. Eliminate currant and gooseberry from vicinity of White Pines, for these plants harbor the fatal blister rust.

Other Useful White Pine Variety

Fastigiate White Pine (*Pinus strobus fastigiata*)

Narrow, columnar. Creates very tall but soft screening. Branches at 45 degree angle. Often three times as high as wide.

Eastern White Pine nursery specimen: 10–12 feet high, 8-foot spread, 4-inch caliber, 42-inch ball.

PINE, JAPANESE BLACK (*Pinus thunbergi*)

A dense, spreading evergreen tree, irregular in habit. This Pine seldom grows a straight trunk and characteristically develops an asymmetric head. Perhaps its most valuable design attribute is that it evidences a strong character or interesting line almost at once.

The Japanese Black Pine is the most tolerant of seashore conditions of all the evergreens in the northeastern United States. It also thrives well under less adverse conditions.

Lower branches are retained longer than in most other varieties, which makes this an extremely effective screening tree. Its irregular habit makes possible a closer planting interval (as close as 6 feet) without creating the appearance of crowding, as would be the case with trees of a more symmetrical shape. Planted in this manner, they will merge as a single, dense mass with an irregular, feathery surface.

Design Use

Probably the most effective evergreen for screening, particularly near the shore. It is used successfully in this manner on most Long Island beaches.

In maturity, it develops an increasingly rugged, almost tortuous outline, particularly in locations exposed to strong sea winds, and can serve well as a specimen tree.

The natural irregularity of this species can also be accentuated by pruning and even training of branches—in the Japanese manner—to create a desired effect. (See Chapter 6.)

Japanese Black Pine nursery specimen: 8–10 feet high, 6–8 feet spread, 3–3½ inch caliber, 36-inch ball.

Data

Height: 20–35 feet. Mature appearance at 20 feet.
Spread: 25 feet (a 20-foot tree would have a 12–15 foot spread.
Form: Irregular, Japanese-like.
Foliage: Evergreen, stiff, dark green needles.
Texture: Coarse.
Rate of growth: Medium.
Culture: Prefers sandy soil. Adapts well to moist loam.
Hardiness zone: 5 (southern portion) to 7.

Transplanting: Easily moved. Safest period is late August in northeast sector of the United States.
Special characteristics: Best seashore evergreen for the northeast. Lends itself to mass planting and close spacing.
Special maintenance requirements: Vulnerable to turpentine beetle, a serious pest requiring annual painting of lower trunk with repellent. Pine tip moth destroys buds, but serves the purpose of pruning.

PINE, MONTEREY (*Pinus radiata*)

A tall, handsome, evergreen tree with deep green foliage and stout, spreading branches, forming a round, open head. Bold, massive, and rapid-growing. The young trees have a more or less regular pyramidal habit, but in maturity they become picturesque, as seen on the Monterey Peninsula of California.

The Monterey Pine is said to be more widely planted throughout the world than any other California tree.

Design Use

Valuable for seaside planting. Its thick, picturesque, dark green foliage and wide-spreading branches, together with its rapid growth, make it popular for a variety of uses, including use as a street tree. Although in its first years it is a spindly, slender tree, it becomes a well-branched tree within 6–7 years. Excellent for background plantings, windbreaks, and specimen.

Data

Height: 60–100 feet.
Spread: 30–40 feet.
Foliage: Dark green; medium green in younger years.
Bark: Gray, with deep furrows and long flat ridges, the inner bark showing in the furrows as reddish brown.
Rate of growth: Rapid, vigorous, bushy when young.
Culture: Sandy soils, medium to heavy. Grows best when given ample water. Very susceptible to the double spotted mite.
Hardiness zone: 7.
Transplanting: Difficult to transplant when large because of tap root.

Other Useful Pine Varieties

Bristlecone Pine (*Pinus aristata*)

Small (to 20 feet), very picturesque even in young specimens. Hardiness zones: 4–7.

Japanese Red or Tanyosho Pine (*Pinus densiflora*)

Horizontal branching, interesting irregular open tree with orange-red bark. Hardiness zones: 3–7.

Lacebark Pine (*Pinus burgeana*)

Interesting exfoliating bark, fragrant needles, matures to flat-topped broad tree. Good as specimen. Hardiness zones: 4–8.

Pitch Pine (*Pinus rigida*)

Good windbreak tree for poor, sandy soils. Hardiness zones: 4–7.

Red Pine (*Pinus resinosa*)

Very hardy (zone 2), adaptable to poor soils and windy conditions. Picturesque, good grove tree.

Scotch Pine (*Pinus sylvestris*)

Picturesque, umbrella-shaped in maturity. lower branches die early, handsome bark (large rough plates). Good specimen tree. Hardiness zones: 2–7.

Swiss Stone Pine (*Pinus cembra*)

Somewhat columnar when young, maturing to picturesque, flat-topped open tree. Very hardy. Good as specimen tree or in groups. Hardiness zones: 4–7.

Western White Pine (*Pinus monticola*)

More compact with a narrower branching habit than Eastern White Pine (*Pinus strobus*). Hardiness zones: 4–7.

REDWOOD, COAST (*Sequoia sempervirens*)

Evergreen tree of narrow habit and great height. Although under cultivation it rarely exceeds 60 feet, specimens as tall as 360 feet are known. Foliage is composed of flat sprays of needles much like those of the Hemlock, dark green and glossy above, silvery underside. Trunk is reddish and rough in appearance. Prefers deep soil, reasonable shelter from strong winds, and water close to the surface.

Design Use

The Redwood, because of its tall, slender, graceful appearance, is an interesting tree for a large property, public or private. In a woodland, it is an excellent tree, particularly when planted in groves.

Data

Height: 50–60 feet as a cultivated tree. 100–360 feet in its native habitat.
Spread: 20–30 feet within the first 50 years.
Form: Pyramidal, straight trunk extends through the tree.
Foliage: Evergreen, dark green and glossy above, silvery underside.
Texture: Fine to medium.
Bark: On old trees, 3 inches to 1 foot thick. Dark red fissured, deeply grooved.
Rate of growth: Rapid.
Culture: Prefers rich, deep soil with water close to surface. Shelter from ocean winds.
Hardiness zone: 7.
Transplanting: Difficult in size.
Special maintenance requirements: High water table.

SPRUCE, NORWAY (*Picea abies*)

An evergreen tree, pyramidal in shape with pendulous branches that turn up softly at the tips. It can reach a height of 100 feet, but usually does not grow beyond 60 feet. Foliage, except in very young plants, is a deep, lustrous green.

Although stiff in appearance as a young tree, it is quite graceful in maturity. It is useful as a lawn specimen or windbreak when planted at 15–30 feet intervals.

Prefers colder climate and sandy as well as acid soil, somewhat moist.

Design Use

There is little use for this tree other than as a specimen tree or windbreak. For the latter use, it must be kept tightly pruned to prevent it from becoming too open.

Data

Height: 40–60 feet; can grow to 100 feet.
Spread: 25–30 feet.
Form: Pyramidal with pendulous branches turning up at tips.
Foliage: Dark green, lustrous.
Texture: Medium.
Rate of growth: Moderately rapid.
Culture: Prefers moderate moisture, sandy acid soil, but adapts readily to other soil if it receives average moisture. Prefers cold climate.

Norway Spruce nursery specimen: 5–6 feet tall, 4–5 foot spread, 2-inch caliber, 24-inch ball.

Hardiness zone: 2–7.
Transplanting: Moves well in large sizes. (Shallow root system.) Should be balled and burlapped.
Special maintenance requirements: May require spraying against red spider, spruce gall, aphid.

P A R T IV

TREE PALETTE

The tree lists that follow are organized by states and classified according to the following design attributes:

State tree
Trees classified by height, branching, and form
Trees classified by color of blossom, color of summer foliage, color of fall
    foliage, interesting bark
Trees for the city, classified by usefulness for wide, medium, and suburban
    streets
Trees tolerating acid soil, moist soil, dry or poor soil
Pest-resistant trees
Trees for seashore planting

Thus, when seeking a tree suitable for a specific design use, on a city street in Indiana, for example, one turns to the Indiana state list and consults the heading "City Trees" for names of trees recommended for this purpose. Trees within each category are listed in alphabetical order according to the Latin names. In all lists, an asterisk indicates that the tree so marked, or a closely related variety, appears in the photographic "Tree Portraits" section of this book.

Every state in the United States, except Alaska and Hawaii, is included. Each list has been reviewed by respective state foresters and university landscape design professors. However, because of the great variation in the topography, climate, temperature extremes, soil and wind conditions, etc., within states (California lies within six zones of hardiness), it is advisable to verify tree selections with local professionals.

ALABAMA

State Tree
*Pine (*Pinus*)

Evergreen Trees
Monkey-Puzzle Tree (*Araucaria araucana*)
Strawberry Tree (*Arbutus unedo*)
Lemon Bottlebrush (*Callistemon elanceolatus*)
Camelia species (*Camellia*)
*Deodar Cedar (*Cedrus deodara*)
Camphor Tree (*Cinnamomum camphora*)
Citrus species (*Citrus*)
Common China Fir (*Cunninghamia lanceolata*)
Cypress species (*Cupressus*)
Loquat (*Eriobotrya japonica*)
Eucalyptus species (*Eucalyptus*)
Brush-Cherry Eugenia (*Eugenia paniculata*)
Loblolly Bay Gordonia (*Gordonia lasianthus*)
Holly species (*Ilex*)
Juniper species (*Juniperus*)
Fortune Keteleeria (*Keteleeria fortunei*)
Paterson Sugar Plum Tree (*Lagunaria patersoni*)
*Southern Magnolia (*Magnolia grandiflora*)
*Pine species (*Pinus*)
Yew Podocarpus (*Podocarpus macrophyllus*)
Portugal Laurel (*Prunus lusitanica*)
Holly Oak (*Quercus ilex*)
*Live Oak (*Quercus virginiana*)
Palmetto (*Sabal palmetto*)
*Hemlock species (*Tsuga*)

Trees Classified by Height

20–35 Feet
Strawberry Tree (*Arbutus unedo*)
Lemon Bottlebrush (*Callistemon lanceolatus*)
Judas Tree (*Cercis siliquastrum*)
American Smoke Tree (*Cotinus americanus*)
*Hawthorn species (*Crataegus*)
Loquat (*Eriobotrya japonica*)
Common Fig (*Ficus carica*)
Dahoon (*Ilex cassine*)
Possum Haw (*Ilex decidua*)
Yaupon (*Ilex vomitoria*)
Crape-Myrtle (*Lagerstroemia indica*)
Yellow Cucumber Tree (*Magnolia cordata*)
Oyama Magnolia (*Magnolia sieboldi*)
Wilson Magnolia (*Magnolia wilsoni*)
*Crab Apple species (*Malus*)
Jerusalem Thorn (*Parkinsonia aculeata*)
*Cherry species (*Prunus*)
*Babylon Weeping Willow (*Salix babylonica*)
Common Jujube or Chinese Date (*Zizyphus jujuba*)

35–75 Feet
Silver Wattle (*Acacia decurrens dealbata*)
Florida Maple (*Acer floridanum*)
Silk Tree (*Albizzia julibrissin*)
Common Camellia (*Camellia japonica*)
Chinese Redbud (*Cercis chinesis*)
Camphor Tree (*Cinnamomum camphora*)
*Flowering Dogwood (*Cornus florida*)
Common China Fir (*Cunninghamia lanceolata*)
Chinese Parasol Tree (*Firmiana simplex*)
Lobolly Bay Gordonia (*Gordonia lasianthus*)
English Holly (*Ilex aquifolium*)
Luster-leaf Holly (*Ilex latifolia*)
Mountain Winterberry (*Ilex montana*)
American Holly (*Ilex opaca*)
Syrian Juniper (*Juniperus drupacea*)
Greek Juniper (*Juniperus excelsa*)
West Indies Juniper (*Juniperus lucayana*)
Alligator Juniper (*Juniperus pachyphloea*)
Paterson Supar Plum Tree (*Lagunaria patersoni*)
Veitch Magnolia (*Magnolia veitchi*)
Sweet Bay (*Magnolia virginiana*)
Chinaberry (*Melia azedorach*)
Chinese Pistache (*Pistacia chinesis*)
Yew Podocarpus (*Podocarpus macrophyllus*)
Holly or Holm Oak (*Quercus ilex*)
Laurel Oak (*Quercus laurifolia*)

Water Oak (*Quercus nigra*)
Willow Oak (*Quercus phellos*)
Cork Oak (*Quercus suber*)
*Live Oak (*Quercus virginiana*)
Clammy Locust (*Robinia viscosa*)
Carolina Hemlock (*Tsuga caroliniana*)

75 Feet or Over
*Red or Swamp Maple (*Acer rubrum*)
Monkey-Puzzle Tree (*Araucaria araucana*)
Campbell Magnolia (*Magnolia campbelli*)
*Southern Magnolia (*Magnolia grandiflora*)
Sabal Palmetto (*Palmetto*)
*Oak species (*Quercus*)

Trees Classified by Form

Pyramidal
*Cedar species (*Cedrus*)
English Holly (*Ilex aquifolium*)
American Holly (*Ilex opaca*)
Juniper or Red Cedar species (*Juniperus*)
Paterson Sugar Plum Tree (*Lagunaria patersoni*)
*Sweet Gum (*Liquidambar styraciflua*)
*Magnolia species (*Magnolia*)
Dawn Redwood (*Metasequoia glyptostroboides*)
*Black Tupelo or Black Gum (*Nyssa sylvatica*)
Turkey Oak (*Quercus cerris*)
*Hemlock species (*Tsuga*)

Columnar
Columnar Red Maple (*Acer rubrum columnare*)
Common Bald Cypress (*Taxodium distichum*)

Weeping
Weeping Red Cedar (*Juniperus virginiana pendula*)
*Babylon Weeping Willow (*Salix babylonica*)

Rounded or Globe-Shaped
Single Seed Hawthorn (*Crataegus monogyna inermis*)
*White Oak (*Quercus alba*)

With Horizontal Branching
Silk Tree (*Albizzia julibrissin*)
Monkey-Puzzle Tree (*Araucaria araucana*)
*Cedar species (*Cedrus*)
*Flowering Dogwood (*Cornus florida*)
*Hawthorn species (*Crataegus*)
*Black Tupelo or Black Gum (*Nyssa sylvatica*)
*White Oak (*Quercus alba*)
*Live Oak (*Quercus virginiana*)
Common Bald Cypress (*Taxodium distichum*)

Trees Classified by Color of Blossom

Yellow
*Golden Rain Tree (*Koelreuteria paniculata*)
*Laburnum (*Laburnum vossi*)

White
Citrus species (*Citrus*)
*Southern Magnolia (*Magnolia grandiflora*)
Mount Fuji Cherry (*Prunus serrulata* "Shirotae")

Pink
Wither's Pink Redbud (*Cercis canadensis* "Wither's Pink Charm")
Red Flowering Dogwood (*Cornus florida rubra*)
Ingleside Crape-Myrtle (*Lagerstroemia indica* "Ingleside Pink")
Japanese Flowering Crab Apple (*Malus floribunda*)
Katherine Crab Apple (*Malus* "Katherine")
Prince Georges Crab Apple (*Malus* "Prince Georges")
*Common Apple (*Malus pumila*)
Sargent Cherry (*Prunus sargenti*)
Blireiana Plum (*Prunus blireiana*)

Red
Crimson Eucalyptus (*Eucalyptus ficifolia*)
Red Crape-Myrtle (*Lagerstroemia indica* "Wm. Toovey")
Alexandrina Magnolia (*Magnolia soulageana* "Alexandrina")

Trees with Bright Red Fruit
*Flowering Dogwood (*Cornus florida*)
Almey Crab Apple (*Malus* "Almey")
Siberian Crab Apple (*Malus baccata*)
Hopa Crab Apple (*Malus* "Hopa")

Trees Classified by Color of Summer Foliage

Blue
Blue Gum (*Eucalyptus globolus*)
Eastern Red Cedar (*Juniperus virginiana var. Burki*)

Silver to Gray
South American Jelly or Pindo Palm (*Butia capitata*)
Russian Olive (*Elaeagnus angustifolia*)
White Popular (*Populus alba*)
Pendent Silver Linden (*Tilia petiolaris*)
*Silver Linden (*Tilia tomentosa*)

Trees Classified by Color of Fall Foliage

Yellow
Fringetree (*Chionanthus virginicus*)
*Willow species (*Salix*)
*Ginkgo (*Ginkgo biloba*)

Red
*Red Maple (*Acer rubrum*)
Chinese Pistache (*Pistacia chinensis*)

Trees with Interesting Bark

Gray
*Red Maple (*Acer rubrum*)
American Holly (*Ilex opaca*)

Corky
Hackberry (*Celtis*)

Flaking
*Eucalyptus species (*Eucalyptus*)
Eastern Red Cedar (*Juniperus virginiana*)
Crape-Myrtle (*Lagerstroemia indica*)
*Plane Tree species (*Platanus*)

Trees for the City
Silk Tree (*Albizzia julibrissin*)
Hackberry (*Celtis*)
*Ginkgo (*Ginkgo biloba*)
Thornless Honey-Locust (*Gleditsia triacanthos inermis*)
*Golden Rain Tree (*Koelreuteria paniculata*)
*Southern Magnolia (*Magnolia grandiflora*)
*Crab Apple (*Malus varieties*)
Chinaberry (*Melia azedarach*)
Red Oak (*Quercus borealis*)
*Japanese Pagoda Tree (*Sophora japonica*)

Trees for Wide Streets
Sugar Hackberry (*Celtis laevigata*)
Camphor Tree (*Cinnamomum camphora*)
Eucalyptus species (*Eucalyptus*)
White Ash (*Fraxinus americana*)
Green Ash (*Fraxunus pennsylvanica lanceolata*)
*Common Honey-Locust (*Gleditsia triacanthos*)
Paterson Sugar Plum Tree (*Lagunaria patersoni*)
*Southern Magnolia (*Magnolia grandiflora*)
Willow Oak (*Quercus phellos*)
*Live Oak (*Quercus virginiana*)

Trees for Medium Streets
Mountain Silverbell (*Halesia monticola*)
*Sweet Gum (*Liquidambar styraciflua*)
Chinaberry (*Melia azerdarach*)
Hop-Hornbeam (*Ostrya virginiana*)
*Sorrel Tree or Sourwood (*Oxydendron arboreum*)
Scarlet Oak (*Quercus coccinea*)
Laurel Oak (*Quercus laurifolia*)
Willow Oak (*Quercus suber*)
Cork Oak (*Quercus suber*)
*Black Locust (*Robinia pseudoacacia*)
Sassafras (*Sassafras albidium officinale*)

Trees for Suburban Streets
American Hornbeam (*Carpinus caroliniana*)
Fringe Tree (*Chionanthus virginicus*)
★Flowering Dogwood (*Cornus florida*)
★Hawthorn species (*Crataegus*)

Soil Tolerance

Trees Tolerating Acid Soil
★Japanese Maple (*Acer palmatum* var.)
Citrus species (*Citrus*)
★Flowering Dogwood (*Cornus florida* var.)
Sweet Bay (*Magnolia virginiana*)
★Black Tupelo (*Nyssa sylvatica*)
★Sorrel Tree or Sourwood (*Oxydendrum arboreum*)
Willow Oak (*Quercus phellos*)

Trees Tolerating Moist Soil
★Red Maple (*Acer rubrum*)
Holly species (*Ilex*)
Sweet Bay (*Magnolia virginiana*)
Common Bald Cypress (*Taxodium distichum*)

Trees Tolerating Dry or Poor Soil
Silk Tree (*Albizzia julibrissin*)
Common Paper-Mulberry (*Broussonetia papyrifera*)
★Eucalyptus (*Eucalyptus* species)
★Honey-Locust (*Gleditsia triacanthos* var.)

★Golden Rain Tree (*Koelreuteria paniculata*)
Australian Tea Tree (*Leptospermum laevigatum*)
Chinaberry (*Melia azedarach*)
Common Olive (*Olea europaea*)
Jerusalem Thorn (*Parkinsonia aculeata*)
Chinese Pistache (*Pistacia chinensis*)
Honey Mesquite (*Prosopis glandulosa*)
Chinese Elm (*Ulmus parvifolia*)

Pest-Resistant Trees

Hornbeam species (*Carpinus*)
Fig species (*Ficus*)
Franklinia (*Franklinia alatamaha*)
Ginkgo (*Ginkgo biloba*)
Juniper species (*Juniperus*)
★Sweet Gum (*Liquidambar styraciflua*)
Hop-Hornbeam species (*Ostrya*)

Trees for Seashore Planting

★Eucalyptus (*Eucalyptus*)
Velvet Ash (*Fraxinus velutina*)
Spiny Greek Juniper (*Juniperus excelsa stricta*)
West Indies Juniper (*Juniperus lucayana*)
Paterson Sugar Plum Tree (*Lagunaria* "Patersoni")
★Southern Magnolia (*Magnolia grandiflora*)
★Common Olive (*Olea europaea*)

Holly Oak (*Quercus ilex*)
Black Jack Oak (*Quercus marilandica*)
★Live Oak (*Quercus virginiana*)
Palmetto (*Sabal palmetto*)
Oriental Arbor-vitae (*Thuja orientalis*)
Chinese Elm (*Ulmus parvifolia*)

Trees for Hedging or Barriers

European Beech (*Fagus sylvatica*) prunes well.
Leyland Cypress (*Cupressocyparis leylandii*) withstands heavy pruning.
Hawthorn varieties (*Crataegus*) easily pruned, advantage of thorns.
Canadian Hemlock (*Tsuga canadensis*) evergreen.
American Holly (*Ilex opaca*) can be pruned.
European Hornbeam (*Carpinus betulus*) prunes well.
Little-leaf Linden (*Tilia cordata*) tolerates heavy pruning.
Hedge Maple (*Acer campestre*) can be pruned.
Austrian Pine (*Pinus nigra*) plant 10–12 feet on centers, staggered row.
Japanese Black Pine (*Pinus thunbergi*) plant 8 feet on centers, staggered row.
Eastern White Pine (*Pinus strobus*) plant 15 feet on centers, staggered row.

ARIZONA

State Tree

Paloverde (*Cercidium*)

Evergreen Trees

Fir species (*Abies*)
Acacia species (*Acacia*)
★Deodar Cedar (*Cedrus deodara*)
Camphor Tree (*Cinnamomum camphora*)
Evergreen Dogwood (*Cornus capitata*)
Common China Fir (*Cunninghamia lanceolata*)
★Cypress species (*Cupressus*)
Juniper species (*Juniperus*)
Spruce species (*Picea*)
★Pine species (*Pinus*)
★Douglas Fir (*Pseudotsuga menziesii*)
★California Live Oak (*Quercus agrifolia*)
Arbor-vitae species (*Thuja*)
★Hemlock species (*Tsuga*)

Trees Classified by Height

20–35 Feet
Huisache (*Acacia farnesiana*)
Blue Paloverde (*Cercidium floridum*)
Judas Tree (*Cercis siliquastrum*)
American Smoke Tree (*Cotinus americanus*)
★Hawthorn species (*Crataegus*)
Modoc Cypress (*Cupressus bakeri*)
Russian Olive (*Elaeagnus angostifolia*)
Loquat (*Eribotrya japonica*)
Common Fig (*Ficus carica*)
Arizona Ash (*Fraxinus velutina*)
★Golden Rain Tree (*Koelreuteria paniculata*)
★Laburnum species (*Laburnum*)
Crape-Myrtle (*Lagerstroemia indica*)
Sweet Bay or Laurel (*Lauris nobilis*)
Australian Tea Tree (*Leptospermum laevigatum*)
★Crab Apple species (*Malus*)
Jerusalem Thorn (*Parkinsonia aculeata*)
Chokecherry (*Prunus virginian melanocarpa*)
Goat Willow (*Salix caprea*)
★Babylon Weeping Willow (*Salix babylonica*)
Snowberry Mountain Ash (*Sorbus discolor*)

35–75 Feet
Korean Fir (*Abies koreana*)
Silver Wattle (*Acacia decurrens dealbata*)
Florida Maple (*Acer floridanum*)
Box-Elder (*Acer negundo*)
Red-fruited Tree of Heaven (*Ailanthus altissima erythrocarpa*)

Silk Tree (*Albizzia julibrissin*)
Red Alder (*Alnus rubra*)
★Shadblow Serviceberry (*Amelanchier laevis*)
Southern Catalpa (*Catalpa bignonioides*)
Bunch Hackberry (*Celtis bungeana*)
Net-leaf Hackberry (*Celtis laevigata*)
Eastern Redbud (*Cercis canadensis*)
Camphor Tree (*Cinnamomum camphora*)
Sour Orange (*Citrus aurantium*)
Delavay Clethra (*Clethra delavayi*)
Giant Dogwood (*Cornus controversa*)
Cockspur Thorn (*Crataegus crus-galli*)
Green Hawthorn (*Crataegus viridis*)
Common China Fir (*Cunninghamia lanceolata*)
Arizona Cypress (*Cupressus arizonica*)
Green Ash (*Fraxinus pennsylvanica lanceolata*)
Hinds Black Walnut (*Juglans hindsi*)
Arizona Black Walnut (*Juglans rupestris*)
Heartnut (*Juglans sieboldiana cordiformis*)
Chinese Juniper (*Juniperus chinensis*)
Alligator Juniper (*Juniperus pachyphloea*)
Western Red Cedar (*Juniperus scopulorum*)
★Crab Apple species (*Malus*)
Chinaberry (*Melia azedarach*)
White Mulberry (*Morus alba*)
★Amur Cork (*Phellodendron amurense*)
Limber Pine (*Pinus flexilis*)
Aleppo Pine (*Pinus halepensis*)
Scotch Pine (*Pinus sylvestris*)
Chinese Pistache (*Pistacia chinensis*)
Yew Podocarpus (*Podocarpus macrophyllus*)
Arizona Sycamore (*Platanus racemosa*)
Freemont Cottonwood (*Populus fremonti*)
Carolina Poplar (*Populus monilifera*)
Simon Poplar (*Populus simoni*)
Honey Mesquite (*Prosopis glandulosa*)
White Willow (*Salix alba*)
★Babylon Weeping Willow (*Salix babylonica*)
American Arbor-vitae (*Thuja occidentalis*)
Carolina Hemlock (*Tsuga caroliniana*)
Chinese Elm (*Ulmus parvifolia*)
Siberian Elm (*Ulmus pumila*)

75 Feet or Over
Fir species (*Abies*)
European Alder (*Alnus glutinosa*)
Pecan (*Carya pecan*)
European Hackberry (*Celtis australis*)
Sugar Hackberry (*Celtis laevigata*)
White Ash (*Fraxinus americana*)

European Ash (*Fraxinus excelsior*)
★Ginkgo or Maidenhair Tree (*Ginkgo biloba*)
★Common Honey-Locust (*Gleditsia triacanthos*)
Kentucky Coffee Tree (*Gymnocladus dioicus*)
English or Persian Walnut (*Juglans regia*)
Palmetto (*Sabal palmetto*)
Spruce species (*Picea*)
★Pine species (*Pinus*)
Italian Stone Pine (*Pinus pinea*)
★Plane Tree species (*Platanus*)
Poplar species (*Populus*)
★Douglas Fir (*Pseudotsuga menziesi*)
★Oak species (*Quercus*)
★Canada Hemlock (*Tsuga canadensis*)
★Elm species (*Ulmus*)
Japanese Zelkova (*Zelkova serrata*)

Trees Classified by Form

Pyramidal
Fir species (*Abies*)
Italian Cypress (*Cupressus sempervirens*)
Arizona Cypress (*Cupressus arizonica*)
Juniper or Red Cedar species (*Juniperus*)
★Hemlock species (*Tsuga*)
Smooth-leaved Elm varieties (*Ulmus carpinifolia*)

Rounded or Globe-Shaped
Bunch Hackberry (*Celtis bungeana*)
Single Seed Hawthorn (*Crataegus monogyna inermis*)
★Crab Apple Species (*Malus*)
Umbrella Black Locust (*Robinia pseudoacacia umbraculifera*)

Columnar
Pyramidal Washington Hawthorn (*Crataegus phaenopyrum fastigiata*)
Sentry Ginkgo (*Ginkgo biloba fastigiata*)
Blue Columnar Chinese Juniper (*Juniperus chinensis columnaris*)
Fastigiate Scotch Pine (*Pinus sylvestris fastigiata*)
Bolleana Poplar (*Populus alba pyramidalis*)
★Lombardy Poplar (*Populus nigra italica*)
Pyramidal Simon Poplar (*Populus simoni fastigiata*)
Shipmast Locust (*Robinia pseudoacacia rectissima*)
Douglas Arbor-vitae (*Thuja occidentalis douglasi pyramidalis*)
Fastigiate American Arbor-vitae (*Thuja occidentalis fastigiata*)
Columnar Giant Arbor-vitae (*Thuja plicata fastigiata*)

Weeping
★Deodar Cedar (*Cedrus deodara*)

"Exzellenz Thiel" Crab Apple (*Malus* "Exzellenz Thiel")
"Oekonomierat Echtermeyer" Crab Apple (*Malus* "Oekonomierat Echtermeyer")
Weeping Mulberry (*Morus alba pendula*)
Brewer Spruce (*Picea breweriana*)
Koster Weeping Blue Spruce (*Picea pungens kosteriana*)
Weeping Douglas Fir (*Pseudotsyga taxifolia pendula*)
Golden Weeping Willow (*Salix alba tristis*)
★Babylon Weeping Willow (*Salix babylonica*)
★Sargent Hemlock (*Tsuga canadensis pendula*)
Weeping American Elm (*Ulmus americana pendula*)

With Horizontal Branching
Fir species (*Abies*)
Silk Tree (*Albizzia julibrissin*)
Monkey-Puzzle Tree (*Araucaria araucana*)
★Hawthorn species (*Crataegus*)
Spruce species (*Picea*)
Italian Stone Pine (*Pinus pinea*)
Yew Podocarpus (*Podocarpus macrophyllus*)

Trees Classified by Color of Blossom

Yellow
Huisache (*Acacia farnesiana*)
Blue Paloverde (*Cercidium floridum*)
★Golden Rain Tree (*Koelreuteria paniculata*)

White
Strawberry Tree (*Arbutus unedo*)
White Redbud (*Cercis canadensis alba*)
Citrus species (*Citrus*)
Arnold Crab Apple (*Malus arnoldiana*)
★Siberian Crab Apple (*Malus baccata*)
Tea Crab Apple (*Malus hupehensis*)
Sargent Crab Apple (*Malus sargenti*)
Chinese Photinia (*Photinia serrulata*)
Thundercloud Plum (*Prunus cerasifera* "Thundercloud")
★Common Pear (*Pyrus communis*)
★Japanese Pagoda Tree (*Sophora japonica*)

Pink
Wither's Pink Redbud (*Cercis canadensis* "Wither's Pink Charm")
Toba Hawthorn (*Crataegus mordenensis* "Toba")
Ingleside Crape-Myrtle (*Lagerstroemia indica* "Ingleside Pink")
★Japanese Flowering Crab Apple (*Malus floribunda*)
Katherine Crab Apple (*Malus* "Katherine")
Prince Georges Crab Apple (*Malus* "Prince Georges")
★Common Apple (*Malus pumila*)

Red
Paul's Scarlet Hawthorn (*Crataegus oxyacantha pauli*)
Crimson Eucalyptus (*Eucalyptus ficifolia*)
Red Crape-Myrtle (*Lagerstroemia indica* var. "William Toovey")
Almey Crab Apple (*Malus* "Almey")
Carmine Crab Apple (*Malus atrosanguinea*)

Trees with Bright Red Fruit
Pacific Dogwood (*Cornus nuttalli*)
Downy Hawthorn (*Crataegus mollis*)
Washington Hawthorn (*Crataegus phaenopyrum*)
Almey Crab Apple (*Malus* "Almey")
★Siberian Crab Apple (*Malus baccata*)
Hopa Crab Apple (*Malus* "Hopa")
★Common Apple (*Malus pumila*)
Sargent Crab Apple (*Malus sargenti*)

Trees Classified by Color of Summer Foliage

Blue
White Fir (*Abies concolor*)
★Blue Atlas Cedar (*Cedrus atlantica glauca*)
Smooth Arizona Cypress (*Cupressus arizonica bonita*)
Blue Gum (*Eucalyptus globulus*)
Western Red Cedar (*Juniperus scopulorum* var. Chandler Blue)
Eastern Red Cedar (*Juniperus virginiana* var. *Burki*)
Colorado Blue Spruce (*Picea pungens* var. *Glauca*)

Silver to Gray
South American Jelly or Pindo Palm (*Butia capitata*)
Russian Olive (*Elaeagnus angustifolia*)
White Poplar (*Populus alba*)
★Silver Linden (*Tilia tomentosa*)

Red to Purple
Rubylace Locust (*Gleditsia triacanthos inermis* "Rubylace")
Purple Crab Apple (*Malus purpurea*)
Blireiana Plum (*Prunus blireiana*)
Pissard Plum (*Prunus cerasifera atropurpurea*)
Woods Myrobalan Plum (*Prunus cerasifera woodi*)
Thundercloud Plum (*Prunus cerasifera nigra* "Thundercloud")

Trees Classified by Color of Fall Foliage

Yellow
Redbud species (*Cercis*)
★Ginkgo (*Ginkgo biloba*)
★Willow species (*Salix*)

Red
Washington Hawthorn (*Crataegus phaenopyrum*)
Dawson Crab Apple (*Malus dansoniana*)
Chinese Pistache (*Pistacia chinensis*)

Purple
★Common Pear (*Pyrus communis*)

Trees with Interesting Bark

Gray
Hackberry species (*Celtis*)
★Hawthorn species (*Crataegus*)
English or Persian Walnut (*Juglans regia*)

White
★European Birch (*Betula pendula*)
★Gray Birch (*Betula populifolia*)
Aspen (*Populus tremuloides*)

Corky
Hackberry species (*Celtis*)

Green
★Babylon Weeping Willow (*Salix babylonica*)

Flaking
Russian Olive (*Elaeagnus angustifolia*)
Crape-Myrtle (*Lagerstroemia indica*)
★Plane Tree species (*Platanus*)

Trees for the City
Box-Elder (*Acer negundo*)
★Tree of Heaven (*Ailanthus*)
Catalpa (*Catalpa*)
Hackberry (*Celtis*)
Downy Hawthorn (*Crataegus mollis*)
Washington Hawthorn (*Crataegus phaenopyrum*)
Russian Olive (*Elaeagus angustifolia*)
Thornless Honey-Locust (*Gleditsia triacanthos inermis*)
★Ginkgo (*Ginkgo biloba*)
★Golden Rain Tree (*Koelreuteria paniculata*)
★Crab Apple (*Malus* var.)
Chinaberry (*Melia azedarach*)

London Plane Tree (*Platanus acerifolia*)
White Poplar (*Populus alba*)
★Black Locust (*Robinia pseudoacacia*)

Trees for Wide Streets
Sugar Hackberry (*Celtis laevigata*)
Green Ash (*Fraxinus pennsylvanica lanceolata*)
★Ginkgo (*Ginkgo biloba*)
★Common Honey-Locust (*Gleditsia triacanthos*)
London Plane Tree (*Platanus acerifolia*)
California Plane Tree (*Platanus racemosa*)
White Poplar (*Populus alba*)
Sargent Cherry (*Prunus sargenti*)

Trees for Medium Streets
Velvet Ash (*Fraxinus velutina*)
★Black Locust (*Robinia pseudoacacia*)

Trees for Suburban Streets
★Hawthorn species (*Crataegus*)
★Golden Rain Tree (*Koelreuteria paniculata*)

Soil Tolerance

Trees Tolerating Moist Soil
Alder species (*Alnus*)
★Willow species (*Salix*)
American Arbor-vitae (*Thuja occidentalis*)

Trees Tolerating Dry or Poor Soil
Silk Tree (*Albizzia julibrissin*)
★Tree of Heaven (*Ailanthus*)
Common Paper-Mulberry (*Broussonetia papyrifera*)
European Hackberry (*Celtis australis*)
Russian Olive (*Elaeagnus angustifolia*)
Modesto Ash (*Fraxinus velutina* "Modesto")
★Honey-Locust (*Gleditsia triacanthos* varieties)
Western Red Cedar (*Juniperus scopulorum*)
★Golden Rain Tree (*Koelreuteria paniculata*)
Chinaberry (*Melia azedarach*)
Piñon Pine (*Pinus edulis*)
Virginia Scrub Pine (*Pinus virginiana*)
White Poplar (*Populus alba*)
Honey Mesquite (*Prosopis glandulosa*)
★Black Locust (*Robinia pseudoacacia*)
★Japanese Pagoda Tree (*Sophora japonica*)
Siberian Elm (*Ulmus pumila*)

Pest-Resistant Trees
★Tree of Heaven (*Ailanthus altissima*)
★Cedar species (*Cedrus*)
European Hackberry (*Celtis australis*)
American Smoke Tree (*Cotinus americanus*)
Russian Olive (*Elaeagnus angustifolia*)
Fig species (*Ficus*)
★Ginkgo (*Ginkgo biloba*)

Trees for Hedging or Barriers
European Beech (*Fagus sylvatica*) prunes well.
Leyland Cypress (*Cupressocyparis leylandii*) withstands heavy pruning.
Hawthorn varieties (*Crataegus*) easily pruned, advantage of thorns.
Canadian Hemlock (*Tsuga canadensis*) evergreen.
American Holly (*Ilex opaca*) can be pruned.
European Hornbeam (*Carpinus betulus*) prunes well.
Little-leaf Linden (*Tilia cordata*) tolerates heavy pruning.
Hedge Maple (*Acer campestre*) can be pruned.
Austrian Pine (*Pinus nigra*) plant 10–12 feet on centers, staggered row.
Japanese Black Pine (*Pinus thunbergi*) plant 8 feet on centers, staggered row.
Eastern White Pine (*Pinus strobus*) plant 15 feet on centers, staggered row.

ARKANSAS

State Tree
★Pine (*Pinus*)

Evergreen Trees
★Cedar species (*Cedrus*)

★Deodar cedar (*Cedrus deodara*)
★Cypress species (*Cupressus*)

Holly species (*Ilex*)
Juniper species (*Juniperus*)
*Southern Magnolia (*Magnolia grandiflora*)
Chinese Photinia (*Photinia serrulata*)
*Pine species (*Pinus*)
Portugal Laurell (*Prunus lusitanica*)
Cork Oak (*Quercus suber*)
Arbor-vitae species (*Thuja*)
Farkleberry (*Vaccinium arboreum*)

Trees Classified by Height

20—35 Feet

Hedge Maple (*Acer campestre*)
Amur Maple (*Acer ginnala*)
*Japanese Maple (*Acer palmatum*)
Ohio Buckeye (*Aesculus glabra*)
Silk Tree (*Albizzia julibrissin*)
Apple Serviceberry (*Amelanchier grandiflora*)
European Hornbeam (*Carpinus betulus globosa*)
Mockernut (*Carya tomentosa*)
Judas Tree (*Cercis siliquastrum*)
Fringe Tree (*Chionanthus virginicus*)
Japanese Dogwood (*Cornus kousa*)
Cornelian Cherry (*Cornus mas*)
American Smoke Tree (*Cotinus americanus*)
Common Smoke Tree (*Cotinus coggygria*)
*Hawthorn species (*Crataegus*)
Russian Olive (*Elaeagnus angustifolia*)
Carolina Silverbell (*Halesia carolina*)
English Holly (*Ilex aquifolium*)
Possom Haw (*Ilex decidua*)
Ilex opaca (*Ilex opaca*)
Yaupon (*Ilex vomitoria*)
*Golden Rain Tree (*Koelreuteria paniculata*)
Crape-Myrtle (*Lagerstroemia indica*)
Yellow Cucumber Tree (*Magnolia cordata*)
*Saucer Magnolia (*Magnolia soulangeana*)
*Star Magnolia (*Magnolia stellata*)
Crab Apple species (*Malus*)
*Cherry species (*Prunus*)
Black Jack Oak (*Quercus marilandica*)
*Babylon Weeping Willow (*Salix babylonica*)
European Mountain Ash (*Sorbus aucuparia*)
Snowbell species (*Styrax*)
Farkleberry (*Vaccinium arboreum*)

35—75 Feet

Box-Elder (*Acer negundo*)
Nikko Maple (*Acer nikoense*)
Striped Maple or Moosewood (*Acer pennsylvanicum*)
*Red-fruited Tree of Heaven (*Ailanthus altissima erythrocarpa*)
Italian Alder (*Alnus cordata*)
Red Alder (*Alnus rubra*)
*Shadblow Serviceberry (*Amelanchier canadensis*)
Allegany Serviceberry (*Amelanchier laevis*)
Dahurian Birch (*Betula davurica*)
Manchurian Birch (*Betula mandshurica szechuanica*)
Common Paper-Mulberry (*Broussonetia papyrifera*)
Common Camellia (*Camellia japonica*)
European Hornbeam (*Carpinus betulus*)
American Hornbeam (*Carpinus caroliniana*)
Japanese Hornbeam (*Carpinus japonica*)
Chinese Chestnut (*Castanea mollissima*)
Southern Catalpa (*Catalpa bignonioides*)
Bunch Hackberry (*Celtis hungeana*)
Eastern Redbud (*Cercis canadensis*)
Chinese Redbud (*Cercis chinensis*)
*American Yellow-wood (*Cladrastis lutea*)
*Flowering Dogwood (*Cornus florida*)
Cockspur Tree (*Crataegus crus-galli*)
Green Hawthorn (*Crataegus viridis*)
Common Persimmon (*Diospyros virginiana*)
Green Ash (*Fraxinus pennsylvanica lanceolata*)
Dahoon (*Ilex cassine*)
Luster-leaf Holly (*Ilex latifolia*)
Mountain Winterberry (*Ilex montana*)
Heartnut (*Juglans sieboldiana cordiformis*)
Chinese Juniper (*Juniperus chinensis*)
Syrian Juniper (*Juniperus drupacea*)
Greek Juniper (*Juniperus excelsa*)

Alligator Juniper (*Juniperus pachyphloca*)
Yulan Magnolia (*Magnolia denudata*)
Fraser Magnolia (*Magnolia fraseri*)
Sweet Bay (*Magnolia virginiana*)
Chinaberry (*Melia azedarach*)
White Mulberry (*Morus alba*)
Empress Tree (*Paulownia tomentosa*)
Dragon Spruce (*Picea asperata*)
Chinese Poplar (*Populus lasiocarpa*)
Simon Poplar (*Populus simoni*)
Portugal Laurel (*Prunus lusitanica*)
Sargent Cherry (*Prunus sargenti*)
Yoshino Cherry (*Prunus yedoensis*)
Red Oak (*Quercus borealis*)
Scarlet Oak (*Quercus coccinea*)
Spanish or Southern Red Oak (*Quercus falcata*)
Water Oak (*Quercus nigra*)
*Pin Oak (*Quercus palustris*)
Willow Oak (*Quercus phellos*)
Cork Oak (*Quercus suber*)
Clammy Locust (*Robinia viscosa*)
Laurel Willow (*Salix pentandra*)
Sassafras (*Sassafras albidum officinale*)
Korean Mountain Ash (*Sorbus alnifolia*)
White Beam Mountain Ash (*Sorbus aria*)
Korean Stewartia (*Stewartia koreana*)
Japanese Stewartia (*Stewartis pseudo-camellia*)
American Arbor-vitae (*Thuja orientalis*)
Japanese Arbor-vitae (*Thuja standishi*)
*Crimean Linden (*Tilia euchlora*)
Winged or Wahoo Elm (*Ulmus alata*)
Chinese Elm (*Ulmus parvifolia*)

75 Feet or Over

Norway Maple (*Acer platanoides*)
Sycamore Maple (*Acer pseudoplatanus*)
*Red or Swamp Maple (*Acer rubrum*)
Hickory species (*Carya*)
European Hackberry (*Celtis australis*)
Sugar Hackberry (*Celtis laevigata*)
False Cypress species (*Chamaecyparis*)
*Beech species (*Fagus*)
*Ginkgo or Maidenhair Tree (*Ginkgo biloba*)
*Common Honey-Locust (*Gleditsia triancanthos*)
Mountain Silverbell (*Halesia monticola*)
English or Persian Walnut (*Juglanus regia*)
*Sweet Gum (*Liquidambar styraciflua*)
Cucumber Tree (*Magnolia acuminata*)
*Southern Magnolia (*Magnolia grandiflora*)
White-leaf Japanese Magnolia (*Magnolia obovata*)
*Black Gum or Black Tupelo (*Nyssa sylvatica*)
*Pine species (*Pinus*)
*Plane Tree species (*Platanus*)
Poplar species (*Populus*)
Caucasian Wing-Nut (*Pterocarya fraxinifolia*)
*Oak species (*Quercus*)
Common Bald Cypress (*Taxodium distichum*)
English Elm (*Ulmus procera*)

Trees Classified by Form

Pyramidal

Italian Cypress (*Cupressus sempervirens*)
*Beech species (*Fagus*)
English Holly (*Ilex aquifolium*)
American Holly (*Ilex opaca*)
Longstalk Holly (*Ilex pedunculosa*)
Juniper or Red Cedar species (*Juniperus*)
*Sweet Gum (*Liquidambar styraciflua*)
*Magnolia species (*Magnolia*)
*Black Tupelo or Black Gum (*Nyssa sylvatica*)
Hop-Hornbeam (*Ostrya virginiana*)
Turkey Oak (*Quercus cerris*)
*Pin Oak (*Quercus palustris*)
Arbor-vitae species (*Thuja*)
*Linden species (*Tilia*)
Smooth-leaved Elm varieties (*Ulmus carpinifolia*)

Columnar

Ascending Norway Maple (*Acer plantanoides ascendens*)
Columnar Norway Maple (*Acer platanoides columnare*)

Erect Norway Maple (*Acer platanoides erectum*)
Columnar Red Maple (*Acer rubrum columnare*)
Fastigiate European Hornbeam (*Carpinus betulus fastigiata*)
Fastigiate Washington Hawthorn (*Crataegus phaenopyrum fastigiata*)
Dawyck Beech (*Fagus sylvatica fastigiata*)
Sentry Ginkgo (*Ginkgo biloba fastigiata*)
Pyramidal Red Cedar (*Juniperus virginiana pyramidalis*)
Schott Red Cedar (*Juniperus virginiana schotti*)
Bolleana Poplar (*Poplulus alba pyramidalis*)
*Lombardy Poplar (*Populus nigra italica*)
"Amanogawa" Cherry (*Prunus serrulata* "Amanogawa")
Pyramidal English Oak (*Quercus robur fastigiata*)
Shipmast Locust (*Robinia pseudoacacia rectissima*)
Common Bald Cypress (*Taxodium distichum*)

Weeping

Weeping European Hornbeam (*Carpinus betulus pendula*)
*Deodar Cedar (*Cedrus deodara*)
*Weeping Beech (*Fagus sylvatica pendula*)
Weeping Red Cedar (*Juniperus virginiana pendula*)
"Exzellenz Thiel" Crab Apple (*Malus* "Exzellenz Thiel")
"Oekonomierat Echtermeyer" Crab Apple (*Malus* "Oekonomierat Echtermeyer")
Weeping Mulberry (*Morus alba pendula*)
Weeping White Pine (*Pinus strobus pendula*)
Weeping Japanese Apricot (*Prunus mume pendula*)
Weeping Black Cherry (*Prunus serotina pendula*)
Weeping Higan Cherry (*Prunus subhirtella pendula*)
"Yaeshidare" Cherry (*Prunus subhirtella pendula flora plena*)
Weeping Yoshino Cherry (*Prunus yedoensis perpendens*)
*Babylon Weeping Willow (*Salix babylonica*)
Weeping Folgner Mountain Ash (*Sorbus folgneri pendula*)
Pendant Silver Linden (*Tilia petiolaris*)
Weeping American Elm (*Ulmus americana pendula*)

Rounded or Globe-Shaped

*Japanese Maple (*Acer palmatum*)
Globe Norway Maple (*Acer platanoides globosum*)
Globe European Hornbeam (*Carpinus betulus globosa*)
Bunch Hackberry (*Celtis bungeana*)
Cornelian Cherry (*Cornus mas*)
Japanese Cornel (*Cornus officinalis*)
Single Seed Hawthorn (*Crataegus monogyna inermis*)
*Saucer Magnolia (*Magnolia soulangeana*)
*Crab Apple species (*Malus*)
*White Oak (*Quercus alba*)
*Umbrella Black Locust (*Robinia pseudoacacia umbraculifera*)

With Horizontal Branching

Silk Tree (*Albizzia julbrissin*)
Eastern Redbud (*Cercis canadensis*)
*Flowering Dogwood (*Cornus florida*)
Japanese Dogwood (*Cornus kousa*)
*Hawthorn species (*Crataegus*)
*Black Tupelo or Black Gum (*Nyssa sylvatica*)
*Eastern White Pine (*Pinus strobus*)
*White Oak (*Quercus alba*)
*Pin Oak (*Quercus palustris*)
Live Oak (*Quercus virginiana*)
Common Bald Cypress (*Taxodium distichum*)

Trees Classified by Color of Blossom

Yellow

*Golden Rain Tree (*Koelreuteria paniculata*)

White

*Shadblow Serviceberry (*Amelanchier canadensis*)
Whitebud (*Cercis candensis alba*)
*American Yellow-wood (*Cladrastis lutea*)
Japanese Dogwood (*Cornus kousa*)
Washington Hawthorn (*Crataegus phaenopyrum*)
Carolina Silverbell (*Halesia carolina*)

Yulan Magnolia (*Magnolia denudata*)
★Southern Magnolia (*Magnolia grandiflora*)
★Star Magnolia (*Magnolia stellata*)
Arnold Crab Apple (*Malus arnoldiana*)
Tea Crab Apple (*Malus hupehensis*)
Sargent Crab Apple (*Malus sargenti*)
★Sorrel Tree (*Oxydendrum arboreum*)
Chinese Photina (*Photinia serrulata*)
Thundercloud Plum (*Prunus cerasifera* "Thundercloud")
Mount Fuji Cherry (*Prunus serrulata* "Shirotae")
Yoshino Cherry (*Prunus yedoensis*)
Bradford Callery Pear (*Pyrus calleryana* "Bradford")
★Common Pear (*Pyrus communis*)
Korean Mountain Ash (*Sorbus alnifolia*)
Japanese Stewartia (*Stewartia pseudocamellia*)
Japanese Snowbell (*Styrax japonica*)

Pink

Wither's Pink Redbud (*Cercis canadensis* "Wither's Pink Charm")
Red Flowering Dogwood (*Cornus florida rubra*)
Toba Hawthorn (*Crataegus mordenensis* "Toba")
Ingleside Crape-Myrtle (*Lagerstroemia indica* "Ingleside Pink")
★Saucer Magnolia (*Magnolia soulangeana*)
Japanese Flowering Crab Apple (*Malus floribunda*)
Katherine Crab Apple (*Malus* "Katherine")
Prince Georges Crab Apple (*Malus* "Prince Georges")
★Common Apple (*Malus pumila*)
Blireiana Plum (*Prunus blireiana*)
Sargent Cherry (*Prunus sargenti*)
Amanogawa Cherry (*Prunus serrulata* "Amanogawa")
Kwanzan Cherry (*Prunus serrulata* "Kwanzan")
Autumn Cherry (*Prunus subhirtella autumnalis*)
Weeping Cherry (*Prunus subhirtella pendula*)

Red

Ruby Horse-Chestnut (*Aesculus carnea briotti*)
Paul's Scarlet Hawthorn (*Crataegus oxyacantha pauli*)
Red Crape-Myrtle (*Lagerstroemia indica* "Wm. Toovey")
Alexandrina Magnolia (*Magnolia soulangeana* "Alexandrina")
Almey Crab Apple (*Malus* "Almey")
Carmine Crab Apple (*Malus atrosanguinea*)

Trees with Bright Red Fruit

★Flowering Dogwood (*Cornus florida*)
Japanese Dogwood (*Cornus kousa*)
Downy Hawthorn (*Crataegus mollis*)
Washington Hawthorn (*Crataegus phaenopyrum*)
American Holly (*Ilex opaca*)
Almey Crab Apple (*Malus* "Almey")
Siberian Crab Apple (*Malus baccata*)
Hopa Crab Apple (*Malus* "Hopa")
★Common Apple (*Malus pumila*)
Sargent Crab Apple (*Malus sargenti*)
Korean Mountain Ash (*Sorbus alnifolia*)
American Mountain Sah (*Sorbus americana*)
European Mountain Ash (*Sorbus aucuparia*)

Trees Classified by Color of Summer Foliage

Blue

Steel Lawson Cypress (*Chamaecyparis lawsonia glauca*)
Western Red Cedar (*Juniperus scopulorum* var. Chandler Blue)
Eastern Red Cedar (*Juniperus virginiana* var. Burki)

Silver to Gray

Russian Olive (*Elaeagnus angustifolia*)
White Poplar (*Populus alba*)
Pendent Silver Linden (*Tilia petiolaris*)
★Silver Linden (*Tilia tomentosa*)

Red to Purple

Broadleaf Japanese Maple (*Acer palmatum atropurpureum*)
Crimson King Maple (*Acer platanoides* "Crimson King")

Schwedler Maple (*Acer platanoides schwedleri*)
Purple Leaf Sycamore Maple (*Acer pseudoplatanus purpureum*)
Purple Beech (*Fagus sylvatica atropunicea*)
Weeping Purple Beech (*Fagus sylvatica purpureopendula*)
River's Purple Beech (*Fagus sylvatica riversi*)
Rubylace Locust (*Gleditsia triacanthos inermis* "Rubylace")
Blireiana Plum (*Prunus blireiana*)
Pissard Plum (*Prunus cerasifera atropurpurea*)
Thundercloud Plum (*Prunus cerasifera nigra* "Thundercloud")
Woods Myrobalan Plum (*Prunus cerasifera woodi*)
Blood-leaf Peach (*Prunus persica atropurpurea*)
Purple English Oak (*Quercus robur atropurpurea*)

Trees Classified by Color of Fall Foliage

Yellow

Big-leaf Maple (*Acer macrophyllum*)
Striped Maple or Moosewood (*Acer pennsylvanicum*)
Norway Maple (*Acer platanoides* var.)
Apple Serviceberry (yellow-orange) (*Amelanchier grandiflora*)
★Birch species (*Betula*)
Hickory species (*Carya*)
Chinese Chestnut (*Castanea mollissima*)
Redbud species (*Cercis*)
Fringetree (*Chionanthus virginicus*)
★American Yellow-wood (*Cladrastis lutea*)
★American Beech (*Fagus grandifolia*)
★European Beech (*Fagus sylvatica*)
White Ash (purple to yellow) (*Fraxinus americana*)
★Ginkgo (*Ginkgo biloba*)
★Star Magnolia (*Magnolia stellata*)
★Willow species (*Salix*)

Red

Amur Maple (*Acer ginnala*)
Manchurian Maple (*Acer mandshuricum*)
Nikko Maple (*Acer nikoense*)
★Japanese Maple (*Acer palmatum* var.)
★Red Maple (*Acer rubrum*)
Tatarian Maple (*Acer tataricum*)
★Shadblow Serviceberry (*Amelanchier canadensis*)
Hornbeam species (*Carpinus*)
★Flowering Dogwood (*Cornus florida*)
Japanese Dogwood (*Cornus kousa*)
American Smoke Tree (*Cotinus americanus*)
Washington Hawthorn (*Crataegus phaenopyrum*)
★Sweet Gum (*Liquidambar styraciflua*)
★Black Tupelo or Black Gum (*Nyssa sylvatica*)
★Cherry species (*Prunus*)
Bradford Callery Pear (*Pyrus calleryana* "Bradford")
Red Oak (*Quercus borealis*)
Scarlet Oak (*Quercus coccinea*)
★Pin Oak (*Quercus palustris*)
Sassafras (*Sassafras albidium*)
Korean Mountain Ash (*Sorbus alnifolia*)
Korean Stewartia (orange to red) (*Stewartis koreana*)

Purple

White Ash (*Fraxinus americana*)
★Sweet Gum (*Liquidambar styraciflua*)
★Common Pear (*Pyrus communis*)
Japanese Stewartia (*Stewartia pseudocamellia*)

Trees with Interesting Bark

Gray

★Red Maple (*Acer rubrum*)
★Serviceberry species (*Amelanchier*)
Hackberry species (*Celtis*)
★American Yellow-wood (*Cladrastis lutea*)
★Hawthorn species (*Crataegus*)
★Beech species (*Fagus*)
American Holly (*Ilex opaca*)
English or Persian Walnut (*Juglans regia*)
Cucumber Tree (*Magnolia acuminata*)
★Saucer Magnolia (*Magnolia soulangeana*)
Red Oak (young trunk and branches) (*Quercus borealis*)

Black Oak (young trunk and branches) (*Quercus velutina*)
Mountain Ash species (*Sorbus*)

Reddish Brown

Chinese Paper Birch (*Betula albo-sinensis*)

Yellow

Wisconsin or Niobe Weeping Willow (*Salix blanda*)

Green

★Babylon Weeping Willow (*Salix babylonica*)

Corky

Cork Oak (*Quercus suber*)

Flaking

Paperbark Maple (*Acer griseum*)
★Birch species (*Betula*)
Shagbark Hickory (*Carya ovata*)
Eastern Red Cedar (*Juniperus virginiana*)
Crape-Myrtle (*Lagerstroemia indica*)
Lace-bark Pine (*Pinus bungeana*)
★Plane Tree species (*Platanus*)
Stewartia species (*Stewartia*)

Trees for the City

Hedge Maple (*Acer campestre*)
Box-Elder (*Acer negundo*)
Norway Maple (*Acer platanoides*)
Sycamore Maple (*Acer pseudoplatanus*)
★Horse-Chestnut Buckeye (*Aesculus*)
★Tree of Heaven (*Ailanthus*)
Silk Tree (*Albizzia julibrissin*)
Catalpa (*Catalpa*)
Hackberry (*Celtis*)
Downy Hawthorn (*Crataegus mollis*)
Washington Hawthorn (*Crataegus phaenopyrum*)
Russian Olive (*Elaegus angustifolia*)
White Ash (*Fraxinus americana*)
European Ash (*Fraxinus excelsior*)
Green Ash (*Fraxinus pennsylvanica*)
★Ginkgo (*Ginkgo biloba*)
Thornless Honey-Locust (*Gleditsia triacanthos*)
★Golden Rain Tree (*Koelreuteria paniculata*)
★Saucer Magnolia (*Magnolia soulangeana*)
★Star Magnolia (*Magnolia stellata*)
★Crab Apple (*Malus* var.)
Chinaberry (*Melia azedarrach*)
London Plane Tree (*Platanus acerfolia*)
White Poplar (*Populus alba*)
★Lombardy Poplar (*Populus nigra italica*)
Bradford Callery Pear (*Pyrus callerana* "Bradford")
Red Oak (*Quercus borealis*)
★Black Locust (*Robinia pseudoacacia*)
★Little-leaf Linden (*Tilia cordata*)
★Crimean Linden (*Tilia euchlora*)
★Silver Linden (*Tilia tomentosa*)

Trees for Wide Streets

Sycamore Maple (*Acer pseudoplatanus*)
Sugar Hackberry (*Celtis laevigata*)
White Ash (*Fraxinus americana*)
Green Ash (*Fraxinus pennsylvanica lanceolata*)
★Ginkgo (*Ginkgo biloba*)
★Common Honey-Locust (*Gleditsia triacanthos*)
★Southern Magnolia (*Magnolia grandiflora*)
Tulip Tree (*Liriodendron tulipifera*)
★Eastern White Pine (*Pinus strobus*)
London Plane Tree (*Platanus acerifola*)
★Oriental Plane Tree (*Platanus orientalis*)
White Poplar (*Populus alba*)
Sargent Cherry (*Prunus sargenti*)
★Pin Oak (*Quercus palustris*)
Willow Oak (*Quercus phellos*)

Trees for Medium Streets

Norway Maple (*Acer platanoides*)
Mountain Silverbell (*Halesia monticola*)
★Sweet Gum (*Liquidambar styraciflua*)
Hop-Hornbeam (*Ostrya virginiana*)
Simon Poplar (*Populus simoni*)
Scarlet Oak (*Quercus coccinea*)
Willow Oak (*Quercus phellos*)
Laurel Oak (*Quercus laurifolia*)

Cork Oak (*Quercus suber*)
★Black Locust (*Robinia pseudoacacia*)
Sassafras (*Sassafras albidium officinale*)
★Linden species (*Tilia*)
Winged Elm (*Ulmus alata*)

Trees for Suburban Streets
Hedge Maple (*Acer campestre*)
Paperbark Maple (*Acer griseum*)
Mountain Maple (*Acer spicatum*)
American Hornbeam (*Carpinus caroliniana*)
Pyramid European Hornbeam (*Carpinus betulus fastigiata*)
Globe European Hornbeam (*Carpinus betulus globosa*)
Fringetree (*Chionanthus virginicus*)
★Flowering Dogwood (*Cornus florida*)
★Hawthorn species (*Crataegus*)
Carolina Silverbell (*Halesia carolina*)
★Golden Rain Tree (*Koelreuteria paniculata*)
Oriental Cherry (*Prunus serrulata*)
Columnar Sargent Cherry (*Prunus sargenti columnaris*)
Japanese Snowbell (*Styrax japonica*)
Fragrant Snowbell (*Styrax obassia*)
Asiatic Sweetleaf (*Symplocos paniculata*)
Smooth-leaved Elm varieties (*Ulmus carpinifolia*)

Soil Tolerance

Trees Tolerating Acid Soil
★Japanese Maple (*Acer palmatum* var.)
★Flowering Dogwood (*Cornus flordia* var.)
Japanese Dogwood (*Cornus kousa*)
★European Beech (*Fagus sylvatica* var.)
Sweet Bay (*Magnolia virginiana*)
★Black Tupelo (*Nyssa sylvatica*)
★Sorrel Tree (*Oxydendrum arboreum*)

Red Oak (*Quercus borealis*)
Scarlet Oak (*Quercus coccinea*)
★Pin Oak (*Quercus palustris*)
Willow Oak (*Quercus phellos*)
Japanese Stewartia (*Stewartia pseudocamellia*)

Trees Tolerating Moist Soil
★Red Maple (*Acer rubrum*)
Alder species (*Alnus*)
Holly species (*Ilex*)
★Sweet Gum (*Liquidambar styraciflua*)
Sweet Bay (*Magnolia virginiana*)
★Black Tupelo or Black Gum (*Nyssa sylvatica*)
Swamp White Oak (*Quercus bicolor*)
★Willow species (*Salix*)
Common Bald Cypress (*Taxodium distichum*)
American Arbor-vitae (*Thuja occidentalis*)

Trees Tolerating Dry or Poor Soil
Box-Elder (*Acer negundo*)
★Tree of Heaven (*Ailanthus*)
Silk Tree (*Albizzia julibrissin*)
Common Paper-Mulberry (*Broussonetia papyrifera*)
European Hackberry (*Celtis australis*)
Russian Olive (*Elaeagnus angustifolia*)
Green Ash (*Fraxinus pennsylvanica*)
Modesto Ash (*Fraxinus velutina* "Modesto")
★Honey-Locust (*Gledistia triacanthos varities*)
Western Red Cedar (*Juniperus scopulorum*)
Eastern Red Cedar (*Juniperus virginiana*)
★Golden Rain Tree (*Koelreuteria paniculata*)
Chinaberry (*Melia azedarach*)
Jack Pine (*Pinus banksiana*)
White Poplar (*Poplulus alba*)
Black Jack Oak (*Quercus marilandica*)
★Black Locust (*Robinia pseudoacacia*)
Sassafras (*Sassafras albidum officinale*)

Pest-Resistant Trees
★Tree of Heaven (*Ailanthus altissima*)
Hornbeam species (*Carpinus*)
Cedar species (*Cedrus*)
European Hackberry (*Celtis australis*)
Cornelian Cherry (*Cornus mas*)
Japanese Cornel (*Cornus officinalis*)
American Smoke Tree (*Cotinus americanus*)
Russian Olive (*Elaeagnus angustifolia*)
★Ginkgo (*Ginkgo biloba*)
Juniper species (*Juniperus*)
★Golden Rain Tree (*Koelreuteria paniculata*)
★Sweet Gum (*Liquidambar styraciflua*)
Anise Magnolia (*Magnolia salicifolia*)
★Star Magnolia (*Magnolia stellata*)
Hop-Hornbeam species (*Ostrya*)

Trees for Hedging or Barriers
European Beech (*Fagus sylvatica*) prunes well.
Leyland Cypress (*Cupressocyparis leylandii*) withstands heavy pruning.
Hawthorn varieties (*Crataegus*) easily pruned, advantage of thorns.
Canadian Hemlock (*Tsuga canadensis*) evergreen.
American Holly (*Ilex opaca*) can be pruned.
European Hornbeam (*Carpinus betulus*) prunes well.
Little-leaf Linden (*Tilia cordata*) tolerates heavy pruning.
Hedge Maple (*Acer campestre*) can be pruned.
Austrian Pine (*Pinus nigra*) plant 10–12 feet on centers, staggered row.
Japanese Black Pine (*Pinus thunbergi*) plant 8 feet on centers, staggered row.
Eastern White Pine (*Pinus strobus*) plant 15 feet on centers, staggered row.

CALIFORNIA

State Tree
★Redwood (*Sequoia sempervirens*)

Evergreen Trees
★Acacia species (*Acacia*)
Pacific Madrone (*Arbutus menziesi*)
Camellia species (*Camellia*)
Horsetail Beefwood (*Casuarina equisetifolia*)
Coast Beefwood (*Casuarina stricta*)
★Carob (*Ceratonia siliqua*)
Camphor Tree (*Cinnamomum camphora*)
Citrus species (*Citrus*)
Evergreen Dogwood (*Cornus capitala*)
Common China Fir (*Cunninghamia lanceolata*)
★Cypress species (*Cupressus*)
Loquat (*Eriobotrya japonica*)
★Eucalyptus species (*Eucalyptus*)
Brush-Cherry Eugenia (*Eugenia paniculata*)
Loblolly Bay Gordonia (*Gordonia lasianthus*)
Silk-Oak Grevillea (*Grevillea robusta*)
Holly species (*Ilex*)
Juniper species (*Juniperus*)
Paterson Suger Plum Tree (*Lagunaria patersoni*)
Sweet Bay (*Laurus nobilis*)
Australian Tea Tree (*Leptospermum laevigatum*)
★Southern Magnolia (*Magnolia grandiflora*)
Chile Mayten Tree (*Maytenus boaria*)
Cajeput Tree (*Melaleuca leucadendron*)
California Bayberry (*Myrica californica*)
★Common Olive (*Olea europaea*)
Chinese Photinia (*Photinia serrulata*)
★Pine species (*Pinus*)
Tarata Pittosporum (*Pittosporum eugenoides*)
Diamond Leaf Pittosporum (*Pittosporum rhombifolium*)
Yew Podocarpus (*Podocarpus macrophyllus*)
Fern Podocarpus (*Podocarpus racemosa*)
★Douglas Fir (*Pseudotsuga menziesii*)
★California Live Oak (*Quercus agrifolia*)

Holly Oak (*Quercus ilex*)
Cork Oak (*Quercus suber*)
Royal Palm (*Roystonea regia*)
Palmetto (*Sabal palmetto*)
★Redwood (*Sequoia sempervirens*)
Giant Sequoia (*Sequoiadendron giganteum*)
Brazil Pepper Tree (*Schinus trebinthifolius*)
Arbor-vitae species (*Thuja*)
California Laurel (*Umbellularia californica*)
Mexican Washington Palm (*Washingtonia robusta*)

Trees Classified by Height
20–35 Feet
Cootamundra Wattle (*Acacia baileyana*)
Gossamer Sydney Acacia (*Acacia longifolia floribunda*)
Weeping Boree Acacia (*Acacia pendula*)
Hedge Maple (*Acer campestre*)
Hornbeam Maple (*Acer carpinifolium*)
Vine Maple (*Acer circinatum*)
Amur Maple (*Acer ginnala*)
Paperback Maple (*Acer griseum*)
★Japanese Maple (*Acer palmatum*)
Mountain Maple (*Acer spicatum*)
Apple Serviceberry (*Amelanchier grandiflora*)
Strawberry Tree (*Arbutus unedo*)
Ohio Buckeye (*Aesculus glabra*)
Buddhist Bauhinia (*Bauhinia variegata*)
European Hornbeam (*Carpinus betulus globosa*)
Golden Shower Senna (*Cassia fistula*)
Coast Beefwood (*Casuarina stricta*)
Judas Tree (*Cercis siliquastrum*)
Lemon Bottlebrush (*Callistemon lanceolatus*)
Japanese Dogwood (*Cornus kousa*)
★Hawthorn species (*Crataegus*)
Russian Olive (*Elaeagnus angustifolia*)
Loquat (*Eriobotrya japonica*)
Blue Erythea (*Erythea armata*)
Common Fig (*Ficus carica*)
Flowering Ash (*Fraxinus ornus*)
★Golden Rain Tree (*Koelreuteria paniculata*)

★Laburnum species (*Laburnum*)
Crape-Myrtle (*Lagerstroemia indica*)
Sweet Bay or Laurel (*Laurus nobilis*)
Australian Tea Tree (*Leptospermum laevigatum*)
Silver Leucadendron (*Leucadendron argenteum*)
Queensland Nut (*Macadamia ternifolia*)
★Saucer Magnolia (*Magnolia soulangeana*)
★Star Magnolia (*Magnolia stellata*)
★Crab Apple species (*Malus*)
Jerusalem Thorn (*Parkinsonia aculeata*)
★Cherry species (*Prunus*)
Madagascar Traveler's Tree (*Ravenala madagascariensis*)
★Babylon Weeping Willow (*Salix babylonica*)
Snowbell species (*Styrax*)
Asiatic Sweetleaf (*Symplocos paniculata*)
Farkleberry (*Vaccinium arboreum*)

35–75 Feet
Korean Fir (*Abies koreana*)
Silver Wattle (*Acacia decurrens dealbata*)
Black Wattle (*Acacia decurrens mollis*)
Box-Elder (*Acer negundo*)
Nikko Maple (*Acer nikoense*)
★Red Fruited Tree of Heaven (*Ailanthus altissima erythrocarpa*)
Silk Tree (*Albizzia julibrissin*)
Italian Alder (*Alnus cordata*)
Common Paper-Mulberry (*Broussonetia papyrifera*)
Common Camellia (*Camellia japonica*)
European Hornbeam (*Carpinus caroliniana*)
Horsetail Beefwood (*Casuarina equisetifolia*)
Southern Catalpa (*Catalpa bignoniodes*)
Bunch Hackberry (*Celtis bungeana*)
★Carob (*Ceratonia siliqua*)
Chinese Redbud (*Cercis sinensis*)
Camphor Tree (*Cinnamomum camphor*)
★American Yellow-wood (*Cladrastis lutea*)
Evergreen Dogwood (*Cornus capitala*)
Giant Dogwood (*Cornus controversa*)

*Flowering Dogwood (*Cornus florida*)
Large-leaf Dogwood (*Cornus macrophylla*)
Cockspur Tree (*Crataegus crus-galli*)
Green Hawthorn (*Crataegus viridis*)
Common China Fir (*Cunninghamia lanceolata*)
Smooth Arizona Cypress (*Cupressus arizonica bonita*)
*Monterey Cypress (*Cupressus macrocarpa*)
Italian Cypress (*Cupressus sempervirens*)
Common Persimmon (*Diospyros virginiana*)
Hardy Rubber Tree (*Eucommia ulmoides*)
Brush-Cherry Eugenia (*Eugenia paniculata*)
Green Ash (*Fraxinus pennsylvanica lanceolata*)
Loblolly Bay Gordonia (*Gordonia lasianthus*)
English Holly (*Ilex aquifolium*)
Luster-leaf Holly (*Ilex latifolia*)
Sharp-leaf Jacaranda (*Jacaranda acutifolia*)
Hinds Black Walnut (*Juglans hindsi*)
Heartnut (*Juglans sieboldiana cordiformis*)
Chinese Juniper (*Juniperus chinensis*)
Western Red Cedar (*Juniperus scopulorum*)
Paterson Sugar Plum Tree (*Lagunaria patersoni*)
Australian Fan Palm (*Livistona australis*)
Fraser Magnolia (*Magnolia fraseri*)
Cajeput Tree (*Malaleuca leucadendron*)
"Cowichan" *Crab Apple* (*Malus* "Cowichan")
"Dolgo" *Crab Apple* (*Malus* "Dolgo")
"Makamik" *Crab Apple* (*Malus* "Makamik")
Cherry Crab Apple (*Malus robusta*)
"Sissipuk" *Crab Apple* (*Malus* "Sissipuk")
Chinaberry (*Melia azedarach*)
White Mulberry (*Morus alba*)
Empress Tree (*Paulownia tomentosa*)
Big Cone or Coulter Pine (*Pinus coulteri*)
*Monterey Pine (*Pinus resinosa*)
Chinese Pistache (*Pistacia chinensis*)
Tarata Pittosporum (*Pittosporum eugenoides*)
Fern Podocarpus (*Podocarpus elongatus*)
Yew Podocarpus (*Podocarpus macrophyllus*)
Hardy Orange (*Poncirus trifoliata*)
Chinese Poplar (*Populus lasiocarpa*)
Sargent Cherry (*Prunus sargenti*)
Yoshino Cherry (*Prunus yedoensis*)
Portugal Laurel (*Prunus lusitanica*)
Fragrant Epaulette Tree (*Pterostyrax hispida*)
Canyon Live or Golden Cup Oak (*Quercus chrysolepis*)
Holly Oak (*Quercus ilex*)
*Pin Oak (*Quercus palustris*)
Cork Oak (*Quercus suber*)
California Pepper Tree (*Schinus molle*)
Korean Mountain Ash (*Sorbus alnifolia*)
Bell Flambeau Tree (*Spathodea campanulata*)
Korean Stewartia (*Stewartia koreana*)
Japanese Stewartia (*Stewartia pseudo-camellia*)
Oriental Arbor-vitae (*Thuja orientalis*)
Japanese Arbor-vitae (*Thuja standishi*)
*Crimean Linden (*Tilia euchlora*)
Winged or Wahoo Elm (*Ulmus alata*)
Chinese Elm (*Ulmus parvifolia*)
California Laurel (*Umbellularia californica*)

75 Feet or Over
Big-leaf Maple (*Acer macrophyllum*)
Norway Maple (*Acer platanoides*)
Sycamore Maple (*Acer pseudoplatanus*)
*Red or Swamp Maple (*Acer rubrum*)
Kapok or Silk Cotton Tree (*Ceiba pentandra*)
European Hackberry (*Celtis australis*)
Sugar Hackberry (*Celtis laevigata*)
False Cypress species (*Chamaecyparis*)
Pacific Dogwood (*Cornus nuttalli*)
Cryptomeria (*Cryptomeria japonica*)
*Eucalyptus species (*Eucalyptus*)
*Beech species (*Fagus*)
Oregon Ash (*Fraxinus oregona*)
*Ginkgo or Maidenhair Tree (*Ginkgo biloba*)
*Common Honey-Locust (*Gleditsia triacanthos*)
Silk-Oak Grevillea (*Grevillea robusta*)
California Incense Cedar (*Libocedrus decurrens*)
*Sweet Gum (*Liquidambar styraciflua*)
*Southern Magnolia (*Magnolia grandiflora*)

White-leaf Japanese Magnolia (*Magnolia obovata*)
Dawn Redwood (*Metasequoia glyptostroboides*)
*Black Gum or Black Tupelo (*Nyssa sylvatica*)
Sabal Palmetto (*Palmetto*)
*Pine species (*Pinus*)
Diamond Leaf Pittosporum (*Pittosporum rhombifoium*)
*Plane Tree species (*Platanus*)
Poplar species (*Populus*)
*Oak species (*Quercus*)
*Redwood (*Sequoia sempervirens*)
Giant Sequoia (*Sequoiadendron giganteum*)
Western Hemlock (*Tsuga heterophylla*)
English Elm (*Ulmus procera*)
Mexican Washington Palm (*Washingtonia robusta*)
Japanese Zelkova (*Zelkova serrata*)

Trees Classified by Form

Pyramidal
Cryptomeria (*Cryptomeria japonica*)
Smooth Arizona Cypress (*Cupressus arizonica bonita*)
Italian Cypress (*Cupressus sempervirens*)
*Beech species (*Fagus*)
English Holly (*Ilex aquifolium*)
American Holly (*Ilex opaca*)
Juniper or Red Cedar species (*Juniperus*)
Paterson Sugar Plum Tree (*Lagunaria patersoni*)
*Sweet Gum (*Liquidambar styraciflua*)
*Magnolia species (*Magnolia*)
Dawn Redwood (*Metasequoia glyptostroboides*)
*Black Gum or Black Tupelo (*Nyssa sylvatica*)
*Pin Oak (*Quercus palustris*)
Giant Sequoia (*Sequoiadendron giganteum*)
Arbor-vitae species (*Thuja*)
*Linden species (*Tilia*)
Smooth-leaved Elm varities (*Ulmus carpinifolia*)

Rounded or Globe-Shaped
*Japanese Maple (*Acer palmatum*)
Globe Norway Maple (*Acer platanoides globosum*)
Globe European Hornbeam (*Carpinus betulus globosa*)
Bunch Hackberry (*Celtis bungeana*)
Single Seed Hawthorn (*Crataegus monogyna inermis*)
*Saucer Magnolia (*Magnolia soulangeana*)
*Crab Apple species (*Malus*)
Umbrella Black Locust (*Robinia pseudoacacia umbraculifera*)

Columnar
Ascending Norway Maple (*Acer platanoides ascendens*)
Columnar Norway Maple (*Acer platanoides columnare*)
Erect Norway Maple (*Acer platanoides columnare*)
Fastigiate European Hornbeam (*Carpinus betulus fastigiata*)
Scarab Lawson Cypress (*Chamaecyparis lawsoniana allumi*)
Erect Lawson Cypress (*Chamaecyparis lawsoniana erecta*)
Fastigiate Washington Hawthorn (*Crataegus phaenopyrum fastigiata*)
Dawyck Beech (*Fagus sylvatica fastigiata*)
Sentry Ginkgo (*Ginkgo biloba fastigiata*)
Bolleana Poplar (*Populus alba pyramidalis*)
*Lombardy Poplar (*Populus nigra italica*)
"Amanogawa" Cherry (*Prunus serrulata* "Amanogawa")
Shipmast Locust (*Robinia pseudoacacia rectissima*)
Common Bald Cypress (*Taxodium distichum*)

Weeping
Weeping Boree Acacia (*Acacia pendula*)
Weeping European Hornbeam (*Carpinus betulus pendula*)
Weeping Lawson Cypress (*Chamaecyparis lawsoniana pendula*)
*Weeping Beech (*Fagus syvatica pendula*)
"Exzellenz Thiel" Crab Apple (*Malus* "Exzellenz Thiel")
"Oekonomierat Echtermeyer" Crab Apple (*Malus* "Oekonomierat Echtermeyer")

Weeping Mulberry (*Morus alba pendula*)
Weeping Japanese Apricot (*Prunus mume pendula*)
Weeping Higan Cherry (*Prunus subhirtella pendula*)
"Yaeshidare" Cherry (*Prunus subhirtella pendula flora plena*)
Weeping Yoshino Cherry (*Prunus yedoensis perpendens*)
*Babylon Weeping Willow (*Salix babylonica*)
California Pepper Tree (*Schinus molle*)
Weeping Japanese Pagoda Tree (*Sophora japonica pendula*)
Pendant Silver Linden (*Tilia petiolaris*)
Weeping American Elm (*Ulmus americana pendula*)

With Horizontal Branching
Silk Tree (*Albizzia julibrissin*)
Giant Dogwood (*Cornus controversa*)
*Flowering Dogwood (*Cornus florida*)
Japanese Dogwood (*Cornus kousa*)
*Hawthorn species (*Crataegus*)
Dawn Redwood (*Metasequoia glyptostroboides*)
*Black Gum or Black Tupelo (*Nyssa sylvatica*)
Yew Podocarpus (*Podocarpus macrophyllos*)
*Pin Oak (*Quercus palustris*)
Common Bald Cypress (*Taxodium distichum*)

Trees Classified by Color of Blossom

Yellow
Cootamundra Wattle (*Acacia baileyana*)
Silver Wattle (*Acacia decurrens dealbata*)
Shower of Gold (*Cassia fistula*)
*Golden Rain Tree (*Koelreutaria paniculata*)
*Laburnum (*Laburnum vossi*)

White
Citrus species (*Citrus*)
American Yellow-wood (*Cladrastis lutea*)
Japanese Dogwood (*Cornus kousa*)
Pacific Dogwood (*Cornus nuttali*)
*Washington Hawthorn (*Craegus phaenopyrum*)
Yulan Magnolia (*Magnolia denudata*)
*Southern Magnolia (*Magnolia grandiflora*)
*Star Magnolia (*Magnolia stellata*)
Arnold Crab Apple (*Malus arnoldiana*)
Tea Crab Apple (*Malus hupehensis*)
Sargent Crab Apple (*Malus sargenti*)
*Sorrel Tree (*Oxydendrum arboreum*)
Thundercloud Plum (*Prunus cerasifera* "Thundercloud")
Mount Fuji Cherry (*Prunus serrulata* "Shirotae")
Yoshino Cherry (*Prunus yedoensis*)
Bradford Callery Pear (*Pyrus calleryana* "Bradford")
*Common Pear (*Pyrus communis*)
*Japanese Pagoda Tree (*Sophora japonica*)
Korean Mountain Ash (*Sorbus alnifolia*)
Japanese Stewartia (*Stewartia pseudocamellia*)
Japanese Snowbell (*Styrax japonica*)

Pink
Wither's Pink Redbud (*Cercis canadensis* "Wither's Pink Charm")
Red Flowering Dogwood (*Cornus florida rubra*)
Toba Hawthorn (*Crataegus mordenensis* "Toba")
Ingleside Crape-Myrtle (*Lagerstroemia indica* "Ingleside Pink")
*Saucer Magnolia (*Magnolia soulangeana*)
Japanese Flowering Crab Apple (*Malus floribunda*)
Katherine Crab Apple (*Malus* "Katherine")
Prince Georges Crab Apple (*Malus* "Prince Georges")
*Common Apple (*Malus pumila*)
Blireiana Plum (*Prunus blireiana*)
Sargent Cherry (*Prunus sargenti*)
Amanogawa Cherry (*Prunus serrulata* "Amanogawa")
Kwanzan Cherry (*Prunus serrulata* "Kwanzan")
Autumn Cherry (*Prunus subhirtella autumnalis*)
Weeping Cherry (*Prunus subhirtella pendula*)

Blue
Purple Orchid Tree (*Bauhinia variegata*)
Sharp-leaf Jacaranda (*Jacaranda acutifolia*)

Red
Ruby Horse-Chestnus (*Aesculus carnea briotti*)
★Carob (*Cerationia siliqua*)
Paul's Scarlet Hawthorn (*Crataegus oxyacantha pauli*)
Crimson Eucalyptus (*Eucalyptus ficifolia*)
Red Crape-Myrtle (*Lagerstroemia indica* "Wm. Toovey")
Alexandrina Magnolia (*Magnolia soulangeana* "Alexandrina")
Carmine Crab Apple (*Malus atrosanguinea*)

Trees with Bright Red Fruit
★Flowering Dogwood (*Cornus florida*)
Japanese Dogwood (*Cornus kousa*)
Pacific Dogwood (*Cornus nuttalli*)
Downy Hawthorn (*Crataegus mollis*)
Washington Hawthorn (*Crataegus phaenopyrum*)
Almey Crab Apple (*Malus* "Almey")
Siberian Crab Apple (*Malus baccata*)
Hopa Crab Apple (*Malus* "Hopa")
★Common Apple (*Malus pumila*)
Sargent Crab Apple (*Malus sargenti*)
Korean Mountain Ash (*Sorbus alnifolia*)
European Mountain Ash (*Sorbus aucuparia*)

Trees Classified by Color of Summer Foliage

Blue
White Fir (*Abies concolor*)
Cootamundra Wattle (*Acacia baileyana*)
Silver Wattle (*Acacia decurrens dealbata*)
Weeping Boree Acacia (*Acacia pendula*)
Blue Gum (*Eucalyptus globulus*)
Western Red Cedar (*Juniperus scopulorum* var. Chandler Blue)

Silver to Gray
Russian Olive (*Elaeagnus angustifolia*)
★Common Olive (*Olea europaea*)
White Poplar (*Populus alba*)
Pendant Silver Linden (*Tilia petiolaris*)
★Silver Linden (*Tilia tomentosa*)

Red to Purple
Blood-leaf Japanese Maple (*Acer palmatum atropurpureum*)
Crimson King Maple (*Acer platanoides* "Crimson King")
Schwedler Maple (*Acer platanoides schwedleri*)
Purple-leaf Sycamore Maple (*Acer pseudo-platanus*)
Purple Beech (*Fagus sylvatica atropunicea*)
Weeping Purple Beech (*Fagus sylvatica purpureopendula*)
River's Purple Beech (*Fagus sylvatica riversi*)
Rubylace Locust (*Gleditsia triacanthos inermmis* "Rubylace")
Purple Crab Apple (*Malus purpurea*)
Blireiana Plum (*Prunus blireiana*)
Pissard Plum (*Prunus cerasifera atropurpurea*)
Thundercloud Plum (*Prunus cerasifera nigra* "Thundercloud")
Wood's Myrobalan Plum (*Prunus cerasifera woodi*)
Blood-leaf Peach (*Prunus persica atropurpurea*)

Trees Classified by Color of Fall Foliage

Yellow
Big-leaf Maple (*Acer macrophyllum*)
Norway Maple (*Acer platanoides varieties*)
Apple Serviceberry (yellow-orange) (*Amelanchier grandiflora*)
Hickory species (*Carya*)
Chinese Chestnut (*Castanea mollissima*)
★Katsura Tree (yellow to scarlet) (*Cercidiphyllum japonicum*)
Redbud species (*Cercis*)
Fringetree (*Chionanthus virginicus*)
★Yellow-wood (*Cladrastis lutea*)
★American Beech (*Fagus grandifolia*)
★European Beech (*Fagus sylvatica*)
White Ash (purple to yellow) (*Fraxinus americana*)

★Ginkgo (*Ginkgo biloba*)
★Star Magnolia (bronze) (*Magnolia stellata*)
★Willow species (*Salix*)

Red
Vine Maple (*Acer circinatum*)
★Japanese Maple (*Acer palmatum*)
★Red Maple (*Acer rubrum*)
Hornbeam species (*Carpinus*)
★Flowering Dogwood (*Cornus florida*)
Japanese Dogwood (*Cornus kousa*)
Pacific Dogwood (*Cornus nuttalli*)
American Smoke Tree (*Cotinus americanus*)
Washington Hawthorn (*Crataegus phaenopyrum*)
Sweet Gum (*Liquidambar styraciflua*)
★Black Gum or Black Tupelo (*Nyssa sylvatica*)
★Sorrel Tree (*Oxydendrum arboreum*)
Chinese Pistache (*Pistacia chinensis*)
★Cherry species (*Prunus*)
Bradford Callery Pear (*Pyrus calleryana* "Bradford")
Red Oak (*Quercus borealis*)
Scarlet Oak (*Quercus coccinea*)
★Pin Oak (*Quercus palustris*)
Sassafras (*Sassafras albidum*)
Korean Mountain Ash (*Sorbus alnifolia*)
Korean Stewartia (orange to red) (*Stewartia koreana*)

Purple
White Ash (*Fraxinus americana*)
★Sweet Gum (*Liquidambar styraciflua*)
★Common Pear (*Pyrus communis*)
★White Oak (*Quercus alba*)

Trees with Interesting Bark

Gray
★Red Maple (*Acer rubrum*)
Serviceberry species (*Amelanchier*)
Kapok or Silk-Cotton Tree (*Ceiba pentandra*)
Hackberry species (*Celtis*)
★American Yellow-wood (*Cladrastis lutea*)
★Hawthorn species (*Crataegus*)
★Beech species (*Fagus*)
American Holly (*Ilex opaca*)
English or Persian Walnut (*Juglans regia*)
Cucumber Tree (*Magnolia acuminata*)
★Saucer Magnolia (*Magnolia soulangeana*)
Royal Palm (*Roystonea regia*)
Mountain Ash species (*Sorbus*)

White
★Gray Birch (*Betula populifolia*)

Red
Japanese Red Pine (*Pinus densiflora*)

Reddish Brown
Chinese Paper Birch (*Betula albo-sinensis*)
Sargent Cherry (*Prunus sargenti*)

Yellow
Wisconsin or Niobe Weeping Willow (*Salix blanda*)

Green
★Babylon Weeping Willow (*Salix babylonica*)

Corky
Hackberry (*Celtis*)
★Amur Cork (*Phellodendron amurense*)
Cork Oak (*Quercus suber*)

Flaking
Paperbark Maple (*Acer griseum*)
★Eucalyptus species (*Eucalyptus*)
Crape-Myrtle (*Lagerstroemia indica*)
★Plane Tree species (*Platanus*)
Lace-bark Pine (*Pinus bungeana*)

Trees for the City
Norway Maple (*Acer platanoides*)
Sycamore Maple (*Acer pseudoplatanus*)
★Horse-Chestnut or Buckeye (*Aesculus*)
★Tree of Heaven (*Ailanthus*)
Silk Tree (*Albizzia julibrissin*)
Catalpa (*Catalpa*)
Hackberry species (*Celtis*)

★Flowering Dogwood (*Cornus florida*)
Downy Hawthorn (*Crataegus mollis*)
Washington Hawthorn (*Crataegus phaenopyrum*)
Russian Olive (*Elaeagnus angustifolia*)
Arizona Ash (*Fraxinus velutina*)
★Ginkgo (*Ginkgo biloba*)
Thornless Honey-Locust (*Gleditsia triacanthos inermis*)
★Golden Rain Tree (*Koelreutaria paniculata*)
★Southern Magnolia (*Magnolia grandiflora*)
★Saucer Magnolia (*Magnolia soulangeana*)
★Star Magnolia (*Magnolia stellata*)
★Crab Apple species (*Malus*)
Chinaberry (*Melia azedarach*)
★Amur Cork (*Phellodendron amurense*)
London Plane Tree (*Platanus acerifolia*)
White Poplar (*Populus alba*)
★Lombardy Poplar (*Populus nigra italica*)
Bradford Callery Pear (*Pyrus calleryana* "Bradford")
Red Oak (*Quercus borealis*)
★Black Locust (*Robinia pseudoacacia*)
★Japanese Pagoda Tree (*Sophora japonica*)
Little-leaf Linden (*Tilia cordata*)
★Crimean Linden (*Tilia euchlora*)
★Silver Linden (*Tilia tomentosa*)
Village Green Zelkova (*Zelkova serrata* "Village Green")

Trees for Wide Streets
Sycamore Maple (*Acer pseudoplatanus*)
Horsetail Beefwood (*Casuarina equisetifolia*)
Sugar Hackberry (*Celtis laevigata*)
★Katsura Tree (*Cercidiphyllum japonicum*)
Camphor Tree (*Cinnamomum camphora*)
Eucalyptus species (*Eucalyptus*)
Velvet Ash (*Fraxinus velutina*)
★Ginkgo (*Ginkgo biloba*)
★Common Honey-Locust (*Gleditsia triacanthos*)
Silk-Oak Grevillea (*Grevillea robusta*)
Paterson Sugar Plum Tree (*Lagunaria patersoni*)
★Southern Magnolia (*Magnolia grandiflora*)
Diamond Leaf Pittosporum (*Pittosporum rhombifolium*)
London Plane Tree (*Platanus acerifolia*)
California Plane Tree (*Platanus racemosa*)
White Poplar (*Populus alba*)
Sargent Cherry (*Prunus sargenti*)
★California Live Oak (*Quercus agrifolia*)
★Pin Oak (*Quercus palustris*)
Willow Oak (*Quercus phellos*)
Japanese Zelkova (*Zelkova serrata*)

Trees for Medium Streets
Norway Maple (*Acer platanoides*)
Velvet Ash (*Fraxinus velutina*)
★Sweet Gum (*Liquidambar styraciflua*)
Chile Mayten Tree (*Maytenus boaria*)
Chinaberry (*Melia azedarach*)
Hop-Hornbeam (*Ostrya virginiana*)
Diamond Leaf Pittosporum (*Pittosporum rhombifolium*)
Simon Poplar (*Populus Simoni*)
Scarlet Oak (*Quercus coccinea*)
Laurel Oak (*Quercus laurifolia*)
Willow Oak (*Quercus phellos*)
Black Oak (*Quercus suber*)
★Black Locust (*Robinia pseudoacacia*)
California Pepper Tree (*Schinus molle*)
Japanese Pagoda Tree (*Sophora japonica*)
★Linden species (*Tilia*)
American Washington Palm (*Washingtonia robusta*)

Trees for Suburban Streets
Paperbark Maple (*Acer griseum*)
Mountain Maple (*Acer spicatum*)
Pyramid European Hornbeam (*Carpinus betulus fastigiata*)
Globe European Hornbeam (*Carpinus betulus globosa*)
Fringe Tree (*Chionanthus virginicus*)
★Flowering Dogwood (*Cornus florida*)
★Hawthorn species (*Crataegus*)

★Golden Rain Tree (*Koelreutaria paniculata*)
Chile Mayten Tree (*Maytenus boaria*)
Oriental Cherry (*Prunus serrulata*)
Columnar Sargent Cherry (*Prunus sargenti columnaris*)
Japanese Snowbell (*Styrax japonica*)
Fragrant Snowbell (*Styrax obassia*)

Soil Tolerance

Trees Tolerating Acid Soil

★Japanese Maple (*Acer palmatum*)
Citrus species (*Citrus*)
★Flowering Dogwood (*Cornus florida*)
Japanese Dogwood (*Cornus kousa*)
★European Beech (*Fagus sylvatica*)
★Black Gum or Black Tupelo (*Nyssa sylvatica*)
★Sorrel Tree (*Oxydendrum arboreum*)
Hardy Orange (*Poncirus trifoliata*)
Red Oak (*Quercus borealis*)
Scarlet Oak (*Quercus coccinea*)
★Pin Oak (*Quercus palustris*)
Willow Oak (*Quercus phellos*)

Trees Tolerating Moist Soil

★Red Maple (*Acer rubrum*)
Alder species (*Alnus*)
Beefwood species (*Casuarina*)
Holly species (*Ilex*)
★Sweet Gum (*Liquidambar styraciflua*)
Sweet Bay (*Magnolia virginiana*)
Cajeput Tree (*Melaleuca leucadendron*)
★Willow species (*Salix*)
Common Bald Cypress (*Taxodium distichum*)

Trees Tolerating Dry or Poor Soil

Cootamundra Wattle (*Acacia baileyana*)
Silver Maple (*Acacia decurrens dealbata*)
Grossamer Sydney Acacia (*Acacia longifolia floribunda*)
★Tree of Heaven (*Ailanthus*)
Silk Tree (*Albizzia julibrissin*)
Orchid Tree (*Bauhinia variegata*)
★Gray Birch (*Betula populifolia*)
Common Paper-Mulberry (*Broussonetia papyrifera*)
Beefwood (*Casuarina*)
European Hackberry (*Celtis australis*)
★Cabro (*Ceratonia siliqua*)
Russian Olive (*Elaeagnus angustifolia*)
Eucalyptus species (*Eucalyptus*)
Fig species (*Ficus*)
Modesto Ash (*Fraxinus velutina* "Modesto")
★Honey-Locust (*Gledistia triacanthos*)
Silk-Oak Grevillea (*Grevillea robusta*)
Western Red Cedar (*Juniperus scopulorum*)
★Golden Rain Tree (*Koelreutaria paniculata*)
Austrawän Tea Tree (*Leptospermum laevigatum*)

Osage-Orange (*Maclura pomifera*)
Cajeput Tree (*Melaleuca leucadendron*)
Chinaberry (*Melia azedarach*)
★Common Olive (*Olea europaea*)
Jerusalem Thorn (*Parkinsonia aculeata*)
Jack Pine (*Pinus Banksiana*)
Torrey Pine (*Pinus torreyana*)
Chinese Pistache (*Pistacia chinensis*)
White Poplar (*Populus alba*)
Fremont Cottonwood (*Populus fremonti*)
★Coast Live Oak (*Quercus agrifolia*)
California Black Oak (*Quercus kelloggi*)
Valley Oak (*Quercus lobata*)
★Black Jack Oak (*Quercus marilandica*)
★Black Locust (*Robinia pseudoacacia*)
Sassafras (*Sassafras albidium officinale*)
California Pepper Tree (*Schinus molle*)
Brazilian Pepper Tree (*Schinus terebinthifolius*)
★Japanese Pagoda Tree (*Sophora japonica*)
Washington Fan Palm (*Washingtonia filifera*)
Mexican Fan Palm (*Washingtonia robusta*)

Pest-Resistant Trees

★Tree of Heaven (*Ailanthus altissima*)
Flame Bottle Tree (*Brachychiton acerifolium*)
Hornbeam species (*Carpinus*)
European Hackberry (*Celtis australis*)
Russian Olive (*Elaeagnus angustifolia*)
Fig species (*Ficus*)
★Ginkgo (*Ginkgo biloba*)
★Honey-Locust (*Gleditsia triacanthos*)
Silk-Oak Tree (*Grevillea robusta*)
Juniper species (*Juniperus*)
★Golden Rain Tree (*Koelreutaria paniculata*)
★Laburnum species (*Laburnum*)
★Sweet Gum (*Liquidambar styraciflua*)
★Star Magnolia (*Magnolia stellata*)
Hop-Hornbeam species (*Ostrya*)

Trees for Seashore Planting

Norway Maple (*Acer platanoides*)
Sycamore Maple (*Acer pseudoplatanus*)
★Tree of Heaven (*Ailanthus*)
Horsetail Beefwood (*Casuarina equisetifolia*)
Coast Beefwood (*Casuarina stricta*)
Cockspur Thorn (*Crataegus crus-galli*)
English Hawthorn (*Crataegus oxyacantha*)
Washington Hawthorn (*Crataegus phaeonopyrum*)
Cryptomeria (*Cryptomeria japonica*)
★Monterey Cypress (*Cupressus macrocarpa*)
Russian Olive (*Elaeagnus angustifolia*)
Eucalyptus species (*Eucalyptus*)
Velvet Ash (*Fraxinus velutina*)

Thornless Honey-Locust (*Gleditsia triacanthos inermis*)
West Indies Juniper (*Juniperus lucayana*)
Paterson Sugar Plum Tree (*Lagunaria patersoni*)
★Southern Magnolia (*Magnolia grandiflora*)
Chile Mayten Tree (*Maytenus boaria*)
Cajeput Tree (*Melaleuca leucadendron*)
★Common Olive (*Olea europaea*)
Aleppo Pine (*Pinus halepensis*)
★Austrian Pine (*Pinus nigra*)
★Monterey Pine (*Pinus radiata*)
Scotch Pine (*Pinus sylvestris*)
★Japanese Black Pine (*Pinus thunbergi*)
Pittosporum (*Pittosporum*)
London Plane Tree (*Platanus acerifolia*)
Hardy Orange (*Poncirus trifoliata*)
White Poplar (*Populus alba*)
Black Cherry (*Prunus serotina*)
★California Live Oak (*Quercus agrifolia*)
★White Oak (*Quercus alba*)
Holly Oak (*Quercus ilex*)
★Black Locust (*Robinia pseudoacacia*)
Royal Palm (*Roystonea regia*)
Golden Weeping Willow (*Salix alba tristis*)
California Pepper Tree (*Schinus molle*)
Brazil Pepper Tree (*Schinus terebinthifolius*)
★Japanese Pagoda Tree (*Sophora japonica*)
Oriental Arbor-vitae (*Thuja orientalis*)
★Little-leaf Linden (*Tilia cordata*)
★Crimean Linden (*Tilia euchlora*)
Chinese Elm (*Ulmus parvifolia*)
California Laurel (*Umbellularia californica*)
Mexican Washington Palm (*Washingtonia robusta*)

Trees for Hedging or Barriers

European Beech (*Fagus sylvatica*) prunes well.
Leyland Cypress (*Cupressocyparis leylandii*) with-stands heavy pruning.
Hawthorn varieties (*Crataegus*) easily pruned, advantage of thorns.
Canadian Hemlock (*Tsuga canadensis*) evergreen.
American Holly (*Ilex opaca*) can be pruned.
European Hornbeam (*Carpinus betulus*) prunes well.
Little-leaf Linden (*Tilia cordata*) tolerates heavy pruning.
Hedge Maple (*Acer campestre*) can be pruned.
Austrian Pine (*Pinus nigra*) plant 10–12 feet on centers, staggered row.
Japanese Black Pine (*Pinus thunbergi*) plant 8 feet on centers, staggered row.
Eastern White Pine (*Pinus strobus*) plant 15 feet on centers, staggered row.

COLORADO

State Tree

Colorado Blue Spruce (*Picea pungens coerulea*)

Evergreen Trees

Fir species (*Abies*)
Juniper species (*Juniperus*)
Eastern Red Cedar (*Juniperus virginiana*)
★Larch species (*Larix*)
Spruce species (*Picea*)
★Pine species (*Pinus*)
★Douglas Fir (*Pseudotsuga menziesii*)
Arbor-vitae species (*Thuja*)
★Hemlock species (*Tsuga*)

Trees Classified by Height

20–35 Feet

Hedge Maple (*Acer campestre*)
Amur Maple (*Acer ginnala*)
Manchurian Maple (*Acer mandshuricum*)
Mountain Maple (*Acer spictam*)
Tatarian Maple (*Acer tataricum*)
Ohio Buckeye (*Aesculus glabra*)
Apple Serviceberry (*Amelanchier grandiflora*)

Mockernut (*Carya tomentosa*)
Fringe Tree (*Chionanthus virginicus*)
Cornelian Cherry (*Cornus mas*)
★Hawthorn species (*Crataegus*)
Russian Olive (*Elaeagnus angustifolia*)
Euonymus species (*Euonymus*)
Carolina Silverbell (*Halesia carolina*)
Common Sea-Buckthorn (*Hippophae rhamnoides*)
★Laburnum species (*Laburnum*)
★Crab Apple species (*Malus*)
★Cherry species (*Prunus*)
Dahurian Buckthorn (*Rhamnus davurica*)
Almond-leaf Willow (*Salix amygdalina*)
Goat Willow (*Salix caprea*)
Showy Mountain Ash (*Sorbus decora*)
Japanese Tree Lilac (*Syringa amurensis japonica*)

35–75 Feet

Box-Elder (*Acer negundo*)
Striped Maple or Moosewood (*Acer pennsylvanicum*)
★Sugar Maple (*Acer saccharum*)
★Red-fruited Tree of Heaven (*Ailanthus altissima erythrocarpa*)

Speckled Alder (*Alnus incana*)
Red Alder (*Alnus rubra*)
★Shadblow Serviceberry (*Amelanchier canadensis*)
Allegany Serviceberry (*Amelanchier laevis*)
Devil's Walking Stick (*Aralia elata*)
Dahurian Birch (*Betula davurica*)
★European Birch (*Betula pendula*)
American Hornbeam (*Carpinus caroliniana*)
Japanese Hornbeam (*Carpinus japonica*)
Chinese Chestnut (*Castanea mollissima*)
Southern Catalpa (*Catalpa bignoniodes*)
★Katsura Tree (*Cercidiphyllum japonicum*)
Eastern Redbud (*Cercis canadensis*)
★Flowering Dogwood (*Cornus florida*)
Turkish Filbert (*Corylus colurna*)
Cockspur Thorn (*Crataegus crus-galli*)
Green Hawthorn (*Crataegus viridis*)
Green Ash (*Fraxinus pennsylvanica lanceolata*)
★Ginkgo or Maidenhair Tree (*Ginkgo biloba*)
Chinese Juniper (*Juniperus chinensis*)
Siberian Crab Apple (*Malus baccata*)
"Cowichan" Crab Apple (*Malus* "Cowichan")
"Dolga" Crab Apple (*Malus* "Dolgo")

"Makamik" Crab Apple (*Malus* "Makamik")
Cherry Crab Apple (*Malus robusta*)
"Sissipuk" Crab Apple (*Malus* "Sissipuk")
White Mulberry (*Morus alba*)
★Amur Cork (*Phellodendron amurense*)
Black Hills spruce (*Picea glauca densata*)
Jack Pine (*Pinus banksiana*)
Lace-bark Pine (*Pinus bungeana*)
Swiss Stone Pine (*Pinus cembra*)
Limber Pine (*Pinus flexilis*)
Scotch Pine (*Pinus sylvestris*)
Simon Poplar (*Populus simoni*)
Amur Choke Cherry (*Prunus maacki*)
Miyama Cherry (*Prunus maximowiczi*)
European Bird Cherry (*Prunus padus*)
Sargent Cherry (*Prunus sargenti*)
Ussurian Pear (*Pyrus ussuriensis*)
Red Oak (*Quercus borealis*)
Scarlet Oak (*Quercus coccinea*)
★Pin Oak (*Quercus palustris*)
White Willow (*Salix alba*)
Wisconsin or Niobe Weeping Willow (*Salix blanda*)
Elaeagnus Willow (*Salix elaeagnus*)
Thurlow Weeping Willow (*Salix eegantissima*)
Laurel Willow (*Salix pentandra*)
European Mountain Ash or Rowan Tree (*Sorbus aucuparia*)
American Arbor-vitae (*Thuja occidentalis*)
Carolina Hemlock (*Tsuga caroliniana*)
Siberian Elm (*Ulmus pumila*)

75 Feet or Over
Fir species (*Abies*)
Norway Maple (*Acer platanoides*)
★Red or Swamp Maple (*Acer rubrum*)
★Baumann Horse-Chestnut (*Aesculus hippocastanum baumanni*)
European Alder (*Alnus glutinosa*)
★Canoe Birch (*Betula papyrifera*)
Hickory species (*Carya*)
Northern Catalpa (*Catalpa speciosa*)
False Cypress species (*Fagus*)
White Ash (*Fraxinus americana*)
European Ash (*Fraxinus excelsior*)
★Common Honey-Locust (*Gleditsia triacanthos*)
Kentucky Coffee Tree (*Cymnocladus dioicus*)
European Larch (*Larix decidua*)
Japanese Larch (*Laris leptolepis*)
★Sweet Gum (*Liquidambar styraciflua*)
★Black Gum or Black Tupelo (*Nyssa sylvatica*)
Spruce species (*Pinus*)
Poplar species (*Populus*)
Sargent Cherry (*Prunus sargenti*)
Black or Rum Cherry (*Prunus serotina*)
★Douglas Fir (*Pseudotsuga menziesii*)
★Oak species (*Quercus*)
Giant Arbor-vitae (*Thuja plicata*)
★Linden species (*Tilia*)
★Canada Hemlock (*Tsuga canadensis*)
★Elm species (*Ulmus*)

Trees Classified by Form

Pyramidal
Fir species (*Abies*)
★Birch species (*Betula*)
Pyramidal European Birch (*Betula pendula fastigiata*)
Pyramidal Washington Hawthorn (*Crataegus phaenopyrum fastigiata*)
False Cypress species (*Chamaecyparis*)
★Beech species (*Fagus*)
Juniper or Red Cedar species (*Juniperus*)
★Larch species (*Larix*)
★Sweet Gum (*Liquidambar styraciflua*)
Spruce species (*Picea*)
Swiss Stone Pine (*Pinus cembra*)
Korean Pine (*Pinus koraiensis*)
Pyramidal Austrian Pine (*Pinus nigra pyramidalis*)
Red Pine or Norway Pine (*Pinus resinosa*)
★Douglas Fir (*Pseudotsuga meziesii*)
★Pin Oak (*Quercus palustris*)
Common Bald Cypress (*Taxodium distichum*)

Arbor-vitae species (*Thuja*)
★Linden species (*Tilia*)
★Hemlock species (*Tsuga*)

Columnar
Ascending Norway Maple (*Acer platanoides ascendens*)
Columnar Norway Maple (*Acer platanoides columnare*)
Erect Norway Maple (*Acer platanoides erectum*)
Columnar Red Maple (*Acer rubrum columnare*)
Sentry Maple (*Acer saccharum monumentale*)
Sentry Ginkgo (*Ginkgo biloba fastigiata*)
Blue Columnar Chinese Juniper (*Juniperus chinensis columnaris*)
Swiss Stone Pine (*Pinus cembra*)
Fastigiate Scotch Pine (*Pinus sylvestris fastigiata*)
Bolleana Poplar (*Populus alba pyramidalis*)
★Lombardy Poplar (*Populus nigra italica*)
Pyramidal Simon Poplar (*Populus simoni fastigiata*)
Columnar Sargent Cherry (*Prunus sargenti columnaris*)
Shipmast Locust (*Robinia pseudoacacia rectissima*)
Upright European Mountain Ash (*Sorbus aucuparia fastigiata*)
Douglas Arbor-vitae (*Thuja occidentalis douglasi pyramidalis*)
Columnar Big-leaf Linden (*Tilia platyphyllos fastigiata*)
★American Elm varieties (*Ulmus americana*)

Weeping
Slender European Birch (*Betula pendula tristis*)
Young's Birch (*Betula pendula youngi*)
Weeping Beech (*Fagus sylvatica pendula*)
Weeping Purple Beech (*Fagus sylvatica purpureo-pendula*)
Weeping Larch (*Larix decidua pendula*)
"Exzellenz Thiel" Crab Apple (*Malus* "Exzellenz Thiel")
"Oekonomierat Echtermeyer" Crab Apple (*Malus* "Oekonomierat Echtermeyer")
Weeping Mulberry (*Morus alba pendula*)
Koster Weeping Willow (*Picea pungens kosteriana*)
Weeping Black Cherry (*Prunus serotina pendula*)
Weeping Douglas Fir (*Pseudotsuga menziesii pendula*)
Golden Weeping Willow (*Salix alba tristis*)
Wisconsin or Niobe Weeping Willow (*Salix blanda*)
Thurlow Weeping Willow (*Salix elegantissima*)
Weeping European Mountain Ash (*Sorbus aucuparia pendula*)
Sargent Hemlock (*Tsuga canadensis pendula*)
Weeping American Elm (*Ulmus americana pendula*)

Rounded or Globe-Shaped
Globe Norway Maple (*Acer platanoides globosum*)
Cornelian Cherry (*Cornus mas*)
Single Seed Hawthorn (*Crataegus monogyna inermis*)
★Crab Apple species (*Malus*)
Umbrella Black Locust (*Robinia pseudoacacia umbraculifera*)
Sargent Hemlock (*Tsuga canadensis sargenti*)
Koopmann Elm (*Ulmus carpinifolia koopmanni*)
Globe Smooth-leaved Elm (*Ulmus carpinifolia umbraculifera*)

With Horizontal Branching
Fir species (*Abies*)
★Hawthorn species (*Crataegus*)
Spruce species (*Picea*)
Japanese Red Pine (*Pinus densiflora*)
★Eastern White Pine (*Pinus strobus*)
★White Oak (*Quercus alba*)
★Pin Oak (*Quercus palustris*)
Common Bald Cypress (*Taxodium distichum*)

Trees Classified by Color of Blossom

White
★Shadblow Serviceberry (*Amelanchier canadensis*)
Washington Hawthorn (*Crataegus phaenopyrum*)
Arnold Crab Apple (*Malus arnoldiana*)
Siberian Crab Apple (*Malus baccata*)
Tea Crab Apple (*Malus hupenhensis*)
Thundercloud Plum (*Prunus cerasifera* "Thundercloud")

Sour Cherry (*Prunus cerasus*)
★Japanese Pagoda Tree (*Sophora japonica*)
American Mountain Ash (*Sorbus americana*)
European Mountain Ash (*Sorbus aucuparia*)
Showy Mountain Ash (*Sorbus decora*)

Pink
Toba Hawthorn (*Crataegus mordenensis* "Toba")
Japanese Flowering Crab Apple (*Malus floribunda*)
Katherine Crab Apple (*Malus* "Katherine")
Prince Georges Crab Apple (*Malus* "Prince Georges")
★Common Apple (*Malus pumila*)
Sargent Cherry (*Prunus sargenti*)

Red
Ruby Horse-Chestnut (*Aesculus carnea briotti*)
Paul's Scarlet Hawthorn (*Crataegus oxyacantha pauli*)
Almey Crab Apple (*Malus* "Almey")
Carmine Crab Apple (*Malus atrosanguinea*)

Trees with Bright Red Fruit
Downy Hawthorn (*Crataegus mollis*)
Washington Hawthorn (*Crataegus phaenopyrum*)
Almey Crab Apple (*Malus* "Almey")
Siberian Crab Apple (*Malus baccata*)
Hopa Crab Apple (*Malus* "Hopa")
★Common Apple (*Malus pumila*)
American Mountain Ash (*Sorbus americana*)
European Mountain Ash (*Sorbus aucuparia*)

Trees Classified by Color of Summer Foliage

Blue
Russian Olive (*Elaeagnus angustifolia*)
Eastern Red Cedar (*Juniperus virginiana* var. *Burki*)
Colorado Blue Spruce (*Picea pungens coerulea*)

Silver–Gray
Russian Olive (*Elaeagnus angustifolia*)
Common Sea-Buckthorn (*Hippophae rhamnoides*)
White Poplar (*Populus alba*)
★Silver Linden (*Tilia tomentosa*)

Red–Purple
Crimson King Maple (*Acer platanoides* "Crimson King")
Schwedler Maple (*Acer platanoides schwedleri*)
Purple Beech (*Fagus sylvatica atropunicea*)
Weeping Purple Beech (*Fagus sylvatica purpureo-pendula*)
River's Purple Beech (*Fagus sylvatica riversi*)
Rubylace Locust (*Gleditsia triacanthos inermis* "Rubylace")
Purple Crab Apple (*Malus purpurea*)
Pissard Plum (*Prunus cerasifera atropurpurea*)
Thundercloud Plum (*Prunus cerasifera nigra* "Thundercloud")
Woods Myrobalan Plum (*Prunus cerasifera woodi*)

Trees Classified by Color of Fall Foliage

Yellow
Striped Maple or Moosewood (*Acer pensylvanicum*)
Norway Maple (*Acer platanoide* var.)
★Sugar Maple (*Acer saccharum*)
Ohio Buckeye (orange) (*Aesculus glabra*)
Apple Serviceberry (yellow-orange) (*Amelanchier grandiflora*)
★Birch species (*Betula*)
Hickory species (*Carya*)
Chinese Chestnut (*Castanea mollissima*)
★Katsura Tree (yellow-scarlet) (*Cercidiphyllum japonicum*)
★American Beech (*Fagus grandifolia*)
★European Beech (*Fagus sylvatica*)
White Ash (purple-yellow) (*Fraxinus americana*)
★Ginkgo (*Ginkgo biloba*)
★Larch (*Larix decidua*)
Tulip Tree (*Liriodendron tulipifera*)
★Willow species (*Salix*)

Red
Amur Maple (*Acer ginnala*)

Manchurian Maple (*Acer mandshuricum*)
*Red Maple (*Acer rubrum*)
*Sugar Maple (*Acer saccharum*)
Tatarian Maple (*Acer tataricum*)
*Shadblow Serviceberry (*Amelanchier canadensis*)
Hornbeam species (*Carpinus*)
Washington Hawthorn (*Crataegus phaenopyrum*)
*Sweet Gum (*Liquidambar styraciflua*)
Dawson Crab Apple (*Malus dawsoniana*)
*Cherry species (*Prunus*)
*Pin Oak (*Quercus palustris*)

Purple
White Ash (*Fraxinus americana*)
*Sweet Gum (*Liquidambar styraciflua*)
*White Oak (*Quercus alba*)

Trees with Interesting Bark

Gray
*Red Maple (*Acer rubrum*)
*Serviceberry species (*Amelanchier*)
Hornbeam species (*Carpinus*)
*Hawthorn species (*Crataegus*)
*Beech species (*Fagus*)
Red Oak (young trunk and branches) (*Quercus borealis*)
Mountain Ash species (*Sorbus*)

White
*Canoe Birch (*Betula papyrifera*)
*European Birch (*Betula pendula*)

Red
Scotch Pine (*Pinus sylvestris*)

Reddish Brown
Sargent Cherry (*Prunus sargenti*)

Yellow
Wisconsin or Niobe Weeping Willow (*Salix blanda*)

Corky
*Amur Cork (*Phellodendron amurense*)

Flaking
*Birch species (*Betula*)
Russian Olive (*Elaeagnus angustifolia*)

Trees for the City
White Fir (*Abies concolor*)
Hedge Maple (*Acer campestre*)
Box-Elder (*Acer negundo*)
Norway Maple (*Acer platanoides*)
*Horse-Chestnut or Buckeye (*Aesculus*)

*Tree of Heaven (*Ailanthus*)
Catalpa (*Catalpa*)
*Washington Hawthorn (*Crataegus phaenopyrum*)
Downy Hawthorn (*Crataegus mollis*)
Russian Olive (*Elaeagnus angustifolia*)
White Ash (*Fraxinus americana*)
European Ash (*Fraxinus excelsior*)
Green Ash (*Fraxinus pennsylvanica*)
*Ginkgo (*Ginkgo biloba*)
Thornless Honey-Locust (*Gleditsia triacanthos inermis*)
*Crab Apple Species (*Malus*)
*Amur Cork (*Phellodendron amurense*)
Colorado Spruce (*Picea pungens*)
White Poplar (*Populus alba*)
*Lombardy Poplar (*Populus nigra italica*)
Red Oak (*Quercus borealis*)
*Black Locust (*Robinia pseudoacacia*)
*Little-leaf Linden (*Tilia cordata*)
*Silver Linden (*Tilia tomentosa*)

Trees for Wide Streets
*Sugar Maple (*Acer saccharum*)
White Ash (*Fraxinus americana*)
Green Ash (*Fraxinus pennsylvanica lanceolata*)
*Ginkgo (*Ginkgo biloba*)
Common Honey-Locust (*Gleditsia triacanthos*)
*Eastern White Pine (*Pinus strobus*)
White Poplar (*Populus alba*)
Sargent Cherry (*Prunus sargenti*)
Red Oak (*Quercus borealis*)
*Pin Oak (*Quercus palustris*)

Trees for Medium Streets
Norway Maple (*Acer platanoides*)
*Sweet Gum (*Liquidambar styraciflua*)
Simon Poplar (*Populus simoni*)
Scarlet Oak (*Quercus coccinea*)
*Black Locust (*Robinia pseudoacacia*)
*Linden species (*Tilia*)

Trees for Suburban Streets
Hedge Maple (*Acer campestre*)
Amur Maple (*Acer ginnala*)
Globe Norway Maple (*Acer platanoides globosum*)
Mountain Maple (*Acer spicatum*)
Tatarian Maple (*Acer tataricum*)
*Hawthorn species (*Crataegus*)
Columnar Sargent Cherry (*Prunus sargenti columnaris*)

Soil Tolerance

Trees Tolerating Acid Soil

*European Beech (*Fagus sylvatica* var.)
Scarlet Oak (*Quercus coccinea*)
*Pin Oak (*Quercus palustris*)

Trees Tolerating Moist Soil
Alder species (*Alnus*)
Eastern Larch (*Larix laricina*)
*Sweet Gum (*Liquidambar styraciflua*)
Swamp White Oak (*Quercus bicolor*)
Willow species (*Salix*)
American Arbor-vitae (*Thuja occidentalis*)

Trees Tolerating Dry or Poor Soil
Box-Elder (*Acer negunda*)
Russian Olive (*Elaeagnus angustifolia*)
Green Ash (*Fraxinus pennsylvanica*)
*Honey-Locust (*Gleditsia triacanthos* var.)
Western Red Cedar (*Juniperus scopulorum*)
Jack Pine (*Pinus banksiana*)
Pitch Pine (*Pinus rigida*)
White Poplar (*Populus alba*)
Chestnut Oak (*Quercus montana*)
*Black Locust (*Robinia pseudoacacia*)
Siberian Elm (*Ulmus pumila*)

Pest-Resistant Trees

Japanese Cornel (*Cornus officinalis*)
Kentucky Coffee Tree (*Gymnocladus dioicus*)
Russian Olive (*Elaeagnus angustifolia*)
*Ginkgo (*Ginkgo biloba*)
*Honey-Locust (*Gleditsia triacanthos*)
Juniper species (*Juniperus*)
*Sweet Gum (*Liquidambar styraciflua*)

Trees for Hedging or Barriers

European Beech (*Fagus sylvatica*) prunes well.
Hawthorn varieties (*Crataegus*) easily pruned, advantage of thorns.
Canadian Hemlock (*Tsuga canadensis*) evergreen.
American Holly (*Ilex opaca*) can be pruned.
European Hornbeam (*Carpinus betulus*) prunes well.
Little-leaf Linden (*Tilia cordata*) tolerates heavy pruning.
Hedge Maple (*Acer campestre*) can be pruned.
Austrian Pine (*Pinus nigra*) plant 10–12 feet on centers, staggered row.
Japanese Black Pine (*Pinus thunbergi*) plant 8 feet on centers, staggered row.
Eastern White Pine (*Pinus strobus*) plant 15 feet on centers, staggered row.

CONNECTICUT

State Tree
*White Oak (*Quercus alba*)

Evergreen Trees
Fir species (*Abies*)
Tree Box (*Buxus sempervirens arborescens*)
*Cedar species (*Cedrus*)
*Cypress species (*Cupressus*)
Holly species (*Ilex*)
Juniper species (*Juniperus*)
*Pine species (*Pinus*)
*Douglas Fir (*Pseudotsuga menziesii*)
Arbor-vitae species (*Thuja*)
*Hemlock species (*Tsuga*)

Trees Classified by Height

20–35 Feet
Hedge Maple (*Acer campestre*)
Hornbeam Maple (*Acer carpinifolium*)
Amur Maple (*Acer ginnala*)
Paper Bark Maple (*Acer griseum*)
*Japanese Maple (*Acer palmatum*)
Mountain Maple (*Acer spicatum*)
Ohio Buckeye (*Aesculus glabra*)
Apple Serviceberry (*Amelanchier grandiflora*)
*Gray Birch (*Betula populifolia*)

European Hornbeam (*Carpinus betulus globosa*)
Mockernut (*Carya tomentosa*)
Fringe Tree (*Chionanthus virginicus*)
Japanese Clethra (*Clethra barbinervis*)
Japanese Dogwood (*Cornus kousa*)
Cornelian Cherry (*Cornus mas*)
Japanese Cornel (*Cornus officinalis*)
American Smoke Tree (*Cotinus americanus*)
*Hawthorn species (*Crataegus*)
Russian Olive (*Elaeagnus angustifolia*)
Euonymus species (*Euonymus*)
Korean Evodia (*Evodia danielli*)
Franklinia (*Franklinia alatamaha*)
Flowering Ash (*Fraxinus ornus*)
Carolina Silverbell (*Halesia carolina*)
Longstalk Holly (*Ilex pedunculosa*)
Perny Holly (*Ilex pernyi*)
Needle Juniper (*Juniperus rigida*)
*Golden Rain Tree (*Koelreuteria paniculata*)
*Laburnum species (*Laburnum*)
Sweet Bay or Laurel (*Laurus nobilis*)
Anise Magnolia (*Magnolia salicifolia*)
Oyama Magnolia (*Magnolia sieboldi*)
*Saucer Magnolia (*Magnolia soulangeana*)
*Star Magnolia (*Magnolia stellata*)
*Crab Apple species (*Malus*)

*Cherry species (*Prunus*)
*Babylon Weeping Willow (*Salix babylonica*)
Snowbell species (*Styrax*)
Asiatic Sweetleaf (*Symplocos paniculata*)

35–75 Feet
Korean Fir (*Abies koreana*)
Box-Elder (*Acer negundo*)
Striped Maple or Moosewood (*Acer pennsylvanicum*)
*Red-fruited Tree of Heaven (*Ailanthus altissima erythrocarpa*)
Italian Alder (*Alnus cordata*)
Red Alder (*Alnus rubra*)
*Shadblow Serviceberry (*Amelanchier canadensis*)
Allegany Serviceberry (*Amelanchier laevis*)
Dahurian Birch (*Betula davurica*)
Manchurian Birch (*Betula mandshurica szechuanica*)
Common Paper-Mulberry (*Brousonetia papyrifera*)
European Hornbeam (*Carinus betulus*)
American Hornbeam (*Carpinus betulus*)
Japanese Hornbeam (*Carpinus japonica*)
Chinese Chestnut (*Castanea mollissima*)
Southern Catalpa (*Catalpa bignoniodes*)
Chinese Toon (*Cedrela sinensis*)
Bunch Hackberry (*Celtis bungeana*)
*Katsura Tree (*Cercidiphyllum japonicum*)

Eastern Redbud (*Cercis canadensis*)
Chinese Redbud (*Cercis chinensis*)
*American Yellow-wood (*Cladrastis lutea*)
*Flowering Dogwood (*Cornus florida*)
Cockspur Tree (*Crataegus crus-galli*)
Green Hawthorn (*Crataegus viridis*)
Dove Tree (*Davidia involucrata*)
Common Persimmon (*Diospyros virginiana*)
Green Ash (*Fraxinus pennsylvanica lanceolata*)
English Holly (*Ilex aquifolium*)
American Holly (*Ilex opaca*)
Heartnut (*Juglans sieboldiana cordiformis*)
Chinese Juniper (*Juniperus chinensis*)
Yulan Magnolia (*Magnolia denudata*)
Kobus Magnolia (*Magnolia kobus borealis*)
Loebner Magnolia (*Magnolia loebneri*)
Bigleaf Magnolia (*Magnolia macrophylla*)
Sweet Bay (*Magnolia virginiana*)
"Cowichan" Crab Apple (*Malus* "Cowichan")
"Dolgo" Crab Apple (*Malus* "Dolgo")
"Makamik" Crab Apple (*Malus* "Makamik")
Cherry Crab Apple (*Malus robusta*)
"Sissipuk" Crab Apple (*Malus* "Sissipuk")
White Mulberry (*Morus alba*)
*Sorrel Tree or Sourwood (*Oxydendrum arboreum*)
Persian Parrotia (*Parrotia persica*)
Empress Tree (*Paulownia tomentosa*)
Dragon Spruce (*Picea asperata*)
Virginia or Scrub Pine (*Pinus virginiana*)
Simon Poplar (*Populus simoni*)
Sargent Cherry (*Prunus sargenti*)
Yoshino Cherry (*Prunus yedoensis*)
Fragrant Epaulette Tree (*Pterostyrax hispida*)
Red Oak (*Quercus borealis*)
Scarlet Oak (*Quercus coccinea*)
Shingle Oak (*Quercus imbricaria*)
*Pin Oak (*Quercus palustris*)
Willow Oak (*Quercus phellos*)
Clammy Locust (*Robinia viscosa*)
Laurel Willow (*Salix pentandra*)
Sassafras (*Sassafras albidum officinale*)
Korean Mountain Ash (*Sorbus alnifolia*)
White Beam Mountain Ash (*Sorbus aria*)
Korean Stewartia (*Stewartia koreana*)
Japanese Stewartia (*Stewartia pseudo-camellia*)
American Arbor-vitae (*Thuja occidentalis*)
Oriental Arbor-vitae (*Thuja orientalis*)
*Crimean Linden (*Tilia euchlora*)
Carolina Hemlock (*Tsuga caroliniana*)
Chinese Elm (*Ulmus parvifolia*)

75 Feet or Over

Fir species (*Abies*)
Norway Maple (*Acer platanoides*)
Sycamore Maple (*Acer pseudoplatanus*)
*Red or Swamp Maple (*Acer rubrum*)
Hickory species (*Carya*)
*Cedar species (*Cedrus*)
Sugar Hackberry (*Celtis laevigata*)
False Cypress species (*Chamaecyparis*)
Cryptomeria (*Cryptomeria japonica*)
*Beech species (*Fagus*)
*Ginkgo or Maidenhair Tree (*Ginkgo biloba*)
*Common Honey-Locust (*Gleditsia triacanthos*)
Mountain Silverbell (*Halesia monticola*)
English or Persian Walnut (*Juglans regia*)
*Sweet Gum (*Liquidambar styraciflua*)
Cucumber Tree (*Magnolia acuminata*)
Dawn Redwood (*Metasequoia glyptostroboides*)
*Black Gum or Black Tupelo (*Nyssa sylvatica*)
*Pine species (*Pinus*)
*Plane Tree species (*Platanus*)
Poplar species (*Populus*)
Golden Larch (*Pseudolarix amabilis*)
*Douglas Fir (*Pseudotsuga menziesii*)
*Oak species (*Quercus*)
Umbrella Pine (*Sciadopitys verticillata*)
Common Bald Cypress (*Taxodium distichum*)
Japanese Zelkova (*Zelkova serrata*)

Trees Classified by Form

Pyramidal

Fir species (*Abies*)
Arbor-vitae species (*Arbor-vitae*)
*Cedar species (*Cedrus*)
Cryptomeria (*Cryptomeria japonica*)
*Beech species (*Fagus*)
English Holly (*Ilex aquifolium*)
American Holly (*Ilex opaca*)
Longstalk Holly (*Ilex pedunculosa*)
Juniper or Red Cedar species (*Juniperus*)
*Sweet Gum (*Liquidambar styraciflua*)
*Magnolia species (*Magnolia*)
Dawn Redwood (*Metasequoia glyptostroboides*)
*Black Tupelo or Black Gum (*Nyssa sylvatica*)
Hop-Hornbeam (*Ostrya virginiana*)
*Sorrel Tree or Sourwood (*Oxydendrum arboreum*)
*Douglas Fir (*Pseudotsuga menziesii*)
*Pin Oak (*Quercus palustris*)
*Linden species (*Tilia*)
*Hemlock species (*Tsuga*)
Smooth-leaved Elm varieties (*Ulmus carpinifolia*)

Columnar

Ascending Norway Maple (*Acer platanoides ascendens*)
Columnar Norway Maple (*Acer platanoides columnare*)
Erect Norway Maple (*Acer platanoides erectum*)
Columnar Red Maple (*Acer rubrum columnare*)
Fastigiate European Hornbeam (*Carpinus betulus fastigiata*)
Fastigiate Washington Hawthorn (*Crataegus phaenopyrum fastigiata*)
Dawyck Beech (*Fagus sylvatica fastigiata*)
Sentry Ginkgo (*Ginkgo biloba fastigiata*)
Schott Red Cedar (*Juniperus virginiana schotti*)
Bolleana Poplar (*Polulus alba pyramidalis*)
*Lombardy Poplar (*Populus nigra italica*)
"Amanogawa" Cherry (*Prunus serrulata* "Amanogawa")
Fastigiate English Oak (*Quercus robur fastigiata*)
Shipmast Locust (*Robinia pseudoacacia rectissima*)
Common Bald Cypress (*Taxodium distichum*)

Weeping

Weeping European Hornbeam (*Carpinus betulus pendula*)
*Weeping Beech (*Fagus sylvatica pendula*)
Weeping Red Cedar (*Juniperus virginiana pendula*)
"Exzellenz Thiel" Crab Apple (*Malus* "Exzellenz Thiel")
"Oekonomierat Echtermeyer" Crab Apple (*Malus* "Oekonomierat Echtermeyer")
Weeping Mulberry (*Morus alba pendula*)
Weeping White Pine (*Pinus strobus pendula*)
Weeping Black Cherry (*Prunus serotina pendula*)
Weeping Higan Cherry (*Prunus subhirtella pendula*)
"Yaeshidare" Cherry (*Prunus subhirtella pendula flora plena*)
Weeping Yoshino Cherry (*Prunus yedoensis perpendens*)
Weeping Douglas Fir (*Pseudotsuga menziesii pendula*)
*Babylon Weeping Willow (*Salix babylonica*)
Weeping Japanese Pagoda Tree (*Sophora japonica pendula*)
Pendant Silver Linden (*Tilia petiolaris*)
Sargent Hemlock (*Tsuga canadensis pendula*)
Weeping American Elm (*Ulmus americana pendula*)

Rounded or Globe-Shaped

*Japanese Maple (*Acer palmatum*)
Globe Norway Maple (*Acer platanoides globosum*)
Globe European Hornbeam (*Carpinus betulus globosa*)
Cornelian Cherry (*Cornus mas*)
Japanese Cornel (*Cornus officinalis*)
Single Seed Hawthorn (*Crataegus monogyna inermis*)
*Saucer Magnolia (*Magnolia soulangeana*)
*Crab Apple species (*Malus*)
*White Oak (*Quercus alba*)
Umbrella Black Locust (*Robinia pseudoacacia umbraculifera*)
Sargent Hemlock (*Tsuga canadensis sargenti*)

With Horizontal Branching

Fir species (*Abies*)
Silk Tree (*Albizzia julibrissin*)
*Cedar species (*Cedrus*)
Eastern Redbud (*Cercis canadensis*)
*Flowering Dogwood (*Cornus florida*)
Japanese Dogwood (*Cornus kousa*)
*Hawthorn species (*Crataegus*)
Dawn Redwood (*Metasequoia glyptostroboides*)
*Black Tupelo or Black Gum (*Nyssa sylvatica*)
*Eastern White Pine (*Pinus strobus*)
*White Oak (*Quercus alba*)
*Pin Oak (*Quercus palustris*)
Common Bald Cypress (*Taxodium distichum*)

Trees Classified by Color of Blossom

Yellow

*Golden Rain Tree (*Koelreuteria paniculata*)
*Laburnum (*Laburnum vossi*)

White

*Shadblow Serviceberry (*Amelanchier canadensis*)
Whitebud (*Cercis canadensis alba*)
*Yellow-wood (*Cladrastis lutea*)
Japanese Dogwood (*Cornus kousa*)
Washington Hawthorn (*Crataegus phaenopyrum*)
Carolina Silverbell (*Halesia carolina*)
Yulan Magnolia (*Magnolia denudata*)
*Star Magnolia (*Magnolia stellata*)
Arnold Crab Apple (*Malus arnoldiana*)
Tea Crab Apple (*Malus hupehensis*)
Sargent Crab Apple (*Malus sargenti*)
*Sorrel Tree (*Oxydendrum arboreum*)
Thundercloud Plum (*Prunus cerasifera* "Thundercloud")
Mount Fuji Cherry (*Prunus serrulata* "Shirotae")
Yoshino Cherry (*Prunus yedoensis*)
Bradford Callery Pear (*Pryus calleryana* "Bradford")
*Common Pear (*Pyrus communis*)
*Japanese Pagoda Tree (*Sophora japonica*)
Korean Mountain Ash (*Sorbus alnifolia*)
Japanese Stewartia (*Stewartia pseudocamellia*)
Japanese Snowbell (*Styrax japonica*)

Pink

Wither's Pink Redbud (*Cercis canadensis* "Wither's Pink Charm")
Red Flowering Dogwood (*Cornus florida rubra*)
Toba Hawthorn (*Crataegus mordenensis*)
*Saucer Magnolia (*Magnolia soulangeana*)
*Japanese Flowering Crab Apple (*Malus floribunda*)
Katherine Crab Apple (*Malus* "Katherine")
Prince Georges Crab Apple (*Malus* "Prince Georges")
*Common Apple (*Malus pumila*)
Blireiana Plum (*Prunus blireiana*)
Sargent Cherry (*Prunus sargenti*)
Amanogawa Cherry (*Prunus serrulata* "Amanogawa")
Kwanzan Cherry (*Prunus serrulata* "Kwanzan")
Autumn Cherry (*Prunus subhirtella autumnalis*)
Weeping Cherry (*Prunus subhirtella pendula*)

Red

Ruby Horse-Chestnut (*Aesculus carnea briotti*)
Paul's Scarlet Hawthorn (*Crataegus oxyacantha pauli*)
Alexandrina Magnolia (*Magnolia soulangeana* "Alexandrina")
Almey Crab Apple (*Malus* "Almey")
Carmine Crab Apple (*Malus atrosanguinea*)

Trees with Bright Red Fruit

*Flowering Dogwood (*Cornus florida*)
Japanese Dogwood (*Cornus kousa*)
Downy Hawthorn (*Crataegus mollis*)
Washington Hawthorn (*Crataegus phaenopyrum*)
American Holly (*Ilex opaca*)
Almey Crab Apple (*Malus* "Almey")
Siberian Crab Apple (*Malus baccata*)
Hopa Crab Apple (*Malus* "Hopa")
*Common Apple (*Malus pumila*)
Sargent Crab Apple (*Malus sargenti*)

Korean Mountain Ash (*Sorbus alnifolia*)
American Mountain Ash (*Sorbus americana*)
European Mountain Ash (*Sorbus aucuparia*)

Trees Classified by Color of Summer Foliage

Blue
White Fir (*Abies concolor*)
*Blue Atlas Cedar (*Cedrus atlantica glauca*)
Steel Lawson Cypress (*Chamaecyparis lawsoniana glauca*)
Eastern Red Cedar (*Juniperus virginiana* var. *Burki*)

Red to Purple
Blood-leaf Japanese Maple (*Acer palmatum atropurpureum*)
Schwedler Maple (*Acer platanoides schwedleri*)
Crimson King Maple (*Acer platanoides* "Crimson King")
Purple-leaf Sycamore Maple (*Acer pseudoplatanus purpureum*)
Purple Beech (*Fagus sylvatica atropunicea*)
Weeping Purple Beech (*Fagus sylvatica purpureopendula*)
River's Purple Beech (*Fagus sylvatica riversi*)
Rubylace Locust (*Gleditsia triacanthos inermis* "Rubylace")
Purple Crab Apple (*Malus purpurea*)
Blireiana Plum (*Prunus blireiana*)
Pissard Plum (*Prunus cerasifera atropurpurea*)
Thundercloud Plum (*Prunus cerasifera nigra* "Thundercloud")
Woods Myrobalan Plum (*Prunus cerasifera woodi*)
Blood-leaf Peach (*Prunus persica atropurpurea*)
Purple English Oak (*Quercus robur atropurpurea*)

Trees Classified by Color of Fall Foliage

Yellow
Striped Maple or Moosewood (*Acer pensylvanicum*)
Norway Maple (*Acer platanoides*)
Apple Serviceberry (yellow-orange) (*Amelanchier grandiflora*)
*Birch species (*Betula*)
Hickory species (*Carya*)
Chinese Chestnut (*Castanea mollissima*)
*Katsura Tree (yellow to scarlet) (*Cercidiphyllum japonicum*)
Redbud species (*Cercis*)
Fringetree (*Chionanthus virginicus*)
*American Yellow-wood (*Cladrastis lutea*)
*American Beech (*Fagus grandifolia*)
*European Beech (*Fagus sylvatica*)
White Ash (purple to yellow) (*Fraxinus americana*)
*Ginkgo (*Ginkgo biloba*)
*Star Magnolia (bronze) (*Magnolia stellata*)
Golden Larch (*Pseudolarix amabilis*)
*Willow species (*Salix*)

Red
Amur Maple (*Acer ginnala*)
Manchurian Maple (*Acer mandshuricum*)
Nikko Maple (*Acer nikoense*)
*Red Maple (*Acer rubrum*)
*Japanese Maple (*Acer palmatum* var.)
Tatarian Maple (*Acer tataricum*)
*Shadblow Serviceberry (*Amelanchier canadensis*)
Hornbeam species (*Carpinus*)
*Flowering Dogwood (*Cornus florida*)
Japanese Dogwood (*Cornus kousa*)
American Smoke Tree (*Cotinus americanus*)
Washington Hawthorn (*Crataegus phaenopyrum*)
*Sweet Gum (*Liquidambar styraciflua*)
*Black Tupelo or Black Gum (*Nyssa sylvatica*)
*Sorrel Tree (*Oxydendrum arboreum*)
*Cherry species (*Prunus*)
Bradford Callery Pear (*Pyrus calleryana* "Bradford")
Red Oak (*Quercus borealis*)
Scarlet Oak (*Quercus coccinea*)
*Pin Oak (*Quercus palustris*)
Sassafras (*Sassafras albidium*)

Korean Mountain Ash (*Sorbus alnifolia*)
Korean Stewartia (orange to red) (*Stewartia koreana*)

Purple
White Ash (*Fraxinus americana*)
*Sweet Gum (*Liquidambar styraciflua*)
*White Oak (*Quercus alba*)
*Common Pear (*Pyrus communis*)
Japanese Stewartia (*Stewartia pseudocamellia*)

Silver to Grayish
Russian Olive (*Elaeagnus angustifolia*)
White Poplar (*Populus alba*)
Pendant Silver Linden (*Tilia petiolaris*)
*Silver Linden (*Tilia tomentosa*)

Trees with Interesting Bark

Gray
*Red Maple (*Acer Rubrum*)
*Serviceberry species (*Amelanchier*)
Hackberry species (*Celtis*)
*American Yellow-wood (*Cladrastis lutea*)
*Hawthorn species (*Crataegus*)
*Beech species (*Fagus*)
American Holly (*Ilex opaca*)
English or Persian Walnut (*Juglans regia*)
Cucumber Tree (*Magnolia acuminata*)
*Saucer Magnolia (*Magnolia soulangeana*)
Red Oak (young trunk and branches) (*Quercus borealis*)
Black Oak (young trunk and branches) (*Quercus velutina*)
Mountain Ash species (*Sorbus*)

White
*Paper or Canoe Birch (*Betula papyrifera*)
*Gray Birch (*Betula populifolia*)

Red
Paperbark Maple (*Acer griseum*)
Japanese Red Pine (*Pinus densiflora*)
Scotch Pine (*Pinus sylvestris*)

Reddish Brown
Chinese Paper Birch (*Betula albo-sinensis*)
River Birch (*Betula nigra*)
Amur Chokecherry (*Prunus maacki*)
Sargent Cherry (*Prunus sargenti*)

Yellow
Wisconsin or Niobe Weeping Willow (*Salix blanda*)

Green
*Babylon Weeping Willow (*Salix babylonica*)

Corky
*Sweet Gum (*Liquidambar sryraciflua*)
*Amur Cork (*Phellodendron amurense*)

Flaking
Paperbark Maple (*Acer griseum*)
*Birch species (*Betula*)
Shagbark Hickory (*Carya ovata*)
*Japanese Dogwood (*Cornus kousa*)
Eastern Red Cedar (*Juniperus virginiana*)
Persian Parrotia (*Parrotia persica*)
*Plane Tree species (*Platanus*)
Lace-bark Pine (*Pinus bungeana*)
Stewartia species (*Stewartia*)

Trees for the City

Hedge Maple (*Acer campestre*)
Box-Elder (*Acer negundo*)
Norway Maple (*Acer platanoides*)
Sycamore Maple (*Acer pseudoplatanus*)
*Horse-Chestnut (Buckeye) (*Aesculus*)
*Tree of Heaven (*Ailanthus*)
Silk Tree (*Albizzia julibrissin*)
Catalpa (*Catalpa*)
Chinese Toon (*Cedrela sinensis*)
Hackberry (*Celtis*)
Downy Hawthorn (*Crataegus mollis*)
Washington Hawthorn (*Crataegus phaenopyrum*)
Russian Olive (*Elaeagus angustifolia*)
White Ash (*Fraxinus americana*)
European Ash (*Fraxinus excelsior*)

Green Ash (*Fraxinus pennsylvanica*)
*Ginkgo (*Ginkgo biloba*)
Thornless Honey-Locust (*Gleditsia triacanthos inermis*)
*Golden Rain Tree (*Koelreuteria paniculata*)
*Saucer Magnolia (*Magnolia soulangeana*)
*Star Magnolia (*Magsnoliastellata*)
*Crab Apple species (*Malus*)
White Poplar (*Popuus alba*)
*Lombardy Poplar (*Populus nigra italica*)
*Amur Cork (*Phellodendron amurense*)
London Plane Tree (*Platanus acerifolia*)
Bradford Callery Pear (*Pyrus calleryana* "Bradford")
Red Oak (*Quercus borealis*)
*Black Locust (*Robinia pseudoacacia*)
*Japanese Pagoda Tree (*Sophora japonica*)
*Little-leaf Linden (*Tilia cordata*)
*Crimean Linden (*Tilia euchlora*)
*Silver Linden (*Tilia tomentosa*)
Village Green Zelkova (*Zelkova serrata* "Village Green")

Trees for Wide Streets
Sycamore Maple (*Acer pseudoplatanus*)
Sugar Hackberry (*Celtis laevigata*)
*Katsura Tree (*Cercidiphyllum japonicum*)
White Ash (*Fraxinus americana*)
Green Ash (*Fraxinus pennsylvanica lanceolata*)
*Ginkgo (*Ginkgo biloba*)
*Common Honey-Locust (*Gleditsia triacanthos*)
Tulip Tree (*Liriodendron tulipifera*)
*Eastern White Pine (*Pinus strobus*)
London Plane Tree (*Platanus acerifola*)
*Oriental Plane Tree (*Platanus orientalis*)
White Poplar (*Populus alba*)
Sargent Cherry (*Prunus sargenti*)
*Pin Oak (*Quercus phellos*)
Japanese Zelkova (*Zelkova serrata*)

Trees for Medium Streets
Norway Maple (*Acer platanoides*)
Mountain Silverbell (*Halesia monticola*)
*Sweet Gum (*Liquidambar styraciflua*)
Hop-Hornbeam (*Ostrya virginiana*)
*Sorrel Tree or Sourwood (*Oxydendrum arboreum*)
Simon Poplar (*Populus simoni*)
Scarlet Oak (*Quercus coccinea*)
Willow Oak (*Quercus phellos*)
*Black Locust (*Robinia pseudoacacia*)
Sassafras (*Sassafras albidum officinale*)
*Japanese Pagoda Tree (*Sophora japonica*)
*Linden species (*Tilia*)
Winged Elm (*Ulmus alata*)

Trees for Suburban Streets
Hedge Maple (*Acer campestre*)
Paperbark Maple (*Acer griseum*)
American Hornbeam (*Carpinus caroliniana*)
Pyramidal European Hornbeam (*Carpinus betulus fastigiata*)
Globe European Hornbeam (*Carpinus betulus globosa*)
Fringetree (*Chionanthus virginicus*)
*Flowering Dogwood (*Cornus florida*)
*Hawthorn species (*Crataegus*)
Korean Evodia (*Evodia danielli*)
Carolina Silverbell (*Halesia carolina*)
*Golden Rain Tree (*Koelreuteria paniculata*)
Columnar Sargent Cherry (*Prunus sargenti columnaris*)
Oriental Cherry (*Prunus serrulata*)
Japanese Snowbell (*Styrax japonica*)
Fragrant Snowbell (*Styrax obassia*)
Asiatic Sweetleaf (*Symplocos paniculata*)
Smooth-leaved Elm varieties (*Ulmus carpinifolia*)

Soil Tolerance

Trees Tolerating Acid Soil
*Japanese Maple (*Acer palmatum* var.)
*Flowering Dogwood (*Cornus florida* var.)
Japanese Dogwood (*Cornus kousa*)
*European Beech (*Fagus sylvatica* var.)
Sweet Bay (*Magnolia virginiana*)
*Black Tupelo (*Nyssa sulvatica*)

*Sorrel Tree (*Oxydendrum arboreum*)
Red Oak (*Quercus borealis*)
Scarlet Oak (*Quercus coccinea*)
*Pin Oak (*Quercus palustris*)
Willow Oak (*Quercus phellos*)
Japanese Stewartia (*Stewartia pseudocamellia*)

Trees Tolerating Moist Soil

*Red Maple (*Acer rubrum*)
Alder species (*Alnus*)
Holly species (*Ilex*)
*Sweet Gum (*Liquidambar styraciflua*)
Sweet Bay (*Magnolia virginiana*)
*Black Tupelo or Black Gum (*Nyssa sylvatica*)
Swamp White Oak (*Quercus bicolor*)
*Willow species (*Salix*)
Common Bald Cypress (*Taxodium distichum*)
American Arbor-vitae (*Thuja occidentalis*)

Trees Tolerating Dry or Poor Soil

Box-Elder (*Acer negunda*)
*Tree of Heaven (*Ailanthus*)
Silk Tree (*Albizzia julibrissin*)
*Gray Birch (*Betula populifolia*)
Common Paper-Mulberry (*Broussonetia papyrifera*)
European Hackberry (*Celtis australis*)
Russian Olive (*Elaeagnus angustifolia*)
Green Ash (*Fraxinus pennsylvanica*)
Modesto Ash (*Fraxinus velutina* "Modesto")
*Honey-Locust (*Gleditsia triacanthos*)
Western Red Cedar (*Juniperus scopulorum*)
Eastern Red Cedar (*Juniperus virginiana*)
*Golden Rain Tree (*Koelreuteria paniculata*)
Jack Pine (*Pinus banksiana*)
White Poplar (*Populus alba*)
*Black Locust (*Robinia pseudoacacia*)
Sassafras (*Sassafras albidum officinale*)

*Japanese Pagoda Tree (*Sophora japonica*)
Chinese Elm (*Ulmus parvifolia*)

Pest-Resistant Trees

*Tree of Heaven (*Ailanthus altissima*)
Hornbeam (*Carpinus*)
*Cedar species (*Cedrus*)
Cornelian Cherry (*Cornus mas*)
Japanese Cornel (*Cornus officinalis*)
American Smoke Tree (*Cotinus americanus*)
Russian Olive (*Elaeagnus angustifolia*)
Franklinia (*Franklinia alatamaha*)
*Ginkgo (*Ginkgo biloba*)
*Honey-Locust (*Gleditsia triacanthos*)
Juniper species (*Juniperus*)
*Golden Rain Tree (*Koelreuteria paniculata*)
*Laburnum species (*Laburnum*)
*Sweet Gum (*Liquidambar styraciflua*)
Anise Magnolia (*Magnolia salicifolia*)
*Star Magnolia (*Magnolia stellata*)
Hop-Hornbeam species (*Ostrya*)

Trees for Seashore Planting

Norway Maple (*Acer platanoides*)
Sycamore Maple (*Acer pseudoplatanus*)
Horse-Chestnut (*Aesculus hippocastanum*)
*Tree of Heaven (*Ailanthus*)
*Shadblow Serviceberry (*Amelanchier canadensis*)
Cockspur Thorn (*Crataegus crus galli*)
English Hawthorn (*Crataegus oxyacantha*)
Washington Hawthorn (*Crataegus phaenopyrum*)
Cryptomeria (*Cryptomeria japonica*)
Russian Olive (*Elaegnus angustifolia*)
Thornless Honey-Locust (*Gleditsia triacanthos inermis* var.)
American Holly (*Ilex opaca*)
Eastern Red Cedar (*Juniperus virginiana*)

*Black Tupelo (*Nyssa sylvatica*)
Colorado Blue Spruce (*Picea pungens glauca*)
*Austrian Pine (*Pinus nigra*)
Pitch Pine (*Pinus rigida*)
Scotch Pine (*Pinus sylvestris*)
*Japanese Black Pine (*Pinus thunbergi*)
London Plane Tree (*Platanus acerifolia*)
White Poplar (*Populus alba*)
Black Cherry (*Prunus serotina*)
*White Oak (*Quercus alba*)
*Black Locust (*Robina pseudoacacia*)
Golden Weeping Willow (*Salix alba tristis*)
*Japanese Pagoda Tree (*Sophora japonica*)
*Little-leaf Linden (*Tilia cordata*)
*Crimean Linden (*Tilia euchlora*)
American Arbor-vitae (*Thuja occidentalis*)
Oriental Arbor-vitae (*Thuja orientalis*)

Trees for Hedging or Barriers

European Beech (*Fagus sylvatica*) prunes well.
Leyland Cypress (*Cupressocyparis leylandii*) withstands heavy pruning.
Hawthorn varieties (*Crataegus*) easily pruned, advantage of thorns.
Canadian Hemlock (*Tsuga canadensis*) evergreen.
American Holly (*Ilex opaca*) can be pruned.
European Hornbeam (*Carpinus betulus*) prunes well.
Little-leaf Linden (*Tilia cordata*) tolerates heavy pruning.
Hedge Maple (*Acer campestre*) can be pruned.
Austrian Pine (*Pinus nigra*) plant 10–12 feet on centers, staggered row.
Japanese Black Pine (*Pinus thunbergi*) plant 8 feet on centers, staggered row.
Eastern White Pine (*Pinus strobus*) plant 15 feet on centers, staggered row.

DELAWARE

State Tree

American Holly (*Ilex opaca*)

Evergreen Trees

*Deodar Cedar (*Cedrus deodara*)
Common China Fir (*Cunninghamia lanceolata*)
Holly species (*Ilex*)
Juniper species (*Juniperus*)
*Southern Magnolia (*Magnolia grandiflora*)
Chinese Photinia (*Photinia serrulata*)
*Pine species (*Pinus*)
Cork Oak (*Quercus suber*)
*Hemlock species (*Tsuga*)

Trees Classified by Height

20–35 Feet

Hedge Maple (*Acer campestre*)
Hornbeam Maple (*Acer carpinifolium*)
Amur Maple (*Acer ginnala*)
Paperbark Maple (*Acer griseum*)
*Japanese Maple (*Acer palmatum*)
Tatarian Maple (*Acer tataricum*)
Apple Serviceberry (*Amelanchier grandiflora*)
European Hornbeam (*Carpinus betulus globosa*)
Mocker-Nut (*Carya tomentosa*)
Eastern Redbud (*Cercis canadensis*)
Chinese Redbud (*Cercis chinensis*)
Judas Tree (*Cercis siliquastrum*)
Japanese Clethra (*Clethra barbinervis*)
Japanese Dogwood (*Cornus kousa*)
Japanese Cornel (*Cornus officinalis*)
American Smoke Tree (*Cotinus americanus*)
*Hawthorn species (*Crataegus*)
Russian Olive (*Elaeagnus angustifolia*)
Eunoymus species (*Eunoymus*)
Korean Evodia (*Evodia danielli*)
Franklinia (*Franklinia alatamaha*)
Flowering Ash (*Fraxinus ornus*)

Carolina Silverbell (*Halesia carolina*)
David Hemiptelea (*Hemiptelea davida*)
Possum Haw (*Ilex decidua*)
Longstalk Holly (*Ilex pendunculosa*)
Perny Holly (*Ilex pernyi*)
Needle Juniper (*Juniperus rigida*)
*Golden Rain Tree (*Koelreuteria paniculata*)
Crape-Myrtle (*Lagerstroemia indica*)
Yellow Cucumber Tree (*Magnolia cordata*)
*Southern Magnolia (*Magnolia grandiflora*)
Anise Magnolia (*Magnolia salicifolia*)
Oyama Magnolia (*Magnolia sieboldi*)
*Saucer Magnolia (*Magnolia soulangeana*)
*Star Magnolia (*Magnolia stellata*)
Watson Magnolia (*Magnolia watsoni*)
Wilson Magnolia (*Magnolia wilsoni*)
*Crab Apple species (*Malus*)
*Cherry species (*Prunus*)
Black Jack Oak (*Quercus marilandica*)
*Babylon Weeping Willow (*Salix babylonica*)
Snowbell species (*Styrax*)
Asiatic Sweet-leaf (*Symplocos paniculata*)
Farkleberry (*Vaccinium arboreum*)

35–75 Feet

Nikko Maple (*Acer nikoense*)
*Red-fruited Tree of Heaven (*Ailanthus altissima erythrocarpa*)
Silk Tree (*Albizzia julibrissin*)
Italian Alder (*Alnus cordata*)
Red Alder (*Alnus rubra*)
*Shadblow Serviceberry (*Amelanchier canadensis*)
Allegany Serviceberry (*Amelanchier laevis*)
Dahurian Birch (*Betula davurica*)
Manchurian Birch (*Betula mandshurica szechuanica*)
Common Paper-Mulberry (*Broussonetia papyrifera*)
European Hornbeam (*Carpinus betulus*)
Japanese Hornbeam (*Carpinus japonica*)
Chinese Chestnut (*Castanea mollissima*)

Southern Catalpa (*Catalpa bignoniodes*)
*Katsura Tree (*Cercidiphyllum japonicum*)
Delavay Clethra (*Clethra delavayi*)
*Flowering Dogwood (*Cornus florida*)
Cockspur Tree (*Crataegus crus-galli*)
Green Hawthorn (*Crataegus virdis*)
Common China Fir (*Cunninghamia lanceolata*)
Dove Tree (*Davidia involucrata*)
Kaki Persimmon (*Diosypros kaki*)
Common Persimmon (*Diospyros virginiana*)
Mountain Silverbell (*Halesia monticola*)
English Holly (*Ilex aquifolium*)
Luster-leaf Holly (*Ilex latifolia*)
Mountain Winterberry (*Ilex montana*)
American Holly (*Ilex opaca*)
Syrian Juniper (*Juniperus drupacea*)
Greek Juniper (*Juniperus excelsa*)
Alligator Juniper (*Juniperus pachyphloea*)
Yulan Magnolia (*Magnolia denudata*)
Fraser Magnolia (*Magnolia fraseri*)
Big-leaf Magnolia (*Magnolia macrophylla*)
Veitch Magnolia (*Magnolia veitchi*)
Sweet Bay (*Magnolia virginiana*)
"Dolgo" Crab Apple (*Malus* "Dolgo")
"Makamik" Crab Apple (*Malus* "Makamik")
Cherry Crab Apple (*Malus robusta*)
"Sissipuk" Crab Apple (*Malus* "Sissipuk")
Chinaberry (*Melia azedarach*)
Persian Parrotia (*Parrotia persica*)
Yoshino Cherry (*Prunus yedoensis*)
Spanish or Southern Red Oak (*Quercus falcata*)
Laurel Oak (*Quercus laurifolia*)
Water Oak (*Quercus nigra*)
Willow Oak (*Quercus phellos*)
Cork Oak (*Quercus suber*)
*Live Oak (*Quercus virginiana*)
Oriental Arbor-vitae (*Thuja orientalis*)
Carolina Hemlock (*Tsuga caroliniana*)

Winged or Wahoo Elm (*Ulmus alata*)

75 Feet or Over
Fir species (*Abies*)
*Red or Swamp Maple (*Acer rubrum*)
*Cedar species (*Cedrus*)
Campbell Magnolia (*Magnolia campbelli*)
*Southern Magnolia (*Magnolia grandiflora*)
White-leaf Japanese Magnolia (*Magnolia obovata*)
Dawn Redwood (*Metasequoia glyptostroboides*)
*Pine species (*Pinus*)
*Plane Tree species (*Platanus*)
Poplar species (*Populus*)
*Oak species (*Quercus*)
Common Bald Cypress (*Taxodium distichum*)

Trees Classified by Form

Pyramidal
*Cedar species (*Cedrus*)
American Holly (*Ilex opaca*)
Juniper or Red Cedar species (*Juniperus*)
*Sweet Gum (*Liquidambar styraciflua*)
*Magnolia species (*Magnolia*)
Dawn Redwood (*Metasequoia glyptostroboides*)
*Black Tupelo or Black Gum (*Nyssa sylvatica*)
Hop-Hornbeam (*Ostrya virginiana*)
*Sorrel Tree or Sourwood (*Oxydendron arboreum*)
Turkey Oak (*Quercus cerris*)
*Hemlock species (*Tsuga*)

Columnar
Columnar Red Maple (*Acer rubrum columnare*)
Fastigiate Washington Hawthorn (*Crataegus phaenopyrum fastigiata*)
Schott Red Cedar (*Juniperus virginiana schotti*)
Bolleana Poplar (*Populus alba pyramidalis*)
Shipmast Locust (*Robinia pseudoacacia rectissima*)
Common Bald Cypress (*Taxodium distichum*)

Weeping
Weeping Red Cedar (*Juniperus virginiana pendula*)
Weeping Black Cherry (*Prunus serotina pendula*)
*Babylon Weeping Willow (*Salix babylonica*)
Pendant Silver Linden (*Tilia petiolaris*)
Weeping American Elm (*Ulmus americana pendula*)

Rounded or Globe-Shaped
*Japanese Maple (*Acer palmatum*)
Single Seed Hawthorn (*Crataegus monogyna inermis*)
*Saucer Magnolia (*Magnolia soulangeana*)
*Crab Apple species (*Malus*)
*White Oak (*Quercus alba*)
Umbrella Black Locust (*Robinia pseudoacacia umbraculifera*)
Sargent Hemlock (*Tsuga canadensis sargenti*)

With Horizontal Branching
Fir species (*Abies*)
Silk Tree (*Albizzia julibrissin*)
*Cedar species (*Cedrus*)
Eastern Redbud (*Cercis canadensis*)
*Flowering Dogwood (*Cornus florida*)
Japanese Dogwood (*Cornus kousa*)
*Hawthorn species (*Crataegus*)
Dawn Redwood (*Metasequoia glyptostroboides*)
*Black Tupelo or Black Gum (*Nyssa sylvatica*)
*Eastern White Pine (*Pinus strobus*)
*White Oak (*Quercus alba*)
*Pin Oak (*Quercus palustris*)
Common Bald Cypress (*Taxodium distichum*)

Trees Classified by Color of Blossom

Yellow
*Golden Rain Tree (*Koelreuteria paniculata*)
*Laburnum (*Laburnum vossi*)

White
*Southern Magnolia (*Magnolia grandiflora*)
*Crab Apple species (*Malus*)
Chinese Photina (*Photinia serrulata*)
Mount Fuji Cherry (*Prunus serrulata* "Shirotae")

Pink
Wither's Pink Redbud (*Cercis canadensis* "Wither's Pink Charm")

Red Flowering Dogwood (*Cornus florida rubra*)
Toba Hawthorn (*Crataegus mordenesis* "Toba")
Ingleside Crape-Myrtle (*Lagerstroemia indica* "Ingleside Pink")
*Saucer Magnolia (*Magnolia soulangeana*)
Katherine Crab Apple (*Malus* "Katherine")
Japanese Flowering Crab Apple (*Malus floribunda*)
Prince Georges Crab Apple (*Malus* "Prince Georges")
*Common Apple (*Malus pumila*)
Blireiana Plum (*Prunus blireiana*)
Sargent Cherry (*Prunus sargenti*)
Autumn Cherry (*Prunus subhirtella autumnalis*)
Weeping Cherry (*Prunus subhirtella pendula*)
Amanogawa Cherry (*Prunus serrulata* "Amanogawa")
Kwanzan Cherry (*Prunus serrulata* "Kwanzan")

Red
Paul's Scarlet Hawthorn (*Crataegus oxyacantha pauli*)
Red Crape-Myrtle (*Lagerstroemia indica* "Wm. Toovey")
Alexandrina Magnolia (*Magnolia soulangeana* "Alexandrina")
Carmine Crab Apple (*Malus atrosanguinea*)

Trees with Bright Red Fruit
*Flowering Dogwood (*Cronus florida*)
Japanese Dogwood (*Cornus kousa*)
Downy Hawthorn (*Crataegus phaenopyrum*)
American Holly (*Ilex opaca*)
Almey Crab Apple (*Malus* "Almey")
Siberian Crab Apple (*Malus baccata*)
Hopa Crab Apple (*Malus* "Hopa")
*Common Apple (*Malus pumila*)
Sargent Crab Apple (*Malus sargenti*)
Korean Mountain Ash (*Sorbus alnifolia*)

Trees Classified by Color of Summer Foliage

Blue
White Fir (*Abies concolor*)
*Blue Atlas Cedar (*Cedrus atlantica glauca*)
Steel Lawson Cypress (*Chamaecyparis lawsonia glauca*)
Western Red Cedar (*Juniperus scopulorum* var. Chandler Blue)
Eastern Red Cedar (*Juniperus virginiana* var. *Burki*)

Silver to Gray
Russian Olive (*Elaeagnus angustifolia*)
White Poplar (*Populus alba*)
Pendant Silver Linden (*Tilia petiolaris*)
*Silver Linden (*Tilia tomentosa*)

Red to Purple
Blood-leaf Japanese Maple (*Acer palmatum atropurpureum*)
Crimson King Maple (*Acer plataoides* "Crimson King")
Schwedler Maple (*Acer platanoides schwedleri*)
Purple-leaf Sycamore Maple (*Acer pseudoplatanus purpureum*)
Purple Beech (*Fagus sylvatica atropunicea*)
Weeping Purple Beech (*Fagus sylvatica purpureopendula*)
River's Purple Beech (*Fagus sylvatica riversi*)
Rubylace Locust (*Gleditsia triacanthos inermis* "Rubylace")
Purple Crab Apple (*Malus purpurea*)
Blireiana Plum (*Prunus blireiana*)
Pissard Plum (*Prunus cerasifera atropurpurea*)
Thundercloud Plum (*Prunus cerasifera nigra* "Thundercloud")
Woods Myrobalan Plum (*Prunus cerasifera woodi*)
Blood-leaf Peach (*Prunus persica atropurpurea*)
Purple English Oak (*Quercus robur atropurpurea*)

Trees Classified by Color of Fall Foliage

Yellow
Apple Serviceberry (yellow-orange) (*Amelanchier grandiflora*)

*Birch species (*Betula*)
Redbud species (*Cercis*)
Fringetree (*Chionanthus virginicus*)
*Yellow-wood (*Cladrastis lutea*)
*American Beech (*Fagus grandifolia*)
*European Beech (*Fagus sylvatica*)
Golden Larch (*Pseudolarix amabilis*)
*Willow species (*Salix*)
Sassafras (*Sassafras albidum officinale*)

Red
*Red Maple (*Acer rubrum*)
*Shadblow Serviceberry (*Amelanchier canadensis*)
*Flowering Dogwood (*Cornus florida*)
Japanese Dogwood (*Cornus kousa*)
Washington Hawthorn (*Crataegus phaenopyrum*)
*Sweet Gum (*Liquidambar styraciflua*)
*Black Tupelo or Black Gum (*Nyssa sylvatica*)
*Sorrel Tree (*Oxydendrum arboreum*)
Bradford Callery Pear (*Pyrus calleryana* "Bradford")
Red Oak (*Quercus borealis*)
Scarlet Oak (*Quercus coccinea*)
*Pin Oak (*Quercus palustris*)
Sassafras (*Sassafras albidum officinale*)
Korean Mountain Ash (*Sorbus alnifolia*)
Korean Stewartia (orange to red) (*Stewartia koreana*)

Trees with Interesting Bark

Gray
*Red Maple (*Acer rubrum*)
*Serviceberry species (*Amelanchier*)
*American Yellow-wood (*Cladrastis lutea*)
*Hawthorn species (*Crataegus*)
*Beech species (*Fagus*)
American Holly (*Ilex opaca*)
Cucumber Tree (*Magnolia acuminata*)
*Saucer Magnolia (*Magnolia soulangeana*)

White
*Canoe Birch (*Betula papyrifera*)
*Gray Birch (*Betula populifolia*)

Reddish Brown
Sargent Cherry (*Prunus sargenti*)

Yellow
Wisconsin or Niobe Weeping Willow (*Salix blanda*)

Green
*Babylon Weeping Willow (*Salix babylonica*)

Flaking
Eastern Red Cedar (*Juniperus virginiana*)
Crape-Myrtle (*Lagerstroemia indica*)
Persian Parrotia (*Parrotia persica*)
*Plane Tree species (*Platanus*)
Stewartia species (*Stewartia*)

Trees for the City
Norway Maple (*Acer platanoides*)
Sycamore Maple (*Acer pseudoplatanus*)
*Horse-Chestnut or Buckeye (*Aesculus*)
*Tree of Heaven (*Ailanthus*)
Silk Tree (*Albizzia julibrissin*)
Catalpa (*Catalpa*)
Hackberry species (*Celtis*)
Downy Hawthorn (*Crataegus mollis*)
Washington Hawthorn (*Crataegus phaenopyrum*)
Russian Olive (*Elaeagus angustifolia*)
White Ash (*Fraxinus americana*)
European Ash (*Fraxinus excelsior*)
Green Ash (*Fraxinus pennsylvanica*)
*Ginkgo (*Ginkgo biloba*)
Thornless Honey-Locust (*Gleditsia triacanthos*)
*Golden Rain Tree (*Koelreuteria paniculata*)
*Southern Magnolia (*Magnolia grandiflora*)
*Saucer Magnolia (*Magnolia soulangeana*)
*Star Magnolia (*Magnolia stellata*)
*Crab Apple species (*Malus*)
*Amur Cork (*Phellodendron amurense*)
London Plane Tree (*Platanus acerifolia*)
White Poplar (*Populus alba*)
*Lombardy Poplar (*Populus nigra italica*)
Bradford Callery Pear (*Pyrus calleryana* "Bradford")

Red Oak (*Quercus borealis*)
★Black Locust (*Robinia pseudoacacia*)
★Japanese Pagoda Tree (*Sophora japonica*)
★Little-leaf Linden (*Tilia cordata*)
★Crimean Linden (*Tilia euchlora*)
★Silver Linden (*Tilia tomentosa*)
  Village Green Zelkova (*Zelkova serrata* "Village Green")

Trees for Wide Streets
Sugar Hackberry (*Celtis laevigata*)
White Ash (*Fraxinus americana*)
Green Ash (*Fraxinus pennsylvanica lanceolata*)
★Common Honey-Locust (*Gleditsia triacanthos*)
★Southern Magnolia (*Magnolia grandiflora*)
★Eastern White Pine (*Pinus strobus*)
London Plane Tree (*Platanus acerifolia*)
★Oriental Plane Tree (*Platanus orientalis*)
★Pin Oak (*Quercus palustris*)
Willow Oak (*Quercus phellos*)

Trees for Medium Streets
Mountain Silverbell (*Halesia monticola*)
★Sweet Gum (*Liquidambar styraciflua*)
Hop-Hornbeam (*Ostrya virginiana*)
★Sorrel Tree or Sourwood (*Oxydendrum arboreum*)
Scarlet Oak (*Quercus coccinea*)
Willow Oak (*Quercus phellos*)
★Black Locust (*Robinia pseudoacacia*)
Sassafras (*Sassafras albidium officinale*)
Winged Elm (*Ulmus alata*)

Trees for Suburban Streets
American Hornbeam (*Carpinus carolinianum*)
Pyramidal European Hornbeam (*Carpinus betulus fastigiata*)
Globe European Hornbeam (*Carpinus betulus globosa*)
Fringetree (*Chionanthus virginicus*)
★Flowering Dogwood (*Cornus florida*)
★Hawthorn species (*Crataegus*)
Carolina Silverbell (*Halesia carolina*)
Oriental Cherry (*Prunus serrulata*)
Columnar Sargent Cherry (*Prunus sargenti columnaris*)
Fragrant Snowbell (*Styrax obassia*)

Soil Tolerance

Trees Tolerating Acid Soil
★Japanese Maple (*Acer palmatum* var.)
★Flowering Dogwood (*Cornus florida* var.)
Japanese Dogwood (*Cornus kousa*)
★European Beech (*Fagus sylvatica* var.)

Sweet Bay (*Magnolia virginiana*)
★Black Tupelo (*Nyssa sylvatica*)
★Sorrel Tree (*Oxydendrum arboreum*)
Red Oak (*Quercus borealis*)
Scarlet Oak (*Quercus coccinea*)
★Pin Oak (*Quercus palustris*)
Willow Oak (*Quercus phellos*)
Japanese Stewartia (*Stewartia pseudocamellia*)

Trees Tolerating Moist Soil
★Red Maple (*Acer rubrum*)
Alder species (*Alnus*)
Holly species (*Ilex*)
★Sweet Gum (*Liquidambar styraciflua*)
Sweet Bay (*Magnolia virginiana*)
★Black Tupelo or Black Gum (*Nyssa sylvatica*)
★Willow species (*Salix*)
Common Bald Cypress (*Taxodium distichum*)
American Arbor-vitae (*Thuja occidentalis*)

Trees Tolerating Dry or Poor Soil
★Tree of Heaven (*Ailanthus*)
Silk Tree (*Albizzia julibrissin*)
★Gray Birch (*Betula populifolia*)
Common Paper-Mulberry (*Broussonetia papyrifera*)
European Hackberry (*Celtis australis*)
Russian Olive (*Elaeagnus angustifolia*)
Green Ash (*Fraxinus pennsylvanica*)
Modesto Ash (*Fraxinus velutina* "Modesto")
★Honey-Locust (*Gleditsia triacanthos* var.)
Western Red Cedar (*Juniperus virginiana*)
★Golden Rain Tree (*Koelreuteria paniculata*)
White Poplar (*Populus alba*)
Black Jack Oak (*Quercus marilandica*)
★Black Locust (*Robinia pseudoacacia*)
Chinese Elm (*Ulmus parvifolia*)

Pest-Resistant Trees
★Tree of Heaven (*Ailanthus altissima*)
Hornbean species (*Carpinus*)
★Cedar species (*Cedrus*)
European Hackberry (*Celtis australis*)
★Katsura Tree (*Cercidiphyllum japonica*)
American Smoke Tree (*Cotinus*)
Franklinia (*Franklinia alatamaha*)
★Ginkgo (*Ginkgo biloba*)
Juniper species (*Juniperus*)
★Sweet Gum (*Liquidambar styraciflua*)
★Star Magnolia (*Magnolia stellata*)
Hop-Hornbeam species (*Ostrya*)

Trees for Seashore Planting

Norway Maple (*Acer platanoides*)
Sycamore Maple (*Acer pseudoplatanus*)
★Tree of Heaven (*Ailanthus*)
★Shadblow Serviceberry (*Amelanchier canadensis*)
English Hawthorn (*Crataegus oxyacantha*)
Cryptomeria (*Cryptomeria japonica*)
Russian Olvie (*Elaeagnus angustifolia*)
American Holly (*Ilex opaca*)
Spiny Greek Juniper (*Juniperus excelsa stricta*)
Eastern Red Cedar (*Juniperus virginiana*)
★Southern Magnolia (*Magnolia grandiflora*)
★Black Tupelo (*Nyssa sylvatica*)
Colorado Blue Spruce (*Picea pungens glauca*)
★Austrian Pine (*Pinus nigra*)
Pitch Pine (*Pinus rigida*)
★Japanese Black Pine (*Pinus thunbergi*)
London Plane Tree (*Platanus acerifolia*)
White Poplar (*Populus alba*)
Black Cherry (*Prunus serotina*)
★White Oak (*Quercus alba*)
Black Jack Oak (*Quercus marilandica*)
★Live Oak (*Quercus virginiana*)
★Black Locust (*Robinia pseudoacacia*)
Golden Weeping Willow (*Salix alba tristis*)
★Japanese Pagoda Tree (*Sophora japonica*)
American Arbor-vitae (*Thuja occidentalis*)
Oriental Arbor-vitae (*Thuja orientalis*)
★Little-leaf Linden (*Tilia cordata*)
★Crimean Linden (*Tilia euchlora*)
Chinese Elm (*Ulmus parvifolia*)

Trees for Hedging or Barriers
European Beech (*Fagus sylvatica*) prunes well.
Leyland Cypress (*Cupressocyparis leylandii*) withstands heavy pruning.
Hawthorn varieties (*Crataegus*) easily pruned, advantage of thorns.
Canadian Hemlock (*Tsuga canadensis*) evergreen.
American Holly (*Ilex opaca*) can be pruned.
European Hornbeam (*Carpinus betulus*) prunes well.
Little-leaf Linden (*Tilia cordata*) tolerates heavy pruning.
Hedge Maple (*Acer campestre*) can be pruned.
Austrian Pine (*Pinus nigra*) plant 10–12 feet on centers, staggered row.
Japanese Black Pine (*Pinus thunbergi*) plant 8 feet on centers, staggered row.
Eastern White Pine (*Pinus strobus*) plant 15 feet on centers, staggered row.

FLORIDA

State Tree
Cabbage Palmetto (*Sabal palmetto*)

Evergreen Trees
★Acacia species (*Acacia*)
Norfolk Island Pine (*Araucaria excelsa*)
Strawberry Tree (*Arbutus unedo*)
Lemon Bottlebrush (*Callistemon lanceolatus*)
Citrus species (*Citrus*)
Coconut (*Cocos nucifera*)
Loblolly Bay Gordonia (*Cordonia lasianthus*)
★Eucalyptus species (*Eucalyptus*)
Brush-Cherry Eugenia (*Eugenia paniculata*)
Silk-Oak Grevillea (*Grevillea robusta*)
Queensland Nut (*Macadamia ternifolia*)
Cajeput Tree (*Melaleuca leucadendron*)
Senegal Date Palm (*Phoenix reclinata*)
★Pine species (*Pinus*)
Yew Podocarpus (*Podocarpus macrophyllus*)
Fern Podocarpus (*Podocarpus racemosa*)
Madagascar Traveler's Tree (*Ravenala madagascariensis*)
Royal Palm (*Roystonea regia*)
Brazil Pepper Tree (*Schinus trebinthifolius*)
Bell Flambeau Tree (*Spathodea campanulata*)

Stinking Cedar (*Torreya taxifolia*)
Mexican Washington Palm (*Washingtonia robusta*)

Trees Classified by Height
20–35 Feet
Lemon Bottlebrush (*Callistemon lanceolatus*)
Golden Shower Senna (*Cassia fistula*)
Coast Beefwood (*Casuarina stricta*)
Loquat (*Eribotrya japonica*)
Queensland Nut (*Macadamia ternifolia*)
★Common Olive (*Olea europaea*)
Jerusalem Thorn (*Parkinsonia aculeata*)
Senegal Date Palm (*Phoenix reclinata*)

35–75 Feet
Florida Maple (*Acer floridanum*)
Horsetail Beefwood (*Casuarina equisetifolia*)
Camphor Tree (*Cinnamomum camphor*)
Royal Poinciana or Flame Tree (*Delonix regia*)
Loblolly Bay Gordonia (*Gordonia lasianthus*)
Sharp-leaf Jacaranda (*Jacaranda acutifolia*)
Southern Red Cedar (*Juniperus silicicola*)
Cajeput Tree (*Malaleuca leucadendron*)
Chinese Pistache (*Pistacia chinensis*)
Fern Podocarpus (*Podocarpus elongatus*)
Yew Podocarpus (*Podocarpus macrophyllus*)

Royal Palm (*Roystonea regia*)
Brazil Pepper Tree (*Schinus terebinthifolius*)
Bell Flambeau Tree (*Spathodea campanulata*)

75 Feet or Over
Norfolk Island Pine (*Araucaria excelsa*)
Coconut (*Cocos nucifera*)
★Eucalyptus species (*Eucalyptus*)
Silk-Oak Grevillea (*Grevillea robusta*)
★Oak species (*Quercus*)
Palmetto (*Sabal palmetto*)
Mexican Washington Palm (*Washington robusta*)

Trees Classified by Form
Pyramidal
Juniper or Red Cedar species (*Juniperus*)

Columnar
Columnar Red Maple (*Acer rubrum columnare*)

Weeping
Brazil Pepper Tree (*Schinus terebinthifolius*)

Trees Classified by Color of Blossom
Yellow
Cootamundra Wattle (*Acacia baileyana*)
White Orchid Tree (*Bauhinia variegata candida*)

Shower of Gold (*Cassia fistula*)
Citrus species (*Citrus*)
★Golden Rain Tree (*Koelreuteria paniculata*)

Red
Crimson Eucalyptus (*Eucalyptus ficifolia*)

Blue
Purple Orchid Tree (*Bauhinia variegata*)
Sharp-leaf Jacaranda (*Jacaranda acutifolia*)

Trees with Bright Red Fruit

Brazilian Pepper Tree (*Schinus terebinthifolius*)

Trees Classified by Color of Summer Foliage

Blue
Cootamundra Wattle (*Acacia baileyana*)
Purple Orchid Tree (*Bauhinia variegata*)
Blue Gum (*Eucalyptus globulus*)
Sharp-leaf Jacaranda (*Jacaranda acutifolia*)

Silver to Gray
South American Jelly or Pindo Palm (*Butia capitata*)
★Common Olive (*Olea europaea*)

Trees Classified by Color of Fall Foliage

Yellow
Fringetree (*Chionanthus virginicus*)
★Willow species (*Salix*)

Trees with Interesting Bark

Gray
★Red Maple (*Acer rubrum*)

American Holly (*Ilex opaca*)
Royal Palm (*Roystonea regia*)

White
Florida Maple (*Acer floridanum*)

Flaking
★Eucalyptus species (*Eucalyptus*)
Eastern Red Cedar (*Juniperus virginiana*)

Trees for the City

Trees for Wide Streets
Horsetail Beefwood (*Casuarina equisetifolia*)
Camphor Tree (*Cinnamomum camphora*)
★Eucalyptus species (*Eucalyptus*)
Silk-Oak Grevillea (*Grevillea robusta*)
★Live Oak (*Quercus virginiana*)
Royal Palm (*Roystonea regia*)

Soil Tolerance

Trees Tolerating Acid Soil
Citrus species (*Citrus*)

Trees Tolerating Moist Soil
★Red Maple (*Acer rubrum*)
Beefwood species (*Casuarina*)
Holly species (*Ilex*)
Cajeput Tree (*Melaleuca leucadendron*)
Common Bald Cypress (*Taxodium distichum*)

Trees Tolerating Dry or Poor Soil
Cootamundra Wattle (*Acacia baileyana*)
Orchid Tree (*Bauhinia variegata*)
South American Jelly or Pindo Palm (*Butia capitata*)
Beefwood (*Casuarina*)
★Eucalyptus (*Eucalyptus* species)

Fig species (*Ficus*)
Silk-Oak Grevillea (*Grevillea robusta*)
Cajeput Tree (*Melaleuca leucadendron*)
Chinaberry (*Melia azedarach*)
★Common Olive (*Olea europeae*)
Jerusalem Thorn (*Parkinsonia aculeata*)
Chinese Pistache (*Pistacia chinensis*)
Brazilian Pepper Tree (*Schinus terebinthifolius*)
Mexican Fan Palm (*Washington robusta*)

Pest-Resistant Trees

★Fig species (*Ficus*)
Silk-Oak Tree (*Grevillea robusta*)

Trees for Seashore Planting

Norfolk Island Pine (*Araucaria excelsa*)
Horsetail Beefwood (*Casuarina equisetifolia*)
★Eucalyptus (*Eucalyptus*)
Southern Red Cedar (*Juniperus silicicola*)
Cajeput Tree (*Melaleuca leucadendron*)
★Common Olive (*Olea europaea*)
Pittosporum (*Pittosporum*)
★Live Oak (*Quercus virginiana*)
Royal Palm (*Roystonea regia*)
Palmetto (*Sabal palmetto*)
Brazil Pepper Tree (*Schinus terebinthifolius*)
Chinese Elm (*Ulmus parviflora*)
Mexican Washington Palm (*Washingtonia robusta*)

Trees for Hedging or Barriers

Leyland Cypress (*Cupressocyparis leylandii*) with-stands heavy pruning.
American Holly (*Ilex opaca*) can be pruned.

GEORGIA

State Tree
★Live Oak (*Quercus virginiana*)

Evergreen Trees

Monkey-Puzzle Tree (*Araucaria araucana*)
Strawberry Tree (*Arbutus unedo*)
Lemon Bottlebrush (*Callistemon lanceolatus*)
Camellia species (*Camellia*)
★Deodar Cedar (*Cedrus deodara*)
Camphor Tree (*Cinnamomum camphora*)
Evergreen Dogwood (*Cornus capitala*)
Common China Fir (*Cunninghamia lanceolata*)
★Cypress species (*Cupressus*)
Loquat (*Eriobotrya japonica*)
Brush-Cherry Eugenia (*Eugenia paniculata*)
Loblolly Bay Gordonia (*Gordonia lasianthus*)
Holly species (*Ilex*)
Juniper species (*Juniperus*)
Fortune Keteleeria (*Keteleeria fortunei*)
★Southern Magnolia (*Magnolia grandiflora*)
★Common Olive (*Olea europaea*)
Chinese Photinia (*Photinia serrulata*)
★Pine species (*Pinus*)
Yew Podocarpus (*Podocarpus macrophyllus*)
Portugal laurel (*Prunus lusitanica*)
Holly Oak (*Quercus ilex*)
★Live Oak (*Quercus virginiana*)
Palmetto (*Sabal palmetto*)
Brazil Pepper Tree (*Schinus terebinthifolius*)
★Hemlock species (*Tsuga*)

Trees Classified by Height

20–35 Feet
★Serviceberry (*Amelanchier canadensis*)
Strawberry Tree (*Arbutus unedo*)
Lemon Bottlebrush (*Callistemon lanceolatus*)
Judas Tree (*Cercis siliquastrum*)
American Smoke Tree (*Cotinus americanus*)
★Hawthorn species (*Crataegus*)
Loquat (*Eriobotrya japonica*)
Common Fig (*Ficus carica*)
Carolina Silverbell (*Halesia carolina*)

Dahoon (*Ilex cassine*)
Possum Haw (*Ilex decidua*)
Yaupon (*Ilex vomitoria*)
Crape-Myrtle (*Lagerstroemia indica*)
Yellow Cucumber Tree (*Magnolia cordata*)
Wilson Magnolia (*Magnolia wilsoni*)
★Crab Apple species (*Malus*)
Jerusalem Thorn (*Parkinsonia aculeata*)
★Cherry species (*Prunus*)
★Babylon Weeping Willow (*Salix babylonica*)
Common Jujube or Chinese Date (*Zizyphus jujuba*)

35–75 Feet
Silver Wattle (*Acacia decurrens dealbata*)
Florida Maple (*Acer floridanum*)
Silk Tree (*Albizzia julibrissin*)
Common Camellia (*Camellia japonica*)
Chinese Red Bud (*Cercis chinensis*)
★Katsura Tree (*Cercidiphyllum japonicum*)
Camphor Tree (*Cinnamomum camphora*)
★Flowering Dogwood (*Cornus florida*)
Common China Fir (*Cunninghamia lanceolata*)
Brush Cherry Eugenia (*Eugenia paniculata*)
Loblolly Bay Gordonia (*Gordonia lasianthus*)
English Holly (*Ilex aquifolium*)
Luster-leaf Holly (*Ilex latifolia*)
Mountain Winterberry (*Ilex montana*)
American Holly (*Ilex opaca*)
Syrian Juniper (*Juniperus drupacea*)
Greek Juniper (*Juniperus excelsa*)
West Indies Juniper (*Juniperus lucayana*)
Paterson Sugar Plum Tree (*Lagunaria patersoni*)
Veitch Magnolia (*Magnolia veitchi*)
Sweet Bay (*Magnolia virginiana*)
Chinaberry (*melia azedarach*)
★Sorrel Tree or Sourwood (*Oxydendrum arboreum*)
Chinese Pistache (*Pistacia chinensis*)
Yew Podocarpus (*Podocarpus macrophyllus*)
Holly Oak or Holm Oak (*Quercus ilex*)
Laurel Oak (*Quercus laurifolia*)
Water Oak (*Quercus nigra*)
★Pin Oak (*Quercus palustris*)
Willow Oak (*Quercus phellos*)

Cork Oak (*Quercus suber*)
★Live Oak (*Quercus virginiana*)
Clammy Locust (*Robinia viscosa*)
Brazil Pepper Tree (*Schinus terebinthifolius*)
Carolina Hemlock (*Tsuga caroliniana*)

75 Feet or Over
★Red or Swamp Maple (*Acer rubrum*)
Monkey-Puzzle Tree (*Araucaria araucana*)
★Ginkgo or Maidenhair Tree (*Ginkgo biloba*)
★Common Honey-Locust (*Gleditsia triacanthos*)
Campbell Magnolia (*Magnolia campbelli*)
★Southern Magnolia (*Magnolia grandiflora*)
Sabal Palmetto (*Palmetto*)
★Oak species (*Quercus*)

Trees Classified by Form

Pyramidal
★Cedar species (*Cedrus*)
English Holly (*Ilex aquifolium*)
American Holly (*Ilex opaca*)
Juniper or Red Cedar species (*Juniperus*)
Paterson Sugar Plum Tree (*Lagunaria patersoni*)
★Sweet Gum (*Liquidambar styraciflua*)
★Magnolia species (*Magnolia*)
Dawn Redwood (*Metasequoia glyptostroboides*)
★Black Tupelo or Black Gum (*Nyssa sylvatica*)
★Sorrel Tree or Sourwood (*Oxydendron arboreum*)
Turkey Oak (*Quercus cerris*)
★Pin Oak (*Quercus palustris*)
★Hemlock species (*Tsuga*)

Columnar
Columnar Red Maple (*Acer rubrum columnare*)
Sentry Ginkgo (*Ginkgo biloba fastigiata*)
Shipmast Locust (*Robinia pseudoacacia rectissima*)
Common Bald Cypress (*Taxodium distichum*)

Weeping
Weeping Red Cedar (*Juniperus virginiana pendula*)
★Babylon Weeping Willow (*Salix babylonica*)

Rounded or Globe-Shaped
Single Seed Hawthorn (*Crataegus monogyna inermis*)

*White Oak (*Quercus alba*)
Umbrella Black Locust (*Robinia pseudoacacia umbraculifera*)

With Horizontal Branching
Silk Tree (*Albizzia julibrissin*)
Monkey-Puzzle Tree (*Araucaria araucana*)
*Cedar species (*Cedrus*)
*Flowering Dogwood (*Cornus florida*)
*Hawthorn species (*Crataegus*)
*Black Tupelo or Black Gum (*Nyssa sylvatica*)
*White Oak (*Quercus alba*)
*Pin Oak (*Quercus palustris*)
*Live Oak (*Quercus virginiana*)
Common Bald Cypress (*Taxodium distichum*)

Trees Classified by Color of Blossom
Yellow
*Golden Rain Tree (*Koelreuteria paniculata*)
*Laburnum (*Laburnum vossi*)

White
*Serviceberry (*Amelanchier canadensis*)
Carolina Silverbell (*Halesia carolina*)
Southern Magnolia (*Magnolia grandiflora*)
*Star Magnolia (*Magnolia stellata*)
Mount Fuji Cherry (*Prunus serrulata* "Shirotae")

Pink
Wither's Pink Redbud (*Cercis canadensis* "Wither's Pink Charm")
Red Flowering Dogwood (*Cornus florida rubra*)
Ingleside Crape-Myrtle (*Lagerstroemia indica* "Ingleside Pink")
Japanese Flowering Crab Apple (*Malus floribunda*)
Katherine Crab Apple (*Malus* "Katherine")
Prince Georges Crab Apple (*Malus* "Prince Georges")
*Common Apple (*Malus pumila*)
Sargent Cherry (*Prunus sargenti*)
Blireiana Plum (*Prunus blireiana*)
Amanogawa Cherry (*Prunus serrulata* "Amanogawa")
Kwanzan Cherry (*Prunus serrulata* "Kwanzan")
Autumn Cherry (*Prunus subhirtella pendula*)
Weeping Cherry (*Prunus subhirtella pendula*)

Red
Crimson Eucalyptus (*Eucalyptus ficifolia*)
Rubylace Locust (*Gleditsia triacanthos inermis* "Rubylace")
Red Crape-Myrtle (*Lagerstroemia indica* "Wm. Toovey")
Alexandrina Magnolia (*Magnolia soulangeana* "Alexandrina")

Trees with Bright Red Fruit
*Flowering Dogwood (*Cornus florida*)
Almey Crab Apple (*Malus* "Almey")
Siberian Crab Apple (*Malus baccata*)
*Common Apple (*Malus floribunda*)
Hopa Crab Apple (*Malus* "Hopa")
Brazil Pepper Tree (*Schinus terebinthifolius*)

Trees Classified by Color of Summer Foliage
Blue
Eastern Red Cedar (*Juniperus virginiana* var. *Burki*)

Silver to Gray
South American Jelly or Pindo Palm (*Butia capitata*)
Russian Olive (*Elaeagnus angustifolia*)
*Common Olive (*Olea europaea*)
White Poplar (*Populus alba*)
Pendent Silver Linden (*Tilia petiolaris*)
*Silver Linden (*Tilia tomentosa*)

Trees Classified by Color of Fall Foliage

Yellow
*Katsura Tree (*Cercidiphyllum japonicum*)
Fringetree (*Chionanthus virginicus*)
*Ginkgo (*Ginkgo biloba*)
Tulip Tree (*Liriodendron tulipifera*)
*Willow species (*Salix*)

Red
*Red Maple (*Acer rubrum*)
*Serviceberry (*Amelanchier canadensis*)
*Sorrel Tree or Sourwood (*Oxydendrum arboreum*)
Chinese Pistache (*Pistacia chinensis*)
*Pin Oak (*Quercus palustris*)

Trees with Interesting Bark
Gray
*Red Maple (*Acer rubrum*)
*Serviceberry (*Amelanchier canadensis*)
American Holly (*Ilex opaca*)

Corky
Hackberry (*Celtis*)

Flaking
*Eucalyptus species (*Eucalyptus*)
Eastern Red Cedar (*Juniperus virginiana*)
Crape-Myrtle (*Lagerstroemia indica*)
*Plane Tree species (*Platanus*)

Trees for the City
Silk Tree (*Albizzia julibrissin*)
Hackberry (*Celtis*)
*Ginkgo (*Ginkgo biloba*)
Thornless Honey-Locust (*Gleditsia triacanthos inermis*)
*Golden Rain Tree (*Koelreuteria paniculata*)
*Southern Magnolia (*Magnolia grandiflora*)
*Crab Apple (*Malus* var.)
Chinaberry (*Melia azedarach*)
Red Oak (*Quercus borealis*)
*Japanese Pagoda Tree (*Sophora japonica*)
Village Green Zelkova (*Zelkova serrata* "Village Green")

Trees for Wide Streets
Sugar Hackberry (*Celtis laevigata*)
*Katsura Tree (*Cercidiphyllum japonicum*)
Camphor Tree (*Cinnamomum camphora*)
White Ash (*Fraxinus americana*)
Green Ash (*Fraxinus pennsylvanica lanceolata*)
*Ginkgo (*Ginkgo biloba*)
*Common Honey-Locust (*Gleditsia triacanthos*)
Paterson Sugar Plum Tree (*Lagunaria patersoni*)
Tulip Tree (*Liriodendron tulipifera*)
*Southern Magnolia (*Magnolia grandiflora*)
Willow Oak (*Quercus phellos*)
*Pin Oak (*Quercus palustris*)
*Live Oak (*Quercus virginiana*)

Trees for Medium Streets
Mountain Silverbell (*Halesia monticola*)
*Sweet Gum (*Liquidambar styraciflua*)
Chinaberry (*Melia azedarach*)
Hop-Hornbeam (*Ostrya virginiana*)
*Sorrel Tree or Sourwood (*Oxydendrum arboreum*)
Scarlet Oak (*Quercus coccinea*)
Laurel Oak (*Quercus laurifolia*)
Willow Oak (*Quercus phellos*)
Cork Oak (*Quercus suber*)
*Black Locust (*Robinia pseudoacacia*)
Sassafras (*Sassafras albidum officinale*)

Trees for Suburban Streets
American Hornbeam (*Carpinus caroliniana*)
Fringetree (*Chionanthus virginicus*)
*Flowering Dogwood (*Cornus florida*)
*Hawthorn species (*Crataegus*)

Soil Tolerance

Trees Tolerating Acid Soil
*Japanese Maple (*Acer palmatum* var.)
Strawberry Tree (*Arbutus unedo*)
*Flowering Dogwood (*Cornus florida* var.)
Sweet Bay (*Magnolia virginiana*)
*Black Tupelo (*Nyssa sylvatica*)
*Sorrel Tree (*Oxydendrum arboreum*)
Willow Oak (*Quercus phellos*)

Trees Tolerating Moist Soil
*Red Maple (*Acer rubrum*)
Holly species (*Ilex*)
Sweet Bay (*Magnolia virginiana*)
Common Bald Cypress (*Taxodium distichum*)

Trees Tolerating Dry or Poor Soil
Silk Tree (*Albizzia julibrissin*)
Common Paper-Mulberry (*Broussonetia papyrifera*)
European Hackberry (*Celtis australis*)
*Eucalyptus (*Eucalyptus species*)
*Honey-Locust (*Gleditsia triacanthos*)
*Golden Rain Tree (*Koelreuteria paniculata*)
Australian Tea Tree (*Leptospermum laevigatum*)
Chinaberry (*Melia azedarach*)
*Common Olive (*Olea europaea*)
Jerusalem Thorn (*Parkinsonia aculeata*)
Chinese Pistache (*Pistacia chinensis*)
Honey Mesquite (*Prosopis glandulosa*)
Brazil Pepper Tree (*Schinus terebinthifolius*)
Chinese Elm (*Ulmus parvifolia*)

Pest-Resistant Trees
Hornbeam species (*Carpinus*)
*Fig species (*Ficus*)
Franklinia (*Franklinia alatamaha*)
*Ginkgo (*Ginkgo biloba*)
*Honey-Locust (*Gleditsia triacanthos*)
Juniper species (*Juniperus*)
Sweet Gum (*Liquidambar styraciflua*)
Hop-Hornbeam species (*Ostrya*)

Trees for Seashore Planting
*Serviceberry (*Amelanchier canadensis*)
*Eucalyptus (*Eucalyptus*)
Velvet Ash (*Fraxinus velutina*)
*Honey-Locust (*Gleditsia triacanthos*)
Spiny Greek Juniper (*Juniperus excelsa stricta*)
West Indies Juniper (*Juniperus lucayana*)
Paterson Sugar Plum Tree (*Lagunaria* "Patersoni")
*Southern Magnolia (*Magnolia grandiflora*)
*Common Olive (*Olea europaea*)
Holly Oak (*Quercus ilex*)
Black Jack Oak (*Quercus marilandica*)
*Live Oak (*Quercus virginiana*)
Palmetto (*Sabal palmetto*)
Brazil Pepper Tree (*Schinus terebinthifolius*)
Oriental Arbor-vitae (*Thuja orientalis*)
Chinese Elm (*Ulmus parvifolia*)

Trees for Hedging or Barriers
European Beech (*Fagus sylvatica*) prunes well.
Leyland Cypress (*Cupressocyparis leylandii*) withstands heavy pruning.
Hawthorn varieties (*Crataegus*) easily pruned, advantage of thorns.
Canadian Hemlock (*Tsuga canadensis*) evergreen.
American Holly (*Ilex opaca*) can be pruned.
European Hornbeam (*Carpinus betulus*) prunes well.
Little-leaf Linden (*Tilia cordata*) tolerates heavy pruning.
Hedge Maple (*Acer campestre*) can be pruned.
Austrian Pine (*Pinus nigra*) plant 10–12 feet on centers, staggered row.
Japanese Black Pine (*Pinus thunbergi*) plant 8 feet on centers, staggered row.
Eastern White Pine (*Pinus strobus*) plant 15 feet on centers, staggered row.

IDAHO

State Tree
*Western White Pine (*Pinus monticola*)

Evergreen Trees

Fir species (*Abies*)
Smooth Arizona Cypress (*Cupressus arizonica bonita*)
Holly species (*Ilex*)
Rocky Mountain Juniper (*Juniperus scopulorum*)
Eastern Red Cedar (*Juniperus virginiana*)
Spruce species (*Picea*)
*Pine species (*Pinus*)
*Douglas Fir (*Pseudotsuga menziesii*)
Arbor-vitae species (*Thuja*)
*Hemlock species (*Tsuga*)

Trees Classified by Height

20–35 Feet

Argutum Maple (*Acer argutum*)
Hedge Maple (*Acer campestre*)
Hornbeam Maple (*Acer carpinifolium*)
Vine Maple (*Acer circinatum*)
Amur Maple (*Acer ginnala*)
Paperbark Maple (*Acer griseum*)
Manchurian Maple (*Acer mandshuricum*)
*Japanese Maple (*Acer palmatum*)
Mountain Maple (*Acer spicatum*)
Tatarian Maple (*Acer tataricum*)
Ohio Buckeye (*Aesculus glabra*)
Apple Serviceberry (*Amelanchier grandiflora*)
*Gray Birch (*Betula populifolia*)
American Smoke Tree (*Cotinus americanus*)
*Hawthorn species (*Crataegus*)
Russian Olive (*Elaeagnus angustifolia*)
Euonymus species (*Euonymus*)
Needle Juniper (*Juniperus rigida*)
Yellow Cucumber Tree (*Magnolia cordata*)
*Saucer Magnolia (*Magnolia soulangeana*)
*Star Magnolia (*Magnolia stellata*)
*Crab Apple species (*Malus*)
*Cherry species (*Prunus*)
Almond-leaf Willow (*Salix amygdalina*)
Goat Willow (*Salix caprea*)
Showy Mountain Ash (*Sorbus decora*)
Snowberry Mountain Ash (*Sorbus discolor*)
Japanese Tree Lilac (*Syringa amurensis japonica*)

35–75 Feet

Box-Elder (*Acer negundo*)
Nikko Maple (*Acer nikoense*)
Striped Maple or Moosewood (*Acer pennsylvanicum*)
*Red-fruited Tree of Heaven (*Ailanthus altissima erythrocarpa*)
Italian Alder (*Alnus cordata*)
Speckled Alder (*Alnus incana*)
Red Alder (*Alnus rubra*)
*Shadblow Serviceberry (*Amelanchier canadensis*)
Allegany Serviceberry (*Amelanchier laevis*)
*European Birch (*Betula pendula*)
American Hornbeam (*Carpinus caroliniana*)
Southern Catalpa (*Catalpa bignonioides*)
Bunch Hackberry (*Celtis bungeana*)
Hackberry (*Celtis occidentalis*)
Eastern Redbud (*Cercis canadensis*)
*Flowering Dogwood (*Cornus florida*)
Cockspur Thorn (*Crataegus crus-galli*)
Green Hawthorn (*Crataegus viridis*)
Common Persimmon (*Diospyros virginiana*)
Green Ash (*Fraxinus pennsylvanica lanceolata*)
Heartnut (*Juglans sieboldiana cordiformis*)
Chinese Juniper (*Juniperus chinensis*)
Rocky Mountain Juniper (*Juniperus sopulorum*)
Osage-Orange (*Maclura pomifera*)
Yulan Magnolia (*Magnolia denudata*)
Kobus Magnolia (*Magnolia kobus borealis*)
Loebner Magnolia (*Magnolia loebneri*)
Sweet Bay (*Magnolia virginiana*)
Siberian Crab Apple (*Malus bacata*)
"Cowichan" (*Malus* "Cowichan")
"Dolgo" Crab Apple (*Malus* "Dolgo")
"Makamik" Crab Apple (*Malus* "Makamik")
Cherry Crab Apple (*Malus robusta*)
"Sissipuk" Crab Apple (*Malus* "Sissipuk")
White Mulberry (*Morus alba*)
Dragon Spruce (*Picea asperata*)

Black Hills Spruce (*Picea glauca densata*)
Jack Pine (*Pinus bankiana*)
Swiss Stone Pine (*Pinus cembra*)
Limber Pine (*Pinus flexilis*)
Scotch Pine (*Pinus sylvestris*)
Chinese Poplar (*Populus lasiocarpa*)
Simon Poplar (*Populus simoni*)
Amur Chokecherry (*Prunus maacki*)
Miyama Cherry (*Prunus maximowiczi*)
Sargent Cherry (*Prunus sargenti*)
Yoshino Cherry (*Prunus yedoensis*)
Shingle Oak (*Quercus imbricaria*)
*Pin Oak (*Quercus palustris*)
Willow Oak (*Quercus phellos*)
White Willow (*Salix alba*)
Wisconsin or Niobe Weeping Willow (*Salix blanda*)
Elaeagnus Willow (*Salix elaeagnos*)
Thurlow Weeping Willow (*Salix elegantissima*)
Laurel Willow (*Salix pentandra*)
Blueberry Elder (*Sambucus coerulea*)
Korean Mountain Ash (*Sorbus alnifolia*)
White Beam Mountain Ash (*Sorbus aria*)
European Mountain Ash or Rowan Tree (*Sorbus aucuparia*)
Japanese Stewartia (*Stewartia pseudo-camellia*)
American Arbor-vitae (*Thuja occidentalis*)
Japanese Arbor-vitae (*Thuja standishi*)
*Crimean Linden (*Tilia euchlora*)
Carolina Hemlock (*Tsuga caroliniana*)
Chinese Elm (*Ulmus parvifolia*)
Siberian Elm (*Ulmus pumila*)

75 Feet and Over

Fir species (*Abies*)
Norway Maple (*Acer platanoides*)
Sycamore Maple (*Acer pseudoplatanus*)
Red or Swamp Maple (*Acer rubrum*)
*Sugar Maple (*Acer saccharum*)
*Baumann Horse-Chestnut (*Aesculus hippocastanum baumanni*)
European Alder (*Alnus glutinosa*)
*Canoe Birch (*Betula papyrifera*)
Hickory species (*Carya*)
Northern Catalpa (*Catalpa speciosa*)
Sugar Hackberry (*Celtis laevigata*)
Cryptomeria (*Cryptomeria japonica*)
*Beech species (*Fagus*)
White Ash (*Fraxinus americana*)
European Ash (*Fraxinus excelsior*)
*Ginkgo or Maidenhair Tree (*Ginkgo biloba*)
*Common Honey-Locust (*Gleditsia triacanthos*)
Kentucky Coffee Tree (*Gymnocladus dioicus*)
English or Persian Walnut (*Juglans regia*)
*European Larch (*Larix dicidua*)
Japanese Larch (*Larix leptolepis*)
*Sweet Gum (*Liquidambar styraciflua*)
Tulip Tree or Yellow Poplar (*Liriodendron tulipifera*)
Cucumber Tree (*Magnolia acuminata*)
White-leaf Japanese Magnolia (*Magnolia obovata*)
Spruce species (*Picea*)
*Pine species (*Pinus*)
*Plane Tree species (*Platanus*)
Poplar species (*Populus*)
Sargent Cherry (*Prunus sargenti*)
Black or Rum Cherry (*Prunus serotina*)
*Douglas Fir (*Pseudotsuga menziesii*)
*Oak species (*Quercus*)
Giant Arbor-vitae (*Thuja plicata*)
*Linden species (*Tilia*)
*Canada Hemlock (*Tsuga canadensis*)
*Elm species (*Ulmus*)

Trees Classified by Form

Pyramidal

Fir species (*Abies*)
Red Alder (*Alnus rubra*)
Arbor-vitae species (*Arbor-vitae*)
*Birch species (*Betula*)
Pyramidal European Birch (*Betula pendula fastigiata*)
Pyramidal Washington Hawthorn (*Crataegus phaenopyrum fastigiata*)

*Beech species (*Fagus*)
American Holly (*Ilex opaca*)
Longstalk Holly (*Ilex pedunculosa*)
Juniper or Red Cedar species (*Juniperus*)
*Larch species (*Larix*)
*Sweet Gum (*Liquidambar styraciflua*)
*Magnolia species (*Magnolia*)
Spruce species (*Picea*)
Swiss Stone Pine (*Pinus cembra*)
Korean Pine (*Pinus koraiensis*)
*Pyramidal Austrian Pine (*Pinus nigra pyramidalis*)
Japanese White Pine (*Pinus parviflora*)
Red or Norway Pine (*Pinus resinosa*)
*Douglas Fir (*Pseudotsuga menziesii*)
*Pin Oak (*Quercus palustris*)
Common Bald Cypress (*Taxodium distichum*)
*Linden species (*Tilia*)
*Hemlock species (*Tsuga*)
Smooth-leaved Elm varieties (*Ulmus carpinifolia*)

Columnar

Ascending Norway Maple (*Acer platanoides ascendens*)
Columnar Norway Maple (*Acer platanoides columnare*)
Erect Norway Maple (*Acer platanoides erectum*)
Columnar Red Maple (*Acer rubrum columnare*)
Sentry Maple (*Acer saccharum monumentale*)
Dawyck Beech (*Fagus sylvatica fastigiata*)
Sentry Ginkgo (*Ginkgo biloba fastigiata*)
Blue Columnar Chinese Juniper (*Juniperus chinensis columnaris*)
Schott Red Cedar (*Juniperus virginiana schotti*)
Swiss Stone Pine (*Pinus cembra*)
Fastigiate Scotch Pine (*Pinus sylvestris fastigiata*)
Bolleana Poplar (*Populus alba pyramidalis*)
*Lombardy Poplar (*Populus nigra italica*)
Pyramidal Simon Poplar (*Populus simoni fastigiata*)
Columnar Sargent Cherry (*Prunus sargenti columaris*)
"Amanogawa" Cherry (*Prunus serrulata* "Amanogawa")
Fastigiate English Oak (*Quercus robur fastigiata*)
Shipmast Locust (*Robinia pseudoacacia rectissima*)
Upright European Mountain Ash (*Sorbus acuparia fastigiata*)
Douglas Arbor-vitae (*Thuja occidentalis douglasi pyramidalis*)
Fastigiate American Arbor-vitae (*Thuja occidentalis fastigiata*)
Columnar Big-leaf Linden (*Tilia platyphyllos fastigiata*)
American Elm varieties (*Ulmus americana*)

Weeping

Slender European Birch (*Betula pendula tristis*)
Young's Birch (*Betula pendula youngi*)
*Weeping Beech (*Fagus sylvatica pendula*)
Weeping Purple Beech (*Fagus sylvatica purpureo-pendula*)
Weeping Larch (*Larix decidua pendula*)
"Exzellenz Thiel" Crab Apple (*Malus* "Exzellenz Thiel")
"Oekonomierat Echtermeyer" Crab Apple (*Malus* "Oekonomierat Echtermeyer")
Weeping Mulberry (*Morus alba pendula*)
Koster Weeping Blue Spruce (*Picea pungens kosteriana*)
Weeping Black Cherry (*Prunus serotina pendula*)
Weeping Higan Cherry (*Prunus subhirtella pendula*)
"Yaeshidare" Cherry (*Prunus subhirtella pendula flora plena*)
Weeping Yoshino Cherry (*Prunus yedoensis perpendens*)
Weeping Douglas Fir (*Pseudotsuga menziesii pendula*)
Golden Weeping Willow (*Salix alba tristis*)
Wisconsin or Niobe Weeping Willow (*Salix blanda*)
Thurlow Weeping Willow (*Salix elegantissima*)
Weeping European Mountain Ash (*Sorbus aucuparia pendula*)
Weeping Folgner Mountain Ash (*Sorbus folgneri pendula*)
Pendant Silver Linden (*Tilia petiolaris*)
Sargent Hemlock (*Tsuga canadensis pendula*)

Weeping American Elm (*Ulmus americana pendula*)

Rounded or Globe-Shaped
*Japanese Maple (*Acer palmatum*)
Globe Norway Maple (*Acer platanoides globosum*)
Globe European Hornbeam (*Carpinus betulus globosa*)
Bunch Hackberry (*Celtis bungeana*)
Cornelian Cherry (*Cornus mas*)
Japanese Cornel (*Cornus officinalis*)
Single Seed Hawthorn (*Crataegus monogyna inermis*)
*Saucer Magnolia (*Magnolia soulangeana*)
*Crab Apple species (*Malus*)
*White Oak (*Quercus alba*)
Umbrella Black Locust (*Robinia pseudoacacia umbraculifera*)
Sargent Hemlock (*Tsuga canadensis sargenti*)
Koopmann Elm (*Ulmus carpinifolia koopmanni*)
Globe Smooth-leaved Elm (*Ulmus carpinifolia umbraculifera*)

With Horizontal Branching
Fir species (*Abies*)
*Flowering Dogwood (*Cornus florida*)
Japanese Dogwood (*Cornus kousa*)
*Hawthorn species (*Crataegus*)
Spruce species (*Picea*)
*Eastern White Pine (*Pinus strobus*)
Golden Larch (*Pseudolarix amabilis*)
*White Oak (*Quercus alba*)
*Pin Oak (*Quercus palustris*)

Trees Classified by Color of Blossom

White
*Shadblow Serviceberry (*Amelanchier canadensis*)
Whitebud (*Cercis canadensis alba*)
*Japanese Dogwood (*Cornus kousa*)
Washington Hawthorn (*Crataegus phaenopyrum*)
Yulan Magnolia (*Magnolia stellata*)
*Star Magnolia (*Magnolia stellata*)
Arnold Crab Apple (*Malus arnoldiana*)
Siberian Crab Apple (*Malus baccata*)
Tea Crab Apple (*Malus hupehensis*)
Sargent Crab Apple (*Malus sargenti*)
Thundercloud Plum (*Prunus cerasifera* "Thundercloud")
Sour Cherry (*Prunus cerasus*)
Yoshino Cherry (*Prunus yedoensis*)
Bradford Callery Pear (*Pyrus calleryana* "Bradford")
*Common Pear (*Pyrus communis*)
Korean Mountain Ash (*Sorbus alnifolia*)
American Mountain Ash (*Sorbus americana*)
European Mountain Ash (*Sorbus aucuparia*)
Showy Mountain Ash (*Sorbus decora*)

Pink
Wither's Pink Redbud (*Cercis canadensis* "Wither's Pink Charm")
*Red Flowering Dogwood (*Cornus florida rubra*)
Toba Hawthorn (*Crataegus mordenensis* "Toba")
*Saucer Magnolia (*Magnolia soulangeana*)
Japanese Flowering Crab Apple (*Malus floribunda*)
Katherine Crab Apple (*Malus* "Katherine")
Prince Georges Crab Apple (*Malus* "Prince Georges")
*Common Apple (*Malus pumila*)
Blireiana Plum (*Prunus blireiana*)
Sargent Cherry (*Prunus sargenti*)
Amanogawa Cherry (*Prunus serrulata* "Amanogawa")
Kwanzan Cherry (*Prunus serrulata* "Kwanzan")
Autumn Cherry (*Prunus subhirtella autumnalis*)
Weeping Cherry (*Prunus subhirtella pendula*)

Red
Ruby Horse-Chestnut (*Aesculus carnea briotti*)
Paul's Scarlet Hawthorn (*Crataegus oxyacantha pauli*)
Alexandrina Magnolia (*Magnolia soulangeana* "Alexandrina")
Almey Crab Apple (*Malus* "Almey")
Carmine Crab Apple (*Malus atrosanguinea*)

Trees with Bright Red Fruit

*Flowering Dogwood (*Cornus florida*)
Japanese Dogwood (*Cornus kousa*)
Downy Hawthorn (*Crataegus mollis*)
Washington Hawthorn (*Crataegus phaenopyrum*)
American Holly (*Ilex opaca*)
Almey Crab Apple (*Malus* "Almey")
Siberian Crab Apple (*Malus baccata*)
Hopa Crab Apple (*Malus* "Hopa")
*Common Apple (*Malus pumila*)
Sargent Crab Apple (*Malus sargenti*)
American Mountain Ash (*Sorbus americana*)
European Mountain Ash (*Sorbus aucuparia*)

Trees Classified by Color of Summer Foliage

Blue
White Fir (*Abies concolor*)
Steel Lawson Cypress (*Chamaecyparis lawsoniana glauca*)
Rocky Mountain Juniper (*Juniperus scopulorum* var. Chandler Blue)
Eastern Red Cedar (*Juniperus virginiana* var. *Burki*)
Colorado Blue Spruce (*Picea pungens* var. *Glauca*)

Silver to Gray
Russian Olive (*Elaeagnus angustifolia*)
White Poplar (*Populus alba*)
Pendant Silver Linden (*Tilia petiolaris*)
*Silver Linden (*Tilia Tomentosa*)

Red to Purple
Blood-leaf Japanese Maple (*Acer palmatum atropurpureum*)
Crimson King Maple (*Acer platanoides* "Crimson King")
Schwedler Maple (*Acer platanoides schwedleri*)
Purple-leaf Sycamore Maple (*Acer pseudoplatanus purpureum*)
Purple Beech (*Fagus sylvatica atropunicea*)
Weeping Purple Beech (*Fagus sylvatica purpureopendula*)
River's Purple Beech (*Fagus sylvatica riversi*)
Rubylace Locust (*Gleditsia triacanthos inermis* "Rubylace")
Purple Crab Apple (*Malus purpurea*)
Blireiana Plum (*Prunus blireiana*)
Pissard Plum (*Prunus cerasifera atropurpurea*)
Thundercloud Plum (*Prunus cerasifera nigra* "Thundercloud")
Woods Myrobalan Plum (*Prunus cerasifera woodi*)
Blood-leaf Peach (*Prunus persica atropurpurea*)
Purple English Oak (*Quercus robur atropurpurea*)

Trees Classified by Color of Fall Foliage

Yellow
Norway Maple (*Acer platanoides* var.)
Striped Maple or Moosewood (*Acer pennsylvanicum*)
*Sugar Maple (*Acer saccharum*)
Ohio Buckeye (orange) (*Aesculus glabra*)
Apple Serviceberry (yellow-orange) (*Amelanchier grandiflora*)
*Birch species (*Betula*)
Hickory species (*Carya*)
Chinese Chestnut (*Castanea mollissima*)
Redbud species (*Cercis*)
*American Beech (*Fagus grandifolia*)
*European Beech (*Fagus sylvatica*)
White Ash (purple to yellow) (*Fraxinus americana*)
*Ginkgo (*Ginkgo biloba*)
Tulip Tree (*Liriodendron tulipifera*)
*Star Magnolia (bronze) (*Magnolia stellata*)
Golden Larch (*Pseudolarix amabilis*)
*Willow species (*Salix*)

Red
Vine Maple (*Acer circinatum*)
Amur Maple (*Acer ginnala*)
Manchurian Maple (*Acer mandshuricum*)
Nikko Maple (*Acer nikoense*)
*Japanese Maple (*Acer palmatum* var.)
*Red Maple (*Acer rubrum*)

*Sugar Maple (*Acer saccharum*)
Tatarian Maple (*Acer tataricum*)
*Shadblow Serviceberry (*Amelanchier canadensis*)
Hornbeam species (*Carpinus*)
*Flowering Dogwood (*Cornus florida*)
Japanese Dogwood (*Cornus kousa*)
American Smoke Tree (*Cotinus americanus*)
Washington Hawthorn (*Crataegus phaenopyrum*)
*Sweet Gum (*Liquidambar styraciflua*)
Dawson Crab Apple (*Malus dawsoniana*)
*Black Tupelo or Black Gum (*Nyssa sylvatica*)
*Sorrel Tree (*Oxydendrum arboreum*)
Persian Parrotia (*Parrotia persica*)
*Cherry species (*Prunus*)
Bradford Callery Pear (*Pyrus calleryana* "Bradford")
Red Oak (*Quercus borealis*)
Scarlet Oak (*Quercus coccinea*)
*Pin Oak (*Quercus palustris*)
Sassafras (*Sassafras albidum*)
Korean Mountain Ash (*Sorbus alnifolia*)
Korean Stewartia (orange to red) (*Stewartia koreana*)

Purple
White Ash (*Fraxinus americana*)
*Sweet Gum (*Liquidambar styraciflua*)
*Common Pear (*Pyrus communis*)
*White Oak (*Quercus alba*)

Trees with Interesting Bark

Gray
*Red Maple (*Acer rubrum*)
*Serviceberry species (*Amelanchier*)
Hornbeam species (*Carpinus*)
Hackberry species (*Celtis*)
*Hawthorn species (*Crataegus*)
*Beech species (*Fagus*)
American Holly (*Ilex opaca*)
English or Persian Walnut (*Juglans regia*)
Cucumber Tree (*Magnolia acuminata*)
*Saucer Magnolia (*Magnolia soulangeana*)
Red Oak (young trunk and branches) (*Quercus borealis*)
Black Oak (young trunk and branches) (*Quercus velutina*)
Mountain Ash species (*Sorbus*)

White
*Canoe Birch (*Betula papyrifera*)
European Birch (*Betula pendula*)
*Gray Birch (*Betula populifolia*)

Red
Japanese Red Pine (*Pinus densiflora*)
Red Norway Pine (*Pinus resinosa*)
Scotch Pine (*Pinus sylvestris*)

Reddish Brown
Chinese Paper Birch (*Betula albo-sinensis*)
Sargent Cherry (*Prunus sargenti*)

Green
*Babylon Weeping Willow (*Salix babylonica*)

Yellow
Wisconsin or Niobe Weeping Willow (*Salix blanda*)

Corky
Hackberry (*Celtis*)

Flaking
Paper Bark Maple (*Acer griseum*)
*Birch species (*Betula*)
Shagbark Hickory (*Carya ovata*)
Russian Olive (*Elaeagnus angustifolia*)
*Plane Tree species (*Platanus*)

Trees for the City

White Fir (*Abies concolor*)
Hedge Maple (*Acer campestre*)
Box-Elder (*Acer negundo*)
Norway Maple (*Acer platanoides*)
Sycamore Maple (*Acer pseudo platanus*)
*Horse-Chestnut or Buckeye (*Aesculus*)
*Tree of Heaven (*Ailanthus*)
Catalpa (*Catalpa*)
Hackberry (*Celtis*)

Downy Hawthorn (*Crataegus mollis*)
Washington Hawthorn (*Crataegus phaenopyrum*)
Russian Olive (*Elaeagnus angustifolia*)
White Ash (*Fraxinus americana*)
European Ash (*Fraxinus excelsior*)
Green Ash (*Fraxinus pennsylvanica*)
*Ginkgo (*Ginkgo biloba*)
Thornless Honey-Locust (*Gleditsia triacanthos inermis*)
*Saucer Magnolia (*Magnolia soulangeana*)
*Star Magnolia (*Magnolia stellata*)
*Crab Apple species (*Malus*)
Colorado Blue Spruce (*Picea pungens*)
London Plane Tree (*Platanus acerifolia*)
White Poplar (*Populus alba*)
*Lombardy Poplar (*Populus nigra italica*)
Red Oak (*Quercus borealis*)
*Black Locust (*Robinia pseudoacacia*)
Little-leaf Linden (*Tilia cordata*)
*Crimean Linden (*Tilia euchlora*)
*Silver Linden (*Tilia tomentosa*)

Trees for Wide Streets

Sycamore Maple (*Acer pseudoplatanus*)
*Sugar Maple (*Acer saccharum*)
Sugar Hackberry (*Celtis laevigata*)
White Ash (*Fraxinus americana*)
Green Ash (*Fraxinus pennsylvanica lanceolata*)
*Ginkgo (*Ginkgo biloba*)
*Common Honey-Locust (*Gleditsia triacanthos*)
Tulip Tree (*Liriodendron tulipifera*)
London Plane Tree (*Platanus acerifolium*)
White Poplar (*Populus alba*)
Sargent Cherry (*Prunus sargenti*)
Red Oak (*Quercus borealis*)
*Pin Oak (*Quercus palustris*)
Willow Oak (*Quercus phellos*)

Trees for Medium Streets

Norway Maple (*Acer platanoides*)
*Sweet Gum (*Liquidambar styraciflua*)
Hop-Hornbeam (*Ostrya virginiana*)
Simon Poplar (*Populus simoni*)
Scarlet Oak (*Quercus coccinea*)
Willow Oak (*Quercus phellos*)
*Black Locust (*Robinia pseudoacacia*)
Sassafras (*Sassafras albidum officinale*)
*Linden species (*Tilia*)

Trees for Suburban Streets

Argutum Maple (*Acer argutum*)
Hedge Maple (*Acer campestre*)
Vine Maple (*Acer circinatum*)
Amur Maple (*Acer ginnala*)
Paperbark Maple (*Acer griseum*)
Globe Norway Maple (*Acer platanoides globosum*)
Mountain Maple (*Acer spicatum*)
Tatarian Maple (*Acer tataricum*)
American Hornbeam (*Carpinus caroliniana*)
Pyramidal European Hornbeam (*Carpinus betulus globosa*)
Globe European Hornbeam (*Carpinus betulus globosa*)
*Hawthorn species (*Crataegus*)
Oriental Cherry (*Prunus serrulata*)
Columnar Sargent Cherry (*Prunus sargenti columnaris*)
Smooth-leaved Elm varieties (*Ulmus carpinifolia*)

Soil Tolerance

Trees Tolerating Acid Soil

*Japanese Maple (*Acer palmatum*)
*Flowering Dogwood (*Cornus kousa*)
*European Beech (*Fagus sylvatica*)
Sweet Bay (*Magnolia virginiana*)
Red Oak (*Quercus borealis*)
Scarlet Oak (*Quercus coccinea*)
*Willow Oak (*Quercus phellos*)
*Pin Oak (*Quercus palustris*)

Trees Tolerating Moist Soil

*Red Maple (*Acer rubrum*)
Alder species (*Alnus*)
Holly species (*Ilex*)
*Sweet Gum (*Liquidambar styraciflua*)
Sweet Bay (*Magnolia virginiana*)
Swamp White Oak (*Quercus bicolor*)
*Willow species (*Salix*)
American Arbor-vitae (*Thuja occidentalis*)

Trees Tolerating Dry or Poor Soil

Box-Elder (*Acer negundo*)
*Tree of Heaven (*Ailanthus*)
*Gray Birch (*Betula populifolia*)
Russian Olive (*Elaeagnus angustifolia*)
Green Ash (*Fraxinus pennsylvanica*)
*Honey-Locust (*Gleditsia triacanthos* var.)
Rocky Mountain Juniper (*Juniperus scopulorum*)

Eastern Red Cedar (*Juniperus virginiana*)
Osage-Orange (*Maclura pomifera*)
Jack Pine (*Pinus banksiana*)
White Poplar (*Populus alba*)
Chestnut Oak (*Quercus montana*)
*Black Locust (*Robinia pseudoacacia*)
Chinese Elm (*Ulmus parvifolia*)
Siberian Elm (*Ulmus pumila*)

Pest-Resistant Trees

*Tree of Heaven (*Ailanthus altissima*)
Hornbeam species (*Carpinus*)
Cornelian Cherry (*Cornus mas*)
Japanese Cornel (*Cornus officinalis*)
American Smoke Tree (*Cotinus americanus*)
Russian Olive (*Elaeagnus angustifolia*)
*Ginkgo (*Ginkgo biloba*)
*Honey-Locust (*Gleditsia triacanthos*)
Kentucky Coffee Tree (*Gymnocladus dioicus*)
Juniper species (*Juniperus*)
*Sweet Gum (*Liquidambar styraciflua*)
Cucumber Tree (*Magnolia acuminata*)
Kobus Magnolia (*Magnolia kobus borealis*)
Anise Magnolia (*Magnolia salicifolia*)
*Star Magnolia (*Magnolia stellata*)
Hop-Hornbeam species (*Ostrya*)

Trees for Hedging or Barriers

European Beech (*Fagus sylvatica*) prunes well.
Leyland Cypress (*Cupressocyparis leylandii*) withstands heavy pruning.
Hawthorn varieties (*Crataegus*) easily pruned, advantage of thorns.
Canadian Hemlock (*Tsuga canadensis*) evergreen.
American Holly (*Ilex opaca*) can be pruned.
European Hornbeam (*Carpinus betulus*) prunes well.
Little-leaf Linden (*Tilia cordata*) tolerates heavy pruning.
Hedge Maple (*Acer campestre*) can be pruned.
Austrian Pine (*Pinus nigra*) plant 10–12 feet on centers, staggered row.
Japanese Black Pine (*Pinus thunbergi*) plant 8 feet on centers, staggered row.
Eastern White Pine (*Pinus strobus*) plant 15 feet on centers, staggered row.

ILLINOIS

State Tree

*Native Oak (*Quercus*)

Evergreen Trees

Fir species (*Abies*)
False Cypress species (*Chamaecyparis*)
Holly species (*Ilex*)
Juniper species (*Juniperus*)
*Larch species (*Larix*)
Spruce species (*Picea*)
*Pine species (*Pinus*)
*Douglas Fir (*Pseudotsuga menziesii*)
Umbrella Pine (*Sciadopitys verticillata*)
Arbor-vitae species (*Thuja*)
*Hemlock species (*Tsuga*)

Trees Classified by Height

20–30 Feet

Argutum Maple (*Acer argutum*)
Hedge Maple (*Acer campestre*)
Hornbeam Maple (*Acer carpinifolium*)
Vine Maple (*Acer circinatum*)
Amur Maple (*Acer ginnala*)
Paperbark Maple (*Acer griseum*)
Manchurian Maple (*Acer mandshuricum*)
*Japanese Maple (*Acer palmatum*)
Striped Maple or Moosewood (*Acer pennsylvanicum*)
Mountain Maple (*Acer spicatum*)

Tatarian Maple (*Acer tataricum*)
Ohio Buckeye (*Aesculus glabra*)
*Serviceberry species (*Amelanchier*)
*Gray Brich (*Betula populifolia*)
European Hornbeam (*Carpinus betulus globosa*)
American Hornbeam (*Carpinus carolineana*)
Mockernut (*Carya tomentosa*)
Chinese Chestnut (*Castanea mollisima*)
Eastern Redbud (*Cercis canadensis*)
Fringetree (*Chionanthus virginicus*)
*Flowering Dogwood (*Cornus florida*)
Japanese Dogwood (*Cornus kousa*)
Cornelian Cherry (*Cornus mas*)
Japanese Cornel (*Cornus officinalis*)
American Smoke Tree (*Cotinus americanus*)
*Hawthorn species (*Crataegus*)
Russian Olive (*Elaeagnus angustifolia*)
Franklinia (*Franklinia alatamaha*)
Flowering Ash (*Fraxinus ornus*)
Carolina Silverbell (*Halesia carolina*)
Common Sea-Buckthorn (*Hippophae rhamnoides*)
Possum Haw (*Ilex decidua*)
*Golden Rain Tree (*Koelreuteria paniculata*)
*Laburnum species (*Laburnum*)
Yellow Cucumber Tree (*Magnolia cordata*)
*Magnolia species (*Magnolia*)
*Crab Apple species (*Malus*)
*Sorrel Tree or Sourwood (*Oxydendrum arboreum*)

*Cherry species (*Prunus*)
European Mountain Ash (*Sorbus aucuparia*)
Snowy Mountain Ash (*Sorbus decora*)
Snowberry Mountain Ash (*Sorbus discolor*)
Folgner Mountain Ash (*Sorbus folgneri*)
Asiatic Sweetleaf (*Symplocos paniculata*)
Japanese Tree Lilac (*Syringa amuerensis japonica*)

35–75 Feet

Korean Fir (*Abies koreana*)
Nikko Maple (*Acer nikoense*)
*Red-fruited Tree of Heaven (*Ailanthus altissima erythrocarpa*)
Italian Alder (*Alnus cordata*)
Speckled Alder (*Alnus incana*)
Red Alder (*Alnus rubra*)
Allegany Serviceberry (*Amelanchier laevis*)
Sweet Birch (*Betula lenta*)
Dahurian Birch (*Betula mandshurica szechuanica*)
River Birch (*Betula nigra*)
*Canoe Birch (*Betula papyrifera*)
*European Birch (*Betula pendula*)
Japanese Hornbeam (*Carpinus japonica*)
Southern Catalpa (*Catalpa bignoniodes*)
Bunch Hackberry (*Celtis bungeana*)
Hackberry (*Celtis occidentalis*)
*Katsura Tree (*Cercidiphyllum japonicum*)
*American Yellow-wood (*Cladrastis lutea*)

*Flowering Dogwood (*Cornus florida*)
Turkish Filbert (*Corylus colurna*)
Green Hawthorn (*Crataegus viridis*)
Common Persimmon (*Diospyros virginiana*)
Green Ash (*Fraxinus pennsylvanica lanceolata*)
Mountain Winterberry (*Ilex montana*)
Heartnut (*Juglans sieboldiana cordiformis*)
Chinese Juniper (*Juniperus chinensis*)
*Amur Cork (*Phellodendron amurense*)
Jack Pine (*Pinus banksiana*)
Lace-bark Pine (*Pinus bungeana*)
Swiss Stone Pine (*Pinus cembra*)
Limper Pine (*Pinus flexilis*)
Pitch Pine (*Pinus rigida*)
Scotch Pine (*Pinus sylvestris*)
Virginia or Scrub Pine (*Pinus virginiana*)
Simon Poplar (*Populus simoni*)
European Bird Cherry (*Prunus padus*)
Golden Larch (*Pseudolarix amabilis*)
Ussurian Pear (*Pyrus ussuriensis*)
Swamp White Oak (*Quercus bicolor*)
Red Oak (*Quercus borealis*)
Scarlet Oak (*Quercus coccinea*)
Shingle Oak (*Quercus imbricaria*)
*Pin Oak (*Quercus palustris*)
Willow Oak (*Quercus phellos*)
White Willow (*Salix alba*)
Wisconsin or Niobe Weeping Willow (*Salix blanda*)
Thurlow Weeping Willow (*Salix elegantissima*)
Laurel Willow (*Salix pentandra*)
Sassafras (*Sassafras albidum officinale*)
American Arbor-vitae (*Thuja occidentalis*)
*Crimean Linden (*Tilia euchlora*)
Carolina Hemlock (*Tsuga caroliniana*)
Chinese Elm (*Ulmus parvifolia*)

75 Feet or Over
Fir species (*Abies*)
Norway maple (*Acer platanoides*)
Sycamore Maple (*Acer pseudoplatanus*)
*Red or Swamp Maple (*Acer rubrum*)
*Sugar Maple (*Acer saccharum*)
*Baumann Horse-Chestnut (*Aesculus hippocastanum baumanni*)
European Alder (*Alnus glutinosa*)
*Canoe Birch (*Betula papyrifera*)
Hickory species (*Carya*)
Sugar Hackberry (*Celtis laevigata*)
*Katsura Tree (*Cercidiphyllum japonicum*)
*Beech species (*Fagus*)
White Ash (*Fraxinus americana*)
European Ash (*Fraxinus excelsior*)
*Ginkgo or Maidenhair Tree (*Ginkgo biloba*)
*Common Honey-Locust (*Gleditsia triacanthos*)
Kentucky Coffee Tree (*Gymnocladus dioicus*)
Mountain Silverbell (*Halesia monticola*)
Eastern Black Walnut (*Juglans nigra*)
English or Persian Walnut (*Juglans regia*)
*European Larch (*Larix decidua*)
Japanese Larch (*Larix leptolepis*)
*Sweet Gum (*Liquidambar styraciflua*)
Tulip Tree or Yellow Poplar (*Liriodendron tulipifera*)
Cucumber Tree (*Magnolia acuminata*)
*Black Gum or Black Tupelo (*Nyssa sylvatica*)
Spruce species (*Picea*)
*Pine species (*Pinus*)
*Plane Tree species (*Platanus*)
Poplar species (*Populus*)
Black or Rum Cherry (*Prunus serotina*)
*Douglas Fir (*Pseudotsuga menziessi*)
Oak species (*Quercus*)
Umbrella Pine (*Sciadopitys verticillata*)
Common Bald Cypress (*Taxodium distichum*)
*Linden species (*Tilia*)
*Canada Hemlock (*Tsuga canadensis*)
*Elm species (*Ulmus*)
Japanese Zelkova (*Zelkova serrata*)

Tree Classified by Form

Pyramidal
Fir species (*Abies*)

Arbor-vitae species (*Arbor-vitae*)
*Birch species (*Betula*)
*Cedar species (*Cedrus*)
False Cypress species (*Chamaecyparis*)
Turkish Filbert (*Corylus colurna*)
American Holly (*Ilex opaca*)
Juniper or Red Cedar species (*Juniperus*)
*Larch species (*Larix*)
*Sweet Gum (*Liquidambar styraciflua*)
*Magnolia species (*Magnolia*)
*Black Tupelo or Black Gum (*Nyssa sylvatica*)
Hop-Hornbeam (*Ostrya virginiana*)
*Sorrel Tree or Sourwood (*Oxydendrum arboreum*)
Spruce species (*Picea*)
Swiss Stone Pine (*Pinus cembra*)
Korean Pine (*Pinus koraiensis*)
Japanese White Pine (*Pinus parviflora*)
Red or Norway Pine (*Pinus resinosa*)
Bolleana Poplar (*Populus alba pyramidalis*)
Golden Larch (*Pseudolarix amabilis*)
Douglas Fir (*Pseudotsuga menziesii*)
*Pin Oak (*Quercus palustris*)
Umbrella Pine (*Sciadopitys verticillata*)
Common Bald Cypress (*Taxodium distichum*)
*Linden species (*Tilia*)
Douglas Arbor-vitae (*Thuja occidentalis douglasi pyramidalis*)
*Hemlock species (*Tsuga*)

Columnar
Ascending Norway Maple (*Acer platanoides ascendens*)
Columnar Norway Maple (*Acer platanoides columnare*)
Erect Norway Maple (*Acer platanoides erectum*)
Columnar Red Maple (*Acer rubrum columnare*)
Sentry Maple (*Acer saccharum monumentale*)
Fastigiate European Birch (*Betula pendula fastigiata*)
Fastigiate European Hornbeam (*Carpinus betulus fastigiata*)
Columnar Hinoki Cypress (*Chamaecyparis obtusa erecta*)
Fastigiate Washington Hawthorn (*Crataegus phaenopyrum fastigiata*)
Dawyck Beech (*Fagus sylvatica fastigiata*)
Sentry Ginkgo (*Ginkgo biloba fastigiata*)
Blue Columnar Chinese Juniper (*Juniperus chinensis columnaris*)
White Pine (*Pinus strobus fastigiata*)
Fastigiata Scotch Pine (*Pinus sylvestris fastigiata*)
Lombardy Poplar (*Populus nigra italica*)
Columnar Sargent Cherry (*Prunus sargenti columnaris*)
"Amanogawa" Cherry (*Prunus serrulata "Amanogawa"*)
Fastigiate English Oak (*Quercus robur fastigiata*)
Common Bald Cypress (*Taxodium distichum*)
Fastigiate American Arbor-vitae (*Thuja occidentalis fastigiata*)
Columnar Big-leaf Linden (*Tilia platyphyllos fastigiata*)
American Elm varieties (*Ulmus americana*)

Weeping
Slender European Birch (*Betula pendula tristis*)
Young's Birch (*Betula pendula youngi*)
Weeping European Hornbeam (*Carpinus betulus pendula*)
*Weeping Beech (*Fagus sylvatica pendula*)
Weeping Purple Beech (*Fagus sylvatica purpureo-pendula*)
Weeping Red Cedar (*Juniperus virginiana pendula*)
Weeping Larch (*Larix decidua pendula*)
"Exzellenz Thiel" Crab Apple (*Malus "Exzellenz Thiel"*)
"Oekonomierat Echtermeyer" Crab Apple (*Malus "Oekonomierat Echtermeyer"*)
Koster Weeping Blue Spruce (*Picea pungens kosteriana*)
Weeping White Pine (*Pinus strobus pendula*)
Weeping Higan Cherry (*Prunus subhirtella pendula*)
"Yaeshidare" Cherry (*Prunus subhirtella pendula flora plena*)

Weeping Yoshino Cherry (*Prunus yedoensis perpendens*)
Weeping Douglas Fir (*Pseudotsuga menziesii pendula*)
Golden Weeping Willow (*Salix alba tristis*)
Wisconsin or Niobe Weeping Willow (*Salix blanda*)
Thurlow Weeping Willow (*Salix elegantissima*)
Weeping Japanese Pagoda Tree (*Sophora japonica pendula*)
Weeping European Mountain Ash (*Sorbus aucuparia pendula*)
Sargent Hemlock (*Tsuga canadensis pendula*)
Weeping American Elm (*Ulmus americana pendula*)

Rounded or Globe-Shaped
*Japanese Maple (*Acer palmatum*)
Globe Norway maple (*Acer platanoides globosum*)
Globe European Hornbeam (*Carpinus betulus globosa*)
Bunch Hackberry (*Celtis bungeana*)
Cornelian Cherry (*Cornus mas*)
Japanese Cornel (*Cornus officinalis*)
Single Seed Hawthorn (*Crataegus monogyna inermis*)
*Saucer Magnolia (*Magnolia soulangeana*)
*Crab Apple species (*Malus*)
*White Oak (*Quercus alba*)
Umbrella Black Locust (*Robinia pseudoacacia umbraculifera*)
Sargent Hemlock (*Tsuga canadensis sargenti*)

With Horizontal Branching
Fir species (*Abies*)
Eastern Redbud (*Cercis canadensis*)
Giant Dogwood (*Cornus controversa*)
*Flowering Dogwood (*Cornus florida*)
Japanese Dogwood (*Cornus kousa*)
*Hawthorn species (*Crataegus*)
*Black Tupelo or Black Gum (*Nyssa sylvatica*)
Japanese Red Pine (*Pinus densiflora*)
*Eastern White Pine (*Pinus strobus*)
Golden Larch (*Pseudolarix amabilis*)
*White Oak (*Quercus alba*)
*Pin Oak (*Quercus palustris*)
Common Bald Cypress (*Taxodium distichum*)

Trees Classified by Color of Blossom
Yellow
*Golden Rain Tree (*Koelreuteria paniculata*)

White
*Shadblow Serviceberry (*Amelanchier canadensis*)
Whitebud (*Cercis canadensis alba*)
*Yellow-wood (*Cladrastis lutea*)
Japanese Dogwood (*Cornus kousa*)
Washington Hawthorn (*Crataegus phaenopyrum*)
Carolina Silverbell (*Halesia carolina*)
Yulan Magnolia (*Magnolia denudata*)
*Star Magnolia (*Magnolia stellata*)
Arnold Crab Apple (*Malus arnoldiana*)
Siberian Crab Apple (*Malus baccata*)
Tea Crab Apple (*Malus hupehensis*)
Sargent Crab Apple (*Malus sargenti*)
*Sorrel Tree (*Oxydendrum arboreum*)
Sour Cherry (*Prunus cerasus*)
Yoshino Cherry (*Prunus yedoensis*)
Bradford Callery Pear (*Pyrus calleryana "Bradford"*)
*Common Pear (*Pyrus communis*)
*Japanese Pagoda Tree (*Sophora japonica*)
Korean Mountain Ash (*Sorbus alnifolia*)
American Mountain Ash (*Sorbus americana*)
European Mountain Ash (*Sorbus aucuparia*)
Showy Mountain Ash (*Sorbus decora*)

Pink
Wither's Pink Redbud (*Cercis canadensis "Wither's Pink Charm"*)
Red Flowering Dogwood (*Cornus florida rubra*)
Toba Hawthorn (*Crataegus mordenensis "Toba"*)
*Saucer Magnolia (*Magnolia soulangeana*)
Japanese Flowering Crab Apple (*Malus floribunda*)
Katherine Crab Apple (*Malus "Katherine"*)
Prince Georges Crab Apple (*Malus "Prince Georges"*)
*Common Apple (*Malus pumila*)

Blireiana Plum (*Prunus blireiana*)
Sargent Cherry (*Prunus sargenti*)
Amanogawa Cherry (*Prunus serrulata* "Amano-gawa")
Kwanzan Cherry (*Prunus serrulata* "Kwanzan")
Autumn Cherry (*Prunus subhirtella autumnalis*)
Weeping Cherry (*Prunus subhirtella pendula*)

Red
Ruby Horse-Chestnut (*Aesculus carnea briotti*)
Paul's Scarlet Hawthorn (*Crataegus oxyacantha pauli*)
Alexandrina Magnolia (*Magnolia soulangeana* "Alexandrina")
Almey Crab Apple (*Malus* "Almey")
Carmine Crab Apple (*Malus atrosanguinea*)

Trees with Bright Red Fruit
★Flowering Dogwood (*Cornus florida*)
Japanese Dogwood (*Cornus kousa*)
Downy Hawthorn (*Crataegus mollis*)
Washington Hawthorn (*Crataegus phaenopyrum*)
American Holly (*Ilex opaca*)
Siberian Crab Apple (*Malus baccata*)
Hopa Crab Apple (*Malus* "Hopa")
★Common Apple (*Malus pumila*)
Sargent Crab Apple (*Malus sargenti*)
Korean Mountain Ash (*Sorbus alnifolia*)
American Mountain Ash (*Sorbus americana*)
European Mountain Ash (*Sorbus aucuparia*)

Trees Classified by Color of Summer Foliage
Blue
White Fir (*Abies concolor*)
Eastern Red Cedar (*Juniperus virginiana* var. *Burki*)
Colorado Blue Spruce (*Picea Purgens* var. *Glauca*)

Silver to Gray
Russian Olive (*Elaeagnus angustifolia*)
Common Sea-Buckthorn (*Hippophae rhamnoides*)
White Poplar (*Populus alba*)
Pendent Silver Linden (*tilia petiolaris*)
★Silver Linden (*Tilia tomentosa*)

Red to Purple
Blood-leaf Japanese Maple (*Acer palatum atropurpureum*)
Crimson King Maple (*Acer platanoides* "Crimson King")
Schwedler Maple (*Acer platanoides schwedleri*)
Purple-leaf Sycamore Maple (*Acer pseudoplatanus*)
Purple Beech (*Fagus sylvatica atropunicea*)
Weeping Purple Beech (*Fagus sylvatica purpureo-pendula*)
River's Purple Beech (*Fagus sylvatica riversi*)
Rubylace Locust (*Gleditsia triacanthos inermis* "Rubylace")
Purple Crab Apple (*Malus purpurea*)
Blireiana Plum (*Prunus blireiana*)
Pissard Plum (*Prunus cerasifera atropurpurea*)
Thundercloud Plum (*Prunus cerasifera nigra* "Thunder-cloud")
Purple English Oak (*Quercus robur atropurpurea*)

Trees Classified by Color of Fall Foliage
Yellow
Striped Maple or Moosewood (*Acer pennsylvanicum*)
Norway Maple (*Acer platanoides*)
★Sugar Maple (*Acer saccharum*)
Ohio Buckeye (orange) (*Aesculus glabra*)
Apple Serviceberry (yellow-orange) (*Amelanchier grandiflora*)
★Birch species (*Betula species*)
Hickory species (*Carya*)
Chinese Chestnut (*Castanea mollissima*)
★Katsura Tree (yellow to scarlet) (*Cercidiphyllum japonicum*)
Redbud species (*Cercis*)
Fringetree (*Chionanthus virginicus*)
★Yellow-wood (*Cladrastis lutea*)
★American Beech (*Fagus grandifolia*)

★Ginkgo (*Ginkgo biloba*)
★Larch (*Larix decidua*)
Tulip Tree (*Liriodendron tulipifera*)
★Star Magnolia (bronze) (*Magnolia stellata*)
Golden Larch (*Pseudolarix amabilis*)
★Willow species (*Salix*)

Red
Amur Maple (*Acer ginnala*)
Manchurian Maple (*Acer mandshuricum*)
Nikko Maple (*Acer nikoense*)
★Japanese Maple (*Acer palmatum*)
★Red Maple (*Acer rubrum*)
★Sugar Maple (*Acer saccharum*)
Tatarian Maple (*Acer tataricum*)
★Shadblow Serviceberry (*Amelanchier canadensis*)
Hornbeam species (*Carpinus*)
★Flowering Dogwood (*Cornus florida*)
Japanese Dogwood (*Cornus kousa*)
American Smoke Tree (*Cotinus americanus*)
Washington Hawthorn (*Crataegus phaenopyrum*)
★Sweet Gum (*Liquidambar styraciflua*)
Dawson Crab Apple (*Malus dawsoniana*)
★Black Tupelo or Black Gum (*Nyssa sylvatica*)
★Sorrel Tree (*Oxydendrum arboreum*)
Persian Parrotia (*Parrotia persica*)
★Cherry species (*Prunus*)
Bradford Callery Pear (*Pyrus calleryana* "Bradford")
Red Oak (*Quercus borealis*)
Scarlet Oak (*Quercus coccinea*)
★Pin Oak (*Quercus palustris*)
Sassafras (*Sassafras albidium*)
Korean Mountain Ash (*Sorbus alnifolia*)

Purple
White Ash (*Fraxinus americana*)
★Sweet Gum (*Liquidambar styraciflua*)
★Common Pear (*Pyrus communis*)
★White Oak (*Quercus alba*)

Trees with Interesting Bark
Gray
★Red Maple (*Acer rubrum*)
★Serviceberry species (*Amelanchier*)
Hornbeam species (*Carpinus*)
Hackberry species (*Celtis*)
★American Yellow-wood (*Cladrastis lutea*)
★Hawthorn species (*Crataegus*)
★Beech species (*Fagus*)
American Holly (*Ilex opaca*)
English or Persian Walnut (*Juglans regia*)
Cucumber Tree (*Magnolia acuminata*)
★Saucer Magnolia (*Magnolia soulangeana*)
Mountain Ash species (*Sorbus*)

White
★Canoe Birch (*Betula papyrifera*)
★European Birch (*Betula pendula*)
★Gray Birch (*Betula populifolia*)

Red
Japanese Red Pine (*Pinus densiflora*)
Scotch Pine (*Pinus sylvestris*)
Red or Norway Pine (*Pinus resinosa*)

Reddish Brown
Sargent Cherry (*Prunus sargenti*)

Yellow
Wisconsin or Niobe Weeping Willow (*Salix blanda*)

Corky
★Amur Cork (*Phellodendron amurense*)

Flaking
Paper Bark Maple (*Acer griseum*)
★Birch species (*Betula*)
Shagbark Hickory (*Carya ovata*)
Russian Olive (*Elaeagnus angustifolia*)
Eastern Red Cedar (*Juniperus virginiana*)
Persian Parrotia (*Parrotia persica*)
★Plane Tree species (*Platanus*)
Lace-bark Pine (*Pinus bungeana*)

Trees for the City
White Fir (*Abies concolor*)

Hedge Maple (*Acer campestre*)
Box-Elder (*Acer negundo*)
Norway Maple (*Acer platanoides*)
Sycamore Maple (*Acer pseudoplatanus*)
Horse-Chestnut (Buckeye) (*Aesculus*)
★Tree of Heaven (*Ailanthus*)
Catalpa (*Catalpa*)
Hackberry (*Celtis*)
★Downy Hawthorn (*Crataegus mollis*)
Washington Hawthorn (*Crataegus phaenopyrum*)
Russian Olive (*Elaeagnus angustifolia*)
White Ash (*Fraxinus americana*)
European Ash (*Fraxinus excelsior*)
Green Ash (*Fraxinus pennsylvanica*)
★Ginkgo (*Ginkgo biloba*)
Thornless Honey-Locust (*Gleditsia triacanthos inermis*)
★Golden Rain Tree (*Koelreuteria paniculata*)
★Saucer Magnolia (*Magnolia soulangeana*)
★Star Magnolia (*Magnolia stellata*)
★Crab Apple (*Malus var.*)
★Amur Cork (*Phellodendron amurense*)
Colorado Spruce (*Picea pungens*)
London Plane Tree (*Platanus acerifolia*)
Bradford Callery Pear (*Pyrus calleryana* "Bradford")
White Poplar (*Populus alba*)
★Lombardy Poplar (*Populus nigra italica*)
Red Oak (*Quercus borealis*)
★Black Locust (*Robinia pseudoacacia*)
Japanese Pagoda Tree (*Sophora japonica*)
Little-leaf Linden (*Tilia cordata*)
★Crimean Linden (*Tilia euchlora*)
★Silver Linden (*Tilia tomentosa*)
Village Green Zelkova (*Zelkova serrata* "Village Green")

Trees for Wide Streets
Sycamore Maple (*Acer pseudoplatanus*)
★Sugar Maple (*Acer saccharum*)
Sugar Hackberry (*Celtis laevigata*)
★Katsura Tree (*Cercidiphyllum japonicum*)
White Ash (*Fraxinus americana*)
Green Ash (*Fraxinus pennsylvanica lanceolata*)
★Ginkgo (*Ginkgo biloba*)
★Common Honey-Locust (*Gleditsia triacanthos*)
Tulip Tree (*Liriodendron tulipifera*)
★Amur Cork (*Phellodendron amurense*)
★Eastern White Pine (*Pinus strobus*)
London Plane Tree (*Platanus acerifolium*)
White Poplar (*Populus alba*)
Sargent Cherry (*Prunus sargenti*)
Red Oak (*Quercus borealis*)
★Pin Oak (*Quercus palustris*)
Willow Oak (*Quercus phellos*)
Japanese Zelkova (*Zelkova serrata*)

Trees for Medium Streets
Norway Maple (*Acer platanoides*)
Mountain Silverbell (*Halesia monticola*)
★Sweet Gum (*Liquidambar styraciflua*)
Hop-Hornbeam (*Ostrya virginiana*)
★Sorrel Tree or Sourwood (*Oxydendrum arboreum*)
Simon Poplar (*Populus simoni*)
Scarlet Oak (*Quercus coccinea*)
Willow Oak (*Quercus phellos*)
★Black Locust (*Robinia pseudoacacia*)
Sassafras (*Sassafras albidum officinale*)
★Japanese Pagoda Tree (*Sophora japonica*)
★Linden species (*Tilia*)

Trees for Suburban Streets
Hedge Maple (*Acer campestre*)
Amur Maple (*Acer ginnala*)
Paperbark Maple (*Acer griseum*)
Globe Norway Maple (*Acer platanoides globosum*)
Mountain Maple (*Acer spicatum*)
Tatarian Maple (*Acer tataricum*)
American Hornbeam (*Carpinus caroliniana*)
Pyramidal European Hornbeam (*Carpinus betulus fastigiata*)
Globe European Hornbeam (*Carpinus betulus globosa*)

Fringetree (*Chionanthus virginicus*)
*Flowering Dogwood (*Cornus florida*)
*Hawthorn species (*Crataegus*)
Korean Evodia (*Evodia danielli*)
Carolina Silverbell (*Halesia carolina*)
*Golden Rain Tree (*Koelreuteria paniculata*)
Oriental Cherry (*Prunus serrulata*)
Columnar Sargent Cherry (*Prunus sargenti columnaris*)
Asiatic Sweetleaf (*Symplocos paniculata*)

Soil Tolerance

Trees Tolerating Acid Soil
*Japanese Maple (*Acer palmatum*)
*Flowering Dogwood (*Cornus florida*)
Japanese Dogwood (*Cornus kousa*)
*European Beech (*Fagus sylvatica*)
*Black Tupelo (*Nyssa sylvatica*)
*Sorrel Tree (*Oxydendrum arboreum*)
Red Oak (*Quercus borealis*)
Scarlet Oak (*Quercus coccinea*)
Willow Oak (*Quercus phellos*)
*Pin Oak (*Quercus palustris*)

Trees Tolerating Moist Soil
*Red Maple (*Acer rubrum*)
Alder species (*Alnus*)
Holly species (*Ilex*)
*Sweet Gum (*Liquidambar styraciflua*)
Sweet Bay (*Magnolia virginiana*)
*Black Tupelo or Black Gum (*Nyssa sylvatica*)
Swamp White Oak (*Quercus bicolor*)
*Willow species (*Salix*)

Common Bald Cypress (*Taxodium distichum*)
American Arbor-vitae (*Thuja occidentalis*)

Trees Tolerating Dry or Poor Soil
Box-Elder (*Acer negundo*)
*Tree of Heaven (*Ailanthus*)
*Gray Birch (*Betula populifolia*)
Russian Olive (*Elaeagnus angustifolia*)
Green Ash (*Fraxinus pennsylvanica*)
*Honey-Locust (*Gleditsia triacanthos*)
Western Red Cedar (*Juniperus scopulorum*)
Eastern Red Cedar (*Juniperus virginiana*)
*Golden Rain Tree (*Koelreuteria paniculata*)
Jack Pine (*Pinus banksiana*)
Pitch Pine (*Pinus rigida*)
Virginia Scrub Pine (*Pinus virginiana*)
White Poplar (*Populus alba*)
Chestnut Oak (*Quercus montana*)
*Black Locust (*Roginia pseudoacacia*)
Sassafras (*Sassafras albidum officinale*)
Chinese Elm (*Ulmus parvifolia*)
Siberian Elm (*Ulmus pumila*)

Pest-Resistant Trees
*Tree of Heaven (*Ailanthus altissima*)
Hornbeam species (*Carpinus*)
*Katsura Tree (*Cercidiphyllum japonicum*)
Cornelian Cherry (*Cornus mas*)
Japanese Cornel (*Cornus officinalis*)
Turkish Filbert (*Corylus columa*)
American Smoke Tree (*Cotinus americanus*)

Russian Olive (*Elaeagnus angustifolia*)
Franklinia (*Franklinia alatamaha*)
*Ginkgo (*Ginkgo biloba*)
*Honey-Locust (*Gleditsia triacanthos*)
Kentucky Coffee Tree (*Gymnocladus dioicus*)
*Golden Rain Tree (*Koelreuteria paniculata*)
*Sweet Gum (*Liquidambar styraciflua*)
Cucumber Tree (*Magnolia acuminata*)
Anise Magnolia (*Magnolia salicifolia*)
*Star Magnolia (*Magnolia stellata*)
Hop-Hornbeam species (*Ostrya*)

Trees for Hedging or Barriers

European Beech (*Fagus sylvatica*) prunes well.
Leyland Cypress (*Cupressocyparis leylandii*) withstands heavy pruning.
Hawthorn varieties (*Crataegus*) easily pruned, advantage of thorns.
Canadian Hemlock (*Tsuga canadensis*) evergreen.
American Holly (*Ilex opaca*) can be pruned.
European Hornbeam (*Carpinus betulus*) prunes well.
Little-leaf Linden (*Tilia cordata*) tolerates heavy pruning.
Hedge Maple (*Acer campestre*) can be pruned.
Austrian Pine (*Pinus nigra*) plant 10–12 feet on centers, staggered row.
Japanese Black Pine (*Pinus thunbergi*) plant 8 feet on centers, staggered row.
Eastern White Pine (*Pinus strobus*) plant 15 feet on centers, staggered row.

INDIANA

State Tree
*Native Oak (*Quercus*)

Evergreen Trees

Fir species (*Abies*)
False Cypress species (*Chamaecyparis*)
American Holly (*Ilex opaca*)
Juniper species (*Juniperus*)
*Larch species (*Larix*)
Spruce species (*Picea*)
*Pine species (*Pinus*)
*Douglas Fir (*Pseudotsuga menziesii*)
Umbrella Pine (*Sciodopitys verticillata*)
Arbor-vitae species (*Thuja*)
*Hemlock species (*Tsuga*)

Trees Classified by Height

20–35 Feet
Argutum Maple (*Acer argutum*)
Hedge Maple (*Acer campestre*)
Hornbeam Maple (*Acer carpinifolium*)
Vine Maple (*Acer circinatum*)
Amur Maple (*Acer ginnala*)
Paperbark Maple (*Acer griseum*)
Manchurian Maple (*Acer mandshuricum*)
*Japanese Maple (*Acer palmatum*)
Striped Maple or Moosewood (*Acer pennsylvanicum*)
Mountain Maple (*Acer spicatum*)
Tatarian Maple (*Acer tataricum*)
Ohio Buckeye (*Aesculus glabra*)
*Serviceberry species (*Amelanchier*)
*Gray Birch (*Betula populifolia*)
*European Birch (*Betula pendula*)
European Hornbeam (*Carpinus betulus globosa*)
American Hornbeam (*Carpinus caroliniana*)
Mockernut (*Carya tomentosa*)
Chinese Chestnut (*Castanea mollissima*)
Fringetree (*Chionanthus virginicus*)
Eastern Redbud (*Cercis canadensis*)
*Flowering Dogwood (*Cornus florida*)
Japanese Dogwood (*Cornus kousa*)
Cornelian Cherry (*Cornus mas*)
Japanese Cornel (*Cornus officinalis*)
American Smoke Tree (*Cotinus americanus*)

*Hawthorn species (*Crataegus*)
Russian Olive (*Elaeagnus angustifolia*)
Franklinia (*Franklinia alatamaha*)
Flowering Ash (*Fraxinus ornus*)
Carolina Silverbell (*Halesia carolina*)
Common Sea-Buckthorn (*Hippophae rhamnoides*)
Possom Haw (*Ilex decidua*)
*Golden Rain Tree (*Koelreuteria paniculata*)
*Laburnum species (*Laburnum*)
*Magnolia species (*Magnolia*)
*Crab Apple species (*Malus*)
*Sorrel Tree or Sourwood (*Oxydendrum arboreum*)
*Cherry species (*Prunus*)
American Mountain Ash (*Sorbus americana*)
Showy Mountain Ash (*Sorbus decora*)
Snowberry Mountain Ash (*Sorbus discolor*)
Folgner Mountain Ash (*Sorbus folgneri*)
Asiatic Sweetleaf (*Symplocos paniculata*)
Japanese Tree Lilac (*Syringa amurensis japonica*)

35–75 Feet
Korean Fir (*Abies koreana*)
Nikko Maple (*Acer nikoense*)
*Red-fruited Tree of Heaven (*Ailanthus altissima erythrocarpa*)
Italian Alder (*Alnus cordata*)
Speckled Alder (*Alnus incana*)
Red Alder (*Alnus rubra*)
Allegany Serviceberry (*Amelanchier laevis*)
Sweet Birch (*Betula lenta*)
River Birch (*Betula nigra*)
*European Birch (*Betula pendula*)
Japanese Hornbeam (*Carpinus japonica*)
Southern Catalpa (*Catalpa bignoniodes*)
Bunch Hackberry (*Celtis bungeana*)
*Katsura Tree (*Cercidiphyllum japonicum*)
*American Yellow-wood (*Cladrastis lutea*)
Turkish Filbert (*Corylus columa*)
Green Hawthorn (*Crataegus virdis*)
Common Persimmon (*Diospyros virginiana*)
Green Ash (*Fraxinus pennsylvanica lanceolata*)
Mountain Winterberry (*Ilex montana*)
Heartnut (*Juglans sieboldiana cordiformis*)
Chinese Juniper (*Juniperus chinensis*)

*Amur Cork (*Phellodendron amurense*)
Jack Pine (*Pinus banksiana*)
Lace-bark Pine (*Pinus bungeana*)
Swiss Stone Pine (*Pinus cembra*)
Limber Pine (*Pinus flexilis*)
Pitch Pine (*Pinus rigida*)
Scotch Pine (*Pinus sylvestris*)
Virginia or Scrub Pine (*Pinus virginiana*)
Simon Poplar (*Populus simoni*)
European Bird Cherry (*Prunus padus*)
Golden Larch (*Pseudolarix amabilis*)
Ussurian Pear (*Pyrus ussuriensis*)
Swamp White Oak (*Quercus bicolor*)
Red Oak (*Quercus borealis*)
Scarlet Oak (*Quercus coccinea*)
Shingle Oak (*Quercus imbricaria*)
*Pin Oak (*Quercus palustris*)
Willow Oak (*Quercus phellos*)
White Willow (*Salix alba*)
Wisconsin or Niobe Weeping Willow (*Salix blanda*)
Thurlow Weeping Willow (*Salix elegantissima*)
Laurel Willow (*Salix pentandra*)
Sassafras (*Sassafras albidum officinale*)
American Arbor-vitae (*Thuja occidentalis*)
*Crimean Linden (*Tilia euchlora*)
Carolina Hemlock (*Tsuga caroliniana*)
Chinese Elm (*Ulmus parvifolia*)

75 Feet or Over
Fir species (*Abies*)
Norway Maple (*Acer platanoides*)
Sycamore Maple (*Acer pseudoplatanus*)
*Red or Swamp Maple (*Acer rubrum*)
*Sugar Maple (*Acer saccharum*)
*Baumann Horse-Chestnut (*Aesculus hippocastanum baumanni*)
European Alder (*Alnus glutinosa*)
Hickory species (*Carya*)
Sugar Hackberry (*Celtis laevigata*)
*Katsura Tree (*Cercidiphyllum japonicum*)
False Cypress species (*Chamaecyparis*)
*Beech species (*Fagus*)
White Ash (*Fraxinus americana*)
European Ash (*Fraxinus excelsior*)

★Ginkgo or Maidenhair Tree (*Ginkgo biloba*)
★Common Honey-Locust (*Gleditsia triacanthos*)
Kentucky Coffee Tree (*Gymnocladus dioicus*)
Mountain Silverbell (*Halesia monticola*)
Eastern Black Walnut (*Juglans nigra*)
English or Persian Walnut (*Juglans regia*)
★European Larch (*Larix decidua*)
Japanese Larch (*Larix leptolepis*)
★Sweet Gum (*Liquidambar styraciflua*)
Tulip Tree or Yellow Poplar (*Liriodendron tulipifera*)
Cucumber Tree (*Magnolia acuminata*)
White-leaf Japanese Magnolia (*Magnolia obovata*)
★Black Gum or Black Tupelo (*Nyssa sylvatica*)
Spruce species (*Picea*)
★Pine species (*Pinus*)
★Plane Tree species (*Platanus*)
Poplar species (*Populus*)
Sargent Cherry (*Prunus sargenti*)
Black or Rum Cherry (*Prunus serotina*)
★Douglas Fir (*Pseudotsuga menziesii*)
Oak species (*Quercus*)
Umbrella Pine (*Sciadopitys verticillata*)
Common Bald Cypress (*Taxodium distichum*)
★Linden species (*Tilia*)
★Canada Hemlock (*Tsuga canadensis*)
★Elm species (*Ulmus*)
Japanese Zelkova (*Zelkova serrata*)

Trees Classified by Form

Pyramidal
Fir species (*Abies*)
Arbor-vitae species (*Arbor-vitae*)
★Birch species (*Betula*)
Pyramidal European Hornbeam (*Carpinus betulus fastigiata*)
★Cedar species (*Cedrus*)
False Cypress species (*Chamaecyparis*)
Turkish Filbert (*Corylus colurna*)
Pyramidal Washington Hawthorn (*Crataegus phaenopyrum fastigiata*)
American Holly (*Ilex opaca*)
Juniper or Red Cedar species (*Juniperus*)
★Larch species (*Larix*)
★Sweet Gum (*Liquidambar styraciflua*)
Magnolia species (*Magnolia*)
★Black Tupelo or Black Gum (*Nyssa sylvatica*)
Hop-Hornbeam (*Ostrya virginiana*)
★Sorrel Tree or Sourwood (*Oxydendrum arboreum*)
Spruce species (*Picea*)
Swiss Stone Pine (*Pinus cembra*)
Korean Pine (*Pinus koraiensis*)
Japanese White Pine (*Pinus parviflora*)
Red or Norway Pine (*Pinus resinosa*)
Golden Larch (*Pseudolarix amabilis*)
★Douglas Fir (*Pseudotsuga menziesii*)
★Pin Oak (*Quercus palustris*)
Umbrella Pine (*Sciadopitys verticillata*)
Common Bald Cypress (*Taxodium distichum*)
★Linden species (*Tilia*)
★Hemlock species (*Tsuga*)

Columnar
Ascending Norway Maple (*Acer platanoides ascendens*)
Columnar Norway Maple (*Acer platanoides columnare*)
Erect Norway Maple (*Acer platanoides erectum*)
Columnar Red Maple (*Acer rubrum columnare*)
Sentry Maple (*Acer saccharum monumentale*)
Fastigiate European Birch (*Betula pendula fastigiata*)
Columnar Hinoki Cypress (*Chamaecyparis obtusa erecta*)
Sentry Ginkgo (*Ginkgo biloba fastigiata*)
Blue Columnar Chinese Juniper (*Juniperus chinensis columnaris*)
Swiss Stone Pine (*Pinus cembra*)
Fastigiate White Pine (*Pinus strobus fastigiata*)
Fastigiate Scotch Pine (*Pinus sylvestris fastigiata*)
Bolleana Poplar (*Populus alba pyramidalis*)
★Lombardy Poplar (*Populus nigra italica*)
Pyramidal Simon Poplar (*Populus simoni fastigiata*)
Columnar Sargent Cherry (*Prunus sargenti columnaris*)

"Amanogawa" Cherry (*Prunus serrulata "Amanogawa"*)
Fastigiate English Oak (*Quercus robur fastigiata*)
Common Bald Cypress (*Taxodium distichum*)
Douglas Arbor-vitae (*Thuja occidentalis douglasi pyramidalis*)
Fastigiate American Arbor-vitae (*Thuja occidentalis fastigiata*)
Columnar Big-leaf Linden (*Tilia platyphyllos fastigiata*)

Weeping
Slender European Birch (*Betula pendula tristis*)
Young's Birch (*Betula pendula youngi*)
Weeping European Hornbeam (*Carpinus betulus pendula*)
★Weeping Beech (*Fagus sylvatica pendula*)
Weeping Purple Beech (*Fagus sylvatica purpureopendula*)
Weeping Red Cedar (*Juniperus virginiana pendula*)
Weeping Larch (*Larix decidua pendula*)
"Exzellenz Thiel" Crab Apple (*Malus "Exzellenz Thiel"*)
"Oekonomierat Echtermeyer" Crab Apple (*Malus "Oekonomierat Echtermeyer"*)
Koster Weeping Blue Spruce (*Picea pungens kosteriana*)
Weeping White Pine (*Pinus strobus pendula*)
Weeping Higan Cherry (*Prunus subhirtella pendula*)
"Yaeshidare" Cherry (*Prunus subhirtella penula flora plena*)
Weeping Yoshino Cherry (*Prunus yedoensis perpendens*)
Weeping Douglas Fir (*Pseudotsuga menziesii pendula*)
Golden Weeping Willow (*Salix alba tristis*)
Wisconsin or Niobe Weeping Willow (*Salix blanda*)
Thurlow Weeping Willow (*Salix elegantissima*)
Weeping Japanese Pagoda Tree (*Sophora japonica pendula*)
Weeping European Mountain Ash (*Sorbus aucuparia pendula*)
Sargent Hemlock (*Tsuga canadensis pendula*)
Weeping American Elm (*Ulmus americana pendula*)

Rounded or Globe-Shaped
★Japanese Maple (*Acer palmatum*)
Globe Norway Maple (*Acer platanoides globosum*)
Globe European Hornbeam (*Carpinus betulus globosa*)
Bunch Hackberry (*Celtis bungeana*)
Cornelian Cherry (*Cornus mas*)
Japanese Cornel (*Cornus officinalis*)
Single Seed Hawthorn (*Crataegus monogyna inermis*)
★Beech species (*Fagus*)
★Saucer Magnolia (*Magnolia soulangeana*)
★Crab Apple species (*Malus*)
Umbrella Black Locust (*Robinia pseudoacacia umbraculifera*)
★Sargent Hemlock (*Tsuga canadensis sargenti*)

With Horizontal Branching
Fir species (*Abies*)
Eastern Redbud (*Cercis canadensis*)
★Flowering Dogwood (*Cornus florida*)
Japanese Dogwood (*Cornus kousa*)
★Hawthorn species (*Crataegus*)
★Black Tupelo or Black Gum (*Nyssa sylvatica*)
Spruce species (*Picea*)
Japanese Red Pine (*Pinus densiflora*)
★Eastern White Pine (*Pinus strobus*)
Golden Larch (*Pseudolarix amabilis*)
★White Oak (*Quercus alba*)
Common Bald Cypress (*Taxodium distichum*)

Trees Classified by Color of Blossom

Yellow
★Golden Rain Tree (*Koelreuteria paniculata*)

White
Shadblow Serviceberry (*Amelanchier canadensis*)
Whitebud (*Cercis canadensis alba*)
★American Yellow-wood (*Cladrastis lutea*)
Japanese Dogwood (*Cornus kousa*)

Washington Hawthorn (*Crataegus phaenopyrum*)
Carolina Silverbell (*Halesia carolina*)
Yulan Magnolia (*Magnolia denudata*)
★Star Magnolia (*Magnolia stellata*)
Arnold Crab Apple (*Malus arnoldiana*)
Siberian Crab Apple (*Malus baccata*)
Tea Crab Apple (*Malus hupehensis*)
Sargent Crab Apple (*Malus sargenti*)
★Sorrel Tree (*Oxydendrum arboreum*)
Sour Cherry (*Prunus cerasus*)
Yoshino Cherry (*Prunus yedoensis*)
Bradford Callery Pear (*Pyrus calleryana "Bradford"*)
★Common Pear (*Pyrus communis*)
★Japanese Pagoda Tree (*Sophora japonica*)
Korean Mountain Ash (*Sorbus alnifolia*)
American Mountain Ash (*Sorbus americana*)
European Mountain Ash (*Sorbus aucuparia*)
Showy Mountain Ash (*Sorbus decora*)

Pink
Wither's Pink Redbud (*Cercis canadensis "Wither's Pink Charm"*)
Red Flowering Dogwood (*Cornus florida rubra*)
Toba Hawthorn (*Crataegus mordenensis "Toba"*)
★Saucer Magnolia (*Magnolia soulangeana*)
Japanese Flowering Crab Apple (*Malus floribunda*)
Katherine Crab Apple (*Malus "Katherine"*)
Prince Georges Crab Apple (*Malus "Prince Georges"*)
★Common Apple (*Malus pumila*)
Blireiana Plum (*Prunus blireiana*)
Sargent Cherry (*Prunus sargenti*)
Amanogawa Cherry (*Prunus serrulata "Amanogawa"*)
Kwanzan Cherry (*Prunus serrulata "Kwanzan"*)
Autumn Cherry (*Prunus subhirtella autumnalis*)
Weeping Cherry (*Prunus subhirtella pendula*)

Red
Ruby Horse-Chestnut (*Aesculus carnea briotti*)
Paul's Scarlet Hawthorn (*Crataegus oxyacantha pauli*)
Alexandrina Magnolia (*Magnolia soulangeana "Alexandrina"*)
Almey Crab Apple (*Malus "Almey"*)
Carmine Crab Apple (*Malus atrosanguinea*)

Trees with Bright Red Fruit
★Flowering Dogwood (*Cornus florida*)
Japanese Dogwood (*Cornus kousa*)
★Downy Hawthorn (*Crataegus mollis*)
Washington Hawthorn (*Crataegus phaenopyrum*)
American Holly (*Ilex opaca*)
Siberian Crab Apple (*Malus baccata*)
Hopa Crab Apple (*Malus "Hopa"*)
★Common Apple (*Malus pumila*)
Sargent Crab Apple (*Malus sargenti*)
Korean Mountain Ash (*Sorbus alnifolia*)
American Mountain Ash (*Sorbus americana*)
European Mountain Ash (*Sorbus aucuparia*)

Trees Classified by Color of Summer Foliage

Blue
White Fir (*Abies concolor*)
Eastern Red Cedar (*Juniperus virginiana* var. *Burki*)
Colorado Blue Spruce (*Picea pungens* var. *Glauca*)

Silver to Gray
Russian Olive (*Elaeagnus angustifolia*)
Common Sea-Buckthorn (*Hippophae rhamnoides*)
White Poplar (*Populus alba*)
★Pendent Silver Linden (*Tilia petiolaris*)
★Silver Linden (*Tilia tomentosa*)

Red to Purple
Blood-leaf Japanese Maple (*Acer palmatum atropurpureum*)
Crimson King Maple (*Acer platanoides "Crimson King"*)
Schwedler Maple (*Acer platanoides schwedleri*)
Purple-leaf Sycamore Maple (*Acer pseudoplatanus purpureum*)
Purple Beech (*Fagus sylvatica atropunicea*)

Weeping Purple Beech (*Fagus sylvatica purpureo-pendula*)
River's Purple Beech (*Fagus sylvatica riversi*)
Rubylace Locust (*Gleditsia triacanthos inermis* "Rubylace")
Purple Crab Apple (*Malus purpurea*)
Blireiana Plum (*Prunus blireiana*)
Pissard Plum (*Prunus cerasifera atropurpurea*)
Thundercloud Plum (*Prunus cerasifera nigra* "Thundercloud")
Purple English Oak (*Quercus robur atropurpurea*)

Trees Classified by Color of Fall Foliage

Yellow
Striped Maple or Moosewood (*Acer pensylvanicum*)
Norway Maple (*Acer platanoides*)
★Sugar Maple (*Acer saccharum*)
Apple Serviceberry (yellow-orange) (*Amelanchier grandiflora*)
★Birch species (*Betula*)
Hickory species (*Carya*)
Chinese Chestnut (*Castanea mollissima*)
★Katsura Tree (yellow to scarlet) (*Cercidiphyllum japonicum*)
Fringetree (*Chionanthus virginicus*)
★Amercian Yellow-wood (*Cladrastis lutea*)
★American Beech (*Fagus grandifolia*)
★Ginkgo (*Ginkgo biloba*)
★Larch (*Larix decidua*)
Tulip Tree (*Liriodendron tulipifera*)
★Star Magnolia (bronze) (*Magnolia stellata*)
Golden Larch (*Pseudolarix amabilis*)
★Willow species (*Salix*)

Red
Amur Maple (*Acer ginnala*)
Manchurian Maple (*Acer mandshuricum*)
Nikko Maple (*Acer nikoense*)
★Japanese Maple (*Acer palmatum*)
★Red Maple (*Acer rubrum*)
★Sugar Maple (*Acer saccharum*)
Tatarian Maple (*Acer tataricum*)
★Shadblow Serviceberry (*Amelanchier canadensis*)
★Flowering Dogwood (*Cornus florida*)
Japanese Dogwood (*Cornus kousa*)
American Smoke Tree (*Cotinus americanus*)
Washington Hawthorn (*Crataegus phaenopyrum*)
★Sweet Gum (*Liquidambar styraciflua*)
★Dawson Crab Apple (*Malus dawsoniana*)
★Black Tupelo or Black Gum (*Nyssa sylvatica*)
★Sorrel Tree (*Oxydendrum arboreum*)
Persian Parrotia (*Parrotia persica*)
★Cherry species (*Prunus*)
Bradford Callery Pear (*Pyrus calleryana* "Bradford")
Red Oak (*Quercus borealis*)
Scarlet Oak (*Quercus coccinea*)
★Pin Oak (*Quercus palustris*)
Sassafras (orange) (*Sassafras albidum*)
Korean Mountain Ash (*Sorbus alnifolia*)
Korean Stewartia (orange to red) (*Stewartia koreana*)

Purple
White Ash (*Fraxinus americana*)
★Sweet Gum (*Liquidambar styraciflua*)
★Common Pear (*Pyrus communis*)
★White Oak (*Quercus alba*)

Trees with Interesting Bark

Gray
★Red Maple (*Acer rubrum*)
★Serviceberry species (*Amelanchier*)
Hornbeam species (*Carpinus*)
Hackberry species (*Celtis*)
★American Yellow-wood (*Cladrastis lutea*)
★Hawthorn species (*Crataegus*)
Beech species (*Fagus*)
American Holly (*Ilex opaca*)
English or Persian Walnut (*Juglans regia*)
Cucumber Tree (*Magnolia acuminata*)
★Saucer Magnolia (*Magnolia soulangeana*)
Mountain Ash species (*Sorbus*)

White
★Canoe Birch (*Betula papyrifera*)
★European Birch (*Betula pendula*)
★Gray Birch (*Betula populifolia*)

Red
Japanese Red Pine (*Pinus densiflora*)
Scotch Pine (*Pinus sylvestris*)
Red or Norway Pine (*Pinus resinosa*)

Reddish Brown
Sargent Cherry (*Prunus sargenti*)

Yellow
Wisconsin or Niobe Weeping Willow (*Salix blanda*)

Corky
★Amur Cork (*Phellodendron amurense*)

Flaking
Paper Bark Maple (*Acer griseum*)
★Birch species (*Betula*)
Shagbark Hickory (*Carya ovata*)
Russian Olive (*Elaeagnus angustifolia*)
Eastern Red Cedar (*Juniperus virginiana*)
Persian Parrotia (*Parrotia persica*)
★Plane Tree species (*Plantanus*)
Lace-bark Pine (*Pinus bungeana*)

Trees for the City
White Fir (*Abies concolor*)
Hedge Maple (*Acer campestre*)
Box-Elder (*Acer negundo*)
Norway Maple (*Acer platanoides*)
Sycamore Maple (*Acer pseudo platanus*)
★Horse-Chestnut (Buckeye) (*Aesculus*)
★Tree of Heaven (*Ailanthus*)
Catalpa (*Catalpa*)
Hackberry (*Celtis*)
★Downy Hawthorn (*Crataegus mollis*)
Washington Hawthorn (*Crataegus phaenopyrum*)
Russian Olive (*Elaeagnus angustifolia*)
White Ash (*Fraxinus americana*)
European Ash (*Fraxinus excelsior*)
Green Ash (*Fraxinus pennsylvanica*)
★Ginkgo (*Ginkgo biloba*)
Thornless Honey-Locust (*Gleditsia triacanthos inermis*)
★Golden Rain Tree (*Koelreuteria paniculata*)
★Saucer Magnolia (*Magnolia soulangeana*)
★Star Magnolia (*Magnolia stellata*)
★Crab Apple (*Malus* var.)
★Amur Cork (*Phellodendron amurense*)
Colorado Spruce (*Picea pungens*)
London Plane Tree (*Platanus acerifolia*)
Bradford Callery Pear (*Pyrus calleryana* "Bradford")
★White Poplar (*Populus alba*)
★Lombardy Poplar (*Populus nigra italica*)
Red Oak (*Quercus borealis*)
★Black Locust (*Robinia pseudoacacia*)
★Japanese Pagoda Tree (*Sophora japonica*)
★Little-leaf Linden (*Tilia cordata*)
★Crimean Linden (*Tilia euchlora*)
★Silver Linden (*Tilia tomentosa*)
Village Green Zelkova (*Zelkova serrata* "Village Green")

Trees for Wide Streets
Sycamore Maple (*Acer pseudoplatanus*)
★Sugar Maple (*Acer saccharum*)
Sugar Hackberry (*Celtis laevigata*)
★Katsura Tree (*Cercidiphyllum japonicum*)
White Ash (*Fraxinus americana*)
Green Ash (*Fraxinus pennsylvanica lanceolata*)
★Ginkgo (*Ginkgo biloba*)
★Common Honey-Locust (*Gleditsia triacanthos*)
Tulip Tree (*Liriodendron tulipifera*)
★Amur Cork (*Phellodendron amurense*)
★Eastern White Pine (*Pinus strobus*)
London Plane Tree (*Platanus acerifolium*)
White Poplar (*Populus alba*)
Sargent Cherry (*Prunus sargenti*)
Red Oak (*Quercus borealis*)
★Pin Oak (*Quercus palustris*)

Willow Oak (*Quercus phellos*)
Japanese Zelkova (*Zelkova serrata*)

Trees for Medium Streets
Norway Maple (*Acer platanoides*)
Mountain Silverbell (*Halesia monticola*)
★Sweet Gum (*Liquidambar styraciflua*)
Hop-Hornbeam (*Ostrya virginiana*)
★Sorrel Tree (Sourwood) (*Oxydendrum arboreum*)
Simon Poplar (*Populus simoni*)
Scarlet Oak (*Quercus coccinea*)
★Willow Oak (*Quercus phellos*)
★Black Locust (*Robinia pseudoacacia*)
Sassafras (*Sassafras albidum officinale*)
★Japanese Pagoda Tree (*Sophora japonica*)
★Linden species (*Tilia*)

Trees for Suburban Streets
Hedge Maple (*Acer campestre*)
Amur Maple (*Acer ginnala*)
Paperbark Maple (*Acer griseum*)
Globe Norway Maple (*Acer platanoides globosum*)
Mountain Maple (*Acer spicatum*)
Tatarian Maple (*Acer tataricum*)
American Hornbeam (*Carpinus caroliniana*)
Pyramidal European Hornbeam (*Carpinus betulus fastigiata*)
Globe European Hornbeam (*Carpinus betulus globosa*)
Fringetree (*Chionanthus virginicus*)
★Flowering Dogwood (*Cornus florida*)
★Hawthorn species (*Crataegus*)
Korean Evodia (*Evodia danielli*)
Carolina Silverbell (*Halesia carolina*)
★Golden Rain Tree (*Koelreuteria paniculata*)
Oriental Cherry (*Prunus serrulata*)
Columnar Sargent Cherry (*Prunus sargenti columnaris*)
Asiatic Sweetleaf (*Symplocos paniculata*)

Soil Tolerance

Trees Tolerating Acid Soil
★Japanese Maple (*Acer palmatum*)
★Flowering Dogwood (*Cornus florida*)
Japanese Dogwood (*Cornus kousa*)
★European Beech (*Fagus sylvatica*)
★Black Tupelo (*Nyssa sylvatica*)
★Sorrel Tree (*Oxydendrum arboreum*)
Red Oak (*Quercus borealis*)
Scarlet Oak (*Quercus coccinea*)
Willow Oak (*Quercus phellos*)
★Pin Oak (*Quercus palustris*)
Japanese Stewartia (*Stewartia pseudocamellia*)

Trees Tolerating Moist Soil
★Red Maple (*Acer rubrum*)
Alder species (*Alnus*)
Holly species (*Ilex*)
★Sweet Gum (*Liquidambar styraciflua*)
Sweet Bay (*Magnolia virginiana*)
★Black Tupelo or Black Gum (*Nyssa sylvatica*)
Swamp White Oak (*Quercus bicolor*)
★Willow species (*Salix*)
Common Bald Cypress (*Taxodium distichum*)
American Arbor-vitae (*Thuja occidentalis*)

Trees Tolerating Dry or Poor Soil
Box-Elder (*Acer negundo*)
★Tree of Heaven (*Ailanthus*)
★Gray Birch (*Betula populifolia*)
Russian Olive (*Elaeagnus angustifolia*)
Green Ash (*Fraxinus pennsylvanica*)
★Honey-Locust (*Gleditsia triacanthos*)
Western Red Cedar (*Juniperus scopulorum*)
Eastern Red Cedar (*Juniperus virginiana*)
★Golden Rain Tree (*Koelreuteria paniculata*)
Jack Pine (*Pinus banksiana*)
Pitch Pine (*Pinus rigida*)
Virginia or Scrub Pine (*Pinus virginiana*)
White Poplar (*Populus alba*)
Chestnut Oak (*Quercus montana*)
★Black Locust (*Robinia pseudoacacia*)
Sassafras (*Sassafras albidum officinale*)

Chinese Elm (*Ulmus parvifolia*)
Siberian Elm (*Ulmus pumila*)

Pest-Resistant Trees

*Tree of Heaven (*Ailanthus altissima*)
Hornbeam species (*Carpinus*)
*Katsura Tree (*Cercidiphyllum japonicum*)
Cornelian Cherry (*Cornus mas*)
Japanese Cornel (*Cornus officinalis*)
Turkish Filbert (*Corylus colurna*)
American Smoke Tree (*Cotinus americanus*)
Franklinia (*Franklinia alatamaha*)
*Ginkgo (*Ginkgo biloba*)
*Honey-Locust (*Gleditsia triacanthos*)

Kentucky Coffee Tree (*Gymnocladus dioicus*)
*Golden Rain Tree (*Koelreuteria paniculata*)
*Sweet Gum (*Liquidambar styraciflua*)
Cucumber Tree (*Magnolia acuminata*)
Anise Magnolia (*Magnolia salicifolia*)
*Star Magnolia (*Magnolia stellata*)
Hop-Hornbeam species (*Ostrya*)

Trees for Hedging or Barriers

European Beech (*Fagus sylvatica*) prunes well.
Leyland Cypress (*Cupressocyparis leylandii*) withstands heavy pruning.
Hawthorn varieties (*Crataegus*) easily pruned, advantage of thorns.

Canadian Hemlock (*Tsuga canadensis*) evergreen.
American Holly (*Ilex opaca*) can be pruned.
European Hornbeam (*Carpinus betulus*) prunes well.
Little-leaf Linden (*Tilia cordata*) tolerates heavy pruning.
Hedge Maple (*Acer campestre*) can be pruned.
Austrian Pine (*Pinus nigra*) plant 10–12 feet on centers, staggered row.
Japanese Black Pine (*Pinus thunbergi*) plant 8 feet on centers, staggered row.
Eastern White Pine (*Pinus strobus*) plant 15 feet on centers, staggered row.

IOWA

State Tree

*Oak (*Quercus*)

Evergreen Trees

Fir species (*Abies*)
Juniper species (*Juniperus*)
Eastern Red Cedar (*Juniperus virginiana*)
Spruce species (*Picea*)
*Pine species (*Pinus*)
Arbor-vitae species (*Thuja*)
*Canada Hemlock (*Tsuga canadensis*)

Trees Classified by Height

20–35 Feet

Hedge Maple (*Acer campestre*)
Amur Maple (*Acer ginnala*)
Manchurian Maple (*Acer mandshuricum*)
Mountain Maple (*Acer spicatum*)
Tatarian Maple (*Acer tataricum*)
Ohio Buckeye (*Aesculus glabra*)
Apple Serviceberry (*Amelanchier grandiflora*)
Mockernut (*Carya tomentosa*)
Eastern Redbud (*Cercis canadensis*)
Fringetree (*Chionanthus virginicus*)
Cornelian Cherry (*Cornus mas*)
*Hawthorn species (*Crataegus*)
Russian Olive (*Elaeagnus angustifolia*)
Euonymus species (*Euonymus*)
*Golden Rain Tree (*Koelreuteria paniculata*)
*Laburnum species (*Laburnum*)
*Saucer Magnolia (*Magnolia soulangeana*)
*Crab Apple species (*Malus*)
*Cherry species (*Prunus*)
Dahurian Buckthorn (*Rhamnus davurica*)
Goat Willow (*Salix caprea*)
Japanese Tree Lilac (*Syringa amurensis japonica*)

35–75 Feet

Striped Maple or Moosewood (*Acer pennsylvanicum*)
*Red-fruited Tree of Heaven (*Ailanthus altissima erythrocarpa*)
Speckled Alder (*Alnus incana*)
Red Alder (*Alnus rubra*)
*Shadblow Serviceberry (*Amelanchier canadensis*)
Devil's Walking Stick (*Aralia elata*)
*European Birch (*Betula pendula*)
Chinese Chestnut (*Castanea mollissima*)
Southern Catalpa (*Catalpa bignoniodes*)
*Katsura Tree (*Cercidiphyllum japonicum*)
Hackberry (*Celtis occidentalis*)
Eastern Redbud (*Cercis canadensis*)
*American Yellow-wood (*Cladrastis lutea*)
*Flowering Dogwood (*Cornus florida*)
Turkish Filbert (*Corylus colurna*)
Cockspur Thorn (*Crataegus crus-galli*)
Green Hawthorn (*Crataegus virdis*)
Common Persimmon (*Diospyros virginiana*)
Green Ash (*Fraxinus pennsylvanica lanceolata*)
Heartnut (*Juglans sieboldiana cordiformis*)
Chinese Juniper (*Juniperus chinensis*)
Kobus Magnolia (*Magnolia kobus borealis*)
Loebner Magnolia (*Magnolia loebneri*)
Siberian Crab Apple (*Malus baccata*)

"Cowichan" Crab Apple (*Malus* "Cowichan")
"Dolgo" Crab Apple (*Malus* "Dolgo")
"Makamik" Crab Apple (*Malus robusta*)
"Sissipuk" Crab Apple (*Malus* "Sissipuk")
White Mulberry (*Morus alba*)
*Sorrel Tree or Sourwood (*Oxydendrum arboreum*)
*Amur Cork (*Phellodendron amurense*)
Black Hills Spruce (*Picea glauca densata*)
Jack Pine (*Pinus banksiana*)
Lace-bark Pine (*Pinus bungeana*)
Scotch Pine (*Pinus sylvestris*)
Simon Poplar (*Populus simoni*)
Miyama Cherry (*Prunus maximowiczi*)
Sargent Cherry (*Prunus sargenti*)
Ussurian Pear (*Pyrus ussuriensis*)
Swamp White Oak (*Quercus bicolor*)
Red Oak (*Quercus borealis*)
Scarlet Oak (*Quercus coccinea*)
*Pin Oak (*Quercus palustris*)
White Willow (*Salix alba*)
Wisconsin or Niobe Weeping Willow (*Salix blanda*)
Elaeagnus Willow (*Salix elaeagnos*)
Thurlow Weeping Willow (*Salix elegantissima*)
Laurel Willow (*Salix pentandra*)
Sassafras (*Sassafras albidum officinale*)
European Mountain Ash or Rowan Tree (*Sorbus aucuparia*)
American Arbor-vitae (*Thuja occidentalis*)
Carolina Hemlock (*Tsuga caroliniana*)

75 Feet or Over

*Fir species (*Abies*)
Norway Maple (*Acer platanoides*)
*Red Swamp Maple (*Acer rubrum*)
*Sugar Maple (*Acer saccharum*)
European Alder (*Alnus glutinosa*)
River Birch (*Betula nigra*)
*Canoe Birch (*Betula papyrifera*)
Hickory species (*Carya*)
Northern Catalpa (*Catalpa speciosa*)
*Katsura Tree (*Cercidiphyllum japonicum*)
*American Beech (*Fagus grandifolia*)
White Ash (*Fraxinus americana*)
European Ash (*Fraxinus excelsior*)
*Ginkgo or Maidenhair Tree (*Ginkgo biloba*)
*Common Honey-Locust (*Gleditsia triacanthos*)
Kentucky Coffee Tree (*Gymnocladus dioicus*)
Eastern Black Walnut (*Juglans nigra*)
Kalopanax (*Kalopanax pictus*)
*European Larch (*Larix decidua*)
*Sweet Gum (*Liquidambar styraciflua*)
*Spruce species (*Picea*)
*Pine species (*Pinus*)
*Plane Tree (*Platanus occidentalis*)
Poplar species (*Populus*)
Black Rum Cherry (*Prunus serotina*)
*Douglas Fir (*Pseudotsuga menziesii*)
*Oak species (*Quercus*)
Common Bald Cypress (*Taxodium distichum*)
Giant Arbor-vitae (*Thuja plicata*)
*Linden species (*Tilia*)
*Canada Hemlock (*Tsuga canadensis*)

*Elm species (*Ulmus*)

Trees Classified by Form

Pyramidal

*Fir species (*Abies*)
*Birch species (*Betula*)
False Cypress species (*Chamaecyparis*)
Turkish Filbert (*Corylus colurna*)
Juniper or Red Cedar species (*Juniperus*)
*Larch species (*Larix*)
*Sweet Gum (*Liquidambar styraciflua*)
*Black Tupelo or Black Gum (*Nyssa sylvatica*)
Hop Hornbeam (*Ostrya virginiana*)
Spruce species (*Picea*)
Korean Pine (*Pinus koraiensis*)
*Pyramidal Austrian Pine (*Pinus nigra pyramidalis*)
Red or Norway Pine (*Pinus resinosa*)
*Douglas Fir (*Pseudotsuga menziesii*)
*Pin Oak (*Quercus palustris*)
Common Bald Cypress (*Taxodium distichum*)
Arbor-vitae species (*Thuja*)
*Linden species (*Tilia*)
*Canada Hemlock (*Tsuga canadensis*)

Columnar

Ascending Norway Maple (*Acer platanoides ascendens*)
Columnar Norway Maple (*Acer platanoides columnare*)
Erect Norway Maple (*Acer platanoides erectum*)
Columnar Red Maple (*Acer rubrum columnare*)
Fastigiate European Birch (*Betula pendula fastigiata*)
Sentry Ginkgo (*Ginkgo biloba fastigiata*)
Blue Columnar Chinese Juniper (*Juniperus chinensis columnaris*)
Fastigiate Red Cedar (*Juniperus virginiana pyramidalis*)
Fastigiate White Pine (*Pinus strobus fastigiata*)
Fastigiate Scotch Pine (*Pinus sylvestris fastigiata*)
Bolleana Poplar (*Populus alba pyramidalis*)
*Lombardy Poplar (*Populus nigra italica*)
Fastigiate Simon Poplar (*Populus simoni fastigiata*)
Shipmast Locust (*Robinia pseudoacacia rectissima*)
Upright European Mountain Ash (*Sorbus aucuparia fastigiata*)
Common Bald Cypress (*Taxodium distichum*)
Columnar Big-Leaf Linden (*Tilia platyphyllos fastigiata*)
*American Elm varieties (*Ulmus americana*)

Weeping

Young's Birch (*Betula pendula youngi*)
Weeping Red Cedar (*Juniperus virginiana pendula*)
Weeping Mulberry (*Morus alba pendula*)
Weeping White Pine (*Pinus strobus pendula*)
Thurlow Weeping Willow (*Salix elegantissima*)
Weeping Japanese Pagoda Tree (*Sophora japonica pendula*)

Rounded or Globe-Shaped

Hackberry (*Celtis occidentalis*)
Cornelian Cherry (*Cornus mas*)
Single Seed Hawthorn (*Crataegus monogyna inermis*)
*Saucer Magnolia (*Magnolia soulangeana*)
*Crab Apple species (*Malus*)
*White Oak (*Quercus alba*)

With Horizontal Branching
*Fir species (*Abies*)
Eastern Redbud (*Cercis canadensis*)
*Flowering Dogwood (*Cornus florida*)
*Hawthorn species (*Crataegus*)
Spruce species (*Picea*)
*Eastern White Pine (*Pinus strobus*)
*White Oak (*Quercus alba*)
*Pin Oak (*Quercus palustris*)
Common Bald Cypress (*Taxodium distichum*)

Trees Classified by Color of Blossom

Yellow
*Golden Rain Tree (*Koelreuteria paniculata*)

White
*Shadblow Serviceberry (*Amelanchier canadensis*)
Carolina Silverbell (*Halesia carolina*)
Arnold Crab Apple ((*Malus arnoldiana*)
*Siberian Crab Apple (*Malus baccata*)
Tea Crab Apple (*Malus hupehensis*)
*Sorrel Tree (*Oxydendrum arboreum*)
Thundercloud Plum (*Prunus cerasifera* "Thunder-cloud")
Sour Cherry (*Prunus cerasus*)
*Japanese Pagoda Tree (*Sophora japonica*)
American Mountain Ash (*Sorbus americana*)
Showy Mountain Ash (*Sorbus decora*)

Pink
Toba Hawthorn (*Crataegus mordenensis* "Toba")
Japanese Flowering Crab Apple (*Malus floribunda*)
Katherine Crab Apple (*Malus* "Katherine")
*Saucer Magnolia (*Magnolia soulangeana*)
*Crab Apple species (*Malus*)

Red
Ruby Horse-Chestnut (*Aesculus carnea briotti*)
Paul's Scarlet Hawthorn (*Crataegus oxyacantha pauli*)
Almey Crab Apple (*Malus* "Almey")
Carmine Crab Apple (*Malus atrosanguinea*)

Trees Classified by Color of Summer Foliage

Blue
Eastern Red Cedar (*Juniperus virginiana* var. *Burki*)

Silver to Gray
Russian Olive (*Elaeagnus angustifolia*)
Common Sea-Buckthorn (*Hippophae rhamnoides*)
White Poplar (*Populus alba*)
*Silver Linden (*Tilia tomentosa*)

Red to Purple
Schwedler Maple (*Acer platanoides schwedleri*)
Purple Crab Apple (*Malus purpurea*)
Pissard Plum (*Prunus cerasifera atropurpurea*)
Thundercloud Plum (*Prunus cerasifera nigra* "Thundercloud")
Woods Myrobalan Plum (*Prunus cerasifera woodi*)

Trees Classified by Color of Fall Foliage

Yellow
Norway Maple (*Acer platanoides* var.)
*Sugar Maple (*Acer saccharum*)
Ohio Buckeye (orange) (*Aesculus glabra*)
Apple Serviceberry (yellow-orange) (*Amelanchier grandiflora*)
*Birch species (*Betula species*)
Hickory species (*Carya*)
Chinese Chestnut (*Castanea mollissima*)
*Katsura Tree (*Cercidiphyllum japonicum*)
Redbud species (*Cercis*)
Fringetree (*Chionanthus virginicus*)
*American Yellow-wood (*Cladrastis lutea*)
White Ash (purple to yellow) (*Fraxinus americana*)
*Ginkgo (*Ginkgo biloba*)
*Larch (*Larix decidua*)
*Willow species (*Salix*)

Red
Amur Maple (*Acer ginnala*)
Manchurian Maple (*Acer mandshuricum*)
*Red Maple (*Acer rubrum*)
*Sugar Maple (*Acer saccharum*)
Shadblow Serviceberry (*Amelanchier canadensis*)
*Flowering Dogwood (*Cornus florida*)
*Sweet Gum (*Liquidambar styraciflua*)
Dawson Crab Apple (*Malus dawsoniana*)
*Black Tupelo or Black Gum (*Nyssa sylvatica*)
*Sorrel Tree (*Oxydendrum arboreum*)
*Cherry species (*Prunus*)
Red Oak (*Quercus borealis*)
Scarlet Oak (*Quercus coccinea*)
*Pin Oak (*Quercus palustris*)

Purple
White Ash (*Fraxinus americana*)
*Sweet Gum (*Liquidambar styraciflua*)
*White Oak (*Quercus alba*)

Trees with Interesting Bark

Gray
*Red Maple (*Acer rubrum*)
*Serviceberry species (*Amelanchier*)
Hornbeam species (*Carpinus*)
Hackberry (*Celtis occidentalis*)
*American Yellow-wood (*Cladrastis lutea*)
Cucumber Tree (*Magnolia acuminata*)
*Saucer Magnolia (*Magnolia soulangeana*)
Red Oak (young trunk and branches) (*Quercus borealis*)
Black Oak (young trunk and branches) (*Quercus velutina*)

White
*Canoe Birch (*Betula papyrifera*)
*European Birch (*Betula pendula*)

Red
Scotch Pine (*Pinus sylvestris*)

Yellow
Wisconsin or Niobe Weeping Willow (*Salix blanda*)

Corky
*Amur Cork (*Phellodendron amurense*)
Hackberry (*Celtis occidentalis*)

Flaking
*Birch species (*Betula*)
Shag Bark Hickory (*Carya ovata*)
Russian Olive (*Elaeagnus angustifolia*)
Eastern Red Cedar (*Juniperus virginiana*)
Lace-bark Pine (*Pinus bungeana*)
*Plane Tree (*Platanus occidentalis*)

Trees for the City
White Fir (*Abies concolor*)
Hedge Maple (*Acer campestre*)
Norway Maple (*Acer platanoides*)
*Tree of Heaven (*Ailanthus*)
Catalpa (*Catalpa*)
*Hawthorn species (*Crataegus*)
Russian Olive (*Elaeagnus angustifolia*)
White Ash (*Fraxinus americana*)
European Ash (*Fraxinus excelsior*)
Green Ash (*Fraxinus pennsylvanica*)
*Ginkgo (*Ginkgo biloba*)
Thornless Honey-Locust (*Gleditsia triacanthos inermis*)
*Golden Rain Tree (*Koelreuteria paniculata*)
*Saucer Magnolia (*Magnolia soulangeana*)
*Crab Apple (*Malus* var.)
*Amur Cork (*Phellodendron amurense*)
*Plane Tree (*Platanus occidentalis*)
White Poplar (*Populus alba*)
*Lombardy Poplar (*Populus nigra italica*)
Red Oak (*Quercus borealis*)
*Japanese Pagoda Tree (*Sophora japonica*)
*Little-leaf Linden (*Tilia cordata*)
*Silver Linden (*Tilia tomentosa*)

Trees for Wide Streets
*Sugar Maple (*Acer saccharum*)
*Katsura Tree (*Cercidiphyllum japonicum*)
White Ash (*Fraxinus americana*)
Green Ash (*Fraxinus pennsylvanica lanceolata*)

*Ginkgo (*Ginkgo biloba*)
*Common Honey-Locust (*Gleditsia triacanthos*)
*Cork (*Phellodendron amurense*)
*Eastern White Pine (*Pinus strobus*)
*Plane Tree (*Platanus occidentalis*)
White Poplar (*Populus alba*)
Red Oak (*Quercus borealis*)
*Pin Oak (*Quercus palustris*)

Trees for Medium Streets
Norway Maple (*Acer platanoides*)
*Sweet Gum (*Liquidambar styraciflua*)
Simon Poplar (*Populus simoni*)
Scarlet Oak (*Quercus coccinea*)
*Black Locust (*Robinia pseudoacacia*)
*Japanese Pagoda Tree (*Sophora japonica*)
*Linden species (*Tilia*)

Trees for Suburban Streets
Hedge Maple (*Acer campestre*)
Amur Maple (*Acer ginnala*)
Fringetree (*Chionanthus virginicus*)
*Flowering Dogwood (*Cornus florida*)
*Hawthorn species (*Crataegus*)
*Golden Rain Tree (*Koelreuteria paniculata*)

Soil Tolerance

Trees Tolerating Acid Soil
*Black Tupelo (*Nyssa sylvatica*)
*Sorrel Tree (*Oxydendrum arboreum*)
Red Oak (*Quercus borealis*)
Scarlet Oak (*Quercus coccinea*)
*Pin Oak (*Quercus palustris*)

Trees Tolerating Dry or Poor Soil
Box-Elder (*Acer negunda*)
*Tree of Heaven (*Ailanthus*)
Hackberry (*Celtis occidentalis*)
Russian Olive (*Elaeagnus angustifolia*)
Green Ash (*Fraxinus pennsylvanica*)
*Honey-Locust (*Gleditsia triacanthos* var.)
Western Red Cedar (*Juniperus scopulorum*)
Eastern Red Cedar (*Juniperus virginiana*)
*Golden Rain Tree (*Koelreuteria paniculata*)
Jack Pine (*Pinus banksiana*)
White Poplar (*Populus alba*)
Chestnut Oak (*Quercus montana*)
*Black Locust (*Robinia pseudoacacia*)
*Japanese Pagoda Tree (*Sophora japonica*)

Pest-Resistant Trees
*Tree of Heaven (*Ailanthus altissima*)
*Katsura Tree (*Cercidiphyllum japonicum*)
Cornelian Cherry (*Cornus mas*)
Turkish Filbert (*Corylus columa*)
Russian Olive (*Elaeagnus angustifolia*)
*Ginkgo (*Ginkgo biloba*)
*Honey-Locust (*Gleditsia triacanthos*)
Kentucky Coffee Tree (*Gymnocladus dioicus*)
Juniper species (*Juniperus*)
Kalopanax (*Kalopanax pictus*)
*Golden Rain Tree (*Koelreuteria paniculata*)
Hop-Hornbeam species (*Ostrya*)

Trees for Hedging or Barriers
European Beech (*Fagus sylvatica*) prunes well.
Leyland Cypress (*Cupressocyparis leylandii*) withstands heavy pruning.
Hawthorn varieties (*Crataegus*) easily pruned, advantage of thorns.
Canadian Hemlock (*Tsuga canadensis*) evergreen.
American Holly (*Ilex opaca*) can be pruned.
European Hornbeam (*Carpinus betulus*) prunes well.
Little-leaf Linden (*Tilia cordata*) tolerates heavy pruning.
Hedge Maple (*Acer campestre*) can be pruned.
Austrian Pine (*Pinus nigra*) plant 10–12 feet on centers, staggered row.
Japanese Black Pine (*Pinus thunbergi*) plant 8 feet on centers, staggered row.
Eastern White Pine (*Pinus strobus*) plant 15 feet on centers, staggered row.

KANSAS

State Tree

Cottonwood (*Populus deltoides*)

Evergreen Trees

Fir species White Fir (*Abies concolor*)
Holly species (*Ilex opaca*)
Eastern Red Cedar (*Juniperus virginiana*)
Colorado Juniper (*Juniperus scopulorum*)
Colorado Spruce (*Picea pungens*)
Norway Spruce (*Picea abies*)
White Spruce (*Picea canadensis*)
★Austrian Pine (*Pinus nigra*)
Western Yellow Pine (*Pinus ponderosa*)
Scotch Pine (*Pinus sylvestris*)
White Pine (*Pinus strobus*)
★Douglas Fir (*Pseudotsuga menziesii*)
Oriental Arbor-vitae (*Thuja orientalis*)

Trees Classified by Height

20—35 Feet

Hedge Maple (*Acer campestre*)
Amur Maple (*Acer ginnala*)
★Japanese Maple (*Acer palmatum*)
Tatarian maple (*Acer tataricum*)
Ohio Buckeye (*Aesculus glabra*)
Texas Buckeye (*Aesculus arguta*)
Red Buckeye (*Aesculus pavia*)
Mockernut (*Carya tomentosa*)
Eastern Redbud (*Cercis canadensis*)
Fringetree (*Chionanthus virginicus*)
Cornelian Cherry (*Cornus mas*)
Japanese Cornel (*Cornus officinalis*)
★Hawthorn (*Crataegus*)
Russian Olive (*Elaeagnus angustifolia*)
Euonymus species (*Euonymus*)
Korean Evodia (*Evodia danielli*)
Flowering Ash (*Fraxinus ornus*)
Possum Haw (*Ilex decidua*)
★Golden Rain Tree (*Koelreuteria paniculata*)
★Saucer Magnolia (*Magnolia soulangeana*)
★Star Magnolia (*Magnolia stellata*)
★Crab Apple species (*Malus*)
★Cherry species (*Prunus*)
Dahurian Buckthorn (*Rhamnus davurica*)
Goat Willow (*Salix caprea*)
Japanese Tree Lilac (*Syringa amurensis japonica*)

35—75 Feet

Box-Elder (*Acer negundo*)
Ohio Buckeye (*Aesulus glabra*)
Horse-Chestnut (*Aesculus hippocastanum*)
★Red-fruited Tree of Heaven (*Ailanthus altissima erythrocarpa*)
★Shadblow Serviceberry (*Amelanchier canadensis*)
Allegany Serviceberry (*Amelanchier laevis*)
★European Birch (*Betula pendula*)
American Hornbeam (*Carpinus caroliniana*)
Southern Catalpa (*Catalba bignoniodes*)
★American Yellow-wood (*Cladrastis lutea*)
★Flowering Dogwood (*Cornus florida*)
Cockspur Thorn (*Crataegus crus-galli*)
Green Hawthorn (*Crataegus viridis*)
Common Persimmon (*Diospyros virginiana*)
Green Ash (*Fraxinus pennsylvanica lanceolata*)
Kentucky Coffee Tree (*Gymnocladus dioicus*)
American Holly (*Ilex opaca*)
Heartnut (*Juglans sieboldiana cordiformis*)
Chinese Juniper (*Juniperus chinensis*)
Kobus Magnolia (*Magnolia kobus borealis*)
Sweet Bay (*Magnolia virginiana*)
Siberian Crab Apple (*Malus bacata*)
"Cowichan" Crab Apple (*Malus "Cowichan"*)
"Dolgo" Crab Apple (*Malus "Dolgo"*)
"Makamik" Crab Apple (*Malus "Makamik"*)
Cherry Crab Apple (*Malus robusta*)
"Sissipuk" Crab Apple (*Malus "Sissipuk"*)
White Mulberry (*Morus alba*)
Hop-Hornbeam (*Ostrya virginiana*)
Empress Tree (*Paulownia tomentosa*)

Jack Pine (*Pinus banksiana*)
Pitch Pine (*Pinus rigida*)
Scotch Pine (*Pinus sylvestris*)
Virginia or Scrub Pine (*Pinus virginiana*)
Simon Poplar (*Populus simoni*)
European Bird Cherry (*Prunus padus*)
Sargent Cherry (*Prunus sargenti*)
Yoshino Cherry (*Prunus yedoensis*)
Swamp White Oak (*Quercus bicolor*)
Red Oak (*Quercus borealis*)
Scarlet Oak (*Quercus coccinea*)
Spanish or Southern Red Oak (*Quercus falcata*)
Shingle Oak (*Quercus imbricaria*)
Willow Oak (*Quercus phellos*)
White Willow (*Salix alba*)
Wisconsin or Niobe Weeping Willow (*Salix blanda*)
Thurlow Weeping Willow (*Salix elegantissima*)
Laurel Willow (*Salix pentandra*)
Western Soapberry (*Sapindus drummondi*)
Sassafras (*Sassafras albidum officinale*)
European Mountain Ash or Rowan Tree (*Sorbus aucuparia*)
★Crimean Linden (*Tilia euchlora*)
Chinese Elm (*Ulmus parvifolia*)
Siberean Elm (*Ulmus pumila*)

75 Feet or Over

Norway Maple (*Acer platanoides*)
★Red or Swamp Maple (*Acer rubrum*)
Silver Maple (*Acer saccharinum*)
★Sugar Maple (*Acer saccharum*)
★Baumann Horse-Chestnut (*Aesculus hippocastanum baumanni*)
River Birch (*Betula nigra*)
Sugar Hackberry (*Celtis laevigata*)
Common Hackberry (*Celtis occidentalis*)
White Ash (*Fraxinus americana*)
★Ginkgo or Maidenhair Tree (*Ginkgo biloba*)
★Common Honey-Locust (*Gleditsia triacanthos*)
Kentucky Coffee Tree (*Gymnocladus dioicus*)
Shellbark Hickory (*Carya laciniosa*)
Shagbark (*Carya ouata*)
Pecan (*Carya illinoensis*)
Eastern Black Walnut (*Juglans nigra*)
English or Persian Walnut (*Juglans regia*)
★European Larch (*Larix decidua*)
★Sweet Gum (*Liquidambar styraciflua*)
Tulip Tree or Yellow Poplar (*Liriodendron tulipifera*)
Cucumber Tree (*Magnolia acuminata*)
Spruce species (*Picea*)
★Pine species (*Pinus*)
★American Plane Tree (*Platanus occidentalis*)
★London Plane Tree (*Platanus acerifolia*)
Poplar species (*Populus*)
Black or Rum Cherry (*Prunus serotina*)
★Douglas Fir (*Pseudotsuga menziesii*)
Bur Oak (*Quercus macrocarpa*)
★Pin Oak (*Quercus palustris*)
★White Oak (*Quercus alba*)
★Japanese Pagoda Tree (*Sophora japonica*)
Common Bald Cypress (*Taxodium distichum*)
American Linden (*Tilia americana*)
★American Elm (*Ulmus americana*)

Trees Classified by Form

Pyramidal

Fir species (*Abies*)
American Holly (*Ilex opaca*)
Eastern Red Cedar (*Juniperus virginiana*)
★Larch species (*Larix*)
★Sweet Gum (*Liquidambar styraciflua*)
★Magnolia species (*Magnolia*)
Hop-Hornbeam (*Ostrya virginiana*)
Colorado Spruce (*Picea pungens*)
Norway Spruce (*Picea abies*)
★Pyramidal Austrian Pine (*Pinus nigra pyramidalis*)
Red or Norway Pine (*Pinus resinosa*)
★Douglas Fir (*Pseudotsuga taxifolia*)
★Pin Oak (*Quercus palustris*)

Common Bald Cypress (*Taxodium distichum*)
★Linden species (*Tilia*)
Arbor-vitae species (*Thuja*)
Smooth-leaved Elm varieties (*Ulmus carpinifolia*)

Columnar

Ascending Norway Maple (*Acer platanoides ascendens*)
Columnar Norway Maple (*Acer platanoides columnare*)
Erect Norway Maple (*Acer platanoides erectum*)
★Columnar Red Maple (*Acer rubrum columnare*)
Sentry Maple (*Acer saccharum monumentale*)
Fastigiate European Hornbeam (*Carpinus betulus fastigiata*)
Fastigiate Washington Hawthorn (*Crataegus phaenopyrum fastigiata*)
★Sentry Ginkgo (*Ginkgo biloba fastigiata*)
Blue Columnar Chinese Juniper (*Juniperus chinensis columnaris*)
Fastigiate Red Cedar (*Juniperus virginiana pyramidalis*)
Schott Red Cedar (*Juniperus virginiana schotti*)
Fastigiate White Pine (*Pinus strobus fastigiata*)
Fastigiate Scotch Pine (*Pinus sylvestris fastigiata*)
Bolleana Poplar (*Populus alba pyramidalis*)
★Lombardy Poplar (*Populus nigra italica*)
Fastigiate Simon Poplar (*Populus simoni fastigiata*)
Fastigiate English Oak (*Quercus robur fastigiata*)
Common Bald Cypress (*Taxodium distichum*)
Columnar Big-leaf Linden (*Tilia platyphyllos fastigiata*)

Weeping

★Slender European Birch (*Betula pendula tristis*)
Young's Birch (*Betula pendula youngi*)
Weeping Red Cedar (*Juniperus virginiana pendula*)
Weeping Mulberry (*Morus alba pendula*)
Koster Weeping Blue Spruce (*Picea pungens kosteriana*)
Weeping White Pine (*Pinus strobus pendula*)
Weeping Black Cherry (*Prunus serotina pendula*)
Weeping Higan Cherry (*Prunus subhirtella pendula*)
"Yaeshidare" Cherry (*Prunus subhirtella pendula flora plena*)
Weeping Douglas Fir (*Pseudotsuga menziesii pendula*)
Golden Weeping Willow (*Salix alba tristis*)
Wisconsin or Niobe Weeping Willow (*Salix blanda*)
Thurlow Weeping Willow (*Salix elegantissma*)
Weeping Japanese Pagoda Tree (*Sophora japonica pendula*)
Weeping European Mountain Ash (*Sorbus aucuparia pendula*)
Weeping American Elm (*Ulmus americana pendula*)

Rounded or Globe-Shaped

Globe Norway Maple (*Acer platanoides globosum*)
Cornelian Cherry (*Cornus mas*)
Japanese Cornel (*Cornus officinalis*)
Single Seed Hawthorn (*Crataegus monogyna inermis*)
★Saucer Magnolia (*Magnolia soulangeana*)
★Crab Apple species (*Malus*)
★White Oak (*Quercus alba*)
Mossycup Oak (*Quercus macrocarpa*)
Umbrella Black Locust (*Robinia pseudoadacia umbraculifera*)
Koopmann Elm (*Ulmus carpinifolia koopmanni*)
Globe Smooth-leaved Elm (*Ulmus carpinifolia umbraculifera*)

With Horizontal Branching

White Fir (*Abies concolor*)
Eastern Redbud (*Cercis canadensis*)
★Flowering Dogwood (*Cornus florida*)
★Hawthorn species (*Crataegus*)
Colorado Spruce (*Picea pungens*)
★Eastern White Pine (*Pinus strobus*)
★White Oak (*Quercus alba*)
★Pin Oak (*Quercus palustris*)
Common Bald Cypress (*Taxodium distichum*)

Trees Classified by Color of Blossom

Yellow

*Golden Rain Tree (*Koelreuteria paniculata*)

White
*Shadblow Serviceberry (*Amelanchier canadensis*)
White Redbud (*Cercis canadensis alba*)
*American Yellow-wood (*Cladrastis lutea*)
*Japanese Dogwood (*Cornus kousa*)
Washington Hawthorn (*Crataegus phaenopyrum*)
*Star Magnolia (*Magnolia stellata*)
Arnold Crab Apple (*Malus arnoldiana*)
*Siberian Crab Apple (*Malus baccata*)
Sargent Crab Apple (*Malus sargenti*)
Thundercloud Plum (*Prunus cerasifera* "Thunder-cloud")
Sour Cherry (*Prunus cerasus*)
Yoshino Cherry (*Prunus yedoensis*)
Bradford Callery Pear (*Pyrus calleryana* "Bradford")
*Common Pear (*Pyrus communis*)
*Japanese Pagoda Tree (*Sophora japonica*)
European Mountain Ash (*Sorbus aucuparia*)

Pink
Wither's Pink Redbud (*Cercis canadensis* "Wither's Pink Charm")
Red Flowering Dogwood (*Cornus florida rubra*)
Toba Hawthorn (*Crataegus mordenensis* "Toba")
*Saucer Magnolia (*Magnolia soulangeana*)
*Japanese Flowering Crab Apple (*Malus floribunda*)
Hopa Crab Apple (*Malus* "Hopa")
Katherine Crab Apple (*Malus* "Katherine")
Prince Georges Crab Apple (*Malus* "Prince Georges")
*Common Apple (*Malus pumila*)
Blireiana Plum (*Prunus blireiana*)
Sargent Cherry (*Prunus sargenti*)
Amanogawa Cherry (*Prunus serrulata* "Amano-gawa")
Kwanzan Cherry (*Prunus serrulata* "Kwanzan")
Autumn Cherry (*Prunus subhirtella autumnalis*)
Weeping Cherry (*Prunus subhirtella pendula*)

Red
Ruby Horse-Chestnut (*Aesculus carnea briotti*)
Red Buckeye (*Aesculus pavia*)
Paul's Scarlet Hawthorn (*Crataegus oxyacantha pauli*)
Alexandrina Magnolia (*Magnolia soulangeana* "Alexandrina")
Almey Crab Apple (*Malus* "Almey")
Carmine Crab Apple (*Malus atrosanguinea*)

Trees with Bright Red Fruit

*Flowering Dogwood (*Cornus florida*)
Kansas Hawthorn (*Crataegus coccinioides*)
Downy Hawthorn (*Crataegus mollis*)
Washington Hawthorn (*Crataegus phaenopyrum*)
American Holly (*Ilex opaca*)
*Siberian Crab Apple (*Malus baccata*)
Almey Crab Apple (*Malus* "Almey")
Hopa Crab Apple (*Malus* "Hopa")
*Common Apple (*Malus pumila*)
Sargent Crab Apple (*Malus sargenti*)

Trees Classified by Color of Summer Foliage

Blue
White Fir (*Abies concolor*)
Western Red Cedar (*Juniperus scopulorum* var. "Chandler Blue")
Eastern Red Cedar (*Juniperus virginiana* var. *Burki*)
Colorado Blue Spruce (*Picea pungens* var. *Glauca*)

Silver to Gray
Russian Olive (*Elaeagnus angustifolia*)
White Poplar (*Populus alba*)

Red to Purple
Crimson King Maple (*Acer platanoides* "Crimson King")
Schwedler Maple (*Acer platanoides schwedleri*)
Rubylace Locust (*Gleditsia triacanthos inermis* "Rubylace")
Purple Crab Apple (*Malus purpurea*)
Pissard Plum (*Prunus cerasifera atropurpurea*)

Thundercloud Plum (*Prunus cerasifera nigra* "Thundercloud")
Woods Myrobalan Plum (*Prunus cerasifera woodi*)
Blood-leaf Peach (*Prunus persica atropurpurea*)
Purple English Oak (*Quercus robur atropurpurea*)

Trees Classified by Color of Fall Foliage

Yellow
Norway Maple (*Acer platanoides* var.)
*Sugar Maple (*Acer saccharum*)
Ohio Buckeye (orange) (*Aesculus glabra*)
Texas Buckeye (*Aesculus arguta*)
*Birch species (*Betula*)
Hickory species (*Carya*)
Chinese Chestnut (*Castanea mollissima*)
Redbud species (*Cercis*)
Fringetree (*Chionanthus virginicus*)
*American Yellow-wood (*Cladrastis lutea*)
White Ash (purple to yellow) (*Fraxinus americana*)
*Ginkgo (*Ginkgo biloba*)
Tulip Tree (*Liriodendron tulipifera*)
*Star Magnolia (bronze) (*Magnolia stellata*)
*Willow species (*Salix*)

Red
Amur Maple (*Acer ginnala*)
*Japanese Maple (*Acer palmatum* var.)
*Red Maple (*Acer rubrum*)
*Sugar Maple (*Acer saccharum*)
Tatarian Maple (*Acer tataricum*)
*Shadblow Serviceberry (*Amelanchier canadensis*)
Hornbeam species (*Carpinus*)
*Flowering Dogwood (*Cornus florida*)
American Smoke Tree (*Cotinus americanus*)
Washington Hawthorn (*Crataegus phaenopyrum*)
*Sweet Gum (*Liquidambar styraciflua*)
Dawson Crab Apple (*Malus dawsoniana*)
*Cherry species (*Prunus*)
Red Oak (*Quercus borealis*)
Scarlet Oak (*Quercus coccinea*)
*Pin Oak (*Quercus palustris*)
Sassafras (*Sassafras albidum*)

Purple
White Ash (*Fraxinus americana*)
*Sweet Gum (*Liquidambar styraciflua*)
*Common Pear (*Pyrus communis*)
*White Oak (*Quercus alba*)

Trees with Interesting Bark

Gray
*Red Maple (*Acer rubrum*)
*Serviceberry species (*Amelanchier*)
Hornbeam species (*Carpinus*)
Hackberry species (*Celtis*)
*American Yellow-wood (*Cladrastis lutea*)
*Hawthorn species (*Crataegus*)
American Holly (*Ilex opaca*)
English or Persian Walnut (*Juglans regia*)
Cucumber Tree (*Magnolia acuminata*)
*Saucer Magnolia (*Magnolia soulangeana*)
Red Oak (young trunk and branches) (*Quercus borealis*)
Black Oak (young trunk and branches) (*Quercus velutina*)
Mountain Ash species (*Sorbus*)

White
*Canoe Birch (*Betula papyrifera*)
*American Plane Tree (*Platanus occidentalis*)
*London Plane Tree (*Platanus acerifolia*)

Red
Japanese Red Pine (*Pinus densiflora*)
Scotch Pine (*Pinus sylvestris*)
Red or Norway Pine (*Pinus resinosa*)

Reddish Brown
Sargent Cherry (*Prunus sargenti*)

Yellow
Wisconsin or Niobe Weeping Willow (*Salix blanda*)

Corky
Corkbark Elm (*Ulmus campestris suberosa*)
Cork Elm (*Ulmus racemosa*)

Flaking
*Birch species (*Betula*)
Shagbark Hickory (*Carya ovata*)
Shellbark Hickory (*Carya laciniosa*)
Russian Olive (*Elaeagnus angustifolia*)
Eastern Red Cedar (*Juniperus virginiana*)
*American Plane Tree (*Platanus occidentalis*)

Trees for the City

White Fir (*Abies concolor*)
Hedge Maple (*Acer campestre*)
Box-Elder (*Acer negundo*)
Norway Maple (*Acer platanoides*)
*Horse-Chestnut (Buckeye) (*Aesculus*)
*Tree of Heaven (*Ailanthus glandulosa*)
Hackberry (*Celtis occidentalis*)
*Downy Hawthorn (*Crataegus mollis*)
*Washington Hawthorn (*Crataegus phaenopyrum*)
Russian Olive (*Elaeagnus angustifolia*)
White Ash (*Fraxinus americana*)
Green Ash (*Fraxinus pennsylvanica*)
*Ginkgo (*Ginkgo biloba*)
Thornless Honey-Locust (*Gleditsia triacanthos inermis*)
*Golden Rain Tree (*Koelreuteria paniculata*)
*Saucer Magnolia (*Magnolia soulangeana*)
*Star Magnolia (*Magnolia stellata*)
*Crab Apple (*Malus* var.)
Colorado Spruce (*Picea pungens*)
*London Plane Tree (*Platanus acerifolia*)
White Poplar (*Populus alba*)
*Lombardy Poplar (*Populus nigra italica*)
Red Oak (*Quercus borealis*)
*Black Locust (*Robinia pseudoacacia*)
*Japanese Pagoda Tree (*Sophora japonica*)
*Little-leaf Linden (*Tilia cordata*)
*Silver Linden (*Tilia tomentosa*)

Trees for Wide Streets
*Sugar Maple (*Acer saccharum*)
Sugar Hackberry (*Celtis laevigata*)
White Ash (*Fraxinus americana*)
Green Ash ((*Fraxinus pennsylvanica lanceolata*)
*Ginkgo (*Ginkgo biloba*)
*Common Honey-Locust (*Gleditsia triacanthos*)
Tulip Tree (*Liriodendron tulipifera*)
*Eastern White Pine (*Pinus strobus*)
*London Plane Tree (*Platanus acerifolia*)
White Poplar (*Populus alba*)
Red Oak (*Quercus borealis*)
*Pin Oak (*Quercus palustris*)
Willow Oak (*Quercus phellos*)

Trees for Medium Streets
Norway Maple (*Acer platanoides*)
*Sweet Gum (*Liquidambar styraciflua*)
Hop-Hornbeam (*Ostrya virginiana*)
Simon Poplar (*Populus simoni*)
Scarlet Oak (*Quercus coccinea*)
Willow Oak (*Quercus phellos*)
*Black Locust (*Robinia pseudoacacia*)
Sassafras (*Sassafras albidum officinale*)
*Japanese Pagoda Tree (*Sophora japonica*)
*Linden species (*Tilia*)

Trees for Suburban Streets
Amur Maple (*Acer ginnala*)
Tatarian Maple (*Acer tataricum*)
American Hornbeam (*Carpinus caroliniana*)
*Flowering Dogwood (*Cornus florida*)
*Hawthorn species (*Crataegus*)
Korean Evodia (*Evodia danielli*)
*Golden Rain Tree (*Koelreuteria paniculata*)
Columnar Sargent Cherry (*Prunus sargenti columnaris*)
Smooth-leaved Elm varieties (*Ulmus carpinifolia*)

Soil Tolerance

Trees Tolerating Acid Soil
*Japanese Maple (*Acer palmatum*)

*Flowering Dogwood (*Cornus florida* var.)
Red Oak (*Quercus borealis*)
Scarlet Oak (*Quercus coccinea*)
*Willow Oak (*Quercus phellos*)
*Pin Oak (*Quercus palustris*)

Trees Tolerating Moist Soil
*Red Maple (*Acer rubrum*)
Alder species (*Alnus*)
Holly species (*Ilex*)
*Sweet Gum (*Liquidambar styraciflua*)
Swamp White Oak (*Quercus bicolor*)
*Willow species (*Salix*)
Common Bald Cypress (*Taxodium distichum*)
American Arbor-vitae (*Thuja occidentalis*)

Trees Tolerating Dry or Poor Soil
Box-Elder (*Acer negundo*)
*Tree of Heaven (*Ailanthus glandulosa*)
Hackberry (*Celtis occidentalis*)
Russian Olive (*Elaeagnus angustifolia*)
Green Ash (*Fraxinus pennsylvanica*)
*Honey-Locust (*Gleditsia triacanthos* var.)
Rocky Mountain Juniper (*Juniperus scopulorum*)

Eastern Red Cedar (*Juniperus virginiana*)
*Golden Rain Tree (*Koelreuteria paniculata*)
Osage-Orange (*Maclura pomifera*)
Jack Pine (*Pinus banksiana*)
Pitch Pine (*Pinus rigida*)
Virginia or Scrub Pine (*Pinus virginiana*)
White Poplar (*Populus alba*)
Chestnut Oak (*Quercus montana*)
*Black Locust (*Robinia pseudoacacia*)
Sassafras (*Sassafras albidum officinale*)
Chinese Elm (*Ulmus parvifolia*)
Siberian Elm (*Ulmus pumila*)

Pest-Resistant Trees
*Tree of Heaven (*Ailanthus altissima*)
Hornbeam species (*Carpinus*)
Cornelian Cherry (*Cornus mas*)
Japanese Cornel (*Cornus officinalis*)
American Smoke Tree (*Cotinus americanus*)
Russian Olive (*Elaeagnus angustifolia*)
*Ginkgo (*Ginkgo biloba*)
Kentucky Coffee Tree (*Gymnocladus dioicus*)
Juniper species (*Juniperus*)
*Golden Rain Tree (*Koelreuteria paniculata*)

*Sweet Gum (*Liquidambar styraciflua*)
Cucumber Tree (*Magnolia acuminata*)
*Star Magnolia (*Magnolia stellata*)
American Hornbeam (*Ostrya virginiana*)

Trees for Hedging or Barriers
European Beech (*Fagus sylvatica*) prunes well.
Leyland Cypress (*Cupressocyparis leylandii*) withstands heavy pruning.
Hawthorn varieties (*Crataegus*) easily pruned, advantage of thorns.
Canadian Hemlock (*Tsuga canadensis*) evergreen.
American Holly (*Ilex opaca*) can be pruned.
European Hornbeam (*Carpinus betulus*) prunes well.
Little-leaf Linden (*Tilia cordata*) tolerates heavy pruning.
Hedge Maple (*Acer campestre*) can be pruned.
Austrian Pine (*Pinus nigra*) plant 10–12 feet on centers, staggered row.
Japanese Black Pine (*Pinus thunbergi*) plant 8 feet on centers, staggered row.
Eastern White Pine (*Pinus strobus*) plant 15 feet on centers, staggered row.

KENTUCKY

State Tree

Tulip Tree or Yellow Poplar (*Liriodendron tulipifera*)

Evergreen Trees

Fir species (*Abies*)
*Cedar species (*Cedrus*)
*Cypress species (*Cupressus*)
Holly species (*Ilex*)
Juniper species (*Juniperus*)
Norway Spruce (*Picea abies*)
*Pine species (*Pinus*)
Arbor-vitae species (*Thuja*)
*Hemlock species (*Tsuga*)

Trees Classified by Height

20–35 Feet
Hedge Maple (*Acer campestre*)
Paperbark Maple (*Acer griseum*)
*Japanese Maple (*Acer palmatum*)
Mountain Maple (*Acer spicatum*)
Tatarian Maple (*Acer tataricum*)
Ohio Buckeye (*Aesculus glabra*)
Apple Serviceberry (*Amelanchier grandiflora*)
*Gray Birch (*Betula populifolia*)
European Hornbeam (*Carpinus betulus globosa*)
Mockernut (*Carya tomentosa*)
Fringetree (*Chionanthus virginicus*)
*Japanese Dogwood (*Cornus kousa*)
Cornealian Cherry (*Cornus mas*)
Japanese Cornel (*Cornus officinalis*)
American Smoke Tree (*Cotinus americanus*)
*Hawthorn species (*Crataegus*)
Russian Olive (*Elaeagnus angustifolia*)
Euonymus species (*Euonymus*)
Korean Evodia (*Evodia danielli*)
Franklinia (*Franklinia alatamaha*)
Flowering Ash (*Fraxinus ornus*)
Carolina Silverbell (*Halesia carolina*)
Possum Haw (*Ilex decidua*)
*Golden Rain Tree (*Koelreuteria paniculata*)
*Laburnum species (*Laburnum*)
Yellow Cucumber Tree (*Magnolia cordata*)
Saucer Magnolia (*Magnolia soulangeana*)
*Star Magnolia (*Magnolia stellata*)
*Crab Apple species (*Malus*)
*Cherry species (*Prunus*)
Black Jack Oak (*Quercus marilandica*)
*Babylon Weeping Willow (*Salix babylonica*)
Japanese Snowbell (*Styrax japonica*)
Asiatic Sweetleaf (*Symplocos paniculata*)

35–75 Feet
Striped Maple or Moosewood (*Acer pennsylvanicum*)
*Red-fruited Tree of Heaven (*Ailanthus altissima erythrocarpa*)
*Shadblow Serviceberry (*Amelanchier canadensis*)
Allegany Serviceberry (*Amelanchier laevis*)
Manchurian Birch (*Betula mandshurica szechuanica*)
Common Paper-Mulberry (*Broussonetia papyrifera*)
European Hornbeam (*Carpinus betulus*)
American Hornbeam (*Carpinus caroliniana*)
Chinese Chestnut (*Castanea mollissima*)
Southern Catalpa (*Catalpa bignoniodes*)
Chinese Toon (*Cedrela sinensis*)
Bunch Hackberry (*Celtis bungeana*)
*Katsura Tree (*Cercidiphyllum japonicum*)
Eastern Redbud (*Cercis canadensis*)
*American Yellow-wood (*Cladrastis lutea*)
*Flowering Dogwood (*Cornus florida*)
Large-leaf Dogwood (*Cornus macrophylla*)
Turkish Filbert (*Corylus columa*)
Cockspur Tree (*Crataegus crus-galli*)
Green Hawthorn (*Crataegus viridis*)
Common Persimmon (*Diospyros virginiana*)
Green Ash (*Fraxinus pennsylvanica lanceolata*)
American Holly (*Ilex opaca*)
Chinese Juniper (*Juniperus chinensis*)
Yulan Magnolia (*Magnolia denudata*)
Kobus Magnolia (*Magnolia kobus borealis*)
Loebner Magnolia (*Magnolia loebneri*)
Big-leaf Magnolia (*Magnolia macrophylla*)
Sweet Bay (*Magnolia virginiana*)
"Cowichan" Crab Apple (*Malus* "Cowichan")
"Dolgo" Crab Apple (*Malus* "Dolgo")
"Makamik" Crab Apple (*Malus* "Makamik")
Cherry Crab Apple (*Malus robusta*)
"Sissipuk" Crab Apple (*Malus* "Sissipuk")
*Sorrel Tree or Sourwood (*Oxydendrum arboreum*)
Empress Tree (*Paulownia tomentosa*)
Virginia or Scrib Pine (*Pinus virginiana*)
Chinese Poplar (*Populus lasiocarpa*)
Simon Poplar (*Populus simoni*)
Sargent Cherry (*Prunus sargenti*)
Yoshino Cherry (*Prunus yedoensis*)
Red Oak (*Quercus borealis*)
Scarlet Oak (*Quercus coccinea*)
Shingle Oak (*Quercus imbricaria*)
*Pin Oak (*Quercus palustris*)
Willow Oak (*Quercus phellos*)
Clammy Locust (*Robinia viscosa*)
Laurel Willow (*Salxi pentandra*)

Sassafras (*Sassafras albidum officinale*)
Korean Mountain Ash (*Sorbus alnifolia*)
Korean Stewartia (*Stewartia koreana*)
American Arbor-vitae (*Thuja occidentalis*)
Oriental Arbor-vitae (*Thuja orientalis*)
*Crimean Linden (*Tilia euchlora*)
*Carolina Hemlock (*Tsuga carolinana*)
Winged or Wahoo Elm (*Ulmus alata*)
Chinese Elm (*Ulmus parvifolia*)

75 Feet or Over
Fir species (*Abies*)
Norway Maple (*Acer platanoides*)
Sycamore Maple (*Acer pseudoplatanus*)
*Red or Swamp Maple (*Acer rubrum*)
Hickory species (*Carya*)
*Cedar species (*Cedrus*)
*Beech species (*Fagus*)
*Ginkgo or Maidenhair Tree (*Ginkgo biloba*)
*Common Honey-Locust (*Gleditsia triacanthos*)
Mountain Silverbell (*Halesia monticola*)
*Sweet Gum (*Liquidambar styraciflua*)
Cucumber Tree (*Magnolia acuminata*)
Dawn Redwood (*Metasequoia glyptostroboides*)
*Black Gum or Black Tupelo (*Nyssa sylvatica*)
*Pine species (*Pinus*)
*Plane Tree species (*Platanus*)
Poplar species (*Populus*)
*Oak species (*Quercus*)
Common Bald Cypress (*Taxodium distichum*)
Japanese Zelkova (*Zelkova serrata*)

Trees Classified by Form

Pyramidal
Fir species (*Abies*)
*Cedar species (*Cedrus*)
*Beech species (*Fagus*)
American Holly (*Ilex opaca*)
Juniper or Red Cedar species (*Juniperus*)
*Sweet Gum (*Liquidambar styraciflua*)
*Magnolia species (*Magnolia*)
Dawn Redwood (*Metasequoia glyptostroboides*)
*Black Tupelo or Black Gum (*Nyssa sylvatica*)
Hop-Hornbeam (*Ostrya virginiana*)
*Sorrel Tree or Sourwood (*Oxydendrum arboreum*)
*Pin Oak (*Quercus palustris*)
*Linden species (*Tilia*)
Arbor-vitae species (*Thuja*)
*Hemlock species (*Tsuga*)
Smooth-leaved Elm varieties (*Ulmus carpinifolia*)

Columnar

Ascending Norway Maple (*Acer platanoides ascendens*)
★Columnar Norway Maple (*Acer platanoides columnare*)
Erect Norway Maple (*Acer platanoides erectum*)
Columnar Red Maple (*Acer rubrum columnare*)
Fastigiate European Hornbeam (*Carpinus betulus fastigiata*)
Fastigiate Washington Hawthorn (*Crataegus phaenopyrum fastigiata*)
Dawyck Beech (*Fagus sylvatica fastigiata*)
★Sentry Ginkgo (*Ginkgo biloba fastigiata*)
Fastigiate Red Cedar (*Juniperus virginiana pyramidalis*)
Schott Red Cedar (*Juniperus virginiana schotti*)
Bolleana Poplar (*Populus alba pyramidalis*)
★Lombardy Poplar (*Populus nigra italica*)
"Amanogawa" Cherry (*Prunus serrulata* "Amanogawa")
Fastigiate English Oak (*Quercus robur fastigiata*)
Shipmast Locust (*Robinia pseudoacacia rectissima*)
Common Bald Cypress (*Taxodium distichum*)

Weeping
Weeping European Hornbeam (*Carpinus betulus pendula*)
★Weeping Beech (*Fagus sylvatica pendula*)
Weeping Red Cedar (*Juniperus virginiana pendula*)
"Exzellenz Thiel" Crab Apple (*Malus* "Exzellenz Thiel")
Weeping White Pine (*Pinus strobus pendula*)
Weeping Black Cherry (*Prunus serotina pendula*)
Weeping Higan Cherry (*Prunus subhirtella pendula flora plena*)
"Yaeshidare" Cherry (*Prunus subhirtella pendula flora plena*)
Weeping Yoshino Cherry (*Prunus yedoensis perpendens*)
Weeping Douglas Fir (*Pseudotsuga menziesii pendula*)
★Babylon Weeping Willow (*Salix babylonica*)
Weeping Japanese Pagoda Tree (*Sophora japonica pendula*)
Pendant Silver Linden (*Tilia petiolaris*)
Sargent Hemlock (*Tsuga canadensis pendula*)
Weeping American Elm (*Ulmus americana pendula*)

Rounded or Globe-Shaped
★Japanese Maple (*Acer palmatum*)
Globe Norway Maple (*Acer platanoides globosum*)
Globe European Hornbeam (*Carpinus betulus globosa*)
Cornelian Cherry (*Cornus mas*)
Japanese Cornel (*Cornus officinalis*)
Single Seed Hawthorn (*Crataegus monogyna inermis*)
★Saucer Magnolia (*Magnolia soulangeana*)
★Crab Apple species (*Malus*)
★White Oak (*Quercus alba*)
Umbrella Black Locust (*Robinia pseudoacacia umbraculifera*)
Sargent Hemlock (*Tsuga canadensis sargenti*)

With Horizontal Branching
Fir species (*Abies*)
Silk Tree (*Albizzia julibrissin*)
★Cedar species (*Cedrus*)
Eastern Redbud (*Cercis canadensis*)
★Flowering Dogwood (*Cornus florida*)
Japanese Dogwood (*Cornus kousa*)
★Hawthorn species (*Crataegus*)
Dawn Redwood (*Metasequoia glyptostroboides*)
★Black Tupelo or Black Gum (*Nyssa sylvatica*)
★Eastern White Pine (*Pinus strobus*)
★White Oak (*Quercus alba*)
★Pin Oak (*Quercus palustris*)
Common Bald Cypress (*Taxodium distichum*)

Trees Classified by Color of Blossom

Yellow
★Golden Rain Tree (*Koelreuteria paniculata*)
★Laburnum (*Laburnum vossi*)

White
★Shadblow Serviceberry (*Amelanchier canadensis*)
White Bud (*Cercis canadensis alba*)
★American Yellow-wood (*Cladrastis lutea*)

★Japanese Dogwood (*Cornus kousa*)
Washington Hawthorn (*Crataegus phaenopyrum*)
Carolina Silverbell (*Halesia carolina*)
Yulan Magnolia (*Magnolia denudata*)
★Star Magnolia (*Magnolia stellata*)
Sweet Bay (*Magnolia virginiana*)
Arnold Crab Apple (*Malus arnoldiana*)
Tea Crab Apple (*Malus hupehensis*)
Sargent Crab Apple (*Malus sargenti*)
★Sorrel Tree (*Oxydendrum arboreum*)
Thundercloud Plum (*Prunus cerasifera* "Thundercloud")
Mount Fuji Cherry (*Prunus serrulata* "Shirotae")
Yoshino Cherry (*Prunus yedoensis*)
Bradford Callery Pear (*Pryus calleryana* "Bradford")
★Common Pear (*Pyrus communis*)
★Japanese Pagoda Tree (*Sophora japonica*)
Korean Mountain Ash (*Sorbus alnifolia*)
Japanese Snowbell (*Styrax japonica*)

Pink
Wither's Pink Redbud (*Cercis canadensis* "Wither's Pink Charm")
Red Flowering Dogwood (*Cornus florida rubra*)
★Saucer Magnolia (*Magnolia soulangeana*)
★Japanese Flowering Crab Apple (*Malus floribunda*)
Katherine Crab Apple (*Malus* "Katherine")
Prince Georges Crab Apple (*Malus* "Prince Georges")
★Common Apple (*Malus pumila*)
Blireiana Plum (*Prunus blireiana*)
Sargent Cherry (*Prunus sargenti*)
Amanogawa Cherry (*Prunus serrulata* "Amanogawa")
Kwanzan Cherry (*Prunus serrulata* "Kwanzan")
Autumn Cherry (*Prunus subhirtella autumnalis*)
Weeping Cherry (*Prunus subhirtella pendula*)

Red
Ruby Horse-Chestnut (*Aesculus carnea briotti*)
Paul's Scarlet Hawthorn (*Crataegus oxyacantha pauli*)
Alexandria Magnolia (*Magnolia soulangeana* "Alexandrina")
Almey Crab Apple (*Malus* "Almey")
Carmine Crab Apple (*Malus atrosanguinea*)

Trees with Bright Red Fruit
★Flowering Dogwood (*Cornus florida*)
Japanese Dogwood (*Cornus kousa*)
Downy Hawthorn (*Crataegus mollis*)
Washington Hawthorn (*Crataegus phaenopyrum*)
American Holly (*Ilex opaca*)
Almey Crab Apple (*Malus* "Almey")
Hopa Crab Apple (*Malus* "Hopa")
★Common Apple (*Malus pumila*)
Sargent Crab Apple (*Malus sargenti*)
Korean Mountain Ash (*Sorbus alnifolia*)

Trees Classified by Color of Summer Foliage

Blue
White Fir (*Abies concolor*)
★Blue Atlas Cedar (*Cedrus atlantica glauca*)
Steel Lawson Cypress (*Chamaecyparis lawsonia glauca*)
Eastern Red Cedar (*Juniperus virginiana* var. *Burki*)

Red to Purple
Blood-leaf Japanese Maple (*Acer palmatum atropurpureum*)
Schwedler Maple (*Acer platanoides schwedleri*)
Crimson King Maple (*Acer platanoides* "Crimson King")
Purple-leaf Sycamore Maple (*Acer pseudoplatanus*)
Purple Beech (*Fagus sylvatica atropunicea*)
Weeping Purple Beech (*Fagus sylvatica purpureopendula*)
River's Purple Beech (*Fagus sylvatica riversi*)
Rubylace Locust (*Gleditsia triacanthos inermis* "Rubylace")
Purple Crab Apple (*Malus purpurea*)
Blireiana Plum (*Prunus blireiana*)
Pissard Plum (*Prunus cerasifera* "Pissard")

Thundercloud Plum (*Prunus cerasifera nigra* "Thundercloud")
Woods Myrobalan Plum (*Prunus cerasifera woodi*)
Blood-leaf Peach (*Prunus persica atropurpurea*)
Purple English Oak (*Quercus robur atropurpurea*)

Trees Classified by Color of Fall Foliage

Yellow
Striped Maple or Moosewood (*Acer pennsylvanicum*)
Norway Maple (*Acer platanoides*)
Apple Serviceberry (yellow-orange) (*Amelanchier grandiflora*)
★Birches (*Betula*)
Hickory species (*Carya*)
Chinese Chestnut (*Castanea mollissima*)
★Katsura Tree (yellow to scarlet) (*Cercidiphyllum japonicum*)
Redbud species (*Cercis*)
Fringetree (*Chionanthus virginicus*)
★American Yellow-wood (*Cladrastis lutea*)
★American Beech (*Fagus grandifolia*)
★European Beech (*Fagus sylvatica*)
White Ash (purple to yellow) (*Fraxinus americana*)
★Ginkgo (*Ginkgo biloba*)
★Star Magnolia (bronze) (*Magnolia stellata*)
★Willow species (*Salix*)

Red
Amur Maple (*Acer ginnala*)
★Red Maple (*Acer rubrum*)
★Japanese Maple (*Acer palmatum varieties*)
Tatarian Maple (*Acer tataricum*)
★Shadblow Serviceberry (*Amelanchier canadensis*)
Hornbeam species (*Carpinus*)
★Flowering Dogwood (*Cornus florida*)
Japanese Dogwood (*Cornus kousa*)
American Smoke Tree (*Cotinus americanus*)
Washington Hawthorn (*Crataegus phaenopyrum*)
★Sweet Gum (*Liquidambar styraciflua*)
★Black Tupelo or Black Gum (*Nyssa sylvatica*)
★Sorrel Tree (*Osydendrum arboreum*)
★Cherry species (*Prunus*)
Bradford Callery Pear (*Pyrus calleryana* "Bradford")
★White Oak (*Quercus alba*)
Red Oak (*Quercus borealis*)
Scarlet Oak (*Quercus coccinea*)
★Pin Oak (*Quercus palustris*)
Sassafras (*Sassafras albidum*)
Korean Stewartia (orange to red) (*Stewartia koreana*)

Purple
White Ash (*Fraxinus americana*)
★Sweet Gum (*Liquidambar styraciflua*)
Common Pear (*Pyrus communis*)

Silver to Grayish
Russian Olive (*Elaeagnus angustifolia*)
White Poplar (*Populus alba*)
★Silver Linden (*Tilia tomentosa*)

Trees with Interesting Bark

Gray
★Red Maple (*Acer rubrum*)
★Serviceberry species (*Amelanchier*)
Hackberry species (*Celtis*)
★American Yellow-wood (*Cladrastis lutea*)
★Hawthorn species (*Crataegus*)
★Beech species (*Fagus*)
American Holly (*Ilex opaca*)
English or Persian Walnut (*Juglans regia*)
Cucumber Tree (*Magnolia acuminata*)
★Saucer Magnolia (*Magnolia soulangeana*)
Red Oak (young trunk and branches) (*Quercus borealis*)
Black Oak (young trunk and branches) (*Quercus veltutina*)
Mountain Ash species (*Sorbus*)

Red
Sargent Cherry (*Prunus sargenti*)

Yellow
Wisconsin or Niobe Weeping Willow (*Salix blanda*)

Green
*Babylon Weeping Willow (*Salix babylonica*)

Corky
*Amur Cork (*Phellodendron amurense*)

Flaking
Paperbark Maple (*Acer griseum*)
Shagbark Hickory (*Carya ovata*)
Eastern Red Cedar (*Juniperus virginiana*)
Plane Tree species (*Platanus*)

Trees for the City

Hedge Maple (*Acer campestre*)
Box-Elder (*Acer negundo*)
Norway Maple (*Acer platanoides*)
Sycamore Maple (*Acer pseudoplatanus*)
*Horse-Chestnut (Buckeye) (*Aesculus*)
*Tree of Heaven (*Ailanthus*)
Silk Tree (*Albizzia julibrissin*)
Catalpa (*Catalpa*)
Chinese Toon (*Cedrela sinensis*)
Hackberry (*Celtis*)
*Downy Hawthorn (*Crataegus mollis*)
Washington Hawthorn (*Crataegus phaenopyrum*)
Russian Olive (*Elaeagnus angustifolia*)
White Ash (*Fraxinus americana*)
Green Ash (*Fraxinus pennsylvanica*)
*Ginkgo (*Ginkgo biloba*)
Thornless Honey-Locust (*Gleditsia triacanthos inermis*)
*Golden Rain Tree (*Koelreuteria paniculata*)
*Saucer Magnolia (*Magnolia soulangeana*)
*Star Magnolia (*Magnolia stellata*)
*Crab Apple (*Malus* var.)
White Poplar (*Populus alba*)
*Lombardy Poplar (*Populus nigra italica*)
*Amur Cork (*Phellodendron amurense*)
*London Plane Tree (*Platanus acerifolia*)
Bradford Callery Pear (*Pyrus calleryana* "Bradford")
Red Oak (*Quercus borealis*)
*Black Locust (*Robinia pseudoacacia*)
*Little-leaf Linden (*Tilia cordata*)
*Crimean Linden (*Tilia euchlora*)
*Silver Linden (*Tilia tomentosa*)

Trees for Wide Streets

White Ash (*Fraxinus americana*)
Green Ash (*Fraxinus pennsylvanica lanceolata*)
*Ginkgo (*Ginkgo biloba*)
*Common Honey-Locust (*Gleditsia triacanthos*)
Tulip Tree (*Liriodendron tulipifera*)
*Eastern White Pine (*Pinus strobus*)
*London Plane Tree (*Platanus acerifola*)
*Oriental Plane Tree (*Platanus orientalis*)
White Poplar (*Populus alba*)
Sargent Cherry (*Prunus sargenti*)

Pin Oak (*Quercus phellos*)
Japanese Zelkova (*Zelkova serrata*)

Trees for Medium Streets
Norway Maple (*Acer platanoides*)
Mountain Silverbell (*Halesia monticola*)
*Sweet Gum (*Liquidambar styraciflua*)
Hop-Hornbeam (*Ostrya virginiana*)
*Sorrel Tree or Sourwood (*Oxydendrum arboreum*)
Simon Poplar (*Populus simoni*)
Scarlet Oak (*Quercus coccinea*)
Willow Oak (*Quercus phellos*)
*Black Locust (*Robinia pseudoacacia*)
*Linden species (*Tilia*)
Winged Elm (*Ulmus alata*)

Trees for Suburban Streets
Hedge Maple (*Acer campestre*)
American Hornbeam (*Carpinus caroliniana*)
Pyramid European Hornbeam (*Carpinus betulus fastigiata*)
Globe European Hornbeam (*Carpinus betulus globosa*)
Fringetree (*Chionanthus virginicus*)
*Flowering Dogwood (*Cornus florida*)
*Hawthorn species (*Crataegus*)
Korean Evodia (*Evodia danielli*)
Carolina Silverbell (*Halesia carolina*)
*Golden Rain Tree (*Koelreuteria paniculata*)
Columnar Sargent Cherry (*Prunus sargenti columnaris*)
Oriental Cherry (*Prunus serrulata*)
Smooth-leaved Elm varieties (*Ulmus carpinifolia*)

Soil Tolerance

Trees Tolerating Acid Soil

*Japanese Maple (*Acer palmatum*)
*Flowering Dogwood (*Cornus florida*)
Japanese Dogwood (*Cornus kousa*)
*European Beech (*Fagus sylvatica*)
Sweet Bay (*Magnolia virginiana*)
*Black Tupelo (*Nyssa sylvatica*)
*Sorrel Tree (*Oxydendrum arboreum*)
Red Oak (*Quercus borealis*)
Scarlet Oak (*Quercus coccinea*)
*Pin Oak (*Quercus palustris*)
Willow Oak (*Quercus phellos*)
Japanese Stewartia (*Stewartia pseudocamellia*)

Trees Tolerating Moist Soil

*Red Maple (*Acer rubrum*)
Alder species (*Alnus*)
River Birch (*Betula nigra*)
*Sweet Gum (*Liquidambar styraciflua*)
Sweet Bay (*Magnolia virginiana*)
*Black Tupelo or Black Gum (*Nyssa sylvatica*)
Swamp White Oak (*Quercus bicolor*)
*Willow species (*Salix*)

Common Bald Cypress (*Taxodium distichum*)
American Arbor-vitae (*Thuja occidentalis*)

Trees Tolerating Dry or Poor Soil
Box-Elder (*Acer negundo*)
*Tree of Heaven (*Ailanthus*)
Silk Tree (*Albizzia julibrissin*)
Common Paper-Mulberry (*Broussonetia papyrifera*)
Russian Olive (*Elaeagnus angustifolia*)
Green Ash (*Fraxinus pennsylvanica*)
Modesto Ash (*Fraxinus velutina* "Modesto")
*Honey-Locust (*Gleditsia triacanthos* var.)
Eastern Red Cedar (*Juniperus virginiana*)
*Golden Rain Tree (*Koelreuteria paniculata*)
White Poplar (*Populus alba*)
Black Jack Oak (*Quercus marilandica*)
*Black Locust (*Robinia pseudoacacia*)
Sassafras (*Sassafras albidum officinale*)
Chinese Elm (*Ulmus parvifolia*)

Pest-Resistant Trees

*Tree of Heaven (*Ailanthus altissima*)
Hornbeam species (*Carpinus*)
*Cedar species (*Cedrus*)
Cornelian Cherry (*Cornus mas*)
Japanese Cornel (*Cornus officinalis*)
American Smoke Tree (*Cotinus americanus*)
Russian Olive (*Elaeagnus angustifolia*)
*Fig species (*Ficus*)
Franklinia (*Franklinia alatamaha*)
*Ginkgo (*Ginkgo biloba*)
*Golden Rain Tree (*Koelreuteria paniculata*)
*Laburnum species (*Laburnum*)
*Sweet Gum (*Liquidambar styraciflua*)
*Star Magnolia (*Magnolia stellata*)
Hop-Hornbeam species (*Ostrya*))

Trees for Hedging or Barriers

European Beech (*Fagus sylvatica*) prunes well.
Leyland Cypress (*Cupressocyparis leylandii*) withstands heavy pruning.
Hawthorn varieties (*Crataegus*) easily pruned, advantage of thorns.
Canadian Hemlock (*Tsuga canadensis*) evergreen.
American Holly (*Ilex opaca*) can be pruned.
European Hornbeam (*Carpinus betulus*) prunes well.
Little-leaf Linden (*Tilia cordata*) tolerates heavy pruning.
Hedge Maple (*Acer campestre*) can be pruned.
Austrian Pine (*Pinus nigra*) plant 10–12 feet on centers, staggered row.
Japanese Black Pine (*Pinus thunbergi*) plant 8 feet on centers, staggered row.
Eastern White Pine (*Pinus strobus*) plant 15 feet on centers, staggered row.

LOUISIANA

State Tree

Bald Cypress (*Taxodium distichum*)

Evergreen Trees

Acacia species (*Acacia*)
Monkey-Puzzle Tree (*Araucaria araucana*)
Strawberry Tree (*Arbutus unedo*)
Lemon Bottlebrush (*Callistemon lanceolatus*)
Camellia species (*Camellia*)
Giant Evergreen Chinquapin (*Castanopsis chrysophylla*)
*Australian Pine (*Casuarina equisetifolia*)
*Deodar Cedar (*Cedrus deodara*)
Camphor Tree (*Cinnamomum camphora*)
Citrus species (*Citrus*)
Evergreen Dogwood (*Cornus capitata*)
Common China Fir (*Cunninghamia lanceolata*)
*Cypress species (*Cupressus*)
Loquat (*Eriobotrya japonica*)

Brush-Cherry Eugenia (*Eugenia paniculata*)
Loblolly Bay Gordonia (*Gordonia lasianthus*)
Holly species (*Ilex*)
Juniper species (*Juniperus*)
Fortune Keteleeria (*Keteleeria fortunei*)
Paterson Sugar Plum Tree (*Lagunaria patersoni*)
Australian Tea Tree (*Leptospermum laevigatum*)
*Southern Magnolia (*Magnolia grandiflora*)
Chile Mayten Tree (*Maytens boaria*)
California Bayberry (*Myrica californica*)
*Common Olive (*Olea europaea*)
Chinese Photinia (*Photinia serrulata*)
*Pine species (*Pinus*)
Yew Podocarpus (*Podocarpus macrophyllus*)
Portugal Laurel (*Prunus lusitanica*)
Holly Oak (*Quercus ilex*)
Cork Oak (*Quercus suber*)
*Live Oak (*Quercus virginiana*)
Palmetto (*Sabal palmetto*)
*Hemlock species (*Tsuga*)

Farkleberry (*Vaccinium arboreum*)

Trees Classified by Height

20–35 Feet
Strawberry Tree (*Arbutus unedo*)
Lemon Bottlebrush (*Callistemon lanceolatus*)
Mockernut (*Carya tomentosa*)
Judas Tree (*Cercis siliquastrum*)
American Smoke Tree (*Cotinus americanus*)
*Hawthorn species (*Crataegus*)
Loquat (*Eriobotrya japonica*)
Common Fig (*Ficus carica*)
Dahoon (*Ilex cassine*)
Possum Haw (*Ilex decidua*)
Yaupon (*Ilex vomitoria*)
Crape-Myrtle (*Lagerstroemia indica*)
Australian Tea Tree (*Leptospermum laevigatum*)
Yellow Cucumber Tree (*Magnolia cordata*)
Oyama Magnolia (*Magnolia sieboldi*)
Wilson Magnolia (*Magnolia wilsoni*)

*Crab Apple species (*Malus*)
Chile Mayten Tree (*Maytenus boaria*)
*Common Olive (*Olea europaea*)
*Cherry species (*Prunus*)
*Babylon Weeping Willow (*Salix babylonica*)
Farkleberry (*Vaccinium arboreum*)

35–75 Feet
Silver Wattle (*Acacia decurrens dealbata*)
Florida Maple (*Acer floridanum*)
Silk Tree (*Albizzia julibrissin*)
Common Camellia (*Camellia japonica*)
Chinese Redbud (*Cercis chinensis*)
Camphor Tree (*Cinnamomum camphora*)
Delavay Clethra (*Clethra delavayi*)
Evergreen Dogwood (*Cornus capitata*)
*Flowering Dogwood (*Cornus florida*)
Common China Fir (*Cunninghamia lanceolata*)
Italian Cypress (*Cupressus sempervirens*)
Kaki Persimmon (*Diospyros kaki*)
Brush-Cherry Eugenia (*Eugenia paniculata*)
Chinese Parasol Tree (*Firmiana simplex*)
Green Ash (*Fraxinus pennsylvanica lanceolata*)
Loblolly Bay Gordonia (*Gordonia lasianthus*)
English Holly (*Ilex aquifolium*)
Dahoon (*Ilex cassine*)
Luster-leaf Holly (*Ilex latifolia*)
Mountain Winterberry (*Ilex montana*)
American Holly (*Ilex opaca*)
Syrian Juniper (*Juniperus drupacea*)
Greek Juniper (*Juniperus excelsa*)
Alligator Juniper (*Juniperus pachyphloea*)
Veitch Magnolia (*Magnolia veitchi*)
Sweet Bay (*Magnolia virginiana*)
Chinaberry (*Pinus halepensis*)
Aleppo Pine (*Pinus halepensis*)
Chinese Pistache (*Pistacia chinensis*)
*Plane Tree species (*Platanus*)
Portugal Laurel (*Prunus lusitanica*)
Holly or Holm Oak (*Quercus ilex*)
Laurel Oak (*Quercus laurifolia*)
Water Oak (*Quercus nigra*)
Willow Oak (*Quercus phellos*)
Cork Oak (*Quercus suber*)
*Live Oak (*Quercus virginiana*)
Clammy Locust (*Robinia viscosa*)
Carolina Hemlock (*Tsuga caroliniana*)

75 Feet or Over
*Red or Swamp Maple (*Acer rubrum*)
Monkey-Puzzle Tree (*Araucaria araucana*)
Shagbark Hickory (*Carya ovata*)
White Ash (*Fraxinus americana*)
Campbell Magnolia (*Magnolia campbelli*)
*Southern Magnoli (*Magnolia grandiflora*)
Palmetto (*Sabal palmetto*)
Italian Stone Pine (*Pinus pinea*)
*Oak species (*Quercus*)
*Elm species (*Ulmus*)

Trees Classified by Form

Pyramidal
Italian Cypress (*Cupressus sempervirens*)
Juniper or Red Cedar species (*Juniperus*)
*Sweet Gum (*Liquidambar styraciflua*)
Magnolia species (*Magnolia*)
Dawn Redwood (*Metasequoia glyptostroboides*)
*Black Tupelo or Black Gum (*Nyssa sylvatica*)
Hop-Hornbeam (*Ostrya virginiana*)
*Sorrel Tree or Sourwood (*Oxydendrum arboreum*)

Columnar
Columnar Red Maple (*Acer rubrum columnare*)
Schott Red Cedar (*Juniperus virginiana schotti*)
Lombardy Poplar (*Populus nigra italica*)
Shipmast Locust (*Robinia pseudoacacia rectissima*)
Common Bald Cypress (*Taxodium distichum*)

Weeping
*Deodar Cedar (*Cedrus deodar*)
Weeping Red Cedar (*Juniperus virginiana pendula*)
*Babylon Weeping Willow (*Salix babylonica*)

Rounded or Globe-Shaped

Single Seed Hawthorn (*Crataegus monogyna inermis*)
*White Oak (*Quercus alba*)
Umbrella Black Locust (*Robinia pseudoacacia umbraculifera*)

With Horizontal Branching
Silk Tree (*Albizzia julibrissin*)
Monkey-Puzzle Tree (*Araucana araucana*)
*Cedar species (*Cedrus*)
*Flowering Dogwood (*Cornus florida*)
*Hawthorn species (*Crataegus*)
*Black Tupelo or Black Gum (*Nyssa sylvatica*)
*White Oak (*Quercus alba*)
*Live Oak (*Quercus virginiana*)
Common Bald Cypress (*Taxodium distichum*)

Trees Classified by Color of Blossom

Yellow
Cootamundra Wattle (*Acacia baileyana*)
Silver Wattle (*Acacia decurrens dealbata*)
Shower of Gold (*Cassia fistula*)
*Golden Rain Tree (*Koelreuteria paniculata*)
*Laburnum (*Laburnum vossi*)

White
Strawberry Tree (*Arbutus unedo*)
Citrus species (*Citrus*)
*Southern Magnolia (*Magnolia grandiflora*)
Chinese Photinia (*Photinia serrulata*)
Mount Fuji Cherry (*Prunus serrulata* "Shirotae")

Pink
Wither's Pink Redbud (*Cercis canadensis* "Wither's Pink Charm")
Red Flowering Dogwood (*Cornus florida rubra*)
Ingleside Crape-Myrtle (*Lagerstroemia indica* "Ingleside Pink")
Japanese Flowering Crab Apple (*Malus floribunda*)
Katherine Crab Apple (*Malus* "Katherine")
Prince Georges Crab Apple (*Malus* "Prince Georges")
*Common Apple (*Malus pumila*)
Sargent Cherry (*Prunus sargenti*)
Blireiana Plum (*Prunus blireiana*)
Amanogawa Cherry (*Prunus serrulata* "Amanogawa")
Kwanzan Cherry (*Prunus serrulata* "Kwanzan")
Autumn Cherry (*Prunus subhirtella autumnalis*)
Weeping Cherry (*Prunus subhirtella pendula*)

Red
Red Crape-Myrtle (*Lagerstroemia indica* "Wm. Toovey")
Alexandrina Magnolia (*Magnolia soulangeana* "Alexandrina")

Trees with Bright Red Fruit
*Flowering Dogwood (*Cornus florida*)
Almey Crab Apple (*Malus* "Almey")
Siberian Crab Apple (*Malus baccata*)
Hopa Crab Apple (*Malus* "Hopa")
Brazil Pepper Tree (*Schinus terebinthifolius*)

Trees Classified by Color of Summer Foliage

Blue
Silver Wattle (*Acacia decurrens dealbata*)
Eastern Red Cedar (*Juniperus virginiana* var. *Burki*)

Silver to Grayish
South American Jelly or Pindo Palm (*Butia capitata*)
Russian Olive (*Elaeagnus angustifolia*)
*Common Olive (*Olea europaea*)
White Poplar (*Populus alba*)
Pendent Silver Linden (*Tilia petiolaris*)
*Silver Linden (*Tilia tomentosa*)

Trees Classified by Color of Fall Foliage

Yellow
Fringetree (*Chionanthus virginicus*)
*Willow species (*Salix*)

Red

*Red Maple (*Acer rubrum*)

Trees with Interesting Bark

Gray
*Red Maple (*Acer rubrum*)
American Holly (*Ilex opaca*)

Corky
Hackberry (*Celtis*)
Cork Oak (*Quercus suber*)

Flaking
Eastern Red Cedar (*Juniperus virginiana*)
Crape-Myrtle (*Lagerstroemia indica*)
*Plane Tree species (*Platanus*)

Trees for the City
Silk Tree (*Albizzia julibrissin*)
Hackberry (*Celtis*)
*Ginkgo (*Ginkgo biloba*)
Thornless Honey-Locust (*Gleditsia triacanthos inermis*)
*Golden Rain Tree (*Koelreuteria paniculata*)
*Southern Magnolia (*Magnolia grandiflora*)
*Crab Apple (*Malus* var.)
Chinaberry (*Melia azedarach*)
Red Oak (*Quercus borealis*)
*Japanese Pagoda Tree (*Sophora japonica*)
Village Green Zelkova (*Zelkova serrata* "Village Green")

Trees for Wide Streets
Sugar Hackberry (*Celtis laevigata*)
Camphor Tree (*Cinnamomum camphora*)
White Ash (*Fraxinus americana*)
Green Ash (*Fraxinus pennsylvanica lanceolata*)
Common Honey-Locust (*Gleditsia triacanthos*)
Paterson Sugar Plum Tree (*Lagunaria patersoni*)
*Southern Magnolia (*Magnolia grandiflora*)
California Plane Tree (*Platanus racemosa*)
Willow Oak (*Quercus phellos*)
*Live Oak (*Quercus virginiana*)

Trees for Medium Streets
Mountain Silverbell (*Halesia monticola*)
*Sweet Gum (*Liquidambar styraciflua*)
Chile Mayten Tree (*Maytenus boaria*)
Chinaberry (*Melia azedarach*)
Hop-Hornbeam (*Ostrya virginiana*)
*Sorrel Tree or Sourwood (*Oxydendrum arboreum*)
Scarlet Oak (*Quercus coccinea*)
Laurel Oak (*Quercus laurifolia*)
Willow Oak (*Quercus phellos*)
Cork Oak (*Quercus suber*)
*Black Locust (*Robinia pseudoacacia*)
Sassafras (*Sassafras albidum officinale*)

Trees for Suburban Streets
American Hornbeam (*Carpinus caroliniana*)
Fringetree (*Chionanthus virginicus*)
*Flowering Dogwood (*Cornus florida*)
*Hawthorn species (*Crataegus*)
Chile Mayten Tree (*Maytenus boaria*)

Soil Tolerance

Trees Tolerating Acid Soil
Strawberry Tree (*Arbutus unedo*)
*Japanese Maple (*Acer palmatum* var.)
Citrus species (*Citrus*)
*Flowering Dogwood (*Cornus florida* var.)
Sweet Bay (*Magnolia virginiana*)
*Black Tupelo (*Nyssa sylvatica*)
*Sorrel Tree (*Oxydendrum arboreum*)
Willow Oak (*Quercus phellos*)

Trees Tolerating Moist Soil
*Red Maple (*Acer rubrum*)
Holly species (*Ilex*)
Sweet Bay (*Magnolia virginiana*)
Common Bald Cypress (*Taxodium distichum*)

Trees Tolerating Dry or Poor Soil
Silver Wattle (*Acacia decurrens dealbata*)
*Tree of Heaven (*Ailanthus*)
Silk Tree (*Albizzia julibrissin*)

Common Paper-Mulberry (*Broussonetia papyrifera*)
South American Jelly Palm (*Butia capitata*)
European Hackberry (*Celtis australis*)
*Honey-Locust (*Gleditsia triacanthos* var.)
*Golden Rain Tree (*Koelreuteria paniculata*)
Australian Tea Tree (*Leptospermum laevigatum*)
Chinaberry (*Melia azedarach*)
Jerusalem Thorn (*Parkinsonia aculeata*)
Canary Pine (*Pinus canariensis*)
Torrey Pine (*Pinus torreyana*)
Honey Mesquit (*Prosopis glandulosa*)

Pest-Resistant Trees

Hornbeam species (*Carpinus*)
*Fig species (*Ficus*)
Franklinia (*Franklinia alatamaha*)
Juniper species (*Juniperus*)
*Sweet Gum (*Liquidambar styraciflua*)
Hop-Hornbeam species (*Ostrya*)

Trees for Seashore Planting

Velvet Ash (*Fraxinus velutina*)
Spiny Greek Juniper (*Juniperus excelsa stricta*)
West Indies Juniper (*Juniperus lucayana*)
*Southern Magnolia (*Magnolia grandiflora*)
Chile Mayten Tree (*Maytenus boaria*)

Aleppo Pine (*Pinus halepensis*)
Cluster Pine (*Pinus pinaster*)
Holly Oak (*Quercus ilex*)
Oriental Arbor-vitae (*Thuja orientalis*)
Chinese Elm (*Ulmus parvifolia*)

Trees for Hedging or Barriers

Leyland Cypress (*Cupressocyparis leylandii*) withstands heavy pruning.
American Holly (*Ilex opaca*) can be pruned.
Hedge Maple (*Acer campestre*) can be pruned.
Eastern White Pine (*Pinus strobus*) plant 15 feet on centers, staggered row.

MAINE

State Tree

*White Pine (*Pinus strobus*)

Evergreen Trees

Fir species (*Abies*)
False Cypress species (*Chamaecyparis*)
Juniper species (*Juniperus*)
Eastern Red Cedar (*Juniperus virginiana*)
*Larch species (*Larix*)
*Spruce species (*Picea*)
*Pine species (*Pinus*)
*Douglas Fir (*Pseudotsuga menziesii*)
Arbor-vitae species (*Thuja*)
*Hemlock species (*Tsuga*)

Trees Classified by Height

20–35 Feet

Hedge Maple (*Acer campestre*)
Amur Maple (*Acer ginnala*)
Manchurian Maple (*Acer mandshuricum*)
Mountain Maple (*Acer spicatum*)
Tatarian Maple (*Acer tataricum*)
Ohio Buckeye (*Aesculus glabra*)
Apple Serviceberry (*Amelanchier grandiflora*)
Mockernut (*Carya tomentosa*)
Fringetree (*Chionanthis virginicus*)
Cornelian Cherry (*Cornus mas*)
*Hawthorn species (*Crataegus*)
Russian Olive (*Elaeagnus angustifolia*)
Euonymus species (*Euonymus*)
Carolina Silverbell (*Halesia carolina*)
Common Sea-Buckthorn (*Hippophae rhamnoides*)
*Laburnum species (*Laburnum*)
*Crab Apple species (*Malus*)
*Cherry species (*Prunus*)
Dahurian Buckthorn (*Rhamnus davurica*)
Almond-leaf Willow (*Salix amygdalina*)
Goat Willow (*Salix caprea*)
Showy Mountain Ash (*Sorbus decora*)
Japanese Tree Lilac (*Syringa amurensis japonica*)

35–75 Feet

Striped Maple or Moosewood (*Acer pennsylvanicum*)
Red-fruited Tree of Heaven (*Ailanthus altissima erythrocarpa*)
Speckled Alder (*Alnus incana*)
Red Alder (*Alnus rubra*)
*Shadblow Serviceberry (*Amelanchier canadensis*)
Allegany Serviceberry (*Amelanchier laevis*)
Devil's Walking Stick (*Aralia elata*)
Dahurian Birch (*Betula davurica*)
*European Birch (*Betula pendula*)
American Hornbeam (*Carpinus caroliniana*)
Japanese Hornbeam (*Carpinus japonica*)
Chinese Chestnut (*Castanea mollissima*)
Southern Catalpa (*Catalpa bignonioides*)
*Katsura Tree (*Cercidiphyllum japonicum*)
Eastern Redbud (*Cercis canadensis*)
*American Yellow-wood (*Cladrastis lutea*)
*Flowering Dogwood (*Cornus florida*)
Turkish Filbert (*Corylus colurna*)
Cockspur Thorn (*Crataegus crus-galli*)
Green Hawthorn (*Crataegus viridis*)
Common Persimmon (*Diospyros virginiana*)

Green Ash (*Fraxinus pennsylvanica lanceolata*)
Heartnut (*Juglans sieboldiana cordiformis*)
Chinese Juniper (*Juniperus chinensis*)
Eastern Larch or Tamarack (*Larix laricina*)
Kobus Magnolia (*Magnolia kobus borealis*)
Loebner Magnolia (*Magnolia loebneri*)
Siberian Crab Apple (*Malus baccata*)
"Makamik" Crab Apple (*Malus robusta*)
White Mulberry (*Morus alba*)
*Sorrel Tree or Sourwood (*Oxydendrum arboreum*)
*Amur Cork (*Phellodendron amurense*)
Black Hills Spruce (*Picea glauca densata*)
Jack Pine (*Pinus banksiana*)
Lace-bark Pine (*Pinus bungeana*)
Swiss Stone Pine (*Pinus cembra*)
Limber Pine (*Pinus flexilis*)
Pitch Pine (*Pinus rigida*)
Scotch Pine (*Pinus sylvestris*)
Virginia or Scrub Pine (*Pinus virginiani*)
Simon Poplar (*Populus simoni*)
Amur Chockecherry (*Prunus maacki*)
Miyama Cherry (*Prunus maximowiczi*)
European Bird Cherry (*Prunus padus*)
Sargent Cherry (*Prunus sargenti*)
Ussurian Pear (*Pyrus ussuriensis*)
Swamp White Oak (*Quercus bicolor*)
Red Oak (*Quercus borealis*)
Scarlet Oak (*Quercus coccinea*)
*Pin Oak (*Quercus palustris*)
White Willow (*Salix alba*)
Wisconsin or Niobe Weeping Willow (*Salix blanda*)
Elaeagnus Willow (*Salix claeagnos*)
Thurlow Weeping Willow (*Salix elegantissima*)
Laurel Willow (*Salix pentandra*)
Sassafras (*Sassafras albidum officinale*)
European Mountain Ash or Rowan Tree (*Sorbus aucuparia*)
American Arbor-vitae (*Thuja occidentalis*)
Carolina Hemlock (*Tsuga caroliniana*)
Siberian Elm (*Ulmus pumila*)

75 Feet or Over

Fir species (*Abies*)
Norway Maple (*Acer platanoides*)
*Red or Swamp Maple (*Acer rubrum*)
*Sugar Maple (*Acer saccharum*)
*Baumann Horse-Chestnut (*Aesculus hippocastanum baumanni*)
European Alder (*Alnus glutinosa*)
Sweet Birch (*Betula lenta*)
River Birch (*Betula nigra*)
*Canoe Birch (*Betula papyrifera*)
Hickory species (*Carya*)
Northern Catalpa (*Catalpa speciosa*)
*Katsura Tree (*Cercidiphyllum japonicum*)
False Cypress species (*Chamaecyparis*)
*Beech species (*Fagus*)
White Ash (*Fraxinus americana*)
European Ash (*Fraxinus excelsior*)
*Ginkgo or Maidenhair Tree (*Ginkgo biloba*)
*Common Honey-Locust (*Gleditsia triacanthos*)
Kentucky Coffee Tree (*Gymnocladus dioicus*)
Eastern Black Walnut (*Juglans nigra*)

Kalopanax (*Kalopanax pictus*)
*European Larch (*Larix decidua*)
Japanese Larch (*Larix leptolepis*)
*Sweet Gum (*Liquidambar styraciflua*)
Tulip Tree or Yellow Poplar (*Liriodendron tulipifera*)
Cucumber Tree (*Magnolia acuminata*)
*Black Gum or Black Tupelo (*Nyssa sylvatica*)
*Spruce species (*Picea*)
*Pine species (*Pinus*)
Poplar species (*Populus*)
Sargent Cherry (*Prunus sargenti*)
Black or Rum Cherry (*Prunus serotina*)
*Douglas Fir (*Pseudotsuga menziesii*)
*Oak species (*Quercus*)
Common Bald Cypress (*Taxodium distichum*)
Giant Arbor-vitae (*Thuja plicata*)
*Linden species (*Tilia*)
*Canada Hemlock (*Tsuga canadensis*)
*Elm species (*Ulmus*)

Trees Classified by Form

Pyramidal

Fir species (*Abies*)
*Birch species (*Betula*)
False Cypress species (*Chamaecyparis*)
Turkish Filbert (*Corylus colurna*)
*Beech species (*Fagus*)
Juniper or Red Cedar species (*Juniperus*)
Pyramidal Red Cedar (*Juniperus virginiana pyramidalis*)
*Larch species (*Larix*)
*Sweet Gum (*Liquidambar styraciflua*)
*Magnolia species (*Magnolia*)
*Black Tupelo or Black Gum (*Nyssa sylvatica*)
Hop-Hornbeam (*Ostrya virginiana*)
*Sorrel Tree or Sourwood (*Oxydendrum arboreum*)
Spruce species (*Picea*)
Swiss Stone Pine (*Pinus cembra*)
Korean Pine (*Pinus koraiensis*)
*Pyramid Austrian Pine (*Pinus nigra pyramidalis*)
Red Pine or Norway Pine (*Pinus resinosa*)
*Douglas Fir (*Pseudotsuga menziesii*)
*Pin Oak (*Quercus palustris*)
Common Bald Cypress (*Taxodium distichum*)
Arbor-vitae species (*Thuja*)
*Linden species (*Tilia*)
*Hemlock species (*Tsuga*)
Smooth-leaved Elm varieties (*Ulmus carpinifolia*)

Columnar

Ascending Norway Maple (*Acer platanoides ascendens*)
Columnar Norway Maple (*Acer platanoides columnare*)
Erect Norway Maple (*Acer platanoides erectum*)
Columnar Red Maple (*Acer rubrum columnare*)
*Sentry Maple (*Acer saccharum monumentale*)
Fastigiate European Birch (*Betula pendula fastigiata*)
Fastigiate Washington Hawthorn (*Crataegus phaenopyrum fastigiata*)
Dawych Beech (*Fagus sylvatica fastigiata*)
Sentry Ginkgo (*Ginkgo biloba fastigiata*)
Blue Columnar Chinese Juniper (*Juniperus chinensis columnaris*)
Schott Red Cedar (*Juniperus virginiana schotti*)

Swiss Stone Pine (*Pinus cembra*)
Fastigiate White Pine (*Pinus strobus fastigiata*)
Fastigiate Scotch Pine (*Pinus sylvestris fastigiata*)
Bolleana Poplar (*Populus alba pyramidalis*)
*Lombardy Poplar (*Populus nigra italica*)
Fastigiate Simon Poplar (*Populus simoni fastigiata*)
*Columnar Sargent Cherry (*Prunus sargenti columnaris*)
Shipmast Locust (*Robinia pseudoacacia rectissima*)
Upright European Mountain Ash (*Sorbus aucoparia fastigiata*)
Common Bald Cypress (*Taxodium distichum*)
Fastigiate American Arbor-vitae (*Thuja occidentalis fastigiata*)
Columnar Big-leaf Linden (*Tilia platyphyllos fastigiata*)
*American Elm varieties (*Ulmus americana*)

Weeping
Slender European Birch (*Betula pendula tristis*)
Young's Birch (*Betula pendula youngi*)
Weeping Beech (*Fagus sylvatica pendula*)
Weeping Purple Beech (*Fagus sylvatica purpureo-pendula*)
Weeping Red Cedar (*Juniperus virginiana pendula*)
Weeping Larch (*Larix decidua pendula*)
Weeping Mulberry (*Morus alba pendula*)
Koster Weeping Blue Spruce (*Picea pungens kosteriana*)
Weeping White Pine (*Pinus strobus pendula*)
Weeping Black Cherry (*Prunus serotina pendula*)
Weeping Douglas Fir (*Pseudotsuga menziesii pendula*)
Golden Weeping Willow (*Salix alba tristis*)
Wisconsin or Niobe Weeping Willow (*Salix blanda*)
Thurlow Weeping Willow (*Salix elegantissima*)
Weeping Japanese Pagoda Tree (*Sophora japonica pendula*)
Weeping European Mountain Ash (*Sorbus aucuparia pendula*)
Sargent Hemlock (*Tsuga canadensis pendula*)
Weeping American Elm (*Ulmus americana pendula*)

Rounded or Globe-Shaped
Globe Norway Maple (*Acer platanoides globosum*)
Cornelian Cherry (*Cornus mas*)
Single Seed Hawthorn (*Crataegus monogyna inermis*)
*Crab Apple species (*Malus*)
*White Oak (*Quercus alba*)
Umbrella Black Locust (*Robinia pseudoacacia umbraculifera*)
Sargent Hemlock (*Tsuga canadensis sargenti*)
Koopmann Elm (*Ulmus carpinifolia koopmanni*)
Globe Smooth-leaved Elm (*Ulmus carpinifolia umbraculifera*)

With Horizontal Branching
Fir species (*Abies*)
Eastern Redbud (*Cercis canadensis*)
*Flowering Dogwood (*Cornus florida*)
*Hawthorn species (*Crataegus*)
*Black Tupelo or Black Gum (*Nyssa sylvatica*)
Spruce species (*Picea*)
Japanese Red Pine (*Pinus densiflora*)
*Eastern White Pine (*Pinus strobus*)
*White Oak (*Quercus alba*)
*Pin Oak (*Quercus palustris*)
Common Bald Cypress (*Taxodium distichum*)

Trees Classified by Color of Blossom
White
*Shadblow Serviceberry (*Amelanchier canadensis*)
*American Yellow-wood (*Cladrastis lutea*)
Washington Hawthorn (*Crataegus phaenopyrum*)
Carolina Silverbell (*Halesia carolina*)
Arnold Crab Apple (*Malus arnoldiana*)
*Siberian Crab Apple (*Malus baccata*)
Tea Crab Apple (*Malus hupehensis*)
*Sorrel Tree (*Oxydendrum arboreum*)
Thundercloud Plum (*Prunus cerasifera* "Thundercloud")
Sour Cherry (*Prunus cerasus*)
*Japanese Pagoda Tree (*Sophora japonica*)
American Mountain Ash (*Sorbus americana*)

European Mountain Ash (*Sorbus aucuparia*)
Showy Mountain Ash (*Sorbus decora*)

Pink
Katherine Crab Apple (*Malus* "Katherine")
*Common Apple (*Malus pumila*)
Sargent Cherry (*Prunus sargenti*)

Red
Ruby Horse-Chestnut (*Aesculus carnea briotti*)
Paul's Scarlet Hawthorn (*Crataegus oxyacantha pauli*)
Carmine Crab Apple (*Malus atrosanguinea*)

Trees Classified by Color of Summer Foliage
Blue
Eastern Red Cedar (*Juniperus virginiana* var. *Burki*)

Silver to Gray
Russian Olive (*Elaeagnus angustifolia*)
Common Sea-Buckthorn (*Hippophae rhamnoides*)
White Poplar (*Populus alba*)
*Silver Linden (*Tilia tomentosa*)

Red to Purple
Crimson King Maple (*Acer platanoides* "Crimson King")
Schwedler Maple (*Acer platanoides schwedleri*)
Purple Beech (*Fagus sylvatica atropunicea*)
Weeping Purple Beech (*Fagus sylvatica purpurea-pendula*)
River's Purple Beech (*Fagus sylvatica riversi*)
Rubylace Locust (*Gleditsia triacanthos inermis* "Rubylace")
Purple Crab Apple (*Malus purpurea*)
Pissard Plum (*Prunus cerasifera atropurpurea*)
Thundercloud Plum (*Prunus cerasifera nigra* "Thundercloud")
Woods Myrobalan Plum (*Prunus cerasifera woodi*)

Trees Classified by Color of Fall Foliage
Yellow
Striped Maple or Moosewood (*Acer pensylvanicum*)
Norway Maple (*Acer platanoides* var.)
*Sugar Maple (*Acer saccharum*)
Ohio Buckeye (orange) (*Aesculus glabra*)
Apple Serviceberry (yellow-orange) (*Amelanchier grandiflora*)
*Birch species (*Betula*)
Hickory species (*Carya*)
Chinese Chestnut (*Castanea mollissima*)
*Katsura Tree (*Cercidiphyllum japonicum*)
Redbud species (*Cercis*)
Fringetree (*Chionanthus virginicus*)
*American Yellow-wood (*Cladrastis lutea*)
*American Beech (*Fagus grandifolia*)
*European Beech (*Fagus sylvatica*)
White Ash (purple to yellow) (*Fraxinus americana*)
*Ginkgo (*Ginkgo biloba*)
*Larch (*Larix decidua*)
Tulip Tree (*Liriodendron tulipifera*)
*Star Magnolia (bronze) (*Magnolia stellata*)
*Willow species (*Salix*)

Red
Amur Maple (*Acer ginnala*)
Manchurian Maple (*Acer mandshuricum*)
*Red Maple (*Acer rubrum*)
*Sugar Maple (*Acer saccharum*)
Tataran Maple (*Acer tataricum*)
*Shadblow Serviceberry (*Amelanchier canadensis*)
Hornbeam species (*Carpinus*)
*Flowering Dogwood (*Cornus florida*)
Washington Hawthorn (*Crataegus phaenopyrum*)
*Sweet Gum (*Liquidambar styraciflua*)
Dawson Crab Apple (*Malus dawsoniana*)
*Black Tupelo or Black Gum (*Nyssa sylvatica*)
*Sorrel Tree (*Oxydendrum arboreum*)
*Cherry species (*Prunus*)
Red Oak (*Quercus borealis*)
Scarlet Oak (*Quercus coccinea*)
*Pin Oak (*Quercus palustris*)

Sassafras (*Sassafras albidum*)
Purple
White Ash (*Fraxinus americana*)
*Sweet Gum (*Liquidambar styraciflua*)
*White Oak (*Quercus alba*)

Trees with Interesting Bark
Gray
*Red Maple (*Acer rubrum*)
*Serviceberry species (*Amelanchier*)
Hornbeam species (*Carpinus*)
*American Yellow-wood (*Cladrastis lutea*)
*Hawthorn species (*Crataegus*)
*Beech species (*Fagus*)
Cucumber Tree (*Magnolia acuminata*)
Red Oak (young trunk and branches) (*Quercus borealis*)
Black Oak (young trunk and branches) (*Quercus velutina*)
Mountain Ash species (*Sorbus*)

White
*Canoe Birch (*Betula papyrifera*)
*European Birch (*Betula pendula*)

Red
Japanese Red Pine (*Pinus densiflora*)
Red Pine or Norway Pine (*Pinus resinosa*)
Scotch Pine (*Pinus sylvestris*)

Reddish Brown
Sargent Cherry (*Prunus sargenti*)

Yellow
Wisconsin or Niobe Weeping Willow (*Salix blanda*)

Corky
*Amur Cork (*Phellodendron amurense*)

Flaking
*Birch species (*Betula*)
Shag Bark Hickory (*Carya ovata*)
Russian Olive (*Elaeagnus angustifolia*)
Eastern Red Cedar (*Juniperus virginiana*)
Lace-bark Pine (*Pinus bungeana*)

Trees for the City
White Fir (*Abies concolor*)
Hedge Maple (*Acer campestre*)
Box-Elder (*Acer negundo*)
Norway Maple (*Acer platanoides*)
Horse-Chestnut or Buckeye (*Aesculus*)
*Tree of Heaven (*Ailanthus*)
Catalpa (*Catalpa*)
Downy Hawthorn (*Crataegus mollis*)
Washington Hawthorn (*Crataegus phaenopyrum*)
Russian Olive (*Elaeagnus angustifolia*)
White Ash (*Fraxinus americana*)
European Ash (*Fraxinus excelsior*)
Green Ash (*Fraxinus pennsylvanica*)
*Ginkgo (*Ginkgo biloba*)
Thornless Honey-Locust (*Gleditsia triacanthos inermis*)
*Crab Apple (*Malus varieties*)
*Amur Cork (*Phellodendron amurense*)
Colorado Spruce (*Picea pungens*)
White Poplar (*Populus alba*)
*Lombardy Poplar (*Populus nigra italica*)
Red Oak (*Quercus borealis*)
*Black Locust (*Robinia pseudoacacia*)
*Japanese Pagoda Tree (*Sophora japonica*)
*Little-leaf Linden (*Tilia cordata*)
*Silver Linden (*Tilia tomentosa*)

Trees for Wide Streets
*Sugar Maple (*Acer saccharum*)
*Katsura Tree (*Cercidiphyllum japonicum*)
White Ash (*Fraxinus americana*)
Green Ash (*Fraxinus pennsylvanica lanceolata*)
*Ginkgo (*Ginkgo biloba*)
*Common Honeylocust (*Gleditsia triacanthos*)
Kalopanax (*Kalopanax pictus*)
Tulip Tree (*Liriodendron tulipifera*)
*Amur Cork (*Phellodendron amurense*)
*Eastern White Pine (*Pinus strobus*)

White Poplar (*Populus alba*)
Sargent Cherry (*Prunus sargenti*)
Red Oak (*Quercus borealis*)
★Pin Oak (*Quercus palustris*)

Trees for Medium Streets
Norway Maple (*Acer platanoides*)
★Sweet Gum (*Liquidambar styraciflua*)
Hop-Hornbeam (*Ostrya virginiana*)
★Sorrel Tree (Sourwood) (*Oxydendrum arboreum*)
Simon Poplar (*Populus simoni*)
Scarlet Oak (*Quercus coccinea*)
★Black Locust (*Robinia pseudoacacia*)
Sassafras (*Sassafras albidum officinale*)
★Japanese Pagoda Tree (*Sophora japonica*)
★Linden species (*Tilia*)

Trees for Suburban Streets
Hedge Maple (*Acer campestre*)
Amur Maple (*Acer ginnala*)
Globe Norway Maple (*Acer spicatum*)
Tatarian Maple (*Acer tataricum*)
American Hornbeam (*Carpinus caroliniana*)
Fringetree (*Chionanthus virginicus*)
★Flowering Dogwood (*Cornus florida*)
★Hawthorn species (*Crataegus*)
Carolina Silverbell (*Halesia carolina*)
Columnar Sargent Cherry (*Prunus sargenti columnaris*)

Soil Tolerance

Trees Tolerating Acid Soil
★Flowering Dogwood (*Cornus florida*)
★European Beech (*Fagus sylvatica*)
Black Tupelo (*Nyssa sylvatica*)
★Sorrel Tree (*Oxydendrum arboreum*)
Red Oak (*Quercus borealis*)
Scarlet Oak (*Quercus coccinea*)
★Pin Oak (*Quercus palustris*)
Willow Oak (*Quercus phellos*)

Trees Tolerating Dry or Poor Soil

Box-Elder (*Acer negunda*)
★Tree of Heaven (*Ailanthus*)
Russian Olive (*Elaeagnus angustifolia*)
Green Ash (*Fraxinus pennsylvanica*)
★Honey-Locust (*Gleditsia triacanthos* var.)
Western Red Cedar (*Juniperus scopulorum*)
Eastern Red Cedar (*Juniperus virginiana*)
Jack Pine (*Pinus banksiana*)
Pitch Pine (*Pinus rigida*)
Virginia or Scrub Pine (*Pinus virginiana*)
White Poplar (*Populus alba*)
Chestnut Oak (*Quercus montana*)
★Black Locust (*Robinia pseudoacacia*)
Sassafras (*Sassafras albidum officinale*)
★Japanese Pagoda Tree (*Sophora japonica*)
Siberian Elm (*Ulmus pumila*)

Pest-Resistant Trees

★Tree of Heaven (*Ailanthus altissima*)
Hornbeam species (*Carpinus*)
★Katsura Tree (*Cercidiphyllum japonicum*)
False Cypress species (*Chamaecyparis*)
Cornelian Cherry (*Cornus mas*)
Japanese Cornel (*Cornus officinalis*)
Turkish Filbert (*Corylus colurna*)
Russian Olive (*Elaeagnus angustifolia*)
★Ginkgo (*Ginkgo biloba*)
★Honey-Locust (*Gleditsia triacanthos*)
Kentucky Coffe Tree (*Gymnocladus dioicus*)
Juniper species (*Juniperus*)
Kalopanax (*Kalopanax pictus*)
★Laburnum species (*Laburnum*)
★Sweet Gum (*Liquidambar styraciflua*)
Cucumber Tree (*Magnolia acuminata*)
Kobus Magnolia (*Magnolia kobus borealis*)
Hop-Hornbeam species (*Ostrya*)

Trees for Seashore Planting

Norway Maple (*Acer platanoides*)
Horse-Chestnut (*Aesculus hippocastanum*)
★Tree of Heaven (*Ailanthus*)

★Shadblow Serviceberry (*Amelanchier canadensis*)
Cockspur Thorn (*Crataegus crus-galli*)
English Hawthorn (*Crataegus oxyacantha*)
Washington Hawthorn (*Crataegus phaenopyrum*)
Russian Olive (*Elaeagnus angustifolia*)
★Honey-Locust (*Gleditsia triacanthos*)
Eastern Red Cedar (*Juniperus virginiana*)
★Black Tupelo (*Nyssa sylvatica*)
Colorado Blue Spruce (*Picea pungens glauca*)
★Austrian Pine (*Pinus nigra*)
Pitch Pine (*Pinus rigida*)
Scotch Pine (*Pinus sylvestris*)
★Japanese Black Pine (*Pinus thunbergi*)
White Poplar (*Populus alba*)
Black Cherry (*Prunus serotina*)
★White Oak (*Quercus alba*)
★Black Locust (*Robinia pseudoacacia*)
Golden Weeping Willow (*Salix alba tristis*)
★Japanese Pagoda Tree (*Sophora japonica*)
American Arbor-vitae (*Thuja occidentalis*)
★Little-leaf Linden (*Tilia cordata*)

Trees for Hedging or Barriers

European Beech (*Fagus sylvatica*) prunes well.
Leyland Cypress (*Cupressocyparis leylandii*) withstands heavy pruning.
Hawthorn varieties (*Crataegus*) easily pruned, advantage of thorns.
Canadian Hemlock (*Tsuga canadensis*) evergreen.
American Holly (*Ilex opaca*) can be pruned.
European Hornbeam (*Carpinus betulus*) prunes well.
Little-leaf Linden (*Tilia cordata*) tolerates heavy pruning.
Hedge Maple (*Acer campestre*) can be pruned.
Austrian Pine (*Pinus nigra*) plant 10–12 feet on centers, staggered row.
Japanese Black Pine (*Pinus thunbergi*) plant 8 feet on centers, staggered row.
Eastern White Pine (*Pinus strobus*) plant 15 feet on centers, staggered row.

MARYLAND

State Tree

★White Oak (*Quercus alba*)

Evergreen Trees

Fir species (*Abies*)
Tree Box (*Buxus sempervirens arborescens*)
★Cedar species (*Cedrus*)
False Cypress species (*Chamaecyparis*)
Common China Fir (*Cunninghamia lanceolata*)
Holly species (*Ilex*)
Juniper species (*Juniperus*)
★Larch species (*Larix*)
★Southern Magnolia (*Magnolia grandiflora*)
Spruce species (*Picea*)
★Pine species (*Pinus*)
★Douglas Fir (*Pseudotsuga menziesii*)
Umbrella Pine (*Sciadopitys verticillata*)
Arbor-vitae species (*Thuja*)
★Hemlock species (*Tsuga*)

Trees Classified by Height

20–35 Feet
Hedge Maple (*Acer campestre*)
Amur Maple (*Acer ginnala*)
Paperbark Maple (*Acer griseum*)
★Japanese Maple (*Acer palmatum*)
Tatarian Maple (*Acer tataricum*)
Ohio Buckeye (*Aesculus glabra*)
Apple Serviceberry (*Amelanchier grandiflora*)
★Gray Birch (*Betula populifolia*)
European Hornbeam (*Carpinus betulus globosa*)
Mockernut (*Carya tomentosa*)
Judas Tree (*Cercis canadensis*)
Fringetree (*Chionanthus virginicus*)

Japanese Dogwood (*Cornus kousa*)
Cornelian Cherry (*Cornus mas*)
Japanese Cornel (*Cornus officinalis*)
American Smoke Tree (*Cotinus americanus*)
★Hawthorn species (*Crataegus*)
Russian Olive (*Elaeagnus angustifolia*)
Korean Evodia (*Evodia danielli*)
Franklinia (*Franklinia alatamaha*)
Flowering Ash (*Fraxinus ornus*)
Carolina Silverbell (*Halesia carolina*)
★Golden Rain Tree (*Koelreuteria paniculata*)
★Laburnum species (*Laburnum*)
Crape-Myrtle (*Lagerstroemia indica*)
Yellow Cucumber Tree (*Magnolia cordata*)
Anise Magnolia (*Magnolia salcifolia*)
Oyama Magnolia (*Magnolia sieboldi*)
★Saucer Magnolia (*Magnolia soulangeana*)
★Star Magnolia (*Magnolia stellata*)
Watson Magnolia (*Magnolia watsoni*)
Wilson Magnolia (*Magnolia wilsoni*)
★Crab Apple species (*Malus*)
★Cherry species (*Prunus*)
Black Jack Oak (*Quercus marilandica*)
Almond-leaf Willow (*Salix amygdalina*)
★Babylon Weeping Willow (*Salix babylonica*)
Showy Mountain Ash (*Sorbus decora*)
Snowbell species (*Styrax*)

35–75 Feet
Silk Tree (*Albizzia julibrissin*)
Box-Elder (*Acer negundo*)
Nikko Maple (*Acer nikoense*)
Striped Maple or Moosewood (*Acer pennsylvanicum*)
★Red-fruited Tree of Heaven (*Ailanthus altissima erythrocarpa*)

★Shadblow Serviceberry (*Amelanchier canadensis*)
Allegany Serviceberry (*Amelanchier laevis*)
Dahurian Birch (*Betula davurica*)
Manchurian Birch (*Betula mandshurica szechuanica*)
★European Birch (*Betula pendula*)
Common Paper-Mulberry (*Broussonetia papyrifera*)
European Hornbeam (*Carpinus betulus*)
American Hornbeam (*Carpinus caroliniana*)
Japanese Hornbeam (*Carpinus japonica*)
Chinese Chestnut (*Castanea mollissima*)
Southern Catalpa (*Catalpa bignoniodes*)
Bunch Hackberry (*Celtis bungeana*)
★Katsura Tree (*Cercidiphyllum japonicum*)
Eastern Redbud (*Cercis chinensis*)
★American Yellow-wood (*Cladrastis lutea*)
★Flowering Dogwood (*Cornus florida*)
Cockspur Tree (*Crataegus crus-galli*)
Green Hawthorn (*Crataegus viridis*)
Common Persimmon (*Diospyros virginiana*)
Green Ash (*Fraxinus pennsylvanica lanceolata*)
English Holly (*Ilex aquifolium*)
Heartnut (*Juglans sieboldiana cordiformis*)
Chinese Juniper (*Juniperus chinensis*)
Western Red Cedar (*Juniperus scopulorum*)
Osage Orange (*Maclura pomifera*)
Yulan Magnolia (*Magnolia denudata*)
Fraser Magnolia (*Magnolia fraseri*)
Kobus Magnolia (*Magnolia kobus borealis*)
Loebner Magnolia (*Magnolia loebneri*)
Big-leaf Magnolia (*Magnolia macrophylla*)
★Siberian Crab Apple (*Malus bacata*)
"Cowichan" Crab Apple (*Malus* "Cowichan")
"Dolgo" Crab Apple (*Malus* "Dolga")
"Makamik" Crab Apple (*Malus* "Makamik")
Cherry Crab Apple (*Malus robusta*)

"Sissipuk" Crab Apple (*Malus* "Sissipuk")
White Mulberry (*Morus alba*)
Persian Parrotia (*Parrotia persica*)
Empress Tree (*Paulownia tomentosa*)
★Amur Cork (*Phellodendron amurense*)
Dragon Spruce (*Picea asperata*)
★Pine species (*Pinus*)
Simon Poplar (*Populus simoni*)
Miyama Cherry (*Prunus maximowiczi*)
Sargent Cherry (*Prunus sargenti*)
Yoshino Cherry (*Prunus yedoensis*)
Fragrant Epaulette Tree (*Pterostyrax hispida*)
Laurel Oak (*Quercus laurifolia*)
★Pin Oak (*Quercus palustris*)
Willow Oak (*Quercus phellos*)
White Willow (*Salix alba*)
Wisconsin or Niobe Weeping Willow (*Salix blanda*)
Eleagnus Willow (*Salix eleagnos*)
Thurlow Weeping Willow (*Salix elegantissima*)
Laurel Willow (*Salix pentandra*)
European Mountain Ash or Rowan Tree (*Sorbus aucuparia*)
Korean Stewartia (*Stewartia koreana*)
Japanese Stewartia (*Stewartia pseudo-camellia*)
American Arbor-vitae (*Thuja standishi*)
★Crimean Linden (*Tilia euchlora*)
Carolina Hemlock (*Tsuga caroliniana*)
Chinese Elm (*Ulmus parvifolia*)
Siberian Elm (*Ulmus pumila*)
Winged Elm (*Ulmus alata*)

75 Feet or Over

Fir species (*Abies*)
Norway Maple (*Acer platanoides*)
Sycamore Maple (*Acer pseudoplatanus*)
Red or Swamp Maple (*Acer rubrum*)
★Sugar Maple (*Acer saccharum*)
★Baumann Horse-Chestnut (*Aesculus hippocastanum baumanni*)
Hickory species (*Carya*)
Northern Catalpa (*Catalpa speciosa*)
★Cedar species (*Cedrus*)
European Hackberry (*Celtis australis*)
Sugar Hackberry (*Celtis laevigata*)
★Katsura Tree (*Cercidiphyllum japonicum*)
False Cypress species (*Chamaecyparis*)
Cryptomeria (*Cryptomeria japonica*)
★Beech species (*Fagus*)
White Ash (*Fraxinus americana*)
European Ash (*Fraxinus excelsior*)
★Ginkgo or Maidenhair Tree (*Ginkgo biloba*)
★Common Honey-Locust (*Gleditsia triacanthos*)
Kentucky Coffee Tree (*Gymnocladus dioicus*)
Mountain Silverbell (*Halesia monticola*)
English or Persian Walnut (*Juglans regia*)
Kalopanax (*Kalopanax pictus*)
Japanese Larch (*Larix leptolepis*)
Tulip Tree or Yellow Poplar (*Liriodendron tulipifera*)
★Sweet Gum (*Liquidambar styraciflua*)
Cucumber Tree (*Magnolia acuminata*)
★Southern Magnolia (*Magnolia grandiflora*)
White-leaf Japanese Magnolia (*Magnolia obovata*)
Dawn Redwood (*Metasequoia glyptostroboides*)
★Black Gum or Black Tupelo (*Nyssa sylvatica*)
Spruce species (*Picea*)
★Pine species (*Pinus*)
★Plane Tree species (*Platanus*)
Poplar species (*Populus*)
Sargent Cherry (*Prunus sargenti*)
Golden Larch (*Pseudolarix amabilis*)
★Douglas Fir (*Pseudotsuga menziesii*)
★Oak species (*Quercus*)
Umbrella Pine (*Sciadopitys verticillata*)
Giant Arbor-vitae (*Thuja plicata*)
★Linden species (*Tilia*)
★Canada Hemlock (*Tsuga canadensis*)
★Elm species (*Ulmus*)
Japanese Zelkova (*Zelkova serrata*)

Trees Classified by Form

Pyramidal

★Birch species (*Betula*)
★Cedar species (*Cedrus*)
False Cypress species (*Chamaecyparis*)
Cryptomeria (*Cryptomeria japonica*)
★Beech species (*Fagus*)
English Holly (*Ilex aquifolium*)
American Holly (*Ilex opaca*)
Juniper or Red Cedar species (*Juniperus*)
Pyramidal Red Cedar (*Juniperus virginiana pyramidalis*)
★Larch species (*Larix*)
★Sweet Gum (*Liquidambar styraciflua*)
★Magnolia species (*Magnolia*)
Dawn Redwood (*Metasequoia glyptostroboides*)
★Black Tupelo or Black Gum (*Nyssa sylvatica*)
Spruce species (*Picea*)
Swiss Stone Pine (*Pinus cembra*)
Pyramid Austrian Pine (*Pinus nigra pyramidalis*)
Japanese White Pine (*Pinus parviflora*)
Golden Larch (*Pseudolarix amabilis*)
★Douglas Fir (*Pseudotsuga menziesii*)
★Pin Oak (*Quercus palustris*)
Umbrella Pine (*Sciadopitys verticillata*)
Korean Stewartia (*Stewartia koreana*)
Common Bald Cypress (*Taxodium distichum*)
★Linden species (*Tilia*)
Arbor-vitae species (*Thuja*)
★Hemlock species (*Tsuga*)
Smooth-leaved Elm varieties (*Ulmus carpinifolia*)

Columnar

Ascending Norway Maple (*Acer platanoides ascendens*)
Columnar Norway Maple (*Acer platanoides columnare*)
Erect Norway Maple (*Acer platanoides erectum*)
Columnar Red Maple (*Acer rubrum columnare*)
Sentry Maple (*Acer saccharum monumentale*)
Fastigiate European Birch (*Betula pendula fastigiata*)
Fastigiate European Hornbeam (*Carpinus betulus fastigiata*)
Fastigiate Washington Hawthorn (*Crataegus phaenopyrum fastigiata*)
Dawyck Beech (*Fagus sylvatica fastigiata*)
Sentry Ginkgo (*Ginkgo biloba fastigiata*)
Blue Columnar Chinese Juniper (*Juniperus chinensis columnaris*)
Schott Red Cedar (*Juniperus virginiana schotti*)
Fastigiate Scotch Pine (*Pinus sylvestris fastigiata*)
Bolleana Poplar (*Populus alba pyramidalis*)
★Lombardy Poplar (*Populus nigra italica*)
Fastigiate Simon Poplar (*Populus simoni fastigiata*)
Columnar Sargent Cherry (*Prunus sargenti columnaris*)
"Amanogawa" Cherry (*Prunus serrulata* "Amanogawa")
Fastigiate English Oak (*Quercus robur fastigiata*)
Shipmast Locust (*Robinia pseudoacacia rectissima*)
Upright European Mountain Ash (*Sorbus acuparia fastigiata*)
Douglas Arbor-vitae (*Thuja occidentalis douglasi pyramidalis*)
Fastigiate American Arbor-vitae (*Thuja occidentalis fastigiata*)
Columnar Big-leaf Linden (*Tilia platyphyllos fastigiata*)
★American Elm varieties (*Ulmus americana*)

Weeping

Slender European Birch (*Betula pendula tristis*)
Young's Birch (*Betula pendula youngi*)
Weeping European Hornbeam (*Carpinus betulus pendula*)
★Weeping Beech (*Fagus sylvatica pendula*)
Weeping Larch (*Larix decidua pendula*)
"Exzellenz Thiel" Crab Apple (*Malus* "Exzellenz Thiel")
"Oekonomierat Echtermeyer" Crab Apple (*Malus* "Oekonomierat Echtermeyer")
Weeping Mulberry (*Morus alba pendula*)
Koster Weeping Blue Spruce (*Picea pungens kosteriana*)
Weeping Japanese Apricot (*Prunus mume pendula*)
Weeping Black Cherry (*Prunus serotina pendula*)

Weeping Higan Cherry (*Prunus subhirtella pendula*)
"Yaeshidare" Cherry (*Prunus subhirtella pendula flora plena*)
Weeping Yoshino Cherry (*Prunus yedoensis perpendens*)
Weeping Douglas Fir (*Pseudotsuga menziesii pendula*)
Golden Weeping Willow (*Salix alba tristis*)
★Babylon Weeping Willow (*Salix babylonica*)
Wisconsin or Niobe Weeping Willow (*Salix blanda*)
Thurlow Weeping Willow (*Salix elegantissima*)
Weeping Japanese Pagoda Tree (*Sophora japonica pendula*)
Weeping European Mountain Ash (*Sorbus aucuparia pendula*)
Pendant Silver Linden (*Tilia petiolaris*)
Sargent Hemlock (*Tsuga canadensis pendula*)
Weeping American Elm (*Ulmus americana pendula*)

Rounded or Globe-Shaped

★Japanese Maple (*Acer palmatum*)
Globe Norway Maple (*Acer platanoides globosum*)
Globe European Hornbeam (*Carpinus betulus globosa*)
Bunch Hackberry (*Celtis bungeana*)
Cornelian Cherry (*Cornus mas*)
Japanese Cornel (*Cornus officinalis*)
Single Seed Hawthorn (*Crataegus monogyna inermis*)
★Saucer Magnolia (*Magnolia soulangeana*)
★Crab Apple species (*Malus*)
★White Oak (*Quercus alba*)
Umbrella Black Locust (*Robinia pseudoacacia umbraculifera*)
Sargent Hemlock (*Tsuga canadensis sargenti*)
Koopman Elm (*Ulmus carpinifolia koopmanni*)
Globe Smooth-leaved Elm (*Ulmus carpinifolia umbraculifera*)

With Horizontal Branching

Fir species (*Abies*)
Silk Tree (*Albizzia julibrissin*)
★Flowering Dogwood (*Cornus florida*)
Japanese Dogwood (*Cornus kousa*)
★Hawthorn species (*Crataegus*)
Dawn Redwood (*Metasequoia glyptostroboides*)
★Black Tupelo or Black Gum (*Nyssa sylvatica*)
Spruce species (*Picea*)
Japanese Red Pine (*Pinus densiflora*)
★Eastern White Pine (*Pinus strobus*)
Golden Larch (*Pseudolarix amabilis*)
★White Oak (*Quercus alba*)
★Pin Oak (*Quercus palustris*)
Common Bald Cypress (*Taxodium distichum*)

Trees Classified by Color of Blossom

Yellow

★Golden Rain Tree (*Koelreuteria paniculata*)
★Laburnum (*Laburnum vossi*)

White

★Shadblow Serviceberry (*Amelanchier canadensis*)
Whitebud (*Cercis canadensis alba*)
★American Yellow-wood (*Cladrastis lutea*)
Japanese Dogwood (*Cornus kousa*)
Washington Hawthorn (*Crataegus phaenop rum*)
Carolina Silverbell (*Halesia carolina*)
Yulan Magnolia (*Magnolia denudata*)
★Southern Magnolia (*Magnolia grandiflora*)
★Star Magnolia (*Magnolia stellata*)
★Arnold Crap Apple (*Malus arnoldiana*)
Siberian Crab Apple (*Malus baccata*)
Tea Crab Apple (*Malus hupehensis*)
Sargent Crab Apple (*Malus sargenti*)
★Sorrel Tree (*Oxydendrum arboreum*)
Thundercloud Plum (*Prunus cerasifera* "Thundercloud")
Sour Cherry (*Prunus cerasus*)
Mount Fuji Cherry (*Prunus serrulata* "Shirotae")
Yoshino Cherry (*Prunus yedoensis*)
Bradford Callery Pear (*Pyrus calleryana* "Bradford")
★Common Pear (*Pyrus communis*)
★Japanese Pagoda Tree (*Sophora japonica*)
Korean Mountain Ash (*Sorbus alnifolia*)

American Mountain Ash (*Sorbus americana*)
European Mountain Ash (*Sorbus aucuparia*)
Showy Mountain Ash (*Sorbus decora*)
Japanese Stewartia (*Stewartia pseudocamellia*)
Japanese Snowbell (*Styrax japonica*)

Pink

Wither's Pink Redbud (*Cercis canadensis* "Wither's Pink Charm")
Red Flowering Dogwood (*Cornus florida rubra*)
Toba Hawthorn (*Crataegus mordenensis* "Toba")
Ingleside Crape-Myrtle (*Lagerstroemia indica* "Ingleside Pink")
★Saucer Magnolia (*Magnolia soulangeana*)
★Japanese Flowering Crab Apple (*Malus floribunda*)
Katherine Crab Apple (*Malus* "Katherine")
Prince Georges Crab Apple (*Malus* "Prince Georges")
★Common Apple (*Malus pumila*)
Blireiana Plum (*Prunus blireiana*)
Sargent Cherry (*Prunus sargenti*)
Amanogawa Cherry (*Prunus serrulata* "Amanogawa")
Kwanzan Cherry (*Prunus serrulata* "Kwanzan")
Autumn Cherry (*Prunus subhirtella autumnalis*)
Weeping Cherry (*Prunus subhirtella pendula*)

Red

Ruby Horse-Chestnut (*Aesculus carnea briotti*)
Paul's Scarlet Hawthorn (*Crataegus oxyacantha pauli*)
Red Crape-Myrtle (*Lagerstroemia indica* "Wm. Toovey")
Alexandrina Magnolia (*Magnolia soulangeana* "Alexandrina")
Almey Crab Apple (*Malus* "Almey")
Carmine Crab Apple (*Malus atrosanguinea*)

Trees with Bright Red Fruit

★Flowering Dogwood (*Cornus florida*)
Japanese Dogwood (*Cornus kousa*)
Downy Hawthorn (*Crataegus mollis*)
Washington Hawthorn (*Crataegus phaenopyrum*)
American Holly (*Ilex opaca*)
Almey Crab Apple (*Malus* "Almey")
Siberian Crab Apple (*Malus baccata*)
Hopa Crab Apple (*Malus* "Hopa")
★Common Apple (*Malus pumila*)
Sargent Crab Apple (*Malus sargenti*)
Korean Mountain Ash (*Sorbus alnifolia*)
American Mountain Ash (*Sorbus americana*)
European Mountain Ash (*Sorbus aucuparia*)

Trees Classified by Color of Summer Foliage

Blue

White Fir (*Abies concolor*)
★Blue Atlas Cedar (*Cedrus atlantica glauca*)
Steel Lawson Cypress (*Chamaecyparis lawsonia glauca*)
Western Red Cedar (*Juniperus scopulorum* var. Chandler Blue)
Eastern Red Cedar (*Juniperus virginiana* var. *Burki*)
Colorado Blue Spruce (*Picea pungens* var. *Glauca*)

Silver to Gray

Russian Olive (*Elaeagnus angustifolia*)
White Poplar (*Populus alba*)
Pendant Silver Linden (*Tilia petiolaris*)
★Silver Linden (*Tilia tomentosa*)

Red to Purple

Blood-leaf Japanese Maple (*Acer palmatum atropurpureum*)
Crimson King Maple (*Acer platanoides* "Crimson King")
Schwedler Maple (*Acer platanoides schwedleri*)
Purple-leaf Sycamore Maple (*Acer pseudoplatanus*)
Purple Beech (*Fagus sylvatica atropunicea*)
Weeping Purple Beech (*Fagus sylvatica purpureopendula*)
River's Purple Beech (*Fagus sylvatica riversi*)
Rubylace Locust (*Gleditsia triacanthos inermis* "Rubylace")
Purple Crab Apple (*Malus purpurea*)

Blireiana Plum (*Prunus blireiana*)
Pissard Plum (*Prunus cerasifera atropurpurea*)
Thundercloud Plum (*Prunus cerasifera nigra* "Thundercloud")
Blood-leaf Peach (*Prunus persica atropurpurea*)
Purple English Oak (*Quercus robur atropurpurea*)

Trees Classified by Color of Fall Foliage

Yellow

Striped Maple or Moosewood (*Acer pensylvanicum*)
Norway Maple (*Acer platanoides* var.)
★Sugar Maple (*Acer saccharum*)
Apple Serviceberry (yellow-orange) (*Amelanchier grandiflora*)
★Birch species (*Betula*)
Hickory species (*Carya*)
Chinese Chestnut (*Castanea mollissima*)
★Katsura Tree (yellow to scarlet) (*Cercidiphyllum japonicum*)
Redbud species (*Cercis*)
Fringetree (*Chionanthus virginicus*)
★American Yellow-wood (*Cladrastis lutea*)
★American Beech (*Fagus grandifolia*)
★European Beech (*Fagus sylvatica*)
White Ash (purple to yellow) (*Fraxinus americana*)
★Ginkgo (*Ginkgo biloba*)
★Star Magnolia (bronze) (*Magnolia stellata*)
Golden Larch (*Pseudolarix amabilis*)
★Willow species (*Salix*)

Red

Amur Maple (*Acer ginnala*)
★Japanese Maple (*Acer palmatum* var.)
★Red Maple (*Acer rubrum*)
★Sugar Maple (*Acer saccharum*)
Tatarian Maple (*Acer tataricum*)
★Shadblow Serviceberry (*Amelanchier canadensis*)
Hornbeam species (*Carpinus*)
★Flowering Dogwood (*Cornus florida*)
Japanese Dogwood (*Cornus kousa*)
American Smoke Tree (*Cotinus americanus*)
Washington Hawthorn (*Crataegus phaenopyrum*)
★Sweet Gum (*Liquidambar styraciflua*)
Dawson Crab Apple (*Malus dawsoniana*)
★Black Tupelo or Black Gum (*Nyssa sylvatica*)
★Sorrel Tree (*Oxydendrum arboreum*)
Persian Parrotia (*Parrotia persica*)
★Cherry species (*Prunus*)
Bradford Callery Pear (*Pyrus calleryana* "Bradford")
Red Oak (*Quercus borealis*)
Scarlet Oak (*Quercus coccinea*)
★Pin Oak (*Quercus palustris*)
Sassafras (*Sassafras albidum*)

Purple

White Ash (*Fraxinus americana*)
★Sweet Gum (*Liquidambar styraciflua*)
★White Oak (*Quercus alba*)
★Common Pear (*Pyrus communis*)
Japanese Stewartia (*Stewartia pseudocamellia*)

Trees with Interesting Bark

Gray

★Red Maple (*Acer rubrum*)
Serviceberry species (*Amelanchier*)
Hornbeam species (*Carpinus*)
Hackberry species (*Celtis*)
★American Yellow-wood (*Cladrastis lutea*)
★Hawthorn species (*Crataegus*)
★Beech species (*Fagus*)
American Holly (*Ilex opaca*)
English or Persian Walnut (*Juglans regia*)
Cucumber Tree (*Magnolia acuminata*)
★Saucer Magnolia (*Magnolia soulangeana*)
Red Oak (young trunk and branches) (*Quercus borealis*)
Black Oak (young trunk and branches) (*Quercus velutina*)
Mountain Ash species (*Sorbus*)

White

★European Birch (*Betula pendula*)
★Gray Birch (*Betula populifolia*)

Red

Japanese Red Pine (*Pinus densiflora*)
Scotch Pine (*Pinus sylvestris*)

Reddish Brown

Sargent Cherry (*Prunus sargenti*)

Yellow

Wisconsin or Niobe Weeping Willow (*Salix blanda*)

Corky

★Amur Cork (*Phellodendron amurense*)

Green

★Babylon Weeping Willow (*Salix babylonica*)

Flaking

Paperbark Maple (*Acer griseum*)
★Birch species (*Betula*)
Shagbark Hickory (*Carya ovata*)
Russian Olive (*Elaeagnus angustifolia*)
Crape-Myrtle (*Lagerstroemia indica*)
Persian Parrotia (*Parrotia persica*)
★Plane Tree species (*Platanus*)
Lace-bark Pine (*Pinus bungeana*)
Stewartia species (*Stewartia*)

Trees for the City

White Fir (*Abies concolor*)
Hedge Maple (*Acer campestre*)
Box-Elder (*Acer negundo*)
Norway Maple (*Acer platanoides*)
Sycamore Maple (*Acer pseudoplatanus*)
★Horse Chestnut or Buckeye (*Aesculus*)
★Tree of Heaven (*Ailanthus*)
Silk Tree (*Albizzia julibrissin*)
Catalpa (*Catalpa*)
Hackberry (*Celtis*)
★Downy Hawthorn (*Crataegus mollis*)
★Washington Hawthorn (*Crataegus phaenopyrum*)
Russian Olive (*Elaeagnus angustifolia*)
White Ash (*Fraxinus americana*)
European Ash (*Fraxinus excelsior*)
Green Ash (*Fraxinus pennsylvanica*)
★Ginkgo (*Ginkgo biloba*)
Thornless Honey-Locust (*Gleditsia triacanthos inermis*)
★Golden Rain Tree (*Koelreuteria paniculata*)
★Southern Magnolia (*Magnolia grandiflora*)
★Saucer Magnolia (*Magnolia soulangeana*)
★Star Magnolia (*Magnolia stellata*)
★Crab Apple (*Malus* var.)
Chinaberry (*Melia azedarach*)
★Amur Cork (*Phellodendron amurense*)
★London Plane Tree (*Platanus acerifolia*)
White Poplar (*Populus alba*)
Lombardy Poplar (*Populus nigra italica*)
Bradford Callery Pear (*Pyrus calleryana* "Bradford")
Red Oak (*Quercus borealis*)
★Black Locust (*Robinia pseudoacacia*)
★Japanese Pagoda Tree (*Sophora japonica*)
★Little-leaf Linden (*Tilia cordata*)
★Crimean Linden (*Tilia euchlora*)
★Silver Linden (*Tilia tomentosa*)
Village Green Zelkova (*Zelkova serrata* "Village Green")

Trees for Wide Streets

Sycamore Maple (*Acer pseudoplatanus*)
★Sugar Maple (*Acer saccharum*)
Sugar Hackberry (*Celtis laevigata*)
★Katsura Tree (*Cercidiphyllum japonicum*)
White Ash (*Fraxinus americana*)
Green Ash (*Fraxinus pennsylvanica lanceolata*)
★Ginkgo (*Ginkgo biloba*)
★Common Honey-Locust (*Gleditsia triacanthos*)
Kalopanax (*Kalopanax pictus*)
Tulip Tree (*Liriodendron tulipifera*)
★Southern Magnolia (*Magnolia grandiflora*)
★Amur Cork (*Phellodendron amurense*)
Eastern White Pine (*Pinus strobus*)

*London Plane Tree (*Platanus acerifolium*)
*Oriental Plane Tree (*Platanus orientalis*)
White Poplar (*Populus alba*)
Sargent Cherry (*Prunus sargenti*)
Red Oak (*Quercus borealis*)
*Pin Oak (*Quercus palustris*)
Willow Oak (*Quercus phellos*)
Japanese Zelkova (*Zelkova serrata*)

Trees for Medium Streets

Norway Maple (*Acer platanoides*)
*Sweet Gum (*Liquidambar styraciflua*)
Chinaberry (*Melia azedarach*)
Hop-Hornbeam (*Ostrya virginiana*)
*Sorrel Tree or Sourwood (*Oxydendrum arboreum*)
Simon Poplar (*Populus simoni*)
Scarlet Oak (*Quercus coccinea*)
Laurel Oak (*Quercus laurifolia*)
Willow Oak (*Quercus phellos*)
*Black Locust (*Robinia pseudoacacia*)
Sassafras (*Sassafras albidum officinale*)
*Japanese Pagoda Tree (*Sophora japonica*)
*Linden species (*Tilia*)

Trees for Suburban Streets

Hedge Maple (*Acer campestre*)
Amur Maple (*Acer ginnala*)
Globe Norway Maple (*Acer platanoides globosum*)
Mountain Maple (*Acer spicatum*)
Tatarian Maple (*Acer tataricum*)
American Hornbeam (*Carpinus caroliniana*)
Pyramidal European Hornbeam (*Carpinus betulus fastigiata*)
Globe European Hornbeam (*Carpinus betulus globosa*)
Fringetree (*Chionanthus virginicus*)
*Hawthorn species (*Crataegus*)
Korean Evodia (*Evodia danielli*)
Carolina Silverbell (*Halesia carolina*)
*Golden Rain Tree (*Koelreuteria paniculata*)
Oriental Cherry (*Prunus serrulata*)
Columnar Sargent Cherry (*Prunus sargenti columnaris*)
Japanese Snowbell (*Styrax japonica*)
Fragrant Snowbell (*Styrax obassia*)
Smooth-leaved Elm varieties (*Ulmus carpinifolia*)

Soil Tolerance

Trees Tolerating Acid Soil

*Japanese Maple (*Acer palmatum*)
*Flowering Dogwood (*Cornus florida*)
Japanese Dogwood (*Cornus kousa*)
*European Beech (*Fagus sylvatica*)
Sweet Bay (*Magnolia virginiana*)
*Black Tupelo (*Nyssa sylvatica*)
*Sorrel Tree (*Oxydendrum arboreum*)
Red Oak (*Quercus borealis*)
Scarlet Oak (*Quercus coccinea*)
*Pin Oak (*Quercus palustris*)
Willow Oak (*Quercus phellos*)
Japanese Stewartia (*Stewartia pseudocamellia*)

Trees Tolerating Moist Soil

*Red Maple (*Acer rubrum*)
Holly species (*Ilex*)
*Sweet Gum (*Liquidambar styraciflua*)
Sweet Bay (*Magnolia virginiana*)
*Black Tupelo or Black Gum (*Nyssa sylvatica*)
Poplar species (*Populus*)
Swamp White Oak (*Quercus bicolor*)
*Willow species (*Salix*)
Common Bald Cypress (*Taxodium distichum*)
American Arbor-vitae (*Thuja occidentalis*)

Trees Tolerating Dry or Poor Soil

Box-Elder (*Acer negunda*)
*Tree of Heaven (*Ailanthus*)
Silk Tree (*Albizzia julibrissin*)
*Gray Birch (*Betula populifolia*)
Common Paper-Mulberry (*Broussonetia papyrifera*)
European Hackberry (*Celtis australis*)
Russian Olive (*Elaeagnus angustifolia*)
Green Ash (*Fraxinus pennsylvanica*)
*Honey-Locust (*Gleditsia triacanthos* var.)
Western Red Cedar (*Juniperus scopulorum*)
Eastern Red Cedar (*Juniperus virginiana*)
*Golden Rain Tree (*Koelreuteria paniculata*)
Osage-Orange (*Maclura pomifera*)
Virginia or Scrub Pine (*Pinus virginiana*)
White Poplar (*Populus alba*)
Black Jack Oak (*Quercus marilandica*)
Chestnut Oak (*Quercus montana*)
*Black Locust (*Robinia pseudoacacia*)
Sassafras (*Sassafras albidum officinale*)
*Japanese Pagoda Tree (*Sophora japonica*)
Chinese Elm (*Ulmus parvifolia*)
Siberian Elm (*Ulmus pumila*)

Pest-Resistant Trees

*Tree of Heaven (*Ailanthus altissima*)
Hornbeam species (*Carpinus*)
*Cedar species (*Cedrus*)
European Hackberry (*Celtis australis*)
*Katsura Tree (*Cercidiphyllum japonicum*)
False Cypress species (*Chamaecyparis*)
Cornelian Cherry (*Cornus mas*)
Japanese Cornel (*Cornus officinalis*)
American Smoke Tree (*Cotinus americanus*)
Russian Olive (*Elaeagnus angustifolia*)
Franklinia (*Franklinia alatamaha*)
*Ginkgo (*Ginkgo biloba*)
*Honey-Locust (*Gleditsia triacanthos*)
Kentucky Coffee Tree (*Gymnocladus dioicus*)
Juniper species (*Juniperus*)
Kalopanax (*Kalopanax pictus*)
*Golden Rain Tree (*Koelreuteria paniculata*)
*Laburnum species (*Laburnum*)
*Sweet Gum (*Liquidambar styraciflua*)
Cucumber Tree (*Magnolia acuminata*)
Kobus Magnolia (*Magnolia kobus borealis*)

Anise Magnolia (*Magnolia salicifolia*)
*Star Magnolia (*Magnolia stellata*)
Hop-Hornbeam species (*Ostrya*)

Trees for Seashore Planting

Norway Maple (*Acer platanoides*)
Sycamore Maple (*Acer pseudoplatanus*)
Horse-Chestnut (*Aesculus hippocastanum*)
*Tree of Heaven (*Ailanthus*)
*Shadblow Serviceberry (*Amelanchier canadensis*)
Cockspur Thorn (*Crataegus crus-galli*)
English Hawthorn (*Crataegus oxyacantha*)
Russian Olive (*Elaeagnus angustifolia*)
Velvet Ash (*Fraxinus vetutina*)
Thornless Honey-Locust (*Gleditsia triacanthos inermis* var.)
American Holly (*Ilex opaca*)
Eastern Red Cedar (*Juniperus virginiana*)
*Southern Magnolia (*Magnolia grandiflora*)
*Black Tupelo (*Nyssa sylvatica*)
Colorado Blue Spruce (*Picea pungens glauca*)
*Austrian Pine (*Pinus nigra*)
Scotch Pine (*Pinus sylvestris*)
*Japanese Black Pine (*Pinus thunbergi*)
*London Plane Tree (*Platanus acerifolia*)
White Poplar (*Populus alba*)
Black Cherry (*Prunus serotina*)
*White Oak (*Quercus alba*)
Black Jack Oak (*Quercus marilandica*)
*Live Oak (*Quercus virginiana*)
*Black Locust (*Robinia pseudoacacia*)
Golden Weeping Willow (*Salix alba tristis*)
*Japanese Pagoda Tree (*Sophora japonica*)
*Little-leaf Linden (*Tilia cordata*)
*Crimean Linden (*Tilia euchlora*)
*Oriental Arbor-vitae (*Thuja orientalis*)
Chinese Elm (*Ulmus parvifolia*)

Trees for Hedging or Barriers

European Beech (*Fagus sylvatica*) prunes well.
Leyland Cypress (*Cupressocyparis leylandii*) withstands heavy pruning.
Hawthorn varieties (*Crataegus*) easily pruned, advantage of thorns.
Canadian Hemlock (*Tsuga canadensis*) evergreen.
American Holly (*Ilex opaca*) can be pruned.
European Hornbeam (*Carpinus betulus*) prunes well.
Little-leaf Linden (*Tilia cordata*) tolerates heavy pruning.
Hedge Maple (*Acer campestre*) can be pruned.
Austrian Pine (*Pinus nigra*) plant 10–12 feet on centers, staggered row.
Japanese Black Pine (*Pinus thunbergi*) plant 8 feet on centers, staggered row.
Eastern White Pine (*Pinus strobus*) plant 15 feet on centers, staggered row.

MASSACHUSETTS

State Tree

*American Elm (*Ulmus americana*)

Evergreen Trees

Fir species (*Abies*)
Holly species (*Ilex*)
Juniper species (*Juniperus*)
*Larch species (*Larix*)
Spruce species (*Picea*)
*Pine species (*Pinus*)
*Douglas Fir (*Pseudotsuga menziesii*)
Arbor-vitae species (*Thuja*)
*Hemlock species (*Tsuga*)

Trees Classified by Height

20–35 Feet

Argutum Maple (*Acer argutum*)
Hedge Maple (*Acer campestre*)
Hornbeam Maple (*Acer carpinifolium*)
Amur Maple (*Acer ginnala*)
Paperbark Maple (*Acer griseum*)
Manchurian Maple (*Acer mandshuricum*)
*Japanese Maple (*Acer palmatum*)
Mountain Maple (*Acer spicatum*)
Tatarian Maple (*Acer tataricum*)
Ohio Buckeye (*Aesculus glabra*)
Apple Serviceberry (*Amelanchier grandiflora*)
*Gray Birch (*Betula populifolia*)
European Hornbeam (*Carpinus betulus globosa*)
Mockernut (*Carya tomentosa*)
Fringetree (*Chionanthus virginicus*)
Japanese Clethra (*Clethra barbinervis*)

Cornelian Cherry (*Cornus mas*)
Japanese Cornel (*Cornus officinalis*)
American Smoke Tree (*Cotinus americanus*)
*Hawthorn species (*Crataegus*)
Russian Olive (*Elaeagnus angustifolia*)
Euonymus species (*Euonymus*)
Korean Evodia (*Evodia danielli*)
Franklinia (*Franklinia alatamaha*)
Flowering Ash (*Fraxinus ornus*)
Carolina Silverbell (*Halesia carolina*)
David Hemiptelea (*Hemiptelea davidi*)
Common Sea-Buckthorn (*Hippophae rhamnoides*)
Possum Haw (*Ilex decidua*)
Longstalk Holly (*Ilex pedunculosa*)
Needle Juniper (*Juniperus rigida*)
*Golden Rain Tree (*Koelreuteria paniculata*)

*Laburnum species (*Laburnum*)
Yellow Cucumber Tree (*Magnolia cordata*)
Anise Magnolia (*Magnolia salicifolia*)
*Saucer Magnolia (*Magnolia soulangeana*)
*Star Magnolia (*Magnolia stellata*)
*Crab Apple species (*Malus*)
*Cherry species (*Prunus*)
Dahurian Buckthorn (*Rhamnus davurica*)
Almond-leaf Willow (*Salix amygdalina*)
*Babylon Weeping Willow (*Salix babylonica*)
Goat Willow (*Salix caprea*)
Showy Mountain Ash (*Sorbus decora*)
Snowberry Mountain Ash (*Sorbus discolor*)
Folgner Mountain Ash (*Sorbus folgneri*)
Snowbell species (*Styrax*)
Asiatic Sweetleaf (*Symplocus paniculata*)
Japanese Tree Lilac (*Syringa amurensis japonica*)

35–75 Feet
Korean Fir (*Abies koreana*)
Box-Elder (*Acer negundo*)
Nikko Maple (*Acer nikoense*)
Striped Maple or Moosewood (*Acer pennsylvanicum*)
*Red-fruited Tree of Heaven (*Ailanthus altissima erythrocarpa*)
Italian Alder (*Alnus cordata*)
Speckled Alder (*Alnus incana*)
Red Alder (*Alnus rubra*)
*Shadblow Serviceberry (*Amelanchier canadensis*)
Allegany Serviceberry (*Amelanchier laevis*)
Devil's Walking Stick (*Aralia elata*)
Dahurian Birch (*Betula davurica*)
Manchurian Birch (*Betula mandshurica szechuanica*)
*European Birch (*Betula pendula*)
Common Paper-Mulberry (*Broussonetia papyrifera*)
European Hornbeam (*Carpinus betula*)
American Hornbeam (*Carpinus caroliniana*)
Japanese Hornbeam (*Carpinus japonica*)
Chinese Chestnut (*Castanea mollissima*)
Southern Catalpa (*Catalpa bignoniodies*)
Chinese Toon (*Cedrela sinensis*)
Bunch Hackberry (*Celtis bungeana*)
*Katsura Tree (*Cercidiphyllum japonicum*)
*American Yellow-wood (*Cladrastis lutea*)
*Flowering Dogwood (*Cornus florida*)
Turkish Filbert (*Corylus coluna*)
Cockspur Thorn (*Crataegus crus-galli*)
Green Hawthorn (*Crataegus viridis*)
Common Persimmon (*Diospyros virginiana*)
Green Ash (*Fraxinus pennsylvanica lanceolata*)
Mountain Winterberry (*Ilex montana*)
American Holly (*Ilex opaca*)
Heartnut (*Juglans sieboldiana cordiformis*)
Chinese Juniper (*Juniperus chinensis*)
Western Red Cedar (*Juniperus scopulorum*)
Osage-Orange (*Maclura pomifera*)
Yulan Magnolia (*Magnolia denudata*)
Fraser Magnolia (*Magnolia fraseri*)
Kobus Magnolia (*Magnolia kobus borealis*)
Loebner Magnolia (*Magnolia loebneri*)
Siberian Crab Apple (*Malus bacata*)
"Cowichan" Crab Apple (*Malus* "Cowichan")
"Dolgo" Crab Apple (*Malus* "Dolgo")
"Makamik" Crab Apple (*Malus* "Makamik")
Cherry Crab Apple (*Malus robusta*)
"Sissipuk" Crab Apple (*Malus* "Sissipuk")
White Mulberry (*Morus alba*)
*Sorrel Tree or Sourwood (*Oxydendrum arboreum*)
Persian Parrotia (*Parrotia persica*)
Empress Tree (*Paulownia tomentosa*)
*Amur Cork (*Phellodendron amurense*)
Dragon Spruce (*Picea asperata*)
Jack Pine (*Pinus banksiana*)
Lace-bark Pine (*Pinus bungeana*)
Swiss Stone Pine (*Pinus cembra*)
Limber Pine (*Pinus flexilis*)
Pitch Pine (*Pinus rigida*)
Scotch Pine (*Pinus sylvestris*)
Hardy Orange (*Poncirus trifoliata*)
Chinese Poplar (*Populus lasiocarpa*)
Simon Poplar (*Populus simoni*)

Miyama Cherry (*Prunus maximowiczi*)
European Bird Cherry (*Prunus padus*)
Sargent Cherry (*Prunus sargenti*)
Yoshino Cherry (*Prunus yedoensis*)
Fragrant Epaulette Tree (*Pterostyrax hispida*)
Ussurian Pear (*Pyrus ussuriensis*)
Swamp White Oak (*Quercus bicolor*)
Red Oak (*Quercus borealis*)
Scarlet Oak (*Quercus coccinea*)
Shingle Oak (*Quercus imbricaria*)
*Pin Oak (*Quercus palustris*)
Willow Oak (*Quercus phellos*)
Clammy Locust (*Robinia viscosa*)
White Willow (*Salix alba*)
Wisconsin or Niobe Weeping Willow (*Salix blanda*)
Elaeagnus Willow (*Salix elaeagnos*)
Thurlow Weeping Willow (*Salix elegantissima*)
Laurel Willow (*Salix pentandra*)
Sassafras (*Sassafras albidum officinale*)
Korean Mountain Ash (*Sorbus alnifolia*)
White Beam Mountain Ash (*Sorbus aria*)
European Mountain Ash or Rowan Tree (*Sorbus aucuparia*)
Korean Stewartia (*Stewartia koreana*)
Japanese Stewartia (*Stewartia pseudo-camellia*)
American Arbor-vitae (*Thuja occidentalis*)
Japanese Arbor-vitae (*Thuja standishi*)
*Crimean Linden (*Tilia euchlora*)
Carolina Hemlock (*Tsuga caroliniana*)
Chinese Elm (*Ulmus parviflora*)
Siberian Elm (*Ulmus pumila*)

75 Feet or Over
Fir species (*Abies*)
Norway Maple (*Acer platanoides*)
Sycamore Maple (*Acer pseudoplatanus*)
*Red or Swamp Maple (*Acer rubrum*)
*Sugar Maple (*Acer saccharum*)
*Baumann Horse-Chestnut (*Aesculus hippocastanum baumanni*)
European Alder (*Alnus glutinosa*)
Sweet Birch (*Betula lenta*)
River Birch (*Betula nigra*)
*Canoe Birch (*Betula papyrifera*)
Hickory species (*Carya*)
Northern Catalpa (*Catalpa speciosa*)
*Cedar species (*Cedrus*)
Sugar Hackberry (*Celtis laevigata*)
*Katsura Tree (*Cercidiphyllum japonicum*)
False Cypress species (*Chamaecyparis*)
*Beech species (*Fagus*)
White Ash (*Fraxinus americana*)
European Ash (*Fraxinus excelsior*)
*Ginkgo or Maidenhair Tree (*Ginkgo biloba*)
*Common Honey-Locust (*Gleditsia triacanthos*)
Kentucky Coffee Tree (*Gymnocladus dioicus*)
Mountain Silverbell (*Halesia monticola*)
Eastern Black Walnut (*Juglans nigra*)
English or Persian Walnut (*Juglans regia*)
Kalopanax (*Kalopanax pictus*)
Japanese Larch (*Larix leptolepis*)
*Sweet Gum (*Liquidambar* (styraciflua))
Tulip Tree or Yellow Poplar (*Liriodendron tulipifera*)
Cucumber Tree (*Magnolia acuminata*)
White-leaf Japanese Magnolia (*Magnolia obovata*)
Dawn Redwood (*Metasequoia glyptostroboides*)
*Black Gum or Black Tupelo (*Nyssa sylvatica*)
Spruce species (*Picea*)
*Pine species (*Pinus*)
*Plane Tree species (*Platanus*)
Poplar species (*Populus*)
Sargent Cherry (*Prunus sargenti*)
Black or Rum Cherry (*Prunus serotina*)
Golden Larch (*Pseudolarix amabilis*)
*Douglas Fir (*Pseudotsuga menziesii*)
*Oak species (*Quercus*)
Umbrella Pine (*Sciadopitys verticillata*)
Common Bald Cypress (*Taxodium distichum*)
*Linden species (*Tilia*)
*Canada Hemlock (*Tsuga canadensis*)
*Elm species (*Ulmus*)
Japanese Zelkova (*Zelkova serrata*)

Trees Classified by Form
Pyramidal
Fir species (*Abies*)
*Birch species (*Betula*)
*Cedar species (*Cedrus*)
False Cypress species (*Chamaecyparis*)
Turkish Filbert (*Corylus coluna*)
Cryptomeria (*Cryptomeria japonica*)
*Beech species (*Fagus*)
English Holly (*Ilex aquifolium*)
American Holly (*Ilex opaca*)
Longstalk Holly (*Ilex pedunculosa*)
Juniper or Red Cedar species (*Juniperus*)
*Larch species (*Larix*)
*Sweet Gum (*Liquidambar styraciflua*)
*Magnolia species (*Magnolia*)
Dawn Redwood (*Metasequoia glyptostroboides*)
*Black Gum or Black Tupelo (*Nyssa sylvatica*)
Hop-Hornbeam (*Ostrya virginiana*)
*Sorrel Tree or Sourwood (*Oxydendrum arboreum*)
Spruce species (*Picea*)
Swiss Stone Pine (*Pinus cembra*)
Korean Pine (*Pinus koraiensis*)
Pyramid Austrian Pine (*Pinus nigra pyramidalis*)
Japanese White Pine (*Pinus parviflora*)
Bolleana Poplar (*Populus alba pyramidalis*)
Golden Larch (*Pseudolarix amabilis*)
*Douglas Fir (*Pseudotsuga menziesii*)
*Pin Oak (*Quercus palustris*)
Korean Stewartia (*Stewartia koreana*)
Common Bald Cypress (*Taxodium distichum*)
Arbor-vitae species (*Thuja*)
*Linden species (*Tilia*)
*Hemlock species (*Tsuga*)
Smooth-leaved Elm (*Ulmus carpinifolia*)

Columnar
Ascending Norway Maple (*Acer platanoides columnare*)
Columnar Norway Maple (*Acer platanoides columnare*)
Erect Norway Maple (*Acer platanoides erectum*)
Columnar Red Maple (*Acer rubrum columnare*)
Sentry maple (*Acer saccharum monumentale*)
Fastigiate European Birch (*Betula pendula fastigiata*)
Fastigiate European Hornbeam (*Carpinus betulus fastigiata*)
Fastigiate Washington Hawthorn (*Crataegus phaenopyrum fastigiata*)
Dawyck Beech (*Fagus sylvatica fastigiata*)
Sentry Ginkgo (*Ginkgo biloba fastigiata*)
Blue Columnar Chinese Juniper (*Juniperus chinensis columnaris*)
Schott Red Cedar (*Juniperus virginiana schotti*)
Swiss Stone Pine (*Pinus cembra*)
Fastigiate White Pine (*Pinus strobus fastigiata*)
*Lombardy Poplar (*Populus nigra italica*)
Fastigiate Simon Poplar (*Populus simoni fastigiata*)
Columnar Sargent Cherry (*Prunus sargenti columnaris*)
"Amanogawa" Cherry (*Prunus serrulata* "Amanogawa")
Fastigiate English Oak (*Quercus robur fastigiata*)
Shipmast Locust (*Robinia pseudoacacia rectissima*)
Upright European Mountain Ash (*Sorbus aucuparia fastigiata*)
Fastigiate American Arbor-vitae (*Thuja occidentalis douglasi pyramidalis*)
Columnar Big-leaf Linden (*Tilia platyphyllos fastigiata*)
*American Elm varieties (*Ulmus americana*)

Weeping
Slender European Birch (*Betula pendula tristis*)
Young's Birch (*Betula pendula youngi*)
Weeping European Hornbeam (*Carpinus betulus pendula*)
*Weeping Beech (*Fagus sylvatica pendula*)
Weeping Purple Beech (*Fagus sylvatica purpureo-pendula*)
Weeping Red Cedar (*Juniperus virginiana pendula*)
Weeping Larch (*Larix decidua pendula*)

"Exzellenz Thiel" Crab Apple (*Malus* "Exzellenz Thiel")

"Oekonomierat Echtermeyer" Crab Apple (*Malus* "Oekonomierat Echtermeyer")

Weeping Mulberry (*Morus alba pendula*)

Koster Weeping Blue Spruce (*Picea pungens kosteriana*)

Weeping White Pine (*Pinus strobus pendula*)

Weeping Black Cherry (*Prunus serotina pendula*)

Weeping Higan Cherry (*Prunus subhirtella pendula*)

"Yaeshidare" Cherry (*Prunus subhirtella pendula flora plena*)

Weeping Yoshino Cherry (*Prunus yedoensis perpendens*)

Weeping Douglas Fir (*Pseudotsuga taxifolia pendula*)

Golden Weeping Willow (*Salix alba tristis*)

★Babylon Weeping Willow (*Salix babylonica*)

Wisconsin or Niobe Weeping Willow (*Salix blanda*)

Thurlow Weeping Willow (*Salix elegantissima*)

Weeping Japanese Pagoda Tree (*Sophora japonica pendula*)

Weeping European Mountain Ash (*Sorbus aucuparia pendula*)

Weeping Folgner Mountain Ash (*Sorbus folgneri pendula*)

Pendant Silver Linden (*Tilia petiolaris*)

Sargent Hemlock (*Tsuga canadensis pendula*)

Weeping American Elm (*Ulmus americana pendula*)

Rounded or Globe-Shaped

★Japanese Maple (*Acer palmatum*)

Globe Norway Maple (*Acer platanoides globosum*)

Globe European Hornbeam (*Carpinus betulus globosa*)

Bunch Hackberry (*Celtis bungeana*)

Cornelian Cherry (*Cornus mas*)

Japanese Cornel (*Cornus officinalis*)

Single Seed Hawthorn (*Crataegus monogyna inermis*)

★Saucer Magnolia (*Magnolia soulangeana*)

★Crab Apple species (*Malus*)

★White Oak (*Quercus alba*)

Umbrella Black Locust (*Robinia pseudoacacia umbraculifera*)

Sargent Hemlock (*Tsuga canadensis sargenti*)

Koopmann Elm (*Ulmus carpinifolia koopmanni*)

Globe Smooth-leaved Elm (*Ulmus carpinifolia umbraculifera*)

With Horizontal Branching

Fir species (*Abies*)

Silk Tree (*Albizzia julibrissin*)

★Cedar species (*Cedrus*)

Eastern Redbud (*Cercis canadensis*)

★Flowering Dogwood (*Cornus florida*)

Japanese Dogwood (*Cornus kousa*)

★Hawthorn species (*Crataegus*)

Dawn Redwood (*Metasequoia glyptostroboides*)

★Black Gum or Black Tupelo (*Nyssa sylvatica*)

Spruce species (*Picea*)

Japanese Red Pine (*Pinus densiflora*)

★Eastern White Pine (*Pinus strobus*)

Golden Larch (*Pseudolarix amabilis*)

★White Oak (*Quercus alba*)

★Pin Oak (*Quercus palustris*)

Common Bald Cypress (*Taxodium distichum*)

Trees Classified by Color of Blossom

Yellow

★Golden Rain Tree (*Koelreuteria paniculata*)

★Laburnum (*Laburnum vossi*)

White

★Shadblow Serviceberry (*Amelanchier canadensis*)

Whitebud (*Cercis canadensis alba*)

★American Yellow-wood (*Cladrastis lutea*)

Japanese Dogwood (*Cornus kousa*)

Washington Hawthorn (*Crataegus phaenopyrum*)

Carolina Silverbell (*Halesia carolina*)

Yulan Magnolia (*Magnolia denudata*)

★Star Magnolia (*Magnolia stellata*)

Arnold Crab Apple (*Malus arnoldiana*)

Siberian Crab Apple (*Malus baccata*)

Tea Crab Apple (*Malus hupehensis*)

Sargent Crab Apple (*Malus sargenti*)

★Sorrel Tree (*Oxydendrum arboreum*)

Hardy Orange (*Poncirus trifoliata*)

Sour Cherry (*Prunus cerasus*)

Thundercloud Plum (*Prunus cerasifera* "Thundercloud")

Mount Fuji Cherry (*Prunus serrulata* "Shirotae")

Yoshino Cherry (*Prunus yedoensis*)

Bradford Callery Pear (*Pyrus calleryana* "Bradford")

★Common Pear (*Pyrus communis*)

★Japanese Pagoda Tree (*Sophora japonica*)

Korean Mountain Ash (*Sorbus alnifolia*)

American Mountain Ash (*Sorbus americana*)

European Mountain Ash (*Sorbus aucuparia*)

Showy Mountain Ash (*Sorbus decora*)

Japanese Stewartia (*Stewartia pseudocamellia*)

Japanese Snowbell (*Styrax japonica*)

Pink

Red Flowering Dogwood (*Cornus florida rubra*)

Toba Hawthorn (*Crataegus mordenensis* "Toba")

★Saucer Magnolia (*Magnolia soulangeana*)

Japanese Flowering Crab Apple (*Malus floribunda*)

Katherine Crab Apple (*Malus* "Katherine")

Prince Georges Crab Apple (*Malus* "Prince Georges")

★Common Apple (*Malus pumila*)

Sargent Cherry (*Prunus sargenti*)

Amanogawa Cherry (*Prunus serrulata* "Amanogawa")

Kwanzan Cherry (*Prunus serrulata* "Kwanzan")

Autumn Cherry (*Prunus subhirtella autumnalis*)

Weeping Cherry (*Prunus subhirtella pendula*)

Red

Ruby Horse-Chestnut (*Aesculus carnea briotti*)

Paul's Scarlet Hawthorn (*Crataegus oxyacantha pauli*)

Alexandrina Magnolia (*Magnolia soulangeana* "Alexandrina")

Almey Crab Apple (*Malus* "Almey")

Carmine Crab Apple (*Malus atrosanguinea*)

Trees with Bright Red Fruit

★Flowering Dogwood (*Cornus florida*)

Japanese Dogwood (*Cornus kousa*)

Downy Hawthorn (*Crataegus mollis*)

Washington Hawthorn (*Crataegus phaenopyrum*)

American Holly (*Ilex opaca*)

Almey Crab Apple (*Malus* "Almey")

★Siberian Crab Apple (*Malus baccata*)

Hopa Crab Apple (*Malus* "Hopa")

★Common Apple (*Malus pumila*)

Sargent Crab Apple (*Malus sargenti*)

Korean Mountain Ash (*Sorbus alnifolia*)

American Mountain Ash (*Sorbus americana*)

European Mountain Ash (*Sorbus aucuparia*)

Trees Classified by Color of Summer Foliage

Blue

White Fir (*Abies concolor*)

Western Red Cedar (*Juniperus scopulorum* var. Chandler Blue)

Eastern Red Cedar (*Juniperus virginiana* var. *Burki*)

Colorado Blue Spruce (*Picea purgens* var. *glauca*)

Silver to Gray

Russian Olive (*Elaeagnus angustifolia*)

Common Sea-Buckthorn (*Hippophae rhamnoides*)

White Poplar (*Populus alba*)

Pendant Silver Linden (*Tilia petiolaris*)

★Silver Linden (*Tilia tomentosa*)

Red to Purple

Blood-leaf Japanese Maple (*Acer palmatum atropurpureum*)

Crimson King Maple (*Acer platanoides* "Crimson King")

Schwedler Maple (*Acer platanoides schwedleri*)

Purple-leaf Sycamore Maple (*Acer pseudoplatanus*)

River's Purple Beech (*Fagus sylvatica riversi*)

Purple Beech (*Fagus sylvatica atropunicea*)

Weeping Purple Beech (*Fagus sylvatica purpureopendula*)

Rubylace Locust (*Gleditsia triacanthos inermis* "Rubylace")

Purple Crab Apple (*Malus purpurea*)

Blireiana Plum (*Prunus blireiana*)

Pissard Plum (*Prunus cerasifera atropurpurea*)

Thundercloud Plum (*Prunus cerasifera nigra* "Thundercloud")

Woods Myrobalan Plum (*Prunus cerasifera woodi*)

Blood-leaf Peach (*Prunus persica atropurpurea*)

Purple English Oak (*Quercus robur atropurpurea*)

Trees Classified by Color of Fall Foliage

Yellow

Striped Maple or Moosewood (*Acer pensylvanicum*)

Norway Maple (*Acer platanoides* var.)

★Sugar Maple (*Acer saccharum*)

Ohio Buckeye (orange) (*Aesculus glabra*)

Apple Serviceberry (yellow-orange) (*Amelanchier grandiflora*)

★Birch species (*Betula*)

Hickory species (*Carya*)

Chinese Chestnut (*Castanea mollissima*)

★Katsura Tree (yellow to scarlet) (*Cercidiphyllum japonicum*)

Redbud species (*Cercis*)

Fringetree (*Chionanthus virginicus*)

★American Yellow-wood (*Cladrastis lutea*)

★American Beech (*Fagus grandifolia*)

★European Beech (*Fagus sylvatica*)

White Ash (purple to yellow) (*Fraxinus americana*)

★Ginkgo (*Ginkgo biloba*)

★Larch (*Larix decidua*)

Tulip Tree (*Liriodendron tulipifera*)

★Star Magnolia (bronze) (*Magnolia stellata*)

Golden Larch (*Pseudolarix amabilis*)

★Willow species (*Salix*)

Red

Vine Maple (*Acer circinatum*)

Amur Maple (*Acer ginnala*)

Manchurian Maple (*Acer mandshuricum*)

Nikko Maple (*Acer nikoense*)

★Japanese Maple (*Acer palmatum* var.)

★Red Maple (*Acer rubrum*)

★Sugar Maple (*Acer saccharum*)

Tatarian Maple (*Acer tataricum*)

★Shadblow Serviceberry (*Amelanchier canadensis*)

Hornbeam species (*Carpinus*)

★Flowering Dogwood (*Cornus florida*)

Japanese Dogwood (*Cornus kousa*)

American Smoke Tree (*Cotinus americanus*)

Washington Hawthorn (*Crataegus phaenopyrum*)

★Sweet Gum (*Liquidambar styraciflua*)

Dawson Crab Apple (*Malus dawsoniana*)

★Black Tupelo or Black Gum (*Nyssa sylvatica*)

★Sorrel Tree (*Oxydendrum arboreum*)

Persian Parrotia (*Parrotia persica*)

★Cherry species (*Prunus*)

Bradford Callery Pear (*Pyrus calleryana* "Bradford")

Red Oak (*Quercus borealis*)

Scarlet Oak (*Quercus coccinea*)

★Pin Oak (*Quercus palustris*)

Sassafras (*Sassafras albidum*)

Korean Mountain Ash (*Sorbus alnifolia*)

Korean Stewartia (orange to red) (*Stewartia koreana*)

Purple

White Ash (*Fraxinus americana*)

★Sweet Gum (*Liquidambar styraciflua*)

★White Oak (*Quercus alba*)

★Common Pear (*Pyrus communis*)

Japanese Stewartia (*Stewartia pseudocamellia*)

Trees with Interesting Bark

Gray

★Red Maple (*Acer rubrum*)

★Serviceberry species (*Amelanchier*)

Hornbeam species (*Carpinus*)

Hackberry species (*Celtis*)
★American Yellow-wood (*Cladrastis lutea*)
★Hawthorn species (*Crataegus*)
★Beech species (*Fagus*)
American Holly (*Ilex opaca*)
English or Persian Walnut (*Juglans regia*)
Cucumber Tree (*Magnolia acuminata*)
★Saucer Magnolia (*Magnolia soulangeana*)
Red Oak (young branches and trunk) (*Quercus borealis*)
Black Oak (young branches and trunk) (*Quercus velutina*)
Mountain Ash species (*Sorbus*)

White
★European Birch (*Betula pendula*)
★Gray Birch (*Betula populifolia*)

Red
Japanese Red Pine (*Pinus densiflora*)
Red or Norway Pine (*Pinus resinosa*)
Scotch Pine (*Pinus sylvestris*)

Reddish Brown
Chinese Paper Birch (*Betula albo-sinensis*)
Sargent Cherry (*Prunus sargenti*)

Yellow
Wisconsin or Niobe Weeping Willow (*Salix blanda*)

Corky
★Amur Cork (*Phellodendron amurense*)

Green
★Babylon Weeping Willow (*Salix babylonica*)

Flaking
Paper Bark Maple (*Acer griseum*)
★Birch species (*Betula*)
Shagbark Hickory (*Carya ovata*)
Russian Olive (*Elaeagnus angustifolia*)
Persian Parrotia (*Parrotia persica*)
★Plane Tree species (*Platanus*)
Lace-bark Pine (*Pinus bungeana*)
Stewartia species (*Stewartia*)

Trees for the City
White Fir (*Abies concolor*)
Hedge Maple (*Acer campestre*)
Box-Elder (*Acer negundo*)
Norway Maple (*Acer platanoides*)
Sycamore Maple (*Acer pseudoplatanus*)
Horse-Chestnut or Buckeye (*Aesculus*)
★Tree of Heaven (*Ailanthus*)
Silk Tree (*Albizzia julibrissin*)
Catalpa (*Catalpa*)
Chinese Toon (*Cedrella sinensis*)
Hackberry (*Celtis*)
Downy Hawthorn (*Crataegus mollis*)
Washington Hawthorn (*Crataegus phaenopyrum*)
Russian Olive (*Elaeagnus angustifolia*)
White Ash (*Fraxinus americana*)
European Ash (*Fraxinus excelsior*)
Green Ash (*Fraxinus pennsylvanica*)
★Ginkgo (*Ginkgo biloba*)
Thornless Honey-Locust (*Gleditsia triacanthos inermis*)
★Golden Rain Tree (*Koelreuteria paniculata*)
★Saucer Magnolia (*Magnolia soulangeana*)
★Star Magnolia (*Magnolia stellata*)
★Crab Apples species (*Malus*)
★Amur Cork (*Phellodendron amurense*)
★London Plane Tree (*Platanus acerifolia*)
White Poplar (*Populus alba*)
★Lombardy Poplar (*Populus nigra italica*)
Red Oak (*Quercus borealis*)
★Black Locust (*Robinia pseudoacacia*)
★Japanese Pagoda Tree (*Sophora japonica*)
★Little-leaf Linden (*Tilia cordata*)
★Crimean Linden (*Tilia euchlora*)
★Silver Linden (*Tilia tomentosa*)
Village Green Zelkova (*Zelkova serrata* "Village Green")

Trees for Wide Streets

Sycamore Maple (*Acer pseudoplatanus*)
★Sugar Maple (*Acer saccharum*)
Sugar Hackberry (*Celtis laevigata*)
★Katsura Tree (*Cercidiphyllum japonicum*)
White Ash (*Fraxinus americana*)
Green Ash (*Fraxinus pennsylvanica lanceolata*)
★Ginkgo (*Ginkgo biloba*)
★Common Honey-Locust (*Gleditsia triacanthos*)
Kalopanax (*Kalopanax pictus*)
Tulip Tree (*Liriodendron tulipifera*)
★Amur Cork (*Phellodendron amurense*)
★Eastern White Pine (*Pinus strobus*)
★London Plane Tree (*Platanus acerifola*)
White Poplar (*Populus alba*)
Sargent Cherry (*Prunus sargenti*)
★Pin Oak (*Quercus palustris*)
Willow Oak (*Quercus phellos*)
Japanese Zelkova (*Zelkova serrata*)

Trees for Medium Streets
Norway Maple (*Acer platanoides*)
Mountain Silverbell (*Halesia monticola*)
★Sweet Gum (*Liquidambar styraciflua*)
Hop-Hornbeam (*Ostrya virginiana*)
★Sorrel Tree or Sourwood (*Oxydendrum arboreum*)
Simon Poplar (*Populus simoni*)
Scarlet Oak (*Quercus coccinea*)
Willow Oak (*Quercus phellos*)
★Black Locust (*Robinia pseudoacacia*)
Sassafras (*Sassafras albidum officinale*)
★Japanese Pagoda Tree (*Sophora japonica*)
★Linden species (*Tilia*)
Winged Elm (*Ulmus alata*)

Trees for Suburban Streets
Hedge Maple (*Acer campestre*)
Amur Maple (*Acer ginnala*)
Paperbark Maple (*Acer griseum*)
Globe Norway Maple (*Acer platanoides globosum*)
Mountain Maple (*Acer spicatum*)
Tatarian Maple (*Acer tataricum*)
Pyramidal European Hornbeam (*Carpinus betulus fastigiata*)
Globe European Hornbeam (*Carpinus betulus globosa*)
American Hornbeam (*Carpinus caroliniana*)
Fringetree (*Chionanthus virginicus*)
★Hawthorn species (*Crataegus*)
Korean Evodia (*Evodia danielli*)
Carolina Silverbell (*Halesia carolina*)
★Golden Rain Tree (*Koelreuteria paniculata*)
Columnar Sargent Cherry (*Prunus sargenti columnaris*)
Oriental Cherry (*Prunus serrulata*)
Japanese Snowbell (*Styrax japonica*)
Asiatic Sweetleaf (*Symplocos paniculata*)
Smooth-leaved Elm varieties (*Ulmus carpinifolia*)

Soil Tolerance

Trees Tolerating Acid Soil
★Japanese Maple (*Acer palmatum*)
★Flowering Dogwood (*Cornus florida*)
Japanese Dogwood (*Cornus kousa*)
★European Beech (*Fagus sylvatica*)
Sweet Bay (*Magnolia virginiana*)
★Black Tupelo (*Nyssa sylvatica*)
★Sorrel Tree (*Oxydendrum arboreum*)
Hardy Orange (*Poncirus trifoliata*)
Red Oak (*Quercus borealis*)
Scarlet Oak (*Quercus coccinea*)
★Pin Oak (*Quercus palustris*)
Willow Oak (*Quercus phellos*)
Japanese Stewartia (*Stewartia pseudocamellia*)

Trees Tolerating Moist Soil
★Red Maple (*Acer rubrum*)
Alder species (*Alnus*)
Holly species (*Ilex*)
★Sweet Gum (*Liquidambar styraciflua*)
Sweet Bay (*Magnolia virginiana*)
★Black Tupelo or Black Gum (*Nyssa sylvatica*)
Swamp White Oak (*Quercus bicolor*)
★Willow species (*Salix*)

Common Bald Cypress (*Taxodium distichum*)
American Arbor-vitae (*Thuja occidentalis*)

Trees Tolerating Dry or Poor Soil
Box-Elder (*Acer negundo*)
★Tree of Heaven (*Ailanthus*)
★Gray Birch (*Betula populifolia*)
Russian Olive (*Elaeagnus angustifolia*)
Green Ash (*Fraxinus pennsylvanica*)
Modesto Ash (*Fraxinus velutina* "Modesto")
★Honey-Locust (*Gleditsia triacanthos* var.)
Western Red Cedar (*Juniperus scopulorum*)
Eastern Red Cedar (*Juniperus virginiana*)
★Golden Rain Tree (*Koelreuteria paniculata*)
Osage-Orange (*Maclura pomifera*)
Jack Pine (*Pinus banksiana*)
Pitch Pine (*Pinus rigida*)
Virginia or Scrub Pine (*Pinus virginiana*)
White Poplar (*Populus alba*)
Chestnut Oak (*Quercus montana*)
★Black Locust (*Robinia pseudoacacia*)
Sassafras (*Sassafras albidum officinale*)
★Japanese Pagoda Tree (*Sophora japonica*)
Chinese Elm (*Ulmus parvifolia*)
Siberian Elm (*Ulmus pumila*)

Pest-Resistant Trees

★Tree of Heaven (*Ailanthus altissima*)
Hornbeam species (*Carpinus*)
★Cedar species (*Cedrus*)
★Katsura Tree (*Cercidiphyllum japonicum*)
False Cypress species (*Chamaecyparis*)
Cornelian Cherry (*Cornus mas*)
Japanese Cornel (*Cornus officinalis*)
Turkish Filbert (*Corylus columa*)
American Smoke Tree (*Cotinus americanus*)
Kentucky Coffee Tree (*Cymnocladus dioicus*)
Russian Olive (*Elaeagnus angustifolia*)
★Fig species (*Ficus*)
Franklinia (*Franklinia alatamaha*)
★Ginkgo (*Ginkgo biloba*)
★Honey-Locust (*Gleditsia triacanthos*)
Juniper species (*Juniperus*)
Kalopanax (*Kalopanax pictus*)
★Golden Rain Tree (*Koelreuteria paniculata*)
★Laburnum species (*Laburnum*)
★Sweet Gum (*Liquidambar styraciflua*)
Cucumber Tree (*Magnolia acuminata*)
Kobus Magnolia (*Magnolia kobus borealis*)
Anise Magnolia (*Magnolia salicifolia*)
★Star Magnolia (*Magnolia stellata*)
Hop-Hornbeam species (*Ostrya*)

Trees for Seashore Planting

Norway Maple (*Acer platanoides*)
Sycamore Maple (*Acer pseudoplatanus*)
★Horse-Chestnut (*Aesculus hippocastanum*)
★Tree of Heaven (*Ailanthus*)
★Shadblow Serviceberry (*Amelanchier canadensis*)
Cockspur Thorn (*Crataegus crus-galli*)
English Hawthorn (*Crataegus oxyacantha*)
Washington Hawthorn (*Crataegus phaenopyrum*)
Cryptomeria (*Cryptomeria japonica*)
Russian Olive (*Elaeagnus angustifolia*)
Thornless Honey-locust (*Gleditsia triacanthos inermis* var.)
American Holly (*Ilex opaca*)
Eastern Red Cedar (*Juniperus virginiana*)
★Black Tupelo (*Nyssa sylvatica*)
Dragon Spruce (*Picea asperata*)
Colorado Blue Spruce (*Picea pungens glauca*)
★Austrian Pine (*Pinus nigra*)
Pitch Pine (*Pinus rigida*)
Scotch Pine (*Pinus sylvestris*)
★Japanese Black Pine (*Pinus thunbergi*)
★London Plane Tree (*Platanus acerifolia*)
Hardy Orange (*Poncirus trifoliata*)
White Poplar (*Populus alba*)
Black Cherry (*Prunus serotina*)
★White Oak (*Quercus alba*)
Black Jack Oak (*Quercus marilandica*)

★Black Locust (*Robina pseudoacacia*)
Golden Weeping Willow (*Salix alba tristis*)
★Japanese Pagoda Tree (*Sophora japonica*)
American Arbor-vitae (*Thuja occidentalis*)
Oriental Arbor-vitae (*Thuja orientalis*)
★Little-leaf Linden (*Tilia cordata*)
★Crimean Linden (*Tilia euchlora*)

Trees for Hedging or Barriers

European Beech (*Fagus sylvatica*) prunes well.
Leyland Cypress (*Cupressocyparis leylandii*) withstands heavy pruning.
Hawthorn varieties (*Crataegus*) easily pruned, advantage of thorns.
Canadian Hemlock (*Tsuga canadensis*) evergreen.
American Holly (*Ilex opaca*) can be pruned.
European Hornbeam (*Carpinus betulus*) prunes well.

Little-leaf Linden (*Tilia cordata*) tolerates heavy pruning.
Hedge Maple (*Acer campestre*) can be pruned.
Austrian Pine (*Pinus nigra*) plant 10–12 feet on centers, staggered row.
Japanese Black Pine (*Pinus thunbergi*) plant 8 feet on centers, staggered row.
Eastern White Pine (*Pinus strobus*) plant 15 feet on centers, staggered row.

MICHIGAN

State Tree

★Apple (*Malus*)

Evergreen Trees

Fir species (*Abies*)
False Cypress species (*Chamaecyparis*)
Holly species (*Ilex*)
Juniper species (*Juniperus*)
★Larch species (*Larix*)
Spruce species (*Picea*)
★Pine species (*Pinus*)
★Douglas Fir (*Pseudotsuga menziesii*)
Arbor-vitae species (*Thuja*)

Trees Classified by Height

20–35 Feet Tall

Hedge Maple (*Acer campestre*)
Hornbeam Maple (*Acer carpinifolium*)
Vine Maple (*Acer circinatum*)
Amur Maple (*Acer ginnala*)
Paperbark Maple (*Acer griseum*)
Manchurian Maple (*Acer mandshuricum*)
Ohio Buckeye (*Aesculus glabra*)
Apple Serviceberry (*Amelanchier grandiflora*)
★Gray Birch (*Betula populifolia*)
European Hornbeam (*Carpinus betulus globosa*)
Mockernut (*Carya Tomentosa*)
Fringetree (*Chionanthus virginicus*)
Japanese Dogwood (*Cornus kousa*)
Cornelian Cherry (*Cornus mas*)
Japanese Cornel (*Cornus officinalis*)
American Smoke Tree (*Cotinus americanus*)
★Hawthorn species (*Crataegus*)
Russian Olive (*Elaeagnus angustifolia*)
Euonymus species (*Euonymus*)
Korean Evodia (*Evodia danielli*)
Franklinia (*Franklinia alatamaha*)
Flowering Ash (*Fraxinus ornus*)
Carolina Silverbell (*Halesia carolina*)
David Hemiptelea (*Hemiptelea davidi*)
Common Sea-Buckthorn (*Hippophae rhamnoides*)
Possum Haw (*Ilex decidua*)
Longstalk Holly (*Ilex pedunculosa*)
Needle Juniper (*Juniperus rigida*)
★Golden Rain Tree (*Koelreuteria paniculata*)
★Laburnum species (*Laburnum*)
Yellow Cucumber Tree (*Magnolia cordata*)
Anise Magnolia (*Magnolia salicifolia*)
★Saucer Magnolia (*Magnolia soulangeana*)
★Star Magnolia (*Magnolia stellata*)
Watson Magnolia (*Magnolia watsoni*)
★Crab Apple species (*Malus*)
★Cherry species (*Prunus*)
Dahurian Buckthorn (*Rhamnus davurica*)
Almond-leaf Willow (*Salix amygdalina*)
Goat Willow (*Salix caprea*)
Showy Mountain Ash (*Sorbus decora*)
Snowberry Mountain Ash (*Sorbus discolor*)
Folgner Mountain Ash (*Sorbus folgneri*)
Asiatic Sweetleaf (*Symplocos paniculata*)
Japanese Tree Lilac (*Syringa amurensis japonica*)

35–75 Feet

Box Elder (*Acer negundo*)
Nikko Maple (*Acer nikoense*)
Striped Maple or Moosewood (*Acer pennsylvanicum*)

★Red-fruited Tree of Heaven (*Ailanthus altissima erythrocarpa*)
Italian Alder (*Alnus cordata*)
Speckled Alder (*Alnus incana*)
Red Alder (*Alnus rubra*)
★Shadblow Serviceberry (*Amelanchier canadensis*)
Allegany Serviceberry (*Amelanchier laevis*)
Devil's Walking Stick (*Aralia elata*)
Dahurian Birch (*Betula mandshurica szechuanica*)
★European Birch (*Betula pendula*)
European Hornbeam (*Carpinus betulus*)
American Hornbeam (*Carpinus caroliniana*)
Japanese Hornbeam (*Carpinus japonica*)
Chinese Chestnut (*Castanea mollissima*)
Southern Catalpa (*Catalpa bignoniodes*)
Bunch Hackberry (*Celtis bungeana*)
★Katsura Tree (*Cercidiphyllum japonicum*)
Eastern Redbud (*Cercis canadensis*)
★American Yellow-wood (*Cladrastis lutea*)
★Flowering Dogwood (*Cornus florida*)
Turkish Filbert (*Corylus colurna*)
Cockspur Thorn (*Crataegus crus-galli*)
Green Hawthorn (*Crataegus viridis*)
Common Persimmon (*Diospyros virginiana*)
Green Ash (*Fraxinus pennsylvanica lanceolata*)
American Holly (*Ilex opaca*)
Heartnut (*Junglans sieboldiana cordiformis*)
Chinese Juniper (*Juniperus chinensis*)
Yulan Magnolia (*Magnolia denudata*)
Fraser Magnolia (*Magnolia fraseri*)
Kobus Magnolia (*Magnolia kobus borealis*)
Loebner Magnolia (*Magnolia loebneri*)
Big-leaf Magnolia (*Magnolia macrophylla*)
Siberian Crab Apple (*Malus bacata*)
"Cowichan" Crab Apple (*Malus* "Cowichan")
"Dolgo" Crab Apple (*Malus* "Dolgo")
"Makamik" Crab Apple (*Malus* "Makamik")
Cherry Crab Apple (*Malus robusta*)
"Sissipuk" Crab Apple (*Malus* "Sissipuk")
White Mulberry (*Morus alba*)
★Sorrel Tree or Sourwood (*Oxydendrum arboreum*)
Persian Parrotia (*Parrotia persica*)
Empress Tree (*Paulownia tomentosa*)
★Amur Cork (*Phellodendron amurense*)
Dragon Spruce (*Picea asperata*)
Jack Pine (*Pinus banksiana*)
Lace-bark Pine (*Pinus bungeana*)
Swiss Stone Pine (*Pinus cembra*)
Limber Pine (*Pinus flexilis*)
Pitch Pine (*Pinus rigida*)
Scotch Pine (*Pinus sylvestris*)
Virginia or Scrub Pine (*Pinus virginiana*)
Chinese Poplar (*Populus lasiocarpa*)
Simon Poplar (*Populus simoni*)
Miyana Cherry (*Prunus maximowiczi*)
European Bird Cherry (*Prunus padus*)
Sargent Cherry (*Prunus sargenti*)
Yoshino Cherry (*Prunus yedoensis*)
Fragrant Epaulette Tree (*Pterostyrax hispida*)
Ussurian Pear (*Pyrus ussuriensis*)
Swamp White Oak (*Quercus bicolor*)
Red Oak (*Quercus borealis*)
Scarlet Oak (*Quercus coccinea*)
Spanish or Southern Red Oak (*Quercus falcata*)
Shingle Oak (*Quercus imbricaria*)

★Pin Oak (*Quercus palustris*)
Willow Oak (*Quercus phellos*)
White Willow (*Salix alba*)
Wisconsin or Niobe Weeping Willow (*Salix blanda*)
Elaeagnus Willow (*Salix elaeagnos*)
Thurlow Weeping Willow (*Salix elegantissima*)
Laurel Willow (*Salix pentandra*)
Sassafras (*Sassafras albidum officinale*)
Korean Mountain Ash (*Sorbus alnifolia*)
White Beam Mountain Ash (*Sornus aria*)
European Mountain Ash or Rowan Tree (*Sorbus aucuparia*)
American Arbor-vitae (*Thuja occidentalis*)
Japanese Arbor-vitae (*Thuja standishi*)
★Crimean Linden (*Tilia euchlora*)
Chinese Elm (*Ulmus parvifolia*)
Siberian Elm (*Ulmus pumila*)

75 Feet or Over

Fir species (*Abies*)
Norway Maple (*Acer platanoides*)
Sycamore Maple (*Acer pseudoplatanus*)
★Red or Swamp Maple (*Acer rubrum*)
★Sugar Maple (*Acer saccharum*)
★Baumann Horse-Chestnut (*Aesculus hippocastanum baumanni*)
European Alder (*Alnus glutinosa*)
Sweet Birch (*Betula lenta*)
River Birch (*Betula nigra*)
★Canoe Birch (*Betula papyrifera*)
Hickory species (*Carya*)
★Cedar species (*Cedrus*)
Sugar Hackberry (*Celtis laevigata*)
★Katsura Tree (*Cercidiphyllum japonicum*)
False Cypress species (*Chamaecyparis*)
★Beech species (*Fagus*)
White Ash (*Fraxinus americana*)
European Ash (*Fraxinus excelsior*)
★Ginkgo or Maidenhair Tree (*Ginkgo biloba*)
Common Honey-Locust (*Gleditsia tricanthos*)
Kentucky Coffee Tree (*Gymnocladus dioicus*)
Mountain Silverbell (*Halesia monticola*)
Eastern Black Walnut (*Juglans nigra*)
English or Persian Walnut (*Juglans regia*)
Kalopanax (*Kalopanax pictus*)
★European Larch (*Larix decidua*)
Japanese Larch (*Larix leptolepis*)
★Sweet Gum (*Liquidambar styraciflua*)
Tulip Tree or Yellow Poplar (*Liriodendron tulipifera*)
Cucumber Tree (*Magnolia acuminata*)
White-leaf Japanese Magnolia (*Magnolia obovata*)
★Black Gum or Black Tupelo (*Nyssa sylvatica*)
Spruce species (*Picea*)
★Pine species (*Pinus*)
★Plane Tree species (*Platanus*)
Poplar species (*Populus*)
Sargent Cherry (*Prunus sargenti*)
Black or Rum Cherry (*Prunus serotina*)
Golden Larch (*Pseudolarix amabilis*)
★Douglas Fir (*Pseudotsuga menziesii*)
★Oak species (*Quercus*)
Common Bald Cypress (*Taxodium distichum*)
★Linden species (*Tilia*)
★Elm species (*Ulmus*)
Japanese Zelkova (*Zelkova serrata*)

Trees Classified by Form

Pyramidal
Fir species (*Abies*)
*Birch species (*Betula*)
False Cypress species (*Chamaecyparis*)
Turkish Filbert (*Corylus colurna*)
*Beech species (*Fagus*)
American Holly (*Ilex opaca*)
Juniper or Red Cedar species (*Juniperus*)
Pyramidal Red Cedar (*Juniperus virginiana pyramidalis*)
*Larch species (*Larix*)
*Sweet Gum (*Liquidambar styraciflua*)
*Magnolia species (*Magnolia*)
*Black Tupelo or Black Gum (*Nyssa sylvatica*)
Hop-Hornbeam (*Ostrya virginiana*)
*Sorrel Tree or Sourwood (*Oxydendrum arboreum*)
Spruce species (*Picea*)
Swiss Stone Pine (*Pinus cembra*)
Korean Pine (*Pinus koraiensis*)
Pyramid Austrian Pine (*Pinus nigra pyramidalis*)
Japanese White Pine (*Pinus parviflora*)
Red or Norway Pine (*Pinus resinosa*)
Golden Larch (*Pseudolarix amabilis*)
*Douglas Fir (*Pseudotsuga menziesii*)
*Pin Oak (*Quercus palustris*)
Common Bald Cypress (*Taxodium distichum*)
Arbor-vitae species (*Thuja*)
*Linden species (*Tilia*)
Smooth-leaved Elm varieties (*Ulmus carpinifolia*)

Columnar
Ascending Norway Maple (*Acer platanoides ascendens*)
Columnar Norway Maple (*Acer platanoides columnare*)
Erect Norway Maple (*Acer platanoides erectum*)
Columnar Red Maple (*Acer rubrum columnare*)
*Sentry Maple (*Acer saccharum monumentale*)
Fastigiate European Birch (*Betula pendula fastigiata*)
Fastigiate European Hornbeam (*Carpinus betulus fastigiata*)
Scarab Lawson Cypress (*Chamaecyparis lawsoniana allumi*)
Erect Lawson Cypress (*Chamaecyparis lawsoniana erecta*)
Column Hinoki Cypress (*Chamaecyparis obtusa erecta*)
Fastigiate Washington Hawthorn (*Crataegus phaenopyrum fastigiata*)
Dawyck Beech (*Fagus sylvatica fastigiata*)
Sentry Ginkgo (*Ginkgo biloba fastigiata*)
Blue Columnar Chinese Juniper (*Juniperus chinensis columnaris*)
Schott Red Cedar (*Juniperus virginiana schotti*)
Swiss Stone Pine (*Pinus cembra*)
*Fastigiate White Pine (*Pinus strobus fastigiata*)
Fastigiate Scotch Pine (*Pinus sylvestris fastigiata*)
Bolleana Poplar (*Populus alba pyramidalis*)
*Lombardy Poplar (*Populus nigra italica*)
Fastigiate Simon Poplar (*Populus simoni fastigiata*)
Columnar Sargent Cherry (*Prunus sargenti columnaris*)
"Amanogawa" Cherry (*Prunus serrulata* "Amanogawa")
Fastigiate English Oak (*Quercus robur fastigiata*)
Common Bald Cypress (*Taxodium distichum*)
Douglas Arbor-vitae (*Thuja occidentalis douglasi pyramidalis*)
Fastigiate American Arbor-vitae (*Thuja occidentalis fastigiata*)
Columnar Big-leaf Linden (*Tilia platyphyllos fastigiata*)
*American Elm varieties (*Ulmus americana*)

Weeping
Slender European Birch (*Betula pendula tristis*)
Young's Birch (*Betula pendula youngi*)
Weeping European Hornbeam (*Carpinus betulus pendula*)
Weeping Beech (*Fagus sylvatica pendula*)

*Weeping Purple Beech (*Fagus sylvatica purpurea-pendula*)
Weeping Red Cedar (*Juniperus virginiana pendula*)
Weeping Larch (*Larix decidua pendula*)
"Exzellenz Thiel" Crab Apple (*Malus* "Exzellenz Thiel")
"Oekonomierat Echtermeyer" Crab Apple (*Malus* "Oekonomierat Echtermeyer")
Weeping Mulberry (*Morus alba pendula*)
Koster Weeping Blue Spruce (*Picea pungens kosteriana*)
Weeping White Pine (*Pinus strobus pendula*)
Weeping Black Cherry (*Prunus serotina pendula*)
Weeping Higan Cherry (*Prunus subhirtella pendula*)
"Yaeshidare" Cherry (*Prunus subhirtella pendula flora plena*)
Weeping Yoshino Cherry (*Prunus yedoensis perpendens*)
Weeping Douglas Fir (*Pseudotsuga menziesii pendula*)
Golden Weeping Willow (*Salix alba tristis*)
Wisconsin or Niobe Weeping Willow (*Salix blanda*)
Thurlow Weeping Willow (*Salix elegantissima*)
Weeping Japanese Pagoda Tree (*Sophora japonica pendula*)
Weeping European Mountain Ash (*Sorbus aucuparia pendula*)
Weeping Folgner Mountain Ash (*Sorbus folgneri pendula*)
Weeping American Elm (*Ulmus americana pendula*)

Rounded or Globe-Shaped
*Japanese Maple (*Acer palmatum*)
Globe Norway Maple (*Acer platanoides globosum*)
Globe European Hornbean (*Carpinus betulus globosa*)
Bunch Hackberry (*Celtis bungeana*)
Cornelian Cherry (*Cornus mas*)
Japanese Cornel (*Cornus officinalis*)
Single Seed Hawthorn (*Crataegus monogyna inermis*)
*Saucer Magnolia (*Magnolia soulangeana*)
*Crab Apple species (*Malus*)
*White Oak (*Quercus alba*)
Umbrella Black Locust (*Robinia pseudoacacia umbraculifera*)
Koopmann Elm (*Ulmus carpinifolia koopmanni*)
Globe Smooth-leaved Elm (*Ulmus carpinifolia umbraculifera*)

With Horizontal Branching
Fir species (*Abies*)
Eastern Redbud (*Cercis canadensis*)
*Flowering Dogwood (*Cornus florida*)
Japanese Dogwood (*Cornus kousa*)
*Hawthorn species (*Crataegus*)
*Black Tupelo or Black Gum (*Nyssa sylvatica*)
Spruce species (*Picea*)
Japanese Red Pine (*Pinus densiflora*)
*Eastern White Pine (*Pinus strobus*)
Golden Larch (*Pseudolarix amabilis*)
*White Oak (*Quercus alba*)
*Pin Oak (*Quercus palustris*)
Common Bald Cypress (*Taxodium distichum*)

Trees Classified by Color of Blossom

Yellow
*Golden Rain Tree (*Koelreuteria paniculata*)

White
*Shadblow Serviceberry (*Amelanchier canadensis*)
White Bud (*Cercis canadensis alba*)
*American Yellow-wood (*Cladrastis lutea*)
Japanese Dogwood (*Cornus kousa*)
Washington Hawthorn (*Crataegus phaenopyrum*)
Carolina Silverbell (*Halesia carolina*)
Yulan Magnolia (*Magnolia denudata*)
*Star Magnolia (*Magnolia stellata*)
Arnold Crab Apple (*Malus arnoldiana*)
Siberian Crab Apple (*Malus baccata*)
Tea Crab Apple (*Malus hupehensis*)
Sargent Crab Apple (*Malus sargenti*)

*Sorrel Tree (*Oxydendrum arboreum*)
Thundercloud Plum (*Prunus cerasifera* "Thundercloud")
Sour Cherry (*Prunus cerasus*)
Yoshino Cherry (*Prunus yedoensis*)
Bradford Callery Pear (*Pyrus calleryana* "Bradford")
*Common Pear (*Pyrus communis*)
*Japanese Pagoda Tree (*Sophora japonica*)
Korean Mountain Ash (*Sorbus alnifolia*)
American Mountain Ash (*Sorbus americana*)
European Mountain Ash (*Sorbus aucuparia*)
Showy Mountain Ash (*Sorbus decora*)

Pink
*Red Flowering Dogwood (*Cornus florida rubra*)
Toba Hawthorn (*Crataegus mordenensis* "Toba")
*Saucer Magnolia (*Magnolia soulangeana*)
Japanese Flowering Crab Apple (*Malus floribunda*)
Katherine Crab Apple (*Malus* "Katherine")
Prince Georges Crab Apple (*Malus* "Prince Georges")
*Common Apple (*Malus pumila*)
Bliereiana Plum (*Prunus blireiana*)
Sargent Cherry (*Prunus sargenti*)
Amanogawa Cherry (*Prunus serrulata* "Amanogawa")
Kwanzan Cherry (*Prunus serrulata* "Kwanzan")
Autumn Cherry (*Prunus subhirtella autumnalis*)
Weeping Cherry (*Prunus subhirtella pendula*)

Red
Ruby Horse-Chestnut (*Aesculus carnea briotti*)
Paul's Scarlet Hawthorn (*Crataegus oxyacantha pauli*)
Alexandrina Magnolia (*Magnolia soulangeana* "Alexandrina")
Almey Crab Apple (*Malus* "Almey")
Carmine Crab Apple (*Malus atrosanguinea*)

Trees with Bright Red Fruit
*Flowering Dogwood (*Cornus florida*)
Japanese Dogwood (*Cornus kousa*)
*Downy Hawthorn (*Crataegus mollis*)
Washington Hawthorn (*Crataegus phaenopyrum*)
American Holly (*Ilex opaca*)
Siberian Crab Apple (*Malus baccata*)
Almey Crab Apple (*Malus* "Almey")
Hopa Crab Apple (*Malus* "Hopa")
*Common Apple (*Malus pumila*)
Sargent Crab Apple (*Malus sargenti*)
Korean Mountain Ash (*Sorbus alnifolia*)
American Mountain Ash (*Sorbus americana*)
European Mountain Ash (*Sorbus aucuparia*)

Trees Classified by Color of Summer Foliage

Blue
White Fir (*Abies concolor*)
Steel Lawson Cypress (*Chamaecyparis lawsonia glauca*)
Western Red Cedar (*Juniperus scopulorum* var. "Chandler Blue")
Eastern Red Cedar (*Juniperus virginiana* var. *Burki*)
Colorado Blue Spruce (*Picea Pungens* var. *Glauca*)

Silver to Gray
Russian Olive (*Elaeagnus angustifolia*)
White Poplar (*Populus alba*)
Pendant Silver Linden (*Tilia petiolaris*)
*Silver Linden (*Tilia tomentosa*)

Red to Purple
Blood-leaf Japanese Maple (*Acer palmatum atropurpureum*)
Crimson King Maple (*Acer platanoides* "Crimson King")
Schwedler Maple (*Acer platanoides schwedleri*)
Purple-leaf Sycamore Maple (*Acer pseudoplatanus*)
Purple Beech (*Fagus sylvatica atropunicea*)
Weeping Purple Beech (*Fagus sylvatica purpureo-pendula*)
River's Purple Beech (*Fagus sylvatica riversi*)

Rubylace Locust (*Gleditsia triacanthos inermis* "Rubylace")
Purple Crab Apple (*Malus purpurea*)
Blireiana Plum (*Prunus blireiana*)
Pissard Plum (*Prunus cerasifera atropurpurea*)
Thundercloud Plum (*Prunus cerasifera nigra* "Thundercloud")
Woods Myrobalan Plum (*Prunus cerasifera woodi*)
Blood-leaf Peach (*Prunus persica atropurpurea*)
Purple English Oak (*Quercus robur atropurpurea*)

Trees Classified by Color of Fall Foliage

Yellow
Striped Maple or Moosewood (*Acer pensylvanicum*)
Norway Maple (*Acer platanoides* var.)
*Sugar Maple (*Acer saccharum*)
Ohio Buckeye (orange) (*Aesculus glabra*)
Apple Serviceberry (yellow-orange) (*Amelanchier grandiflora*)
*Birch species (*Betula*)
Hickory species (*Carya*)
Chinese Chestnut (*Castanea mollissima*)
*Katsura Tree (yellow to scarlet) (*Cercidiphyllum japonicum*)
Redbud species (*Cercis*)
Fringetree (*Chionanthus virginicus*)
*American Yellow-wood (*Cladrastis lutea*)
*American Beech (*Fagus grandifolia*)
*European Beech (*Fagus sylvatica*)
White Ash (purple to yellow) (*Fraxinus americana*)
*Ginkgo (*Ginkgo biloba*)
*Larch (*Larix decidua*)
Tulip Tree (*Liriodendron tulipifera*)
*Star Magnolia (bronze) (*Magnolia stellata*)
Golden Larch (*Pseudolarix amabilis*)
*Willow species (*Salix*)

Red
Amur Maple (*Acer ginnala*)
Manchurian Maple (*Acer mandshuricum*)
Nikko Maple (*Acer nikoense*)
*Japanese Maple (*Acer palmatum* var.)
*Red Maple (*Acer rubrum*)
*Sugar Maple (*Acer sacchrum*)
Tatarian Maple (*Acer tataricum*)
*Shadblow Serviceberry (*Amelanchier canadensis*)
Hornbeam species (*Carpinus*)
*Flowering Dogwood (*Cornus florida*)
Japanese Dogwood (*Cornus kousa*)
American Smoke Tree (*Cotinus americanus*)
Washington Hawthorn (*Crataegus phaenopyrum*)
*Sweet Gum (*Liquidambar styraciflua*)
Dawson Crab Apple (*Malus dawsoniana*)
*Black Tupelo or Black-Gum (*Nyssa sylvatica*)
*Sorrel Tree (*Oxydendrum arboreum*)
Persian Parrotia (*Parrotia persica*)
*Cherry species (*Prunus*)
Bradford Callery Pear (*Pyrus calleryana* "Bradford")
Red Oak (*Quercus borealis*)
Scarlet Oak (*Quercus coccinea*)
*Pin Oak (*Quercus palustris*)
Sassafras (*Sassafras albidum*)
Korean Mountain Ash (*Sorbus alnifolia*)
Korean Stewartia (orange to red) (*Stewartia koreana*)

Purple
White Ash (*Fraxinus americana*)
*Sweet Gum (*Liquidambar styraciflua*)
*Common Pear (*Pyrus communis*)
*White Oak (*Quercus alba*)

Trees with Interesting Bark

Gray
*Red Maple (*Acer rubrum*)
*Serviceberry species (*Amelanchier*)
Hornbeam species (*Carpinus*)
Hackberry species (*Celtis*)
*American Yellow-wood (*Cladrastis lutea*)
Hawthorn species (*Crataegus*)
*Beech species (*Fagus*)
American Holly (*Ilex opaca*)

English or Persian Walnut (*Juglans regia*)
Cucumber Tree (*Magnolia acuminata*)
*Saucer Magnolia (*Magnolia soulangeana*)
Red Oak (young trunk and branches) (*Quercus borealis*)
Black Oak (young trunk and branches) (*Quercus velutina*)
Mountain Ash species (*Sorbus*)

White
*Canoe Birch (*Betula papyrifera*)
*European Birch (*Betula pendula*)
*Gray Birch (*Betula populifolia*)

Red
Japanese Red Pine (*Pinus densiflora*)
Scotch Pine (*Pinus sylvestris*)
Red or Norway Pine (*Pinus resinosa*)

Reddish Brown
Chinese Paper Birch (*Betula albo-sinensis*)
Sargent Cherry (*Prunus sargenti*)

Yellow
Wisconsin or Niobe Weeping Willow (*Salix blanda*)

Corky
*Amur Cork (*Phellodendron amurense*)

Flaking
Paper Bark Maple (*Acer griseum*)
*Birch species (*Betula*)
Shagbark Hickory (*Carya ovata*)
Russian Olive (*Eleagnus angustifolia*)
Eastern Red Cedar (*Juniperus virginiana*)
Persian Parrotia (*Parrotia persica*)
*Plane Tree species (*Platanus*)
Lace-bark Pine (*Pinus bungeana*)

Trees for the City
White Fir (*Abies concolor*)
Hedge Maple (*Acer campestre*)
Box-Elder (*Acer negundo*)
Norway Maple (*Acer platanoides*)
Sycamore Maple (*Acer pseudoplatanus*)
Horse-Chestnut or Buckeye (*Aesculus*)
*Tree of Heaven (*Ailanthus*)
Catalpa (*Catalpa*)
Hackberry (*Celtis*)
Downy Hawthorn (*Crataegus mollis*)
Washington Hawthorn (*Crataegus phaenopyrum*)
Russian Olive (*Elaeagnus angustifolia*)
White Ash (*Fraxinus americana*)
European Ash (*Fraxinus excelsior*)
Green Ash (*Fraxinus pennsylvanica*)
*Ginkgo (*Ginkgo biloba*)
Thornless Honey-Locust (*Gleditsia triacanthos inermis*)
*Golden Rain Tree (*Koelreuteria paniculata*)
*Saucer Magnolia (*Magnolia soulangeana*)
*Star Magnolia (*Magnolia stellata*)
*Crab Apple (*Malus* var.)
*Amur Cork (*Phellodendron amurense*)
Colorado Spruce (*Picea pungens*)
*London Plane Tree (*Platanus acerifolia*)
Bradford Callery Pear (*Pyrus calleryana* "Bradford")
White Poplar (*Populus alba*)
*Lombardy Poplar (*Populus nigra italica*)
Red Oak (*Quercus borealis*)
*Black Locust (*Robinia pseudoacacia*)
*Japanese Pagoda Tree (*Sophora japonica*)
*Little-leaf Linden (*Tilia cordata*)
Crimean Linden (*Tilia euchlora*)
*Silver Linden (*Tilia tomentosa*)
Village Green Zelkova (*Zelkova serrata* "Village Green")

Trees for Wide Streets
Sycamore Maple (*Acer pseudoplatanus*)
*Sugar Maple (*Acer saccharum*)
Sugar Hackberry (*Celtis laevigata*)
*Katsura Tree (*Cercidiphyllum japonicum*)
White Ash (*Fraxinus americana*)

Green Ash (*Fraxinus pennsylvanica lanceolata*)
*Ginkgo (*Ginkgo biloba*)
*Common Honey-Locust (*Gleditsia triacanthos*)
Kalopanax (*Kalopanax pictus*)
Tulip Tree (*Liriodendron tulipifera*)
Amur Cork (*Phellodendron amurense*)
*Eastern White Pine (*Pinus strobus*)
*London Plane Tree (*Platanus acerifolium*)
White Poplar (*Populus alba*)
Sargent Cherry (*Prunus sargenti*)
Red Oak (*Quercus borealis*)
*Pin Oak (*Quercus palustris*)
Willow Oak (*Quercus phellos*)
Japanese Zelkova (*Zelkova serrata*)

Trees for Medium Streets
Norway Maple (*Acer platanoides*)
Mountain Silverbell (*Halesia monticola*)
*Sweet Gum (*Liquidambar styraciflua*)
Hop-Hornbeam (*Ostrya virginiana*)
*Sorrel Tree or Sourwood (*Oxydendron arboreum*)
Simon Poplar (*Populus simoni*)
Scarlet Oak (*Quercus coccinea*)
Willow Oak (*Quercus phellos*)
*Black Locust (*Robinia pseudoacacia*)
Sassafras (*Sassafras albidum officinale*)
*Japanese Pagoda Tree (*Sophora japonica*)
*Linden species (*Tilia*)

Trees for Suburban Streets
Hedge Maple (*Acer campestre*)
Amur Maple (*Acer ginnala*)
Paperbark Maple (*Acer griseum*)
Globe Norway Maple (*Acer platanoides globosum*)
Mountain Maple (*Acer spicatum*)
Tatarian Maple (*Acer tataricum*)
American Hornbeam (*Carpinus caroliniana*)
Pyramid European Hornbeam (*Carpinus betulus fastigiata*)
Globe European Hornbeam (*Carpinus betulus globosa*)
Fringetree (*Chionanthus virginicus*)
*Flowering Dogwood (*Cornus florida*)
*Hawthorn species (*Crataegus*)
Korean Evodia (*Evodia danielli*)
Carolina Silverbell (*Halesia carolina*)
*Golden Rain Tree (*Koelreuteria paniculata*)
Oriental Cherry (*Prunus serrulata*)
Columnar Sargent Cherry (*Prunus sargenti columnaris*)
Smooth-leaved Elm varieties (*Ulmus carpinifolia*)

Soil Tolerance

Trees Tolerating Acid Soil
*Japanese Maple (*Acer palmatum*)
*Flowering Dogwood (*Cornus florida*)
Japanese Dogwood (*Cornus kousa*)
*European Beech (*Fagus sylvatica*)
Sweet Bay (*Magnolia virginiana*)
*Black Tupelo (*Nyssa sylvatica*)
*Sorrel Tree (*Oxydendrum arboreum*)
Red Oak (*Quercus borealis*)
Scarlet Oak (*Quercus coccinea*)
Willow Oak (*Quercus phellos*)
*Pin Oak (*Quercus palustris*)

Trees Tolerating Moist Soil
*Red Maple (*Acer rubrum*)
Alder species (*Alnus*)
Holly species (*Ilex*)
*Sweet Gum (*Liquidambar styraciflua*)
Sweet Bay (*Magnolia virginiana*)
*Black Tupelo or Black Gum (*Nyssa sylvatica*)
Swamp White Oak (*Quercus bicolor*)
*Willow species (*Salix*)
Common Bald Cypress (*Taxodium distichum*)
American Arbor-vitae (*Thuja occidentalis*)

Trees Tolerating Dry or Poor Soil
Box-Elder (*Acer negundo*)
*Tree of Heaven (*Ailanthus*)
*Gray Birch (*Betulapopulifolia*)
Russian Olive (*Elaeagnus angustifolia*)

Green Ash (*Fraxinus pennsylvanica*)
Modesto Ash (*Fraxinus velutina* "Modesto")
*Honey-Locust (*Gleditsia triacanthos* var.)
Western Red Cedar (*Juniperus scopulorum*)
Eastern Red Cedar (*Juniperus virginiana*)
*Golden Rain Tree (*Koelreuteria paniculata*)
Osage-Orange (*Maclura pomifera*)
Jack Pine (*Pinus banksiana*)
Pitch Pine (*Pinus rigida*)
Virginia Scrub Pine (*Pinus virginiana*)
White Poplar (*Populus alba*)
Chestnut Oak (*Quercus montana*)
*Black Locust (*Robinia pseudoacacia*)
Sassafras (*Sassafras albidum officinale*)
Chinese Elm (*Ulmus parvifolia*)
Siberian Elm (*Ulmus pumila*)

Pest-Resistant Trees

*Tree of Heaven (*Ailanthus altissima*)
Hornbeam species (*Carpinus*)

*Katsura Tree (*Cercidiphyllum japonicum*)
False Cypress species (*Chamaecyparis*)
Cornelian Cherry (*Cornus mas*)
Japanese Cornel (*Cornus officinalis*)
American Smoke Tree (*Cotinus americanus*)
Russian Olive (*Elaeagnus angustifolia*)
Franklinia (*Franklinia alatamaha*)
*Ginkgo (*Ginkgo biloba*)
Honey-Locust (*Gleditsia triacanthos*)
Kentucky Coffee Tree (*Gymnocladus dioicus*)
Juniper species (*Juniperus*)
Kalopanax (*Kalopanax pictus*)
*Golden Rain Tree (*Koelreuteria paniculata*)
*Laburnum species (*Laburnum*)
*Sweet Gum (*Liquidambar styraciflua*)
Cucumber Tree (*Magnolia acuminata*)
Kobus Magnolia (*Magnolia kobus borealis*)
Anise Magnolia (*Magnolia salicifolia*)
*Star Magnolia (*Magnolia stellata*)
Hop-Hornbeam species (*Ostrya*)

Trees for Hedging or Barriers

European Beech (*Fagus sylvatica*) prunes well.
Leyland Cypress (*Cupressocyparis leylandii*) withstands heavy pruning.
Hawthorn varieties (*Crataegus*) easily pruned, advantage of thorns.
Canadian Hemlock (*Tsuga canadensis*) evergreen.
American Holly (*Ilex opaca*) can be pruned.
European Hornbeam (*Carpinus betulus*) prunes well.
Little-leaf Linden (*Tilia cordata*) tolerates heavy pruning.
Hedge Maple (*Acer campestre*) can be pruned.
Austrian Pine (*Pinus nigra*) plant 10–12 feet on centers, staggered row.
Japanese Black Pine (*Pinus thunbergi*) plant 8 feet on centers, staggered row.
Eastern White Pine (*Pinus strobus*) plant 15 feet on centers, staggered row.

MINNESOTA

State Tree

Norway Pine (*Pinus resinosa*)

Evergreen Trees

White Fir (*Abies concolor*)
Balsam (*Abies balsamea*)
Eastern Red Cedar (*Juniperus virginiana*)
*Larch species (*Larix*)
Spruce species (*Picea*)
*Pine species (*Pinus*)
Arbor-vitae species (*Thuja*)

Trees Classified by Height

20–35 Feet

Amur Maple (*Acer ginnala*)
Ohio Buckeye (*Aesculus glabra*)
Russian Olive (*Elaeagnus angustifolia*)
*Crab Apple species (*Malus*)
*Cherry species (*Prunus*)
Dahurian Buckthorn (*Rhamnus davurica*)
Showy Mountain Ash (*Sorbus decora*)

35–75 Feet

Box-Elder (*Acer negundo*)
Striped Maple or Moosewood (*Acer pennsylvanicum*)
Norway Maple (*Acer platanoides*)
*Red Maple (*Acer rubrum*)
Devil's Walking Stick (*Aralia elata*)
*European Birch (*Betula pendula*)
American Hornbeam (*Carpinus caroliniana*)
Green Ash (*Fraxinus pennsylvanica lanceolata*)
Eastern Larch or Tamarack (*Larix laricina*)
*Siberian Crab Apple (*Malus baccata*)
"Dolgo" Crab Apple (*Malus* "Dolgo")
Cherry Crab Apple (*Malus robusta*)
*Amur Cork (*Phellodendron amurense*)
Black Hills Spruce (*Picea glauca densata*)
Jack Pine (*Pinus banksiana*)
Swiss Stone Pine (*Pinus cembra*)
Limber Pine (*Pinus flexilis*)
Scotch Pine (*Pinus sylvestris*)
Simon Poplar (*Populus simoni*)
Amur Chokecherry (*Prunus maacki*)
European Bird Cherry (*Prunus padus*)
Swamp White Oak (*Quercus bicolor*)
White Willow (*Salix alba*)
European Mountain Ash or Rowan Tree (*Sorbus aucuparia*)
American Arbor-vitae (*Thuja occidentalis*)

75 Feet or Over

Fir species (*Abies*)
*Sugar Maple (*Acer saccharum*)
*Baumann Horse-Chestnut (*Aesculus hippocastanum baumanni*)

European Alder (*Alnus glutinosa*)
*Canoe Birch (*Betula papyrifera*)
False Cypress species (*Chamaecyparis*)
White Ash (*Fraxinus americana*)
*European Larch (*Larix decidua*)
Spruce species (*Picea*)
*Pine species (*Pinus*)
Poplar species (*Populus*)
Black or Rum Cherry (*Prunus serotina*)
*Linden species (*Tilia*)
*Elm species (*Ulmus*)

Trees Classified by Form

Pyramidal

Fir species (*Abies*)
*Birch species (*Betula*)
False Cypress species (*Chamaecyparis*)
Juniper or Red Cedar species (*Juniperus*)
*Larch species (*Larix*)
Spruce species (*Picea*)
Swiss Stone Pine (*Pinus cembra*)
Korean Pine (*Pinus koraiensis*)
Pyramidal Austrian Pine (*Pinus nigra pyramidalis*)
Red or Norway Pine (*Pinus resinosa*)
Bolleana poplar (*Populus alba pyramidalis*)
Arbor-vitae species (*Thuja*)
*Linden species (*Tilia*)

Columnar

Ascending Norway Maple (*Acer platanoides ascendens*)
Columnar Norway Maple (*Acer platanoides columnare*)
Erect Norway Maple (*Acer platanoides erectum*)
Columnar Red Maple (*Acer rubrum columnare*)
Sentry Maple (*Acer saccharum monumentale*)
Fastigiate European Birch (*Betula pendula fastigiata*)
Fastigiate Red Cedar (*Juniperus virginiana schotti*)
Swiss Stone Pine (*Pinus cembra*)
Fastigiate Scotch Pine (*Pinus sylvestris fastigiata*)
Fastigiate Simon Poplar (*Populus simoni fastigiata*)
Shipmast Locust (*Robinia pseudoacacia rectissima*)
Upright European Mountain Ash (*Sorbus aucuparia fastigiata*)
Douglas Arbor-vitae (*Thuja occidentalis douglasi pyramidalis*)
Fastigiate American Arbor-vitae (*Thuja occidentalis fastigiata*)
Columnar Big-leaf Linden (*Tilia platyphyllos fastigiata*)
*American Elm varieties (*Ulmus americana*)

Weeping

Slender European Birch (*Betula pendula tristis*)
Young's Birch (*Betula pendula youngi*)
*Weeping Larch (*Larix decidua pendula*)

Koster Weeping Blue Spruce (*Picea pungens kosteriana*)
Weeping Black Cherry (*Prunus serotina pendula*)
Golden Weeping Willow (*Salix alba tristis*)
Weeping European Mountain Ash (*Sorbus aucuparia pendula*)
Sargent Hemlock (*Tsuga canadensis pendula*)
Weeping American Elm (*Ulmus americana pendula*)

Rounded or Globe-Shaped

Globe Norway Maple (*Acer platanoides globosum*)
Umbrella Black Locust (*Robinia pseudoacacia umbraculifera*)
Sargent Hemlock (*Tsuga canadensis sargenti*)

With Horizontal Branching

Fir species (*Abies*)
Spruce species (*Picea*)
*Eastern White Pine (*Pinus strobus*)

Trees Classified by Color of Blossom

White

*Siberian Crab Apple (*Malus baccata*)
Sour Cherry (*Prunus cerasus*)
American Mountain Ash (*Sorbus americana*)
European Mountain Ash (*Sorbus aucuparia*)
Showy Mountain Ash (*Sorbus decora*)

Pink

Toba Hawthorn (*Crataegus mordenensis* "Toba")
*Common Apple (*Malus pumila*)

Red

*Ruby Horse-Chestnut (*Aesculus carnea briotti*)
Almey Crab Apple (*Malus* "Almey")

Trees with Bright Red Fruit

Almey Crab Apple (*Malus* "Almey")
Siberian Crab Apple (*Malus baccata*)
*Common Apple (*Malus pumila*)
American Mountain Ash (*Sorbus americana*)
European Mountain Ash (*Sorbus aucuparia*)

Trees Classified by Color of Summer Foliage

Blue

Eastern Red Cedar (*Juniperus virginiana* var. *Burki*)

Silver to Gray

Russian Olive (*Elaeagnus angustifolia*)
Common Sea-Buckthorn (*Hippophae rhamnoides*)
White Poplar (*Populus alba*)

Red to Purple

Schwedler Maple (*Acer platanoides schwedleri*)

Trees Classified by Color of Fall Foliage

Yellow

Norway Maple (*Acer platanoides* var.)
*Sugar Maple (*Acer saccharum*)
Ohio Buckeye (orange) (*Aesculus glabra*)
*Birch species (*Betula*)
White Ash (purple to yellow) (*Fraxinus americana*)
*Larch (*Larix decidua*)
Woods Myrobalan Plum (*Prunus cerasifera woodi*)
*Willow species (*Salix*)

Red
Amur Maple (*Acer ginnala*)
*Red Maple (*Acer rubrum*)
*Sugar Maple (*Acer saccharum*)
Mountain Maple (*Acer spicatum*)
Hornbeam species (*Carpinus*)
*Cherry species (*Prunus*)

Purple
White Ash (*Fraxinus americana*)

Trees with Interesting Bark

Gray
*Red Maple (*Acer rubrum*)
Hornbeam species (*Carpinus*)
*American Yellow-wood (*Cladrastis lutea*)
Mountain Ash species (*Sorbus*)

White
*Canoe Birch (*Betula papyrifera*)
*European Birch (*Betula pendula*)

Red
Red or Norway Pine (*Pinus resinosa*)
Scotch Pine (*Pinus sylvestris*)

Corky
*Amur Cork (*Phellodendron amurense*)

Flaking

*Birch species (*Betula*)
Russian Olive (*Elaeagnus angustifolia*)

Trees for the City
Box-Elder (*Acer negundo*)
Norway Maple (*Acer platanoides*)
*Horse-Chestnut or Buckeye (*Aesculus*)
Russian Olive (*Elaeagnus angustifolia*)
White Ash (*Fraxinus americana*)
Green Ash (*Fraxinus pennsylvanica*)
*Siberian Crab Apple (*Malus baccata*)
*Amur Cork (*Phellodendron amurense*)
Colorado Spruce (*Picea pungens*)
White Poplar (*Populus alba*)
*Black Locust (*Robinia pseudoacacia*)
Little-leaf Linden (*Tilia cordata*)

Trees for Wide Streets
*Sugar Maple (*Acer saccharum*)
White Ash (*Fraxinus americana*)
Green Ash (*Fraxinus pennsylvanica lanceolata*)
*Amur Cork (*Phellodendron amurense*)
*Eastern White Pine (*Pinus strobus*)
White Poplar (*Populus alba*)

Trees for Medium Streets
Norway Maple (*Acer platanoides*)
Simon Poplar (*Populus simoni*)
*Black Locust (*Robinia pseudoacacia*)
*Linden species (*Tilia*)

Trees for Suburban Streets
Amur Maple (*Acer ginnala*)
Globe Norway Maple (*Acer platanoides globosum*)
Mountain Maple (*Acer spicatum*)
American Hornbeam (*Carpinus caroliniana*)
*Hawthorn species (*Crataegus*)

Soil Tolerance

Trees Tolerating Moist Soil
*Red Maple (*Acer rubrum*)
Alder species (*Alnus*)
Eastern Larch (*Larix laricina*)
Swamp White Oak (*Quercus bicolor*)
American Arbor-vitae (*Thuja occidentalis*)

Trees Tolerating Dry or Poor Soil
Box-Elder (*Acer negundo*)
Russian Olive (*Elaeagnus angustifolia*)
Green Ash (*Fraxinus pennsylvanica*)
Eastern Red Cedar (*Juniperus virginiana*)
Jack Pine (*Pinus banksiana*)
White Poplar (*Populus alba*)
*Black Locust (*Robinia pseudoacacia*)

Pest-Resistant Trees
Hornbeam species (*Carpinus*)
False Cypress species (*Chamaecyparis*)
Russian Olive (*Elaeagnus angustifolia*)

Trees for Hedging or Barriers
European Beech (*Fagus sylvatica*) prunes well.
Hawthorn varieties (*Crataegus*) easily pruned, advantage of thorns.
Canadian Hemlock (*Tsuga canadensis*) evergreen.
European Hornbeam (*Carpinus betulus*) prunes well.
Little-leaf Linden (*Tilia cordata*) tolerates heavy pruning.
Hedge Maple (*Acer campestre*) can be pruned.
Austrian Pine (*Pinus nigra*) plant 10–12 feet on centers, staggered row.
Eastern White Pine (*Pinus strobus*) plant 15 feet on centers, staggered row.

MISSISSIPPI

State Tree
*Southern Magnolia (*Magnolia grandiflora*)

Evergreen Trees
Strawberry Tree (*Arbutus unedo*)
Lemon Bottlebrush (*Callistemon lanceolatus*)
Camellia species (*Camellia*)
*Deodar Cedar (*Cedrus deodara*)
Camphor Tree (*Cinnamomum camphora*)
Citrus species (*Citrus*)
*Flowering Dogwood (*Cornus florida*)
Common China Fir (*Cunninghamia lanceolata*)
Loblolly Bay Gordonia (*Gordonia lasianthus*)
Holly species (*Ilex*)
Juniper species (*Juniperus*)
*Southern Magnolia (*Magnolia grandiflora*)
Southern Waxmyrtle (*Myrica cerifera*)
Chinese Photinia (*Photinia serrulata*)
Pine species (*Pinus*)
Yew Podocarpus (*Podocarpus macrophyllus*)
Cork Oak (*Quercus suber*)
*Live Oak (*Quercus virginiana*)
Palmetto (*Sabal palmetto*)

Trees Classified by Height

20–35 Feet
Strawberry Tree (*Arbutus unedo*)
Lemon Bottlebrush (*Callistemon lanceolatus*)
Judas Tree (*Cercis canadensis*)
American Smoke Tree (*Cotinus americanus*)
*Hawthorn species (*Crataegus*)
Loquat (*Eribotrya japonica*)
Common Fig (*Ficus carica*)
Dahoon (*Ilex cassine*)
Possum Haw (*Ilex decidua*)
Yaupon (*Ilex vomitoria*)
Crape-Myrtle (*Lagerstroemia indica*)
Yellow Cucumber Tree (*Magnolia cordata*)
*Crab Apple species (*Malus*)
Jerusalem Thorn (*Parkinsonia aculeata*)

*Cherry species (*Prunus*)
*Babylon Weeping Willow (*Salix babylonica*)

35–75 Feet
Camphor Tree (*Cinnamomum camphora*)
*Flowering Dogwood (*Cornus florida*)
Common China Fir (*Cunninghamia lanceolata*)
Kaki Persimmon (*Diospyros kaki*)
Brush Cherry Eugenia (*Eugenia paniculta*)
Chinese Parasol Tree (*Firmiana simplex*)
Lobolly Bay Gordonia (*Gordonia lasianthus*)
English Holly (*Ilex aquifolium*)
Dahoon (*Ilex cassine*)
Luster-leaf Holly (*Ilex latifolia*)
American Holly (*Ilex opaca*)
Greek Juniper (*Juniperus excelsa*)
Sweet Bay (*Magnolia virginiana*)
Chinaberry (*Melia azedarach*)
Yew Podocarpus (*Podocarpus macrophyllus*)
Laurel Oak (*Quercus laurifolia*)
Water Oak (*Quercus nigra*)
Willow Oak (*Quercus phellos*)
Cork Oak (*Quercus suber*)
*Live Oak (*Quercus virginiana*)

75 Feet or Over
*Red or Swamp Maple (*Acer rubrum*)
*Silver Maple (*Acer saccharinum*)
*Sugar Maple (*Acer saccharum*)
*Eucalyptus species (*Eucalyptus*)
*American Beech (*Fagus grandifolia*)
Tulip Tree or Yellow Poplar (*Liriodendron tulipifera*)
*Southern Magnolia (*Magnolia grandiflora*)
*Black Tupelo or Black Gum (*Nyssa sylvatica*)
Sabal Palmetto (*Palmetto*)
*Oak species (*Quercus*)

Trees Classified by Form

Pyramidal
*Cedar species (*Cedrus*)
Smooth Arizona Cypress (*Cupressus arizonica bonita*)

Italian Cypress (*Cupressus sempervirens*)
American Holly (*Ilex opaca*)
Juniper or Red Cedar species (*Juniperus*)
*Sweet Gum (*Liquidambar styraciflua*)
*Magnolia species (*Magnolia*)
Dawn Redwood (*Metasequoia glyptostroboides*)
*Black Tupelo or Black Gum (*Nyssa sylvatica*)

Columnar
Columnar Red Maple (*Acer rubrum columnare*)
Common Bald Cypress (*Taxodium distichum*)

Weeping
*Deodar Cedar (*Cedrus deodar*)
*Babylon Weeping Willow (*Salix babylonica*)

Rounded or Globe-Shaped
*White Oak (*Quercus alba*)
Umbrella Black Locust (*Robinia pseudoacacia umbraculifera*)

With Horizontal Branching
*Cedar species (*Cedrus*)
*Flowering Dogwood (*Cornus florida*)
*Hawthorn species (*Crataegus*)
*Black Tupelo or Black Gum (*Nyssa sylvatica*)
*White Oak (*Quercus alba*)
*Live Oak (*Quercus virginiana*)
Common Bald Cypress (*Taxodium distichum*)

Trees Classified by Color of Blossom

Yellow
Cootamundra Wattle (*Acacia baileyana*)
Shower of Gold (*Cassia fistula*)
*Golden Rain Tree (*Koelreuteria paniculata*)
*Laburnum (*Laburnum vossi*)

White
Strawberry Tree (*Arbutus unedo*)
White Redbud (*Cercis canadensis alba*)
Citrus species (*Citrus*)
Hawthorn (*Crataegus species*)
Silverbell (*Halesia diptera*)

*Southern Magnolia (*Magnolia grandiflora*)
Bigleaf Magnolia (*Magnolia macrophylla*)
Mount Fuji Cherry (*Prunus serrulata* "Shirotae")
Western Soapberry (*Sapindus drummondi*)

Pink
Red Flowering Dogwood (*Cornus florida rubra*)
Ingleside Crape-Myrtle (*Lagerstroemia indica* "Ingleside Pink")
*Saucer Magnolia (*Magnolia soulangeana*)
Japanese Flowering Crab Apple (*Malus floribunda*)
Katherine Crab Apple (*Malus* "Katherine")
Prince Georges Crab Apple (*Malus* "Prince Georges")
*Common Apple (*Malus pumila*)
Weeping Cherry (*Prunus subhirtella pendula*)

Red
Crimson Eucalyptus (*Eucalyptus ficifolia*)
Red Crape-Myrtle (*Lagerstroemia indica* "Wm. Toovey")
Alexandrina Magnolia (*Magnolia soulangeana* "Alexandrina")

Trees with Bright Red Fruit
*Flowering Dogwood (*Cornus florida*)
*Hawthorn species (*Crataegus*)
Holly species (*Ilex*)
*Magnolia species (*Magnolia*)
Almey Crab Apple (*Malus* "Almey")
Siberian Crab Apple (*Malus baccata*)
Hopa Crab Apple (*Malus* "Hopa")

Trees Classified by Color of Summer Foliage

Silver to Gray
Russian Olive (*Elaeagnus angustifolia*)
White Poplar (*Populus alba*)

Trees Classified by Color of Fall Foliage

Yellow
*Sugar Maple (*Acer saccharum*)
Fringetree (*Chionanthus virginicus*)
Tulip Tree or Yellow Poplar (*Liriodendron tulipifera*)
*Willow species (*Salix*)

Red
Japanese Maple (*Acer palmatum*)
*Red Maple (*Acer rubrum*)
*Sweet Gum (*Liquidambar styraciflua*)

Trees with Interesting Bark

Gray
*Red Maple (*Acer rubrum*)
Hackberry species (*Celtis*)
*American Beech (*Fagus grandifolia*)
American Holly (*Ilex opaca*)

Corky
Cork Oak (*Quercus suber*)
Cork-bark Elm (*Ulmus alata*)

Flaking
River Birch (*Betula nigra*)
Shagbark Hickory (*Carya ovata*)
Eucalyptus species (*Eucalyptus*)
Eastern Red Cedar (*Juniperus virginiana*)
Crape-Myrtle (*Lagerstroemia indica*)
*Plane Tree species (*Platanus*)

Trees for the City
Hackberry (*Celtis*)
*Ginkgo (*Ginkgo biloba*)
Thornless Honey-Locust (*Gleditsia triacanthos inermis*)
*Golden Rain Tree (*Koelreuteria paniculata*)
*Southern Magnolia (*Magnolia grandiflora*)
*Crab Apple (*Malus varieties*)
Chinaberry (*Melia azedarach*)
Red Oak (*Quercus borealis*)
*Japanese Pagoda Tree (*Sophora japonica*)

Trees for Wide Streets
Sugar Hackberry (*Celtis laevigata*)
Camphor Tree (*Cinnamomum camphora*)
*Eucalyptus species (*Eucalyptus*)
White Ash (*Fraxinus americana*)
Green Ash (*Fraxinus pennsylvanica lanceolata*)
*Common Honey-Locust (*Gleditsia triacanthos*)
*Southern Magnolia (*Magnolia grandiflora*)
Willow Oak (*Quercus phellos*)
*Live Oak (*Quercus virginiana*)

Trees for Medium Streets
Silverbell (*Halesia diptera*)
*Sweet Gum (*Liquidambar styraciflua*)
Chinaberry (*Melia azedarach*)
*Sorrel Tree or Sourwood (*Oxydendrum arboreum*)
Scarlet Oak (*Quercus coccinea*)
Laurel Oak (*Quercus laurifolia*)
Willow Oak (*Quercus phellos*)
Cork Oak (*Quercus suber*)
*Black Locust (*Robinia pseudoacacia*)
Sassafras (*Sassafras albidum officinale*)

Trees for Suburban Streets
American Hornbeam (*Carpinus caroliniana*)
Fringetree (*Chionanthus virginicus*)
*Flowering Dogwood (*Cornus florida*)
*Hawthorn species (*Crataegus*)
Crape-Myrtle (*Lagerstroemia indica*)

Soil Tolerance

Trees Tolerating Acid Soil
*Japanese Maple (*Acer palmatum*)
Strawberry Tree (*Arbutus unedo*)
Citrus species (*Citrus*)
*Flowering Dogwood (*Cornus florida*)
Sweet Bay (*Magnolia virginiana*)
*Black Tupelo (*Nyssa sylvatica*)
*Sorrel Tree (*Oxydendrum arboreum*)
Willow Oak (*Quercus phellos*)

Trees Tolerating Moist Soil
*Red Maple (*Acer rubrum*)
River Birch (*Betula nigra*)
Catalpa (*Catalpa bignonioides*)
Holly species (*Ilex*)
*Southern Magnolia (*Magnolia grandiflora*)
Sweet Bay (*Magnolia virginana*)
Common Bald Cypress (*Taxodium distichum*)

Trees Tolerating Dry or Poor Soil
Silver Wattle (*Acacia decurrens dealbata*)
Common Paper-Mulberry (*Broussonetia papyrifera*)
*Cedar species (*Cedrus*)
European Hackberry (*Celtis australis*)
Sugar Hackberry (*Celtis laevigata*)
*Honey-Locust (*Gleditsia triacanthos var.*)
*Golden Rain Tree (*Koelreuteria paniculata*)
Chinaberry (*Melia azedarach*)
Jerusalem Thorn (*Parkinsonia aculeata*)
Chinese Elm (*Ulmus parvifolia*)

Pest-Resistant Trees
Hornbeam species (*Carpinus*)
*Fig species (*Ficus*)
Franklinia (*Franklinia alatamaha*)
*Sweet Gum (*Liquidambar styraciflua*)
Hop-Hornbeam species (*Ostrya*)

Trees for Seashore Planting
*Eucalyptus (*Eucalyptus*)
Spiny Greek Juniper (*Juniperus excelsa stricta*)
*Southern Magnolia (*Magnolia grandiflora*)
Holly Oak (*Quercus ilex*)
Black Jack Oak (*Quercus marilandica*)
*Live Oak (*Quercus virginiana*)
Palmetto (*Sabal palmetto*)
Oriental Arbor-vitae (*Thuja orientalis*)
Chinese Elm (*Ulmus parvifolia*)

Trees for Hedging or Barriers
European Beech (*Fagus sylvatica*) prunes well.
Leyland Cypress (*Cupressocyparis leylandii*) withstands heavy pruning.
Hawthorn varieties (*Crataegus*) easily pruned, advantage of thorns.
Canadian Hemlock (*Tsuga canadensis*) evergreen.
American Holly (*Ilex opaca*) can be pruned.
European Hornbeam (*Carpinus betulus*) prunes well.
Little-leaf Linden (*Tilia cordata*) tolerates heavy pruning.
Hedge Maple (*Acer campestre*) can be pruned.
Austrian Pine (*Pinus nigra*) plant 10–12 feet on centers, staggered row.
Japanese Black Pine (*Pinus thunbergi*) plant 8 feet on centers, staggered row.
Eastern White Pine (*Pinus strobus*) plant 15 feet on centers, staggered row.

MISSOURI

State Tree
*Hawthorn (*Crataegus*)

Evergreen Trees
White Fir (*Abies concolor*)
Tree Box (*Buxus sempervirens arborescens*)
American Holly (*Ilex opaca*)
Eastern Red Cedar (*Juniperus virginiana*)
Spruce species (*Picea*)
*Pine species (*Pinus*)
*Douglas Fir (*Pseudotsuga menziesii*)
Arbor-vitae (*Thuja*)
*Canadian Hemlock (*Tsuga canadensis*)

Trees Classified by Height

20–35 Feet
Hedge Maple (*Acer campestre*)
Hornbeam Maple (*Acer carpinifolium*)
Amur Maple (*Acer ginnala*)
Paperbark Maple (*Acer griseum*)
Manchurian Maple (*Acer mandshuricum*)
*Japanese Maple (*Acer palmatum*)
Mountain Maple (*Acer spicatum*)
Tatarian Maple (*Acer tataricum*)
Ohio Buckeye (*Aesculus glabra*)
*Shadblow Serviceberry (*Amelanchier canadensis*)
Apple Serviceberry (*Amelanchier grandiflora*)
*Gray Birch (*Betula populifolia*)
European Hornbeam (*Carpinus betulus globosa*)
Mockernut (*Carya tomentosa*)
Eastern Redbud (*Cercis canadensis*)
Fringetree (*Chionanthus virginicus*)
Cornelian Cherry (*Cornus mas*)
Japanese Cornel (*Cornus officinalis*)
American Smoke Tree (*Cotinus americanus*)
*Hawthorn species (*Crataegus*)
Russian Olive (*Elaeagnus angustifolia*)
Euonymus species (*Euonymus*)
Franklinia (*Franklinia alatamaha*)
Carolina Silverbell (*Halesia carolina*)
Possum Haw (*Ilex decidua*)
Needle Juniper (*Juniperus rigida*)
*Golden Rain Tree (*Koelreuteria paniculata*)
*Laburnum species (*Laburnum*)
*Saucer Magnolia (*Magnolia soulangeana*)
*Star Magnolia (*Magnolia stellata*)
*Crab Apple species (*Malus*)
*Cherry species (*Prunus*)

Black Jack Oak (*Quercus marilandica*)
Almond-leaf Willow (*Salix amygdalina*)
★Babylon Weeping Willow (*Salix babylonica*)
Goat Willow (*Salix caprea*)
Snowberry Mountain Ash (*Sorbus discolor*)
Showy Mountain Ash (*Sorbus decora*)
Folgner Mountain Ash (*Sorbus folgneri*)
Japanese Tree Lilac (*Syringa amurensis japonica*)

35–75 Feet
Box-Elder (*Acer negundo*)
Striped Maple or Moosewood (*Acer pennsylvanicum*)
★Red-fruited Tree of Heaven (*Ailanthus altissima erythrocarpa*)
Red Alder (*Alnus rubra*)
Allegany Serviceberry (*Amelanchier laevis*)
Devil's Walking Stick (*Aralia elata*)
★European Birch (*Betula pendula*)
European Hornbeam (*Carpinus betula*)
American Hornbeam (*Carpinus caroliniana*)
Japanese Hornbeam (*Carpinus japonica*)
Chinese Chestnut (*Castanea mollissima*)
Southern Catalpa (*Catalpa bignoniodies*)
Bunch Hackberry (*Celtis bungeana*)
★Katsura Tree (*Cercidiphyllum japonicum*)
Eastern Redbud (*Cercis canadensis*)
Chinese Redbud (*Cercis chinensis*)
★American Yellow-wood (*Cladrastis lutea*)
★Flowering Dogwood (*Cornus florida*)
Largeleaf Dogwood (*Cornus macrophylla*)
Cockspur Thorn (*Crataegus crus-galli*)
Green Hawthorn (*Crataegus viridis*)
Common Persimmon (*Diospyros virginiana*)
Green Ash (*Fraxinus pennsylvanica lanceolata*)
American Holly (*Ilex opaca*)
Heartnut (*Juglans sieboldiana cordiformis*)
Chinese Juniper (*Juniperus chinensis*)
Western Red Cedar (*Juniperus scopulorum*)
Osage-Orange (*Maclura pomifera*)
★Siberian Crab Apple (*Malus baccata*)
"Cowichan" Crab Apple (*Malus* "Cowichan")
"Dolgo" Crab Apple (*Malus* "Dolgo")
"Makamik" Crab Apple (*Malus* "Makamik")
Cherry Crab Apple (*Malus robusta*)
"Sissipuk" Crab Apple (*Malus* "Sissipuk")
White Mulberry (*Morus alba*)
★Sorrel Tree or Sourwood (*Oxydendrum arboreum*)
Empress Tree ((*Paulownia tomentosa*)
★Amur Cork (*Phellodendron amurense*)
Jack Pine (*Pinus banksiana*)
Swiss Stone Pine (*Pinus cembra*)
Limber Pine (*Pinus flexilis*)
Pitch Pine (*Pinus rigida*)
Scotch Pine (*Pinus sylvestris*)
Simon Poplar (*Populus simoni*)
Miyama Cherry (*Prunus maximowiczi*)
European Bird Cherry (*Prunus padus*)
Sargent Cherry (*Prunus sargenti*)
Yoshino Cherry (*Prunus yedoensis*)
Ussurian Pear (*Pyrus ussuriensis*)
Swamp White Oak (*Quercus bicolor*)
Red Oak (*Quercus borealis*)
Scarlet Oak (*Quercus coccinea*)
Shingle Oak (*Quercus imbricaria*)
Water Oak (*Quercus nigra*)
★Pin Oak (*Quercus palustris*)
Willow Oak (*Quercus phellos*)
White Willow (*Salix alba*)
Wisconsin or Niobe Weeping Willow (*Salix blanda*)
Elaeagnus Willow (*Salix elaeagnus*)
Thurlow Weeping Willow (*Salix elegantissima*)
Laurel Willow (*Salix pentandra*)
Sassafras (*Sassafras albidum officinale*)
Korean Mountain Ash (*Sorbus alnifolia*)
White Beam Mountain Ash (*Sorbus aria*)
European Mountain Ash or Rowan Tree (*Sorbus aucuparia*)
American Arbor-vitae (*Thuja occidentalis*)
Oriental Arbor-vitae (*Thuja orientalis*)

Japanese Arbor-vitae (*Thuja standishi*)
★Crimean Linden (*Tilia euchlora*)
Chinese Elm (*Ulmus parvifolia*)
Siberian Elm (*Ulmus pumila*)

75 Feet or Over
White Fir (*Abies concolor*)
Big-leaf Maple (*Acer macrophyllum*)
Norway Maple (*Acer platanoides*)
Sycamore Maple (*Acer pseudoplatanus*)
★Red or Swamp Maple (*Acer rubrum*)
★Sugar Maple (*Acer saccharum*)
★Baumann Horse-Chestnut (*Aesculus hippocastanum baumanni*)
Sweet Birch (*Betula lenta*)
River Birch (*Betula nigra*)
★Canoe Birch (*Betula papyrifera*)
Hickory species (*Carya*)
Northern Catalpa (*Catalpa speciosa*)
Sugar Hackberry (*Celtis laevigata*)
★Katsura Tree (*Cercidiphyllum japonicum*)
★Beech species (*Fagus*)
White Ash (*Fraxinus americana*)
European Ash (*Fraxinus excelsior*)
★Ginkgo or Maidenhair Tree (*Ginkgo biloba*)
★Common Honey-Locust (*Gleditsia triacanthos*)
Kentucky Coffee Tree (*Gymnocladus dioicus*)
Mountain Silverbell (*Halesia monticola*)
English or Persian Walnut (*Juglans regia*)
Kalopanax (*Kalopanax pictus*)
★Sweet Gum (*Liquidambar styraciflua*)
Tulip Tree or Yellow Poplar (*Liriodendron tulipifera*)
Cucumber Tree (*Magnolia acuminata*)
Dawn Redwood (*Metasequoia glyptostroboides*)
★Black Gum or Black Tupelo (*Nyssa sylvatica*)
Spruce species (*Picea*)
★Pine species (*Pinus*)
★Plane Tree species (*Platanus*)
Poplar species (*Populus*)
Sargent Cherry (*Prunus sargenti*)
Black or Rum Cherry (*Prunus serotina*)
★Douglas Fir (*Pseudotsuga menziesii*)
★Oak species (*Quercus*)
Common Bald Cypress (*Taxodium distichum*)
★Linden species (*Tilia*)
★Canada Hemlock (*Tsuga canadensis*)
★Elm species (*Ulmus*)
Japanese Zelkova (*Zelkova serrata*)

Trees Classified by Form
Pyramidal
White Fir (*Abies concolor*)
★Birch species (*Betula*)
★Beech species (*Fagus*)
American Holly (*Ilex opaca*)
Juniper or Red Cedar species (*Juniperus*)
★Larch species (*Larix*)
★Sweet Gum (*Liquidambar styraciflua*)
★Magnolia species (*Magnolia*)
Dawn Redwood (*Metasequoia glyptostroboides*)
★Black Gum or Black Tupelo (*Nyssa sylvatica*)
Hop-Hornbeam (*Ostrya virginiana*)
★Sorrel Tree or Sourwood (*Oxydendrum arboreum*)
Spruce species (*Picea*)
Korean Pine (*Pinus koraiensis*)
Pyramid Austrian Pine (*Pinus nigra pyramidalis*)
Japanese White Pine (*Pinus parviflora*)
★Douglas Fir (*Pseudotsuga menziesii*)
★Pin Oak (*Quercus palustris*)
Common Bald Cypress (*Taxodium distichum*)
Arbor-vitae species (*Thuja*)
★Linden species (*Tilia*)
★Hemlock species (*Tsuga*)
Smooth-leaved Elm (*Ulmus carpinifolia*)

Columnar
Ascending Norway Maple (*Acer platanoides ascendens*)
Columnar Norway Maple (*Acer platanoides columnare*)
Erect Norway Maple (*Acer platanoides erectum*)
Columnar Red Maple (*Acer rubrum columnare*)

Sentry Maple (*Acer saccharum monumentale*)
Pyramidal European Birch (*Betula pendula fastigiata*)
Fastigiate European Hornbeam (*Carpinus betulus fastigiata*)
Fastigiate Washington Hawthorn (*Crataegus phaenopyrum fastigiata*)
Dawyck Beech (*Fagus sylvatica fastigiata*)
Sentry Ginkgo (*Ginkgo biloba fastigiata*)
Blue Columnar or Chinese Juniper (*Juniperus chinensis columnaris*)
Schott Red Cedar (*Juniperus virginiana schotti*)
Swiss Stone Pine (*Pinus cembra*)
Fastigiate White Pine (*Pinus strobus fastigiata*)
Bolleana Poplar (*Populus alba pyramidalis*)
★Lombardy Poplar (*Populus nigra italica*)
Fastigiate Simon Poplar (*Populus simoni fastigiata*)
Columnar Sargent Cherry (*Prunus sargenti columnaris*)
"Amanogawa" Cherry (*Prunus serrulata* "Amanogawa")
Fastigiate English Oak (*Quercus robur fastigiata*)
Shipmast Locust (*Robinia pseudoacacia rectissima*)
Upright European Mountain Ash (*Sorbus aucuparia fastigiata*)
Fastigiate American Arbor-vitae (*Thuja occidentalis douglasi pyramidalis*)
Columnar Big-leaf Linden (*Tilia platyphyllos fastigiata*)
★American Elm varieties (*Ulmus americana*)

Weeping
Slender European Birch (*Betula pendula tristis*)
Young's Birch (*Betula pendula youngi*)
Weeping European Hornbeam (*Carpinus betulus pendula*)
★Weeping Beech (*Fagus sylvatica pendula*)
Weeping Purple Beech (*Fagus sylvatica purpureo-pendula*)
Weeping Red Cedar (*Juniperus virginiana pendula*)
"Exzellenz Thiel" Crab Apple (*Malus* "Exzellenz Thiel")
"Oekonomierat Echtermeyer" Crab Apple (*Malus* "Oekonomierat Echtermeyer")
Weeping Mulberry (*Morus alba pendula*)
Koster Weeping Blue Spruce (*Picea pungens kosteriana*)
Weeping White Pine (*Pinus strobus pendula*)
Weeping Japanese Apricot (*Prunus mume pendula*)
Weeping Black Cherry (*Prunus serotina pendula*)
Weeping Higan Cherry (*Prunus subhirtella pendula*)
"Yaeshidare" Cherry (*Prunus subhirtella pendula flora plena*)
Weeping Yoshino Cherry (*Prunus yedoensis perpendens*)
Weeping Douglas Fir (*Pseudotsuga menziesii pendula*)
Golden Weeping Willow (*Salix alba tristis*)
★Babylon Weeping Willow (*Salix babylonica*)
Wisconsin or Niobe Weeping Willow (*Salix blanda*)
Thurlow Weeping Willow (*Salix elegantissima*)
Weeping Japanese Pagoda Tree (*Sophora japonica pendula*)
Weeping European Mountain Ash (*Sorbus aucuparia pendula*)
Weeping Folgner Mountain Ash (*Sorbus folgneri pendula*)
Pendant Silver Linden (*Tilia petiolaris*)
Sargent Hemlock (*Tsuga canadensis sargenti*)
Weeping American Elm (*Ulmus americana pendula*)

Rounded or Globe-Shaped
★Japanese Maple (*Acer palmatum*)
Globe Norway Maple (*Acer platanoides globosum*)
Globe European Hornbeam (*Carpinus betulus globosa*)
Bunch Hackberry (*Celtis bungeana*)
Cornelian Cherry (*Cornus mas*)
Japanese Cornel (*Cornus officinalis*)
Single Seed Hawthorn (*Crataegus monogyna inermis*)

*Saucer Magnolia (*Magnolia soulangeana*)
*Crab Apple species (*Malus*)
*White Oak (*Quercus alba*)
Umbrella Black Locust (*Robinia pseudoacacia umbraculifera*)
Sargent Hemlock (*Tsuga canadensis sargenti*)
Koopmann Elm (*Ulmus carpinifolia koopmanni*)
Globe Smooth-leaved Elm (*Ulmus carpinifolia umbraculifera*)

With Horizontal Branching
White Fir (*Abies concolor*)
Silk Tree (*Albizzia julibrissin*)
Eastern Redbud (*Cercis canadensis*)
*Flowering Dogwood (*Cornus florida*)
Japanese Dogwood (*Cornus kousa*)
*Hawthorn species (*Crataegus*)
Dawn Redwood (*Metasequoia glyptostroboides*)
*Black Gum or Black Tupelo (*Nyssa sylvatica*)
Spruce species (*Picea*)
Japanese Red Pine (*Pinus densiflora*)
*Eastern White Pine (*Pinus strobus*)
*White Oak (*Quercus alba*)
*Pin Oak (*Quercus palustris*)
Common Bald Cypress (*Taxodium distichum*)

Trees Classified by Color of Blossom

Yellow
*Golden Rain Tree (*Koelreuteria paniculata*)
*Laburnum (*Laburnum vossi*)

White
*Shadblow Serviceberry (*Amelanchier canadensis*)
Whitebud (*Cercis canadensis alba*)
*American Yellow-wood (*Cladrastis lutea*)
Japanese Dogwood (*Cornus kousa*)
Washington Hawthorn (*Crataegus phaenopyrum*)
Carolina Silverbell (*Halesia carolina*)
*Star Magnolia (*Magnolia stellata*)
Arnold Crab Apple (*Malus arnoldiana*)
*Siberian Crab Apple ((*Malus baccata*)
Tea Crab Apple (*Malus hupehensis*)
Sargent Crab Apple (*Malus sargenti*)
*Sorrel Tree (*Oxydendrum arboreum*)
Sour Cherry (*Prunus cerasus*)
Thundercloud Plum (*Prunus cerasifera* "Thundercloud")
Mount Fuji Cherry (*Prunus serrulata* "Shirotae")
Yoshino Cherry (*Prunus yedoensis*)
Bradford Callery Pear (*Pyrus calleryana bradfordi*)
*Common Pear (*Pyrus communis*)
*Japanese Pagoda Tree (*Sophora japonica*)
Korean Mountain Ash (*Sorbus alnifolia*)
American Mountain Ash (*Sorbus americana*)
European Mountain Ash (*Sorbus aucuparia*)
Showy Mountain Ash (*Sorbus decora*)

Pink
Wither's Pink Redbud (*Cercis canadensis* "Wither's Pink Charm")
Red Flowering Dogwood (*Cornus florida rubra*)
Toba Hawthorn (*Crataegus mordenensis* "Toba")
*Saucer Magnolia (*Magnolia soulangeana*)
Japanese Flowering Crab Apple (*Malus floribunda*)
Katherine Crab Apple (*Malus* "Katherine")
Prince Georges Crab Apple (*Malus* "Prince Georges")
*Common Apple (*Malus pumila*)
Blireiana Plum (*Prunus sargenti*)
Amanogawa Cherry (*Prunus serrulata* "Amanogawa")
Kwanzan Cherry (*Prunus serrulata* "Kwanzan")
Autumn Cherry (*Prunus subhirtella autumnalis*)
Weeping Cherry (*Prunus subhirtella pendula*)

Red
Ruby Horse-Chestnut (*Aesculus carnea briotti*)
Paul's Scarlet Hawthorn (*Crataegus oxyacantha pauli*)
Alexandrina Magnolia (*Magnolia soulangeana* "Alexandrina")
Almey Crab Apple (*Malus* "Almey")
Carmine Crab Apple (*Malus atrosanguinea*)

Trees with Bright Red Fruit
*Flowering Dogwood (*Cornus florida*)
Japanese Dogwood (*Cornus kousa*)
Downy Hawthorn (*Crataegus mollis*)
Washington Hawthorn (*Crataegus phaenopyrum*)
American Holly (*Ilex opaca*)
Almey Crab Apple (*Malus* "Almey")
Siberian Crab Apple (*Malus baccata*)
Hopa Crab Apple (*Malus* "Hopa")
*Common Apple (*Malus pumila*)
Sargent Crab Apple (*Malus sargenti*)
Korean Mountain Ash (*Sorbus alnifolia*)
American Mountain Ash (*Sorbus americana*)
European Mountain Ash (*Sorbus aucuparia*)

Trees Classified by Color of Summer Foliage

Blue
White Fir (*Abies concolor*)
*Blue Atlas Cedar (*Cedrus atlantica glauca*)
Russian Olive (*Elaeagnus angustifolia*)
Western Red Cedar var. Chandler Blue (*Juniperus scopulorum* var. Chandler Blue)
Eastern Red Cedar (*Juniperus virginiana* var. *Burki*)
Colorado Blue Spruce (*Picea pungens* var. *Glauca*)

Silver to Gray
Russian Olive (*Elaeagnus angustifolia*)
Common Sea-Buckthorn (*Hippophae rhamnoides*)
White Poplar (*Populus alba*)
Pendent Silver Linden (*Tilia petiolaris*)
*Silver Linden (*Tilia tomentosa*)

Red to Purple
Blood-leaf Japanese Maple (*Acer palmatum atropurpureum*)
Crimson King Maple (*Acer platanoides* "Crimson King")
Schwedler Maple (*Acer platanoides schwedleri*)
Purple-leaf Sycamore Maple (*Acer pseudoplatanus purpureum*)
River's Purple Beech (*Fagus sylvatica riversi*)
Purple Beech (*Fagus sylvatica atropunicea*)
Weeping Purple Beech (*Fagus sylvatica purpureopendula*)
Rubylace Locust (*Gleditsia triacanthos inermis* "Rubylace")
Purple Crab Apple (*Malus purpurea*)
Blireiana Plum (*Prunus blireiana*)
Pissard Plum (*Prunus cerasifera atropurpurea*)
Thundercloud Plum (*Prunus cerisfera nigra* "Thundercloud")
Woods Myrobalan Plum (*Prunus cerasifera woodi*)
Blood-leaf Peach (*Prunus persica atropurpurea*)
Purple English Oak (*Quercus robur atropurpurea*)

Trees Classified by Color of Fall Foliage

Yellow
Striped Maple or Moosewood (*Acer pennsylvanicum*)
Norway Maple (*Acer platanoides* var.)
*Sugar Maple (*Acer saccharum*)
Ohio Buckeye (orange) (*Aesculus glabra*)
Apple Serviceberry (yellow-orange) (*Amelanchier grandiflora*)
*Birch species (*Betula*)
Hickory species (*Carya*)
Chinese Chestnut (*Castanea mollissima*)
*Katsura Tree (yellow to scarlet) (*Cercidiphyllum japonicum*)
Redbud species (*Cercis*)
Fringetree (*Chionanthus virginicus*)
*American Yellow-wood (*Cladrastis lutea*)
*American Beech (*Fagus grandifolia*)
*European Beech (*Fagus sylvatica*)
White Ash (purple to yellow) (*Fraxinus americana*)
*Ginkgo (*Ginkgo biloba*)
*Larch (*Larix decidua*)
Tulip Tree (*Liriodendron tulipifera*)
*Star Magnolia (bronze) (*Magnolia stellata*)

Willow species (*Salix*)

Red
Vine Maple (*Acer circinatum*)
Amur Maple (*Acer ginnala*)
Manchurian Maple (*Acer mandshuricum*)
Nikko Maple (*Acer nikoense*)
*Japanese Maple (*Acer palmatum* var.)
*Red Maple (*Acer rubrum*)
*Sugar Maple (*Acer saccharum*)
Tatarian Maple (*Acer tataricum*)
*Shadblow Serviceberry (*Amelanchier canadensis*)
Hornbeam species (*Carpinus*)
*Flowering Dogwood (*Cornus florida*)
Japanese Dogwood (*Cornus kousa*)
American Smoke Tree (*Cotinus americanus*)
Washington Hawthorn (*Crataegus phaenopyrum*)
*Sweet Gum (*Liquidambar styraciflua*)
Dawson Crab Apple (*Malus dawsoniana*)
*Black Tupelo or Black Gum (*Nyssa sylvatica*)
*Sorrel Tree (*Oxydendrum arboreum*)
*Cherry species (*Prunus*)
Bradford Callery Pear (*Pyrus calleryana bradfordi*)
Red Oak (*Quercus borealis*)
Scarlet Oak (*Quercus coccinea*)
*Pin Oak (*Quercus palustris*)
Sassafras (*Sassafras albidium*)
Korean Mountain Ash (*Sorbus alnifolia*)

Purple
White Ash (*Fraxinus americana*)
*Sweet Gum (*Liquidambar styraciflua*)
*White Oak (*Quercus alba*)
*Common Pear (*Pyrus communis*)

Trees with Interesting Bark

Gray
*Red Maple (*Acer rubrum*)
*Serviceberry species (*Amelanchier*)
Hornbeam species (*Carpinus*)
Hackberry species (*Celtis*)
*American Yellow-wood (*Cladrastis lutea*)
*Hawthorn species (*Crataegus*)
*Beech species (*Fagus*)
American Holly (*Ilex opaca*)
Cucumber Tree (*Magnolia acuminata*)
*Saucer Magnolia (*Magnolia soulangeana*)
Red Oak (young branches and trunk) (*Quercus borealis*)
Black Oak (young branches and trunk) (*Quercus velutina*)
Mountain Ash species (*Sorbus*)

White
*European Birch (*Betula pendula*)
*Gray Birch (*Betula populifolia*)

Red
Japanese Red Pine (*Pinus densiflora*)
Red or Norway Pine (*Pinus resinosa*)
Scotch Pine (*Pinus sylvestris*)

Reddish Brown
Chinese Paper Birch (*Betula albo-sinensis*)
Sargent Cherry (*Prunus sargenti*)

Yellow
Wisconsin or Niobe Weeping Willow (*Salix blanda*)

Corky
*Amur Cork (*Phellodendron amurense*)

Green
*Babylon Weeping Willow (*Salix babylonica*)

Flaking
Paperbark Maple (*Acer griseum*)
*Birch species (*Betula*)
Shadbark Hickory (*Carya ovata*)
Russian Olive (*Elaeagnus angustifolia*)
Native Sycamore (*Platanus occidentalis*)

Trees for the City
White Fir (*Abies concolor*)
Hedge Maple (*Acer campestre*)

Box-Elder (*Acer negundo*)
Norway Maple (*Acer platanoides*)
Sycamore Maple (*Acer pseudoplatanus*)
*Horse-Chestnut or Buckeye (*Aesculus*)
*Tree of Heaven (*Ailanthus*)
Silk Tree (*Albizzia julibrissin*)
Catalpa (*Catalpa*)
Hackberry (*Celtis*)
Downy Hawthorn (*Crataegus mollis*)
Washington Hawthorn (*Crataegus phaenopyrum*)
Russian Olive (*Elaeagnus angustifolia*)
White Ash (*Fraxinus americana*)
European Ash (*Fraxinus americana*)
Green Ash (*Fraxinus pennsylvanica*)
*Ginkgo (*Ginkgo biloba*)
Thornless Honey-Locust (*Gleditsia triacanthos inermis*)
*Golden Rain Tree (*Koelreuteria paniculata*)
*Saucer Magnolia (*Magnolia soulangeana*)
*Star Magnolia (*Magnolia stellata*)
*Crab Apple (*Malus var.*)
*Amur Cork (*Phellodendron amurense*)
London Plane Tree (*Platanus acerifolia*)
White Poplar (*Populus alba*)
*Lombardy Poplar (*Populus nigra italica*)
Red Oak (*Quercus borealis*)
*Black Locust (*Robinia pseudoacacia*)
*Japanese Pagoda Tree (*Sophora japonica*)
*Little-leaf Linden (*Tilia cordata*)
*Crimean Linden (*Tilia euchlora*)
*Silver Linden (*Tilia tomentosa*)
Village Green Zelkova (*Zelkova serrata* "Village Green")

Trees for Wide Streets
Sycamore Maple (*Acer pseudoplatanus*)
*Sugar Maple (*Acer saccharum*)
Sugar Hackberry (*Celtis laevigata*)
*Katsura Tree (*Cercidiphylllum japonicum*)
White Ash (*Fraxinus americana*)
Green Ash (*Fraxinus pennsylvanica lanceolata*)
*Ginkgo (*Ginkgo biloba*)
*Common Honey-Locust (*Gleditsia triacanthos*)
Kalopanax (*Kalopanax pictus*)
Tulip Tree (*Liriodendron tulipifera*)
*Amur Cork (*Phellodendron amurense*)
*Eastern White Pine (*Pinus strobus*)
*London Plane Tree (*Platanus acerifola*)
*Oriental Plane Tree (*Platanus orientalis*)
White Poplar (*Populus alba*)
Sargent Cherry (*Prunus sargenti*)
*Pin Oak (*Quercus palustris*)
Willow Oak (*Quercus phellos*)
Japanese Zelkova (*Zelkova serrata*)

Trees for Medium Streets
Norway Maple (*Acer platanoides*)
Mountain Silverbell (*Halesia monticola*)
*Sweet Gum (*Liquidambar styraciflua*)
Hop-Hornbeam (*Ostrya virginiana*)
*Sorrel Tree or Sourwood (*Oxydendrum arboreum*)
Simon Poplar (*Populus simoni*)

Scarlet Oak (*Quercus coccinea*)
Willow Oak (*Quercus phellos*)
*Black Locust (*Robinia pseudoacacia*)
Sassafras (*Sassafras albidum officinale*)
*Japanese Pagoda Tree (*Sophora japonica*)
*Linden species (*Tilia*)
Winged Elm (*Ulmus alata*)

Trees for Suburban Streets
Hedge Maple (*Acer campestre*)
Amur Maple (*Acer ginnala*)
Paperbark Maple (*Acer griseum*)
Globe Norway Maple (*Acer platanoides globosum*)
Mountain Maple (*Acer spicatum*)
Tatarian Maple (*Acer tataricum*)
American Hornbeam (*Carpinus caroliniana*)
Pyramid European Hornbeam (*Carpinus betulus fastigiata*)
Globe European Hornbeam (*Carpinus betulus globosa*)
Fringetree (*Chionanthus virginicus*)
*Hawthorn species (*Crataegus*)
Carolina Silverbell (*Halesia carolina*)
*Golden Rain Tree (*Koelrueteria paniculata*)
Oriental Cherry (*Prunus serrulata*)
Columnar Sargent Cherry (*Prunus sargenti columnaris*)
Smooth-leaved Elm varieties (*Ulmus carpinifolia*)

Soil Tolerance
Trees Tolerating Acid Soil
*Japanese Maple (*Acer palmatum*)
*Flowering Dogwood (*Cornus florida*)
Japanese Dogwood (*Cornus kousa*)
*European Beech (*Fagus sylvatica*)
*Black Tupelo (*Nyssa sylvatica*)
*Sorrel Tree (*Oxydendrum arboreum*)
Red Oak (*Quercus borealis*)
Scarlet Oak (*Quercus coccinea*)
*Pin Oak (*Quercus palustris*)
Willow Oak (*Quercus phellos*)

Trees Tolerating Moist Soil
*Red Maple (*Acer rubrum*)
Alder species (*Alnus*)
Holly species (*Ilex*)
*Sweet Gum (*Liquidambar styraciflua*)
*Black Tupelo or Black Gum (*Nyssa sylvatica*)
Swamp White Oak (*Quercus bicolor*)
*Willow species (*Salix*)
Common Bald Cypress (*Taxodium distichum*)
American Arbor-vitae (*Thuja occidentalis*)

Trees Tolerating Dry or Poor Soil
Box-Elder (*Acer negundo*)
*Tree of Heaven (*Ailanthus*)
*Gray Birch (*Betula populifolia*)
Common Paper-Mulberry (*Broussonetia papyrifera*)
European Hackberry (*Celtis australis*)
Russian Olive (*Elaeagnus angustifolia*)
Green Ash (*Fraxinus pennsylvanica*)
Modesto Ash (*Fraxinus velutina* "Modesto")

*Honey-Locust (*Gleditsia triacanthos* var.)
Western Red Cedar (*Juniperus scopulorum*)
Eastern Red Cedar (*Juniperus virginiana*)
*Golden Rain Tree (*Koelreuteria paniculata*)
Osage-Orange (*Maclura pomifera*)
Jack Pine (*Pinus banksiana*)
Pitch Pine (*Pinus rigida*)
Virginia or Scrub Pine (*Pinus virginiana*)
White Poplar (*Populus alba*)
Black Jack Oak (*Quercus marilandica*)
Chestnut Oak (*Quercus montana*)
*Black Locust (*Robinia pseudoacacia*)
Sassafras (*Sassafras albidum officinale*)
*Japanese Pagoda Tree (*Sophora japonica*)
Chinese Elm (*Ulmus parvifolia*)
Siberian Elm (*Ulmus pumila*)

Pest-Resistant Trees
*Tree of Heaven (*Ailanthus altissima*)
Hornbeam species (*Carpinus*)
*Cedar species (*Cedrus*)
European Hackberry (*Celtis australis*)
*Katsura Tree (*Cercidiphyllum japonicum*)
False Cypress species (*Chamaecyparis*)
Cornelian Cherry (*Cornus mas*)
Japanese Cornel (*Cornus officinalis*)
American Smoke Tree (*Cotinus americanus*)
Russian Olive (*Elaeagnus angustifolia*)
Franklinia (*Franklinia alatamaha*)
*Ginkgo (*Ginkgo biloba*)
*Honey-Locust (*Gleditsia triacanthos*)
Kentucky Coffee Tree (*Gymnocladus dioicus*)
Juniper species (*Juniperus*)
Kalopanax (*Kalopanax pictus*)
*Golden Rain Tree (*Koelreuteria paniculata*)
*Laburnum species (*Laburnum*)
*Sweet Gum (*Liquidambar styraciflua*)
Cucumber Tree (*Magnolia acuminata*)
*Star Magnolia (*Magnolia stellata*)
Hop-Hornbeam species (*Ostrya*)

Trees for Hedging or Barriers
European Beech (*Fagus sylvatica*) prunes well.
Leyland Cypress (*Cupressocyparis leylandii*) withstands heavy pruning.
Hawthorn varieties (*Crataegus*) easily pruned, advantage of thorns.
Canadian Hemlock (*Tsuga canadensis*) evergreen.
American Holly (*Ilex opaca*) can be pruned.
European Hornbeam (*Carpinus betulus*) prunes well.
Little-leaf Linden (*Tilia cordata*) tolerates heavy pruning.
Hedge Maple (*Acer campestre*) can be pruned.
Austrian Pine (*Pinus nigra*) plant 10—12 feet on centers, staggered row.
Japanese Black Pine (*Pinus thunbergi*) plant 8 feet on centers, staggered row.
Eastern White Pine (*Pinus strobus*) plant 15 feet on centers, staggered row.

MONTANA

State Tree
Ponderosa or Western Yellow Pine (*Pinus ponderosa*)

Evergreen Trees
Fir species (*Abies*)
Juniper species (*Juniperus*)
Eastern Red Cedar (*Juniperus virginiana*)
*Larch species (*Larix*)
Spruce species (*Picea*)
*Pine species (*Pinus*)
*Douglas Fir (*Pseudotsuga menziesii* var. *Glauca*)
Arbor-vitae species (*Thuja*)
*Hemlock species (*Tsuga*)

Trees Classified by Height

20—35 Feet
Hedge Maple (*Acer campestre*)
Amur Maple (*Acer ginnala*)
Manchurian Maple (*Acer mandshuricum*)
Mountain Maple (*Acer spicatum*)
Tatarian Maple (*Acer tataricum*)
Ohio Buckeye (*Aesculus glabra*)
Apple Serviceberry (*Amelanchier grandiflora*)
*Hawthorn species (*Crataegus*)
Russian Olive (*Elaeagnus angustifolia*)
Euonymus species (*Euonymus*)
Common Sea-Buckthorn (*Hippophae rhamnoides*)
*Laburnum species (*Laburnum*)
*Crab Apple species (*Malus*)

*Cherry species (*Prunus*)
Dahurian Buckthorn (*Rhamnus davurica*)
Almond-leaf Willow (*Salix amygdalina*)
Goat Willow (*Salix caprea*)
Showy Mountain Ash (*Sorbus decora*)
Japanese Tree Lilac (*Syringa amurensis japonica*)

35—75 Feet
Box-Elder (*Acer negundo*)
Striped Maple or Moosewood (*Acer pennsylvanicum*)
*Sugar Maple (*Acer saccharum*)
Speckled Alder (*Alnus incana*)
Red Alder (*Alnus rubra*)
*Shadblow Serviceberry (*Amelanchier canadensis*)
Allegany Serviceberry (*Amelanchier laevis*)

Devil's Walking Stick (*Aralia elata*)
Dahurian Birch (*Betula davurica*)
★European Birch (*Betula pendula*)
American Hornbeam (*Carpinus caroliniana*)
Japanese Hornbeam (*Carpinus japonica*)
Chinese Chestnut (*Castanea mollissima*)
Southern Catalpa (*Catalpa bignoniodes*)
★Katsura Tree (*Cercidiphyllum japonicum*)
★Flowering Dogwood (*Cornus florida*)
Cockspur Thorn (*Crataegus crus-galli*)
Green Hawthorn (*Crataegus viridis*)
Green Ash (*Fraxinus pennsylvanica lanceolata*)
★Ginkgo or Maidenhair Tree (*Ginkgo biloba*)
Chinese Juniper (*Juniperus chinensis*)
Siberian Crab Apple (*Malus baccata*)
"Cowichan" Crab Apple (*Malus* "Cowichan")
"Dolgo" Crab Apple (*Malus* "Dolgo")
"Makamik" Crab Apple (*Malus* "Makamik")
Cherry Crab Apple (*Malus robusta*)
"Sissipuk" Crab Apple (*Malus* "Sissipuk")
White Mulberry (*Morus alba*)
★Amur Cork (*Phellodendron amurense*)
Black Hills Spruce (*Picea glauca densata*)
Lace-bark Pine (*Pinus bungeana*)
Swiss Stone Pine (*Pinus cembra*)
Limber Pine (*Pinus flexilis*)
Scotch Pine (*Pinus sylvestris*)
Simon Poplar (*Populus simoni*)
Amur Choke Cherry (*Prunus maacki*)
Miyama Cherry (*Prunus maximowiczi*)
European Bird Cherry (*Prunus padus*)
Sargent Cherry (*Prunus sargenti*)
Ussurian Pear (*Pyrus ussuriensis*)
Scarlet Oak (*Quercus coccinea*)
★Pin Oak (*Quercus palustris*)
White Willow (*Salix alba*)
Wisconsin or Niobe Weeping Willow (*Salix blanda*)
Elaeagnus Willow (*Salix elaeagnos*)
Thurlow Weeping Willow (*Salix elegantissima*)
Laurel Willow (*Salix pentandra*)
European Mountain Ash or Rowan Tree (*Sorbus aucuparia*)
American Arbor-vitae (*Thuja occidentalis*)
Carolina Hemlock (*Tsuga caroliniana*)
Siberian Elm (*Ulmus pumila*)

75 Feet or Over
Fir species (*Abies*)
Norway maple (*Acer platanoides*)
★Red or Swamp Maple (*Acer rubrum*)
★Baumann Horse-Chestnut (*Aesculus hippocastanum baumanni*)
European Adler (*Alnus glutinosa*)
★Canoe Birch (*Betula papyrifera*)
Northern Catalpa (*Catalpa speciosa*)
White Ash (*Fraxinus americana*)
European Ash (*Fraxinus excelsior*)
★Common Honey-Locust (*Gleditsia triacanthos*)
Kentucky Coffee Tree (*Gymnocladus dioicus*)
★European Larch (*Larix decidua*)
Japanese Larch (*Larix leptolepis*)
★Sweet Gum (*Liquidambar styraciflua*)
★Spruce species (*Pinus*)
Poplar species (*Populus*)
Sargent Cherry (*Prunus sargenti*)
Black or Rum Cherry (*Prunus serotina*)
★Douglas Fir (*Pseudotsuga menziesii*)
★Oak species (*Quercus*)
Giant Arbor-vitae (*Thuja plicata*)
★Linden species (*Tilia*)
★Canada Hemlock (*Tsuga canadensis*)
★Elm species (*Ulmus*)

Trees Classifed by Form

Pyramidal
Fir species (*Abies*)
★Birch species (*Betula*)
False Cypress species (*Chamaecyparis*)
★Beech species (*Fagus*)
Juniper or Red Cedar species (*Juniperus*)
★Larch species (*Larix*)

★Sweet Gum (*Liquidambar styraciflua*)
Spruce species (*Picea*)
Swiss Stone Pine (*Pinus cembra*)
Korean Pine (*Pinus koraiensis*)
Pyramidal Austrian Pine (*Pinus nigra pyramidalis*)
Red or Norway Pine (*Pinus resinosa*)
★Douglas Fir (*Pseudotsuga menziesii*)
★Pin Oak (*Quercus palustris*)
Common Bald Cypress (*Taxodium distichum*)
Arbor-vitae species (*Thuja*)
★Linden species (*Tilia*)
★Hemlock species (*Tsuga*)

Columnar
Ascending Norway Maple (*Acer platanoides ascendens*)
Columnar Norway Maple (*Acer platanoides columnare*)
Erect Norway Maple (*Acer platanoides erectum*)
Columnar Red Maple (*Acer rubrum columnare*)
★Sentry Maple (*Acer saccharum monumentale*)
Fastigiate European Birch (*Betula pendula fastigiata*)
Fastigiate Washington Hawthorn (*Crataegus phaenopyrum fastigiata*)
Dawyck Beech (*Fagus sylvatica fastigiata*)
Sentry Ginkgo (*Ginkgo biloba fastigiata*)
Blue Columnar Chinese Juniper (*Juniperus chinensis columnaris*)
Swiss Stone Pine (*Pinus cembra*)
Fastigiate Scotch Pine (*Pinus sylvestris fastigiata*)
Bolleana Poplar (*Populus alba pyramidalis*)
★Lombardy Poplar (*Populus nigra italica*)
Fastigiate Simon Poplar (*Populus simoni fastigiata*)
Columnar Sargent Cherry (*Prunus sargenti columnaris*)
Shipmast Locust (*Robinia pseudoacacia rectissima*)
Upright European Mountain Ash (*Sorbus aucuparia fastigiata*)
Douglas Arbor-vitae (*Thuja occidentalis douglasi pyramidalis*)
Columnar Big-leaf Linden (*Tilia platyphyllos fastigiata*)
★American Elm varieties (*Ulmus americana*)

Weeping
Slender European Birch (*Betula pendula tristis*)
Young's Birch (*Betula pendula youngi*)
★Weeping Beech (*Fagus sylvatica pendula*)
Weeping Purple Beech (*Fagus sylvatica purpureo-pendula*)
Weeping Larch (*Larix decidua pendula*)
"Exzellenz Thiel" Crab Apple (*Malus* "Exzellenz Thiel")
"Oekonomierat Echtermeyer" Crab Apple (*Malus* "Oekonomierat Echtermeyer")
Weeping Mulberry (*Morus alba pendula*)
Koster Weeping Willow (*Picea pungens kosteriana*)
Weeping Black Cherry (*Prunus serotina pendula*)
Weeping Douglas Fir (*Pseudotsuga menziesii pendula*)
Golden Weeping Willow (*Salix alba tristis*)
Wisconsin or Niobe Weeping Willow (*Salix blanda*)
Thurlow Weeping Willow (*Salix elegantissima*)
Weeping European Mountain Ash (*Sorbus aucuparia pendula*)
Sargent Hemlock (*Tsuga canadensis pendula*)
Weeping American Elm (*Ulmus americana pendula*)

Rounded or Globe-Shaped
Globe Norway Maple (*Acer platanoides globosum*)
Cornelian Cherry (*Cornus mas*)
Single Seed Hawthorn (*Crataegus monogyna inermis*)
★Crab Apple species (*Malus*)
★White Oak (*Quercus alba*)
Umbrella Black Locust (*Robinia pseudoacacia umbraculifera*)
Sargent Hemlock (*Tsuga canadensis sargenti*)
Koopmann Elm (*Ulmus carpinifolia koopmanni*)
Globe Smooth-leaved Elm (*Ulmus carpinifolia umbraculifera*)

With Horizontal Branching
Fir species (*Abies*)
★Hawthorn species (*Crataegus*)
Spruce species (*Picea*)
Japanese Red Pine (*Pinus densiflora*)

★Eastern White Pine (*Pinus strobus*)
★White Oak (*Quercus alba*)
★Pin Oak (*Quercus palustris*)

Trees Classified by Color of Blossom

White
★Shadblow Serviceberry (*Amelanchier canadensis*)
Washington Hawthorn (*Crataegus phaenopyrum*)
Arnold Crab Apple (*Malus arnoldiana*)
★Siberian Crab Apple (*Malus baccata*)
Tea Crab Apple (*Malus hupehensis*)
Thundercloud Plum (*Prunus cerasifera* "Thundercloud")
Sour Cherry (*Prunus cerasus*)
★Japanese Pagoda Tree (*Sophora japonica*)
American Mountain Ash (*Sorbus americana*)
European Mountain Ash (*Sorbus aucuparia*)
Showy Mountain Ash (*Sorbus decora*)

Pink
Toba Hawthorn (*Crataegus mordenensis* "Toba")
Japanese Flowering Crab Apple (*Malus floribunda*)
Katherine Crab Apple (*Malus* "Katherine")
Prince Georges Crab Apple (*Malus* "Prince Georges")
★Common Apple (*Malus pumila*)
Sargent Cherry (*Prunus sargenti*)

Red
Ruby Horse-Chestnut (*Aesculus carnea briotti*)
Paul's Scarlet Hawthorn (*Crataegus oxyacantha pauli*)
Almey Crab Apple (*Malus* "Almey")
Carmine Crab Apple (*Malus atrosanguinea*)

Trees with Bright Red Fruit

Downy Hawthorn (*Crataegus mollis*)
Washington Hawthorn (*Crataegus phaenopyrum*)
Almey Crab Apple (*Malus* "Almey")
Siberian Crab Apple (*Malus baccata*)
Hopa Crab Apple (*Malus* "Hopa")
★Common Apple (*Malus pumila*)
American Mountain Ash (*Sorbus americana*)
European Mountain Ash (*Sorbus aucuparia*)

Trees Classified by Color of Summer Foliage

Blue
Russian Olive (*Elaeagnus angustifolia*)
Eastern Red Cedar (*Juniperus virginiana* var. *Burki*)

Silver to Gray
Russian Olive (*Elaeagnus angustifolia*)
Common Sea-Buckthorn (*Hippophae rhamnoides*)
White Poplar (*Populus alba*)
★Silver Linden (*Tilia tomentosa*)

Red to Purple
Crimson King Maple (*Acer platanoides* "Crimson King")
Schwedler Maple (*Acer platanoides schwedleri*)
Purple Beech (*Fagus sylvatica atropunicea*)
Weeping Purple Beech (*Fagus sylvatica purpureo-pendula*)
River's Purple Beech (*Fagus sylvatica riversi*)
Rubylace Locust (*Gleditsia triacanthos inermis* "Rubylace")
Purple Crab Apple (*Malus purpurea*)
Pissard Plum (*Prunus cerasifera atropurpurea*)
Thundercloud Plum (*Prunus cerasifera nigra* "Thundercloud")
Woods Myrobalan Plum (*Prunus cerasifera woodi*)

Trees Classified by Color of Fall Foliage

Yellow
Striped Maple or Moosewood (*Acer pennsylvanicum*)
Norway Maple (*Acer platanoides* var.)
★Sugar Maple (*Acer saccharum*)
Ohio Buckeye (orange) (*Aesculus glabra*)
Apple Serviceberry (yellow-orange) (*Amelanchier grandiflora*)
★Birches (*Betula species*)
Hickory species (*Carya*)

Chinese Chestnut (*Castanea mollissima*)
*Katsura Tree (yellow to scarlet) (*Cercidiphyllum japonicum*)
*American Beech (*Fagus grandifolia*)
*European Beech (*Fagus sylvatica*)
White Ash (purple to yellow) (*Fraxinus americana*)
*Ginkgo (*Ginkgo biloba*)
*Larch (*Larix decidua*)
Tulip Tree (*Liriodendron tulipifera*)
*Willow species (*Salix*)

Red
Amur Maple (*Acer ginnala*)
Manchurian Maple (*Acer mandshuricum*)
*Red Maple (*Acer rubrum*)
*Sugar maple (*Acer saccharum*)
Tatarian Maple (*Acer tataricum*)
*Shadblow Serviceberry (*Amelanchier canadensis*)
Hornbeam species (*Carpinus*)
Washington Hawthorn (*Crataegus phaenopyrum*)
*Sweet Gum (*Liquidambar styraciflua*)
Dawson Crab Apple (*Malus dawsoniana*)
*Cherry species (*Prunus*)
*Pin Oak (*Quercus palustris*)

Purple
White Ash (*Fraxinus americana*)
*Sweet Gum (*Liquidambar styraciflua*)
*White Oak (*Quercus alba*)

Trees with Interesting Bark

Gray
*Red Maple (*Acer rubrum*)
*Serviceberry species (*Amelanchier*)
Hornbeam species (*Carpinus*)
*Hawthorn species (*Crataegus*)
*Beech species (*Fagus*)
Red Oak (young trunk and branches) (*Quercus borealis*)
Mountain Ash species (*Sorbus*)

White
*Canoe Birch (*Betula papyrifera*)
*European Birch (*Betula pendula*)

Red
Scotch Pine (*Pinus sylvestris*)

Reddish Brown
Sargent Cherry (*Prunus sargenti*)

Yellow
Wisconsin or Niobe Weeping Willow (*Salix blanda*)

Corky
*Amur Cork (*Phellodendron amurense*)

Flaking
*Birch species (*Betula*)
Russian Olive (*Elaeagnus angustifolia*)

Trees for the City
White Fir (*Abies concolor*)
Hedge Maple (*Acer campestre*)
Box-Elder (*Acer negundo*)
Norway Maple (*Acer platanoides*)
*Horse-Chestnut or Buckeye (*Aesculus*)
Catalpa (*Catalpa*)
Washington Hawthorn (*Crataegus phaenopyrum*)
*Downy Hawthorn (*Crataegus mollis*)
Russian Olive (*Elaeagnus angustifolia*)
White Ash (*Fraxinus americana*)
European Ash (*Fraxinus excelsior*)
Green Ash (*Fraxinus pennsylvanica*)
*Ginkgo (*Ginkgo biloba*)
Thornless Honey-Locust (*Gleditsia triacanthos inermis*)
*Crab Apple (*Malus* var.)
*Amur Cork (*Phellodendron amurense*)
Colorado Spruce (*Picea pungens*)
White Poplar (*Populus alba*)
*Lombardy Poplar (*Populus nigra italica*)
*Black Locust (*Robinia pseudoacacia*)
*Little-leaf Linden (*Tilia cordata*)
*Silver Linden (*Tilia tomentosa*)

Trees for Wide Streets
*Sugar Maple (*Acer saccharum*)
White Ash (*Fraxinus americana*)
Green Ash (*Fraxinus pennsylvanica lanceolata*)
*Ginkgo (*Ginkgo biloba*)
*Common Honey-Locust (*Gleditsia triacanthos*)
*Eastern White Pine (*Pinus strobus*)
White Poplar (*Populus alba*)
Sargent Cherry (*Prunus sargenti*)
Red Oak (*Quercus borealis*)
*Pin Oak (*Quercus palustris*)

Trees for Medium Streets
Norway Maple (*Acer platanoides*)
*Sweet Gum (*Liquidambar styraciflua*)
Simon Poplar (*Populus simoni*)
Scarlet Oak (*Quercus coccinea*)
*Black Locust (*Robinia pseudoacacia*)
*Linden species (*Tilia*)

Trees for Suburban Streets
Hedge Maple (*Acer campestre*)
Amur Maple (*Acer ginnala*)
Globe Norway Maple (*Acer platanoides globosum*)
Mountain Maple (*Acer spicatum*)
Tatarian Maple (*Acer tataricum*)

*Hawthorn species (*Crataegus*)
Columnar Sargent Cherry (*Prunus sargenti columnaris*)

Soil Tolerance

Trees Tolerating Acid Soil
*European Beech (*Fagus sylvatica varieties*)
Scarlet Oak (*Quercus coccinea*)
*Pin Oak (*Quercus palustris*)

Trees Tolerating Moist Soil
Alder species (*Alnus*)
Eastern Larch (*Larix laricina*)
*Sweet Gum (*Liquidambar styraciflua*)
*Willow species (*Salix*)
American Arbor-vitae (*Thuja occidentalis*)
Swamp White Oak (*Quercus bicolor*)

Trees Tolerating Dry or Poor Soil
Box-Elder (*Acer negundo*)
Russian Olive (*Elaeagnus angustifolia*)
Green Ash (*Fraxinus pennsylvanica*)
*Honey-Locust (*Gleditsia triacanthos*)
Western Red Cedar (*Juniperus scopulorum*)
Jack Pine (*Pinus banksiana*)
Pitch Pine (*Pinus rigida*)
White Poplar (*Populus alba*)
Chestnut Oak (*Quercus montana*)
*Black Locust (*Robinia pseudoacacia*)
Siberian Elm (*Ulmus pumila*)

Pest-Resistant Trees

Japanese Cornel (*Cornus officinalis*)
Russian Olive (*Elaeagnus angustifolia*)
*Ginkgo (*Ginkgo biloba*)
*Honey-Locust (*Gleditsia triacanthos*)
Kentucky Coffee Tree (*Gymnocladus dioicus*)
Juniper species (*Juniperus*)
*Sweet Gum (*Liquidambar styraciflua*)

Trees for Hedging or Barriers

European Beech (*Fagus sylvatica*) prunes well.
Hawthorn varieties (*Crataegus*) easily pruned, advantage of thorns.
Canadian Hemlock (*Tsuga canadensis*) evergreen.
American Holly (*Ilex opaca*) can be pruned.
European Hornbeam (*Carpinus betulus*) prunes well.
Little-leaf Linden (*Tilia cordata*) tolerates heavy pruning.
Hedge Maple (*Acer campestre*) can be pruned.
Austrian Pine (*Pinus nigra*) plant 10–12 feet on centers, staggered row.
Japanese Black Pine (*Pinus thunbergi*) plant 8 feet on centers, staggered row.
Eastern White Pine (*Pinus strobus*) plant 15 feet on centers, staggered row.

NEBRASKA

State Tree

*American Elm (*Ulmus americana*)

Evergreen Trees

Fir species (*Abies*)
Juniper species (*Juniperus*)
Eastern Red Cedar (*Juniperus virginiana*)
Spruce species (*Picea*)
*Pine species (*Pinus*)
*Douglas Fir (*Pseudotsuga menziesii*)
Arbor-vitae species (*Thuja*)

Trees Classified by Height

20–35 Feet

Hedge Maple (*Acer campestre*)
Amur Maple (*Acer ginnala*)
Manchurian Maple (*Acer mandshuricum*)
Mountain Maple (*Acer spicatum*)
Tatarian Maple (*Acer tataricum*)
Ohio Buckeye (*Aesculus glabra*)
Apple Serviceberry (*Amelanchier grandiflora*)
Mockernut (*Carya tomentosa*)
Fringetree (*Chionanthus virginicus*)
Cornelian Cherry (*Cornus mas*)
*Hawthorn species (*Crataegus*)
Russian Olive (*Elaeagnus angustifolia*)
Euonymus species (*Euonymus*)
*Golden Rain Tree (*Koelreuteria paniculata*)
*Laburnum species (*Laburnum*)
*Saucer Magnolia (*Magnolia soulangeana*)
*Crab Apple species (*Malus*)
*Cherry species (*Prunus*)
Dahurian Buckthorn (*Rhamnus davurica*)
Goat Willow (*Salix caprea*)
Japanese Tree Lilac (*Syringa amurensis japonica*)

35–75 Feet

Striped Maple or Moosewood (*Acer pennsylvanicum*)
*Red-fruited Tree of Heaven (*Ailanthus altissima erytharocarpa*)
Speckled Alder (*Alnus incana*)
Red Alder (*Alnus rubra*)
*Shadblow Serviceberry (*Amelanchier canadensis*)
Devil's Walking Stick (*Aralia elata*)
*European Birch (*Betula pendula*)
Chinese Chestnut (*Castanea mollissima*)
Southern Catalpa (*Catalpa bignonioides*)
*Katsura Tree (*Celtis occidentalis*)
Eastern Redbud (*Cercis canadensis*)
*Flowering Dogwood (*Cornus florida*)
Turkish Filbert (*Corylus coluna*)
Cockspur Thorn (*Crataegus crus-galli*)
Green Hawthorn (*Crataegus viridis*)
Common Persimmon (*Diospyros virginiana*)
Green Ash (*Fraxinus pennsylvanica lanceolata*)
Heartnut (*Juglans sieboldiana cordiformis*)
Chinese Juniper (*Juniperus chinensis*)
Kobus Magnolia (*Magnolia kobus borealis*)
Loebner Magnolia (*Magnolia loebneri*)
Siberian Crab Apple (*Malus baccata*)
"Cowichan" Crab Apple (*Malus* "Cowichan")
"Dolgo" Crab Apple (*Malus* "Dolgo")
"Makamik" Crab Apple (*Malus* "Makamik")
"Sissipuk" Crab Apple (*Malus* "Sissipuk")
White Mulberry (*Morus alba*)
*Sorrel Tree or Sourwood (*Oxydendrum arboreum*)
*Amur Cork (*Phellodendron amurense*)
Black Hills Spruce (*Picea glauca densata*)

Jack Pine (*Pinus banksiana*)
Lace-bark Pine (*Pinus bungeana*)
Scotch Pine (*Pinus sylvestris*)
Simon Poplar (*Populus simoni*)
Miyama Cherry (*Prunus maximowiczi*)
Sargent Cherry (*Prunus sargenti*)
Ussurian Pear (*Pyrus ussuriensis*)
Swamp White oak (*Quercus bicolor*)
Red Oak (*Quercus borealis*)
Scarlet Oak (*Quercus coccinea*)
*Pin Oak (*Quercus palustris*)
White Willow (*Salix alba*)
Wisconsin or Niobe Weeping Willow (*Salix blanda*)
Elaeagnus Willow (*Salix elaeagnos*)
Thurlow Weeping Willow (*Salix elegantissima*)
Laurel Willow (*Salix pentandra*)
Sassafras (*Sassafras albidum officinale*)
European Mountain Ash or Rowan Tree (*Sorbus aucuparia*)
American Arbor-vitae (*Thuja occidentalis*)
Carolina Hemlock (*Tsuga caroliniana*)

75 Feet or Over

Fir species (*Abies*)
Norway maple (*Acer platanoides*)
Red or Swamp Maple (*Acer rubrum*)
*Sugar Maple (*Acer saccharum*)
European Adler (*Alnus glutinosa*)
River Birch (*Betula nigra*)
*Canoe Birch (*Betula papyrifera*)
Hickory species (*Carya*)
Northern Catalpa (*Catalpa speciosa*)
*Katsura Tree (*Cercidiphyllum japonicum*)
White Ash (*Fraxinus americana*)
European Ash (*Fraxinus excelsior*)
*Ginkgo or Maidenhair Tree (*Ginkgo biloba*)
*Common Honey-Locust (*Gleditsia triacanthos*)
Kentucky Coffee Tree (*Gymnocladus dioicus*)
Eastern Black Walnut (*Juglans nigra*)
Kalopanax (*Kalopanax pictus*)
*European Larch (*Larix decidua*)
*Sweet Gum (*Liquidambar styraciflua*)
Spruce species (*Picea*)
*Pine species (*Pinus*)
Sycamore (*Platanus occidentalis*)
Poplar species (*Populus*)
Black or Rum Cherry (*Prunus serotina*)
*Douglas Fir (*Pseudotsuga menziesii*)
*Oak species (*Quercus*)
Common Bald Cypress (*Taxodium distichum*)
Giant Arbor-vitae (*Thuja plicata*)
*Linden species (*Tilia*)
*Canada Hemlock (*Tsuga canadensis*)
*Elm species (*Ulmus*)

Trees Classifed by Form

Pyramidal

Fir species (*Abies*)
*Birch species (*Betula*)
False Cypress species (*Chamaecyparis*)
Turkish Filbert (*Corylus coluna*)
Juniper or Red Cedar species (*Juniperus*)
Pyramidal Red Cedar (*Juniperus virginiana pyramidalis*)
*Larch species (*Larix*)
*Sweet Gum (*Liquidambar styraciflua*)
*Black Tupelo or Black Gum (*Nyssa sylvatica*)
Hop-Hornbeam (*Ostrya virginiana*)

Spruce species (*Picea*)
Korean Pine (*Pinus koraiensis*)
*Pyramidal Austrian Pine (*Pinus nigra pyramidalis*)
Red or Norway Pine (*Pinus resinosa*)
*Douglas Fir (*Pseudotsuga menziesii*)
*Pin Oak (*Quercus palustris*)
Common Bald Cypress (*Taxodium distichum*)
Arbor-vitae species (*Thuja*)
*Linden species (*Tilia*)

Columnar

Ascending Norway Maple (*Acer platanoides ascendens*)
Columnar Norway Maple (*Acer platanoides columnare*)
Erect Norway Maple (*Acer platanoides erectum*)
Columnar Red Maple (*Acer rubrum columnare*)
Fastigiate European Birch (*Betula pendula fastigiata*)
Sentry Ginkgo (*Ginkgo biloba fastigiata*)
Blue Columnar Chinese Juniper (*Juniperus chinensis columnaris*)
Fastigiate White Pine (*Pinus strobus fastigiata*)
Fastigiate Scotch Pine (*Pinus sylvestris fastigiata*)
Bolleana Poplar (*Populus alba pyramidalis*)
*Lombardy Poplar (*Populus nigra italica*)
Fastigiate Simon Poplar (*Populus simoni fastigiata*)
Upright European Mountain Ash (*Sorbus aucuparia fastigiata*)
Common Bald Cypress (*Taxodium distichum*)
Columnar Big-leaf Linden (*Tilia platyphyllos fastigiata*)
*American Elm varieties (*Ulmus americana*)

Weeping

Young's Birch (*Betula pendula youngi*)
*Weeping Red Cedar (*Juniperus virginiana pendula*)
Weeping Mulberry (*Morus alba pendula*)
Weeping White Pine (*Pinus strobus pendula*)
Thurlow Weeping Willow (*Salix elegantissima*)
Wisconsin or Niobe Weeping Willow (*Salix blanda*)
Weeping Japanese Pagoda Tree (*Sophora japonica pendula*)

Rounded or Globe-Shaped

Hackberry (*Celtis occidentalis*)
Cornelian Cherry (*Cornus mas*)
Single Seed Hawthorn (*Crataegus monogyna inermis*)
*Saucer Magnolia (*Magnolia soulangeana*)
*Crab Apple species (*Malus*)
*White Oak (*Quercus alba*)

With Horizontal Branching

Fir species (*Abies*)
Eastern Redbud (*Cercis canadensis*)
*Flowering Dogwood (*Cornus florida*)
*Hawthorn species (*Crataegus*)
Spruce species (*Picea*)
*Eastern White Pine (*Pinus strobus*)
*White Oak (*Quercus alba*)
*Pin Oak (*Quercus palustris*)
Common Bald Cypress (*Taxodium distichum*)

Trees Classified by Color of Blossom

Yellow

*Golden Rain Tree (*Koelreuteria paniculata*)

White

*Shadblow Serviceberry (*Amelanchier canadensis*)
Carolina Silverbell (*Halesia carolina*)
Arnold Crab Apple (*Malus arnoldiana*)

Siberian Crab Apple (*Malus baccata*)
Tea Crab Apple (*Malus hupehensis*)
*Sorrel Tree (*Oxydendrum arboreum*)
Thundercloud Plum (*Prunus cerasifera* "Thundercloud")
Sour Cherry (*Prunus cerasus*)
*Japanese Pagoda Tree (*Sophora japonica*)
American Mountain Ash (*Sorbus americana*)
Showy Mountain Ash (*Sorbus decora*)

Pink
*Saucer Magnolia (*Magnolia soulangeana*)
*Crab Apple varieties (*Malus*)

Red
Ruby Horse-Chestnut (*Aesculus carnea briotti*)
Paul's Scarlet Hawthorn (*Crataegus oxyacantha pauli*)
Almey Crab Apple (*Malus* "Almey")
Carmine Crab Apple (*Malus atrosanguinea*)

Trees Classified by Color of Summer Foliage

Blue
Eastern Red Cedar (*Juniperus virginiana* var. *Burki*)

Silver to Gray
Russian Olive (*Elaeagnus angustifolia*)
Common Sea-Buckthorn (*Hippophae rhamnoides*)
White Poplar (*Populus alba*)
*Silver Linden (*Tilia tomentosa*)

Red to Purple
Schwedler Maple (*Acer platanoides schwedleri*)
Purple Crab Apple (*Malus purpurea*)
Pissard Plum (*Prunus cerasifera atropurpurea*)
Thundercloud Plum (*Prunus cerasifera nigra* "Thundercloud")
Woods Myrobalan Plum (*Prunus cerasifera woodi*)

Trees Classified by Color of Fall Foliage

Yellow
Norway Maple (*Acer platanoides* var.)
*Sugar Maple (*Acer saccharum*)
Ohio Buckeye (orange) (*Aesculus glabra*)
Apple Serviceberry (yellow-orange) (*Amelanchier grandiflora*)
*Birch species (*Betula species*)
Hickory species (*Carya*)
Chinese Chestnut (*Castanea mollissima*)
*Katsura Tree (yellow to scarlet) (*Cercidiphyllum japonicum*)
Redbud species (*Cercis*)
Fringetree (*Chionanthus virginicus*)
*American Yellow-wood (*Cladrastis lutea*)
*White Ash (purple to yellow) (*Fraxinus americana*)
*Ginkgo (*Ginkgo biloba*)
*Larch (*Larix decidua*)
*Willow species (*Salix*)

Red
Amur Maple (*Acer ginnala*)
Manchurian Maple (*Acer mandshuricum*)
*Red Maple (*Acer rubrum*)
*Sugar Maple (*Acer saccharum*)
*Shadblow Serviceberry (*Amelanchier canadensis*)
*Flowering Dogwood (*Cornus florida*)
*Sweet Gum (*Liquidambar styraciflua*)
Dawson Crab Apple (*Malus dawsoniana*)
*Black Tupelo or Black Gum (*Nyssa sylvatica*)
*Sorrel Tree (*Oxydendrum arboreum*)
*Cherry species (*Prunus*)
Red Oak (*Quercus borealis*)
Scarlet Oak (*Quercus coccinea*)
*Pin Oak (*Quercus palustris*)

Purple
White Ash (*Fraxinus americana*)
*Sweet Gum (*Liquidambar styraciflua*)
*White Oak (*Quercus alba*)

Trees with Interesting Bark

Gray
*Red Maple (*Acer rubrum*)
*Serviceberry species (*Amelanchier*)
Hornbeam species (*Carpinus*)
Hackberry (*Celtis occidentalis*)
Cucumber Tree (*Magnolia acuminata*)
*Saucer Magnolia (*Magnolia soulangeana*)
Red Oak (young trunk and branches) (*Quercus borealis*)
Black Oak (young trunk and branches) (*Quercus velutina*)

White
*Canoe Birch (*Betula papyrifera*)
*European Birch (*Betula pendula*)

Yellow
Wisconsin or Niobe Weeping Willow (*Salix blanda*)

Corky
*Amur Cork (*Phellodendron amurense*)
Hackberry (*Celtis*)

Flaking
*Birch species (*Betula*)
Shagbark Hickory (*Carya ovata*)
Russian Olive (*Elaeagnus angustifolia*)
Eastern Red Cedar (*Juniperus virginiana*)
Lace-bark Pine (*Pinus bungeana*)
*American Plane Tree (*Platanus occidentalis*)

Trees for the City
White Fir (*Abies concolor*)
Hedge Maple (*Acer campestre*)
Norway Maple (*Acer platanoides*)
*Tree of Heaven (*Ailanthus*)
Catalpa (*Catalpa*)
Hackberry (*Celtis occidentalis*)
*Hawthorn species (*Crataegus*)
Russian Olive (*Elaeagnus angustifolia*)
White Ash (*Fraxinus americana*)
European Ash (*Fraxinus excelsior*)
Green Ash (*Fraxinus pennsylvanica*)
*Ginkgo (*Ginkgo biloba*)
Thornless Honey-Locust (*Gleditsia triacanthos inermis*)
*Golden Rain Tree (*Koelreuteria paniculata*)
*Saucer Magnolia (*Magnolia soulangeana*)
*Crab Apple species (*Malus*)
*Amur Cork (*Phellodendron amurense*)
*American Plane Tree (*Platanus occidentalis*)
White Poplar (*Populus alba*)
*Lombardy Poplar (*Populus nigra italica*)
Red Oak (*Quercus borealis*)
*Japanese Pagoda Tree (*Sophora japonica*)
*Little-leaf Linden (*Tilia cordata*)
*Silver Linden (*Tilia tomentosa*)

Trees for Wide Streets
*Sugar Maple (*Acer saccharum*)
*Katsura Tree (*Cercidiphyllum japonicum*)
White Ash (*Fraxinus americana*)
Green Ash (*Fraxinus pennsylvanica lanceolata*)
*Ginkgo (*Ginkgo biloba*)
*Common Honey-Locust (*Gleditsia triacanthos*)
Amur Cork (*Phellodendron amurense*)
*Eastern White Pine (*Pinus strobus*)
*American Plane Tree (*Platanus occidentalis*)
White Poplar (*Populus alba*)
Red Oak (*Quercus borealis*)

*Pin Oak (*Quercus palustris*)

Trees for Medium Streets
Norway Maple (*Acer platanoides*)
Sweet Gum (*Liquidambar styraciflua*)
Simon Poplar (*Populus simoni*)
Scarlet Oak (*Quercus coccinea*)
*Black Locust (*Robinia pseudoacacia*)
*Japanese Pagoda Tree (*Sophora japonica*)
*Linden species (*Tilia*)

Trees for Suburban Streets
Hedge Maple (*Acer campestre*)
Amur Maple (*Acer ginnala*)
Fringetree (*Chionanthus virginicus*)
*Flowering Dogwood (*Cornus florida*)
*Hawthorn species (*Crataegus*)
*Golden Rain Tree (*Koelreuteria paniculata*)

Soil Tolerance

Trees Tolerating Acid Soil
*Black Tupelo (*Nyssa sylvatica*)
*Sorrel Tree (*Oxydendrum arboreum*)
Red Oak (*Quercus borealis*)
Scarlet Oak (*Quercus coccinea*)
*Pin Oak (*Quercus palustris*)

Trees Tolerating Dry or Poor Soil
Box-Elder (*Acer negundo*)
*Tree of Heaven (*Ailanthus*)
Hackberry (*Celtis occidentalis*)
Russian Olive (*Elaeagnus angustifolia*)
Green Ash (*Fraxinus pennsylvanica*)
*Honey-Locust (*Gleditsia triacanthos* var.)
Western Red Cedar (*Juniperus scopulorum*)
Eastern Red Cedar (*Juniperus virginiana*)
*Golden Rain Tree (*Koelreuteria paniculata*)
White Poplar (*Populus alba*)
Chestnut Oak (*Quercus montana*)
*Black Locust (*Robinia pseudoacacia*)
*Japanese Pagoda Tree (*Sophora japonica*)

Pest-Resistant Trees
*Tree of Heaven (*Ailanthus altissima*)
*Katsura Tree (*Cercidiphyllum japonicum*)
Cornelian Cherry (*Cornus mas*)
Turkish Filbert (*Corylus colurna*)
Russian Olive (*Elaeagnus angustifolia*)
*Ginkgo (*Ginkgo biloba*)
*Honey-Locust (*Gleditsia triacanthos*)
Kentucky Coffee Tree (*Gymnocladus dioicus*)
Juniper species (*Juniperus*)
Kalopanax (*Kalopanax pictus*)
*Golden Rain Tree (*Koelreuteria paniculata*)
Hop-Hornbeam species (*Ostrya*)

Trees for Hedging or Barriers
European Beech (*Fagus sylvatica*) prunes well.
Hawthorn varieties (*Crataegus*) easily pruned, advantage of thorns.
Canadian Hemlock (*Tsuga canadensis*) evergreen.
American Holly (*Ilex opaca*) can be pruned.
European Hornbeam (*Carpinus betulus*) prunes well.
Little-leaf Linden (*Tilia cordata*) tolerates heavy pruning.
Hedge Maple (*Acer campestre*) can be pruned.
Austrian Pine (*Pinus nigra*) plant 10–12 feet on centers, staggered row.
Japanese Black Pine (*Pinus thunbergi*) plant 8 feet on centers, staggered row.
Eastern White Pine (*Pinus strobus*) plant 15 feet on centers, staggered row.

NEVADA

State Tree
Quaking Aspen (*Populus tremuloides*)

Evergreen Trees

Fir species (*Abies*)
Tree Box (*Buxus sempervirens arborescens*)
*Cedar species (*Cedrus*)
*Deodar Cedar (*Cedrus deodara*)

False Cypress species (*Chamaecyparis*)
Cypress species (*Cupressus*)
Loquat (*Eriobotrya japonica*)
Holly species (*Ilex*)

Juniper species (*Juniperus*)
California incense Cedar (*Libocedrus decurrens*)
*Southern Magnolia (*Magnolia grandiflora*)
Chinese Photinia (*Photinia serrulata*)
Spruce species (*Picea*)
*Pine species (*Pinus*)
*Live Oak (*Quercus virginiana*)
Arbor-vitae species (*Thuja*)
*Hemlock species (*Tsuga*)

Trees Classified by Height

20–35 Feet
*Japanese Maple (*Acer palmatum*)
Ohio Buckeye (*Aesculus glabra*)
Apple Serviceberry (*Amelanchier grandiflora*)
*Gray Birch (*Betula populifolia*)
Mocker-Nut (*Carya tomentosa*)
Japanese Dogwood (*Cornus kousa*)
Cornelian Cherry (*Cornus mas*)
Japanese Cornel (*Cornus officinalis*)
American Smoke Tree (*Cotinus americanus*)
*Hawthorn species (*Crataegus*)
Russian Olive (*Elaeagnus angustifolia*)
Loquat (*Eriobotrya japonica*)
Euonymus species (*Euonymus*)
Common Fig (*Ficus carica*)
Flowering Ash (*Fraxinus ornus*)
Possum Haw (*Ilex decidua*)
Yaupon (*Ilex vomitoria*)
*Golden Rain Tree (*Koelreutaria paniculata*)
Crape-Myrtle (*Lagerstroemia indica*)
*Crab Apple species (*Malus*)
*Cherry species (*Prunus*)
Almond-leaf Willow (*Salix amygdalina*)
*Babylon Weeping Willow (*Salix babylonica*)
Goat Willow (*Salix caprea*)
Showy Mountain Ash (*Sorbus decora*)
Snowberry Mountain Ash (*Sorbus discolor*)
Folgner Mountain Ash (*Sorbus folgneri*)
Japanese Tree Lilac (*Syringa amurensis japonica*)

35–75 Feet
Korean Fir (*Abies koreana*)
Box-Elder (*Acer negundo*)
*Red-fruited Tree of Heaven (*Ailanthus altissima erythrocarpa*)
Silk Tree (*Albizzia julibrissin*)
Red Alder (*Alnus rubra*)
*Shadblow Serviceberry (*Amelanchier laevis*)
*European Birch (*Betula pendula*)
Chinese Chestnut (*Castanea mollissima*)
Southern Catalpa (*Catalpa bignonioides*)
Bunch Hackberry (*Celtis bungeana*)
Eastern Redbud (*Cercis canadensis*)
Chinese Redbud (*Cercis chinensis*)
*Flowering Dogwood (*Cornus florida*)
Large-leaf Dogwood (*Cornus macrophylla*)
Green Hawthorn (*Crataegus viridis*)
Italian Cypress (*Cupressus sempervirens*)
Common Persimmon (*Diospyros virginiana*)
Green Ash (*Fraxinus pennsylvanica lanceolata*)
English Holly (*Ilex aquifolium*)
Luster-leaf Holly (*Ilex latifolia*)
Heartnut (*Juglans sieboldiana cordiformis*)
Chinese Juniper (*Juniperus chinensis*)
Syrian Juniper (*Juniperus drupacea*)
Greek Juniper (*Juniperus excelsa*)
Alligator Juniper (*Juniperus pachyphloea*)
Osage-Orange (*Maclura pomifera*)
Siberian Crab Apple (*Malus baccata*)
"Cowichan" Crab Apple (*Malus* "Cowichan")
"Dolgo" Crab Apple (*Malus* "Dolgo")
"Makamik" Crab Apple (*Malus* "Makamik")
Cherry Crab Apple (*Malus robusta*)
"Sissipuk" Crab Apple (*Malus* "Sissipuk")
Chinaberry (*Melia azedarach*)
White Mulberry (*Morus alba*)
Empress Tree (*Paulownia tomentosa*)
Dragon Spruce (*Picea asperata*)
Swiss Stone Pine (*Pinus cembra*)
Limber Pine (*Pinus flexilis*)

Scotch Pine (*Pinus sylvestris*)
Hardy Orange (*Poncirus trifoliata*)
Chinese Poplar (*Populus lasiocarpa*)
Simon Poplar (*Populus simoni*)
Sargent Cherry (*Prunus sargenti*)
Ussurian Pear (*Pyrus ussuriensis*)
Red Oak (*Quercus borealis*)
Scarlet Oak (*Quercus coccinea*)
*Pin Oak (*Quercus palustris*)
Canyon Live or Golden Cup Oak (*Quercus falcata*)
White Willow (*Salix alba*)
Wisconsin or Niobe Weeping Willow (*Salix blanda*)
Elaeagnus Willow (*Salix elaeagnos*)
Thurlow Weeping Willow (*Salix elegantissima*)
Laurel Willow (*Salix pentandra*)
Korean Mountain Ash (*Sorbus alnifolia*)
American Arbor-vitae (*Thuja occidentalis*)
Oriental Arbor-vitae (*Thuja orientalis*)
Japanese Arbor-vitae (*Thuja standishi*)
Carolina Hemlock (*Tsuga caroliniana*)
Winged or Wahoo Elm (*Ulmus alata*)
Chinese Elm (*Ulmus parvifolia*)
Siberian Elm (*Ulmus pumila*)

75 Feet or Over
Fir species (*Abies*)
Norway Maple (*Acer platanoides*)
Sycamore Maple (*Acer pseudoplatanus*)
*Red or Swamp Maple (*Acer rubrum*)
*Sugar Maple (*Acer saccharum*)
*Baumann Horse-Chestnut (*Aesculus hippocastanum baumanni*)
European Adler (*Alnus glutinosa*)
*Canoe Birch (*Betula papyrifera*)
Hickory species (*Carya*)
*Cedar species (*Cedrus*)
Sugar Hackberry (*Celtis laevigata*)
Pacific Dogwood (*Cornus nuttali*)
Cryptomeria (*Cryptomeria japonica*)
White Ash (*Fraxinus americana*)
European Ash (*Fraxinus excelsior*)
Oregon Ash (*Fraxinus oregona*)
*Ginkgo or Maidenhair Tree (*Ginkgo biloba*)
*Common Honey-Locust (*Gleditsia triacanthos*)
Kentucky Coffee Tree (*Gymnocladus dioicus*)
English or Persian Walnut (*Juglans regia*)
*Sweet Gum (*Liquidambar styraciflua*)
Tulip Tree or Yellow Poplar (*Liriodendron tulipfera*)
*Southern Magnolia (*Magnolia grandiflora*)
Spruce species (*Picea*)
*Pine species (*Pinus*)
*Plane Tree species (*Platanus*)
*Poplar species (*Populus*)
Sargent Cherry (*Prunus sargenti*)
Black or Rum Cherry (*Prunus serotina*)
Caucasian Walnut (*Pterocarya fraxinifolia*)
*Oak species (*Quercus*)
Giant Arbor-vitae (*Thuja plicata*)
*Linden species (*Tilia*)
*Canada Hemlock (*Tsuga canadensis*)
Western Hemlock (*Tsuga heterophylla*)
*Elm species (*Ulmus*)

Trees Classified by Form

Pyramidal
Fir species (*Abies*)
*Birch species (*Betula*)
*Cedar species (*Cedrus*)
Crytomeria (*Cryptomeria japonica*)
Italian Cypress (*Cupressus sumpervirens*)
English Holly (*Ilex aquifolium*)
American Holly (*Ilex opaca*)
Juniper or Red Cedar species (*Juniperus*)
*Sweet Gum (*Liquidambar styraciflua*)
*Magnolia species (*Magnolia*)
Spruce species (*Picea*)
Swiss Stone Pine (*Pinus cembra*)
Korean Pine (*Pinus koraiensis*)
*Pyramidal Austrian Pine (*Pinus nigra pyramidalis*)
Japanese White Pine (*Pinus parviflora*)

Red or Norway Pine (*Pinus resinosa*)
Bolleana Poplar (*Populus alba pyramidalis*)
*Pin Oak (*Quercus palustris*)
Arbor-vitae species (*Thuja*)
*Linden species (*Tilia*)
*Hemlock species (*Tsuga*)
Smooth-leaved Elm varieties (*Ulmus carpinifolia*)

Columnar
Ascending Norway Maple (*Acer platanoides ascendens*)
Columnar Norway Maple (*Acer platanoides columnare*)
Erect Norway Maple (*Acer platanoides erectum*)
Columnar Red Maple (*Acer rubrum columnare*)
Sentry Maple (*Acer saccharum columnare*)
Fastigiate European Birch (*Betula pendula fastigiata*)
Fastigiate Washington Hawthorn (*Crataegus phaenopyrum fastigiata*)
Sentry Ginkgo (*Ginkgo biloba fastigiata*)
Blue Columnar Chinese Juniper (*Juniperus chinensis columnaris*)
Schott Red Cedar (*Juniperus virginiana schotti*)
Swiss Stone Pine (*Pinus cembra*)
Fastigiate Scotch Pine (*Pinus sylvestris fastigiata*)
*Lombardy Poplar (*Populus nigra italica*)
Fastigiate Simon Poplar (*Populus simoni fastigiata*)
Columnar Sargent Cherry (*Prunus sargenti columnaris*)
"Amanogawa" Cherry (*Prunus serrulata* "Amanogawa")
Shipmast Locust (*Robinia pseudoacacia rectissima*)
Common Bald Cypress (*Taxodium distichum*)
Douglas Arbor-vitae (*Thuja occidentalis douglasi pyramidalis*)
Fastigiate American Arbor-vitae (*Thuja occidentalis fastigiata*)
*American Elm varieties (*Ulmus americana*)

Weeping
Slender European Birch (*Betula pendula tristis*)
Young's Birch (*Betula pendula youngi*)
*Deodar Cedar (*Cedrus deodara*)
"Exzellenz Thiel" Crab Apple (*Malus* "Exzellenz Thiel")
"Oekonomierat Echtermeyer" Crab Apple (*Malus* "Oekonomierat Echtermeyer")
Weeping Mulberry (*Morus alba pendula*)
Koster Weeping Blue Spruce (*Picea pungens kosteriana*)
Weeping Black Cherry (*Prunus serotina pendula*)
Weeping Higan Cherry (*Prunus subhirtella pendula*)
"Yaeshidare" Cherry (*Prunus subhirtella pendula flora plena*)
Weeping Yoshino Cherry (*Prunus yedoensis perpendens*)
Golden Weeping Willow (*Salix alba tristis*)
*Babylon Weeping Willow (*Salix babylonica*)
Wisconsin or Niobe Weeping Willow (*Salix blanda*)
Thurlow Weeping Willow (*Salix elegantissima*)
*Weeping Japanese Pagoda Tree (*Sophora japonica pendula*)
Weeping European Mountain Ash (*Sorbus aucuparia pendula*)
Weeping Folgner Mountain Ash (*Sorbus folgneri pendula*)
Sargent Hemlock (*Tsuga canadensis pendula*)
Weeping American Elm (*Ulmus americana pendula*)

Rounded or Globe-Shaped
*Japanese Maple (*Acer palmatum*)
Globe Norway Maple (*Acer platanoides globosum*)
Bunch Hackberry (*Celtis bungeana*)
Cornelian Cherry (*Cornus mas*)
*Crab Apple species (*Cornus mas*)
Umbrella Black Locust (*Robinia pseudoacacia umbraculifera*)
Sargent Hemlock (*Tsuga canadnesis sargenti*)
Koopmann Elm (*Ulmus carpinifolia koopmanni*)
Globe Smooth-leaved Elm (*Ulmus carpinifolia umbraculifera*)

With Horizontal Branching
Fir species (*Abies*)
Silk Tree (*Albizzia julibrissin*)
*Cedar species (*Cedrus*)
*Flowering Dogwood (*Cornus florida*)
Japanese Dogwood (*Cornus kousa*)
*Hawthorn species (*Crataegus*)
Spruce species (*Picea*)
Japanese Red Pine (*Pinus densiflora*)
*Pin Oak (*Quercus palustris*)
*Live Oak (*Quercus virginiana*)

Trees Classified by Color of Blossom
Yellow
*Golden Rain Tree (*Koelreuteria paniculata*)

White
*Shadblow Serviceberrry (*Amelanchier canadensis*)
Strawberry Tree (*Arbutus unedo*)
White Redbud (*Cercis canadensis alba*)
Japanese Dogwood (*Cornus kousa*)
Pacific Dogwood (*Cornus nuttalli*)
Washington Hawthorn (*Crataegus phaenopyrum*)
*Southern Magnolia (*Magnolia grandiflora*)
Arnold Crab Apple (*Malus arnoldiana*)
Siberian Crab Apple (*Malus baccata*)
Tea Crab Apple (*Malus hupehensis*)
Sargent Crab Apple (*Malus sargenti*)
Chinese Photinia (*Photinia serrulata*)
Hardy-Orange (*Poncirus trifoliata*)
Thundercloud Plum (*Prunus cerasifera* "Thunder-cloud")
Sour Cherry (*Prunus cerasus*)
Mount Fuji Cherry (*Prunus serrulata* "Shirotae")
Yoshino Cherry (*Prunus yedoensis*)
Bradford Callery Pear (*Pyrus calleryana bradfordi*)
*Common Pear (*Pyrus communis*)
*Japanese Pagoda Tree (*Sophora japonica*)
American Mountain Ash (*Sorbus americana*)
European Mountain Ash (*Sorbus aucuparia*)
Showy Mountain Ash (*Sorbus decora*)

Pink
Wither's Pink Redbud (*Cercis canadensis* "Wither's Pink Charm")
Red Flowering Dogwood (*Cornus florida rubra*)
Ingleside Crape-Myrtle (*Lagerstroemia indica* "Ingleside Pink")
Katherine Crab Apple (*Malus* "Katherine")
Prince Georges Crab Apple (*Malus* "Prince Georges")
*Common Apple (*Malus pumila*)
Blireiana Plum (*Prunus blireiana*)
Sargent Cherry (*Prunus sargenti*)
Amanogawa Cherry (*Prunus serrulata* "Amanogawa")
Kwanzan Cherry (*Prunus serrulata* "Kwanzan")
Autumn Cherry (*Prunus subhirtella autumnalis*)
Weeping Cherry (*Prunus subhirtella pendula*)

Red
Paul's Scarlet Hawthorn (*Crataegus oxyacantha pauli*)
Red Crape-Myrtle (*Lagerstroemia indica* "Wm. Toovey")
Almey Crab Apple (*Malus* "Almey")
Carmine Crab Apple (*Malus atrosanguinea*)

Trees with Bright Red Fruit
*Flowering Dogwood (*Cornus florida*)
Japanese Dogwood (*Cornus kousa*)
Downy Hawthorn (*Crataegus mollis*)
Washington Hawthorn (*Crataegus phaenopyrum*)
American Holly (*Ilex opaca*)
Almey Crab Apple (*Malus* "Almey")
Siberian Crab Apple (*Malus baccata*)
Hopa Crab Apple (*Malus* "Hopa")
*Common Apple (*Malus pumila*)
Sargent Crab Apple (*Malus sargenti*)
Korean Mountain Ash (*Sorbus alnifolia*)
American Mountain Ash (*Sorbus americana*)

Trees Classified by Color of Summer Foliage
Blue
White Fir (*Abies concolor*)
Blue Atlas Cedar (*Cedrus atlantica glauca*)
Western Red Cedar (*Juniperus scopulorum* var. Chandler Blue)
Eastern Red Cedar (*Juniperus virginiana* var. *Burki*)
Blue Spruce (*Picea pungens*)

Silver to Gray
Russian Olive (*Elaeagnus angustifolia*)
White Poplar (*Populus alba*)

Red to Purple
Blood-leaf Japanese Maple (*Acer palmatum atropurpureum*)
Crimson King Maple (*Acer platanoides* "Crimson King")
Schwedler Maple (*Acer platanoides schwedleri*)
Purple-leaf Sycamore Maple (*Acer pseudoplatanus*)
Rubylace Honey-Locust (*Gleditsia triacanthos inermis* "Rubylace")
Purple Crab Apple (*Malus purpurea*)
Blireiana Plum (*Prunus blireiana*)
Pissard Plum (*Prunus cerasifera atropurpurea*)
Thundercloud Plum (*Prunus cerasifera nigra* "Thundercloud")
Woods Myrobalan Plum (*Prunus cerasifera woodi*)

Trees Classified by Color of Fall Foliage
Yellow
Norway Maple (*Acer platanoides*)
*Sugar Maple (*Acer saccharum*)
Ohio Buckeye (orange) (*Aesculus glabra*)
Apple Serviceberry (yellow-orange) (*Amelanchier grandiflora*)
*Birch species (*Betula*)
Hickory species (*Carya*)
Chinese Chestnut (*Castanea mollissima*)
Redbud species (*Cercis*)
White Ash (purple to yellow) (*Fraxinus americana*)
*Ginkgo (*Ginkgo biloba*)
Tulip Tree (*Liriodendron tulipfera*)
Quaking Aspen (*Populus tremuloides*)
*Willow species (*Salix*)

Red
Amur Maple (*Acer ginnala*)
*Japanese Maple (*Acer palmatum*)
*Red Maple (*Acer rubrum*)
*Sugar Maple (*Acer saccharum*)
Tatarian Maple (*Acer tataricum*)
*Shadblow Serviceberry (*Amelanchier canadensis*)
*Flowering Dogwood (*Cornus florida*)
Japanese Dogwood (*Cornus kousa*)
Pacific Dogwood (*Cornus nuttalli*)
American Smoke Tree (*Cotinus americanus*)
Washington Hawthorn (*Crataegus phaenopyrum*)
*Sweet Gum (*Liquidambar styraciflua*)
Dawson Crab Apple (*Malus dawsoniana*)
Cherry species (*Prunus*)
Red Oak (*Quercus borealis*)
Scarlet Oak (*Quercus coccinea*)
*Pin Oak (*Quercus palustris*)

Purple
White Ash (*Fraxinus americana*)
*Sweet Gum (*Liquidambar styraciflua*)
*Common Pear (*Pyrus communis*)

Trees with Interesting Bark
Gray
*Red Maple (*Acer rubrum*)
*Serviceberry species (*Amelanchier*)
Hackberry species (*Celtis*)
*Hawthorn species (*Crataegus*)
American Holly (*Ilex opaca*)
English or Persian Walnut (*Juglans regia*)
Mountain Ash species (*Sorbus*)

White
*Paper Birch (*Betula papyrifera*)
*European Birch (*Betula pendula*)
*Gray Birch (*Betula populifolia*)
Quaking Aspen (*Populus tremuloides*)

Red
Japanese Red Pine (*Pinus densiflora*)
Red or Norway Pine (*Pinus resinosa*)
Scotch Pine (*Pinus sylvestris*)

Reddish Brown
Sargent Cherry (*Prunus sargenti*)

Yellow
Wisconsin or Niobe Weeping Willow (*Salix blanda*)

Green
*Babylon Weeping Willow (*Salix babylonica*)

Flaking
*Birch species (*Betula*)
Russian Olive (*Elaeagnus angustifolia*)
Crape-Myrtle (*Lagerstroemia indica*)
*Plane Tree species (*Platanus*)

Trees for the City
White Fir (*Abies concolor*)
Box-Elder (*Acer negundo*)
Norway Maple (*Acer platanoides*)
Sycamore Maple (*Acer pseudoplatanus*)
*Horse-Chestnut or Buckeye (*Aesculus*)
*Tree of Heaven (*Ailanthus*)
Silk Tree (*Albizzia julibrissin*)
Catalpa (*Catalpa*)
Hackberry (*Celtis*)
Downy Hawthorn (*Crataegus mollis*)
Washington Hawthorn (*Crataegus phaenopyrum*)
Russian Olive (*Elaeagnus angustifolia*)
White Ash (*Fraxinus americana*)
European Ash (*Fraxinus excelsior*)
Green Ash (*Fraxinus pennsylvanica lanceolata*)
*Ginkgo (*Ginkgo biloba*)
*Thornless Honey-Locust (*Gleditsia triacanthos inermis*)
*Golden Rain Tree (*Koelreutaria paniculata*)
*Southern Magnolia (*Magnolia grandiflora*)
*Crab Apple species (*Malus*)
Chinaberry (*Melia azedarach*)
Colorado Spruce (*Picea pungens*)
*London Plane Tree (*Platanus acerifolia*)
Bradford Callery Pear (*Pyrus calleryana bradfordi*)
*Japanese Pagoda Tree (*Sophora japonica*)
Village Green Zelkova (*Zelkova serrata* "Village Green")

Trees for Wide Streets
Sycamore Maple (*Acer pseudoplatanus*)
*Sugar Maple (*Acer saccharum*)
Sugar Hackberry (*Celtis laevigata*)
White Ash (*Fraxinus americana*)
Green Ash (*Fraxinus pennsylvanica lanceolata*)
*Ginkgo (*Ginkgo biloba*)
*Common Honey-Locust (*Gleditsia triacanthos*)
Tulip Tree (*Liriodendron tulipfera*)
*Southern Magnolia (*Magnolia grandiflora*)
*London Plane Tree (*Platanus acerifolia*)
*Oriental Plane Tree (*Platanus orientalis*)
California Plane Tree (*Platanus racemosa*)
White Poplar (*Populus alba*)
Sargent Cherry (*Prunus sargenti*)
*Pin Oak (*Quercus palustris*)

Trees for Medium Streets
Norway Maple (*Acer platanoides*)
*Sweet Gum (*Liquidambar styraciflua*)
Chinaberry (*Melia azedarach*)
Simon Poplar (*Populus simoni*)
Scarlet Oak (*Quercus coccinea*)
*Black Locust (*Robinia pseudoacacia*)
*Japanese Pagoda Tree (*Sophora japonica*)
*Linden species (*Tilia*)
Winged Elm (*Ulmus alata*)

Trees for Suburban Streets
Globe Norway Maple (*Acer platanoides globosum*)
*Flowering Dogwood (*Cornus florida*)
*Hawthorn species (*Crataegus*)
*Golden Rain Tree (*Koelreutaria paniculata*)
Columnar Sargent Cherry (*Prunus sargenti columnare*)
Oriental Cherry (*Prunus serrulata*)
Smooth-leaved Elm varieties (*Ulmus carpinifolia*)

Soil Tolerance

Trees Tolerating Moist Soil
*Red Maple (*Acer rubrum*)
Alder species (*Alnus*)
Holly species (*Ilex*)
*Sweet Gum (*Liquidambar styraciflua*)
*Willow species (*Salix*)
American Arbor-vitae (*Thuja occidentalis*)

Trees Tolerating Dry or Poor Soil
Box-Elder (*Acer negundo*)
*Tree of Heaven (*Ailanthus*)
Silk Tree (*Albizzia julibrissin*)
*Gray Birch (*Betula populifolia*)
European Hackberry (*Celtis australis*)

Russian Olive (*Elaeagnus angustifolia*)
Green Ash (*Fraxinus pennsylvanica lanceolata*)
Modesto Ash (*Fraxinus velutina* "Modesto")
*Honey-Locust (*Gleditsia triacanthos*)
Western Red Cedar (*Juniperus scopulorum*)
Eastern Red Cedar (*Juniperus virginiana*)
*Golden Rain Tree (*Koelreuteria paniculata*)
Chinaberry (*Melia azedarach*)
Jack Pine (*Pinus banksiana*)
Piñon Pine (*Pinus edulis*)
Ponderosa Pine (*Pinus ponderosa*)
*Black Locust (*Robinia pseudoacacia*)
*Japanese Pagoda Tree (*Sophora japonica*)
Siberian Elm (*Ulmus pumila*)

Pest-Resistant Trees
*Tree of Heaven (*Ailanthus altissima*)
*Cedar species (*Cedrus*)
European Hackberry (*Celtis australis*)
Cornelian Cherry (*Cornus mas*)
Japanese Cornel (*Cornus officinalis*)
American Smoke Tree (*Cotinus americanus*)
Russian Olive (*Elaeagnus angustifolia*)
*Fig species (*Ficus*)
*Ginkgo (*Ginkgo biloba*)

*Honey-Locust (*Gleditsia triacanthos*)
Kentucky Coffee Tree (*Gymnocladus dioicus*)
Juniper species (*Juniperus*)
*Golden Rain Tree (*Koelreuteria paniculata*)
*Sweet Gum (*Liquidambar styraciflua*)

Trees for Hedging or Barriers
European Beech (*Fagus sylvatica*) prunes well.
Leyland Cypress (*Cupressocyparis leylandii*) withstands heavy pruning.
Hawthorn varieties (*Crataegus*) easily pruned, advantage of thorns.
Canadian Hemlock (*Tsuga canadensis*) evergreen.
American Holly (*Ilex opaca*) can be pruned.
European Hornbeam (*Carpinus betulus*) prunes well.
Little-leaf Linden (*Tilia cordata*) tolerates heavy pruning.
Hedge Maple (*Acer campestre*) can be pruned.
Austrian Pine (*Pinus nigra*) plant 10–12 feet on centers, staggered row.
Japanese Black Pine (*Pinus thunbergi*) plant 8 feet on centers, staggered row.
Eastern White Pine (*Pinus strobus*) plant 15 feet on centers, staggered row.

NEW HAMPSHIRE

State Tree
*Canoe Birch (*Betula papyrifera*)

Evergreen Trees
Fir species (*Abies*)
False Cypress species (*Chamaecyparis*)
Juniper species (*Juniperus*)
Eastern Red Cedar (*Juniperus virginiana*)
*Larch species (*Larix*)
Spruce species (*Picea*)
*Pine species (*Pinus*)
*Douglas Fir (*Pseudotsuga menziesii*)
Arbor-vitae species (*Thuja*)
*Hemlock species (*Tsuga*)

Trees Classified by Height

20–35 Feet
Hedge Maple (*Acer campestre*)
*Amur Maple (*Acer ginnala*)
Manchurian Maple (*Acer mandshuricum*)
Mountain Maple (*Acer spicatum*)
Tatarian Maple (*Acer tataricum*)
Ohio Buckeye (*Aesculus glabra*)
*Shadblow or Shadbush (*Amelanchier canadensis*)
Mockernut (*Carya tomentosa*)
Cornelian Cherry (*Cornus mas*)
*Hawthorn species (*Crataegus*)
Russian Olive (*Elaeagnus angustifolia*)
Euonymus species (*Euonymus*)
Common Sea-Buckthorn (*Hippophae rhamnoides*)
*Laburnum species (*Laburnum*)
*Crab Apple species (*Malus*)
*Cherry species (*Prunus*)
Dahurian Buckthorn (*Rhamnus davurica*)
Almond-leaf Willow (*Salix amygdalina*)
Goat Willow (*Salix caprea*)
Showy Mountain Ash (*Sorbus decora*)
Japanese Tree Lilac (*Syringa amurensis japonica*)

35–75 Feet
Box-Elder (*Acer negundo*)
Striped Maple or Moosewood (*Acer pennsylvanicum*)
Speckled Alder (*Alnus incana*)
*Shadblow Serviceberry (*Amelanchier canadensis*)
Allegany Serviceberry (*Amelanchier laevis*)
Devil's Walking Stick (*Aralia elata*)
Dahurian Birch (*Betula davurica*)
*European Birch (*Betula pendula*)
American Hornbeam (*Carpinus caroliniana*)

Japanese Hornbeam (*Carpinus japonica*)
Southern Catalpa (*Catalpa bignoniodes*)
*Katsura Tree (*Cercidiphyllum japonicum*)
*American Yellow-wood (*Cladrastis lutea*)
Turkish Filbert (*Corylus colurna*)
Cockspur Thorn (*Crataegus crus-galli*)
Green Hawthorn (*Crataegus viridis*)
Green Ash (*Fraxinus pennsylvanica lanceolata*)
Heartnut (*Juglans sieboldiana cordiformis*)
Chinese Juniper (*Juniperus chinensis*)
Eastern Larch or Tamarack (*Larix laricina*)
Kobus Magnolia (*Magnolia kobus borealis*)
Siberian Crab Apple (*Malus baccata*)
"Cowichan" Crab Apple (*Malus* "Cowichan")
"Dolgo" Crab Apple (*Malus* "Dolgo")
"Makamik" Crab Apple (*Malus* "Makamik")
"Sissipuk" Crab Apple (*Malus* "Sissipuk")
White Mulberry (*Morus alba*)
*Amur Cork (*Phellodendron amurense*)
Black Hills Spruce (*Picea glauca densata*)
Jack Pine (*Pinus banksiana*)
Lace-bark Pine (*Pinus bungeana*)
Swiss Stone Pine (*Pinus cembra*)
Pitch Pine (*Pinus rigida*)
Scotch Pine (*Pinus sylvestris*)
Simon Poplar (*Populus simoni*)
Amur Chokecherry (*Prunus maacki*)
European Bird Cherry (*Prunus padus*)
Sargent Cherry (*Prunus sargenti*)
Ussurian Pear (*Pyrus ussuriensis*)
Swamp White Oak (*Quercus bicolor*)
Red Oak (*Quercus borealis*)
Scarlet Oak (*Quercus coccinea*)
*Pin Oak (*Quercus palustris*)
White Willow (*Salix alba*)
Wisconsin or Niobe Weeping Willow (*Salix blanda*)
Elaeagnus Willow (*Salix elaeagnos*)
Thurlow Weeping Willow (*Salix elegantissima*)
Laurel Willow (*Salix pentandra*)
Sassafras (*Sassafras albidum officinale*)
European Mountain Ash or Rowan Tree (*Sorbus aucuparia*)
American Arbor-vitae (*Thuja occidentalis*)
Carolina Hemlock (*Tsuga caroliniana*)
Siberian Elm (*Ulmus pumila*)

75 Feet or Over
Fir species (*Abies*)
Norway Maple (*Acer platanoides*)
Red or Swamp Maple (*Acer rubrum*)

*Sugar Maple (*Acer saccharum*)
*Baumann Horse-Chestnus (*Aesculus hippocastanum baumanni*)
European Alder (*Alnus glutinosa*)
Sweet Birch (*Betula lenta*)
River Birch (*Betula nigra*)
*Canoe Birch (*Betula papyrifera*)
Hickory species (*Carya*)
Northern Catalpa (*Catalpa speciosa*)
*Katsura Tree (*Cercidiphyllum japonicum*)
False Cypress species (*Chamaecyparis*)
*Beech species (*Fagus*)
White Ash (*Fraxinus americana*)
European Ash (*Fraxinus excelsior*)
*Ginkgo or Maidenhair Tree (*Ginkgo biloba*)
*Common Honey-Locust (*Gleditsia triacanthos*)
Eastern Black Walnut (*Juglans nigra*)
*European Larch (*Larix decidua*)
Japanese Larch (*Larix leptolepis*)
Tulip Tree or Yellow Poplar (*Liriodendron tulipifera*)
Cucumber Tree (*Magnolia acuminata*)
*Black Gum or Black Tupelo (*Nyssa sylvatica*)
Spruce species (*Picea*)
*Pine species (*Pinus*)
Poplar species (*Populus*)
Sargent Cherry (*Prunus sargenti*)
Black or Rum Cherry (*Prunus serotina*)
*Douglas Fir (*Pseudotsuga menziesii*)
*Oak species (*Quercus*)
Giant Arbor-vitae (*Thuja plicata*)
*Linden species (*Tilia*)
*Canada Hemlock (*Tsuga canadensis*)
*Elm species (*Ulmus*)

Trees Classified by Form

Pyramidal
Fir species (*Abies*)
*Birch species (*Betula*)
False Cypress species (*Chamaecyparis*)
Turkish Filbert (*Corylus colurna*)
*Beech species (*Fagus*)
Juniper or Red Cedar species (*Juniperus*)
*Larch species (*Larix*)
*Magnolia species (*Magnolia*)
*Black Tupelo or Black Gum (*Nyssa sylvatica*)
Hop-Hornbeam (*Ostrya virginiana*)
Spruce species (*Picea*)
Swiss Stone Pine (*Pinus cembra*)
Korean Pine (*Pinus koraiensis*)
Pyramid Austrian Pine (*Pinus nigra pyramidalis*)

Red or Norway Pine (*Pinus resinosa*)
*Douglas Fir (*Pseudotsuga menziesii*)
*Pin Oak (*Quercus palustris*)
Arbor-vitae species (*Thuja*)
*Linden species (*Tilia*)
*Hemlock species (*Tsuga*)
Smooth-leaved Elm varieties (*Ulmus carpinifolia*)

Columnar
Ascending Norway Maple (*Acer platanoides ascendens*)
Columnar Norway Maple (*Acer platanoides columnare*)
Erect Norway Maple (*Acer platanoides erectum*)
Columnar Red Maple (*Acer rubrum columnare*)
Sentry Maple (*Acer saccharum monumentale*)
Fastigiate European Birch (*Betula pendula fastigiata*)
Fastigiate Washington Hawthorn (*Crataegus phaenopyrum fastigiata*)
Dawyck Beech (*fagus sylvatica fastigiata*)
Sentry Ginkgo (*Ginkgo biloba fastigiata*)
Blue Columnar Chinese Juniper (*Juniperus chinensis columnaris*)
Schott Red Cedar (*Juniperus virginiana schotti*)
Swiss Stone Pine (*Pinus cembra*)
Fastigiate White Pine (*Pinus strobus fastigiata*)
Fastigiate Scotch Pine (*Pinus sylvestris fastigiata*)
Bolleana Poplar (*Populus alba pyramidalis*)
*Lombardy Poplar (*Populus nigra italica*)
Fastigiate Simon Poplar (*Populus simoni fastigiata*)
Columnar Sargent Cherry (*Prunus sargenti columnaris*)
Shipmast Locust (*Robinia pseudoacacia rectissima*)
Upright European Mountain Ash (*Sorbus aucuparia fastigiata*)
Douglas Arbor-vitae (*Thuja occidentalis douglasi pyramidalis*)
Fastigiate American Arbor-vitae (*Thuja occidentalis fastigiata*)
Columnar Big-leaf Linden (*Tilia platyphyllos fastigiata*)
*American Elm varieties (*Ulmus americana*)

Weeping
Slender European Birch (*Betula pendula tristis*)
Young's Birch (*Betula pendula youngi*)
*Weeping Beech (*Fagus sylvatica pendula*)
Weeping Purple Beech (*Fagus sylvatica purpureo-pendula*)
Weeping Red Cedar (*Juniperus virginiana pendula*)
*Weeping Larch (*Larix decidua pendula*)
"Exzellenz Thiel" Crab Apple (*Malus* "Exzellenz Thiel")
"Oekonomierat Echtermeyer" Crab Apple (*Malus* "Oekonomierat Echtermeyer")
Weeping Mulberry (*Morus alba pendula*)
Koster Weeping Blue Spruce (*Picea pungens kosteriana*)
Weeping White Pine (*Pinus strobus pendula*)
Weeping Black Cherry (*Prunus serotina pendula*)
*Weeping Douglas Fir (*Pseudotsuga menziesii pendula*)
Golden Weeping Willow (*Salix alba tristis*)
Wisconsin or Niobe Weeping Willow (*Salix blanda*)
Thurlow Weeping Willow (*Salix elegantissima*)
Weeping European Mountain Ash (*Sorbus aucuparia pendula*)
Sargent Hemlock (*Tsuga canadensis pendula*)
Weeping American Elm (*Ulmus americana pendula*)

Rounded or Globe-Shaped
Globe Norway Maple (*Acer platanoides globosum*)
Cornelian Cherry (*Cornus mas*)
Single Seed Hawthorn (*Crataegus monogyna inermis*)
*Crab Apple species (*Malus*)
*White Oak (*Quercus alba*)
Umbrella Black Locust (*Robinia pseudoacacia umbraculifera*)
Sargent Hemlock (*Tsuga canadensis sargenti*)
Koopmann Elm (*Ulmus carpinifolia koopmanni*)

Globe Smooth-leaved Elm (*Ulmus carpinifolia umbraculifera*)

With Horizontal Branching
Fir species (*Abies*)
*Hawthorn species (*crataegus*)
*Black Tupelo or Black Gum (*Nyssa sylvatica*)
Spruce species (*Picea*)
Japanese Red Pine (*Pinus densiflora*)
*Eastern White Pine (*Pinus strobus*)
*White Oak (*Quercus alba*)
*Pin Oak (*Quercus palustris*)

Trees Classified by Color of Blossom

White
*Shadblow Serviceberry (*Amelanchier canadensis*)
*American Yellow-wood (*Cladrastis lutea*)
Washington Hawthorn (*Crataegus phaenopyrum*)
Arnold Crab Apple (*Malus arnoldiana*)
Siberian Crab Apple (*Malus accata*)
Tea Crab Apple (*Malus hupehensis*)
Sour Cherry (*Prunus cerasus*)
American Mountain Ash (*Sorbus americana*)
European Mountain Ash (*Sorbus aucuparia*)
Show Mountain Ash (*Sorbus decora*)

Pink
Toba Hawthorn (*Crataegus mordenensis* "Toba")
Japanese Flowering Crab Apple (*Malus floribunda*)
Katherine Crab Apple (*Malus* "Katherine")
*Common Apple (*Malus pumila*)
Prince Georges Crab Apple (*Malus* "Prince Georges")
Sargent Cherry (*Prunus sargenti*)

Red
Ruby Horse-Chestnut (*Aesculus carnea briotti*)
Paul's Scarlet Hawthorn (*Crataegus oxyacantha pauli*)
Almey Crab Apple (*Malus* "Almey")
Carmine Crab Apple (*Malus atrosanguinea*)

Trees Classified by Color of Summer Foliage

Blue
Eastern Red Cedar (*Juniperus virginiana* var. *Burki*)

Silver to Gray
Russian Olive (*Elaeagnus angustifolia*)
Common Sea-Buckthorn (*Hippophae rhamnoides*)
White Poplar (*Populus alba*)
*Silver Linden (*Tilia tomentosa*)

Red to Purple
Crimson King Maple (*Acer platanoides* "Crimson King")
Schwedler Maple (*Acer platanoides schwedleri*)
Purple Beech (*Fagus sylvatica atropunicea*)
Weeping Purple Beech (*Fagus sylvatica purpurea-pendula*)
River's Purple Beech (*Fagus sylvatica riversi*)
Rubylace Locust (*Gleditsia triacanthos inermis* "Rubylace")
Purple Crab Apple (*Malus purpurea*)
Pissard Plum (*Prunus cerasifera atropurpurea*)

Trees Classified by Color of Fall Foliage

Yellow
Striped Maple or Moosewood (*Acer pennsylvanicum*)
Norway Maple (*Acer platanoides* var.)
*Sugar Maple (*Acer saccharum*)
Ohio Buckeye (orange) (*Aesculus glabra*)
Apple Serviceberry (yellow-orange) (*Amelanchier grandiflora*)
*Birch speices (*Betula*)
Hickory species (*Carya*)
*Katsura Tree (*Cercidiphyllum japonicum*)
Redbud species (*Cercis*)
*American Yellow-wood (*Cladrastis lutea*)
*American Beech (*Fagus grandifolia*)
*European Beech (*Fagus sylvatica*)
White Ash (purple to yellow) (*Fraxinus americana*)

*Ginkgo (*Ginkgo biloba*)
*Larch (*Larix decidua*)
Tulip Tree (*Liriodendron tulipifera*)
*Star Magnolia (bronze) (*Magnolia stellata*)
*Willow species (*Salix*)

Red
Amur Maple (*Acer ginnala*)
Manuchurian Maple (*Acer mandshuricum*)
*Red Maple (*Acer rubrum*)
*Sugar Maple (*Acer saccharum*)
Tatarian Maple (*Acer tataricum*)
*Shadblow Serviceberry (*Amelanchier canadensis*)
Hornbeam species (*Carpinus*)
*Flowering Dogwood (*Cornus florida*)
Washington Hawthorn (*Crataegus phaenopyrum*)
Dawson Crab Apple (*Malus dawsoniana*)
*Black Tupelo or Black Gum (*Nyssa sylvatica*)
*Cherry species (*Prunus*)
Red Oak (*Quercus borealis*)
Scarlet Oak (*Quercus coccinea*)
*Pin Oak (*Quercus palustris*)
Sassafras (*Sassafras albidum*)

Purple
White Ash (*Fraxinus americana*)
*White Oak (*Quercus alba*)

Trees with Interesting Bark

Gray
*Red Maple (*Acer rubrum*)
Serviceberry species (*Amelanchier*)
Hornbeam species (*Carpinus*)
*American Yellow-wood (*Cladrastis lutea*)
*Hawthorn species (*Crataegus*)
*Beech species (*Fagus*)
Cucumber Tree (*Magnolia acuminata*)
Red Oak (young trunk and branches) (*Quercus borealis*)
Black Oak (young trunk and branches) (*Quercus velutina*)
Mountain Ash species (*Sorbus*)

White
*Canoe Birch (*Betula papyrifera*)
*European Birch (*Betula pendula*)

Red
Japanese Red Pine (*Pinus densiflora*)
Red or Norway Pine (*Pinus resinosa*)
Scotch Pine (*Pinus sylvestris*)

Reddish Brown
Sargent Cherry (*Prunus sargenti*)

Yellow
Wisconsin or Niobe Weeping Willow (*Salix blanda*)

Corky
*Amur Cork (*Phellodendron amurense*)

Flaking
*Birch species (*Betula*)
Shagbark Hickory (*Carya ovata*)
Russian Olive (*Elaeagnus angustifolia*)
Eastern Red Cedar (*Juniperus virginiana*)
Lace-bark Pine (*Pinus bungeana*)

Trees for the City
White Fir (*Abies concolor*)
Hedge Maple (*Acer campestre*)
Box-Elder (*Acer negundo*)
Norway Maple (*Acer platanoides*)
Horse-Chestnut or Buckeye (*Aesculus*)
Catalpa (*Catalpa*)
Downy Hawthorn (*Crataegus mollis*)
Washington Hawthorn (*Crataegus phaenopyrum*)
Russian Olive (*Elaeagnus angustifolia*)
White Ash (*Fraxinus americana*)
European Ash (*Fraxinus excelsior*)
Green Ash (*Fraxinus pennsylvanica*)
*Ginkgo (*Ginkgo biloba*)
Thornless Honey-Locust (*Gleditsia triacanthos inermis*)

*Crab Apple (*Malus* var.)
*Amur Cork (*Phellodendron amurense*)
Colorado Spruce (*Picea pungens*)
White Poplar (*Populus alba*)
*Lombardy Poplar (*Populus nigra italica*)
Red Oak (*Quercus borealis*)
*Black Locust (*Robinia pseudoacacia*)
*Little-leaf Linden (*Tilia cordata*)
*Silver Linden (*Tilia tomentosa*)

Trees for Wide Streets

*Sugar Maple (*Acer saccharum*)
*Katsura Tree (*Cercidiphyllum japonicum*)
White Ash (*Fraxinus americana*)
Green Ash (*Fraxinus pennsylvanica lanceolata*)
*Ginkgo (*Ginkgo biloba*)
*Common Honey-Locust (*Gleditsia triacanthos*)
Tulip Tree (*Liriodendron tulipifera*)
*Amur Cork (*Phellodendron amurense*)
*Eastern White Pine (*Pinus strobus*)
White Poplar (*Populus alba*)
Sargent Cherry (*Prunus sargenti*)
Red Oak (*Quercus borealis*)
*Pin Oak (*Quercus palustris*)

Trees for Medium Streets

Norway Maple (*Acer platanoides*)
Hop-Hornbeam (*Ostrya virginiana*)
Simon Poplar (*Populus simoni*)
Scarlet Oak (*Quercus coccinea*)
*Black Locust (*Robinia pseudoacacia*)
Sassafras (*Sassafras albidum officinale*)
*Linden species (*Tilia*)

Trees for Suburban Streets

Hedge Maple (*Acer campestre*)
Amur Maple (*Acer ginnala*)
Globe Norway Maple (*Acer spicatum*)
Tatarian Maple (*Acer tataricum*)
American Hornbeam (*Carpinus caroliniana*)
*Hawthorn species (*Crataegus*)
Columnar Sargent Cherry (*Prunus sargenti columnaris*)

Soil Tolerance

Trees Tolerating Acid Soil

*European Beech (*Fagus sylvatica*)
*Black Tupelo (*Nyssa sylvatica*)
Red Oak (*Quercus borealis*)
Scarlet Oak (*Quercus coccinea*)
*Pin Oak (*Quercus palustris*)
Willow Oak (*Quercus phellos*)

Trees Tolerating Dry or Poor Soil

Box-Elder (*Acer negunda*)
*Tree of Heaven (*Ailanthus*)
Russian Olive (*Elaeagnus angustifolia*)
Green Ash (*Fraxinus pennsylvanica*)
*Honey-Locust (*Gleditsia triacanthos*)
Western Red Cedar (*Juniperus scopulorum*)
Eastern Red Cedar (*Juniperus virginiana*)
Jack Pine (*Pinus banksiana*)
Pitch Pine (*Pinus rigida*)
Virginia or Scrub Pine (*Pinus virginiana*)
White Poplar (*Populus alba*)
Chestnut Oak (*Quercus montana*)
*Black Locust (*Robinia pseudoacacia*)
Sassafras (*Sassafras albidum officinale*)
Siberian Elm (*Ulmus pumila*)

Pest-Resistant Trees

Hornbeam species (*Carpinus*)
*Katsura Tree (*Cercidiphyllum japonicum*)
False Cypress species (*Chamaecyparis*)
Cornelian Cherry (*Cornus mas*)
Japanese Cornel (*Cornus officinalis*)
Turkish Filbert (*Corylus columa*)
Russian Olive (*Elaeagnus angustifolia*)
*Ginkgo (*Ginkgo biloba*)
*Honey-Locust (*Gleditsia triacanthos*)
Juniper species (*Juniperus*)
*Laburnum species (*Laburnum*)
Cucumber Tree (*Magnolia acuminata*)
Kobus Magnolia (*Magnolia kobus borealis*)
Hop-Hornbeam species (*Ostrya*)

Trees for Seashore Planting

Norway Maple (*Acer platanoides*)
*Horse-Chestnut (*Aesculus hippocastanum*)
*Shadblow Serviceberry (*Amelanchier canadensis*)
Cockspur Thorn (*Crataegus crus-galli*)
English Hawthorn (*Crataegus oxyacantha*)
Washington Hawthorn (*Crataegus phaenopyrum*)
Russian Olive (*Elaeagnus angustifolia*)
*Thornless Honey-Locust (*Gleditsia triacanthos inermis* var.)
Eastern Red Cedar (*Juniperus virginiana*)
*Black Tupelo (*Nyssa sylvatica*)
Colorado Blue Spruce (*Picea pungens glauca*)
Austrian Pine (*Pinus nigra*)
Scotch Pine (*Pinus sylvestris*)
*Japanese Black Pine (*Pinus thunbergi*)
White Poplar (*Populus alba*)
Black Cherry (*Prunus serotina*)
*White Oak (*Quercus alba*)
*Black Locust (*Robinia pseudoacacia*)
Golden Weeping Willow (*Salix alba tristis*)
*Little-leaf Linden (*Tilia cordata*)

Trees for Hedging or Barriers

European Beech (*Fagus sylvatica*) prunes well.
Hawthorn varieties (*Crataegus*) easily pruned, advantage of thorns.
Canadian Hemlock (*Tsuga canadensis*) evergreen.
American Holly (*Ilex opaca*) can be pruned.
European Hornbeam (*Carpinus betulus*) prunes well.
Little-leaf Linden (*Tilia cordata*) tolerates heavy pruning.
Hedge Maple (*Acer campestre*) can be pruned.
Austrian Pine (*Pinus nigra*) plant 10–12 feet on centers, staggered row.
Japanese Black Pine (*Pinus thunbergi*) plant 8 feet on centers, staggered row.
Eastern White Pine (*Pinus strobus*) plant 15 feet on centers, staggered row.

NEW JERSEY

State Tree

*Red Oak (*Quercus borealis*)

Evergreen Trees

Fir species (*Abies*)
*Cedar species (*Cedrus*)
Holly species (*Ilex*)
Juniper species (*Juniperus*)
Spruce species (*Picea*)
*Pine species (*Pinus*)
*Douglas Fir (*Pseudotsuga menziesii*)
Arbor-vitae species (*Thuja*)
*Hemlock species (*Tsuga*)

Trees Classified by Height

20–35 Feet

Hedge Maple (*Acer campestre*)
Amur Maple (*Acer ginnala*)
Paperbark Maple (*Acer griseum*)
*Japanese Maple (*Acer palmatum*)
Ohio Buckeye (*Aesculus glabra*)
*Gray Birch (*Betula populifolia*)
European Hornbeam (*Carpinus betulus globosa*)
Judas Tree (*Cercis siliquastrum*)
Japanese Dogwood (*Cornus kousa*)
Cornelian Cherry (*Cornus mas*)
American Smoke Tree (*Cotinus americanus*)
*Hawthorn species (*Crataegus*)
Russian Olive (*Elaeagnus angustifolia*)
Korean Evodia (*Evodia danielli*)
Franklinia (*Franklinia alatamaha*)
Flowering Ash (*Fraxinus ornus*)
Carolina Silverbell (*Halesia carolina*)
*Golden Rain Tree (*Koelreuteria paniculata*)

*Laburnum species (*Laburnum*)
Yellow Cucumber Tree (*Magnolia cordata*)
*Saucer Magnolia (*Magnolia soulangeana*)
*Star Magnolia (*Magnolia stellata*)
*Crab Apple species (*Malus*)
*Cherry species (*Prunus*)
*Babylon Weeping Willow (*Salix babylonica*)

35–75 Feet

Box-Elder (*Acer negundo*)
Striped Maple or Moosewood (*Acer pennsylvanicum*)
*Red-fruited Tree of Heaven (*Ailanthus altissima erythrocarpa*)
Silk Tree (*Albizzia julibrissin*)
Italian Alder (*Alnus cordata*)
Red Alder (*Alnus rubra*)
*Shadblow Serviceberry (*Amelanchier canadensis*)
Allegany Serviceberry (*Amelanchier laevis*)
*European Birch (*Betula pendula*)
European Hornbeam (*Carpinus betulus*)
American Hornbeam (*Carpinus caroliniana*)
Chinese Chestnut (*Castanea mollissima*)
Southern Catalpa (*Catalpa bignoniodes*)
Bunch Hackberry (*Celtis bungeana*)
*Katsura Tree (*Cercidiphyllum japonicum*)
Eastern Redbud (*Cercis canadensis*)
Chinese Redbud (*Cercis chinensis*)
*American Yellow-wood (*Cladrastis lutea*)
*Flowering Dogwood (*Cornus florida*)
Cockspur Tree (*Crataegus crus-galli*)
Green Ash (*Fraxinus pennsylvanica lanceolata*)
American Holly (*Ilex opaca*)
Chinese Juniper (*Juniperus chinensis*)

Fraser Magnolia (*Magnolia fraseri*)
Kobus Magnolia (*Magnolia kobus borealis*)
Sweet Bay (*Magnolia virginiana*)
"Cowichan" Crab Apple (*Malus* "Cowichan")
"Dolgo" Crab Apple (*Malus* "Dolgo")
"Makamik" Crab Apple (*Malus* "Makamik")
Cherry Crab Apple (*Malus robusta*)
"Sissipuk" Crab Apple (*Malus* "Sissipuk")
White Mulberry (*Morus alba*)
*Sorrel Tree or Sourwood (*Oxydendrum arboreum*)
Empress Tree (*Paulownia tomentosa*)
Simon Poplar (*Populus simoni*)
Sargent Cherry (*Prunus sargenti*)
Yoshino Cherry (*Prunus yedoensis*)
Red Oak (*Quercus borealis*)
Scarlet Oak (*Quercus coccinea*)
*Pin Oak (*Quercus palustris*)
Willow Oak (*Quercus phellos*)
Laurel Willow (*Salix pentandra*)
Sassafras (*Sassafras albidum officinale*)
Korean Mountain Ash (*Sorbus alnifolia*)
Japanese Stewartia (*Stewartia pseudo-camellia*)
American Arbor-vitae (*Thuja orientalis*)
Japanese Arbor-vitae (*Thuja standishi*)
*Crimean Linden (*Tilia euchlora*)
Carolina Hemlock (*Tsuga caroliniana*)
Winged or Wahoo Elm (*Ulmus alata*)
Chinese Elm (*Ulmus parvifolia*)

75 Feet or Over

Fir species (*Abies*)
Norway Maple (*Acer platanoides*)
Sycamore Maple (*Acer pseudoplatanus*)
*Red or Swamp Maple (*Acer rubrum*)

Hickory species (*Carya*)
★Cedar species (*Cedrus*)
European Hickory (*Celtis australis*)
Sugar Hackberry (*Celtis laevigata*)
False Cypress species (*Chamaecyparis*)
Cryptomeria (*Cryptomeria japonica*)
★Beech species (*Fagus*)
★Ginkgo or Maidenhair Tree (*Ginkgo biloba*)
★Common Honey-Locust (*Gleditsia triacanthos*)
Mountain Silverbell (*Halesia monticola*)
★Sweet Gum (*Liquidambar styraciflua*)
Cucumber Tree (*Magnolia acuminata*)
Dawn Redwood (*Metasequoia glyptostroboides*)
★Black Gum or Black Tupelo (*Nyssa sylvatica*)
★Pine species (*Pinus*)
★Plane Tree species (*Platanus*)
Poplar species (*Populus*)
Golden Larch (*Pseudolarix amabilis*)
★Douglas Fir (*Pseudotsuga menziesii*)
★Oak species (*Quercus*)
Common Bald Cypress (*Taxodium distichum*)
English Elm (*Ulmus procera*)
Japanese Zelkova (*Zelkova serrata*)

Trees Classified by Form

Pyramidal
Fir species (*Abies*)
Arbor-vitae species (*Thuja*)
★Cedar species (*Cedrus*)
Cryptomeria (*Cryptomeria japonica*)
★Beech species (*Fagus*)
American Holly (*Ilex opaca*)
Juniper or Red Cedar species (*Juniperus*)
★Sweet Gum (*Liquidambar styraciflua*)
★Magnolia species (*Magnolia*)
Dawn Redwood (*Metasequoia glyptostroboides*)
★Black Tupelo or Black Gum (*Nyssa sylvatica*)
Hop-Hornbeam (*Ostrya virginiana*)
★Sorrel Tree or Sourwood (*Oxydendrum arboreum*)
★Douglas Fir (*Pseudotsuga menziesii*)
★Pin Oak (*Quercus palustris*)
★Linden species (*Tilia*)
★Hemlock species (*Tsuga*)
Smooth-leaved Elm varieties (*Ulmus carpinifolia*)

Columnar
Ascending Norway Maple (*Acer platanoides ascendens*)
Columnar Norway Maple (*Acer platanoides columnare*)
Erect Norway Maple (*Acer platanoides erectum*)
Columnar Red Maple (*Acer rubrum columnare*)
Fastigiate European Hornbeam (*Carpinus betulus fastigiata*)
Fastigiate Washington Hawthorn (*Crataegus phaenopyrum fastigiata*)
Dawyck Beech (*Fagus sylvatica fastigiata*)
Sentry Ginkgo (*Ginkgo biloba fastigiata*)
Schott Red Cedar (*Juniperus virginiana schotti*)
Bolleana Poplar (*Populus alba pyramidalis*)
★Lombardy Poplar (*Populus nigra italica*)
"Amanogawa" Cherry (*Prunus serrulata* "Amanogawa")
Fastigiate English Oak (*Quercus robur fastigiata*)
Shipmast Locust (*Robinia pseudoacacia rectissima*)
Common Bald Cypress (*Taxodium distichum*)

Weeping
★European Birch (*Betula pendula*)
Weeping European Hornbeam (*Carpinus betulus pendula*)
★Weeping Beech (*Fagus sylvatica pendula*)
Weeping Red Cedar (*Juniperus virginiana pendula*)
"Exzellenz Thiel" Crab Apple (*Malus* "Exzellenz Thiel")
"Oekonomierat Echtermeyer" Crab Apple (*Malus* "Oekonomierat Echtermeyer")
Weeping Mulberry (*Morus alba pendula*)
Weeping White Pine (*Pinus strobus pendula*)
Weeping Black Cherry (*Prunus serotina pendula*)
Weeping Higan Cherry (*Prunus subhirtella pendula*)

"Yaeshidare" Cherry (*Prunus subhirtella pendula flora plena*)
Weeping Yoshino Cherry (*Prunus yedoensis perpendens*)
Weeping Douglas Fir (*Pseudotsuga menziesii pendula*)
★Babylon Weeping Willow (*Salix babylonica*)
Weeping Japanese Pagoda Tree (*Sophora japonica pendula*)
Pendant Silver Linden (*Tilia petiolaris*)
Sargent Hemlock (*Tsuga canadensis pendula*)
Weeping American Elm (*Ulmus americana pendula*)

Rounded or Globe-Shaped
★Japanese Maple (*Acer palmatum*)
Globe Norway Maple (*Acer platanoides globosum*)
Globe European Hornbeam (*Carpinus betulus globosa*)
Bunch Hackberry (*Celtis bungeana*)
Cornelian Cherry (*Cornus mas*)
Japanese Cornel (*Cornus officinalis*)
Single Seed Hawthorn (*Crataegus monogyna inermis*)
★Saucer Magnolia (*Magnolia soulangeana*)
★Crab Apple species (*Malus*)
★White Oak (*Quercus alba*)
Umbrella Black Locust (*Robinia pseudoacacia umbraculifera*)
Sargent Hemlock (*Tsuga canadensis sargenti*)

With Horizontal Branching
Fir species (*Abies*)
Silk Tree (*Albizzia julibrissin*)
★Cedar species (*Cedrus*)
Eastern Redbud (*Cercis canadensis*)
★Flowering Dogwood (*Cornus florida*)
Japanese Dogwood (*Cornus kousa*)
★Hawthorn species (*Crataegus*)
Dawn Redwood (*Metasequoia glyptostroboides*)
★Black Tupelo or Black Gum (*Nyssa sylvatica*)
★Eastern White Pine (*Pinus strobus*)
★White Oak (*Quercus alba*)
★Pin Oak (*Quercus palustris*)
Common Bald Cypress (*Taxodium distichum*)

Trees Classified by Color of Blossom

Yellow
★Golden Rain Tree (*Koelreuteria paniculata*)
★Laburnum (*Laburnum vossi*)

White
★Shadblow Serviceberry (*Amelanchier canadensis*)
White Redbud (*Cercis canadensis alba*)
★American Yellow-wood (*Cladrastis lutea*)
Japanese Dogwood (*Cornus kousa*)
Washington Hawthorn (*Crataegus phaenopyrum*)
Carolina Silverbell (*Halesia carolina*)
Yulan Magnolia (*Magnolia denudata*)
★Star Magnolia (*Magnolia stellata*)
Arnold Crab Apple (*Malus arnoldiana*)
Tea Crab Apple (*Malus hupehensis*)
Sargent Crab Apple (*Malus sargenti*)
★Sorrel Tree (*Oxydendrum arboreum*)
Thundercloud Plum (*Prunus cerasifera* "Thundercloud")
Mount Fuji Cherry (*Prunus serrulata* "Shirotae")
Yoshino Cherry (*Prunus yedoensis*)
Bradford Callery Pear (*Pyrus calleryana bradfordi*)
★Common Pear (*Pyrus communis*)
★Japanese Pagoda Tree (*Sophora japonica*)
Japanese Stewartia (*Stewartia pseudocamellia*)
Japanese Snowbell (*Styrax japonica*)

Pink
Wither's Pink Redbud (*Cercis canadensis* "Wither's Pink Charm")
Red Flowering Dogwood (*Cornus florida rubra*)
Toba Hawthorn (*Crataegus mordenensis* "Toba")
★Saucer Magnolia (*Magnolia soulangeana*)
Japanese Flowering Crab Apple (*Malus floribunda*)
Katherine Crab Apple (*Malus* "Katherine")
Prince Georges Crab Apple (*Malus* "Prince Georges")

★Common Apple (*Malus pumila*)
Blireiana Plum (*Prunus blireiana*)
Sargent Cherry (*Prunus sargenti*)
Amanogawa Cherry (*Prunus serrulata* "Amanogawa")
Kwanzan Cherry (*Prunus serrulata* "Kwanzan")
Autumn Cherry (*Prunus subhirtella autumnalis*)
Weeping Cherry (*Prunus subhirtella pendula*)

Red
Ruby Horse-Chestnut (*Aesculus carnea briotti*)
Paul's Scarlet Hawthorn (*Crataegus oxyacantha pauli*)
Alexandrina Magnolia (*Magnolia soulangeana* "Alexandrina")
Almey Crab Apple (*Malus* "Almey")
Carmine Crab Apple (*Malus atrosanguinea*)

Trees with Bright Red Fruit
★Flowering Dogwood (*Cornus florida*)
Japanese Dogwood (*Cornus kousa*)
Washington Hawthorn (*Crataegus phaenopyrum*)
American Holly (*Ilex opaca*)
Almey Crab Apple (*Malus* "Almey")
Siberian Crab Apple (*Malus baccata*)
Hopa Crab Apple (*Malus* "Hopa")
★Common Apple (*Malus pumila*)
Sargent Crab Apple (*Malus sargenti*)
Korean Mountain Ash (*Sorbus alnifolia*)
American Mountain Ash (*Sorbus americana*)
European Mountain Ash (*Sorbus aucuparia*)

Trees Classified by Color of Summer Foliage

Blue
White Fir (*Abies concolor*)
★Blue Atlas Cedar (*Cedrus atlantica glauca*)
Eastern Red Cedar (*Juniperus virginiana* var. *Burki*)
Steel Lawson Cypress (*Chamaecyparis lawsonia glauca*)

Silver to Gray
Russian Olive (*Elaeagnus angustifolia*)
White Poplar (*Populus alba*)
Pendent Silver Linden (*Tilia petiolaris*)
★Silver Linden (*Tilia tomentosa*)

Red to Purple
Blood-leaf Japanese Maple (*Acer palmatum atropurpureum*)
Crimson King Maple (*Acer platanoides* "Crimson King")
Schwedler Maple (*Acer platanoides schwedleri*)
Purple-leaf Sycamore Maple (*Acer pseudoplatanus*)
Purple Beech (*Fagus sylvatica atropunicea*)
Weeping Purple Beech (*Fagus sylvatica purpurea-pendula*)
River's Purple Beech (*Fagus sylvatica riversi*)
Rubylace Locust (*Gleditsia triacanthos inermis* "Rubylace")

Trees Classified by Color of Fall Foliage

Red
Amur Maple (*Acer ginnala*)
★Japanese Maple (*Acer palmatum* var.)
★Red Maple (*Acer rubrum*)
★Shadblow Serviceberry (*Amelanchier canadensis*)
Hornbeam species (*Carpinus*)
★Flowering Dogwood (*Cornus florida*)
Japanese Dogwood (*Cornus kousa*)
American Smoke Tree (*Cotinus americanus*)
Washington Hawthorn (*Crataegus phaenopyrum*)
★Sweet Gum (*Liquidambar styraciflua*)
★Black Tupelo or Black Gum (*Nyssa sylvatica*)
★Sorrel Tree (*Oxydendrum arboreum*)
★Cherry species (*Prunus*)
Bradford Callery Pear (*Pyrus calleryana bradfordi*)
Red Oak (*Quercus borealis*)
Scarlet Oak (*Quercus coccinea*)
★Pin Oak (*Quercus palustris*)
Sassafras (*Sassafras albidum*)

Korean Mountain Ash (*Sorbus alnifolia*)

Purple
White Ash (*Fraxinus americana*)
*Sweet Gum (*Liquidambar styraciflua*)
*Common Pear (*Pyrus communis*)

Trees with Interesting Bark

Gray
*Red Maple (*Acer rubrum*)
*Serviceberry species (*Amelanchier*)
Hackberry species (*Celtis*)
*American Yellow-wood (*Cladrastis lutea*)
*Hawthorn species (*Crataegus*)
*Beech species (*Fagus*)
American Holly (*Ilex opaca*)
Cucumber Tree (*Magnolia acuminata*)
*Saucer Magnolia (*Magnolia soulangeana*)
Red Oak (young trunk and branches) (*Quercus borealis*)
Mountain Ash species (*Sorbus*)

White
*European Birch (*Betula pendula*)
*Gray Birch (*Betula populifolia*)

Red
Japanese Red Pine (*Pinus densiflora*)

Reddish Brown
Chinese Paper Birch (*Betula albo-sinensis*)

Yellow
Wisconsin or Niobe Weeping Willow (*Salix blanda*)

Green
*Babylon Weeping Willow (*Salix babylonica*)

Corky
Hackberry (*Celtis*)
*Amur Cork (*Phellodendron amurense*)

Flaky
Paperbark Maple (*Acer griseum*)
*Birch species (*Betula*)
Shagbark Hickory (*Carya ovata*)
Eastern Red Cedar (*Juniperus virginiana*)
Lace-bark Pine (*Pinus bungeana*)
*Plane Tree species (*Platanus*)
Stewartia species (*Stewartia*)

Trees for the City

White Fir (*Abies concolor*)
Hedge Maple (*Acer campestre*)
Box-Elder (*Acer negundo*)
Norway Maple (*Acer platanoides*)
Sycamore Maple (*Acer pseudoplatanus*)
*Horse-Chestnut or Buckeye (*Aesculus*)
*Tree of Heaven (*Ailanthus*)
Silk Tree (*Albizzia julibrissin*)
Catalpa (*Catalpa*)
Hackberry (*Celtis*)
Washington Hawthorn (*Crataegus phaenopyrum*)
Russian Olive (*Elaeagnus angustifolia*)
White Ash (*Fraxinus americana*)
European Ash (*Fraxinus excelsior*)
Green Ash (*Fraxinus pennsylvanica*)
*Ginkgo (*Ginkgo biloba*)
Thornless Honey-Locust (*Gleditsia triacanthos*)
*Golden Rain Tree (*Koelreuteria paniculata*)
*Saucer Magnolia (*Magnolia soulangeana*)
*Star Magnolia (*Magnolia stellata*)
*Crab Apple (*Malus* var.)
*Amur Cork (*Phellodendron amurense*)
*London Plane Tree (*Platanus acerifolia*)
White Poplar (*Populus alba*)
*Lombardy Poplar (*Populus nigra italica*)
Bradford Callery Pear (*Pyrus calleryana bradfordi*)
Red Oak (*Quercus borealis*)
*Black Locust (*Robinia pseudoacacia*)
*Japanese Pagoda Tree (*Sophora japonica*)
*Little-leaf Linden (*Tilia cordata*)
*Crimean Linden (*Tilia euchlora*)
*Silver Linden (*Tilia tomentosa*)

Village Green Zelkova (*Zelkova serrata* "Village Green")

Trees for Wide Streets
Sycamore Maple (*Acer pseudoplatanus*)
Sugar Hackberry (*Celtis laevigata*)
*Katsura Tree (*Cercidiphyllum japonicum*)
White Ash (*Fraxinus americana*)
Green Ash (*Fraxinus pennsylvanica lanceolata*)
*Ginkgo (*Ginkgo biloba*)
Common Honey-Locust (*Gleditsia triacanthos*)
Tulip Tree (*Liriodendron tulipifera*)
*Eastern White Pine (*Pinus strobus*)
*London Plane Tree (*Platanus acerifolia*)
*Oriental Plane Tree (*Platanus orientalis*)
White Poplar (*Populus alba*)
Sargent Cherry (*Prunus sargenti*)
*Pin Oak (*Quercus palustris*)
Willow Oak (*Quercus phellos*)
Japanese Zelkova (*Zelkova serrata*)

Trees for Medium Streets
Norway Maple (*Acer platanoides*)
Mountain Silverbell (*Halesia monticola*)
*Sweet Gum (*Liquidambar styraciflua*)
Hop-Hornbeam (*Ostrya virginiana*)
*Sorrel Tree or Sourwood (*Oxydendrum arboreum*)
Simon Poplar (*Populus simoni*)
Scarlet Oak (*Quercus coccinea*)
Willow Oak (*Quercus phellos*)
*Black Locust (*Robinia pseudoacacia*)
Sassafras (*Sassafras albidum officinale*)
*Japanese Pagoda Tree (*Sophora japonica*)
*Linden species (*Tilia*)
Winged Elm (*Ulmus alata*)

Trees for Suburban Streets
Hedge Maple (*Acer campestre*)
Paperbark Maple (*Acer griseum*)
American Hornbeam (*Carpinus caroliniana*)
Pyramid European Hornbeam (*Carpinus betulus fastigiata*)
Globe European Hornbeam (*Carpinus betulus globosa*)
*Flowering Dogwood (*Cornus florida*)
*Hawthorn species (*Crataegus*)
Korean Evodia (*Evodia danielli*)
Carolina Silverbell (*Halesia carolina*)
*Golden Rain Tree (*Koelreuteria paniculata*)
Oriental Cherry (*Prunus serrulata*)
Columnar Sargent Cherry (*Prunus sargenti columnaris*)
Japanese Snowbell (*Styrax japonica*)
Fragrant Snowbell (*Styrax obassia*)
Smooth-leaved Elm varieties (*Ulmus carpinifolia*)

Soil Tolerance

Trees Tolerating Acid Soil
*Japanese Maple (*Acer palmatum* var.)
*Flowering Dogwood (*Cornus florida* var.)
Japanese Dogwood (*Cornus kousa*)
*European Beech (*Fagus sylvatica* var.)
Sweet Bay (*Magnolia virginiana*)
*Black Tupelo (*Nyssa sylvatica*)
*Sorrel Tree (*Oxydendrum arboreum*)
Red Oak (*Quercus borealis*)
Scarlet Oak (*Quercus coccinea*)
*Pin Oak (*Quercus palustris*)
Willow Oak (*Quercus phellos*)

Trees Tolerating Moist Soil
*Red Maple (*Acer rubrum*)
Alder species (*Alnus*)
Holly species (*Ilex*)
*Sweet Gum (*Liquidambar styraciflua*)
Sweet Bay (*Magnolia virginiana*)
*Black Tupelo or Black Gum (*Nyssa sylvatica*)
Swamp White Oak (*Quercus bicolor*)
*Willow species (*Salix*)
Common Bald Cypress (*Taxodium distichum*)
American Arbor-vitae (*Thuja occidentalis*)

Trees Tolerating Dry or Poor Soil
Box-Elder (*Acer negundo*)

*Tree of Heaven (*Ailanthus*)
Silk Tree (*Albizzia julibrissin*)
*Gray Birch (*Betula populifolia*)
European Hackberry (*Celtis australis*)
Russian Olive (*Elaeagnus angustifolia*)
Green Ash (*Fraxinus pennsylvanica*)
Modesto Ash (*Fraxinus velutina* "Modesto")
*Honey-Locust (*Gleditsia triacanthos* var.)
Western Red Cedar (*Juniperus scopulorum*)
Eastern Red Cedar (*Juniperus virginiana*)
*Golden Rain Tree (*Koelreuteria paniculata*)
Jack Pine (*Pinus banksiana*)
White Poplar (*Populus alba*)
*Black Locust (*Robinia pseudoacacia*)
Sassafras (*Sassafras albidum officinale*)
*Japanese Pagoda Tree (*Sophora japonica*)

Pest-Resistant Trees

*Tree of Heaven (*Ailanthus altissima*)
Hornbeam species (*Carpinus*)
*Cedar species (*Cedrus*)
European Hackberry (*Celtis australis*)
Cornelian Cherry (*Cornus mas*)
Japanese Cornel (*Cornus officinalis*)
American Smoke Tree (*Cotinus americanus*)
Russian Olive (*Elaeagnus angustifolia*)
Franklinia (*Franklinia alatamaha*)
*Ginkgo (*Ginkgo biloba*)
*Honey-Locust (*Gleditsia triacanthos*)
Juniper species (*Juniperus*)
*Golden Rain Tree (*Koelreuteria paniculata*)
*Laburnum species (*Laburnum*)
*Sweet Gum (*Liquidambar styraciflua*)
*Star Magnolia (*Magnolia stellata*)
Hop-Hornbeam species (*Ostrya*)

Trees for Seashore Planting

Norway Maple (*Acer platanoides*)
Sycamore Maple (*Acer pseudoplatanus*)
*Tree of Heaven (*Ailanthus*)
*Shadblow Serviceberry (*Amelanchier canadensis*)
Cockspur Thorn (*Crataegus crus-galli*)
English Hawthorn (*Crataegus oxyacantha*)
Washington Hawthorn (*Crataegus phaenopyrum*)
Cryptomeria (*Cryptomeria japonica*)
Russian Olive (*Elaeagnus angustifolia*)
Velvet Ash (*Fraxinus velutina*)
Thornless Honey-Locust (*Gleditsia triacanthos inermis* var.)
American Holly (*Ilex opaca*)
Eastern Red Cedar (*Juniperus virginiana*)
*Black Tupelo (*Nyssa sylvatica*)
Colorado Blue Spruce (*Picea pungens glauca*)
*Austrian Pine (*Pinus nigra*)
Pitch Pine (*Pinus rigida*)
Scotch Pine (*Pinus sylvestris*)
*Japanese Black Pine (*Pinus thunbergi*)
*London Plane Tree (*Platanus acerifolia*)
White Poplar (*Populus alba*)
Black Cherry (*Prunus serotina*)
*White Oak (*Quercus alba*)
*Black Locust (*Robinia pseudoacacia*)
Golden Weeping Willow (*Salix alba tristis*)
*Japanese Pagoda Tree (*Sophora japonica*)
American Arbor-vitae (*Thuja occidentalis*)
Oriental Arbor-vitae (*Thuja orientalis*)
*Little-leaf Linden (*Tilia cordata*)
*Crimean Linden (*Tilia euchlora*)
Chinese Elm (*Ulmus parvifolia*)

Trees for Hedging or Barriers

European Beech (*Fagus sylvatica*) prunes well.
Leyland Cypress (*Cupressocyparis leylandii*) withstands heavy pruning.
Hawthorn varieties (*Crataegus*) easily pruned, advantage of thorns.
Canadian Hemlock (*Tsuga canadensis*) evergreen.
American Holly (*Ilex opaca*) can be pruned.
European Hornbeam (*Carpinus betulus*) prunes well.

Little-leaf Linden (*Tilia cordata*) tolerates heavy pruning.
Hedge Maple (*Acer campestre*) can be pruned.

Austrian Pine (*Pinus nigra*) plant 10–12 feet on centers, staggered row.
Japanese Black Pine (*Pinus thunbergi*) plant 8 feet

on centers, staggered row.
Eastern White Pine (*Pinus strobus*) plant 15 feet on centers, staggered row.

NEW MEXICO

State Tree

Pinon Nut Pine (*Pinus edulis*)

Evergreen Trees

Fir species (*Abies*)
Tree Box (*Buxus sempervirens arborescens*)
★Deodar Cedar (*Cedrus deodara*)
False Cypress species (*Chamaecyparis*)
Arizona Cypress (*Cupressus arizonica bonita*)
Italian Cypress (*Cupressus sempervirens*)
Loquat (*Eriobotrya japonica*)
Holly species (*Ilex*)
Juniper species (*Juniperus*)
★Southern Magnolia (*Magnolia grandiflora*)
Chinese Photinia (*Photinia serrulata*)
★Spruce species (*Picea*)
★Pine species (*Pinus*)
★Live Oak (*Quercus virginiana*)
Arbor-vitae species (*Thuja*)
★Hemlock species (*Tsuga*)

Trees Classified by Height

20–35 Feet

★Japanese Maple (*Acer palmatum*)
Ohio Buckeye (*Aesculus glabra*)
Apple Serviceberry (*Amelanchier grandiflora*)
★Gray Birch (*Betula populifolia*)
European Hornbeam (*Carpinus betulus globosa*)
Mocker-Nut (*Carya tomentosa*)
Japanese Dogwood (*Cornus kousa*)
Cornelian Cherry (*Cornus mas*)
Japanese Cornel (*Cornus officinalis*)
American Smoke Tree (*Cotinus americanus*)
★Hawthorn species (*Crataegus*)
Russian Olive (*Elaeagnus angustifolia*)
Loquat (*Eriobotrya japonica*)
Euonymus species (*Euonymus*)
Common Fig (*Ficus carica*)
Flowering Ash (*Fraxinus ornus*)
Possum Haw (*Ilex decidua*)
Yaupon (*Ilex vomitoria*)
★Golden Rain Tree (*Koelreuteria paniculata*)
Crape-Myrtle (*Lagerstroemia indica*)
★Crab Apple species (*Malus*)
Choke Cherry (*Prunus virginiana melanocarpa*)
Almond-leaf Willow (*Salix amygdalina*)
★Babylon Weeping Willow (*Salix babylonica*)
Goat Willow (*Salix caprea*)
Showy Mountain Ash (*Sorbus decora*)
Snowberry Mountain Ash (*Sorbus discolor*)
Folgner Mountain Ash (*Sorbus folgneri*)
Japanese Tree Lilac (*Syringa amurensis japonica*)
Common Jujube or Chinese Date (*Zizyphus jujuba*)

35–75 Feet

Korean Fir (*Abies koreana*)
Box-Elder (*Acer negundo*)
★Red-fruited Tree of Heaven (*Ailanthus altissima erythrocarpa*)
Silk Tree (*Albizzia julibrissin*)
Red Alder (*Alnus rubra*)
★Shadblow Serviceberry (*Amelanchier laevis*)
★European Birch (*Betula pendula*)
Southern Catalpa (*Catalpa bignoniodes*)
Bunch Hackberry (*Celtis bungeana*)
Eastern Redbud (*Cercis canadensis*)
Chinese Redbud (*Cercis chinensis*)
★Flowering Dogwood (*Cornus florida*)
Largeleaf Dogwood (*Cornus macrophylla*)
Green Hawthorn (*Crataegus viridis*)
Arizona Cypress (*Cupressus arizonica*)
Italian Cypress (*Cupressus sempervirens*)

Common Persimmon (*Diospyros virginiana*)
Green Ash (*Fraxinus pennsylvanica lanceolata*)
English Holly (*Ilex aquifolium*)
Luster-leaf Holly (*Ilex latifolia*)
Heartnut (*Juglans sieboldiana cordiformis*)
Chinese Juniper (*Juniperus chinensis*)
Syrian Juniper (*Juniperus drupacea*)
Greek Juniper (*Juniperus excelsa*)
Alligator Juniper (*Juniperus pachyphloea*)
Osage-Orange (*Maclura pomifera*)
Siberian Crab Apple (*Malus baccata*)
"Cowichan" Crab Apple (*Malus* "Cowichan")
"Dolgo" Crab Apple (*Malus* "Dolgo")
"Makamik" Crab Apple (*Malus* "Makamik")
Cherry Crab Apple (*Malus robusta*)
"Sissipuk" Crab Apple (*Malus* "Sissipuk")
Chinaberry (*Melia azedarach*)
White Mulberry (*Morus alba*)
Dragon Spruce (*Picea asperata*)
Swiss Stone Pine (*Pinus cembra*)
Limber Pine (*Pinus flexilis*)
Scotch Pine (*Pinus sylvestris*)
Hardy Orange (*Poncirus trifoliata*)
Chinese Poplar (*Populus lasiocarpa*)
Simon Poplar (*Populus simoni*)
Sargent Cherry (*Prunus sargenti*)
Ussurian Pear (*Pyrus ussuriensis*)
Red Oak (*Quercus borealis*)
Scarlet Oak (*Quercus coccinea*)
★Pin Oak (*Quercus palustris*)
Willow Oak (*Quercus phellos*)
Canyon Live or Golden Cup Oak (*Quercus falcata*)
White Willow (*Salix alba*)
Wisconsin or Niobe Weeping Willow (*Salix blanda*)
Korean Mountain Ash (*Sorbus alnifolia*)
American Arbor-vitae (*Thuja occidentalis*)
Oriental Arbor-vitae (*Thuja orientalis*)
Japanese Arbor-vitae (*Thuja standishi*)
Winged or Wahoo Elm (*Ulmus alata*)
Chinese Elm (*Ulmus parvifolia*)
Siberian Elm (*Ulmus pumila*)

75 Feet or Over

Fir species (*Abies*)
Norway Maple (*Acer platanoides*)
★Red or Swamp Maple (*Acer rubrum*)
★Sugar Maple (*Acer saccharum*)
★Baumann Horse-Chestnut (*Aesculus hippocastanum baumanni*)
European Alder (*Alnus glutinosa*)
Pecan (*Carya pecan*)
★Cedar species (*Cedrus*)
Sugar Hackberry (*Celtis laevigata*)
White Ash (*Fraxinus americana*)
European Ash (*Fraxinus excelsior*)
Oregon Ash (*Fraxinus oregona*)
★Ginkgo or Maidenhair Tree (*Ginkgo biloba*)
★Common Honey-Locust (*Gleditsia triacanthos*)
Kentucky Coffee Tree (*Gymnocladus dioicus*)
English or Persian Walnut (*Juglans regia*)
Mexican Walnut (*Juglans major*)
★Sweet Gum (*Liquidambar styraciflua*)
Tulip Tree or Yellow Poplar (*Liriodendron tulipifera*)
★Southern Magnolia (*Magnolia grandiflora*)
★Black Gum or Black Tupelo (*Nyssa sylvatica*)
Spruce species (*Picea*)
★Pine species (*Pinus*)
★Plane Tree species (*Platanus wrightii*)
Poplar species (*Populus*)
Sargent Cherry (*Prunus sargenti*)
Black or Rum Cherry (*Prunus serotina*)
★Oak species (*Quercus*)

Giant Arbor-vitae (*Thuja plicata*)
★Linden species (*Tilia*)
★Canada Hemlock (*Tsuga canadensis*)
Western Hemlock (*Tsuga heterophylla*)
★Elm species (*Ulmus*)
Japanese Zelkova (*Zelkova serrata*)

Trees Classified by Form

Pyramidal

Fir species (*Abies*)
★Birch species (*Betula*)
★Cedar species (*Cedrus*)
Italian Cypress (*Cupressus sempervirens*)
English Holly (*Ilex aquifolium*)
American Holly (*Ilex opaca*)
Rocky Mountain Juniper (*Juniperus scopulorum*)
★Sweet Gum (*Liquidambar styraciflua*)
★Magnolia species (*Magnolia*)
Spruce species (*Picea*)
Swiss Stone Pine (*Pinus cembra*)
Korean Pine (*Pinus koraiensis*)
Pyramid Austrian Pine (*Pinus nigra pyramidalis*)
Japanese White Pine (*Pinus parviflora*)
Red or Norway Pine (*Pinus resinosa*)
Bolleana Poplar (*Populus alba pyramidalis*)
★Pin Oak (*Quercus palustris*)
Arbor-vitae species (*Thuja*)
★Linden species (*Tilia*)
★Hemlock species (*Tsuga*)

Columnar

Ascending Norway Maple (*Acer platanoides ascendens*)
Columnar Norway Maple (*Acer platanoides columnare*)
Erect Norway Maple (*Acer platanoides erectum*)
Columnar Red Maple (*Acer rubrum columnare*)
Sentry Maple (*Acer saccharum columnare*)
Fastigiate Washington Hawthorn (*Crataegus phaenopyrum fastigiata*)
Sentry Ginkgo (*Ginkgo biloba fastigiata*)
Blue Columnar Chinese Juniper (*Juniperus chinensis columnaris*)
Schott Red Cedar (*Juniperus virginiana schotti*)
Swiss Stone Pine (*Pinus cembra*)
Fastigiate Scotch Pine (*Pinus sylvestris fastigiata*)
Lombardy Poplar (*Populus nigra italica*)
Fastigiate Simon Poplar (*Populus simoni fastigiata*)
Columnar Sargent Cherry (*Prunus sargenti columnaris*)
"Amanogawa" Cherry (*Prunus serrulata* "Amanogawa")
Shipmast Locust (*Robinia pseudoacacia rectissima*)
Douglas Arbor-vitae (*Thuja occidentalis douglasi pyramidalis*)
Fastigiate American Arbor-vitae (*Thuja occidentalis fastigiata*)
★American Elm varieties (*Ulmus americana*)

Weeping

Slender European Birch (*Betula pendula tristis*)
Young's Birch (*Betula pendula youngi*)
★Deodar Cedar (*Cedrus deodara*)
"Excellenz Thiel" Crab Apple (*Malus* "Excellenz Thiel")
"Oekonomierat Echtermeyer" Crab Apple (*Malus* "Oekonomierat Echtermeyer")
Weeping Mulberry (*Morus alba pendula*)
Koster Weeping Blue Spruce (*Picea pungens kosteriana*)
Weeping Black Cherry (*Prunus serotina pendula*)
Weeping Higan Cherry (*Prunus subhirtella pendula*)
"Yaeshidare" Cherry (*Prunus subhirtella pendula flora*)

Weeping Yoshino Cherry (*Prunus yedoensis perpendens*)
Golden Weeping Willow (*Salix alba tristis*)
*Babylon Weeping Willow (*Salix babylonica*)
Wisconsin or Niobe Weeping Willow (*Salix blanda*)
Thurlow Weeping Willow (*Salix elegantissima*)
Weeping European Mountain Ash (*Sorbus aucuparia pendula*)
Weeping American Elm (*Ulmus americana pendula*)

Rounded or Globe-Shaped
*Japanese Maple (*Acer palmatum*)
Globe Norway Maple (*Acer platanoides globosum*)
Bunch Hackberry (*Celtis bungeana*)
Cornelian Cherry (*Cornus mas*)
*Crab Apple species (*Malus*)
Umbrella Black Locust (*Robinia pseudoacacia umbraculifera*)
Globe Smooth-leaved Elm (*Ulmus carpinifolia umbraculifera*)

With Horzontal Branching
Fir species (*Abies*)
Silk Tree (*Albizzia julibrissin*)
*Cedar species (*Cedrus*)
*Flowering Dogwood (*Cornus florida*)
Japanese Dogwood (*Cornus kousa*)
*Hawthorn species (*Crataegus*)
*Black Gum or Black Tupelo (*Nyssa sylvatica*)
Spruce species (*Picea*)
Japanese Red Pine (*Pinus densiflora*)
*Pin Oak (*Quercus palustris*)
*Live Oak (*Quercus virginiana*)

Trees Classified by Color of Blossom

Yellow
*Golden Rain Tree (*Koelreuteria paniculata*)

White
*Shadblow Serviceberry (*Amelanchier canadensis*)
Strawberry Tree (*Arbutus unedo*)
White Redbud (*Cercis canadensis alba*)
Japanese Dogwood (*Cornus kousa*)
Washington Hawthorn (*Crataegus phaenopyrum*)
*Southern Magnolia (*Magnolia grandiflora*)
Arnold Crab Apple (*Malus arnoldiana*)
Siberian Crab Apple (*Malus baccata*)
Tea Crab Apple (*Malus hupehensis*)
Sargent Crab Apple (*Malus sargenti*)
Chinese Photinia (*Photinia serrulata*)
Hardy-Orange (*Poncirus trifoliata*)
Thundercloud Plum (*Prunus cerasifera* "Thundercloud")
Sour Cherry (*Prunus cerasus*)
Mount Fuji Cherry (*Prunus serrulata* "Shirotae")
Yoshino Cherry (*Prunus yedoensis*)
Bradford Callery Pear (*Pyrus calleryana bradfordi*)
*Common Pear (*Pyrus communis*)
*Japanese Pagoda Tree (*Sophora japonica*)
American Mountain Ash (*Sorbus americana*)
European Mountain Ash (*Sorbus aucuparia*)
Showy Mountain Ash (*Sorbus decora*)

Pink
Wither's Pink Redbud (*Cercis canadensis* "Wither's Pink Charm")
Red Flowering Dogwood (*Cornus florida rubra*)
Ingleside Crape-Myrtle (*Lagerstroemia indica* "Ingleside Pink")
Katherine Crab Apple (*Malus* "Katherine")
Prince Georges Crab Apple (*Malus* "Prince Georges")
*Common Apple (*Malus pumila*)
Blireiana Plum (*Prunus blireiana*)
Sargent Cherry (*Prunus sargenti*)
Amanogawa Cherry (*Prunus serrulata* "Amanogawa")
Kwanzan Cherry (*Prunus serrulata* "Kwanzan")
Autumn Cherry (*Prunus subhirtella autumnalis*)
Weeping Cherry (*Prunus subhirtella pendula*)

Red
Paul's Scarlet Hawthorn (*Crataegus oxyacantha pauli*)
Red Crape-Myrtle (*Lagerstroemia indica* "Wm. Toovey")
Almey Crab Apple (*Malus* "Almey")
Carmine Crab Apple (*Malus atrosanguinea*)

Trees with Bright Red Fruit
*Flowering Dogwood (*Cornus florida*)
Japanese Dogwood (*Cornus kousa*)
Downy Hawthorn (*Crataegus mollis*)
Washington Hawthorn (*Crataegus phaenopyrum*)
American Holly (*Ilex opaca*)
Almey Crab Apple (*Malus* "Almey")
*Siberian Crab Apple (*Malus baccata*)
Hopa Crab Apple (*Malus* "Hopa")
*Common Apple (*Malus pumila*)
Sargent Crab Apple (*Malus sargenti*)
Korean Mountain Ash (*Sorbus alnifolia*)

Trees Classified by Color of Summer Foliage

Blue
White Fir (*Abies concolor*)
Blue Atlas Cedar (*Cedrus atlantica glauca*)
Western Red Cedar (*Juniperus scopulorum* var. Chandler Blue)
Eastern Red Cedar (*Juniperus virginiana* var. *Burki*)
Blue Spruce (*Picea pungens*)

Silver to Gray
Russian Olive (*Elaeagnus angustifolia*)
White Poplar (*Populus alba*)

Red to Purple
Blood-leaf Japanese Maple (*Acer palmatum atropurpureum*)
Crimson King Maple (*Acer platanoides* "Crimson King")
Schwedler Maple (*Acer platanoides schwedleri*)
Purple-leaf Sycamore Maple (*Acer pseudoplatanus*)
Rubylace Honey-Locust (*Gleditsia triacanthos inermis* "Rubylace")
Purple Crab Apple (*Malus purpurea*)
Blireiana Plum (*Prunus blireiana*)
Pissard Plum (*Prunus cerasifera atropurpurea*)
Thundercloud Plum (*Prunus cerasifera nigra* "Thundercloud")

Trees Classified by Color of Fall Foliage

Yellow
Norway Maple (*Acer platanoides*)
*Sugar Maple (*Acer saccharum*)
Apple Serviceberry (yellow-orange) (*Amelanchier grandiflora*)
*Birch species (*Betula*)
Hickory species (*Carya*)
Chinese Chestnut (*Castanea mollissima*)
Redbud species (*Cercis*)
White Ash (purple to yellow) (*Fraxinus americana*)
*Ginkgo (*Ginkgo biloba*)
Quaking Aspen (*Populus tremuloides*)
*Willow species (*Salix*)

Red
Amur Maple (*Acer ginnala*)
*Japanese Maple (*Acer palmatum*)
*Red Maple (*Acer rubrum*)
*Sugar Maple (*Acer saccharum*)
*Shadblow Serviceberry (*Amelanchier canadensis*)
*Flowering Dogwood (*Cornus florida*)
Japanese Dogwood (*Cornus kousa*)
Pacific Dogwood (*Cornus nuttalli*)
American Smoke Tree (*Cotinus americanus*)
Washington Hawthorn (*Crataegus phaenopyrum*)
*Sweet Gum (*Liquidambar styraciflua*)
Dawson Crab Apple (*Malus dawsoniana*)
*Black Gum or Black Tupelo (*Nyssa sylvatica*)
*Cherry species (*Prunus*)
Red Oak (*Quercus borealis*)

*Pin Oak (*Quercus palustris*)

Purple
White Ash (*Fraxinus americana*)
*Sweet Gum (*Liquidambar styraciflua*)
*Common Pear (*Pyrus communis*)

Trees with Interesting Bark

Gray
*Red Maple (*Acer rubrum*)
*Serviceberry species (*Amelanchier*)
Hackberry species (*Celtis*)
*Hawthorn species (*Crataegus*)
American Holly (*Ilex opaca*)
English or Persian Walnut (*Juglans regia*)
Red Oak (*Quercus borealis*)
Black Oak (*Quercus velutina*)
Mountain Ash species (*Sorbus*)

White
*European Birch (*Betula pendula*)
Quaking Aspen (*Populus tremuloides*)

Red
Japanese Red Pine (*Pinus densiflora*)
Red or Norway Pine (*Pinus resinosa*)
Scotch Pine (*Pinus sylvestris*)

Reddish Brown
Sargent Cherry (*Prunus sargenti*)

Yellow
Wisconsin or Niobe Weeping Willow (*Salix blanda*)

Green
*Babylon Weeping Willow (*Salix babylonica*)

Flaking
Russian Olive (*Elaeagnus angustifolia*)
Crape-Myrtle (*Lagerstroemia indica*)
*Plane Tree species (*Platanus*)

Trees for the City
White Fir (*Abies concolor*)
Box-Elder (*Acer negundo*)
Norway Maple (*Acer platanoides*)
Sycamore Maple (*Acer pseudoplatanus*)
*Horse-Chestnut or Buckeye (*Aesculus*)
*Tree of Heaven (*Ailanthus*)
Silk Tree (*Albizzia julibrissin*)
Catalpa (*Catalpa*)
Hackberry (*Celtis*)
Washington Hawthorn (*Crataegus phaenopyrum*)
Russian Olive (*Elaeagnus angustifolia*)
White Ash (*Fraxinus americana*)
European Ash (*Fraxinus excelsior*)
Green Ash (*Fraxinus pennsylvanica lanceolata*)
*Ginkgo (*Ginkgo biloba*)
Thornless Honey-Locust (*Gleditsia triacanthos inermis*)
*Golden Rain Tree (*Koelreuteria paniculata*)
*Southern Magnolia (*Magnolia grandiflora*)
*Crab Apple species (*Malus*)
Chinaberry (*Melia azedarach*)
Colorado Blue Spruce (*Picea pungens*)
London Plane Tree (*Platanus acerifolia*)
Bradford Callery Pear (*Pyrus calleryana bradfordi*)
*Japanese Pagoda Tree (*Sophora japonica*)
Village Green Zelkova (*Zelkova serrata* "Village Green")

Trees for Wide Streets
Sycamore Maple (*Acer pseudoplatanus*)
Sugar Hackberry (*Celtis laevigata*)
White Ash (*Fraxinus americana*)
Green Ash (*Fraxinus pennsylvanica lanceolata*)
*Ginkgo (*Ginkgo biloba*)
Common Honey-Locust (*Gleditsia triacanthos*)
*Southern Magnolia (*Magnolia grandiflora*)
*Eastern White Pine (*Pinus strobus*)
*London Plane Tree (*Platanus acerifolia*)
*Oriental Plane Tree (*Platanus orientalis*)
California Plane Tree (*Platanus racemosa*)
White Poplar (*Populus alba*)

Sargent Cherry (*Prunus sargenti*)
*Pin Oak (*Quercus palustris*)
Japanese Zelkova (*Zelkova serrata*)

Trees for Medium Streets
Norway Maple (*Acer platanoides*)
*Sweet Gum (*Liquidambar styraciflua*)
Chinaberry (*Melia azedarach*)
Simon Poplar (*Populus simoni*)
*Black Locust (*Robinia pseudoacacia*)
*Japanese Pagoda Tree (*Sophora japonica*)
*Linden species (*Tilia*)
Winged Elm (*Ulmus alata*)

Trees for Suburban Streets
Globe Norway Maple (*Acer platanoides globosum*)
*Flowering Dogwood (*Cornus florida*)
*Hawthorn species (*Crataegus*)
*Golden Rain Tree (*Koelreuteria paniculata*)
Columnar Sargent Cherry (*Prunus sargenti columnare*)
Oriental Cherry (*Prunus serrulata*)
Smooth-leaved Elm varieties (*Ulmus carpinifolia*)

Soil Tolerance

Trees Tolerating Moist Soil
*Red Maple (*Acer rubrum*)
Alder species (*Alnus*)
Holly species (*Ilex*)
*Sweet Gum (*Liquidambar styraciflua*)

*Black Gum or Black Tupelo (*Nyssa sylvatica*)
*Willow species (*Salix*)
American Arbor-vitae (*Thuja occidentalis*)

Trees Tolerating Dry or Poor Soil
Box-Elder (*Acer negundo*)
*Tree of Heaven (*Ailanthus*)
Silk Tree (*Albizzia julibrissin*)
*Gray Birch (*Betula populifolia*)
European Hackberry (*Celtis australis*)
Russian Olive (*Elaeagnus angustifolia*)
Green Ash (*Fraxinus pennsylvanica lanceolata*)
Modesto Ash (*Fraxinus pennsylvanica lanceolata*)
*Honey-Locust (*Gleditsia triacanthos*)
Western Red Cedar (*Juniperus scopulorum*)
Eastern Red Cedar (*Juniperus virginiana*)
*Golden Rain Tree (*Koelreuteria paniculata*)
Chinaberry (*Melia azedarach*)
Jack Pine (*Pinus banksiana*)
Piñon Pine (*Pinus edulis*)
White Poplar (*Populus alba*)
*Black Locust (*Robinia pseudoacacia*)
*Japanese Pagoda Tree (*Sophora japonica*)
Siberian Elm (*Ulmus pumila*)

Pest-Resistant Trees
*Tree of Heaven (*Ailanthus altissima*)
*Cedar species (*Cedrus*)
European Hackberry (*Celtis australis*)
Cornelian Cherry (*Cornus mas*)

Japanese Cornel (*Cornus officinalis*)
American Smoke Tree (*Cotinus americanus*)
Russian Olive (*Elaeagnus angustifolia*)
Fig species (*Ficus*)
*Ginkgo (*Ginkgo biloba*)
*Honey-Locust (*Gleditsia triacanthos*)
Kentucky Coffee Tree (*Gymnocladus dioicus*)
Juniper species (*Juniperus*)
*Golden Rain Tree (*Koelreuteria paniculata*)
*Sweet Gum (*Liquidambar styraciflua*)

Trees for Hedging or Barriers
European Beech (*Fagus sylvatica*) prunes well.
Leyland Cypress (*Cupressocyparis leylandii*) withstands heavy pruning.
Hawthorn varieties (*Crataegus*) easily pruned, advantage of thorns.
Canadian Hemlock (*Tsuga canadensis*) evergreen.
American Holly (*Ilex opaca*) can be pruned.
European Hornbeam (*Carpinus betulus*) prunes well.
Little-leaf Linden (*Tilia cordata*) tolerates heavy pruning.
Hedge Maple (*Acer campestre*) can be pruned.
Austrian Pine (*Pinus nigra*) plant 10–12 feet on centers, staggered row.
Japanese Black Pine (*Pinus thunbergi*) plant 8 feet on centers, staggered row.
Eastern White Pine (*Pinus strobus*) plant 15 feet on centers, staggered row.

NEW YORK

State Tree
*Sugar Maple (*Acer saccharum*)

Evergreen Trees

Fir species (*Abies*)
Tree Box (*Buxus sempervirens arborescens*)
*Cedar species (*Cedrus*)
False Cypress species (*Chamaecyparis*)
Holly species (*Ilex opaca*)
Juniper species (*Juniperus*)
*Larch species (*Larix*)
Spruce species (*Picea*)
*Pine species (*Pinus*)
*Douglas Fir (*Pseudotsuga menziesii*)
Umbrella Pine (*Sciadopitys verticillata*)
Arbor-vitae species (*Thuja*)
*Hemlock species (*Tsuga*)

Trees Classified by Height

20–35 Feet
Argutum Maple (*Acer argutum*)
Hedge Maple (*Acer campestre*)
Hornbeam Maple (*Acer carpinifolium*)
Amur Maple (*Acer ginnala*)
Paperbark Maple (*Acer griseum*)
Manchurian Maple (*Acer mandshuricum*)
*Japanese Maple (*Acer palmatum*)
Mountain Maple (*Acer spicatum*)
Tatarian Maple (*Acer tataricum*)
Ohio Buckeye (*Aesculus glabra*)
*Shadblow Serviceberry (*Amelanchier canadensis*)
Apple Serviceberry (*Amelanchier laevis*)
*Gray Birch (*Betula populifolia*)
European Hornbeam (*Carpinus betulus globosa*)
Redbud (*Cercis canadensis*)
Japanese Dogwood (*Cornus kousa*)
*Hawthorn species (*Crataegus*)
Russian Olive (*Elaeagnus angustifolia*)
Franklinia (*Franklinia alatamaha*)
Flowering Ash (*Fraxinus ornus*)
Carolina Silverbell (*Halesia carolina*)
Longstalk Holly (*Ilex pedunculosa*)
Needle Juniper (*Juniperus rigida*)
*Golden Rain Tree (*Koelreuteria paniculata*)
*Laburnum species (*Laburnum*)

*Saucer Magnolia (*Magnolia soulangeana*)
*Star Magnolia (*Magnolia stellata*)
*Crab Apple species (*Malus*)
*Sorrel Tree (*Oxydendrum arboreum*)
*Cherry species (*Prunus*)
*Babylon Weeping Willow (*Salix babylonica*)
Laurel Willow (*Salix pentandra*)
Sassafras (*Sassafras albidum officinale*)
Showy Mountain Ash (*Sorbus decora*)

35–75 Feet
Box-Elder (*Acer negundo*)
Striped Maple or Moosewood (*Acer pennsylvanicum*)
Norway Maple (*Acer platanoides*)
Sycamore Maple (*Acer pseudoplatanus*)
Red or Swamp Maple (*Acer rubrum*)
*Baumann Horse-Chestnut (*Aesculus hippocastanum baumanni*)
*Red-fruited Tree of Heaven (*Ailanthus altissima erythrocarpo*)
Italian Alder (*Alnus cordata*)
European Alder (*Alnus glutinosa*)
Sweet Birch (*Betula lenta*)
River Birch (*Betula nigra*)
*European Birch (*Betula pendula*)
Common Paper-Mulberry (*Broussonetia papyrifera*)
European Hornbeam (*Carpinus betulus*)
American Hornbeam (*Carpinus caroliniana*)
Japanese Hornbeam (*Carpinus japonica*)
Chinese Chestnut (*Castanea mollissima*)
Southern Catalpa (*Catalpa bignonioides*)
*Katsura Tree (*Cercidiphyllum japonicum*)
*American Yellow-wood (*Cladrastis lutea*)
*Flowering Dogwood (*Cornus florida*)
Turkish Filbert (*Corylus columa*)
Cockspur Thorn (*Crataegus crus-galli*)
Green Ash (*Fraxinus pennsylvanica lanceolata*)
Eastern Larch or Tamarack (*Larix laricina*)
Yulan Magnolia (*Magnolia denudata*)
Fraser Magnolia (*Magnolia fraseri*)
Kobus Magnolia (*Magnolia kobus borealis*)
Sweet Bay (*Magnolia virginiana*)
White Mulberry (*Morus alba*)

Persian Parrotia (*Parrotia persica*)
Empress Tree (*Paulownia tomentosa*)
*Amur Cork (*Phellodendron amurense*)
Black Hills Spruce (*Picea glauca densata*)
Jack Pine (*Pinus banksiana*)
Lacebark Pine (*Pinus bungeana*)
Swiss Stone Pine (*Pinus cembra*)
Limber Pine (*Pinus flexilis*)
Pitch Pine (*Pinus rigida*)
Scotch Pine (*Pinus sylvestris*)
Simon Poplar (*Populus simoni*)
Sargent Cherry (*Prunus sargenti*)
Yoshino Cherry (*Prunus yedoensis*)
Swamp White Oak (*Quercus bicolor*)
Red Oak (*Quercus borealis*)
Scarlet Oak (*Quercus coccinea*)
Shingle Oak (*Quercus imbricaria*)
*Pin Oak (*Quercus palustris*)
Willow Oak (*Quercus phellos*)
White Willow (*Salix alba*)
Wisconsin or Niobe Weeping Willow (*Salix blanda*)
Elaeagnus Willow (*Salix elaeagnos*)
Thurlow Weeping Willow (*Salix elegantissima*)
Korean Mountain Ash (*Sorbus alnifolia*)
White Beam Mountain Ash (*Sorbus aria*)
European Mountain Ash or Rowan Tree (*Sorbus aucuparia*)
Korean Stewartia (*Stewartia koreana*)
Japanese Stewartia (*Stewartia pseudo-camellia*)
American Arbor-vitae (*Thuja occidentalis*)
Japanese Arbor-vitae (*Thuja standishi*)
*Crimean Linden (*Tilia euchlora*)
Carolina Hemlock (*Tsuga caroliniana*)
Chinese Elm (*Ulmus parvifolia*)
Siberian Elm (*Ulmus pumila*)

75 Feet or Over
Fir species (*Abies*)
*Sugar Maple (*Acer saccharum*)
*Canoe Birch (*Betula papyrifera*)
Hickory species (*Carya*)
*Cedar species (*Cedrus*)
European Hackberry (*Celtis australis*)
Sugar Hackberry (*Celtis laevigata*)

*Katsura Tree (*Cercidiphyllum japonicum*)
False Cypress species (*Chamaecyparis*)
*Beech species (*Fagus*)
White Ash (*Fraxinus americana*)
*Ginkgo or Maidenhair Tree (*Ginkgo biloba*)
*Common Honey-Locust (*Gleditsia triacanthos*)
Kentucky Coffee Tree (*Gymnocladus dioicus*)
Eastern Black Walnut (*Juglans nigra*)
Kalopanax (*Kalopanax pictus*)
*European Larch (*Larix decidua*)
Japanese Larch (*Larix leptolepis*)
*Sweet Gum (*Liquidambar styraciflua*)
Tulip Tree or Yellow Poplar (*Liriodendron tulipifera*)
Cucumber Tree (*Magnolia acuminata*)
Dawn Redwood (*Metasequoia glyptostroboides*)
*Black Gum or Black Tupelo (*Nyssa sylvatica*)
Spruce species (*Picea*)
*Pine species (*Pinus*)
*Plane Tree species (*Platanus*)
Poplar species (*Populus*)
Black or Rum Cherry (*Prunus serotina*)
*Douglas Fir (*Pseudotsuga menziesii*)
*Oak species (*Quercus*)
*Linden species (*Tilia*)
*Canada Hemlock (*Tsuga canadensis*)
*Elm species (*Ulmus*)

Trees Classified by Form

Pyramidal
Fir species (*Abies*)
*Birch species (*Betula*)
*Cedar species (*Cedrus*)
False Cypress species (*Chamaecyparis*)
Crytomeria (*Cryptomeria japonica*)
American Holly (*Ilex opaca*)
Juniper or Red Cedar species (*Juniperus*)
*Larch species (*Larix*)
*Sweet Gum (*Liquidambar styraciflua*)
*Magnolia species (*Magnolia*)
Dawn Redwood (*Metasequoia glyptostroboides*)
Hop-Hornbeam (*Ostrya virginiana*)
Spruce species (*Picea*)
Swiss Stone Pine (*Pinus cembra*)
Korean Pine (*Pinus koraiensis*)
Pyramidal Austrian Pine (*Pinus nigra pyramidalis*)
Japanese White Pine (*Pinus parviflora*)
Red or Norway Pine (*Pinus resinosa*)
Golden Larch (*Pseudolarix amabilis*)
*Douglas Fir (*Pseudotsuga menziesii*)
Turkey Oak (*Quercus cerris*)
*Pin Oak (*Quercus palustris*)
Umbrella Pine (*Sciadopitys verticillata*)
Korean Stewartia (*Stewartia koreana*)
Common Bald Cypress (*Taxodium distichum*)
Arbor-vitae species (*Thuja*)
*Linden species (*Tilia*)
*Hemlock species (*Tsuga*)
Smooth-leaved Elm varieties (*Ulmus carpinifolia*)

Columnar
Ascending Norway Maple (*Acer platanoides ascendens*)
Columnar Norway Maple (*Acer platanoides columnare*)
Erect Norway Maple (*Acer platanoides erectum*)
Columnar Red Maple (*Acer rubrum columnare*)
Sentry Maple (*Acer saccharum monumentale*)
Fastigiate European Birch (*Betula pendula fastigiata*)
Fastigiate European Hornbeam (*Carpinus betulus fastigiata*)
Column Hinoki Cypress (*Chamaecyparis obtusa erecta*)
Fastigiate Washington Hawthorn (*Crataegus phaenopyrum fastigiata*)
Dawyck Beech (*Fagus sylvatica fastigiata*)
Sentry Ginkgo (*Ginkgo biloba fastigiata*)
Blue Columnar Chinese Juniper (*Juniperus chinensis columnaris*)
Schott Red Cedar (*Juniperus virginiana schotti*)
Swiss Stone Pine (*Pinus cembra*)
Fastigiate White Pine (*Pinus strobus fastigiata*)

Fastigiate Scotch Pine (*Pinus sylvestris fastigiata*)
Bolleana Poplar (*Populus alba pyramidalis*)
*Lombardy Poplar (*Populus nigra italica*)
Fastigiate Simon Poplar (*Populus simoni fastigiata*)
Columnar Sargent Cherry (*Prunus sargenti columnaris*)
"Amanogawa" Cherry (*Prunus serrulata* "Amanogawa")
Fastigiate English Oak (*Quercus robur fastigiata*)
Shipmast Locust (*Robinia pseudoacacia rectissima*)
Upright European Mountain Ash (*Sorbus aucuparia fastigiata*)
Common Bald Cypress (*Taxodium distichum*)
Douglas Arbor-vitae (*Thuja occidentalis douglasi pyramidalis*)
Fastigiate American Arbor-vitae (*Thuja occidentalis fastigiata*)
Columnar Big-leaf Linden (*Tilia platyphyllos fastigiata*)

Weeping
Slender European Birch (*Bteula pendula tristis*)
Weeping European Hornbeam (*Carpinus betulus pendula*)
*Weeping Beech (*Fagus sylvatica pendula*)
Weeping Purple Beech (*Fagus sylvatica purpureopendula*)
Weeping Red Cedar (*Juniperus virginiana pendula*)
Weeping Larch (*Larix decidua pendula*)
"Exzellenz Thiel" Crab Apple (*Malus* "Exzellenz Thiel")
"Oekonomierat Echtermeyer" Crab Apple (*Malus* "Oekonomierat Echtermeyer")
Weeping Mulberry (*Morus alba pendula*)
Koster Weeping Blue Spruce (*Picea pungens kosteriana*)
Weeping White Pine (*Pinus strobus pendula*)
Weeping Japanese Apricot (*Prunus mume pendula*)
Weeping Black Cherry (*Prunus serotina pendula*)
Weeping Higan Cherry (*Prunus subhirtella pendula*)
"Yaeshidare" Cherry (*Prunus subhirtella pendula flora plena*)
Weeping Yoshino Cherry (*Prunus yedoensis perpendens*)
Weeping Douglas Fir (*Pseudotsuga menziesii pendula*)
Golden Weeping Willow (*Salix alba tristis*)
*Babylon Weeping Willow (*Salix babylonica*)
Wisconsin or Niobe Weeping Willow (*Salix blanda*)
Thurlow Weeping Willow (*Salix elegantissima*)
Weeping Japanese Pagoda Tree (*Sophora japonica pendula*)
Weeping European Mountain Ash (*Sorbus aucuparia pendula*)
Weeping Folgner Mountain Ash (*Sorbus folgneri pendula*)
Pendant Silver Linden (*Tilia petiolaris*)
Sargent Hemlock (*Tsuga canadensis pendula*)
Weeping American Elm (*Ulmus americana pendula*)

Rounded or Globe-Shaped
*Japanese Maple (*Acer palmatum*)
Globe Norway Maple (*Acer platanoides globosum*)
Globe European Hornbeam (*Carpinus betulus globosa*)
Bunch Hackberry (*Celtis bungeana*)
Single Seed Hawthorn (*Crataegus monogyna inermis*)
*Beech species (*Fagus*)
*Saucer Magnolia (*Magnolia soulangeana*)
*Crab Apple species (*Malus*)
*White Oak (*Quercus alba*)
Umbrella Black Locust (*Robinia pseudoacacia umbraculifera*)
Sargent Hemlock (*Tsuga canadensis sargenti*)
Koopmann Elm (*Ulmus carpinifolia koopmanni*)
Globe Smooth-leaved Elm (*Ulmus carpinifolia umbraculifera*)

With Horizontal Branching
Fir species (*Abies*)

Silk Tree (*Albizzia julibrissin*)
*Cedar species (*Cedrus*)
Eastern Redbud (*Cercis canadensis*)
*Flowering Dogwood (*Cornus florida*)
Japanese Dogwood (*Cornus kousa*)
*Hawthorn species (*Crataegus*)
Dawn Redwood (*Metasequoia glyptostroboides*)
*Black Tupelo or Black Gum (*Nyssa sylvatica*)
Spruce species (*Picea*)
Japanese Red Pine (*Pinus densiflora*)
*Eastern White Pine (*Pinus strobus*)
*White Oak (*Quercus alba*)
*Pin Oak (*Quercus palustris*)
Common Bald Cypress (*Taxodium distichum*)

Trees Classified by Color of Blossom

Yellow
*Golden Rain Tree (*Koelreuteria paniculata*)
*Laburnum (*Larbunum vossi*)

White
*Shadblow Serviceberry (*Amelanchier canadensis*)
Whitebud (*Cercis canadensis alba*)
*American Yellow-wood (*Cladrastis lutea*)
Japanese Dogwood (*Cornus kousa*)
Washington Hawthorn (*Crataegus phaenopyrum*)
Carolina Silverbell (*Halesia carolina*)
Yulan Magnolia (*Magnolia denudata*)
*Star Magnolia (*Magnolia stellata*)
Arnold Crab Apple (*Malus arnoldiana*)
*Siberian Crab Apple (*Malus baccata*)
Tea Crab Apple (*Malus hupehensis*)
Sargent Crab Apple (*Malus sargenti*)
*Sorrel Tree (*Oxydendrum arboreum*)
Hardy Orange (*Poncirus trifoliata*)
Thundercloud Plum (*Prunus cerasifera* "Thundercloud")
Sour Cherry (*Prunus cerasus*)
Mount Fiji Cherry (*Prunus serrulata* "Shirotae")
Yoshino Cherry (*Prunus yedoensis*)
Bradford Callery Pear (*Pyrus calleryana bradfordi*)
*Common Pear (*Pyrus communis*)
*Japanese Pagoda Tree (*Sophora japonica*)
Korean Mountain Ash (*Sorbus alnifolia*)
American Mountain Ash (*Sorbus americana*)
European Mountain Ash (*Sorbus aucuparia*)
Showy Mountain Ash (*Sorbus decora*)
Japanese Stewartia (*Stewartia pseudocamellia*)
Japanese Snowbell (*Styrax japonica*)

Pink
Wither's Pink Redbud (*Cercis canadensis* "Wither's Pink Charm")
Red Flowering Dogwood (*Cornus florida rubra*)
Toba Hawthorn (*Crataegus mordenensis* "Toba")
*Saucer Magnolia (*Magnolia soulangeana*)
Japanese Flowering Crab Apple (*Malus floribunda*)
Katherine Crab Apple (*Malus* "Katherine")
Prince Georges Crab Apple (*Malus* "Prince Georges")
*Common Apple (*Malus pumila*)
Blireiana Plum (*Prunus blireiana*)
Sargent Cherry (*Prunus sargenti*)
Kwanzan Cherry (*Prunus serrulata* "Kwanzan")
Autumn Cherry (*Prunus subhirtella autumnalis*)
Weeping Cherry (*Prunus subhirtella pendula*)

Red
Ruby Horse-Chestnut (*Aesculus carnea briotti*)
Paul's Scarlet Hawthorn (*Crataegus oxyacantha pauli*)
Alexandrina Magnolia (*Magnolia soulangeana* "Alexandrina")
Almey Crab Apple (*Malus* "Almey")
Carmine Crab Apple (*Malus atrosanguinea*)

Trees with Bright Red Fruit
*Flowering Dogwood (*Cornus florida*)
Japanese Dogwood (*Cornus kousa*)
Downy Hawthorn (*Crataegus phaenopyrum*)
American Holly (*Ilex opaca*)
Almey Crab Apple (*Malus* "Almey")

Siberian Crab Apple (*Malus baccata*)
Hopa Crab Apple (*Malus* "Hopa")
*Common Apple (*Malus pumila*)
Sargent Crab Apple (*Malus sargenti*)
Korean Mountain Ash (*Sorbus alnifolia*)
American Mountain Ash (*Sorbus americana*)
European Mountain Ash (*Sorbus aucuparia*)
Showy Mountain Ash (*Sorbus decora*)

Trees Classified by Color of Summer Foliage

Blue
White Fir (*Abies concolor*)
*Blue Atlas Cedar (*Cedrus atlantica glauca*)
Western Red Cedar (*Juniperus scopulorum* var. Chandler Blue)
Eastern Red Cedar (*Juniperus virginiana* var. *Burki*)
Colorado Blue Spruce (*Picea pungens* var. Glauca)

Silver to Gray
Russian Olive (*Elaeagnus angustifolia*)
White Poplar (*Populus alba*)
Pendant Silver Linden (*Tilia petiolaris*)
*Silver Linden (*Tilia tomentosa*)

Red to Purple
Blood-leaf Japanese Maple (*Acer palmatum atropurpureum*)
Crimson King Maple (*Acer platanoides* "Crimson King")
Schwedler Maple (*Acer platanoides schwedleri*)
Purple-leaf Sycamore Maple (*Acer pseudoplatanus purpureum*)
Purple Beech (*Fagus sylvatica atropunicea*)
Weeping Purple Beech (*Fagus sylvatica purpureopendula*)
River's Purple Beech (*Fagus sylvatica riversi*)
Rubylace Locust (*Gleditsia triacanthos inermis* "Rubylace")
Purple Crab Apple (*Malus purpurea*)
Blireiana Plum (*Prunus blireiana*)
Pissard Plum (*Prunus cerasifera atropurpurea*)
Thundercloud Plum (*Prunus cerasifera nigra* "Thundercloud")
Woods Myrobalan Plum (*Prunus cerasifera woodi*)
Blood-leaf Peach (*Prunus persica atropurpurea*)
Purple English Oak (*Quercus robur atropurpurea*)

Trees Classified by Color of Fall Foliage

Yellow
Striped Maple or Moosewood (*Acer pensylvanicum*)
Norway Maple (*Acer platanoides* var.)
*Sugar Maple (*Acer saccharum*)
Ohio Buckeye (orange) (*Aesculus glabra*)
Apple Serviceberry (yellow-orange) (*Amelanchier grandiflora*)
*Birch species (*Betula*)
Hickory species (*Carya*)
Chinese Chestnut (*Castanea mollissima*)
*Katsura Tree (yellow to scarlet) (*Cercidiphyllum japonicum*)
Redbud species (*Cercis*)
*American Yellow-wood (*Cladrastis lutea*)
*American Beech (*Fagus grandifolia*)
*European Beech (*Fagus sylvatica*)
White Ash (purple to yellow) (*Fraxinus americana*)
*Ginkgo (*Ginkgo biloba*)
Tulip Tree (*Liriodendron tulipifera*)
*Star Magnolia (bronze) (*Magnolia stellata*)
Golden Larch (*Pseudolarix amabilis*)
*Willow species (*Salix*)

Red
Amur Maple (*Acer ginnala*)
Manchurian Maple (*Acer mandshuricum*)
*Japanese Maple (*Acer palmatum* var.)
*Red Maple (*Acer rubrum*)
*Sugar Maple (*Acer saccharum*)
Tatarian Maple (*Acer tataricum*)
*Shadblow Serviceberry (*Amelanchier canadensis*)
Hornbeam species (*Carpinus*)

*Flowering Dogwood (*Cornus florida*)
Japanese Dogwood (*Cornus kousa*)
American Smoke Tree (*Cotinus americanus*)
Washington Hawthorn (*Crataegus phaenopyrum*)
*Sweet Gum (*Liquidambar styraciflua*)
Dawson Crab Apple (*Malus dawsoniana*)
*Black Tupelo or Black Gum (*Nyssa sylvatica*)
*Sorrel Tree (*Oxydendrum arboreum*)
*Cherry species (*Prunus*)
Bradford Callery Pear (*Pyrus calleryana bradfordi*)
Red Oak (*Quercus borealis*)
Scarlet Oak (*Quercus coccinea*)
*Pin Oak (*Quercus palustris*)
Sassafras (*Sassafras albidum*)
Korean Stewartia (orange to red) (*Stewartia koreana*)

Purple
White Ash (*Fraxinus americana*)
*Sweet Gum (*Liquidambar styraciflua*)
*Common Pear (*Pyrus communis*)
*White Oak (*Quercus alba*)
Japanese Stewartia (*Stewartia pseudocamellia*)

Trees with Interesting Bark

Gray
*Red Maple (*Acer rubrum*)
*Serviceberry species (*Amelanchier*)
Hornbeam species (*Carpinus*)
Hackberry species (*Celtis*)
*American Yellow-wood (*Cladrastis lutea*)
*Hawthorn species (*Crataegus*)
*Beech species (*Fagus*)
American Holly (*Ilex opaca*)
Cucumber Tree (*Magnolia acuminata*)
Saucer Magnolia (*Magnolia soulangeana*)
*White Oak (*Quercus alba*)
Mountain Ash species (*Sorbus*)

White
*Canoe Birch (*Betula papyrifera*)
*European Birch (*Betula pendula*)
*Gray Birch (*Betula populifolia*)

Reddish
Japanese Red Pine (*Pinus densiflora*)
Red or Norway Pine (*Pinus resinosa*)
Scotch Pine (*Pinus sylvestris*)

Reddish Brown
Chinese Paper Birch (*Betula albo-sinensis*)
Sargent Cherry (*Prunus sargenti*)

Yellow
Wisconsin or Niobe Weeping Willow (*Salix blanda*)

Corky
*Amur Cork (*Phellodendron amurense*)
Hackberry (*Celtis occidentalis*)

Flaking
Paperbark Maple (*Acer griseum*)
*Birch species (*Betula*)
Shagbark Hickory (*Carya ovata*)
Russian Olive (*Elaeagnus angustifolia*)
Eastern Red Cedar (*Juniperus virginiana*)
Lace-bark Pine (*Pinus bungeana*)
*Plane Tree species (*Platanus*)
Stewartia species (*Stewartia*)

Trees for the City
White Fir (*Abies concolor*)
Hedge Maple (*Acer campestre*)
Box-Elder (*Acer negundo*)
Norway Maple (*Acer platanoides*)
Sycamore Maple (*Acer pseudoplatanus*)
*Horse-Chestnut or Buckeye (*Aesculus*)
*Tree of Heaven (*Ailanthus*)
Silk Tree (*Albizzia julibrissin*)
Catalpa (*Catalpa*)
Hackberry (*Celtis occidentalis*)
Washington Hawthorn (*Crataegus phaenopyrum*)
Russian Olive (*Elaeagnus angustifolia*)
White Ash (*Fraxinus americana*)
European Ash (*Fraxinus excelsior*)

Green Ash (*Fraxinus pennsylvanica*)
*Ginkgo (*Ginkgo biloba*)
Thornless Honey-Locust (*Gleditsia triacanthos inermis*)
*Golden Rain Tree (*Koelreuteria paniculata*)
*Saucer Magnolia (*Magnolia soulangeana*)
*Star Magnolia (*Magnolia stellata*)
*Crab Apple (*Malus* var.)
Colorado Spruce (*Picea pungens*)
*Amur Cork (*Phellodendron amurense*)
*London Plane Tree (*Platanus acerifolia*)
White Poplar (*Populus alba*)
*Lombardy Poplar (*Populus nigra italica*)
Bradford Callery Pear (*Pyrus calleryana bradfordi*)
Red Oak (*Quercus borealis*)
*Black Locust (*Robinia pseudoacacia*)
*Japanese Pagoda Tree (*Sophora japonica*)
*Little-leaf Linden (*Tilia cordata*)
*Crimean Linden (*Tilia euchlora*)
*Silver Linden (*Tilia tomentosa*)
Village Green Zelkova (*Zelkova serrata* "Village Green")

Trees for Wide Streets
Sycamore Maple (*Acer pseudoplatanus*)
*Sugar Maple (*Acer saccharum*)
Sugar Hackberry (*Celtis laevigata*)
*Katsura Tree (*Cercidiphyllum japonicum*)
White Ash (*Fraxinus americana*)
Green Ash (*Fraxinus pennsylvanica lanceolata*)
*Ginkgo (*Ginkgo biloba*)
*Common Honey-Locust (*Gleditsia triacanthos*)
Kalopanax (*Kalopanax pictus*)
Tulip Tree (*Liriodendron tulipifera*)
*Amur Cork (*Phellodendron amurense*)
*Eastern White Pine (*Pinus strobus*)
London Plane Tree (*Platanus acerifolium*)
*Oriental Plane Tree (*Platanus orientalis*)
White Poplar (*Populus alba*)
Sargent Cherry (*Prunus sargenti*)
Red Oak (*Quercus borealis*)
*Pin Oak (*Quercus palustris*)
Willow Oak (*Quercus phellos*)
Japanese Zelkova (*Zelkova serrata*)

Trees for Medium Streets
Norway Maple (*Acer platanoides*)
Mountain Silverbell (*Halesia monticola*)
*Sweet Gum (*Liquidambar styraciflua*)
Hop-Hornbeam (*Ostrya virginiana*)
*Sorrel Tree or Sourwood (*Oxydendrum arboreum*)
Simon Poplar (*Populus simoni*)
Scarlet Oak (*Quercus coccinea*)
Willow Oak (*Quercus phellos*)
*Black Locust (*Robinia pseudoacacia*)
Sassafras (*Sassafras albidum officinale*)
*Japanese Pagoda Tree (*Sophora japonica*)
*Linden species (*Tilia*)

Trees for Suburban Streets
Hedge Maple (*Acer campestre*)
Amur Maple (*Acer ginnala*)
Paperbark Maple (*Acer griseum*)
Globe Norway Maple (*Acer platanoides globosum*)
American Hornbeam (*Carpinus caroliniana*)
Pyramidal European Hornbeam (*Carpinus betulus fastigiata*)
Globe European Hornbeam (*Carpinus betulus globosa*)
*Flowering Dogwood (*Cornus florida*)
*Hawthorn species (*Crataegus*)
Korean Evodia (*Evodia danielli*)
Carolina Silverbell (*Halesia carolina*)
*Golden Rain Tree (*Koelreuteria paniculata*)
Columnar Sargent Cherry (*Prunus sargenti columnaris*)
Oriental Cherry (*Prunus serrulata*)
Japanese Snowbell (*Styrax japonica*)
Smooth-leaved Elm varieties (*Ulmus carpinifolia*)

Soil Tolerance

Trees Tolerating Acid Soil
*Japanese Maple (*Acer palmatum* var.)

*Flowering Dogwood (*Cornus florida* var.)
Japanese Dogwood (*Cornus kousa*)
*European Beech (*Fagus sylvatica* var.)
Sweet Bay (*Magnolia virginiana*)
*Black Tupelo (*Nyssa sylvatica*)
*Sorrel Tree (*Oxydendrum arboreum*)
Hardy Orange (*Poncirus trifoliata*)
Red Oak (*Quercus borealis*)
Scarlet Oak (*Quercus coccinea*)
Willow Oak (*Quercus phellos*)
*Pin Oak (*Quercus palustris*)
Japanese Stewartia (*Stewartia pseudocamellia*)

Trees Tolerating Moist Soil
Red Maple (*Acer rubrum*)
Alder species (*Alnus*)
Holly species (*Ilex*)
Eastern Larch (*Larix laricina*)
*Sweet Gum (*Liquidambar styraciflua*)
Sweet Bay (*Magnolia virginiana*)
*Black Tupelo or Black Gum (*Nyssa sylvatica*)
Swamp White Oak (*Quercus bicolor*)
*Willow species (*Salix*)
Common Bald Cypress (*Taxodium distichum*)
American Arbor-vitae (*Thuja occidentalis*)

Trees Tolerating Dry or Poor Soil
Box-Elder (*Acer negundo*)
*Tree of Heaven (*Ailanthus*)
Silk Tree (*Albizzia julibrissin*)
*Gray Birch (*Betula populifolia*)
Common Paper-Mulberry (*Broussonetia papyrifera*)
European Hackberry (*Celtis australis*)
Russian Olive (*Elaeagnus angustifolia*)
Green Ash (*Fraxinus pennsylvanica*)
Modesto Ash (*Fraxinus velutina* "Modesto")
*Honey-Locust (*Gleditsia triacanthos* var.)
Eastern Red Cedar (*Juniperus virginiana*)
*Golden Rain Tree (*Koelreuteria paniculata*)
Jack Pine (*Pinus banksiana*)
Pitch Pine (*Pinus rigida*)
White Poplar (*Populus alba*)

Black Jack Oak (*Quercus marilandica*)
Chestnut Oak (*Quercus montana*)
*Black Locust (*Robinia pseudoacacia*)
Sassafras (*Sassafras albidum officinale*)
*Japanese Pagoda Tree (*Sophora japonica*)
Chinese Elm (*Ulmus parvifolia*)
Siberian Elm (*Ulmus pumila*)

Pest-Resistant Trees
*Tree of Heaven (*Ailanthus altissima*)
Hornbeam species (*Carpinus*)
*Cedar species (*Cedrus*)
European Hackberry (*Celtis australis*)
*Katsura Tree (*Cercidiphyllum japonicum*)
False Cypress species (*Chamaecyparis*)
Cornelian Cherry (*Cornus mas*)
American Smoke Tree (*Cotinus americanus*)
Russian Olive (*Elaeagnus angustifolia*)
Franklinia (*Franklinia alatamaha*)
*Ginkgo (*Ginkgo biloba*)
*Honey-Locust (*Gleditsia triacanthos*)
Kentucky Coffee Tree (*Gymnocladus dioicus*)
Juniper species (*Juniperus*)
Kalopanax (*Kalopanax pictus*)
*Golden Rain Tree (*Koelreuteria paniculata*)
*Laburnum species (*Laburnum*)
*Sweet Gum (*Liquidambar styraciflua*)
Cucumber Tree (*Magnolia acuminata*)
*Star Magnolia (*Magnolia stellata*)
Hop-Hornbeam species (*Ostrya*)

Trees for Seashore Planting
Norway Maple (*Acer platanoides*)
Sycamore Maple (*Acer pseudoplatanus*)
*Horse-Chestnut (*Aesculus hippocastanum*)
*Tree of Heaven (*Ailanthus*)
*Shadblow Serviceberry (*Amelanchier canadensis*)
Cockspur Thorn (*Crataegus crus-galli*)
English Hawthorn (*Crataegus oxyacantha*)
Washington Hawthorn (*Crataegus phaenopyrum*)
Cryptomeria (*Cryptomeria japonica*)

Russian Olive (*Elaeagnus angustifolia*)
Thornless Honey-Locust (*Gleditsia triacanthos inermis* var.)
American Holly (*Ilex opaca*)
Eastern Red Cedar (*Juniperus virginiana*)
*Black Tupelo (*Nyssa sylvatica*)
Colorado Blue Spruce (*Picea pungens glauca*)
*Austrian Pine (*Pinus nigra*)
Pitch Pine (*Pinus rigida*)
Scotch Pine (*Pinus sylvestris*)
*Japanese Black Pine (*Pinus thunbergi*)
*London Plane Tree (*Platanus acerifolia*)
Hardy Orange (*Poncirus trifoliata*)
White Poplar (*Populus alba*)
Black Cherry (*Prunus serotina*)
*White Oak (*Quercus alba*)
*Black Locust (*Robinia pseudoacacia*)
Golden Weeping Willow (*Salix alba tristis*)
*Japanese Pagoda Tree (*Sophora japonica*)
American Arbor-vitae (*Thuja occidentalis*)
*Little-leaf Linden (*Tilia cordata*)
*Crimean Linden (*Tilia euchlora*)

Trees for Hedging or Barriers
European Beech (*Fagus sylvatica*) prunes well.
Leyland Cypress (*Cupressocyparis leylandii*) withstands heavy pruning.
Hawthorn varieties (*Crataegus*) easily pruned, advantage of thorns.
Canadian Hemlock (*Tsuga canadensis*) evergreen.
American Holly (*Ilex opaca*) can be pruned.
European Hornbeam (*Carpinus betulus*) prunes well.
Little-leaf Linden (*Tilia cordata*) tolerates heavy pruning.
Hedge Maple (*Acer campestre*) can be pruned.
Austrian Pine (*Pinus nigra*) plant 10–12 feet on centers, staggered row.
Japanese Black Pine (*Pinus thunbergi*) plant 8 feet on centers, staggered row.
Eastern White Pine (*Pinus strobus*) plant 15 feet on centers, staggered row.

NORTH CAROLINA

State Tree
Long-leaf Pine (*Pinus palustris*)

Evergreen Trees
Camellia species (*Camellia*)
*Deodar Cedar (*Cedrus deodara*)
Common China Fir (*Cunninghammia lanceolata*)
*Cypress species (*Cupressus*)
Holly species (*Ilex*)
Juniper species (*Juniperus*)
*Southern Magnolia (*Magnolia grandiflora*)
Chinese Photinia (*Photinia serrulata*)
*Pine species (*Pinus*)
Cork Oak (*Quercus suber*)
*Live Oak (*Quercus virginiana*)
Palmetto (*Sabal palmetto*)
*Hemlock species (*Tsuga*)

Trees Classified by Height

20–35 Feet
Hedge Maple (*Acer campestre*)
*Japanese Maple (*Acer palmatum*)
Apple Serviceberry (*Amelanchier grandiflora*)
European Hornbeam (*Carpinus betulus globosa*)
Mocker-Nut (*Carya tomentosa*)
Japanese Dogwood (*Cornus kousa*)
American Smoke Tree (*Cotinus americanus*)
*Hawthorn species (*Crataegus*)
Russian Olive (*Elaeagnus angustifolia*)
Euonymus species (*Euonymus*)
Korean Evodia (*Evodia danielli*)
Franklinia (*Franklinia alatamaha*)
Common Fig (*Ficus carica*)

Flowering Ash (*Fraxinus ornus*)
Carolina Silverbell (*Halesia carolina*)
Yaupon (*Ilex vomitoria*)
Needle Juniper (*Juniperus rigida*)
*Golden Rain Tree (*Koelreuteria paniculata*)
Crape-Myrtle (*Lagerstroemia indica*)
*Southern Magnolia (*Magnolia grandiflora*)
*Saucer Magnolia (*Magnolia soulangeana*)
*Star Magnolia (*Magnolia stellata*)
*Crab Apple species (*Malus*)
*Cherry species (*Prunus*)
Black Jack Oak (*Quercus marilandica*)
*Babylon Weeping Willow (*Salix babylonica*)
Snowbell species (*Styrax*)

35–75 Feet
Box-Elder (*Acer negundo*)
*Red Maple (*Acer rubrum*)
*Sugar Maple (*Acer saccharum*)
*Red-fruited Tree of Heaven (*Ailanthus altissima erythrocarpa*)
Silk Tree (*Albizzia julibrissin*)
Italian Alder (*Alnus cordata*)
Red Alder (*Alnus rubra*)
*Shadblow Serviceberry (*Amelanchier canadensis*)
Allegany Serviceberry (*Amelanchier laevis*)
Common Paper-Mulberry (*Broussonetia papyrifera*)
European Hornbeam (*Carpinus betulus*)
Japanese Hornbeam (*Carpinus japonica*)
Chinese Chestnut (*Castanea mollissima*)
Southern Catalpa (*Catalpa bignonioides*)
Hackberry (*Celtis*)

*Katsura Tree (*Cercidiphyllum japonicum*)
Eastern Redbud (*Cercis canadensis*)
Chinese Redbud (*Cercis chinensis*)
*Flowering Dogwood (*Cornus florida*)
Cockspur Tree (*Crataegus crus-galli*)
Green Hawthorn (*Crataegus viridis*)
Common China Fir (*Cunninghamia lanceolata*)
Italian Cypress (*Cupressus sempervirens*)
Common Persimmon (*Diospyros virginiana*)
Loblolly Bay Gordonia (*Gordonia lasianthus*)
English Holly (*Ilex aquifolium*)
Dahoon (*Ilex cassine*)
Luster-leaf Holly (*Ilex latifolia*)
Mountain Winterberry (*Ilex montana*)
American Holly (*Ilex opaca*)
Fraser Magnolia (*Magnolia fraseri*)
Sweet Bay (*Magnolia virginiana*)
"Dolgo" Crab Apple (*Malus* "Dolgo")
"Makamik" Crab Apple (*Malus* "Makamik")
Cherry Crab Apple (*Malus robusta*)
"Sissipuk" Crab Apple (*Malus* "Sissipuk")
Chinaberry (*Melia azedarach*)
Yoshino Cherry (*Prunus yedoensis*)
Spanish or Southern Red Oak (*Quercus falcata*)
Laurel Oak (*Quercus laurifolia*)
Water Oak (*Quercus nigra*)
Willow Oak (*Quercus phellos*)
Cork Oak (*Quercus suber*)
*Live Oak (*Quercus virginiana*)
Clammy Locust (*Robinia viscosa*)
Oriental Arbor-vitae (*Thuja orientalis*)
Carolina Hemlock (*Tsuga caroliniana*)
Winged or Wahoo Elm (*Ulmus alata*)

75 Feet or Over
*Red or Swamp Maple (*Acer rubrum*)
*Cedar species (*Cedrus*)
Mountain Silverbell (*Halesia monticola*)
*Southern Magnolia (*Magnolia grandiflora*)
Dawn Redwood (*Metasequoia glyptostroboides*)
*Pine species (*Pinus*)
*Plane Tree species (*Platanus*)
Poplar species (*Populus*)
*Oak species (*Quercus*)
Common Bald Cypress (*Taxodium distichum*)

Trees Classified by Form

Pyramidal
*Cedar species (*Cedrus*)
Italian Cypress (*Cupressus sumpervirens*)
American Holly (*Ilex opaca*)
Juniper or Red Cedar species (*Juniperus*)
*Sweet Gum (*Liquidambar styraciflua*)
*Magnolia species (*Magnolia*)
Dawn Redwood (*Metasequoia glyptostroboides*)
*Black Tupelo or Black Gum (*Nyssa sylvatica*)
Hop-Hornbeam (*Ostrya virginiana*)
*Sorrel Tree or Sourwood (*Oxydendrum arboreum*)
Bolleana Poplar (*Populus alba pyramidalis*)
Turkey Oak (*Quercus cerris*)
Common Bald Cypress (*Taxodium distichum*)
*Hemlock species (*Tsuga*)

Columnar
Columnar Red Maple (*Acer rubrum columnare*)
Fastigiate Washington Hawthorn (*Crataegus phaenopyrum fastigiata*)
Italian Cypress (*Cupressus sempervirens*)
Schott Red Cedar (*Juniperus virginiana schotti*)
Shipmast Locust (*Robinia pseudoacacia rectissima*)

Weeping
*Deodar Cedar (*Cedrus deodara*)
Weeping Red Cedar (*Juniperus virginiana pendula*)
Weeping Black Cherry (*Prunus serotina pendula*)
*Babylon Weeping Willow (*Salix babylonica*)
Pendant Silver Linden (*Tilia petiolaris*)
Weeping American Elm (*Ulmus americana pendula*)

Rounded or Globe-Shaped
*Japanese Maple (*Acer palmatum*)
Single Seed Hawthorn (*Crataegus monogyna inermis*)
*Saucer Magnolia (*Magnolia soulangeana*)
*Crab Apple species (*Malus*)
*White Oak (*Quercus alba*)
Umbrella Black Locust (*Robinia pseudoacacia umbraculifera*)

With Horizontal Branching
Fir species (*Abies*)
Silk Tree (*Albizzia julibrissin*)
*Cedar species (*Cedrus*)
Eastern Redbud (*Cercis canadensis*)
*Flowering Dogwood (*Cornus florida*)
Japanese Dogwood (*Cornus kousa*)
*Hawthorn species (*Crataegus*)
Dawn Redwood (*Metasequoia glyptostroboides*)
*Black Tupelo or Black Gum (*Nyssa sylvatica*)
*Eastern White Pine (*Pinus strobus*)
*White Oak (*Quercus alba*)
*Pin Oak (*Quercus palustris*)
*Live Oak (*Quercus virginiana*)
Common Bald Cypress (*Taxodium distichum*)

Trees Classified by Color of Blossom

Yellow
*Golden Rain Tree (*Koelreuteria paniculata*)
*Laburnum (*Laburnum vossi*)

White
*Flowering Dogwood (*Cornus florida*)
Carolina Silverbell (*Halesia carolina*)
*Southern Magnolia (*Magnolia grandiflora*)
Chinese Photina (*Photinia serrulata*)
Mount Fuji Cherry (*Prunus serrulata* "Shirotae")

Pink
Wither's Pink Redbud (*Cercis canadensis* "Wither's Pink Charm")
Red Flowering Dogwood (*Cornus florida rubra*)
Toba Hawthorn (*Crataegus mordenensis* "Toba")
Ingleside Crape-Myrtle (*Lagerstroemia indica* "Ingleside Pink")
*Saucer Magnolia (*Magnolia soulangeana*)
Katherine Crab Apple (*Malus* "Katherine")
Japanese Flowering Crab Apple (*Malus floribunda*)
Prince Georges Crab Apple (*Malus* "Prince Georges")
*Common Apple (*Malus pumila*)
Blireiana Plum (*Prunus blireiana*)
Sargent Cherry (*Prunus sargenti*)
Autumn Cherry (*Prunus subhirtella autumnalis*)
Weeping Cherry (*Prunus subhirtella pendula*)
Amanogawa Cherry (*Prunus serrulata* "Amano-gawa")
Kwanzan Cherry (*Prunus serrulata* "Kwanzan")
Shirofugen Cherry (*Prunus serrulata* "Shiro-fugen")

Red
Paul's Scarlet Hawthorn (*Crataegus oxyacantha pauli*)
Red Crape-Myrtle (*Lagerstroemia indicia* "Wm. Toovey")
Alexandrina Magnolia (*Magnolia soulangeana* "Alexandrina")
Carmine Crab Apple (*Malus atrosanguinea*)

Trees with Bright Red Fruit
*Flowering Dogwood (*Cornus florida*)
Japanese Dogwood (*Cornus kousa*)
Downy Hawthorn (*Crataegus phaenopyrum*)
American Holly (*Ilex opaca*)
Almey Crab Apple (*Malus* "Almey")
Siberian Crab Apple (*Malus baccata*)
Hopa Crab Apple (*Malus* "Hopa")
*Common Apple (*Malus pumila*)
Sargent Crab Apple (*Malus sargenti*)
Korean Mountain Ash (*Sorbus alnifolia*)

Trees Classified by Color of Summer Foliage

Blue
Steel Lawson Cypress (*Chamaecyparis lawsonia glauca*)
Western Red Cedar (*Juniperus scopulorum* var. Chandler Blue)
Eastern Red Cedar (*Juniperus virginiana* var. *Burki*)

Silver to Gray
Russian Olive (*Elaeagnus angustifolia*)
White Poplar (*Populus alba*)
Pendant Silver Linden (*Tilia petiolaris*)
*Silver Linden (*Tilia tomentosa*)

Red to Purple
Blood-leaf Japanese Maple (*Acer palmatum atro-purpureum*)
Crimson King Maple (*Acer platanoides* "Crimson King")
Schwedler Maple (*Acer platanoides schwedleri*)
Purple-leaf Sycamore Maple (*Acer pseudoplatanus purputeum*)
Purple Beech (*Fagus sylvatica atropunicea*)
Weeping Purple Beech (*Fagus sylvatica purpureo-pendula*)
River's Purple Beech (*Fagus sylvatica riversi*)
Rubylace Locust (*Gleditsia triacanthos inermis* "Rubylace")
Purple Crab Apple (*Malus purpurea*)
Blireiana Plum (*Prunus blireiana*)
Pissard Plum (*Prunus cerasifera atropurpurea*)
Thundercloud Plum (*Purnus cerasifera nigra* "Thundercloud")
Woods Myrobalan Plum (*Prunus cerasifera woodi*)
Blood-leaf Peach (*Prunus persica atropurpurea*)
Purple English Oak (*Quercus robur atropurpurea*)

Trees Classified by Color of Fall Foliage

Yellow
*Sugar Maple (*Acer saccharum*)
Apple Serviceberry (yellow-orange) (*Amelanchier grandiflora*)
*Birches (*Betula species*)
Redbud species (*Cercis*)
Fringetree (*Chionanthus virginicus*)
*American Yellow-wood (*Cladrastis lutea*)
*American Beech (*Fagus grandifolia*)
*European Beech (*Fagus sylvatica*)
*Ginkgo (*Ginkgo biloba*)
*Willow species (*Salix*)

Red
*Red Maple (*Acer rubrum*)
*Shadblow Serviceberry (*Amelanchier canadensis*)
*Flowering Dogwood (*Cornus florida*)
Japanese Dogwood (*Cornus kousa*)
Washington Hawthorn (*Crataegus phaenopyrum*)
*Sweet Gum (*Liquidambar styraciflua*)
*Black Tupelo or Black Gum (*Nyssa sylvatica*)
*Sorrel Tree (*Oxydendrum arboreum*)
Bradford Callery Pear (*Pyrus calleryana bradfordi*)
Red Oak (*Quercus borealis*)
Scarlet Oak (*Quercus coccinea*)
*Japanese Maple (*Quercus palustris*)
Sassafras (*Sassafras albidum*)
Korean Mountain Ash (*Sorbus alnifolia*)
Korean Stewartia (orange to red) (*Stewartia koreana*)

Trees with Interesting Bark

Gray
*Red Maple (*Acer rubrum*)
*Serviceberry species (*Amelanchier*)
*American Yellow-wood (*Cladrastis lutea*)
*Hawthorn species (*Crataegus*)
*Beech species (*Fagus*)
American Holly (*Ilex opaca*)
Cucumber Tree (*Magnolia acuminata*)
*Saucer Magnolia (*Magnolia soulangeana*)

White
*Gray Birch (*Betula populifolia*)

Reddish Brown
Sargent Cherry (*Prunus sargenti*)

Yellow
Wisconsin or Niobe Weeping Willow (*Salix blanda*)

Green
*Babylon Weeping Willow (*Salix babylonica*)

Corky
Hackberry (*Celtis*)
Cork Oak (*Quercus suber*)

Flaking
Eastern Red Cedar (*Juniperus virginiana*)
Crape-Myrtle (*Lagerstroemia indica*)
*Plane Tree species (*Platanus*)
Stewartia species (*Stewartia*)

Trees for the City
Box-Elder (*Acer negundo*)
Norway Maple (*Acer platanoides*)
Sycamore Maple (*Acer pseudoplatanus*)
*Horse-Chestnut or Buckeye (*Aesculus*)
*Tree of Heaven (*Ailanthus*)
Silk Tree (*Albizzia julibrissin*)
Catalpa (*Catalpa*)
Hackberry species (*Celtis*)
Downy Hawthorn (*Crataegus mollis*)
Washington Hawthorn (*Crataegus phaenopyrum*)
Russian Olive (*Elaeagnus angustifolia*)
White Ash (*Fraxinus americana*)
European Ash (*Fraxinus excelsior*)
Green Ash (*Fraxinus pennsylvanica*)
*Ginkgo (*Ginkgo biloba*)
Thornless Honey-Locust (*Gleditsia triacanthos*)
*Golden Rain Tree (*Koelreuteria paniculata*)

*Southern Magnolia (*Magnolia grandiflora*)
*Saucer Magnolia (*Magnolia soulangeana*)
*Star Magnolia (*Magnolia stellata*)
*Crab Apple (*Malus* var.)
 Chinaberry (*Melia azedarrach*)
*Amur Cork (*Phellodendron amurense*)
*London Plane Tree (*Platanus acerifolia*)
 White Poplar (*Populus alba*)
*Lombardy Poplar (*Populus nigra italica*)
 Bradford Callery Pear (*Pyrus calleryana bradfordi*)
 Red Oak (*Quercus borealis*)
Black Locust ((Robinia pseudoacacia*)
*Japanese Pagoda Tree (*Sophora japonica*)
*Little-leaf Linden (*Tilia cordata*)
*Crimean Linden (*Tilia euchlora*)
*Silver Linden (*Tilia tomentosa*)
 Village Green Zelkova (*Zelkova serrata* "Village Green")

Trees for Wide Streets
 Sugar Hackberry (*Celtis laevigata*)
 White Ash (*Fraxinus americana*)
 Green Ash (*Fraxinus pennsylvanica lanceolata*)
*Common Honey-Locust (*Gleditsia triacanthos*)
*Southern Magnolia (*Magnolia grandiflora*)
*Eastern White Pine (*Pinus strobus*)
 London Plane Tree (*Platanus acerifolia*)
*Oriental Plane Tree (*Platanus orientalis*)
 Willow Oak (*Quercus phellos*)

Trees for Medium Streets
 Mountain Silverbell (*Halesia monticola*)
*Sweet Gum (*Liquidambar styraciflua*)
 Chinaberry (*Melia azedarach*)
 Hop-Hornbeam (*Ostrya virginiana*)
*Sorrel Tree or Sourwood (*Oxydendrum arboreum*)
 Scarlet Oak (*Quercus coccinea*)
 Laurel Oak (*Quercus laurifolia*)
 Willow Oak (*Quercus phellos*)
 Cork Oak (*Quercus suber*)
*Black Locust (*Robinia pseudoacacia*)
 Sassafras (*Sassafras albidum officinale*)
 Winged Elm (*Ulmus alata*)

Trees for Suburban Streets
 American Hornbeam (*Carpinus caroliniana*)
 Pyramidal European Hornbeam (*Carpinus betulus fastigiata*)
 Globe European Hornbeam (*Carpinus betulus globosa*)
 Fringetree (*Chionanthus virginicus*)
*Flowering Dogwood (*Cornus florida*)
*Hawthorn species (*Crataegus*)
 Carolina Silverbell (*Halesia carolina*)
 Oriental Cherry (*Prunus serrulata*)
 Columnar Sargent Cherry (*Prunus sargenti columnaris*)

Fragrant Snowbell (*Styrax obassia*)

Soil Tolerance

Trees Tolerating Acid Soil
*Japanese Maple (*Acer palmatum* var.)
*Flowering Dogwood (*Cornus florida* var.)
 Japanese Dogwood (*Cornus kousa*)
*European Beech (*Fagus sylvatica* var.)
 Sweet Bay (*Magnolia virigniana*)
*Black Tupelo (*Nyssa sylvatica*)
*Sorrel Tree (*Oxydendrum arboreum*)
 Red Oak (*Quercus borealis*)
 Scarlet Oak (*Quercus coccinea*)
*Pin Oak (*Quercus palustris*)
 Willow Oak (*Quercus phellos*)

Trees Tolerating Moist Soil
*Red Maple (*Acer rubrum*)
 Alder species (*Alnus*)
 Holly species (*Ilex*)
*Sweet Gum (*Liquidambar styraciflua*)
 Sweet Bay (*Magnolia virginiana*)
*Black Tupelo or Black Gum (*Nyssa sylvatica*)
*Willow species (*Salix*)
 Common Bald Cypress (*Taxodium distichum*)
 American Arbor-vitae (*Thuja occidentalis*)

Trees Tolerating Dry or Poor Soil
*Tree of Heaven (*Ailanthus*)
 Silk Tree (*Albizzia julibrissin*)
*Gray Birch (*Betula populifolia*)
 Common Paper-Mulberry (*Broussonetia papyrifera*)
 European Hackberry (*Celtis australis*)
 Russian Olive (*Elaeagnus angustifolia*)
 Green Ash (*Fraxinus pennsylvanica*)
 Modesto Ash (*Fraxinus velutina* "Modesto")
*Honey-Locust (*Gleditsia triacanthos* var.)
 Western Red Cedar (*Juniperus virginiana*)
*Golden Rain Tree (*Koelreuteria paniculata*)
 Chinaberry (*Melia azedarach*)
 White Poplar (*Populus alba*)
 Black Jack Oak (*Quercus marilandica*)
*Black Locust (*Robinia pseudoacacia*)
 Chinese Elm (*Ulmus parvifolia*)

Pest-Resistant Trees
*Tree of Heaven (*Ailanthus altissima*)
 Hornbeam species (*Carpinus*)
*Cedar species (*Cedrus*)
 European Hackberry (*Celtis australis*)
 American Smoke Tree (*Cotinus*)
*Fig species (*Ficus*)
 Franklinia (*Franklinia alatamaha*)
*Ginkgo (*Ginkgo biloba*)
 Juniper species (*Juniperus*)

*Sweet Gum (*Liquidambar styraciflua*)
*Star Magnolia (*Magnolia stellata*)
 Hop-Hornbeam species (*Ostrya*)
*Oak species (*Quercus*)

Trees for Seashore Planting
 Norway Maple (*Acer platanoides*)
 Sycamore Maple (*Acer pseudoplatanus*)
*Tree of Heaven (*Ailanthus*)
*Shadblow Serviceberry (*Amelanchier canadensis*)
 English Hawthorn (*Crataegus oxyacantha*)
 Cryptomeria (*Cryptomeria japonica*)
 Russian Olive (*Elaeagnus angustifolia*)
 Velvet Ash (*Fraxinus velutina*)
 American Holly (*Ilex opaca*)
*Southern Magnolia (*Magnolia grandiflora*)
*Black Tupelo (*Nyssa sylvatica*)
 Colorado Blue Spruce (*Picea pungens glauca*)
*Austrian Pine (*Pinus nigra*)
 Cluster Pine (*Pinus pinaster*)
 Pitch Pine (*Pinus rigida*)
*Japanese Black Pine (*Pinus thunbergi*)
*London Plane Tree (*Platanus acerifolia*)
 White Poplar (*Populus alba*)
 Black Cherry (*Prunus serotina*)
*White Oak (*Quercus alba*)
 Black Jack Oak (*Quercus marilandica*)
*Live Oak (*Quercus virginiana*)
*Black Locust (*Robina pseudoacacia*)
 Golden Weeping Willow (*Salix alba tristis*)
*Japanese Pagoda Tree (*Sophora japonica*)
 American Arbor-vitae (*Thuja occidentalis*)
 Oriental Arbor-vitae (*Thuja orientalis*)
*Little-leaf Linden (*Tilia cordata*)
*Crimean Linden (*Tilia euchlora*)
 Chinese Elm (*Ulmus parvifolia*)

Trees for Hedging or Barriers
 European Beech (*Fagus sylvatica*) prunes well.
 Leyland Cypress (*Cupressocyparis leylandii*) withstands heavy pruning.
 Hawthorn varieties (*Crataegus*) easily pruned, advantage of thorns.
 Canadian Hemlock (*Tsuga canadensis*) evergreen.
 American Holly (*Ilex opaca*) can be pruned.
 European Hornbeam (*Carpinus betulus*) prunes well.
 Little-leaf Linden (*Tilia cordata*) tolerates heavy pruning.
 Hedge Maple (*Acer campestre*) can be pruned.
 Austrian Pine (*Pinus nigra*) plant 10–12 feet on centers, staggered row.
 Japanese Black Pine (*Pinus thunbergi*) plant 8 feet on centers, staggered row.
 Eastern White Pine (*Pinus strobus*) plant 15 feet on centers, staggered row.

NORTH DAKOTA

State Tree
*American Elm (*Ulmus americana*)

Evergreen Trees
 Fir species (*Abies*)
 Eastern Red Cedar (*Juniperus virginiana*)
 Rocky Mountain Juniper (*Juniperus scopulorum*)
*Larch species (*Larix*)
 Spruce species (*Picea*)
*Pine species (*Pinus*)
 Arbor-vitae species (*Thuja*)

Trees Classified by Height

20–30 Feet
 Amur Maple (*Acer ginnala*)
 Ohio Buckeye (*Aesculus glabra*)
 Russian Olive (*Elaeagnus angustifolia*)
*Crab Apple species (*Malus*)
*Cherry and Plum species (*Prunus*)

 Dahurian Buckthorn (*Rhamnus davurica*)
 Showy Mountain Ash (*Sorbus decora*)
 European Mountain Ash (*Sorbus aucuparia*)
 Nannyberry (*Viburnum lentago*)

35–75 Feet
 Fir species (*Abies*)
 Box-Elder (*Acer negundo*)
*Sugar Maple (*Acer saccharum*)
 Speckled Alder (*Alnus incana*)
*Canoe Birch (*Betula papyrifera*)
*European Birch (*Betula pendula*)
 Common Hackberry (*Celtis occidentalis*)
 Green Ash (*Fraxinus pennsylvanica lanceolata*)
*European Larch (*Larix decidua*)
 Eastern Larch or Tamarack (*Larix laricina*)
 Siberian Crab Apple (*Malus baccata*)
 "Dolgo" Crab Apple (*Malus* "Dolgo")
 Spruce species (*Picea*)
 Black Hills Spruce (*Picea glauca densata*)

*Pine species (*Pinus*)
 Jack Pine (*Pinus banksiana*)
 Swiss Stone Pine (*Pinus cembra*)
 Limber Pine (*Pinus flexilis*)
 Scotch Pine (*Pinus sylvestris*)
 Simon Poplar (*Populus simoni*)
 Amur Chokecherry (*Prunus maacki*)
 European Bird Cherry (*Prunus padus*)
 Black or Rum Cherry (*Prunus serotina*)
 Bur Oak (*Quercus macrocarpa*)
 White Willow (*Salix alba*)
 European Mountain Ash or Rowan Tree (*Sorbus aucuparia*)
*Linden species (*Tilia*)
 American Arbor-vitae (*Thuja occidentalis*)
*Elm species (*Ulmus*)

75 Feet or Over
 Poplar species (*Populus*)

Trees Classified by Form

Pyramidal
Fir species (*Abies balsamea*)
*Birch species (*Betula*)
Juniper or Red Cedar species (*Juniperus*)
*Larch species (*Larix*)
Spruce species (*Picea*)
Swiss Stone Pine (*Pinus cembra*)
Arbor-vitae species (*Thuja*)
*Linden species (*Tilia*)

Columnar
Sentry Maple (*Acer saccharum monumentale*)
Fastigiate European Birch (*Betula pendula fastigiata*)
Columnar Siberian Crab (*Malus baccata columnaris*)
Swiss Stone Pine (*Pinus cembra*)
Fastigiate Scotch Pine (*Pinus sylvestris fastigiata*)
*Lombardy Poplar (*Populus nigra italica*)
Fastigiate Simon Poplar (*Populus simoni fastigiata*)
Shipmast Locust (*Robinia pseudoacacia rectissima*)
Upright European Mountain Ash (*Sorbus aucuparia fastigiata*)
Douglas Arbor-vitae (*Thuja occidentalis douglasi pyramidalis*)
Fastigiate American Arbor-vitae (*Thuja occidentalis fastigiata*)
*American Elm varieties (*Ulmus americana*)

Weeping
Slender European Birch (*Betula pendula tristis*)
Weeping Larch (*Larix decidua pendula*)
Koster Weeping Blue Spruce (*Picea pungens kosteriana*)
Weeping Black Cherry (*Prunus serotina pendula*)
Golden Weeping Willow (*Salix alba tristis*)
Weeping European Mountain Ash (*Sorbus aucuparia pendula*)
Weeping American Elm (*Ulmus americana pendula*)

Rounded or Globe-Shaped
*Flowering Crab Apple (*Malus*)
Umbrella Black Locust (*Robinia pseudoacacia umbraculifera*)

With Horizontal Branching
Fir species (*Abies*)
Spruce species (*Picea*)
*Pine species (*Pinus*)

Trees Classified by Color of Blossom

White
*Siberian Crab Apple (*Malus baccata* var.)
European Birdcherry (*Prunus padus*)
Pin Cherry (*Prunus pennsylvanica*)
American Mountain Ash (*Sorbus americana*)
European Mountain Ash (*Sorbus aucuparia*)
Showy Mountain Ash (*Sorbus decora*)

Pink
Toba Hawthorn (*Crataegus mordenensis* "Toba")
*Common Apple (*Malus pumila*)
"Rosybloom" Flowering Crabs (*Malus* hybrids "Rudolph," "Garry," "Red Splendor")

Red
Almey Crab Apple (*Malus* "Almey")

Trees with Bright Red Fruit

Almey Crab Apple (*Malus* "Almey")
Red Splendor Crab Apple (*Malus* "Red Splendor")
Siberian Crab Apple (*Malus baccata*)
*Common Apple (*Malus pumila*)
American Mountain Ash (*Sorbus americana*)
European Mountain Ash (*Sorbus aucuparia*)
Showy Mountain Ash (*Sorbus decora*)

Trees Classified by Color of Summer Foliage

Blue
Eastern Red Cedar (*Juniperus virginiana* var. *Burki*)
Colorado Blue Spruce (*Picea pungens*)

Silver to Gray
Russian Olive (*Elaeagnus angustifolia*)
Common Sea-Buckthorn (*Hippophae rhamnoides*)
White Poplar (*Populus alba*)

Red to Purple
"Crimson King" Maple (*Acer platanoides* "Crimson King")
Newport Plum (*Prunus cerasifera atropurpurea* hybrid)
Royalty Crab (*Malus* "Royalty")

Trees Classified by Color of Fall Foliage

Yellow
Striped Maple or Moosewood (*Acer pennsylvanicum*)
Silver Maple (*Acer saccharinum*)
*Sugar Maple (*Acer saccharum*)
Ohio Buckeye (orange) (*Aesculus glabra*)
*Birches (*Betula* species)
Common Hackberry (*Celtis occidentalis*)
White Ash (purple to yellow) (*Fraxinus americana*)
*Larch (*Larix decidua*)
*Lombardy Poplar (*Populus nigra italica*)
*Willow species (*Salix*)
*American Elm (*Ulmus americana*)

Red
Amur Maple (*Acer ginnala*)
*Sugar Maple (*Acer saccharum*)
*Cherry species (*Prunus*)
Nannyberry (*Viburnum lentago*)

Trees with Interesting Bark

White
*Canoe Birch (*Betula papyrifera*)
*European Birch (*Betula pendula*)

Red
Scotch Pine (*Pinus sylvestris*)

Corky
*Amur Cork (*Phellodendron amurense*)

Flaking
*Birch species (*Betula*)

Russian Olive (*Elaeagnus angustifolia*)

Trees for the City

Ohio Buckeye (*Aesculus glabra*)
Common Hackberry (*Celtis occidentalis*)
Russian Olive (*Elaeagnus angustifolia*)
Green Ash (*Fraxinus pennsylvanica*)
Siberian Crab Apple (*Malus baccata*)
*Flowering Crabs (*Malus* hybrids)
*Amur Cork (*Phellodendron amurense*)
Colorado Spruce (*Picea pungens*)
White Poplar (*Populus alba*)
*Lombardy Poplar (*Populus nigra italica*)
*Black Locust (*Robinia pseudoacacia*)
*Little-leaf Linden (*Tilia cordata*)

Trees for Wide Streets
*Sugar Maple (*Acer saccharum*)
Green Ash (*Fraxinus pennsylvanica lanceolata*)
Cork Tree (*Phellodendron amurense*)
White Poplar (*Populus alba*)

Trees for Medium Streets
Simon Poplar (*Populus simoni*)
*Black Locust (*Robinia pseudoacacia*)
*Linden species (*Tilia*)

Trees for Suburban Streets
Amur Maple (*Acer ginnala*)
*Hawthorn species (*Crataegus*)

Soil Tolerance

Trees Tolerating Moist Soil
Alder species (*Alnus*)
Eastern Larch (*Larix laricina*)
American Arbor-vitae (*Thuja occidentalis*)
*Willow species (*Salix*)

Trees Tolerating Dry or Poor Soil
Box-Elder (*Acer negunda*)
Russian Olive (*Elaeagnus angustifolia*)
Green Ash (*Fraxinus pennsylvanica*)
Eastern Red Cedar (*Juniperus virginiana*)
Jack Pine (*Pinus banksiana*)
White Poplar (*Populus alba*)
*Black Locust (*Robinia pseudoacacia*)

Pest-Resistant Trees

Russian Olive (*Elaeagnus angustifolia*)

Trees for Hedging or Barriers

European Beech (*Fagus sylvatica*) prunes well.
Hawthorn varieties (*Crataegus*) easily pruned, advantage of thorns.
Canadian Hemlock (*Tsuga canadensis*) evergreen.
European Hornbeam (*Carpinus betulus*) prunes well.
Little-leaf Linden (*Tilia cordata*) tolerates heavy pruning.
Hedge Maple (*Acer campestre*) can be pruned.
Austrian Pine (*Pinus nigra*) plant 10–12 feet on centers, staggered row.
Eastern White Pine (*Pinus strobus*) plant 15 feet on centers, staggered row.

OHIO

State Tree

Ohio Buckeye (*Aesculus glabra*)

Evergreen Trees

Fir species (*Abies*)
False Cypress species (*Chamaecyparis*)
American Holly (*Ilex opaca*)
Juniper species (*Juniperus*)
*Larch species (*Larix*)
Spruce species (*Picea*)
*Pine species (*Pinus*)
*Douglas Fir (*Pseudotsuga menziesi*)
Umbrella Pine (*Sciadopitys verticillata*)
Arbor-vitae species (*Thuja*)
*Hemlock species (*Tsuga*)

Trees Classified by Height

20–35 Feet
Argutum Maple (*Acer argutum*)
Hedge Maple (*Acer campestre*)
Hornbeam Maple (*Acer carpinifolium*)
Vine Maple (*Acer circinatum*)
Amur Maple (*Acer ginnala*)
Paperbark Maple (*Acer griseum*)
Manchurian Maple (*Acer mandshuricum*)
*Japanese Maple (*Acer palmatum*)
Striped Maple or Moosewood (*Acer pennsylvanicum*)
Mountain Maple (*Acer spicatum*)
Tatarian Maple (*Acer tataricum*)

Ohio Buckeye (*Aesculus glabra*)
Serviceberry species (*Amelanchier*)
*Gray Birch (*Betula populifolia*)
European Hornbeam (*Carpinus betulus*)
American Hornbeam (*Carpinus caroliniana*)
Mockernut (*Carya tomentosa*)
Chinese Chestnut (*Castanea mollissima*)
Eastern Redbud (*Circus canadensis*)
Fringetree (*Chionanthus virginicus*)
*Flowering Dogwood (*Cornus florida*)
Japanese Dogwood (*Cornus kousa*)
Cornelian Cherry (*Cornus mas*)
Japanese Cornel (*Cornus officinalis*)
American Smoke Tree (*Cotinus americanus*)
*Hawthorn species (*Crataegus*)

Russian Olive (*Elaeagnus angustifolia*)
Franklinia (*Franklinia alatamaha*)
Flowering Ash (*Fraxinus ornus*)
Carolina Silverbell (*Halesia carolina*)
Common Sea-Buckthorn (*Hippophae rhannoides*)
Possum Haw (*Ilex decidua*)
*Golden Rain Tree (*Koelreuteria paniculata*)
*Laburnum species (*Laburnum*)
Yellow Cucumber Tree (*Magnolia cordata*)
*Magnolia species (*Magnolia*)
*Crab Apple species (*Malus*)
*Sorrel Tree or Sourwood (*Oxydendrum arboreum*)
*Cherry species (*Prunus*)
European Mountain Ash (*Sorbus aucuparia*)
Showy Mountain Ash (*Sorbus decora*)
Snowberry Mountain Ash (*Sorbus discolor*)
Folgner Mountain Ash (*Sorbus folgneri*)
Asiatic Sweetleaf (*Symplocos paniculata*)
Japanese Tree Lilac (*Syringa amurensis japonica*)

35—75 Feet
Korean Fir (*Abies koreana*)
Nikko Maple (*Acer nikoense*)
*Red-fruited Tree of Heaven (*Ailanthus altissima erythrocarpa*)
Italian Alder (*Alnus cordata*)
Speckled Alder (*Alnus incana*)
Red Alder (*Alnus rubra*)
Allegany Serviceberry (*Amelanchier laevis*)
Sweet Birch (*Betula lenta*)
Dahurian Birch (*Betula mandshurica szechuanica*)
River Birch (*Betula nigra*)
*Canoe Birch (*Betula papyrifera*)
*European Birch (*Betula pendula*)
Japanese Hornbeam (*Carpinus japonica*)
Southern Catalpa (*Catalpa bignoniodes*)
Bunch Hackberry (*Celtis bungeana*)
*Katsura Tree (*Cercidiphyllum japonicum*)
*American Yellow-wood (*Cladrastis lutea*)
Turkish Filbert (*Corylus colurna*)
Green Hawthorn (*Crataegus viridis*)
Common Persimmon (*Diospyros virginiana*)
Green Ash (*Fraxinus pennsylvanica lanceolata*)
Mountain Winterberry (*Ilex montana*)
Heartnut (*Juglans sieboldiana cordiformis*)
Chinese Juniper (*Juniperus chinensis*)
*Amur Cork (*Phellodendron amurense*)
Jack Pine (*Pinus banksiana*)
Lace-bark Pine (*Pinus bungeana*)
Swiss Stone Pine (*Pinus cembra*)
Limber Pine (*Pinus flexilis*)
Pitch Pine (*Pinus rigida*)
Scotch Pine (*Pinus sylvestris*)
Virginia or Scrub Pine (*Pinus virginiana*)
Simon Poplar (*Populus simoni*)
European Bird Cherry (*Prunus padus*)
Golden Larch (*Pseudolarix amabilis*)
Ussurian Pear (*Pyrus ussuriensis*)
Swamp White Oak (*Quercus bicolor*)
Red Oak (*Quercus borealis*)
Scarlet Oak (*Quercus coccinea*)
Shingle Oak (*Quercus imbricaria*)
*Pin Oak (*Quercus palustris*)
Willow Oak (*Quercus phellos*)
White Willow (*Salix alba*)
Wisconsin or Niobe Weeping Willow (*Salix blanda*)
Thurlow Weeping Willow (*Salix elegantissima*)
Laurel Willow (*Salix pentandra*)
Sassafras (*Sassafras albidum officinale*)
American Arbor-vitae (*Thuja occidentalis*)
*Crimean Linden (*Tilia euchlora*)
Carolina Hemlock (*Tsuga caroliniana*)
Chinese Elm (*Ulmus parvifolia*)

75 Feet or Over
Fir species (*Abies*)
Norway Maple (*Acer platanoides*)
*Red or Swamp Maple (*Acer rubrum*)
*Sugar Maple (*Acer saccharum*)

*Baumann Horse-Chestnut (*Aesculus hippocastanum baumanni*)
European Alder (*Alnus glutinosa*)
*Canoe Birch (*Betula papyrifera*)
Hickory species (*Carya*)
Sugar Hackberry (*Celtis laevigata*)
*Katsura Tree (*Cercidiphyllum japonicum*)
*Beech species (*Fagus*)
White Ash (*Fraxinus americana*)
European Ash (*Fraxinus excelsior*)
*Ginkgo or Maidenhair Tree (*Ginkgo biloba*)
*Common Honey-Locust (*Gleditsia triacanthos*)
Kentucky Coffee Tree (*Gymnocladus dioicus*)
Mountain Silverbell (*Halesia monticola*)
Eastern Black Walnut (*Juglans nigra*)
English or Persian Walnut (*Juglans regia*)
*European Larch (*Larix decidua*)
Japanese Larch (*Larix leptolepis*)
*Sweet Gum (*Liquidambar styraciflua*)
Tulip Tree (*Liriodendron tulipifera*)
Cucumber Tree (*Magnolia acuminata*)
*Black Gum or Black Tupelo (*Nyssa sylvatica*)
Spruce species (*Picea*)
*Pine species (*Pinus*)
*Plane Tree species (*Platanus*)
Poplar species (*Populus*)
Black or Rum Cherry (*Prunus serotina*)
*Douglas Fir (*Pseudotsuga menziesii*)
*Oak species (*Quercus*)
Umbrella Pine (*Sciadopitys verticillata*)
Common Bald Cypress (*Taxodium distichum*)
*Linden species (*Tilia*)
*Canada Hemlock (*Tsuga canadensis*)
*Elm species (*Ulmus*)
Japanese Zelkova (*Zelkova serrata*)

Trees Classified by Form

Pyramidal
Fir species (*Abies*)
Arbor-vitae species (*Arbor-vitae*)
*Birch species (*Betula*)
*Cedar species (*Cedrus*)
False Cypress species (*Chamaecyparis*)
Turkish Filbert (*Corylus colurna*)
American Holly (*Ilex opaca*)
Juniper or Red Cedar species (*Juniperus*)
*Larch species (*Larix*)
*Sweet Gum (*Liquidambar styraciflua*)
*Magnolia species (*Magnolia*)
*Black Tupelo or Black Gum (*Nyssa sylvatica*)
Hop-Hornbeam (*Ostrya virginiana*)
*Sorrel Tree or Sourwood (*Oxydendrum arboreum*)
Spruce species (*Picea*)
Swiss Stone Pine (*Pinus cembra*)
Korean Pine (*Pinus koraiensis*)
Japanese White Pine (*Pinus parviflora*)
Red or Norway Pine (*Pinus resinosa*)
Golden Larch (*Pseudolarix amabilis*)
*Douglas Fir (*Pseudotsuga menziesii*)
*Pin Oak (*Quercus palustris*)
Umbrella Pine (*Sciadopitys verticillata*)
Common Bald Cypress (*Taxodium distichum*)
*Linden species (*Tilia*)
*Hemlock species (*Tsuga*)

Columnar
Ascending Norway Maple (*Acer platanoides ascendens*)
Columnar Norway Maple (*Acer platanoides columnare*)
Erect Norway Maple (*Acer platanoides erectum*)
Columnar Red Maple (*Acer rubrum columnare*)
Sentry Maple (*Acer saccharum monumentale*)
Fastigiate European Birch (*Betula pendula fastigiata*)
Fastigiate European Hornbeam (*Carpinus betulus fastigiata*)
Column Hinoki Cypress (*Chamaecyparis obtusa erecta*)
Fastigiate Washington Hawthorn (*Crataegus phaenopyrum fastigiata*)
Sentry Ginkgo (*Ginkgo biloba fastigiata*)

Blue Columnar Chinese Juniper (*Juniperus chinensis columnaris*)
Swiss Stone Pine (*Pinus cembra*)
Fastigiate White Pine (*Pinus strobus fastigiata*)
Fastigiate Scotch Pine (*Pinus sylvestris fastigiata*)
*Lombardy Poplar (*Populus nigra italica*)
Columnar Sargent Cherry (*Prunus sargenti columnaris*)
"Amanogawa" Cherry (*Prunus serrulata* "Amanogawa")
Fastigiate English Oak (*Quercus robur fastigiata*)
Common Bald Cypress (*Taxodium distichum*)
Douglas Arbor-vitae (*Thuja occidentalis douglasi pyramidalis*)
Fastigiate American Arbor-vitae (*Thuja occidentalis fastigiata*)
Columnar Big-leaf Linden (*Tilia platyphyllos fastigiata*)
*American Elm varieties (*Ulmus americana*)

Weeping
Slender European Birch (*Betula pendula tristis*)
Young's Birch (*Betula pendula youngi*)
Weeping European Hornbeam (*Carpinus betulus pendula*)
*Weeping Beech (*Fagus sylvatica pendula*)
Weeping Purple Beech (*Fagus sylvatica purpureopendula*)
Weeping Red Cedar (*Juniperus virginiana pendula*)
Weeping Larch (*Larix decidua pendula*)
"Exzellenz Thiel" Crab Apple (*Malus* "Exzellenz Thiel")
"Oekonomierat Echtermeyer" Crab Apple (*Malus* "Okeonomierat Echtermeyer")
Koster Weeping Blue Spruce (*Picea pungens kosteriana*)
Weeping White Pine (*Pinus strobus pendula*)
Weeping Higan Cherry (*Prunus subhirtella pendula*)
"Yaeshidare" Cherry (*Prunus subhirtella pendula flora plena*)
Weeping Yoshino Cherry (*Prunus yedoensis perpendens*)
Weeping Douglas Fir (*Pseudotsuga menziesii pendula*)
Golden Weeping Willow (*Salix alba tristis*)
Wisconsin or Niobe Weeping Willow (*Salix blanda*)
Thurlow Weeping Willow (*Salix elegantissima*)
Weeping Japanese Pagoda Tree (*Sophora japonica pendula*)
Weeping European Mountain Ash (*Sorbus aucuparia pendula*)
Sargent Hemlock (*Tsuga canadensis pendula*)
Weeping American Elm (*Ulmus americana pendula*)

Rounded or Globe-Shaped
Japanese Maple (*Acer palmatum*)
Globe Norway Maple (*Acer platanoides globosum*)
Globe European Hornbeam (*Carpinus betulus globosa*)
Bunch Hackberry (*Celtis bungeana*)
Cornelian Cherry (*Cornus mas*)
Japanese Cornel (*Cornus officinalis*)
Single Seed Hawthorn (*Crataegus monogyna inermis*)
*Beech species (*Fagus*)
*Saucer Magnolia (*Magnolia soulangeana*)
*Crab Apple species (*Malus*)
Umbrella Black Locust (*Robinia pseudoacacia umbraculifera*)
Sargent Hemlock (*Tsuga canadensis sargenti*)

With Horizontal Branching
Fir species (*Abies*)
Eastern Redbud (*Cercis canadensis*)
*Flowering Dogwood (*Cornus florida*)
Japanese Dogwood (*Cornus kousa*)
*Hawthorn species (*Crataegus*)
*Black Tupelo or Black Gum (*Nyssa sylvatica*)
Japanese Red Pine (*Pinus densiflora*)
*Eastern White Pine (*Pinus strobus*)
Golden Larch (*Pseudolarix amabilis*)

★White Oak (*Quercus alba*)
Common Bald Cypress (*Taxodium distichum*)

Trees Classified by Color of Blossom

Yellow
★Golden Rain Tree (*Koelreuteria paniculata*)

White
★Shadblow Serviceberry (*Amelanchier canadensis*)
Whitebud (*Cercis canadensis alba*)
★American Yellow-wood (*Cladrastis lutea*)
Japanese Dogwood (*Cornus kousa*)
Washington Hawthorn (*Crataegus phaenopyrum*)
Carolina Silverbell (*Halesia carolina*)
Yulan Magnolia (*Magnolia denudata*)
★Star Magnolia (*Magnolia stellata*)
Arnold Crab Apple (*Malus arnoldiana*)
Siberian Crab Apple (*Malus baccata*)
Tea Crab Apple (*Malus hupehensis*)
Sargent Crab Apple (*Malus sargenti*)
★Sorrel Tree (*Oxydendrum arboreum*)
Sour Cherry (*Prunus cerasus*)
Yoshino Cherry (*Prunus yedoensis*)
Bradford Callery Pear (*Pyrus calleryana bradfordi*)
★Common Pear (*Pyrus communis*)
★Japanese Pagoda Tree (*Sophora japonica*)
Korean Mountain Ash (*Sorbus alnifolia*)
American Mountain Ash (*Sorbus americana*)
European Mountain Ash (*Sorbus aucuparia*)
Showy Mountain Ash (*Sorbus decora*)

Pink
Wither's Pink Redbud (*Cercis canadenis* "Wither's Pink Charm")
Red Flowering Dogwood (*Cornus florida rubra*)
Toba Hawthorn (*Crataegus mordenensis* "Toba")
★Saucer Magnolia (*Magnolia soulangeana*)
Japanese Flowering Crab Apple (*Malus floribunda*)
Katherine Crab Apple (*Malus* "Katherine")
Prince Georges Crab Apple (*Malus* "Prince Georges")
★Common Apple (*Malus pumila*)
Bliereiana Plum (*Prunus blireiana*)
Sargent Cherry (*Prunus sargenti*)
Amanogawa Cherry (*Prunus serrulata* "Amanogawa")
Kwanzan Cherry (*Prunus serrulata* "Kwanzan")
Autumn Cherry (*Prunus subhirtella autumnalis*)
Weeping Cherry (*Prunus subhirtella pendula*)

Red
Ruby Horse-Chestnut (*Aesculus carnea briotti*)
Paul's Scarlet Hawthorn (*Crataegus oxyacantha pauli*)
Alexandrina Magnolia (*Magnolia soulangeana* "Alexandrina")
Almey Crab Apple (*Malus* "Almey")
Carmine Crab Apple (*Malus atrosanguinea*)

Trees with Bright Red Fruit
★Flowering Dogwood (*Cornus florida*)
Japanese Dogwood (*Cornus kousa*)
Downy Hawthorn (*Crataegus mollis*)
Washington Hawthorn (*Crataegus phaenopyrum*)
American Holly (*Ilex opaca*)
Siberian Crab Apple (*Malus baccata*)
Hopa Crab Apple (*Malus* "Hopa")
Sargent Crab Apple (*Malus sargenti*)
Korean Mountain Ash (*Sorbus alnifolia*)
American Mountain Ash (*Sorbus americana*)
European Mountain Ash (*Sorbus aucuparia*)

Trees Classified by Color of Summer Foliage

Blue
White Fir (*Abies concolor*)
Eastern Red Cedar (*Juniperus virginiana* var. *Burki*)
Colorado Blue Spruce (*Picea pungens* var. *Glauca*)
Willow-leaf Pear (*Pyrus salicifolia*)

Silver to Gray
Russian Olive (*Elaeagnus angustifolia*)
Common Sea-Buckthorn (*Hippophae rhamnoides*)

White Poplar (*Populus alba*)
Pendant Silver Linden (*Tilia petiolaris*)
★Silver Linden (*Tilia tomentosa*)

Red to Purple
Blood-leaf Japanese Maple (*Acer palmatum atropurpureum*)
Crimson King Maple (*Acer platanoides* "Crimson King")
Schwedler Maple (*Acer platanoides schwedleri*)
Purple-leaf Sycamore Maple (*Acer pseudoplatanus*)
Purple Beech (*Fagus sylvatica atropunicea*)
Weeping Purple Beech (*Fagus sylvatica purpureopendula*)
River's Purple Beech (*Fagus sylvatica riversi*)
Rubylace Locust (*Gleditsia triacanthos inermis* "Rubylace")
Purple Crab Apple (*Malus purpurea*)
Blireiana Plum (*Prunus blireiana*)
Pissard Plum (*Prunus cerasifera atropurpurea*)
Thundercloud Plum (*Prunus cerasifera nigra* "Thundercloud")
Purple English Oak (*Quercus robur atropurpurea*)

Trees Classified by Color of Fall Foliage

Yellow
Striped Maple or Moosewood (*Acer pensylvanicum*)
Norway Maple (*Acer platanoides* var.)
★Sugar Maple (*Acer saccharum*)
Apple Serviceberry (yellow-orange) (*Amelanchier grandiflora*)
★Birch species (*Betula*)
Hickory species (*Carya*)
Chinese Chestnut (*Castinaea mollissima*)
★Katsura Tree (yellow to scarlet) (*Cercidiphyllum japonicum*)
Fringetree (*Chionanthus virginicus*)
★American Yellow-wood (*Cladrastis lutea*)
★American Beech (*Fagus grandifolia*)
★Ginkgo (*Ginkgo biloba*)
★Larch (*Larix decidua*)
Tulip Tree (*Liriodendron tulipifera*)
★Star Magnolia (bronze) (*Magnolia stellata*)
Golden Larch (*Pseudolarix amabilis*)
★Willow species (*Salix*)

Red
Amur Maple (*Acer ginnala*)
Manchurian Maple (*Acer mandshuricum*)
Nikko Maple (*Acer nikoense*)
★Japanese Maple (*Acer palmatum* var.)
★Red Maple (*Acer rubrum*)
★Sugar Maple (*Acer saccharum*)
Tatarian Maple (*Acer tataricum*)
★Shadblow Serviceberry (*Amelanchier canadensis*)
★Flowering Dogwood (*Cornus florida*)
Japanese Dogwood (*Cornus kousa*)
American Smoke Tree (*Cotinus americanus*)
Washington Hawthorn (*Crataegus phaenopyrum*)
★Sweet Gum (*Liquidambar styraciflua*)
Dawson Crab Apple (*Malus dawsoniana*)
★Black Tupelo or Black Gum (*Nyssa sylvatica*)
★Sorrel Tree (*Oxydendrum arboreum*)
Persian Parrotia (*Parrotia persica*)
★Cherry species (*Prunus*)
Bradford Callery Pear (*Pyrus calleryana bradfordi*)
Red Oak (*Quercus borealis*)
Scarlet Oak (*Quercus coccinea*)
★Pin Oak (*Quercus palustris*)
Sassafras (orange) (*Sassafras albidum*)
Korean Mountain Ash (*Sorbus alnifolia*)

Purple
White Ash (*Fraxinus americana*)
Sweet Gum (*Liquidambar styraciflua*)
★Common Pear (*Pyrus communis*)
★White Oak (*Quercus alba*)

Trees with Interesting Bark

Gray
★Red Maple (*Acer rubrum*)

Serviceberry species (*Amelanchier*)
Hornbeam species (*Carpinus*)
Hackberry species (*Celtis*)
★American Yellow-wood (*Cladrastis lutea*)
★Hawthorn species (*Crataegus*)
★Beech species (*Fagus*)
American Holly (*Ilex opaca*)
English or Persian Walnut (*Juglans regia*)
Cucumber Tree (*Magnolia acuminata*)
★Saucer Magnolia (*Magnolia soulangeana*)
Mountain Ash species (*Sorbus*)

White
★Canoe Birch (*Betula papyrifera*)
★European Birch (*Betula pendula*)
★Gray Birch (*Betula populifolia*)

Red
Japanese Red Pine (*Pinus densiflora*)
Scotch Pine (*Pinus sylvestris*)
Red or Norway Pine (*Pinus resinosa*)

Reddish Brown
Sargent Cherry (*Prunus sargenti*)

Yellow
Wisconsin or Niobe Weeping Willow (*Salix blanda*)

Corky
★Amur Cork (*Phellodendron amurense*)

Flaking
Paperbark Maple (*Acer griseum*)
★Birch species (*Betula*)
Shagbark Hickory (*Carya ovata*)
Russian Olive (*Eleagnus angustifolia*)
Eastern Red Cedar (*Juniperus virginiana*)
Persian Parrotia (*Parrotia persica*)
Plane Tree species (*Platanus*)
Lace-bark Pine (*Pinus bungeana*)

Trees for the City
White Fir (*Abies concolor*)
Hedge Maple (*Acer campestre*)
Box-Elder (*Acer negundo*)
Norway Maple (*Acer platanoides*)
Sycamore Maple (*Acer pseudoplatanus*)
Horse-Chestnut or Buckeye (*Aesculus*)
★Tree of Heaven (*Ailanthus*)
Catalpa (*Catalpa*)
Hackberry (*Celtis*)
Downy Hawthorn (*Crataegus mollis*)
Washington Hawthorn (*Crataegus phaenopyrum*)
Russian Olive (*Elaeagnus angustifolia*)
White Ash (*Fraxinus americana*)
European Ash (*Fraxinus excelsior*)
Green Ash (*Fraxinus pennsylvanica*)
★Ginkgo (*Ginkgo biloba*)
Thornless Honey-Locust (*Gleditsia triacanthos inermis*)
★Golden Rain Tree (*Koelreuteria paniculata*)
★Saucer Magnolia (*Magnolia soulangeana*)
★Star Magnolia (*Magnolia stellata*)
★Crab Apple (*Malus* var.)
★Amur Cork (*Phellodendron amurense*)
Colorado Spruce (*Picea pungens*)
★London Plane Tree (*Platanus acerifolia*)
Bradford Callery Pear (*Pyrus calleryana bradfordi*)
White Poplar (*Populus alba*)
★Lombardy Poplar (*Populus nigra italica*)
Red Oak (*Quercus borealis*)
★Black Locust (*Robinia pseudoacacia*)
★Japanese Pagoda Tree (*Sophora japonica*)
★Little-leaf Linden (*Tilia cordata*)
★Crimean Linden (*Tilia euchlora*)
★Silver Linden (*Tilia tomentosa*)
Village Green Zelkova (*Zelkova serrata* "Village Green")

Trees for Wide Streets
Sycamore Maple (*Acer pseudoplatanus*)
★Sugar Maple (*Acer saccharum*)
Sugar Hackberry (*Celtis laevigata*)
★Katsura Tree (*Cercidiphyllum japonicum*)

White Ash (*Fraxinus americana*)
Green Ash (*Fraxinus pennsylvanica lanceolata*)
★Ginkgo (*Ginkgo biloba*)
★Common Honey-Locust (*Gleditsia triacanthos*)
Tulip Tree (*Liriodendron tulipifera*)
★Amur Cork (*Phellodendrum amurense*)
★Eastern White Pine (*Pinus strobus*)
★London Plane Tree (*Platanus acerifolium*)
White Poplar (*Populus alba*)
Sargent Cherry (*Prunus sargenti*)
Red Oak (*Quercus borealis*)
★Pin Oak (*Quercus palustris*)
Willow Oak (*Quercus phellos*)
Japanese Zelkova (*Zelkova serrata*)

Trees for Medium Streets
Norway Maple (*Acer platanoides*)
Mountain Silverbell (*Halesia monticola*)
★Sweet Gum (*Liquidambar styraciflua*)
Hop-Hornbeam (*Ostrya virginiana*)
★Sorrel Tree or Sourwood (*Oxydendrum arboreum*)
Simon Poplar (*Populus simoni*)
Scarlet Oak (*Quercus coccinea*)
Willow Oak (*Quercus phellos*)
★Black Locust (*Robinia pseudoacacia*)
Sassafras (*Sassafras albidum officinale*)
★Japanese Pagoda Tree (*Sophora japonica*)
★Linden species (*Tilia*)

Trees for Suburban Streets
Hedge Maple (*Acer campestre*)
Amur Maple (*Acer ginnala*)
Paperbark Maple (*Acer griseum*)
Globe Norway Maple (*Acer platanoides globosum*)
Mountain Maple (*Acer spicatum*)
Tatarian Maple (*Acer tataricum*)
American Hornbeam (*Carpinus caroliniana*)
Pyramidal European Hornbeam (*Carpinus betulus fastigiata*)
Globe European Hornbeam (*Carpinus betulus globosa*)
Fringetree (*Chionanthus virginicus*)
★Flowering Dogwood (*Cornus florida*)
★Hawthorn species (*Crataegus*)
Korean Evodia (*Evodia danielli*)

Carolina Silverbell (*Halesia carolina*)
★Golden Rain Tree (*Koelreuteria paniculata*)
Oriental Cherry (*Prunus serrulata*)
Columnar Sargent Cherry (*Prunus sargenti columnaris*)
Asiatic Sweetleaf (*Symplocos paniculata*)

Soil Tolerance

Trees Tolerating Acid Soil
★Japanese Maple (*Acer palmatum* var.)
★Flowering Dogwood (*Cornus florida* var.)
Japanese Dogwood (*Cornus kousa*)
★European Beech (*Fagus sylvatica* var.)
★Black Tupelo (*Nyssa sylvatica*)
★Sorrel Tree (*Oxydendrum arboreum*)
Red Oak (*Quercus borealis*)
Scarlet Oak (*Quercus coccinea*)
Willow Oak (*Quercus phellos*)
★Pin Oak (*Quercus palustris*)

Trees Tolerating Moist Soil
★Red Maple (*Acer rubrum*)
Alder species (*Alnus*)
Holly species (*Ilex*)
★Sweet Gum (*Liquidambar styraciflua*)
Sweet Bay (*Magnolia virginiana*)
★Black Tupelo or Black Gum (*Nyssa sylvatica*)
Swamp White Oak (*Quercus bicolor*)
★Willow species (*Salix*)
Common Bald Cyress (*Taxodium distichum*)
American Arbor-vitae (*Thuja occidentalis*)

Trees Tolerating Dry or Poor Soil
Box-Elder (*Ace negunda*)
★Tree of Heaven (*Ailanthus*)
★Gray Birch (*Betula populifolia*)
Russian Olive (*Elaeagnus angustifolia*)
Green Ash (*Fraxinus pennsylvanica*)
★Honey-Locust (*Gleditsia triacanthos* var.)
Western Red Cedar (*Juniperus scopulorum*)
Eastern Red Cedar (*Juniperus virginiana*)
★Golden Rain Tree (*Koelreuteria paniculata*)
Jack Pine (*Pinus banksiana*)
Pitch Pine (*Pinus rigida*)
Virginia or Scrub Pine (*Pinus virginiana*)
White Poplar (*Populus alba*)

Chestnut Oak (*Quercus montana*)
★Black Locust (*Robinia pseudoacacia*)
Sassafras (*Sassafras albidum officinale*)
Chinese Elm (*Ulmus parvifolia*)
Siberian Elm (*Ulmus pumila*)

Pest-Resistant Trees

★Tree of Heaven (*Ailanthus altissma*)
Hornbeam species (*Carpinus*)
★Katsura Tree (*Cercidipyllum japonicum*)
Cornelian Cherry (*Cornus mas*)
Japanese Cornel (*Cornus officinalis*)
Turkish Filbert (*Corylus colurna*)
American Smoke Tree (*Cotinus americanus*)
Franklinia (*Franklinia alatamaha*)
★Ginkgo (*Ginkgo biloba*)
★Honey-Locust (*Gleditsia triacanthos*)
Kentucky Coffee Tree (*Gymnocladus dioicus*)
★Golden Rain Tree (*Koelreuteria paniculata*)
Sweet Gum (*Liquidambar styraciflua*)
Cucumber Tree (*Magnolia acuminata*)
Anise Magnolia (*Magnolia salicifolia*)
★Star Magnolia (*Magnolia stellata*)
Hop-Hornbeam species (*Ostrya*)

Trees for Hedging or Barriers

European Beech (*Fagus sylvatica*) prunes well.
Leyland Cypress (*Cupressocyparis leylandii*) withstands heavy pruning.
Hawthorn varieties (*Crataegus*) easily pruned, advantage of thorns.
Canadian Hemlock (*Tsuga canadensis*) evergreen.
American Holly (*Ilex opaca*) can be pruned.
European Hornbeam (*Carpinus betulus*) prunes well.
Little-leaf Linden (*Tilia cordata*) tolerates heavy pruning.
Hedge Maple (*Acer campestre*) can be pruned.
Austrian Pine (*Pinus nigra*) plant 10–12 feet on centers, staggered row.
Japanese Black Pine (*Pinus thunbergi*) plant 8 feet on centers, staggered row.
Eastern White Pine (*Pinus strobus*) plant 15 feet on centers, staggered row.

OKLAHOMA

State Tree

Redbud (*Cercis canadensis*)

Evergreen Trees

★Cedar species (*Cedrus*)
★Deodar Cedar (*Cedrus deodara*)
Holly species (*Ilex*)
Juniper species (*Juniperus*)
★Southern Magnolia (*Magnolia grandiflora*)
Chinese Photinia (*Photinia serrulata*)
Spruce species (*Picea*)
★Pine species (*Pinus*)
Arbor-vitae species (*Thuja*)
Farkleberry (*Vaccinium arboreum*)

Trees Classified by Height

20–35 Feet
Amur Maple (*Acer ginnala*)
Ohio Buckeye (*Aesculus glabra*)
Downy or Shadblow Serviceberry (*Amelanchier arborea*)
★Gray Birch (*Betula populifolia*)
American Hornbeam (*Carpinus caroliniana*)
Eastern Redbud (*Cercis canadensis*)
Chinese Redbud (*Cercis chinensis*)
★Flowering Dogwood (*Cornus florida*)
Japanese Dogwood (*Cornus kousa*)
Cornelian Cherry (*Cornus mas*)
American Smoke Tree (*Cotinus americanus*)
Common Smoke Tree (*Cotinus coggygria*)
★Hawthorn species (*Crataegus*)

Russian Olive (*Elaeagnus angustifolia*)
Euonymus species (*Euonymus*)
Carolina Silverbell (*Halesia carolina*)
English Holly (*Ilex aquifolium*)
Possum Haw (*Ilex decidua*)
American Holly (*Ilex opaca*)
★Golden Rain Tree (*Koelreuteria paniculata*)
Crape-Myrtle (*Lagerstroemia indica*)
★Crab Apple species (*Malus*)
Almond-leaf or Peach-leaf Willow (*Salix amygdalina*)
★Babylon Weeping Willow (*Salix babylonica*)
European Mountain Ash (*Sorbus aucuparia*)

35–75 Feet
Silk Tree (*Albizzia julibrissin*)
★Red-fruited Tree of Heaven (*Ailanthus altissima erythrocarpa*)
Speckled Alder (*Alnus incana*)
River Birch (*Betula nigra*)
Common Paper-Mulberry (*Broussonetia papyrifera*)
American Hornbeam (*Carpinus caroliniana*)
Mockernut or Mockernut Hickory (*Carya tomentosa*)
Chinese Chestnut (*Castanea mollissima*)
Southern Catalpa (*Catalpa bignoniodes*)
Northern Catalpa (*Catalpa speciosa*)
Sugar Hackberry (*Celtis laevigata*)
Hackberry (*Celtis occidentalis*)
★American Yellow-wood (*Cladrastis lutea*)

Green Hawthorn (*Crataegus viridis*)
Common Persimmon (*Diospyros virginiana*)
Hardy Rubber Tree (*Eucommia ulmoides*)
Green Ash (*Fraxinus pennsylvanica lanceolata*)
Black Walnut (*Juglans nigra*)
Chinese Juniper (*Juniperus chinensis*)
Western Red Cedar (*Juniperus scopulorum*)
Osage Orange (*Maclura pomifera*)
Cucumber Tree (*Magnolia acuminata*)
★Southern Magnolia (*Magnolia grandiflora*)
White Mulberry (*Morus alba*)
Empress Tree (*Paulownia tomentosa*)
★Amur Cork (*Phellodendron amurense*)
Spruce species (*Picea*)
★Pine species (*Pinus*)
Hardy-Orange (*Poncirus trifoliata*)
Black Jack Oak (*Quercus marilandica*)
★Pin Oak (*Quercus palustris*)
Willow Oak (*Quercus phellos*)
★Babylon Weeping Willow (*Salix babylonica*)
Corkscrew Willow (*Salix matsudana tortuosa*)
European Mountain Ash or Rowan Tree (*Sorbus aucuparia*)
Oriental Arbor-vitae (*Thuja orientalis*)
Chinese Elm (*Ulmus parvifolia*)
Siberian Elm (*Ulmus pumila*)

75 Feet or Over
Norway Maple (*Acer platanoides*)
★Red or Swamp Maple (*Acer rubrum*)
★Sugar Maple (*Acer saccharum*)

Hickory species (*Carya*)
Sugar Hackberry (*Celtis laevigata*)
★Beech species (*Fagus*)
White Ash (*Fraxinus americana*)
★Ginkgo or Maidenhair Tree (*Ginkgo biloba*)
★Common Honey-Locust (*Gleditsia triacanthos*)
Kentucky Coffee Tree (*Gymnocladus dioicus*)
Mountain Silverbell (*Halesia monticola*)
Tulip Tree or Yellow Poplar (*Liriodendron tulipifera*)
★Sweet Gum (*Liquidambar styraciflua*)
Cucumber Tree (*Magnolia acuminata*)
Dawn Redwood (*Metasequoia glyptostroboides*)
★Black Gum or Black Tupelo (*Nyssa sylvatica*)
Spruce species (*Picea*)
★Pine species (*Pinus*)
★Plane Tree species (*Platanus*)
Poplar species (*Populus*)
★Oak species (*Quercus*)
★Linden species (*Tilia*)
★Elm species (*Ulmus*)

Trees Classified by Form

Pyramidal
★Birch species (*Betula*)
Italian Cypress (*Cupressus sempervirens*)
English Holly (*Ilex aquifolium*)
American Holly (*Ilex opaca*)
Juniper or Red Cedar species (*Juniperus*)
★Sweet Gum (*Liquidambar styraciflua*)
★Magnolia species (*Magnolia*)
★Black Tupelo or Black Gum (*Nyssa sylvatica*)
Spruce species (*Picea*)
Bolleana Poplar (*Populus alba pyramidalis*)
★Douglas Fir (*Pseudotsuga menziesii*)
Common Bald Cypress (*Taxidium distichum*)
Arbor-vitae species (*Thuja*)
★Linden species (*Tilia*)

Columnar
Sentry Ginkgo (*Ginkgo biloba fastigiata*)
Blue Columnar Chinese Juniper (*Juniperus chinensis columnaris*)
★Lombardy Poplar (*Populus nigra italica*)
Fastigiate Simon Poplar (*Prunus simoni fastigiata*)
Shipmast Locust (*Robinia pseudoacacia rectissima*)
Upright European Mountain Ash (*Sorbus acuparia fastigiata*)
Douglas Arbor-vitae (*Thuja occidentalis douglasi pyramidalis*)
Fastigiate American Arbor-vitae (*Thuja occidentalis fastigiata*)
★American Elm varieties (*Ulmus americana*)

Weeping
"Exzellentz Thiel" Crab Apple (*Malus* "Exzellenz Thiel")
"Oekonomierat Echtermeyer" Crab Apple (*Malus* "Oekonomierat Echtermeyer")
Weeping Mulberry (*Morus alba pendula*)
Koster Weeping Blue Spruce (*Picea pungens kosteriana*)
★Babylon Weeping Willow (*Salix babylonica*)
Weeping European Mountain Ash (*Sorbus aucuparia pendula*)
Weeping American Elm (*Ulmus americana pendula*)

Rounded or Globe-Shaped
★Saucer Magnolia (*Magnolia souangeana*)
★Crab Apple species (*Malus*)
★White Oak (*Quercus alba*)

With Horizontal Branching
Silk Tree (*Albizzia julibrissin*)
★Flowering Dogwood (*Cornus florida*)
★Hawthorn species (*Crataegus*)
★Black Tupelo or Black Gum (*Nyssa sylvatica*)
Spruce species (*Picea*)
Japanese Red Pine (*Pinus densiflora*)
★Eastern White Pine (*Pinus strobus*)
★White Oak (*Quercus alba*)
★Pin Oak (*Quercus palustris*)
Common Bald Cypress (*Taxodium distichum*)

Trees Classified by Color of Blossom

Yellow
★Golden Rain Tree (*Koelreuteria paniculata*)

White
★Shadblow Serviceberry (*Amelanchier canadensis*)
Whitebud (*Cercis canadensis alba*)
★American Yellow-wood (*Cladrastis lutea*)
Carolina Silverbell (*Halesia carolina*)
★Southern Magnolia (*Magnolia grandiflora*)
Arnold Crab Apple (*Malus arnoldiana*)
Siberian Crab Apple (*Malus baccata*)
Tea Crab Apple (*Malus hupehensis*)
Sargent Crab Apple (*Malus sargenti*)
Hardy Orange (*Poncirus trifoliata*)
Sour Cherry (*Prunus cerasus*)
★Common Pear (*Pyrus communis*)
★Japanese Pagoda Tree (*Sophora japonica*)
American Mountain Ash (*Sorbus americana*)

Pink
Wither's Pink Redbud (*Cercis canadensis* "Wither's Pink Charm")
Red Flowering Dogwood (*Cornus florida rubra*)
Toba Hawthorn (*Crataegus mordenensis* "Toba")
Ingleside Crape-Myrtle (*Lagerstroemia indica* "Ingleside Pink")
Japanese Flowering Crab Apple (*Malus floribunda*)
Hopa Crab Apple (*Malus* "Hopa")
Katherine Crab Apple (*Malus* "Katherine")
Prince Georges Crab Apple (*Malus* "Prince Georges")
★Common Apple (*Malus pumila*)

Red
Red Crape-Myrtle (*Lagerstroemia indica* "Wm. Toovey")
Almey Crab Apple (*Malus* "Almey")
Carmine Crab Apple (*Malus atrosanguinea*)

Trees with Bright Red Fruit
★Flowering Dogwood (*Cornus florida*)
American Holly (*Ilex opaca*)
★Siberian Crab Apple (*Malus baccata*)
Hopa Crab Apple (*Malus* "Hopa")
★Common Apple (*Malus pumila*)
Sargent Crab Apple (*Malus sargenti*)
American Mountain Ash (*Sorbus americana*)
European Mountain Ash (*Sorbus aucuparia*)

Trees Classified by Color of Summer Foliage

Blue
Western Red Cedar (*Juniperus scopulorum* var. Chandler Blue)
Eastern Red Cedar (*Juniperus virginiana* var. *Burki*)
Colorado Blue Spruce (*Picea pungens* var. *Glauca*)

Silver to Gray
Russian Olive (*Elaeagnus angustifolia*)
White Poplar (*Populus alba*)
★Silver Linden (*Tilia tomentosa*)

Red to Purple
Schwedler Maple (*Acer platanoides schwedleri*)
Rubylace Locust (*Gleditsia tiracanthos inermis* "Rubylace")
Purple Crab Apple (*Malus purpurea*)

Trees Classified by Color of Fall Foliage

Yellow
Norway Maple (*Acer platanoides* var.)
★Sugar Maple (*Acer saccharum*)
★Birches (*Betula* species)
Hickory species (*Carya*)
Chinese Chestnut (*Castanea mollissima*)
Redbud species (*Cercis*)
Fringetree (*Chiananthus virginicus*)
★American Yellow-wood (*Cladrastis lutea*)
★American Beech (*Fagus grandifolia*)
White Ash (purple to yellow) (*Fraxinus americana*)
★Ginkgo (*Ginkgo biloba*)

★Willow species (*Salix*)

Red
★Red Maple (*Acer rubrum*)
★Sugar Maple (*Acer saccharum*)
★Shadblow Serviceberry (*Amelanchier canadensis*)
Hornbeam species (*Carpinus*)
★Flowering Dogwood (*Cornus florida*)
American Smoke Tree (*Cotinus americanus*)
★Sweet gum (*Liquidambar styraciflua*)
Black Tupelo or Black Gum (*Nyssa sylvatica*)
★Cherry species (*Prunus*)
Red Oak (*Quercus borealis*)
Scarlet Oak (*Quercus coccinea*)
★Pin Oak (*Quercus palustris*)
Sassafras (*Sassafras albidum*)

Purple
White Ash (*Fraxinus americana*)
★Sweet Gum (*Liquidambar styraciflua*)
★White Oak (*Quercus alba*)
★Common Pear (*Pyrus communis*)

Trees with Interesting Bark

Gray
★Red Maple (*Acer rubrum*)
★Serviceberry species (*Amelanchier*)
Hackberry species (*Celtis*)
★American Yellow-wood (*Cladrastis lutea*)
★Hawthorn species (*Crataegus*)
★Beech species (*Fagus*)
American Holly (*Ilex opaca*)
English or Persian Walnut (*Juglans regia*)
Cucumber Tree (*Magnolia acuminata*)
★Saucer Magnolia (*Magnolia soulangeana*)
Red Oak (young trunk and branches) (*Quercus borealis*)
Black Oak (young trunk and branches) (*Quercus velutina*)
Mountain Ash species (*Sorbus*)

Red
Japanese Red Pine (*Pinus densiflora*)
Scotch Pine (*Pinus sylvestris*)

Corky
Hackberry (*Celtis*)

Green
★Babylon Weeping Willow (*Salix babylonica*)

Flaking
★Birch species (*Betula*)
Shagbark Hickory (*Carya ovata*)
Russian Olive (*Elaeagnus angustifolia*)
Crape-Myrtle (*Lagerstroemia indica*)
★Plane Tree species (*Platanus*)

Trees for the City
Box-Elder (*Acer negundo*)
Norway Maple (*Acer platanoides*)
★Horse-Chestnut or Buckeye (*Aesculus*)
★Tree of Heaven (*Ailanthus*)
Silk Tree (*Albizzia julibrissin*)
Catalpa (*Catalpa*)
Hackberry (*Celtis*)
Russian Olive (*Elaeagnus angustifolia*)
White Ash (*Fraxinus americana*)
Green Ash (*Fraxinus pennsylvanica*)
★Ginkgo (*Ginkgo biloba*)
Thornless Honey-Locust (*Gleditsia triacanthos inermis*)
★Golden Rain Tree (*Koelreuteria paniculata*)
★Southern Magnolia (*Magnolia grandiflora*)
★Saucer Magnolia (*Magnolia soulangeana*)
★Crab Apple (*Malus* var.)
Chinaberry (*Melia azedarach*)
White Poplar (*Populus alba*)
★Lombardy Poplar (*Populus nigra italica*)
Red Oak (*Quercus borealis*)
★Black Locust (*Robinia pseudoacacia*)
★Japanese Pagoda Tree (*Sophora japonica*)

Trees for Wide Streets
★Sugar Maple (*Acer saccharum*)

Sugar Hackberry (*Celtis laevigata*)
White Ash (*Fraxinus americana*)
Green Ash (*Fraxinus pennsylvanica lanceolata*)
★Ginkgo (*Ginkgo biloba*)
★Common Honey-Locust (*Gleditsia triacanthos*)
Tulip Tree (*Liriodendron tulipifera*)
★Southern Magnolia (*Magnolia grandiflora*)
★Eastern White Pine (*Pinus strobus*)
★London Plane Tree (*Platanus acerifolia*)
White Poplar (*Populus alba*)
Red Oak (*Quercus borealis*)
★Pin Oak (*Quercus palustris*)
Willow Oak (*Quercus phellos*)

Trees for Medium Streets
Norway Maple (*Acer platanoides*)
★Sweet Gum (*Liquidambar styraciflua*)
Chinaberry (*Melia azedarach*)
Hop-Hornbeam (*Ostrya virginiana*)
Simon Poplar (*Populus simoni*)
Scarlet Oak (*Quercus coccinea*)
Laurel Oak (*Quercus laurifolia*)
Willow Oak (*Quercus phellos*)
★Black Locust (*Robinia pseudoacacia*)
Sassafras (*Sassafras albidum officinale*)
★Linden species (*Tilia*)

Trees for Suburban Streets
Fringetree (*Chionanthus virginicus*)
★Hawthorn species (*Crataegus*)
Carolina Silverbell (*Halesia carolina*)
★Golden Rain Tree (*Koelreuteria paniculata*)

Soil Tolerance

Trees Tolerating Acid Soil
★Flowering Dogwood (*Cornus florida*)
★Black Tupelo (*Nyssa sylvatica*)

Hardy Orange (*Poncirus trifoliata*)
Red Oak (*Quercus borealis*)
Scarlet Oak (*Quercus coccinea*)
★Pin Oak (*Quercus palustris*)
Willow Oak (*Quercus phellos*)

Trees Tolerating Moist Soil
★Red Maple (*Acer rubrum*)
Holly species (*Ilex*)
★Sweet Gum (*Liquidambar styraciflua*)
★Black Tupelo or Black Gum (*Nyssa sylvatica*)
Poplar species (*Populus*)
Swamp White Oak (*Quercus bicolor*)
★Willow species (*Salix*)
Common Bald Cypress (*Taxodium distichum*)
American Arbor-vitae (*Thuja occidentalis*)

Trees Tolerating Dry or Poor Soil
Box-Elder (*Acer negunda*)
★Tree of Heaven (*Ailanthus*)
Silk Tree (*Albizzia julibrissin*)
Common Paper-Mulberry (*Broussonetia papyrifera*)
Russian Olive (*Elaeagnus angustifolia*)
Green Ash (*Fraxinus pennsylvanica*)
★Honey-Locust (*Gleditsia triacanthos* var.)
Western Red Cedar (*Juniperus scopulorum*)
Eastern Red Cedar (*Juniperus virginiana*)
★Golden Rain Tree (*Koelreuteria paniculata*)
Osage-Orange (*Maclura pomifera*)
White Poplar (*Populus alba*)
Black Jack Oak (*Quercus marilandica*)
★Black Locust (*Robinia pseudoacacia*)
Sassafras (*Sassafras albidum officinale*)
★Japanese Pagoda Tree (*Sophora japonica*)
Chinese Elm (*Ulmus parvifolia*)

Siberian Elm (*Ulmus pumila*)

Pest-Resistant Trees
★Tree of Heaven (*Ailanthus altissima*)
American Smoke Tree (*Cotinus americanus*)
Russian Olive (*Elaeagnus angustifolia*)
Fig species (*Ficus*)
★Ginkgo (*Ginkgo biloba*)
★Honey-Locust (*Gleditsia triacanthos*)
Kentucky Coffee Tree (*Gymnocladus dioicus*)
Juniper species (*Juniperus*)
★Golden Rain Tree (*Koelreuteria paniculata*)
★Sweet Gum (*Liquidambar styraciflua*)
Cucumber Tree (*Magnolia acuminata*)
Hop-Hornbeam species (*Ostrya*)

Trees for Hedging or Barriers
European Beech (*Fagus sylvatica*) prunes well.
Leyland Cypress (*Cupressocyparis leylandii*) withstands heavy pruning.
Hawthorn varieties (*Crataegus*) easily pruned, advantage of thorns.
Canadian Hemlock (*Tsuga canadensis*) evergreen.
American Holly (*Ilex opaca*) can be pruned.
European Hornbeam (*Carpinus betulus*) prunes well.
Little-leaf Linden (*Tilia cordata*) tolerates heavy pruning.
Hedge Maple (*Acer campestre*) can be pruned.
Austrian Pine (*Pinus nigra*) plant 10–12 feet on centers, staggered row.
Japanese Black Pine (*Pinus thunbergi*) plant 8 feet on centers, staggered row.
Eastern White Pine (*Pinus strobus*) plant 15 feet on centers, staggered row.

OREGON

State Tree
★Douglas Fir (*Pseudotsuga menziesii*)

Evergreen Trees

Fir species (*Abies*)
★Acacia species (*Acacia*)
Monkey-Puzzle Tree (*Araucaria araucana*)
Pacific Madrone (*Arbutus menziesi*)
Strawberry Tree (*Arbutus unedo*)
Camellia species (*Camellia*)
Giant Evergreen Chinquapin (*Castonopsis chrysophylla*)
False Cypress species (*Chamaecyparis*)
★Deodar Cedar (*Cedrus deodara*)
Evergreen Dogwood (*Cornus capitata*)
Common China Fir (*Cunninghamia lanceolata*)
★Cypress species (*Cupressus*)
Loquat (*Eriobotrya japonica*)
Eucalyptus species (*Eucalyptus*)
Brush-Cherry Eugenia (*Eugenia paniculata*)
Holly species (*Ilex*)
Juniper species (*Juniperus*)
★Larch species (*Larix*)
California Incense Cedar (*Libocedrus decurrens*)
★Southern Magnolia (*Magnolia grandiflora*)
California Bayberry (*Myrica californica*)
Chinese Photinia (*Photinia serrulata*)
Spruce species (*Picea*)
★Pine species (*Pinus*)
Yew Podocarpus (*Podocarpus macrophyllus*)
Portugal Laurel (*Prunus lusitanica*)
★Douglas Fir (*Pseudotsuga menziesii*)
★California Live Oak (*Quercus agrifolia*)
Canyon Live or Golden Cup Oak (*Quercus chrysolepis*)
★Redwood (*Sequoia sempervirens*)
Umbrella Pine (*Sciadopitys verticillata*)
Arbor-vitae species (*Thuja*)
★Hemlock species (*Tsuga*)

California Laurel (*Umbellularia californica*)

Trees Classified by Height

20–35 Feet
Argutum Maple (*Acer argutum*)
Hedge Maple (*Acer campestre*)
Hornbeam Maple (*Acer carpinifolium*)
Vine Maple (*Acer circinatum*)
Amur Maple (*Acer ginnala*)
Paperback Maple (*Acer griseum*)
Manchurian Maple (*Acer mandshuricum*)
★Japanese Maple (*Acer palmatum*)
Mountain Maple (*Acer spicatum*)
Tatarian Maple (*Acer tataricum*)
Ohio Buckeye (*Aesculus glabra*)
Apple Serviceberry (*Amelanchier grandiflora*)
★Gray Birch (*Betula populifolia*)
Lemon Bottlebrush (*Callistemon lanceolatus*)
European Hornbeam (*Carpinus betulus globosa*)
Mockernut (*Carya tomentosa*)
Judas Tree (*Cercis siliquastrum*)
Fringetree (*Chionanthus virginicus*)
Japanese Clethra (*Clethra barbinervis*)
Japanese Dogwood (*Cornus kousa*)
Cornelian Cherry (*Cornus mas*)
Japanese Cornel (*Cornus officinalis*)
American Smoke Tree (*Cotinus americanus*)
★Hawthorn species (*Crataegus*)
Modoc Cypress (*Cupressus bakeri*)
Russian Olive (*Elaeagnus angustifolia*)
Euonymus species (*Euonymus*)
Flowering Ash (*Fraxinus ornus*)
Carolina Silverbell (*Halesia carolina*)
Dahoon (*Ilex cassine*)
Possum Haw (*Ilex decidua*)
Longstalk Holly (*Ilex pedunculosa*)
Perny Holly (*Ilex pernyi*)
Yaupon (*Ilex vomitoria*)
Neddle Juniper (*Juniperus rigida*)

★Golden Rain Tree (*Koelreuteria paniculata*)
Laburnum species (*Laburnum*)
Anise Magnolia (*Magnolia salicifolia*)
Oyama Magnolia (*Magnolia sieboldi*)
★Saucer Magnolia (*Magnolia soulangeana*)
★Star Magnolia (*Magnolia stellata*)
Watson Magnolia (*Magnolia watsoni*)
Wilson Magnolia (*Magnolia wilsoni*)
★Crab Apple species (*Malus*)
★Cherry species (*Prunus*)
Black Jack Oak (*Quercus marilandica*)
Almond-leaf Willow (*Salix amygdalina*)
Goat Willow (*Salix caprea*)
★Babylon Weeping Willow (*Salix babylonica*)
Showy Mountain Ash (*Sorbus decora*)
Snowberry Mountain Ash (*Sorbus discolor*)
Folgner Mountain Ash (*Sorbus folgneri*)
Snowbell species (*Styrax*)
Asiatic Sweetleaf (*Symplocos paniculata*)
Japanese Tree Lilac (*Syringa amurensis japonica*)

35–75 Feet
Korean Fir (*Abies koreana*)
Silver Wattle (*Acacia decurrens dealbata*)
Box-Elder (*Acer negudo*)
Nikko Maple (*Acer nikoense*)
Striped Maple or Moosewood (*Acer pennsylvanicum*)
Red-fruited Tree of Heaven (*Ailanthus altissima erythrocarpa*)
Silk Tree (*Albizzia julibrissin*)
Italian Alder (*Alnus cordata*)
Speckled Alder (*Alnus incana*)
Red Alder (*Alnus rubra*)
★Shadblow Serviceberry (*Amelanchier laevis*)
Devil's Walking Stick (*Aralia elata*)
Dahurian Birch (*Betula davurica*)
Manchurian Birch (*Betula mandshurica szechuanica*)
★European Birch (*Betula pendula*)

European Hornbeam (*Carpinus betulus*)
American Hornbeam (*Carpinus caroliniana*)
Japanese Hornbeam (*Carpinus japonica*)
Chinese Chestnut (*Castanea mollissima*)
Southern Catalpa (*Catalpa bignoniodes*)
Chinese Toon (*Cedrela sinensis*)
Bunch Hackberry (*Celtis bungeana*)
★Katsura Tree (*Cercidiphyllum japonicum*)
Eastern Redbud (*Cercis canadensis*)
Chinese Redbud (*Cercis chinensis*)
★American Yellow-wood (*Cladrastis lutea*)
Delavay Clethra (*Clethra delavayi*)
Giant Dogwood (*Cornus controversa*)
★Flowering Dogwood (*Cornus florida*)
Turkish Filbert (*Corylus coluna*)
Cockspur Thorn (*Crataegus crus-galli*)
Green Hawthorn (*Crataegus viridis*)
Common China Fir (*Cunninghamia lanceolata*)
Italian Cypress (*Cupressus sempervirens*)
Kaki Persimmon (*Diospyros kaki*)
Common Persimmon (*Diospyros virginiana*)
Brush-Cherry Eugenia (*Eugenia paniculata*)
Chinese Parasol Tree (*Firmiana simpley*)
Green Ash (*Fraxinus pennsylvanica lanceolata*)
English Holly (*Ilex aquifolium*)
Dahoon (*Ilex cassine*)
Lustreleaf Holly (*Ilex latifolia*)
Mountain Winterberry (*Ilex montana*)
American Holly (*Ilex opaca*)
Hinds Black Walnut (*Juglans hindsi*)
Heartnut (*Juglans sieboldiana cordiformis*)
Chinese Juniper (*Juniperus chinensis*)
Syrian Juniper (*Juniperus drupacea*)
Greek Juniper (*Juniperus excelsa*)
Alligator Juniper (*Juniperus pachyphloea*)
Rocky Mountain Red Cedar (*Juniperus scopulorum*)
Yulan Magnolia (*Magnolia denudata*)
Fraser Magnolia (*Magnolia fraseri*)
Kobus Magnolia (*Magnolia kobus borealis*)
Loebner Magnolia (*Magnolia loebneri*)
Big-leaf Magnolia (*Magnolia macrophylla*)
Veitch Magnolia (*Magnolia veitchi*)
Sweet Bay (*Magnolia virginiana*)
Siberian Crab Apple (*Malus baccata*)
"Cowichan" Crab Apple (*Malus "Cowichan"*)
"Dolgo" Crab Apple (*Malus "Dolgo"*)
"Makamik" Crab Apple (*Malus "Makamik"*)
Cherry Crab Apple (*Malus robusta*)
"Sissipuk" Crab Apple (*Malus "Sissipuk"*)
Chinaberry (*Melia azedarach*)
White Mulberry (*Morus alba*)
Persian Parrotia (*Parrotia persica*)
Empress Tree (*Paulownia tomentosa*)
★Amur Cork (*Phellodendron amurense*)
Dragon Spruce (*Picea asperata*)
Jack Pine (*Pinus banksiana*)
Lace-bark Pine (*Pinus bungeana*)
Swiss Stone Pine (*Pinus cembra*)
Limber Pine (*Pinus flexilis*)
Aleppo Pine (*Pinus halepensis*)
Scotch Pine (*Pinus sylvestris*)
Torrey Pine (*Pinus torreyana*)
Yew Podocarpus (*Podocarpus macrophyllus*)
Chinese Poplar (*Populus lasiocarpa*)
Simon Poplar (*Populus simoni*)
Honey Mesquite (*Prosopis glandulosa*)
Portugal Laurel (*Prunus lusitanica*)
Miyama Cherry (*Prunus maximowiczi*)
Sargent Cherry (*Prunus sargenti*)
Yoshino Cherry (*Prunus yedoensis*)
Ussurian Pear (*Pyrus ussuriensis*)
Canyon Live or Golden Cup Oak (*Quercus chrysolepis*)
Laurel Oak (*Quercus laurifolia*)
Shingle Oak (*Quercus imbricaria*)
Water Oak (*Quercus nigra*)
★Pin Oak (*Quercus palustris*)
Willow Oak (*Quercus phellos*)
Clammy Locust (*Robinia viscosa*)

White Willow (*Salix alba*)
Wisconsin or Niobe Weeping Willow (*Salix blanda*)
Elaeagnus Willow (*Salix elaeagnos*)
Thurlow Weeping Willow (*Salix elegantissima*)
Laurel Willow (*Salix pentandra*)
Blueberry Elder (*Sambucus coerulea*)
Korean Mountain Ash (*Sorbus alnifolia*)
White Beam Mountain Ash (*Sorbus aria*)
European Mountain Ash or Rowan Tree (*Sorbus aucuparia*)
Korean Stewartia (*Stewartia koreana*)
Japanese Stewartia (*Stewartia pseudo-camellia*)
American Arbor-vitae (*Thuja occidentalis*)
Japanese Arbor-vitae (*Thuja standishi*)
★Crimean Linden (*Tilia euchlora*)
Carolina Hemlock (*Tsuga caroliniana*)
Chinese Elm (*Ulmus parvifolia*)
Siberian Elm (*Ulmus pumila*)

75 Feet or Over
Fir species (*Abies*)
Norway Maple (*Acer platanoides*)
Sycamore Maple (*Acer pseudoplatanus*)
★Red or Swamp Maple (*Acer rubrum*)
★Sugar Maple (*Acer saccharum*)
★Baumann Horse-Chestnut (*Aesculus hippocastanum baumanni*)
European Alder (*Alnus glutinosa*)
Monkey-Puzzle Tree (*Araucaria araucana*)
Hickory species (*Carya*)
★Cedar species (*Cedrus*)
European Hackberry (*Celtis australis*)
Sugar Hackberry (*Celtis laevigata*)
★Katsura Tree (*Cercidiphyllum japonicum*)
False Cypress species (*Chamaecyparis*)
Pacific Dogwood (*Cornus nuttalli*)
Cryptomeria (*Cryptomeria japonica*)
Eucalyptus species (*Eucalyptus*)
★Beech species (*Fagus*)
White Ash (*Fraxinus americana*)
European Ash (*Fraxinus excelsior*)
★Ginkgo or Maidenhair Tree (*Ginkgo biloba*)
★Common Honey-Locust (*Gleditsia triacanthos*)
Kentucky Coffee Tree (*Gymnocladus dioicus*)
Mountain Silverbell (*Halesia monticola*)
English or Persian Walnut (*Juglans regia*)
Japanese Larch (*Larix leptolepis*)
California Incense Cedar (*Libocedrus decurrens*)
★Sweet Gum (*Liquidambar styraciflua*)
Tulip Tree or Yellow Poplar (*Liriodendron tulipfera*)
Cucumber Tree (*Magnolia acuminata*)
Cambell Magnolia (*Magnolia cambelli*)
★Southern Magnolia (*Magnolia grandiflora*)
White-Leaf Japanese Magnolia (*Magnolia obovata*)
★Black Gum or Black Tupelo (*Nyssa sylvatica*)
Dawn Redwood (*Metasequoia glyptostroboides*)
Spruce species (*Picea*)
★Pine species (*Pinus*)
Italian Stone Pine (*Pinus pinea*)
★Plane Tree species (*Platanus*)
★Poplar species (*Populus*)
Sargent Cherry (*Prunus sargenti*)
Golden Larch (*Pseudolarix amabilia*)
★Douglas Fir (*Pseudotsuga menziesii*)
Caucasian Wingnut (*Pterocarya fraxinifolia*)
★Oak species (*Quercus*)
Umbrella Pine (*Sciadopitys verticillata*)
Giant Arbor-vitae (*Thuja plicata*)
★Linden species (*Tilia*)
★Canada Hemlock (*Tsuga canadensis*)
★Elm species (*Ulmus*)
Japanese Zelkova (*Zelkova serrata*)

Trees Classified by Form

Pyramidal
Fir species (*Abies*)
Red Alder (*Alnus rubra*)
★Birch species (*Betula*)
★Cedar species (*Cedrus*)
False Cypress species (*Chamaecyparis*)

Turkish Filbert (*Corylus coluna*)
Cryptomeria (*Cryptomeria japonica*)
Italian Cypress (*Cupressus sempervirens*)
★Beech species (*Fagus*)
English Holly (*Ilex aquifolia*)
American Holly (*Ilex opaca*)
Longstalk Holly (*Ilex pedunculosa*)
Juniper or Red Cedar species (*Juniperus*)
★Larch species (*Larix*)
★Sweet Gum (*Liquidambar styraciflua*)
★Magnolia species (*Magnolia*)
Dawn Redwood (*Metasequoia glyptostroboides*)
★Black Tupelo or Black Gum (*Nyssa sylvatica*)
Spruce species (*Picea*)
Swiss Stone Pine (*Pinus cembra*)
Korean Pine (*Pinus koraiensis*)
★Pyramidal Austrian Pine (*Pinus nigra pyramidalis*)
Japanese White Pine (*Pinus parviflora*)
Golden larch (*Pseudolarix amabilis*)
Bolleana Poplar (*Populus alba pyramidalis*)
★Douglas Fir (*Pseudotsuga menziesii*)
Turkey Oak (*Quercus cerris*)
★Pin Oak (*Quercus palustris*)
Umbrella Pine (*Sciadopitys verticillata*)
Korean Stewartia (*Stewartia koreana*)
★Linden species (*Tilia*)
Arbor-vitae species (*Thuja*)
★Hemlock species (*Tsuga*)
Smooth-leaved Elm varieties (*Ulmus carpinifolia*)

Rounded or Globe-Shaped
★Japanese Maple (*Acer palmatum*)
Globe Norway Maple (*Acer platanoides globosum*)
Globe European Hornbeam (*Carpinus betulus globosa*)
Bunch Hackberry (*Celtis bungeana*)
Cornelian Cherry (*Cornus mas*)
Japanese Cornel (*Cornus officinalis*)
Single Seed Hawthorn (*Crataegus monogyna inermis*)
★Saucer Magnolia (*Magnolia soulangeana*)
★Crab Apple Species (*Malus*)
★White Oak (*Quercus alba*)
Umbrella Black Locust (*Robinia pseudoacacia umbraculifera*)
Sargent Hemlock (*Tsuga canadensis sargenti*)
Koopmann Elm (*Ulmus carpinifolia koopmanni*)
Globe Smooth-leaved Elm (*Ulmus carpinifolia umbraculifera*)

Columnar
Ascending Norway Maple (*Acer platanoides ascendens*)
Columnar Norway Maple (*Acer platanoides columnare*)
Erect Norway Maple (*Acer platanoides erectum*)
Columnar Red Maple (*Acer rubrum columnare*)
Sentry Maple (*Acer saccharum monumentale*)
Fastigiate European Hornbeam (*Carpinus betulus fastigiata*)
Scarab Lawson Cypress (*Chamaecyparis lawsoniana allumi*)
Erect Lawson Cypress (*Chamaecyparis lawsoniana erecta*)
Column Hinoki Cypress (*Chamaecyparis obtusa erecta*)
Fastigiate Washington Hawthorn (*Crataegus phaenopyrum fastigiata*)
Dawyck Beech (*Fagus sylvatica fastigiata*)
Sentry Ginkgo (*Ginkgo biloba fastigiata*)
Blue Columnar Chinese Juniper (*Juniperus chinensis columnaris*)
Schott Red Cedar (*Juniperus virginiana schotti*)
Fastigiate Scotch Pine (*Pinus sylvestris fastigiata*)
★Lombardy Poplar (*Populus nigra italica*)
Fastigiate Simon Poplar (*Populus simoni fastigiata*)
Columnar Sargent Cherry (*Prunus sargenti columnaris*)
"Amanogawa" Cherry (*Prunus serrulata "Amanogawa"*)
Fastigiate English Oak (*Quercus robur fastigiata*)
Shipmast Locust (*Robinia pseudoacacia rectissima*)

Upright European Mountain Ash (*Sorbus aucuparia fastigiata*)
Common Bald Cypress (*Taxodium distichum*)
Douglas Arbor-vitae (*Thuja occidentalis douglasi pyramidalis*)
Fastigiate American Arbor-vitae (*Thuja occidentalis fastigiata*)
Columnar Giant Arbor-vitae (*Thuja plicata fastigiata*)
Columnar Big-leaf Linden (*Tilia platyphyllos fastigiata*)
★American Elm varieties (*Ulmus americana*)

Weeping
Slender European Birch (*Betula pendula tristis*)
Young's Birch (*Betula pendula youngi*)
Weeping European Hornbeam (*Carpinus betulus pendula*)
★Deodar Cedar (*Cedrus deodara*)
Weeping Lawson Cypress (*Chamaecyparis lawsoniana pendula*)
★Weeping Beech (*Fagus sylvatica pendula*)
Weeping Purple Beech (*Fagus sylvatica purpureo-pendula*)
Weeping Red Cedar (*Juniperus virginiana pendula*)
Weeping Larch (*Larix decidua pendula*)
"Exzellenz Thiel" Crab Apple (*Malus* "Exzellenz Thiel")
"Oekonomierat Echtermeyer" Crab Apple (*Malus* "Oekonomierat Echtermeyer")
Weeping Mulberry (*Morus alba pendula*)
Brewer Spruce (*Picea breweriana*)
Koster Weeping Blue Spruce (*Picea pungens kosteriana*)
Weeping White Pine (*Pinus strobus pendula*)
Weeping Black Cherry (*Prunus serotina pendula*)
Weeping Higan Cherry (*Prunus subhirtella pendula*)
"Yaeshidare" Cherry (*Prunus subhirtella pendula flora plena*)
Weeping Yoshino Cherry (*Prunus yedoensis perpendens*)
Weeping Douglas Fir (*Pseudotsuga menziesii pendula*)
Golden Weeping Willow (*Salix alba tristis*)
★Babylon Weeping Willow (*Salix babylonica*)
Wisconsin or Niobe Weeping Willow (*Salix blanda*)
Thurlow Weeping Willow (*Salix elegantissima*)
Weeping Japanese Pagoda Tree (*Sophora japonica pendula*)
Weeping European Mountain Ash (*Sorbus aucuparia pendula*)
Weeping Folgner Mountain Ash (*Sorbus folgneri pendula*)
Pendant Silver Linden (*Tilia petiolaris*)
Sargent Hemlock (*Tsuga canadensis pendula*)
Weeping American Elm (*Ulmus americana pendula*)

With Horizontal Branching
Fir species (*Abies*)
Silk Tree (*Albizzia julibrissin*)
Monkey-Puzzle Tree (*Araucaria araucana*)
★Cedar species (*Cedrus*)
Eastern Redbud (*Cercis canadensis*)
Giant Dogwood (*Cornus controversa*)
★Flowering Dogwood (*Cornus florida*)
Japanese Dogwood (*Cornus kousa*)
★Hawthorn species (*Crataegus*)
Dawn Redwood (*Metasequoia glyprostroboides*)
★Black Tupelo or Black Gum (*Nyssa sylvatica*)
Spruce species (*Picea*)
Japanese Red Pine (*Pinus densiflora*)
★Eastern White Pine (*Pinus strobus*)
Yew Podocarpus (*Podocarpus macrophyllus*)
Golden Larch (*Pseudolarix amabilis*)
★White Oak (*Quercus alba*)
★Pin Oak (*Quercus palustris*)
Common Bald Cypress (*Taxodium distichum*)

Trees Classified by Color of Blossom
Yellow
★Golden Rain Tree (*Koelreuteria paniculata*)

★Laburnum (*Laburnum vossi*)
White
★Shadblow Serviceberry (*Amelanchier canadensis*)
Strawberry Tree (*Arbutus unedo*)
Whitebud (*Cercis canadensis alba*)
American Yellow-wood (*Cladrastis lutea*)
Japanese Dogwood (*Cornus kousa*)
Washington Hawthorn (*Crataegus phaenopyrum*)
Carolina Silverbell (*Halesia carolina*)
Yulan Magnolia (*Magnolia denudata*)
★Southern Magnolia (*Magnolia grandiflora*)
★Star Magnolia (*Magnolia stellata*)
Arnold Crab Apple (*Malus arnoldiana*)
Siberian Crab Apple (*Malus baccata*)
Tea Crab Apple (*Malus hupehensis*)
Sargent Crab Apple (*Malus sargenti*)
Chinese Photinia (*Photinia serrulata*)
Thundercloud Plum Lt. Pink (*Prunus cerasifera* "Thundercloud")
Sour Cherry (*Prunus cerasus*)
Mount Fuji Cherry (*Prunus serrulata* "Shirotae")
Yoshino Cherry (*Prunus yedoensis*)
Bradford Callery Pear (*Pyrus calleryana bradfordi*)
★Common Pear (*Pyrus communis*)
★Japanese Pagoda Tree (*Sophora japonica*)
American Mountain Ash (*Sorbus americana*)
European Mountain Ash (*Sorbus aucuparia*)
Showy Mountain Ash (*Sorbus decora*)
Japanese Stewartia (*Stewartia pseudocamellia*)

Pink
Wither's Pink Redbud (*Cercis canadensis* "Wither's Pink Charm")
Red Flowering Dogwood (*Cornus florida rubra*)
Toba Hawthorn (*Crataegus mordenensis* "Toba")
Saucer Magnolia (*Magnolia soulangeana*)
Japanese Flowering Crab Apple (*Malus floribunda*)
Katherine Crab Apple (*Malus* "Katherine")
Prince Georges Crab Apple (*Malus* "Prince Georges")
★Common Apple (*Malus pumila*)
Amanogawa Cherry (*Prunus serrulata* "Amanogawa")
Autumn Cherry (*Prunus subhirtella autumnalis*)
Blireiana Plum (*Prunus blireiana*)
Kwanzan Cherry (*Prunus serrulata* "Kwanzan")
Weeping Cherry (*Prunus subhirtella pendula*)
Sargent Cherry (*Prunus sargenti*)

Red
Ruby Horse-Chestnut (*Aesculus carnea briotti*)
Paul's Scarlet Hawthorn (*Crataegus oxyacantha pauli*)
Alexandrina Magnolia (*Magnolia soulangeana* "Alexandrina")
Almey Crab Apple (*Malus* "Almey")
Carmine Crab Apple (*Malus atrosanguinea*)

Trees with Bright Red Fruit
★Flowering Dogwood (*Cornus florida*)
Japanese Dogwood (*Cornus kousa*)
Pacific Dogwood (*Cornus nuttalli*)
Downy Hawthorn (*Crataegus mollis*)
Washington Hawthorn (*Crataegus phaenopyrum*)
American Holly (*Ilex opaca*)
Almey Crab Apple (*Malus* "Almey")
★Siberian Crab Apple (*Malus baccata*)
Hopa Crab Aple (*Malus* "Hopa")
★Common Apple (*Malus pumila*)
Sargent Crab Apple (*Malus sargenti*)
California Pepper Tree (*Schinus molle*)
Korean Mountain Ash (*Sorbus alnifolia*)
American Mountain Ash (*Sorbus americana*)
European Mountain Ash (*Sorbus aucuparia*)

Trees Classified by Color of Summer Foliage
Blue
White Fir (*Abies concolor*)
Silver Wattle (*Acacia decurrens dealbata*)
★Blue Atlas Cedar (*Cedrus atlantica glauca*)

Steel Lawson Cypress (*Chamaecyparis lawsonia glauca*)
Smooth Arizona Cypress (*Cupressus arizonica bonita*)
Blue Gum (*Eucalyptus globulus*)
Western Red Cedar (*Juniperus scopulorum* var. Chandler Blue)
Eastern Red Cedar (*Juniperus virginiana* var. *Burki*)
Colorado Blue Spruce (*Picea pungens* var. *Glauca*)

Silver to Gray
Russian Olive (*Elaeagnus angustifolia*)
White Poplar (*Populus alba*)
Pendant Silver Linden (*Tilia petiolaris*)
★Silver Linden (*Tilia tomentosa*)

Red to Purple
Blood-leaf Japanese Maple (*Acer palmatum atro-purpureum*)
Crimson King Maple (*Acer platanoides* "Crimson King")
Schwedler Maple (*Acer platanoides schwedleri*)
Purple-leaf Sycamore Maple (*Acer pseudoplatanus*)
Purple Beech (*Fagus sylvatica atropunica*)
Weeping Purple Beech (*Fagus sylvatica purpureo-pendula*)
River's Purple Beech (*Fagus sylvatica riversi*)
Rubylace Locust (*Gleditsia triacanthos inermis* "Rubylace")
Purple Crab Apple (*Malus purpurea*)
Blireiana Plum (*Prunus blireiana*)
Pissard Plum (*Prunus cerasifera atropurpurea*)
Woods Myrobalan Plum (*Prunus cerasifera woodi*)
Thundercloud Plum (*Prunus cerasifera nigra* "Thundercloud")
Blood-leaf Peach (*Prunus persica atropurpurea*)
Purple English Oak (*Quercus robur atropurpurea*)

Trees Classified by Color of Fall Foliage
Yellow
Norway Maples (*Acer platanoides* var.)
★Sugar Maple (*Acer saccharum*)
Big-leaf Maple (*Acer macrophyllum*)
Striped Maple or Moosewood (*Acer pensylvanicum*)
Ohio Buckeye (*Aesculus glabra*)
Apple Serviceberry (yellow-orange) (*Amelanchier grandiflora*)
★Birches (*Betula species*)
Hickory species (*Carya*)
Chinese Chestnut (*Castanea mollissima*)
★Katsura Tree (yellow to scarlet) (*Cercidiphyllum japonicum*)
Redbud species (*Cercis*)
Fringetree (*Chionanthus virginicus*)
★American Yellow-wood (*Cladrastis lutea*)
★American Beech (*Fagus grandifolia*)
★European Beech (*Fagus sylvatica*)
White Ash (purple to yellow) (*Fraxinus americana*)
★Ginkgo (*Ginkgo biloba*)
★Star Magnolia (bronze) (*Magnolia stellata*)
Golden Larch (*Pseudolarix amabilis*)
★Willow species (*Salix*)

Red
Vine Maple (*Acer circinatum*)
Amur Maple (*Acer ginnala*)
Manchurian Maple (*Acer mandshuricum*)
Nikko Maple (*Acer nikoense*)
★Japanese Maple (*Acer palmatum* var.)
★Red Maple (*Acer rubrum*)
★Sugar Maple (*Acer saccharum*)
Tatarian Maple (*Acer tataricum*)
★Shadblow Serviceberry (*Amelanchier canadensis*)
Hornbeam species (*Carpinus*)
American Smoke Tree (*Cotinus americanus*)
★Flowering Dogwood (*Cornus florida*)
Japanese Dogwood (*Cornus kousa*)
Pacific Dogwood (*Cornus nuttalli*)
Washington Hawthorn (*Crataegus phaenopyrum*)
★Sweet Gum (*Liquidambar styraciflua*)
Dawson Crab Apple (*Malus dawsoniana*)
★Black Tupelo or Black Gum (*Nyssa sylvatica*)

Persian Parrotia (*Parrotia persica*)
Chinese Pistache (*Pistacia chinensis*)
★Cherry species (*Prunus*)
Bradford Callery Pear (*Pyrus calleryana bradfordi*)
Red Oak (*Quercus borealis*)
Scarlet Oak (*Quercus coccinea*)
★Pin Oak (*Quercus palustris*)
Sassafras (*Sassafras albidum*)
Korean Mountain Ash (*Sorbus alnifolia*)
Korean Stewartia (orange-red) (*Stewartia koreana*)

Purple
White Ash (*Fraxinus americana*)
★Sweet Gum (*Liquidambar styraciflua*)
★Common Pear (*Pyrus communis*)
★White Oak (*Quercus alba*)
Japanese Stewartia (*Stewartia pseudocamellia*)

Trees with Interesting Bark

Gray
★Red Maple (*Acer rubrum*)
Serviceberry species (*Amelanchier*)
Hornbeam species (*Carpinus*)
Hackberry species (*Celtis*)
★American Yellow-wood (*Cladrastis lutea*)
★Hawthorn species (*Crataegus*)
★Beech species (*Fagus*)
American Holly (*Ilex opaca*)
English or Persian Walnut (*Juglans regia*)
Cucumber Tree (*Magnolia acuminata*)
★Saucer Magnolia (*Magnolia soulangeana*)
Red Oak (young trunk and branches) (*Quercus borealis*)
Black Oak (young trunk and branches) (*Quercus velutina*)
Mountain Ash species (*Sorbus*)

White
★European Birch (*Betula pendula*)
★Gray Birch (*Betula populifolia*)

Red
Japanese Red Pine (*Pinus densiflora*)
Scotch Pine (*Pinus sylvestris*)

Reddish Brown
Chinese Paper Birch (*Betula albo-sinensis*)
Sargent Cherry (*Prunus sargenti*)

Yellow
Wisconsin or Niobe Weeping Willow (*Salix blanda*)

Corky
★Amur Cork (*Phellodendron amurense*)

Green
★Babylon Weeping Willow (*Salix babylonica*)

Flaking
Paperbark Maple (*Acer griseum*)
★Birch species (*Betula*)
Shagbark Hickory (*Carya ovata*)
Russian Olive (*Elaeagnus angustifolia*)
★Eucalyptus species (*Eucalyptus*)
Persian Parrotia (*Parrotia persica*)
★Plane Tree species (*Platanus*)
Lace-bark Pine (*Pinus bungeana*)
Stewartia species (*Stewartia*)

Trees for the City
White Fir (*Abies concolor*)
Silk Tree (*Albizzia julibrissin*)
Hedge Maple (*Acer campestre*)
Box-Elder (*Acer negundo*)
Norway Maple (*Acer platanoides*)
Sycamore Maple (*Acer pseudoplatanus*)
★Horse-Chestnut or Buckeye (*Aesculus*)
★Tree of Heaven (*Ailanthus*)
Catalpa (*Catalpa*)
Chinese Toon (*Cedrela sinensis*)
Hackberry (*Celtis*)
Downy Hawthorn (*Crataegus mollis*)
Washington Hawthorn (*Crataegus phaenopyrum*)
Russian Olive (*Elaeagus angustifolia*)

White Ash (*Fraxinus americana*)
European Ash (*Fraxinus excelsior*)
Green Ash (*Fraxinus pennsylvanica*)
Thornless Honey-Locust (*Gleditsia triacanthos inermis*)
★Ginkgo (*Ginkgo biloba*)
★Golden Rain Tree (*Koelreuteria paniculata*)
★Southern Magnolia (*Magnolia grandiflora*)
★Saucer Magnolia (*Magnolia soulangeana*)
★Star Magnolia (*Magnolia stellata*)
★Crab Apple (*Malus var.*)
★Amur Cork (*Phellodendron amurense*)
★London Plane Tree (*Platanus acerifolia*)
White Poplar (*Populus alba*)
★Lombardy Poplar (*Populus nigra italica*)
Bradford Callery Pear (*Pyrus calleryana bradfordi*)
Red Oak (*Quercus borealis*)
★Japanese Pagoda Tree (*Sophora japonica*)
★Black Locust (*Robinia pseudoacacia*)
Little-leaf Linden (*Tilia cordata*)
★Crimean Linden (*Tilia euchlora*)
★Silver Linden (*Tilia tomentosa*)
Village Green Zelkova (*Zelkova serrata* "Village Green")

Trees for Wide Streets
Sycamore Maple (*Acer pseudoplatanus*)
★Sugar Maple (*Acer saccharum*)
Sugar Hackberry (*Celtis laevigata*)
★Katsura Tree (*Cercidiphyllum japonicum*)
White Ash (*Fraxinus americana*)
Green Ash (*Fraxinus pennsylvanica lanceolata*)
★Ginkgo (*Ginkgo biloba*)
★Common Honey-Locust (*Gleditsia triacanthos*)
Tulip Tree (*Liriodendron tulipifera*)
★Southern Magnolia (*Magnolia grandiflora*)
★Amur Cork (*Phellodendron amurense*)
★Eastern White Pine (*Pinus strobus*)
★London Plane Tree (*Platanus acerifolia*)
California Plane Tree (*Platanus racemosa*)
White Poplar (*Populus alba*)
Sargent Cherry (*Prunus sargenti*)
Red Oak (*Quercus borealis*)
★Pin Oak (*Quercus palustris*)
Willow Oak (*Quercus phellos*)
Japanese Zelkova (*Zelkova serrata*)

Trees for Medium Streets
Norway Maple (*Acer platanoides*)
Mountain Silverbell (*Halesia monticola*)
Velvet Ash (*Fraxinus velutina*)
★Sweet Gum (*Liquidambar styraciflua*)
Hop-Hornbeam (*Ostrya virginiana*)
Simon Poplar (*Populus simoni*)
Scarlet Oak (*Quercus coccinea*)
Laurel Oak (*Quercus laurifolia*)
Willow Oak (*Quercus phellos*)
★Black Locust (*Robinia pseudoacacia*)
★Japanese Pagoda Tree (*Sophora japonica*)
★Linden species (*Tilia*)

Trees for Suburban Streets
Argutum Maple (*Acer argutum*)
Hedge Maple (*Acer campestre*)
Paperbark Maple (*Acer griseum*)
Globe Norway Maple (*Acer platanoides globosum*)
Mountain Maple (*Acer spicatum*)
Tatarian Maple (*Acer tataricum*)
American Hornbeam (*Carpinus caroliniana*)
Pyramidal European Hornbeam (*Carpinus betulus fastigiata*)
Globe European Hornbeam (*Carpinus betulus globosa*)
Fringetree (*Chionanthus virginicus*)
★Hawthorn species (*Crataegus*)
Korean Evodia (*Evodia danielli*)
Carolina Silverbell (*Halesia carolina*)
★Golden Rain Tree (*Koelreuteria paniculata*)
Oriental Cherry (*Prunus serrulata*)
Columnar Sargent Cherry (*Prunus sargenti columnaris*)
Japanese Snowbell (*Styrax japonica*)
Fragrant Snowbell (*Styrax obassia*)

Asiatic Sweetleaf (*Symplocos paniculata*)
Smooth-leaved Elm varieties (*Ulmus carpinifolia*)

Soil Tolerance

Trees Tolerating Acid Soil
★Japanese Maple (*Acer palmatum*)
Strawberry Tree (*Arbutus unedo*)
★Flowering Dogwood (*Cornus florida*)
Japanese Dogwood (*Cornus kousa*)
★European Beech (*Fagus sylvatica*)
Sweet Bay (*Magnolia virginiana*)
★Black Tupelo (*Nyssa sylvatica*)
Red Oak (*Quercus borealis*)
Scarlet Oak (*Quercus coccinea*)
★Pin Oak (*Quercus palustris*)
Willow Oak (*Quercus phellos*)
Japanese Stewartia (*Stewartia pseudocamellia*)

Trees Tolerating Moist Soil
★Red Maple (*Acer rubrum*)
Alder species (*Alnus*)
Holly species (*Ilex*)
★Sweet Gum (*Liquidambar styraciflua*)
Sweet Bay (*Magnolia virginiana*)
★Black Tupelo or Black Gum (*Nyssa sylvatica*)
Swamp White Oak (*Quercus bicolor*)
★Willow species (*Salix*)
Common Bald Cypress (*Taxodium distichum*)
American Arbor-vitae (*Thuja occidentalis*)

Trees Tolerating Dry or Poor Soil
Silver Wattle (*Acacia decurrens dealbata*)
Box-Elder (*Acer negunda*)
Silk Tree (*Albizzia julibrissin*)
★Tree of Heaven (*Ailanthus*)
★Gray Birch (*Betula populifolia*)
Common Paper-Mulberry (*Broussonetia papyrifera*)
European Hackberry (*Celtis australis*)
Russian Olive (*Elaeagnus angustifolia*)
★Eucalyptus species (*Eucalyptus*)
Green Ash (*Fraxinus pennsylvanica*)
Modesto Ash (*Fraxinus velutina* "Modesto")
★Honey-Locust (*Gleditsia tricanthos var.*)
Rocky Mountain Juniper (*Juniperus scopulorum*)
Eastern Red Cedar (*Juniperus virginiana*)
★Golden Rain Tree (*Koelreuteria paniculata*)
Osage-Orange (*Maclura pomifera*)
Jerusalem Thorn (*Parkinsonia aculeata*)
Canary Pine (*Pinus canariensis*)
Jack Pine (*Pinus banksiana*)
Pitch Pine (*Pinus rigida*)
Torrey Pine (*Pinus torreyana*)
White Poplar (*Populus alba*)
Black Jack Oak (*Qurcus marilandica*)
Chestnut Oak (*Quercus montana*)
★Blcak Locust (*Robinia pseudoacacia*)
Sassafras (*Sassafras albidum officinale*)
California Pepper Tree (*Schinus molle*)
★Japanese Pagoda Tree (*Sophora japonica*)
Siberian Elm (*Ulmus pumila*)

Pest-Resistant Trees
★Tree of Heaven (*Ailanthus altissima*)
Hornbeam species (*Carpinus*)
★Cedar species (*Cedrus*)
★Katsura Tree (*Cercidiphyllum japonicum*)
European Hackberry (*Celtis australis*)
Cornelian Cherry (*Cornus mas*)
Japanese Cornel (*Cornus officinalis*)
Turkish Filbert (*Corylus colurna*)
American Smoke Tree (*Cotinus americanus*)
Russian Olive (*Elaeagnus angustifolia*)
★Ginkgo (*Ginkgo biloba*)
★Honey-Locust (*Gleditisia triacanthos*)
Kentucky Coffee Tree (*Gymnocladus dioicus*)
Juniper species (*Juniperus*)
★Golden Rain Tree (*Koelreuteria paniculata*)
★Laburnum species (*Laburnum*)
California Incense Cedar (*Libocedrus decurrens*)
★Sweet Gum (*Liquidamba styraciflua*)
Cucumber Tree (*Magnolia acuminata*)

Kobus Magnolia (*Magnolia kobus borealis*)
Anise Magnolia (*Magnolia salicifolia*)
★Star Magnolia (*Magnolia stellata*)
Hop-Hornbeam species (*Ostrya*)

Trees for Seashore Planting

Norway Maple (*Acer platanoides*)
Sycamore Maple (*Acer pseudoplatanus*)
★Horse-Chestnut (*Aesculus hippocastanum*)
★Tree of Heaven (*Ailanthus*)
★Shadblow Serviceberry (*Amelanchier canadensis*)
Washington Hawthorn (*Crataegus phaenopyrum*)
English Hawthorn (*Crataegus oxyacantha*)
Cockspur Thorn (*Crataegus crus-galli*)
Cryptomeria (*Cryptomeria japonica*)
Monterey Cypress (*Cupressus macrocarpa*)
Russian Olive (*Elaeagnus angustifolia*)
★Eucalyptus (*Eucalyptus*)
Velvet Ash (*Fraxinus velutina*)
Thornless Honey-Locust (*Gleditsia triacanthos inermis* var.)
American Holly (*Ilex opaca*)
Spiny Green Juniper (*Juniperus excelsa stricata*)

West Indies Juniper (*Juniperus lucayana*)
Eastern Red Cedar (*Juniperus virginiana*)
★Southern Magnolia (*Magnolia grandiflora*)
★Black Tupelo (*Nyssa sylvatica*)
★London Plane Tree (*Platanus acerifolia*)
Aleppo Pine (*Pinus halepensis*)
Dragon Spruce (*Picea asperata*)
Colorado Blue Spruce (*Picea pungens glauca*)
★Austrian Pine (*Pinus nigra*)
★Japanese Black Pine (*Pinus thunbergi*)
Cluster Pine (*Pinus pinaster*)
★Monterey Pine (*Pinus radiata*)
Scotch Pine (*Pinus sylvestris*)
White Poplar (*Populus alba*)
Black Cherry (*Prunus serotina*)
★California Live Oak (*Quercus agrifolia*)
★White Oak (*Quercus alba*)
Black Jack Oak (*Quercus marilandica*)
★Black Locust (*Robinia pseudoacacia*)
Golden Weeping Willow (*Salix alba tristis*)
California Pepper Tree (*Schinus molle*)
★Japanese Pagoda Tree (*Sophora japonica*)
Oriental Arbor-vitae (*Thuja orientalis*)
★Little-leaf Linden (*Tilia cordata*)

★Crimean Linden (*Tilia euchlora*)
Chinese Elm (*Ulmus parvifolia*)
California Laurel (*Umbellularia californica*)

Trees for Hedging or Barriers

European Beech (*Fagus sylvatica*) prunes well.
Leyland Cypress (*Cupressocyparis leylandii*) withstands heavy pruning.
Hawthorn varieties (*Crataegus*) easily pruned, advantage of thorns.
Canadian Hemlock (*Tsuga canadensis*) evergreen.
American Holly (*Ilex opaca*) can be pruned.
European Hornbeam (*Carpinus betulus*) prunes well.
Little-leaf Linden (*Tilia cordata*) tolerates heavy pruning.
Hedge Maple (*Acer campestre*) can be pruned.
Austrian Pine (*Pinus nigra*) plant 10–12 feet on centers, staggered row.
Japanese Black Pine (*Pinus thunbergi*) plant 8 feet on centers, staggered row.
Eastern White Pine (*Pinus strobus*) plant 15 feet on centers, staggered row.

PENNSYLVANIA

State Tree

★Eastern Hemlock (*Tsuga canadensis*)

Evergreen Trees

Fir species (*Abies*)
Tree Box (*Buxus sempervirens arborescens*)
★Cedar species (*Cupressus*)
Holly species (*Ilex*)
Juniper species (*Juniperus*)
Spruce species (*Picea*)
★Pine species (*Pinus*)
★Douglas Fir (*Pseudotsuga menziesii*)
Umbrella Pine (*Sciadopitys verticillata*)
Arbor-vitae (*Thuja*)
★Hemlock species (*Tsuga*)

Trees Classified by Height

20–35 Feet
Hedge Maple (*Acer campestre*)
Hornbeam Maple (*Acer carpinifolium*)
Vine Maple (*Acer circinatum*)
Amur Maple (*Acer ginnala*)
Paperbark Maple (*Acer griseum*)
Manchurian Maple (*Acer mandshuricum*)
★Japanese Maple (*Acer palmatum*)
Mountain Maple (*Acer spicatum*)
Tatarian Maple (*Acer tataricum*)
Ohio Buckeye (*Aesculus glabra*)
Apple Serviceberry (*Amelanchier grandiflora*)
★Gray Birch (*Betula populifolia*)
European Hornbeam (*Carpinus betulus globosa*)
Mockernut (*Carya tomentosa*)
Chinese Chestnut (*Castanea mollisima*)
Fringetree (*Chionanthus virginicus*)
Cornelian Cherry (*Cornus mas*)
Japanese Cornel (*Cornus officinalis*)
American Smoke Tree (*Cotinus americanus*)
★Hawthorn species (*Crataegus*)
Russian Olive (*Elaeagnus angustifolia*)
Euonymus species (*Euonymus*)
Franklinia (*Franklinia alatamaha*)
Flowering Ash (*Fraxinus ornus*)
Carolina Silverbell (*Halesia carolina*)
Possum Haw (*Ilex decidua*)
Longstalk Holly (*Ilex pedunculosa*)
Needle Juniper (*Juniperus rigida*)
★Golden Rain Tree (*Koelreuteria paniculata*)
★Laburnum species (*Laburnum*)
Yellow Cucumber Tree (*Magnolia cordata*)
★Saucer Magnolia (*Magnolia soulangeana*)
★Star Magnolia (*Magnolia stellata*)
Watson Magnolia (*Magnolia watsoni*)

★Crab Apple species (*Malus*)
★Cherry species (*Prunus*)
Dahurian Buckthorn (*Rhamnus davurica*)
Almond-leaf Willow (*Salix amygdalina*)
★Babylon Weeping Willow (*Salix babylonica*)
Goat Willow (*Salix caprea*)
Snowberry Mountain Ash (*Sorbus discolor*)
Showy Mountain Ash (*Sorbus decora*)
Snowbell species (*Styrax*)
Asiatic Sweetleaf (*Symplocus paniculata*)
Japanese Tree Lilac (*Syringa amurensis japonica*)

35–75 Feet
Korean Fir (*Abies koreana*)
Nikko Maple (*Acer nikoense*)
Striped Maple or Moosewood (*Acer pennsylvanicum*)
★Red-fruited Tree of Heaven (*Ailanthus altissima erythrocarpa*)
Speckled Alder (*Alnus incana*)
Red Alder (*Alnus rubra*)
★Shadblow Serviceberry (*Amelanchier canadensis*)
Allegany Serviceberry (*Amelanchier laevis*)
Devil's Walking Stick (*Aralia elata*)
Dahurian Birch (*Betula davurica*)
Manchurian Birch (*Betula mandshurica szechuanica*)
★European Birch (*Betula pendula*)
Common Paper-Mulberry (*Broussonetia papyrifera*)
European Hornbeam (*Carpinus betula*)
American Hornbeam (*Carpinus caroliniana*)
Japanese Hornbeam (*Carpinus japonica*)
Chinese Chestnut (*Castanea mollissima*)
Southern Catalpa (*Catalpa bignoniodies*)
Bunch Hackberry (*Celtis bungeana*)
★Katsura Tree (*Cercidiphyllum japonicum*)
Eastern Redbud (*Cercis canadensis*)
Chinese Redbud (*Cercis chinensis*)
★American Yellow-wood (*Cladrastis lutea*)
★Flowering Dogwood (*Cornus florida*)
Cockspur Thorn (*Crataegus crus-galli*)
Green Hawthorn (*Crataegus viridis*)
Dove Tree (*Davidia involucrata*)
Common Persimmon (*Diospyros virginiana*)
Green Ash (*Fraxinus pennsylvanica lanceolata*)
English Holly (*Ilex aquifolium*)
Mountain Winterberry (*Ilex montana*)
American Holly (*Ilex opaca*)
Chinese Juniper (*Juniperus chinensis*)
Western Red Cedar (*Juniperus scopulorum*)
Osage-Orange (*Maclura pomifera*)
Kobus Magnolia (*Magnolia kobus borealis*)

★Siberian Crab Apple (*Malus baccata*)
"Cowichan" Crab Apple (*Malus* "Cowichan")
"Dolgo" Crab Apple (*Malus* "Dolgo")
"Makamik" Crab Apple (*Malus* "Makamik")
Cherry Crab Apple (*Malus robusta*)
"Sissipuk" Crab Apple (*Malus* "Sissipuk")
White Mulberry (*Morus alba*)
★Sorrel Tree or Sourwood (*Oxydendrum arboreum*)
Empress Tree (*Paulownia tomentosa*)
★Amur Cork (*Phellodendron amurense*)
Dragon Spruce (*Picea asperata*)
Jack Pine (*Pinus banksiana*)
Lace-bark Pine (*Pinus bungeana*)
Swiss Stone Pine (*Pinus cembra*)
Limber Pine (*Pinus flexilis*)
Pitch Pine (*Pinus rigida*)
Scotch Pine (*Pinus sylvestris*)
Simon Poplar (*Populus simoni*)
European Bird Cherry (*Prunus padus*)
Sargent Cherry (*Prunus sargenti*)
Yoshino Cherry (*Prunus yedoensis*)
Ussurian Pear (*Pyrus ussuriensis*)
Swamp White Oak (*Quercus bicolor*)
Red Oak (*Quercus borealis*)
Scarlet Oak (*Quercus coccinea*)
Spanish Oak (*Quercus falcata*)
Shingle Oak (*Quercus imbricaria*)
★Pin Oak (*Quercus palustris*)
Willow Oak (*Quercus phellos*)
Clammy Locust (*Robinia viscosa*)
White Willow (*Salix alba*)
Wisconsin or Niobe Weeping Willow (*Salix blanda*)
Elaeagnus Willow (*Salix eleagnos*)
Thurlow Weeping Willow (*Salix elegantissima*)
Laurel Willow (*Salix pentandra*)
Sassafras (*Sassafras albidum officinale*)
Korean Mountain Ash (*Sorbus alnifolia*)
White Beam Mountain Ash (*Sorbus aria*)
European Mountain Ash or Rowan Tree (*Sorbus aucuparia*)
Korean Stewartia (*Stewartia koreana*)
American Arbor-vitae (*Thuja occidentalis*)
Oriental Arbor-vitae (*Thuja orientalis*)
Japanese Arbor-vitae (*Thuja standishi*)
Carolina Hemlock (*Tsuga caroliniana*)
Siberian Elm (*Ulmus pumila*)

75 Feet or Over
Fir species (*Abies*)
Big-leaf Maple (*Acer macrophyllum*)
Norway Maple (*Acer platanoides*)

Sycamore Maple (*Acer pseudoplatanus*)
*Red or Swamp Maple (*Acer rubrum*)
*Sugar Maple (*Acer saccharum*)
*Baumann Horse-Chestnut (*Aesculus hippocastanum baumanni*)
European Alder (*Alnus glutinosa*)
Sweet Birch (*Betula lenta*)
River Birch (*Betula nigra*)
*Canoe Birch (*Betula papyrifera*)
Hickory species (*Carya*)
Northern Catalpa (*Catalpa speciosa*)
*Cedar species (*Cedrus*)
Sugar Hackberry (*Celtis laevigata*)
*Katsura Tree (*Cercidiphyllum japonicum*)
False Cypress species (*Chamaecyparis*)
Cryptomeria (*Cryptomeria japonica*)
*Beech species (*Fagus*)
White Ash (*Fraxinus americana*)
European Ash (*Fraxinus excelsior*)
*Ginkgo or Maidenhair Tree (*Ginkgo biloba*)
*Common Honey-Locust (*Gleditsia triacanthos*)
Kentucky Coffee Tree (*Gymnocladus dioicus*)
Mountain Silverbell (*Halesia monticola*)
Eastern Black Walnut (*Juglans nigra*)
English or Persian Walnut (*Juglans regia*)
Kalopanax (*Kalopanax pictus*)
Japanese Larch (*Larix leptolepis*)
*Sweet Gum (*Liquidambar styraciflua*)
Tulip Tree or Yellow Poplar (*Liriodendron tulipifera*)
Cucumber Tree (*Magnolia acuminata*)
White-leaf Japanese Magnolia (*Magnolia obovata*)
Dawn Redwood (*Metasequoia glyptostroboides*)
*Black Gum or Black Tupelo (*Nyssa sylvatica*)
Spruce species (*Picea*)
*Pine species (*Pinus*)
Plane Tree species (*Platanus*)
*Poplar species (*Populus*)
Sargent Cherry (*Prunus sargenti*)
Black or Rum Cherry (*Prunus serotina*)
*Douglas Fir (*Pseudotsuga menziesii*)
*Oak species (*Quercus*)
Umbrella Pine (*Sciadopitys verticillata*)
Common Bald Cypress (*Taxodium distichum*)
*Linden species (*Tilia*)
*Eastern Hemlock (*Tsuga canadensis*)
Elm species (*Ulmus*)
Japanese Zelkova (*Zelkova serrata*)

Trees Classified by Form

Pyramidal
Fir species (*Abies*)
*Birch species (*Betula*)
*Cedar species (*Cedrus*)
False Cypress species (*Chamaecyparis*)
Cryptomeria (*Cryptomeria japonica*)
*Beech species (*Fagus*)
American Holly (*Ilex opaca*)
Juniper or Red Cedar species (*Juniperus*)
*Larch species (*Larix*)
*Sweet Gum (*Liquidambar styraciflua*)
*Magnolia species (*Magnolia*)
Dawn Redwood (*Metasequoia glyptostroboides*)
*Black Gum or Black Tupelo (*Nyssa sylvatica*)
Hop-Hornbeam (*Ostrya virginiana*)
*Sorrel Tree or Sourwood (*Oxydendrum arboreum*)
Spruce species (*Picea*)
Swiss Stone Pine (*Pinus cembra*)
Korean Pine (*Pinus koraiensis*)
Pyramidal Austrian Pine (*Pinus nigra pyramidalis*)
Japanese White Pine (*Pinus parviflora*)
Bolleana Poplar (*Populus alba pyramidalis*)
*Pin Oak (*Quercus palustris*)
Umbrella Pine (*Sciadopitys verticillata*)
Common Bald Cypress (*Taxodium distichum*)
Arbor-vitae species (*Thuja*)
*Linden species (*Tilia*)
*Hemlock species (*Tsuga*)

Columnar
Ascending Norway Maple (*Acer platanoides ascendens*)
Columnar Norway Maple (*Acer platanoides columnare*)
Erect Norway Maple (*Acer platanoides erectum*)
Columnar Red Maple (*Acer rubrum columnare*)
Sentry Maple (*Acer saccharum monumentale*)
Fastigiate European Birch (*Betula pendula fastigiata*)
Fastigiate European Hornbeam (*Carpinus betulus fastigiata*)
Fastigiate Washington Hawthorn (*Crataegus phaenopyrum fastigiata*)
Dawyck Beech (*Fagus syolvatica fastigiata*)
Sentry Ginkgo (*Ginkgo biloba fastigiata*)
Blue Columnar Chinese Juniper (*Juniperus chinensis columnaris*)
Schott Red Cedar (*Juniperus virginiana schotti*)
Swiss Stone Pine (*Pinus cembra*)
Fastigiate White Pine (*Pinus strobus fastigiata*)
*Lombardy Poplar (*Populus nigra italica*)
Fastigiate Simon Poplar (*Populus simoni fastigiata*)
Columnar Sargent Cherry (*Prunus sargenti columnaris*)
"Amanogawa" Cherry (*Prunus serruata* "Amanogawa")
Fastigiate English Oak (*Quercus robur fastigiata*)
Shipmast Locust (*Robinia pseudoacacia rectissima*)
Upright European Mountain Ash (*Sorbus aucuparia fastigiata*)
Fastigiate American Arbor-vitae (*Thuja occidentalis douglasi pyramidalis*)
Columnar Big-leaf Linden (*Tilia platyphyllos fastigiata*)
*American Elm varieties (*Ulmus americana*)

Weeping
Slender European Birch (*Betula pendula tristis*)
Young's Birch (*Betula pendula youngi*)
Weeping European Hornbeam (*Carpinus betulus pendula*)
*Weeping Beech (*Fagus sylvatica pendula*)
Weeping Purple Beech (*Fagus sylvatica purpureo-pendula*)
Weeping Red Cedar (*Juniperus virginiana pendula*)
Weeping Larch (*Larix decidua pendula*)
"Exzellenz Thiel" Crab Apple (*Malus* "Exzellenz Thiel")
"Oekonomierat Echtermeyer" Crab Apple (*Malus* "Oekonomierat Echtermeyer")
Weeping Mulberry (*Morus alba pendula*)
Koster Weeping Blue Spruce (*Picea pungens kosteriana*)
Weeping White Pine (*Pinus strobus pendula*)
Weeping Black Cherry (*Prunus serotina pendula*)
Weeping Higan Cherry (*Prunus subhirtella pendula*)
"Yaeshidare" Cherry (*Prunus subhirtella pendula flora plena*)
Weeping Yoshino Cherry (*Prunus yedoensis perpendens*)
*Weeping Douglas Fir (*Pseudotsuga menziesii pendula*)
Golden Weeping Willow (*Salix alba tristis*)
*Babylon Weeping Willow (*Salix babylonica*)
Wisconsin or Niobe Weeping Willow (*Salix blanda*)
Thurlow Weeping Willow (*Salix elegantissima*)
Weeping Japanese Pagoda Tree (*Sophora japonica pendula*)
Weeping European Mountain Ash (*Sorbus aucuparia pendula*)
Weeping Folgner Mountain Ash (*Sorbus folgneri pendula*)
Pendant Silver Linden (*Tilia petiolaris*)
Sargent Hemlock (*Tsuga canadensis pendula*)
Weeping American Elm (*Ulmus americana pendula*)

Rounded or Globe-Shaped
*Japanese Maple (*Acer palmatum*)
Globe Norway Maple (*Acer platanoides globosum*)
Globe European Hornbeam (*Carpinus betulus globosa*)
Bunch Hackberry (*Celtis bungeana*)
Cornelian Cherry (*Cornus mas*)

Japanese Cornel (*Cornus officinalis*)
Single Seed Hawthorn (*Crataegus monogyna inermis*)
*Saucer Magnolia (*Magnolia soulangeana*)
*Crab Apple species (*Malus*)
*White Oak (*Quercus alba*)
Umbrella Black Locust (*Robinia pseudoacacia umbraculifera*)
Sargent Hemlock (*Tsuga canadensis sargenti*)

With Horizontal Branching
Fir species (*Abies*)
Silk Tree (*Albizzia julibrissin*)
*Cedar species (*Cedrus*)
Eastern Redbud (*Cercis canadensis*)
*Flowering Dogwood (*Cornus florida*)
Japanese Dogwood (*Cornus kousa*)
*Hawthorn species (*Crataegus*)
Dawn Redwood (*Metasequoia glyptostroboides*)
*Black Gum or Black Tupelo (*Nyssa sylvatica*)
Spruce species (*Picea*)
Japanese Red Pine (*Pinus densiflora*)
*Eastern White Pine (*Pinus strobus*)
Golden Larch (*Pseudolarix amabilis*)
*White Oak (*Quercus alba*)
*Pin Oak (*Quercus palustris*)
Common Bald Cypress (*Taxodium distichum*)

Trees Classified by Color of Blossom

Yellow
*Golden Rain Tree (*Koelreuteria paniculata*)
*Laburnum (*Laburnum vossi*)

White
*Shadblow Serviceberry (*Amelanchier canadensis*)
White Redbud (*Cercis canadensis alba*)
*American Yellow-wood (*Cladrastis lutea*)
Japanese Dogwood (*Cornus kousa*)
Washington Hawthorn (*Crataegus phaenopyrum*)
Carolina Silverbell (*Halesia carolina*)
Yulan Magnolia (*Magnolia denudata*)
*Star Magnolia (*Magnolia stellata*)
Arnold Crab Apple (*Malus arnoldiana*)
*Siberian Crab Apple (*Malus baccata*)
Tea Crab Apple (*Malus hupehensis*)
Sargent Crab Apple (*Malus sargenti*)
*Sorrel Tree (*Oxydendrum arboreum*)
Sour Cherry (*Prunus cerasus*)
Thundercloud Plum (*Prunus cerasifera* "Thundercloud")
Mount Fuji Cherry (*Prunus serrulata* "Shirotae")
Yoshino Cherry (*Prunus yedoensis*)
Bradford Callery Pear (*Pyruis calleryana bradfordi*)
*Common Pear (*Pyrus communis*)
*Japanese Pagoda Tree (*Sophora japonica*)
Korean Mountain Ash (*Sorbus alnifolia*)
American Mountain Ash (*Sorbus americana*)
European Mountain Ash (*Sorbus aucuparia*)
Showy Mountain Ash (*Sorbus decora*)
Japanese Stewartia (*Stewartia pseudocamellia*)
Japanese Snowbell (*Styrax japonica*)

Pink
Wither's Pink Redbud (*Cercis canadensis* "Wither's Pink Charm")
Red Flowering Dogwood (*Cornus florida rubra*)
Toba Hawthorn (*Crataegus mordenensis* "Toba")
*Saucer Magnolia (*Magnolia soulangeana*)
Japanese Flowering Crab Apple (*Malus floribunda*)
Katherine Crab Apple (*Malus* "Katherine")
Prince Georges Crab Apple (*Malus* "Prince Georges")
*Common Apple (*Malus pumila*)
Blireiana Plum (*Prunus sargenti*)
Amanogawa Cherry (*Prunus serrulata* "Amanogawa")
Kwanzan Cherry (*Prunus serrulata* "Kwanzan")
Autumn Cherry (*Prunus subhirtella autumnalis*)
Weeping Cherry (*Prunus subhirtella pendula*)

Red
Ruby Horse-Chestnut (*Aesculus carnea briotti*)
Paul's Scarlet Hawthorn (*Crataegus oxyacantha pauli*)

Alexandrina Magnolia (*Magnolia soulangeana* "Alexandrina")
Almey Crab Apple (*Malus* "Almey")
Carmine Crab Apple (*Malus atrosanguinea*)

Trees with Bright Red Fruit

*Flowering Dogwood (*Cornus florida*)
Japanese Dogwood (*Cornus kousa*)
Downy Hawthorn (*Crataegus mollis*)
Washington Hawthorn (*Crataegus phaenopyrum*)
American Holly (*Ilex opaca*)
Almey Crab Apple (*Malus* "Almey")
Siberian Crab Apple (*Malus baccata*)
Hopa Crab Apple (*Malus* "Hopa")
*Common Apple (*Malus pumila*)
Sargent Crab Apple (*Malus sargenti*)
Korean Mountain Ash (*Sorbus alnifolia*)
American Mountain Ash (*Sorbus americana*)
European Mountain Ash (*Sorbus aucuparia*)

Trees Classified by Color of Summer Foliage

Blue
White Fir (*Abies concolor*)
*Blue Atlas Cedar (*Cedrus atlantica glauca*)
Steel Lawson Cypress (*Chamaecyparis lawsonia glauca*)
Western Red Cedar (*Juniperus scopulorum* var. Chandler Blue)
Eastern Red Cedar (*Juniperus virginiana* var. *Burki*)
Colorado Blue Spruce (*Picea pungens* var. *Glauca*)

Silver to Gray
Russian Olive (*Elaeagnus angustifolia*)
White Poplar (*Populus alba*)
Pendant Silver Linden (*Tilia petiolaris*)
*Silver Linden (*Tilia tomentosa*)

Red to Purple
Blood-leaf Japanese Maple (*Acer palmatum atropurpureum*)
Crimson King Maple (*Acer platanoides* "Crimson King")
Schwedler Maple (*Acer platanoides schwedleri*)
Purple-leaf Sycamore Maple (*Acer pseudoplatanus*)
River's Purple Beech (*Fagus sylvatica riversi*)
Purple Beech (*Fagus sylvatica atropunicea*)
Weeping Purple Beech (*Fagus sylvatica purpureopendula*)
Rubylace Locust (*Gleditsia triacanthos inermis* "Rubylace")
Purple Crab Apple (*Malus purpurea*)
Blireiana Plum (*Prunus blireiana*)
Pissard Plum (*Prunus cerasifera atropurpurea*)
Thundercloud Plum (*Prunus cerasifera nigra* "Thundercloud")
Woods Myrobalan Plum (*Prunus cerasifera woodi*)
Blood-leaf Peach (*Prunus persica atropurpurea*)
Purple English Oak (*Quercus robur atropurpurea*)

Trees Classified by Color of Fall Foliage

Yellow
Striped Maple or Moosewood (*Acer pennsylvanicum*)
Norway Maple (*Acer platanoides* var.)
*Sugar Maple (*Acer saccharum*)
Ohio Buckeye (orange) (*Aesculus glabra*)
Apple Serviceberry (yellow-orange) (*Amelanchier grandiflora*)
*Birch species (*Betula species*)
Hickory species (*Carya*)
Chinese Chestnut (*Castanea mollissima*)
*Katsura Tree (yellow to scarlet) (*Cercidiphyllum japonicum*)
Redbud species (*Cercis*)
Fringetree (*Chionanthus virginicus*)
*American Yellow-wood (*Cladrastis lutea*)
*American Beech (*Fagus grandifolia*)
*European Beech (*Fagus sylvatica*)
White Ash (purple to yellow) (*Fraxinus americana*)
*Ginkgo (*Ginkgo biloba*)

*Larch (*Larix decidua*)
Tulip Tree (*Liriodendron tulipifera*)
*Star Magnolia (bronze) (*Magnolia stellata*)
*Willow species (*Salix*)

Red
Amur Maple (*Acer ginnala*)
Manchurian Maple (*Acer mandshuricum*)
Nikko Maple (*Acer nikoense*)
*Japanese Maple (*Acer palmatum* var.)
*Red Maple (*Acer rubrum*)
*Sugar Maple (*Acer saccharum*)
Tatarian Maple (*Acer tataricum*)
*Shadblow Serviceberry (*Amelanchier canadensis*)
Hornbeam species (*Carpinus*)
*Flowering Dogwood (*Cornus florida*)
Japanese Dogwood (*Cornus kousa*)
American Smoke Tree (*Cotinus americanus*)
Washington Hawthorn (*Crataegus phaenopyrum*)
*Sweet Gum (*Liquidambar styraciflua*)
Dawson Crab Apple (*Malus dawsoniana*)
*Black Tupelo or Black Gum (*Nyssa sylvatica*)
*Sorrel Tree (*Oxydendrum arboreum*)
Persian Parrotia (*Parrotia persica*)
*Cherry species (*Prunus*)
Bradford Callery Pear (*Pyrus calleryana bradfordi*)
Red Oak (*Quercus borealis*)
Scarlet Oak (*Quercus coccinea*)
*Pin Oak (*Quercus palustris*)
Sassafras (*Sassafras albidum*)
Korean Mountain Ash (*Sorbus alnifolia*)
Korean Stewartia (orange to red) (*Stewartia koreana*)

Purple
White Ash (*Fraxinus americana*)
*Sweet Gum (*Liquidambar styraciflua*)
*White Oak (*Quercus alba*)
*Common Pear (*Pyrus communis*)

Trees with Interesting Bark

Gray
*Red Maple (*Acer rubrum*)
Serviceberry species (*Amelanchier*)
Hornbeam species (*Carpinus*)
Hackberry species (*Celtis*)
*American Yellow-wood (*Cladrastis lutea*)
*Hawthorn species (*Crataegus*)
*Beech species (*Fagus*)
American Holly (*Ilex opaca*)
English or Persian Walnut (*Juglans regia*)
*Saucer Magnolia (*Magnolia soulangeana*)
Red Oak (young branches and trunk) (*Quercus borealis*)
Black Oak (young branches and trunk) (*Quercus velutina*)
Mountain Ash species (*Sorbus*)

White
*European Birch (*Betula pendula*)
*Gray Birch (*Betula populifolia*)

Red
Japanese Red Pine (*Pinus densiflora*)
Red or Norway Pine (*Pinus resinosa*)
Scotch Pine (*Pinus sylvestris*)

Reddish Brown
Chinese Paper Birch (*Betul albo-sinensis*)
Sargent Cherry (*Prunus sargenti*)

Yellow
Wisconsin or Niobe Weeping Willow (*Salix blanda*)

Corky
*Amur Cork (*Phellodendron amurense*)

Green
Striped Maple (*Acer pennsylvanicum*)
*Babylon Weeping Willow (*Salix babylonica*)

Flaking
Paperbark Maple (*Acer griseum*)
*Birch species (*Betula*)
Shagbark Hickory (*Carya ovata*)
Russian Olive (*Elaeagnus angustifolia*)

Persian Parrotia (*Parrotia persica*)
*Plane Tree species (*Platanus*)
Lace-bark Pine (*Pinus bungeana*)
Stewartia species (*Stewartia*)

Trees for the City

White Fir (*Abies concolor*)
Hedge Maple (*Acer campestre*)
Norway Maple (*Acer platanoides*)
Sycamore Maple (*Acer pseudoplatanus*)
*Horse Chestnut or Buckeye (*Aesculus*)
*Tree of Heaven (*Ailanthus*)
Silk Tree (*Albizzia julibrissin*)
Catalpa (*Catalpa*)
Hackberry (*Celtis*)
Downy Hawthorn (*Crataegus mollis*)
Washington Hawthorn (*Crataegus phaenopyrum*)
Russian Olive (*Elaeagnus angustifolia*)
White Ash (*Fraxinus americana*)
European Ash (*Fraxinus americana*)
Green Ash (*Fraxinus pennsylvanica*)
*Ginkgo (*Ginkgo biloba*)
Thornless Honey-Locust (*Gleditsia triacanthos inermis*)
*Golden Rain Tree (*Koelreuteria paniculata*)
*Saucer Magnolia (*Magnolia soulangeana*)
*Star Magnolia (*Magnolia stellata*)
*Crab Apple (*Malus* var.)
*Amur Cork (*Phellodendron amurense*)
*London Plane Tree (*Platanus acerifolia*)
White Poplar (*Populus alba*)
*Lombardy Poplar (*Populus nigra italica*)
Red Oak (*Quercus borealis*)
*Black Locust (*Robinia pseudoacacia*)
*Japanese Pagoda Tree (*Sophora japonica*)
*Little-leaf Linden (*Tilia cordata*)
*Crimean Linden (*Tilia euchlora*)
*Silver Linden (*Tilia tomentosa*)
Village Green Zelkova (*Zelkova serrata* "Village Green")

Trees for Wide Streets
Sycamore Maple (*Acer pseudoplatanus*)
*Sugar Maple (*Acer saccharum*)
Sugar Hackberry (*Celtis laevigata*)
*Katsura Tree (*Cercidiphyllum japonicum*)
White Ash (*Fraxinus americana*)
Green Ash (*Fraxinus pennsylvanica lanceolata*)
*Ginkgo (*Ginkgo biloba*)
*Common Honey-Locust (*Gleditsia triacanthos*)
Kalopanax (*Kalopanax pictus*)
Tulip Tree (*Liriodendron tulipifera*)
*Amur Cork (*Phellodendron amurense*)
*Eastern White Pine (*Pinus strobus*)
*London Plane Tree (*Platanus acerifola*)
*Oriental Plane Tree (*Platanus orientalis*)
White Poplar (*Populus alba*)
Sargent Cherry (*Prunus sargenti*)
*Pin Oak (*Quercus palustris*)
Willow Oak (*Quercus phellos*)
Japanese Zelkova (*Zelkova serrata*)

Trees for Medium Streets
Norway Maple (*Acer platanoides*)
Mountain Silverbell (*Halesia monticola*)
*Sweet Gum (*Liquidambar styraciflua*)
Hop-Hornbeam (*Ostrya virginiana*)
*Sorrel Tree or Sourwood (*Oxydendron arboreum*)
Simon Poplar (*Populus simoni*)
Scarlet Oak (*Quercus coccinea*)
Willow Oak (*Quercus phellos*)
*Black Locust (*Robinia pseudoacacia*)
Sassafras (*Sassafras albidum officinale*)
*Japanese Pagoda Tree (*Sophora japonica*)
*Linden species (*Tilia*)
Winged Elm (*Ulmus alata*)

Trees for Suburban Streets
Hedge Maple (*Acer campestre*)
Amur Maple (*Acer ginnala*)
Paperbark Maple (*Acer griseum*)
Globe Norway Maple (*Acer platanoides globosum*)

Mountain Maple (*Acer spicatum*)
Tatarian Maple (*Acer tataricum*)
American Hornbeam (*Carpinus caroliniana*)
Pyramidal European Hornbeam (*Carpinus betulus fastigiata*)
Globe European Hornbeam (*Carpinus betulus globosa*)
Fringetree (*Chionanthus virginicus*)
★Hawthorn species (*Crataegus*)
Korean Evodia (*Evodia danielli*)
Carolina Silverbell (*Halesia carolina*)
★Golden Rain Tree (*Koelreuteria paniculata*)
Oriental Cherry (*Prunus serrulata*)
Columnar Sargent Cherry (*Prunus sargenti columnaris*)
Japanese Snowbell (*Styrax japonica*)
Asiatic Sweetleaf (*Symplocos paniculata*)
Smooth-leaved Elm varieties (*Ulmus carpinifolia*)

Soil Tolerance

Trees Tolerating Acid Soil
★Japanese Maple (*Acer palmatum*)
★Flowering Dogwood (*Cornus florida*)
Japanese Dogwood (*Cornus kousa*)
★European Beech (*Fagus sylvatica*)
Sweet Bay (*Magnolia virginiana*)
★Black Tupelo (*Nyssa sylvatica*)
★Sorrel Tree (*Oxydendrum arboreum*)
Red Oak (*Quercus borealis*)
Scarlet Oak (*Quercus coccinea*)
★Pin Oak (*Quercus palustris*)
Willow Oak (*Quercus phellos*)
Japanese Stewartia (*Stewartia pseudocamellia*)

Trees Tolerating Moist Soil
★Red Maple (*Acer rubum*)
Alder species (*Alnus*)
Holly species (*Ilex*)
★Sweet Gum (*Liquidambar styraciflua*)

Sweet Bay (*Magnolia virginiana*)
★Black Tupelo or Black Gum (*Nyssa sylvatica*)
Swamp White Oak (*Quercus bicolor*)
★Willow species (*Salix*)
Common Bald Cypress (*Taxodium distichum*)
American Arbor-vitae (*Thuja occidentalis*)

Trees Tolerating Dry or Poor Soil
Box-Elder (*Acer negundo*)
★Tree of Heaven (*Ailanthus*)
★Gray Birch (*Betula populifolia*)
Common Paper-Mulberry (*Broussonetia papyrifera*)
Russian Olive (*Elaeagnus angustifolia*)
Green Ash (*Fraxinus pennsylvanica*)
Modesto Ash (*Fraxinus velutina* "Modesto")
★Honey-Locust (*Gleditsia triacanthos* var.)
Western Red Cedar (*Juniperus scopulorum*)
Eastern Red Cedar (*Juniperus virginiana*)
Golden Red Cedar (*Juniperus virginiana*)
★Golden Rain Tree (*Koelreuteria paniculata*)
Osage-Orange (*Maclura pomifera*)
Jack Pine (*Pinus banksiana*)
Red Pine (*Pinus resinosa*)
Pitch Pine (*Pinus rigida*)
Virginia or Scrub Pine (*Pinus virginiana*)
Scotch Pine (*Pinus sylvestris*)
White Poplar (*Populus alba*)
Chestnut Oak (*Quercus montana*)
★Black Locust (*Robinia pseudoacacia*)
Sassafras (*Sassafras albidum officinale*)
★Japanese Pagoda Tree (*Sophora japonica*)
Chinese Elm (*Ulmus parvifolia*)
Siberian Elm (*Ulmus pumila*)

Pest-Resistant Trees
★Tree of Heaven (*Ailanthus altissima*)
Hornbeam species (*Carpinus*)
★Cedar species (*Cedrus*)
★Katsura Tree (*Cercidiphyllum japonicum*)

False Cypress species (*Chamaecyparis*)
Cornelian Cherry (*Cornus mas*)
Japanese Cornel (*Cornus officinalis*)
American Smoke Tree (*Cotinus americanus*)
Russian Olive (*Elaeagnus angustifolia*)
Franklinia (*Franklinia alatamaha*)
★Ginkgo (*Ginkgo biloba*)
★Honey-Locust (*Gleditsia triacanthos*)
Kentucky Coffee Tree (*Gymnocladus dioicus*)
Juniper species (*Juniperus*)
Kalopanax (*Kalopanax pictus*)
★Golden Rain Tree (*Koelreuteria paniculata*)
★Laburnum species (*Laburnum*)
★Sweet Gum (*Liquidambar styraciflua*)
Cucumber Tree (*Magnolia acuminata*)
Kobus Magnolia (*Magnolia kobus borealis*)
Anise Magnolia (*Magnolia salicifolia*)
★Star Magnolia (*Magnolia stellata*)
Hop-Hornbeam species (*Ostrya*)

Trees for Hedging or Barriers

European Beech (*Fagus sylvatica*) prunes well.
Leyland Cypress (*Cupressocyparis leylandii*) withstands heavy pruning.
Hawthorn varieties (*Crataegus*) easily pruned, advantage of thorns.
Canadian Hemlock (*Tsuga canadensis*) evergreen.
American Holly (*Ilex opaca*) can be pruned.
European Hornbeam (*Carpinus betulus*) prunes well.
Little-leaf Linden (*Tilia cordata*) tolerates heavy pruning.
Hedge Maple (*Acer campestre*) can be pruned.
Austrian Pine (*Pinus nigra*) plant 10–12 feet on centers, staggered row.
Japanese Black Pine (*Pinus thunbergi*) plant 8 feet on centers, staggered row.
Eastern White Pine (*Pinus strobus*) plant 15 feet on centers, staggered row.

RHODE ISLAND

State Tree
★Sugar Maple (*Acer saccharum*)

Evergreen Trees

Fir species (*Abies*)
Tree Box (*Buxus sempervirens arborescens*)
★Cedar species (*Cedrus*)
Holly species (*Ilex*)
Juniper species (*Juniperus*)
★Pine species (*Pinus*)
★Douglas Fir (*Pseudotsuga menziesii*)
Umbrella Pine (*Sciadopitys verticillata*)
Arbor-vitae species (*Thuja*)
★Hemlock species (*Tsuga*)

Trees Classified by Height

20–35 Feet
Hedge Maple (*Acer campestre*)
Hornbeam Maple (*Acer carpinifolium*)
Amur Maple (*Acer ginnala*)
Paperbark Maple (*Acer griseum*)
★Japanese Maple (*Acer palmatum*)
Mountain Maple (*Acer spicatum*)
Tatarian Maple (*Acer tataricum*)
Ohio Buckeye (*Aesculus glabra*)
Apple Serviceberry (*Amelanchier grandiflora*)
★Gray Birch (*Betula populifolia*)
European Hornbeam (*Carpinus betulus globosa*)
Judas Tree (*Cercis siliquastrum*)
Japanese Dogwood (*Cornus kousa*)
Cornelian Cherry (*Cornus mas*)
Japanese Cornel (*Cornus officinalis*)
American Smoke Tree (*Cotinus americanus*)
★Hawthorn species (*Crataegus*)
Russian Olive (*Elaeagnus angustifolia*)
Euonymus species (*Euonymus*)
Korean Evodia (*Evodia danielli*)

Franklinia (*Franklinia alatamaha*)
Flowering Ash (*Fraxinus ornus*)
Carolina Silverbell (*Halesia carolina*)
Longstalk Holly (*Ilex pernyi*)
Perny Holly (*Ilex pernyi*)
★Golden Rain Tree (*Koelreuteria paniculata*)
★Laburnum species (*Laburnum*)
★Saucer Magnolia (*Magnolia soulangeana*)
★Star Magnolia (*Magnolia stellata*)
★Crab Apple species (*Malus*)
★Cherry species (*Prunus*)
★Babylon Weeping Willow (*Salix babylonica*)

35–75 Feet
Korean Fir (*Abies koreana*)
Box-Elder (*Acer negundo*)
Nikko Maple (*Acer nikoense*)
Striped Maple or Moosewood (*Acer pennsylvanicum*)
★Red-fruited Tree of Heaven (*Ailanthus altissima erythrocarpa*)
Italian Alder (*Alnus cordata*)
Red Alder (*Alnus rubra*)
★Shadblow Serviceberry (*Amelanchier canadensis*)
Allegany Serviceberry (*Amelanchier laevis*)
Manchurian Birch (*Betula mandshurica szechuanica*)
European Hornbeam (*Carpinus betulus*)
American Hornbeam (*Carpinus caroliniana*)
Chinese Chestnut (*Castanea mollissima*)
Bunch Hackberry (*Celtis bungeana*)
★Katsura Tree (*Cercidiphyllum japonicum*)
Eastern Redbud (*Cercis canadensis*)
Chinese Redbud (*Cercis chinensis*)
★American Yellow-wood (*Cladrastis lutea*)
★Flowering Dogwood (*Cornus florida*)
Turkish Filbert (*Corylus colurna*)
Cockspur Thorn (*Crataegus crus-galli*)
Green Hawthorn (*Crataegus viridis*)

Dove Tree (*Davidia involucrata*)
Green Ash (*Fraxinus pennsylvanica lanceolata*)
English Holly (*Ilex aquifolium*)
Mountain Winterberry (*Ilex montana*)
American Holly (*Ilex opaca*)
Chinese Juniper (*Juniperus chinensis*)
Yulan Magnolia (*Magnolia denudata*)
Kobus Magnolia (*Magnolia kobus borealis*)
"Cowichan" Crab Apple (*Malus* "Cowichan")
"Dolgo" Crab Apple (*Malus* "Dolgo")
"Makamik" Crab Apple (*Malus* "Makamik")
Cherry Crab Apple (*Malus robusta*)
"Sissipuk" Crab Apple (*Malus* "Sissipuk")
White Mulberry (*Morus alba*)
★Sorrel Tree or Sourwood (*Oxydendrum arboreum*)
Empress Tree (*Paulownia tomentosa*)
Dragon Spruce (*Picea asperata*)
Sargent Cherry (*Prunus sargenti*)
Yoshino Cherry (*Prunus yedoensis*)
Red Oak (*Quercus borealis*)
Scarlet Oak (*Quercus coccinea*)
★Pin Oak (*Quercus palustris*)
Laurel Willow (*Salix pentandra*)
Sassafras (*Sassafras albidum officinale*)
Korean Mountain Ash (*Sorbus alnifolia*)
White Beam Mountain Ash (*Sorbus aria*)
Korean Stewartia (*stewartia koreana*)
Japanese Stewartia (*Stewartia pseudo-camellia*)
American Arbor-vitae (*Thuja occidentalis*)
Oriental Arbor-vitae (*Thuja orientalis*)
★Crimean Linden (*Tilia euchlora*)
Carolina Hemlock (*Tsuga caroliniana*)
Winged or Wahoo Elm (*Ulmus alata*)
Chinese Elm (*Ulmus parvifolia*)

75 Feet or Over
Fir species (*Abies*)
Norway Maple (*Acer platanoides*)

Sycamore Maple (*Acer pseudoplatanus*)
Red or Swamp Maple (*Acer rubrum*)
Hickory species (*Carya*)
★Cedar species (*Cedrus*)
False Cypress species (*Chamaecyparis*)
Crytomeria (*Cryptomeria japonica*)
★Beech species (*Fagus*)
★Ginkgo or Maidenhair Tree (*Ginkgo biloba*)
★Common Honey-Locust (*Gleditsia triacanthos*)
★Sweet Gum (*Liquidambar styraciflua*)
Cucumber Tree (*Magnolia acuminata*)
Dawn Redwood (*Metasequoia glyptostroboides*)
★Black Gum or Black Tupelo (*Nyssa sylvatica*)
★Pine species (*Pinus*)
★Plane Tree species (*Platanus*)
Poplar species (*Populus*)
Golden Larch (*Pseudolarix amabilis*)
★Douglas Fir (*Pseudotsuga menziesii*)
★Oak species (*Quercus*)
Umbrella Pine (*Sciadopitys verticillata*)
Common Bald Cypress (*Taxodium distichum*)
English Elm (*Ulmus procera*)
Japanese Zelkova (*Zelkova serrata*)

Trees Classifed by Form

Pyramidal
Fir species (*Abies*)
Arbor-vitae species (*Arbor-vitae*)
★Cedar species (*Cedrus*)
Cryptomeria (*Cryptomeria japonica*)
★Beech species (*Fagus*)
English Holly (*Ilex aquifolium*)
American Holly (*Ilex opaca*)
Longstalk Holly (*Ilex pedunculosa*)
Juniper or Red Cedar species (*Juniperus*)
★Sweet Gum (*Liquidambar styraciflua*)
★Magnolia species (*Magnolia*)
Dawn Redwood (*Metasequoia glytostroboides*)
★Black Tupelo or Black Gum (*Nyssa sylvatica*)
Hop-Hornbeam (*Ostrya virginiana*)
★Sorrel Tree or Sourwood (*Oxydendrum arboreum*)
Bolleana Poplar (*Populus alba pyramidalis*)
★Douglas Fir (*Pseudotsuga menziesii*)
Turkey Oak (*Quercus cerris*)
★Pin Oak (*Quercus palustris*)
Umbrella Pine (*Sciadopitys verticillata*)
★Linden species (*Tilia*)
★Hemlock species (*Tsuga*)
Smooth-leaved Elm varieties (*Ulmus carpinifolia*)

Columnar
Ascending Norway Maple (*Acer platanoides ascendens*)
Columnar Norway Maple (*Acer platanoides columnare*)
Erect Norway Maple (*Acer platanoides erectum*)
Columnar Red Maple (*Acer rubrum columnare*)
Fastigiate European Hornbeam (*Carpinus betulus fastigiata*)
Fastigiate Washington Hawthorn (*Crataegus phaenopyrum fastigiata*)
Dawyck Beech (*Fagus sylvatica fastigiata*)
Sentry Ginkgo (*Ginkgo biloba fastigiata pyramidalis*)
★Lombardy Poplar (*Populus nigra italica*)
"Amanogawa" Cherry (*Prunus serrulata* "Amanogawa")
Fastigiate English Oak (*Quercus robur fastigiata*)
Shipmast Locust (*Robinia pseudoacacia rectissima*)

Weeping
Weeping European Hornbeam (*Carpinus betulus pendula*)
★Weeping Beech (*Fagus sylvatica pendula*)
Weeping Red Cedar (*Juniperus virginiana pendula*)
"Exzellenz Thiel" Crab Apple (*Malus* "Exzellenz Thiel")
"Oekonomierat Echtermeyer" Crab Apple (*Malus* "Oekonomierat Echtermeyer")
Weeping Mulberry (*Morus alba pendula*)
Weeping White Pine (*Pinus strobus pendula*)
Weeping Black Cherry (*Prunus serotina pendula*)
Weeping Higan Cherry (*Prunus subhirtella pendula*)

"Yaeshidare" Cherry (*Prunus subhirtella pendula flora plena*)
Weeping Yoshino Cherry (*Prunus yedoensis perpendens*)
Weeping Douglas Fir (*Pseudotsuga menziesii pendula*)
★Babylon Weeping Willow (*Salix babylonica*)
Weeping Japanese Pagoda Tree (*Sophora japonica pendula*)
Weeping Folgner Mountain Ash (*Sorbus folgneri pendula*)
Pendant Silver Linden (*Tilia petiolaris*)
Sargent Hemlock (*Tsuga canadensis pendula*)
Weeping American Elm (*Ulmus americana pendula*)

Rounded or Globe-Shaped
★Japanese Maple (*Acer palmatum*)
Globe Norway Maple (*Acer platanoides globosum*)
Globe European Hornbeam (*Carpinus betulus globosa*)
Bunch Hackberry (*Celtis bungeana*)
Cornelian Cherry (*Cornus mas*)
Japanese Cornel (*Cornus officinalis*)
Single Seed Hawthorn (*Crataegus monogyna inermis*)
★Saucer Magnolia (*Magnolia soulangeana*)
★Crab Apple species (*Malus*)
★White Oak (*Quercus alba*)
Umbrella Black Locust (*Robinia pseudoacacia umbraculifera*)
Sargent Hemlock (*Tsuga canadensis sargenti*)

With Horizontal Branching
Fir species (*Abies*)
★Cedar species (*Cedrus*)
Eastern Redbud (*Cercis canadensis*)
★Flowering Dogwood (*Cornus florida*)
Japanese Dogwood (*Cornus kousa*)
★Hawthorn species (*Crataegus*)
Dawn Redwood (*Metasequoia glytostroboides*)
★Black Tupelo or Black Gum (*Nyssa sylvatica*)
★Eastern White Pine (*Pinus strobus*)
White Oak (*Quercus alba*)
★Pin Oak (*Quercus palustris*)
Common Bald Cypress (*Taxodium distichum*)

Trees Classified by Color of Blossom

Yellow
★Golden Rain Tree (*Koelreuteria paniculata*)
★Laburnum (*Laburnum vossi*)

White
★Shadblow Serviceberry (*Amelanchier canadensis*)
Whitebud (*Cercis canadensis alba*)
★American Yellow-wood (*Cladrastis lutea*)
Japanese Dogwood (*Cornus kousa*)
Washington Hawthorn (*Crataegus phaenopyrum*)
Carolina Silberbell (*Halesia carolina*)
Yulan Magnolia (*Magnolia denudata*)
★Star Magnolia (*Magnolia stellata*)
Arnold Crab Apple (*Malus arnoldiana*)
Tea Crab Apple (*Malus hupehensis*)
Sargent Crab Apple (*Malus sargenti*)
★Sorrel Tree (*Oxydendrum arboreum*)
Thundercloud Plum (*Prunus cerasifera* "Thundercloud")
Mount Fuji Cherry (*Prunus serrulata* "Shirotae")
Yoshino Cherry (*Prunus yedoensis*)
Bradford Callery Pear (*Pryus calleryana bradfordi*)
★Common Pear (*Pyrus communis*)
★Japanese Pagoda Tree (*Sophora japonica*)
Korean Mountain Ash (*Sorbus alnifolia*)
Japanese Stewartia (*Stewartia pseudocamellia*)
Japanese Snowbell (*Styrax japonica*)

Pink
Wither's Pink Redbud (*Cercis canadensis* "Wither's Pink Charm")
Red Flowering Dogwood (*Cornus florida rubra*)
★Saucer Magnolia (*Magnolia soulangeana*)
Japanese Flowering Crab Apple (*Malus floribunda*)
Katherine Crab Apple (*Malus* "Katherine")

Prince Georges Crab Apple (*Malus* "Prince Georges")
★Common Apple (*Malus pumila*)
Blireiana Plum (*Prunus blireiana*)
Sargent Cherry (*Prunus sargenti*)
Amanogawa Cherry (*Prunus serrulata* "Amanogawa")
Kwanzan Cherry (*Prunus serrulata* "Kwanzan")
Autumn Cherry (*Prunus subhirtella autumnalis*)
Weeping Cherry (*Prunus subhirtella pendula*)

Red
Ruby Horse-Chestnut (*Aesculus carnea briotti*)
Paul's Scarlet Hawthorn (*Crataegus oxyacantha pauli*)
Alexandrina Magnolia (*Magnolia soulangeana* "Alexandrina")
Almey Crab Apple (*Malus* "Almey")
Carmine Crab Apple (*Malus atrosanguinea*)

Trees with Bright Red Fruit
★Flowering Dogwood (*Cornus florida*)
Japanese Dogwood (*Cornus kousa*)
Downy Hawthorn (*Crataegus mollis*)
Washington Hawthorn (*Crataegus phaenopyrum*)
American Holly (*Ilex opaca*)
Almey Crab Apple (*Malus* "Almey")
★Siberian Crab Apple (*Malus baccata*)
Hopa Crab Apple (*Malus* "Hopa")
★Common Apple (*Malus pumila*)
Sargent Crab Apple (*Malus sargenti*)
Korean Mountain Ash (*Sorbus alnifolia*)
American Mountain Ash (*Sorbus americana*)
European Mountain Ash (*Sorbus aucuparia*)

Trees Classified by Color of Summer Foliage

Blue
White Fir (*Abies concolor*)
★Blue Atlas Cedar (*Cedrus atlantica glauca*)
Steel Lawson Cypress (*Chamaecyparis lawsonia glauca*)
Eastern Red Cedar (*Juniperus virginiana* var. *Burki*)

Red to Purple
Blood-leaf Japanese Maple (*Acer palmatum atropurureum*)
Schwedler Maple (*Acer platanoides schwedleri*)
Crimson King Maple (*Acer platanoides* "Crimson King")
Purple-leaf Sycamore Maple (*Acer pseudoplatanus*)
Purple Beech (*Fagus sylvatica atropunicea*)
Weeping Purple Beech (*Fagus sylvatica purpureopendula*)
River's Purple Beech (*Fagus sylvatica riversi*)
Rubylace Locust (*Gleditsia triacanthos inermis* "Rubylace")
Purple Crab Apple (*Malus purpurea*)
Blireiana Plum (*Prunus blireiana*)
Pissard Plum (*Prunus cerasifera atropurpurea*)
Thundercloud Plum (*Prunus cerasifera nigra* "Thundercloud")
Blood-leaf Peach (*Prunus persica atropurpurea*)

Trees Classified by Color of Fall Foliage

Yellow
Striped Maple or Moosewood (*Acer pennsylvanicum*)
Norway Maples (*Acer platanoides* var.)
Apple Serviceberry (yellow-orange) (*Amelanchier grandiflora*)
★Birch species (*Betula*)
Hickory species (*Carya*)
Chinese Chestnut (*Castanea mollisima*)
★Katsura Tree (yellow to scarlet) (*Cercidiphyllum japonicum*)
Redbud species (*Cercis*)
Fringetree (*Chionanthus virginicus*)
★American Yellow-wood (*Cladrastis lutea*)
★American Beech (*Fagus grandifolia*)
★European Beech (*Fagus sylvatica*)

White Ash (purple to yellow) (*Fraxinus americana*)
*Ginkgo (*Ginkgo biloba*)
*Star Magnolia (bronze) (*Magnolia stellata*)
Golden Larch (*Pseudolarix amabilis*)
*Willow species (*Salix*)

Red
Amur Maple (*Acer ginnala*)
Nikko Maple (*Acer nikoense*)
*Red Maple (*Acer rubrum*)
*Japanese Maple (*Acer palmatum* var.)
Tatarian Maple (*Acer tataricum*)
*Shadblow Serviceberry (*Amelanchier canadensis*)
Hornbeam species (*Carpinus*)
*Flowering Dogwood (*Cornus florida*)
Japanese Dogwood (*Cornus kousa*)
American Smoke Tree (*Cotinus americanus*)
Washington Hawthorn (*Crataegus phaenopyrum*)
*Sweet Gum (*Liquidambar styraciflua*)
*Black Tupelo or Black Gum (*Nyssa sylvatica*)
*Sorrel Tree (*Oxydendrum arboreum*)
*Cherry species (*Prunus*)
Bradford Callery Pear (*Pyrus calleryana bradfordi*)
Red Oak (*Quercus borealis*)
Scarlet Oak (*Quercus coccinea*)
*Pin Oak (*Quercus palustris*)
Sassafras (*Sassafras albidum*)
Korean Mountain Ash (*Sorbus alnifolia*)
Korean Stewartia (orange to red) (*Stewartia koreana*)

Purple
White Ash (*Fraxinus americana*)
*Sweet Gum (*Liquidambar styraciflua*)
*Common Pear (*Pyrus communis*)
*White Oak (*Quercus alba*)
Japanese Stewartia (*Stewartia pseudocamellia*)

Silver to Grayish
Russian Olive (*Elaeagnus angustifolia*)
White Poplar (*Populus alba*)
Pendant Silver Linden (*Tilia petiolaris*)
*Silver Linden (*Tilia tomentosa*)

Trees with Interesting Bark

Gray
*Red Maple (*Acer rubrum*)
Serviceberry species (*Amelanchier*)
Hackberry species (*Celtis*)
*American Yellow-wood (*Cladrastis lutea*)
*Hawthorn species (*Crataegus*)
*Beech species (*Fagus*)
American Holly (*Ilex opaca*)
English or Persian Walnut (*Juglans regia*)
Cucumber Tree (*Magnolia acuminata*)
*Saucer Magnolia (*Magnolia soulangeana*)
Red Oak (young trunk and branches) (*Quercus borealis*)
Black Oak (young trunk and branches) (*Quercus velutina*)

White
*Gray Birch (*Betula populifolia*)

Red
Japanese Red Pine (*Pinus densiflora*)

Reddish Brown
Chinese Paper Birch (*Betula albo-sinensis*)
Sargent Cherry (*Prunus sargenti*)

Yellow
Wisconsin or Niobe Weeping Willow (*Salix blanda*)

Green
*Babylon Weeping Willow (*Salix babylonica*)

Corky
*Amur Cork (*Phellodendron amurense*)

Flaking
Paperbark Maple (*Acer griseum*)
*Birch species (*Betula*)
Shagbark Hickory (*Carya ovata*)
Eastern Red Cedar (*Juniperus virginiana*)
Persian Parrotia (*Parrotia persica*)

*Plane Tree species (*Platanus*)
Lace-bark Pine (*Pinus bungeana*)
Stewartia species (*Stewartia*)

Trees for the City

Hedge Maple (*Acer campestre*)
Box-Elder (*Acer negundo*)
Norway Maple (*Acer platanoides*)
Sycamore Maple (*Acer pseudoplatanus*)
*Horse-Chestnut Buckeye (*Aesculus*)
*Tree of Heaven (*Ailanthus*)
Silk Tree (*Albizzia julibrissin*)
Catalpa (*Catalpa*)
Hackberry (*Celtis*)
Downy Hawthorn (*Crataegus mollis*)
Washington Hawthorn (*Crataegus phaenopyrum*)
Russian Olive (*Elaeagnus angustifolia*)
White Ash (*Fraxinus americana*)
European Ash (*Fraxinus excelsior*)
Green Ash (*Fraxinus pennsylvanica*)
*Ginkgo (*Ginkgo biloba*)
Thornless Honey-Locust (*Gleditsia triacanthos inermis*)
*Golden Rain Tree (*Koelreuteria paniculata*)
*Saucer Magnolia (*Magnolia soulangeana*)
*Star Magnolia (*Magnolia stellata*)
*Crab Apple (*Malus* var.)
White Poplar (*Populus alba*)
*Lombardy Poplar (*Populus nigra italica*)
*Amur Cork (*Phellodendron amurense*)
*London Plane Tree (*Platanus acerifolia*)
Bradford Callery Pear (*Pyrus calleryana bradfordi*)
Red Oak (*Quercus borealis*)
*Black Locust (*Robinia pseudoacacia*)
*Japanese Pagoda Tree (*Sophora japonica*)
*Little-leaf Linden (*Tilia cordata*)
*Crimean Linden (*Tilia euchlora*)
*Silver Linden (*Tilia tomentosa*)
Village Green Zelkova (*Zelkova serrata* "Village Green")

Trees for Wide Streets
Sycamore Maple (*Acer pseudoplatanus*)
Sugar Hackberry (*Celtis laevigata*)
*Katsura Tree (*Cercidiphyllum japonicum*)
White Ash (*Fraxinus americana*)
Green Ash (*Fraxinus pennsylvanica lanceolata*)
*Ginkgo (*Ginkgo biloba*)
*Common Honey-Locust (*Gleditsia triacanthos*)
Tulip Tree (*Liriodendron tulipifera*)
*Eastern White Pine (*Pinus strobus*)
*London Plane Tree (*Platanus acerifola*)
*Oriental Plane Tree (*Platanus orientalis*)
White Poplar (*Populus alba*)
Sargent Cherry (*Prunus sargenti*)
*Pin Oak (*Quercus palustris*)
Japanese Zelkova (*Zelkova serrata*)

Trees for Medium Streets
Norway Maple (*Acer platanoides*)
Mountain Silverbell (*Halesia monticola*)
Sweet Gum (*Liquidambar styraciflua*)
Hop-Hornbeam (*Ostrya virginiana*)
*Sorrel Tree or Sourwood (*Oxydendrum arboreum*)
Simon Poplar (*Populus simoni*)
Scarlet Oak (*Quercus coccinea*)
*Black Locust (*Robinia pseudoacacia*)
Sassafras (*Sassafras albidum officinale*)
*Japanese Pagoda Tree (*Sophora japonica*)
*Linden species (*Tilia*)
Winged Elm (*Ulmus alata*)

Trees for Suburban Streets
Hedge Maple (*Acer campestre*)
Paperbark Maple (*Acer griseum*)
Mountain Maple (*Acer spicatum*)
American Hornbeam (*Carpinus caroliniana*)
Pyramidal European Hornbeam (*Carpinus betulus fastigiata*)
Globe European Hornbeam (*Carpinus betulus globosa*)

Fringetree (*Chionanthus virginicus*)
*Flowering Dogwood (*Cornus florida*)
*Hawthorn species (*Crataegus*)
Korean Evodia (*Evodia danielli*)
Carolina Silverbell (*Halesia carolina*)
*Golden Rain Tree (*Koelreuteria paniculata*)
Columnar Sargent Cherry (*Prunus sargenti columnaris*)
Oriental Cherry (*Prunus serrulata*)
Japanese Snowbell (*Styrax japonica*)
Fragrant Snowbell (*Styrax obassia*)
Asiatic Sweetleaf (*Symplocos paniculata*)
Smooth-leaved Elm varieties (*Ulmus carpinifolia*)

Soil Tolerance
Trees Tolerating Acid Soil
*Japanese Maple (*Acer palmatum*)
*Flowering Dogwood (*Cornus florida*)
Japanese Dogwood (*Cornus kousa*)
*European Beech (*Fagus sylvatica*)
Sweet Bay (*Magnolia virginiana*)
*Black Tupelo (*Nyssa sylvatica*)
*Sorrel Tree (*Oxydendrum arboreum*)
Hardy Orange (*Poncirus trifoliata*)
Red Oak (*Quercus borealis*)
Scarlet Oak (*Quercus coccinea*)
*Pin Oak (*Quercus palustris*)
Willow Oak (*Quercus phellos*)
Japanese Stewartia (*Stewartia pseudocamellia*)

Trees Tolerating Moist Soil
*Red Maple (*Acer rubrum*)
Alder species (*Alnus*)
Holly species (*Ilex*)
Sweet Gum (*Liquidambar styraciflua*)
Sweet Bay (*Magnolia virginiana*)
*Black Tupelo or Black Gum (*Nyssa sylvatica*)
Swamp White Oak (*Quercus bicolor*)
*Willow species (*Salix*)
Common Bald Cypress (*Taxodium distichum*)
American Arbor-vitae (*Thuja occidentalis*)

Trees Tolerating Dry or Poor Soil
Box-Elder (*Acer negundo*)
*Tree of Heaven (*Ailanthus*)
Silk Tree (*Albizzia julibrissin*)
*Gray Birch (*Betula populifolia*)
Russian Olive (*Elaeagnus angustifolia*)
Green Ash (*Fraxinus pennsylvanica*)
Modesto Ash (*Fraxinus velutina* "Modesto")
*Honey-Locust (*Gleditsia triacanthos* var.)
Eastern Red Cedar (*Juniperus virginiana*)
*Golden Rain Tree (*Koelreuteria paniculata*)
Jack Pine (*Pinus banksiana*)
White Poplar (*Populus alba*)
*Black Locust (*Robinia pseudoacacia*)
Sassafras (*Sassafras albidum officinale*)
*Japanese Pagoda Tree (*Sophora japonica*)
Chinese Elm (*Ulmus parvifolia*)

Pest-Resistant Trees
*Tree of Heaven (*Ailanthus altissima*)
Hornbeam species (*Carpinus*)
*Cedar species (*Cedrus*)
European Hackberry (*Celtis australis*)
Cornelian Cherry (*Cornus mas*)
Japanese Cornel (*Cornus officinalis*)
American Smoke Tree (*Cotinus americanus*)
Russian Olive (*Elaeagnus angustifolia*)
Franklinia (*Franklinia alatamaha*)
*Ginkgo (*Ginkgo biloba*)
*Honey-Locust (*Gleditsia triacanthos*)
Juniper species (*Juniperus*)
*Golden Rain Tree (*Koelreuteria paniculata*)
*Laburnum species (*Laburnum*)
*Sweet Gum (*Liquidambar styraciflua*)
Anise Magnolia (*Magnolia salicifolia*)
*Star Magnolia (*Magnolia stellata*)
Hop-Hornbeam species (*Ostrya*)

Trees for Seashore Planting
Norway Maple (*Acer platanoides*)
Sycamore Maple (*Acer pseudoplatanus*)

★Horse-Chestnut (*Aesculus hippocastanum*)
★Tree of Heaven (*Ailanthus*)
★Shadblow Serviceberry (*Amelanchier canadensis*)
  Cockspur Thorn (*Crataegus crus-galli*)
  English Hawthorn (*Crataegus oxyacantha*)
  Washington Hawthorn (*Crataegus phaenopyrum*)
  Cryptomeria (*Cryptomeria japonica*)
  Russian Olive (*Elaeagnus angustifolia*)
  Thornless Honey-Locust (*Gleditsia triacanthos inermis* var.)
  American Holly (*Ilex opaca*)
  Eastern Red Cedar (*Juniperus virginiana*)
★Black Tupelo (*Nyssa sylvatica*)
  Colorado Blue Spruce (*Picea pungens glauca*)
★Austrian Pine (*Pinus nigra*)
  Pitch Pine (*Pinus rigida*)
  Scotch Pine (*Pinus sylvestris*)

★Japanese Black Pine (*Pinus thunbergi*)
★London Plane Tree (*Platanus acerifolia*)
  White Poplar (*Populus alba*)
  Hardy Orange (*Poncirus trifoliata*)
  Black Cherry (*Prunus serotina*)
★White Oak (*Quercus alba*)
  Black Jack Oak (*Quercus marilandica*)
★Black Locust (*Robinia pseudoacacia*)
  Golden Weeping Willow (*Salix alba tristis*)
★Japanese Pagoda Tree (*Sophora japonica*)
★Little-leaf Linden (*Tilia cordata*)
★Crimean Linden (*Tilia euchlora*)
  American Arbor-vitae (*Thuja occidentalis*)
  Oriental Arbor-vitae (*Thuja orientalis*)
  Cork Elm (*Ulmus alata*)

Trees for Hedging or Barriers

European Beech (*Fagus sylvatica*) prunes well.
Leyland Cypress (*Cupressocyparis leylandii*) withstands heavy pruning.
Hawthorn varieties (*Crataegus*) easily pruned, advantage of thorns.
Canadian Hemlock (*Tsuga canadensis*) evergreen.
American Holly (*Ilex opaca*) can be pruned.
European Hornbeam (*Carpinus betulus*) prunes well.
Little-leaf Linden (*Tilia cordata*) tolerates heavy pruning.
Hedge Maple (*Acer campestre*) can be pruned.
Austrian Pine (*Pinus nigra*) plant 10–12 feet on centers, staggered row.
Japanese Black Pine (*Pinus thunbergi*) plant 8 feet on centers, staggered row.
Eastern White Pine (*Pinus strobus*) plant 15 feet on centers, staggered row.

SOUTH CAROLINA

State Tree

Cabbage Palmetto (*Sabal palmetto*)

Evergreen Trees

  Camellia species (*Camellia*)
★Deodar Cedar (*Cedrus deodara*)
  Camphor Tree (*Cinnamomum camphora*)
  Common China Fir (*Cunninghamia lanceolata*)
★Cypress species (*Cupressus*)
  Eucalyptus species (*Eucalyptus*)
  Loblolly Bay Gordonia (*Gordonia lasianthus*)
  Holly species (*Ilex*)
  Juniper species (*Juniperus*)
★Southern Mangolia (*Magnolia grandiflora*)
  Chinese Photinia (*Photinia serrulata*)
★Pine species (*Pinus*)
  Yew Podocarpus (*Podocarpus macrophyllus*)
  Holly Oak (*Quercus ilex*)
  Cork Oak (*Quercus suber*)
★Live Oak (*Quercus virginiana*)
  Palmetto (*Sabal palmetto*)
★Hemlock species (*Tsuga*)

Trees Classified by Height

20–35 Feet

★Japanese Maple (*Acer palmatum*)
  Strawberry Tree (*Arbutus unedo*)
  American Smoke Tree (*Cotinus americanus*)
★Hawthorn species (*Crataegus*)
  Loquat (*Eriobotrya japonica*)
  Common Fig (*Ficus carica*)
  Dahoon (*Ilex cassine*)
  Possum Haw (*Ilex decidua*)
  Yaupon (*Ilex vomitoria*)
  Crape-Myrtle (*Lagerstroemia indica*)
  Yellow Cucumber Tree (*Magnolia cordata*)
  Oyama Magnolia (*Magnolia sieboldi*)
★Crab Apple species (*Malus*)
★Cherry species (*Prunus*)
★Babylon Weeping Willow (*Salix babylonica*)
  Farkleberry (*Vaccinium-arboreum*)
  Common Jujuba or Chinese Date (*Zizyphus jujuba*)

35–75 Feet

★Red Maple (*Acer rubrum*)
★Sugar Maple (*Acer saccharum*)
★Florida Maple (*Acer floridanum*)
  Silk Tree (*Albizzia julibrissin*)
  Common Camellia (*Camellia japonica*)
  Hackberry (*Celtis*)
  Chinese Redbud (*Cercis chinensis*)
  Camphor Tree (*Cinnamomum camphora*)
★Flowering Dogwood (*Cornus florida*)
  Common China Fir (*Cunninghamia lanceolata*)
  Malian Cypress (*Cupressus sempervirens*)
  Kaki Persimmon (*Diospyros kaki*)
  Chinese Parasol Tree (*Firmiana simplex*)
  Loblolly Bay Gordonia (*Gordonia lasianthus*)

  English Holly (*Ilex aquifolium*)
  Dahoon (*Ilex cassine*)
  Luster-leaf Holly (*Ilex latifolia*)
  Mountain Winterberry (*Ilex montana*)
  American Holly (*Ilex opaca*)
  Greek Juniper (*Juniperus excelsa*)
  Sweet Bay (*Magnolia virginiana*)
  Chinaberry (*Melia azedarach*)
  Aleppo Pine (*Pinus halepensis*)
  Chinese Pistache (*Pistacia chinensis*)
  Yew Podocarpus (*Podocarpus macrophyllus*)
  Holly or Holm Oak (*Quercus ilex*)
  Laurel Oak (*Quercus laurifolia*)
  Water Oak (*Quercus nigra*)
  Willow Oak (*Quercus phellos*)
  Cork Oak (*Quercus suber*)
★Live Oak (*Quercus virginiana*)
  Clammy Locust (*Robinia viscosa*)
  Carolina Hemlock (*Tsuga caroliniana*)

75 Feet or Over

  Red or Swamp Maple (*Acer rubrum*)
  Monkey-Puzzle Tree (*Araucaria araucana*)
  Eucalyptus species (*Eucalyptus*)
★Southern Magnolia (*Magnolia grandiflora*)
  Palmetto (*Sabal palmetto*)
  Italian Stone Pine (*Pinus pinea*)
★Oak species (*Quercus*)

Trees Classified by Form

Pyramidal

  Juniper or Red Cedar species (*Juniperus*)
★Sweet Gum (*Liquidambar styraciflua*)
★Magnolia species (*Magnolia*)
  Chinaberry (*Malia azedarach*)
  Dawn Redwood (*Metasequoia glyptostroboides*)
★Black Tupelo or Black Gum (*Nyssa sylvatica*)
  Hop-Hornbeam (*Ostrya virginiana*)
★Sorrel Tree or Sourwood (*Oxydendrum arboreum*)
  Common Bald Cypress (*Taxodium distichum*)

Columnar

  Columnar Red Maple (*Acer rubrum columnare*)
  Italian Cypress (*Cupressus sempervirens*)
  Pyramidal Red Cedar (*Juniperus virginiana pyramidalis*)
  Schott Red Cedar (*Juniperus virginiana schotti*)
  Shipmast Locust (*Robinia pseudoacacia rectissima*)

Weeping

★Deodar Cedar (*Cedrus deodar*)
  Weeping Red Cedar (*Juniperus virginiana pendula*)
★Babylon Weeping Willow (*Salix babylonica*)
  Weeping Cherry (*Prunus pendula*)

Rounded or Globe-Shaped

  Single Seed Hawthorn (*Crataegus monogyna inermis*)
★White Oak (*Quercus alba*)

  Umbrella Black Locust (*Robinia pseudoacacia umbraculifera*)

With Horizontal Branching

  Silk Tree (*Albizzia julibrissin*)
★Cedar species (*Cedrus*)
★Flowering Dogwood (*Cornus florida*)
★Hawthorn species (*Crataegus*)
★Black Tupelo or Black Gum (*Nyssa sylvatica*)
★White Oak (*Quercus alba*)
★Live Oak (*Quercus virginiana*)
  Common Bald Cypress (*Taxodium distichum*)

Trees Classified by Color of Blossom

Yellow

★Golden Rain Tree (*Koelreuteria paniculata*)
★Laburnum (*Laburnum vossi*)

White

  Strawberry Tree (*Arbutus unedo*)
★Flowering Dogwood (*Cornus florida*)
  Carolina Silverbell (*Halesia carolina*)
★Southern Magnolia (*Magnolia grandiflora*)
  Chinese Photinia (*Photinia serrulata*)
  Bradford Pear (*Pyrus bradfordi*)
  Mount Fuji Cherry (*Prunus serrulata* "Shirotae")

Pink

  Wither's Pink Redbud (*Cercis canadensis* "Wither's Pink Charm")
  Red Flowering Dogwood (*Cornus florida rubra*)
  Ingleside Crape-Myrtle (*Lagerstroemia indica* "Ingleside Pink")
  Japanese Flowering Crab Apple (*Malus floribunda*)
  Katherine Crab Apple (*Malus* "Katherine")
  Prince Georges Crab Apple (*Malus* "Prince Georges")
★Common Apple (*Malus pumila*)
  Sargent Cherry (*Prunus sargenti*)
  Blireiana Plum (*Prunus blireiana*)
  Amanogawa Cherry (*Prunus serrulata* "Amanogawa")
  Kwanzan Cherry (*Prunus serrulata* "Kwanzan")
  Shiro-fugen Cherry (*Prunus serrulata* "Shirofugen")
  Autumn Cherry (*Prunus subhirtella autumnalis*)
  Weeping Cherry (*Prunus subhirtella pendula*)

Red

  Red Crape-Myrtle (*Lagerstroemia indica* "Wm. Toovey")
  Carmine Crab Apple (*Malus atrosanguinea*)

Trees with Bright Red Fruit

★Flowering Dogwood (*Cornus florida*)
  Almey Crab Apple (*Malus* "Almey")
★Siberian Crab Apple (*Malus baccata*)
  Hopa Crab Apple (*Malus* "Hopa")

Trees Classified by Color of Summer Foliage

Blue
Eastern Red Cedar (*Juniperus virginiana* var. *Burki*)

Silver to Grayish
Russian Olive (*Elaeagnus angustifolia*)
*Common Olive (*Olea europaea*)
White Poplar (*Populus alba*)
Pendant Silver Linden (*Tilia petiolaris*)
*Silver Linden (*Tilia tomentosa*)

Trees Classified by Color of Fall Foliage

Yellow
*Sugar Maple (*Acer saccharum*)
Fringetree (*Chionanthus virginicus*)
*Willow species (*Salix*)

Red
*Japanese Maple (*Acer palmatum*)
*Red Maple (*Acer rubrum*)
Chinese Pistache (*Pistacia chinensis*)

Trees with Interesting Bark

Gray
*Red Maple (*Acer rubrum*)
*Beech (*Fagus grandifolia*)
American Holly (*Ilex opaca*)

Corky
Sugar Hackberry (*Celtis laevigata*)
Cork Oak (*Quercus suber*)

Flaking
Eastern Red Cedar (*Juniperus virginiana*)
Crape-Myrtle (*Lagerstroemia indica*)
*Plane Tree species (*Platanus*)
Chinese Elm (*Ulmus parvifolia*)

Trees for the City

Silk Tree (*Albizzia julibrissin*)
Hackberry (*Celtis*)
*Ginkgo (*Ginkgo biloba*)
Thornless Honey-Locust (*Gleditsia triacanthos inermis*)
*Golden Rain Tree (*Koelreuteria paniculata*)
*Southern Magnolia (*Magnolia grandiflora*)
*Crab Apple (*Malus* var.)
Chinaberry (*Melia azedarach*)

Red Oak (*Quercus borealis*)
*Japanese Pagoda Tree (*Sophora japonica*)
Village Green Zelkova (*Zelkova serrata* "Village Green")

Trees for Wide Streets
Sugar Hackberry (*Celtis laevigata*)
Camphor Tree (*Cinnamomum camphora*)
*Eucalyptus species (*Eucalyptus*)
White Ash (*Fraxinus americana*)
Green Ash (*Fraxinus pennsylvanica lanceolata*)
*Common Honey-Locust (*Gleditsia triacanthos*)
*Southern Magnolia (*Magnolia grandiflora*)
Willow Oak (*Quercus phellos*)
*Live Oak (*Quercus virginiana*)

Trees for Medium Streets
Mountain Silverbell (*Halesia monticola*)
*Sweet Gum (*Liquidambar styraciflua*)
Chinaberry (*Melia azedarach*)
Hop-Hornbeam (*Ostrya virginiana*)
*Sorrel Tree or Sourwood (*Oxydendrum arboreum*)
Scarlet Oak (*Quercus coccinea*)
Laurel Oak (*Quercus laurifolia*)
Willow Oak (*quercus phellos*)
Cork Oak (*Quercus suber*)
*Black Locust (*Robinia pseudoacacia*)
Sassafras (*Sassafras albidum officinale*)

Trees for Suburban Streets
American Hornbeam (*Carpinus caroliniana*)
Fringetree (*Chionanthus virginicus*)
*Flowering Dogwood (*Cornus florida*)
*Hawthorn species (*Crataegus*)

Soil Tolerance

Trees Tolerating Acid Soil
Strawberry Tree (*Arbutus unedo*)
*Japanese Maple (*Acer palmatum*)
*Flowering Dogwood (*Cornus florida*)
Sweet Bay (*Magnolia virginiana*)
*Black Tupelo (*Nyssa sylvatica*)
*Sorrel Tree (*Oxydendrum arboreum*)
Willow Oak (*Quercus phellos*)

Trees Tolerating Moist Soil
*Red Maple (*Acer rubrum*)
Holly species (*Ilex*)
Sweet Bay (*Magnolia virginiana*)
Common Bald Cypress (*Taxodium distichum*)
*Willow species (*Salix*)

Trees Tolerating Dry or Poor Soil
Silk Tree (*Albizzia julibrissin*)
Common Paper-Mulberry (*Broussonetia papyrifera*)
Eucalyptus (*Eucalyptus species*)
*Honey-Locust (*Gleditsia triacanthos* var.)
*Golden Rain Tree (*Koelreuteria paniculata*)
Chinaberry (*Melia azedarach*)
*Common Olive (*Olea europaea*)
Jerusalem Thorn (*Parkinsonia aculeata*)
Torrey Pine (*Pinus torreyana*)

Pest-Resistant Trees

Hornbeam species (*Carpinus*)
Franklinia (*Franklinia alatamaha*)
Juniper species (*Juniperus*)
*Sweet Gum (*Liquidambar styraciflua*)
Hop-Hornbeam species (*Ostrya*)
*Oak species (*Quercus*)

Trees for Seashore Planting

Velvet Ash (*Fraxinus velutina*)
*Southern Magnolia (*Magnolia grandiflora*)
Aleppo Pine (*Pinus halepensis*)
Cluster Pine (*Pinus pinaster*)
Holly Oak (*Quercus ilex*)
*Live Oak (*Quercus virginiana*)
Oriental Arbor-vitae (*Thuja orientalis*)
Chinese Elm (*Ulmus parvifolia*)

Trees for Hedging or Barriers

European Beech (*Fagus sylvatica*) prunes well.
Leyland Cypress (*Cupressocyparis leylandii*) withstands heavy pruning.
Hawthorn varieties (*Crataegus*) easily pruned, advantage of thorns.
Canadian Hemlock (*Tsuga canadensis*) evergreen.
American Holly (*Ilex opaca*) can be pruned.
European Hornbeam (*Carpinus betulus*) prunes well.
Little-leaf Linden (*Tilia cordata*) tolerates heavy pruning.
Hedge Maple (*Acer campestre*) can be pruned.
Austrian Pine (*Pinus nigra*) plant 10–12 feet on centers, staggered row.
Japanese Black Pine (*Pinus thunbergi*) plant 8 feet on centers, staggered row.
Eastern White Pine (*Pinus strobus*) plant 15 feet on centers, staggered row.

SOUTH DAKOTA

State Tree

Cottonwood (*Populus*)

Evergreen Trees

Eastern Red Cedar (*Juniperus virginiana*)
*Larch species (*Larix*)
Spruce species (*Picea*)
*Pine species (*Pinus*)
Arbor-vitae species (*Tsuga*)

Trees Classified by Height

20–35 Feet
Amur Maple (*Acer ginnala*)
Ohio Buckeye (*Aesculus glabra*)
Russian Olive (*Elaeagnus angustifolia*)
*Crab Apple species (*Malus*)

35–75 Feet
Box-Elder (*Acer negundo*)
Speckled Alder (*Alnus incana*)
American Hornbeam (*Carpinus caroliniana*)
Green Ash (*Fraxinus pennsylvanica lanceolata*)
Eastern Larch or Tamarack (*Larix laricina*)
Siberian Crab Apple (*Malus baccata*)
"Dolgo" Crab Apple (*Malus* "Dolgo")
Cherry Crab Apple (*Malus robusta*)
Black Hills Spruce (*Picea glauca densata*)

Jack Pine (*Pinus banksiana*)
Scotch Pine (*Pinus sylvestris*)
White Willow (*Salix alba*)
European Mountain Ash or Rowan Tree (*Sorbus aucuparia*)

75 Feet or Over
White Fir (*Abies concolor*)
Norway Maple (*Acer platanoides*)
Red or Swamp Maple (*Acer rubrum*)
European Alder (*Alnus glutinosa*)
Canoe Birch (*Betula papyrifera*)
*Beech species (*Fagus*)
European Ash (*Fraxinus excelsior*)
*European Larch (*Larix decidua*)
Spruce species (*Picea*)
*Pine species (*Pinus*)
Poplar species (*Populus*)
Black or Rum Cherry (*Prunus serotina*)
*Linden species (*Tilia*)
*Elm species (*Ulmus*)

Trees Classified by Form

Pyramidal
Fir species (*Abies*)
Paper Birch (*Betula papyrifera*)
*Beech species (*Fagus*)
Juniper or Red Cedar species (*Juniperus*)

*Larch species (*Larix*)
Spruce species (*Picea*)
Arbor-vitae species (*Thuja*)
*Linden species (*Tilia*)

Columnar
Ascending Norway Maple (*Acer platanoides ascendens*)
Columnar Norway Maple (*Acer platanoides columnare*)
Erect Norway Maple (*Acer platanoides erectum*)
Columnar Red Maple (*Acer rubrum columnare*)
Fastigiate European Birch (*Betula pendula fastigiata*)
Schott Red Cedar (*Juniperus virginiana schotti*)
Swiss Stone Pine (*Pinus cembra*)
Fastigiate Scotch Pine (*Pinus sylvestris fastigiata*)
Fastigiate Simon Poplar (*Populus simoni fastigiata*)
Shipmast Locust (*Robinia pseudoacacia rectissima*)
Upright European Mountain Ash (*Sorbus aucuparia fastigiata*)
Douglas Arbor-vitae (*Thuja occidentalis douglasi pyramidalis*)
Fastigiate American Arbor-vitae (*Thuja occidentalis fastigiata*)
*American Elm varieties (*Ulmus americana*)

Weeping
Slender European Birch (*Betula pendula tristis*)

Young's Birch (*Betula pendula youngi*)
Weeping Larch (*Larix decidua pendula*)
Koster Weeping Blue Spruce (*Picea pungens kosteriana*)
Weeping Black Cherry (*Prunus serotina pendula*)
Golden Weeping Willow (*Salix alba tristis*)
Weeping European Mountain Ash (*Sorbus aucuparia pendula*)
Sargent Hemlock (*Tsuga canadensis pendula*)
Weeping American Elm (*Ulmus americana pendula*)

Rounded or Globe-Shaped
Globe Norway Maple (*Acer platanoides globosum*)
Umbrella Black Locust (*Robinia pseudoacacia umbraculifera*)
Sargent Hemlock (*Tsuga canadensis sargenti*)

With Horizontal Branching
Fir species (*Abies*)
Spruce species (*Picea*)
*Eastern White Pine (*Pinus strobus*)

Trees Classified by Color of Blossom

White
*Siberian Crab Apple (*Malus baccata*)
European Mountain Ash (*Sorbus aucuparia*)

Pink
Toba Hawthorn (*Crataegus mordenensis* "Toba")

Red
Almey Crab Apple (*Malus* "Almey")

Trees with Bright Red Fruit

Almey Crab Apple (*Malus* "Almey")
*Siberian Crab Apple (*Malus baccata*)
American Mountain Ash (*Sorbus americana*)

Trees Classified by Color of Summer Foliage

Blue
Eastern Red Cedar (*Juniperus virginiana* var. *Burki*)

Silver to Gray
Russian Olive (*Elaeagnus angustifolia*)
White Poplar (*Populus alba*)

Trees Classified by Color of Fall Foliage

Yellow
Norway Maple (*Acer platanoides*)
Ohio Buckeye (orange) (*Aesculus glabra*)
*Birch species (*Betula*)
*Larch (*Larix decidua*)
*Willow species (*Salix*)

Red
Amur Maple (*Acer ginnala*)
*Red Maple (*Acer rubrum*)
Hornbeam species (*Carpinus*)
*Cherry species (*Prunus*)

Trees with Interesting Bark

Gray
*Red Maple (*Acer rubrum*)
Hornbeam species (*Carpinus*)
*Beech species (*Fagus*)
Mountain Ash species (*Sorbus*)

White
*Canoe Birch (*Betula papyrifera*)

Red
Red or Norway Pine (*Pinus resinosa*)
Scotch Pine (*Pinus sylvestris*)

Flaking
*Birch species (*Betula*)
Russian Olive (*Elaeagnus angustifolia*)

Trees for the City

Box-Elder (*Acer negundo*)
Norway Maple (*Acer platanoides*)
Russian Olive (*Elaeagnus angustifolia*)
European Ash (*Fraxinus excelsior*)
Green Ash (*Fraxinus pennsylvanica lanceolata*)
*Crab Apple species (*Malus*)
Colorado Spruce (*Picea pungens*)
*Lombardy Poplar (*Populus nigra italica*)
*Black Locust (*Robinia pseudoacacia*)

Trees for Wide Streets
Green Ash (*Fraxinus pennsylvanica lanceolata*)
*Eastern White Pine (*Pinus strobus*)
White Poplar (*Populus alba*)

Trees for Medium Streets
Norway Maple (*Acer platanoides*)
*Black Locust (*Robinia pseudoacacia*)

*Linden species (*Tilia*)

Trees for Suburban Streets
Amur Maple (*Acer ginnala*)
Globe Norway Maple (*Acer platanoides globosum*)
American Hornbeam (*Carpinus caroliniana*)
*Hawthorn species (*Crataegus*)

Soil Tolerance

Trees Tolerating Moist Soil
*Red Maple (*Acer rubrum*)
Alder species (*Alnus*)
Eastern Larch (*Larix larcina*)
American Arbor-vitae (*Thuja occidentalis*)

Trees Tolerating Dry or Poor Soil
Box-Elder (*Acer negundo*)
Russian Olive (*Elaeagnus angustifolia*)
Green Ash (*Fraxinus pennsylvanica lanceolata*)
Eastern Red Cedar (*Juniperus virginiana*)
Jack Pine (*Pinus banksiana*)
White Poplar (*Populus alba*)
*Black Locust (*Robinia pseudoacacia*)

Pest-Resistant Trees

Russian Olive (*Elaeagnus angustifolia*)
Hornbeam species (*Carpinus*)

Trees for Hedging or Barriers

European Beech (*Fagus sylvatica*) prunes well.
Hawthorn varieties (*Crataegus*) easily pruned, advantage of thorns.
Canadian Hemlock (*Tsuga canadensis*) evergreen.
American Holly (*Ilex opaca*) can be pruned.
European Hornbeam (*Carpinus betulus*) prunes well.
Little-leaf Linden (*Tilia cordata*) tolerates heavy pruning.
Hedge Maple (*Acer campestre*) can be pruned.
Austrian Pine (*Pinus nigra*) plant 10–12 feet on centers, staggered row.
Japanese Black Pine (*Pinus thunbergi*) plant 8 feet on centers, staggered row.
Eastern White Pine (*Pinus strobus*) plant 15 feet on centers, staggered row.

TENNESSEE

State Tree

Tulip Tree or Yellow Poplar (*Liriodendron tulipifera*)

Evergreen Trees

Holly species (*Ilex*)
Juniper species (*Juniperus*)
*Southern Magnolia (*Magnolia grandiflora*)
*Pine species (*Pinus*)
*Douglas Fir (*Pseudotsuga menziesii*)
Arbor-vitae species (*Thuja*)
*Hemlock species (*Tsuga*)

Trees Classified by Height

20–35 Feet
Hedge Maple (*Acer campestre*)
Hornbeam Maple (*Acer carpinifolium*)
Amur Maple (*Acer ginnala*)
Paperbark Maple (*Acer griseum*)
*Japanese Maple (*Acer palmatum*)
Ohio Buckeye (*Aesculus glabra*)
Apple Serviceberry (*Amelanchier grandiflora*)
*Gray Birch (*Betula poplifolia*)
European Hornbeam (*Carpinus betulus globosa*)
Mockernut (*Carya tomentosa*)
Judas Tree (*Cercis siliquastrum*)
Japanese Dogwood (*Cornus kousa*)
Cornelian Cherry (*Cornus mas*)
Japanese Cornel (*Cornus officinalis*)
American Smoke Tree (*Cotinus americanus*)

*Hawthorn species (*Crataegus*)
Russian Olive (*Elaeagnus angustifolia*)
Korean Evodia (*Evodia danielli*)
Franklinia (*Franklinia alatamaha*)
Carolina Silverbell (*Halesia carolina*)
*Golden Rain Tree (*Koelreuteria paniculata*)
*Laburnum species (*Laburnum*)
*Saucer Magnolia (*Magnolia soulangeana*)
*Star Magnolia (*Magnolia stellata*)
*Crab Apple species (*Malus*)
*Cherry species (*Prunus*)
Black Jack Oak (*Quercus marilandica*)
*Babylon Weeping Willow (*Salix babylonica*)
Snowbell species (*Styrax*)
35–75 Feet
Box-Elder (*Acer negundo*)
Striped Maple or Moosewood (*Acer pennsylvanicum*)
*Red-fruited Tree of Heaven (*Ailanthus altissima erythrocarpa*)
Silk Tree (*Albizzia julibrissin*)
Red Alder (*Alnus rubra*)
*Shadblow Serviceberry (*Amelanchier canadensis*)
Allegany Serviceberry (*Amelanchier laevis*)
European Hornbeam (*Carpinus betulus*)
American Hornbeam (*Carpinus caroliniana*)
Japanese Hornbeam (*Carpinus japonica*)
Chinese Chestnut (*Castanea mollissima*)
Southern Catalpa (*Catalpa bignoniodes*)

Bunch Hackberry (*Celtis bungeana*)
*Katsura Tree (*Cercidiphyllum japonicum*)
Eastern Redbud (*Cercis canadensis*)
Chinese Redbud (*Cercis chinensis*)
*American Yellow-wood (*Cladrastis lutea*)
*Flowering Dogwood (*Cornus florida*)
Cockspur Thorn (*Crataegus crus-galli*)
Green Ash (*Fraxinus pennsylvanica lanceolata*)
English Holly (*Ilex aquifolium*)
American Holly (*Ilex opaca*)
Heartnut (*Juglans sieboldiana cordiformis*)
Chinese Juniper (*Juniperus chinensis*)
Fraser Magnolia (*Magnolia fraseri*)
Kobus Mangolia (*Magnolia kobus borealis*)
Sweet Bay (*Magnolia virginiana*)
"Cowichan" Crab Apple (*Malus* "Cowichan")
"Dolgo" Crab Apple (*Malus* "Dolgo")
"Makamik" Crab Apple (*Malus* "Makamik")
Cherry Crab Apple (*Malus robusta*)
"Sissipuk" Crab Apple (*Malus* "Sissipuk")
White Mulberry (*Morus alba*)
*Sorrel Tree or Sourwood (*Oxydendrum arboreum*)
Empress Tree (*Paulownia tomentosa*)
Virginia or Scrub Pine (*Pinus virginiana*)
Simon Poplar (*Populus simoni*)
Sargent Cherry (*Prunus sargenti*)
Yoshino Cherry (*Prunus yedoensis*)
Red Oak (*Quercus borealis*)
Scarlet Oak (*Quercus coccinea*)

*Pin Oak (*Quercus palustris*)
Willow Oak (*Quercus phellos*)
Laurel Willow (*Salix pentandra*)
Sassafras (*Sassafras albidum officinale*)
Korean Mountain Ash (*Sorbus alnifolia*)
Japanese Stewartia (*Stewartia pseudo-camellia*)
American Arbor-vitae (*Thuja orientalis*)
Japanese Arbor-vitae (*Thuja standishi*)
*Crimean Linden (*Tilia euchlora*)
Carolina Hemlock (*Tsuga caroliniana*)
Chinese Elm (*Ulmus parvifolia*)

75 Feet or Over
Norway Maple (*Acer platanoides*)
Sycamore Maple (*Acer pseudoplatanus*)
Red or Swamp Maple (*Acer rubrum*)
Hickory species (*Carya*)
European Hackberry (*Celtis australis*)
Sugar Hackberry (*Celtis laevigata*)
*American Beech (*Fagus grandifolia*)
*Ginkgo or Maidenhair Tree (*Ginkgo biloba*)
Common Honey-Locust (*Gleditsia triacanthos*)
Kentucky Coffee Tree (*Gymnocladus dioicus*)
Mountain Silverbell (*Halesia monticola*)
English or Persian Walnut (*Juglans regia*)
*Sweet Gum (*Liquidambar styraciflua*)
*Southern Magnolia (*Magnolia grandiflora*)
Dawn Redwood (*Metasequoia glyptostroboides*)
*Black Gum or Black Tupelo (*Nyssa sylvatica*)
*Pine species (*Pinus*)
*Plane Tree species (*Platanus*)
Poplar species (*Populus*)
*Oak species (*Quercus*)
Common Bald Cypress (*Taxodium distichum*)
English Elm (*Ulmus procera*)
Japanese Zelkova (*Zelkova serrata*)

Trees Classified by Form
Pyramidal
*American Beech (*Fagus grandifolia*)
English Holly (*Ilex aquifolium*)
American Holly (*Ilex opaca*)
Juniper or Red Cedar species (*Juniperus*)
*Sweet Gum (*Liquidambar styraciflua*)
*Magnolia species (*Magnolia*)
Dawn Redwood (*Metasequoia glyptostroboides*)
*Black Tupelo or Black Gum (*Nyssa sylvatica*)
Hop-Hornbeam (*Ostrya virginiana*)
*Sorrel Tree or Sourwood (*Oxydendrum arboreum*)
*Pin Oak (*Quercus palustris*)
Bolleana Poplar (*Populus alba pyramidalis*)
Arbor-vitae species (*Thuja*)
*Linden species (*Tilia*)
*Hemlock species (*Tsuga*)
Smooth-leaved Elm varieties (*Ulmus carpinifolia*)

Columnar
Ascending Norway Maple (*Acer platanoides ascendens*)
Columnar Norway Maple (*Acer platanoides columnare*)
Erect Norway Maple (*Acer platanoides erectum*)
Columnar Red Maple (*Acer rubrum columnare*)
Fastigiate European Hornbeam (*Carpinus betulus fastigiata*)
Fastigiate Washington Hawthorn (*Crataegus phaenopyrum fastigiata*)
Sentry Ginkgo (*Ginkgo biloba fastigiata*)
Schott Red Cedar (*Juniperus virginiana schotti*)
*Lombardy Poplar (*Populus nigra italica*)
"Amanogawa" Cherry (*Prunus serrulata* "Amanogawa")
Fastigiate English Oak (*Quercus robur fastigiata*)
Shipmast Locust (*Robinia pseudoacacia rectissima*)
Common Bald Cypress (*Taxodium distichum*)

Weeping
*European Birch (*Betula pendula*)
Weeping European Hornbeam (*Carpinus betulus pendula*)
Weeping Red Cedar (*Juniperus virginiana pendula*)
"Exzellenz Thiel" Crab Apple (*Malus* "Exzellenz Thiel")

"Oekonomierat Echtermeyer" Crab Apple (*Malus* "Oekonomierat Echtermeyer")
Weeping Mulberry (*Morus alba pendula*)
Weeping White Pine (*Pinus strobus pendula*)
Weeping Japanese Apricot (*Prunus mume pendula*)
Weeping Black Cherry (*Prunus serotina pendula*)
Weeping Higan Cherry (*Prunus subhirtella pendula*)
"Yaeshidare" Cherry (*Prunus subhirtella pendula flora plena*)
Weeping Yoshino Cherry (*Prunus yedoensis perpendens*)
Weeping Douglas Fir (*Pseudotsuga menziesii pendula*)
*Babylon Weeping Willow (*Salix babylonica*)
Weeping Japanese Pagoda Tree (*Sophora japonica pendula*)
Pendant Silver Linden (*Tilia petiolaris*)
Sargent Hemlock (*Tsuga canadensis pendula*)
Weeping American Elm (*Ulmus americana pendula*)

Rounded or Globe-Shaped
*Japanese Maple (*Acer palmatum*)
Globe Norway Maple (*Acer platanoides globosum*)
Globe European Hornbeam (*Carpinus betulus globosa*)
Bunch Hackberry (*Celtis bungeana*)
Cornelian Cherry (*Cornus mas*)
Japanese Cornel (*Cronus officinalis*)
*Saucer Magnolia (*Magnolia soulangeana*)
*Crab Apple species (*Malus*)
*White Oak (*Quercus alba*)
Umbrella Black Locust (*Robinia pseudoacacia umbraculifera*)
Sargent Hemlock (*Tsuga canadensis sargenti*)

With Horizontal Branching
Silk Tree (*Albizzia julbrissin*)
Eastern Redbud (*Cercis canadensis*)
*Flowering Dogwood (*Cornus florida*)
Japanese Dogwood (*Cornus kousa*)
*Hawthorn species (*Crataegus*)
Dawn Redwood (*Metasequoia glyptostroboides*)
*Black Tupelo or Black Gum (*Nyssa sylvatica*)
*Eastern White Pine (*Pinus strobus*)
*White Oak (*Quercus alba*)
*Pin Oak (*Quercus palustris*)
*Live Oak (*Quercus virginiana*)
Common Bald Cypress (*Taxodium distichum*)

Trees Classified by Color of Blossom
Yellow
*Golden Rain Tree (*Koelreuteria paniculata*)
*Laburnum (*Laburnum vossi*)

White
*Shadblow Serviceberry (*Amelanchier canadensis*)
White Redbud (*Cercis canadensis alba*)
*American Yellow-wood (*Cladrastis lutea*)
Japanese Dogwood (*Cornus kousa*)
Washington Hawthorn (*Crataegus phaenopyrum*)
Carolina Silverbell (*Halesia carolina*)
*Southern Magnolia (*Magnolia grandiflora*)
*Star Magnolia (*Magnolia stellata*)
Arnold Crab Apple (*Malus arnoldiana*)
Tea Crab Apple (*Malus hupehensis*)
Sargent Crab Apple (*Malus sargenti*)
*Sorrel Tree (*Oxydendrum arboreum*)
Thundercloud Plum (*Prunus cerasifera* "Thundercloud")
Mount Fuji Cherry (*Prunus serrulata* "Shirotae")
Yoshino Cherry (*Prunus yedoensis*)
Bradford Callery Pear (*Pyrus calleryana bradfordi*)
*Common Pear (*Pyrus communis*)
*Japanese Pagoda Tree (*Sophora japonica*)
Korean Mountain Ash (*Sorbus alnifolia*)

Pink
Wither's Pink Redbud (*Cercis canadensis* "Wither's Pink Charm")
Red Flowering Dogwood (*Cornus florida rubra*)
Toba Hawthorn (*Crataegus mordenensis* "Toba")
*Saucer Magnolia (*Magnolia soulangeana*)

Japanese Flowering Crab Apple (*Malus floribunda*)
Katherine Crab Apple (*Malus* "Katherine")
Prince Georges Crab Apple (*Malus* "Prince Georges")
*Common Apple (*Malus pumila*)
Blireiana Plum (*Prunus blireiana*)
Sargent Cherry (*Prunus sargenti*)
Amanogawa Cherry (*Prunus serrulata* "Amanogawa")
Kwanzan Cherry (*Prunus serrulata* "Kwanzan")
Autumn Cherry (*Prunus subhirtella autumnalis*)
Weeping Cherry (*Prunus subhirtella pendula*)

Red
Ruby Horse-Chestnut (*Aesculus carnea briotti*)
Paul's Scarlet Hawthorn (*Crataegus oxyacantha pauli*)
Alexandrina Magnolia (*Magnolia soulangeana* "Alexandrina")
Almey Crab Apple (*Malus* "Almey")
Carmine Crab Apple (*Malus atrosanguinea*)

Trees with Bright Red Fruit
*Flowering Dogwood (*Cornus florida*)
Japanese Dogwood (*Cornus kousa*)
Washington Hawthorn (*Crataegus phaenopyrum*)
American Holly (*Ilex opaca*)
Almey Crab Apple (*Malus* "Almey")
*Siberian Crab Apple (*Malus baccata*)
Hopa Crab Apple (*Malus* "Hopa")
*Common Apple (*Malus pumila*)
Sargent Crab Apple (*Malus sargenti*)
Korean Mountain Ash (*Sorbus alnifolia*)
American Mountain Ash (*Sorbus americana*)
European Mountain Ash (*sorbus aucuparia*)

Trees Classified by Color of Summer Foliage
Blue
Western Red Cedar (*Juniperus scopulorum* var. Chandler Blue)
Eastern Red Cedar (*Juniperus virginiana* var. Burki)

Silver to Gray
Russian Olive (*Elaeagnus angustifolia*)
White Poplar (*Populus alba*)
Pendant Silver Linden (*Tilia petiolaris*)
*Silver Linden (*Tilia tomentosa*)

Red to Purple
Blood-leaf Japanese Maple (*Acer palmatum atropurpureum*)
Crimson King Maple (*Acer platanoides* "Crimson King")
Schwedler Maple (*Acer platanoides schwedleri*)
Purple-leaf Sycamore Maple (*Acer pseudoplatanus*)
Rubylace Locust (*Gleditsia triacanthos inermis* "Rubylace")
Blireiana Plum (*Prunus blireiana*)
Pissard Plum (*Prunus cerasifera atropurpurea*)
Thundercloud Plum (*Prunus cerasifera nigra* "Thundercloud")
Woods Myrobalan Plum (*Prunus cerasifera woodi*)
Blood-leaf Peach (*Prunus persica atropurpurea*)
Purple English Oak (*Quercus robur atropurpurea*)

Trees Classified by Color of Fall Foliage
Yellow
Striped Maple or Moosewood (*Acer pennsylvanicum*)
Norway Maple (*Acer platanoides* var.)
Apple Serviceberry (yellow-orange) (*Amelanchier grandiflora*)
*Birch species (*Betula species*)
Hickory species (*Carya*)
Chinese Chestnut (*Castanea mollissima*)
*Katsura Tree (yellow to scarlet) (*Cercidiphyllum japonicum*)
Redbud species (*Cercis*)
*American Yellow-wood (*Cladrastis lutea*)
*American Beech (*Fagus grandifolia*)

White Ash (purple to yellow) (*Fraxinus americana*)
*Ginkgo (*Ginkgo biloba*)
*Star Magnolia (bronze) (*Magnolia stellata*)
*Willow species (*Salix*)

Red

Amur Maple (*Acer ginnala*)
*Japanese Maple (*Acer palmatum* var.)
*Red Maple (*Acer rubrum*)
*Shadblow Serviceberry (*Amelanchier canadensis*)
Hornbeam species (*Carpinus*)
*Flowering Dogwood (*Cornus florida*)
Japanese Dogwood (*Cornus kousa*)
American Smoke Tree (*Cotinus americanus*)
Washington Hawthorn (*Crataegus phaenopyrum*)
*Sweet Gum (*Liquidambar styraciflua*)
*Black Tupelo or Black Gum (*Nyssa sylvatica*)
*Sorrel Tree (*Oxydendrum arboreum*)
*Cherry species (*Prunus*)
Bradford Callery Pear (*Pyrus calleryana bradfordi*)
Red Oak (*Quercus borealis*)
Scarlet Oak (*Quercus coccinea*)
*Pin Oak (*Quercus palustris*)
Sassafras (*Sassafras albidum*)
Korean Mountain Ash (*Sorbus alnifolia*)

Purple

White Ash (*Fraxinus americana*)
*Sweet Gum (*Liquidambar styraciflua*)
*Common Pear (*Pyrus communis*)

Trees with Interesting Bark

Gray

*Red Maple (*Acer rubrum*)
Serviceberry species (*Amelanchier*)
Hackberry species (*Celtis*)
*American Yellow-wood (*Cladrastis lutea*)
*Hawthorn species (*Crataegus*)
*American Beech (*Fagus grandifolia*)
American Holly (*Ilex opaca*)
English or Persian Walnut (*Juglans regia*)
Cucumber Tree (*Magnolia acuminata*)
*Saucer Magnolia (*Magnolia soulangeana*)
Red Oak (young trunk and branches) (*Quercus borealis*)
Black Oak (young trunk and branches) (*Quercus velutina*)
Mountain Ash species (*Sorbus*)

White

*Gray Birch (*Betula populifolia*)
*European Birch (*Betula pendula*)

Reddish Brown

Chinese Paper Birch (*Betula albo-sinensis*)

Yellow

Wisconsin or Niobe Weeping Willow (*Salix blanda*)

Green

*Babylon Weeping Willow (*Salix babylonica*)

Corky

*Amur Cork (*Phellodendron amurense*)

Flaking

Paperbark Maple (*Acer griseum*)
*Birch species (*Betula*)
Shagbark Hickory (*Carya ovata*)
Eastern Red Cedar (*Juniperus virginiana*)
Lace-bark Pine (*Pinus bungeana*)
*Plane Tree species (*Platanus*)

Trees for the City

Hedge Maple (*Acer campestre*)
Box-Elder (*Acer negundo*)
Norway Maple (*Acer platanoides*)
Sycamore Maple (*Acer pseudoplatanus*)
*Horse-Chestnut or Buckeye (*Aesculus*)
*Tree of Heaven (*Ailanthus*)
Silk Tree (*Albizzia julibrissin*)

Catalpa (*Catalpa*)
Hackberry (*Celtis*)
Washington Hawthorn (*Crataegus phaenopyrum*)
Russian Olive (*Elaeagnus angustifolia*)
White Ash (*Fraxinus americana*)
European Ash (*Fraxinus excelsior*)
Green Ash (*Fraxinus pennsylvanica*)
*Ginkgo (*Ginkgo biloba*)
Thornless Honey-Locust (*Gleditsia triacanthos*)
*Golden Rain Tree (*Koelreuteria paniculata*)
*Saucer Magnolia (*Magnolia soulangeana*)
*Star Magnolia (*Magnolia stellata*)
*Crab Apple (*Malus* var.)
Chinaberry (*Melia azedarach*)
*Amur Cork (*Phellodendron amurense*)
London Plane Tree (*Platanus acerifolia*)
White Poplar (*Populus alba*)
*Lombardy Poplar (*Populus nigra italica*)
Bradford Callery Pear (*Pyrus calleryana bradfordi*)
Red Oak (*Quercus borealis*)
*Black Locust (*Robinia pseudoacacia*)
*Japanese Pagoda Tree (*Sophora japonica*)
*Little-leaf Linden (*Tilia cordata*)
*Crimean Linden (*Tilia euchlora*)
*Silver Linden (*Tilia tomentosa*)
Village Green Zelkova (*Zelkova serrata* "Village Green")

Trees for Wide Streets

Sycamore Maple (*Acer pseudoplatanus*)
Sugar Hackberry (*Celtis laevigata*)
*Katsura Tree (*Cercidiphyllum japonicum*)
White Ash (*Fraxinus americana*)
Green Ash (*Fraxinus pennsylvanica lanceolata*)
*Ginkgo (*Ginkgo biloba*)
Common Honey-Locust (*Gleditsia triacanthos*)
*Southern Magnolia (*Magnolia grandiflora*)
Tulip Tree (*Liriodendron tulipifera*)
*Eastern White Pine (*Pinus strobus*)
London Plane Tree (*Platanus acerifola*)
*Oriental Plane Tree (*Platanus orientalis*)
White Poplar (*Populus alba*)
*Pin Oak (*Quercus palustris*)
Willow Oak (*Quercus phellos*)
Japanese Zelkova (*Zelkova serrata*)

Trees for Medium Streets

Norway Maple (*Acer platanoides*)
Mountain Silverbell (*Halesia monticola*)
*Sweet Gum (*Liquidambar styraciflua*)
Hop-Hornbeam (*Ostrya virginiana*)
*Sorrel Tree or Sourwood (*Oxydendrum arboreum*)
Simon Poplar (*Populus simoni*)
Scarlet Oak (*Quercus coccinea*)
Willow Oak (*Quercus phellos*)
*Black Locust (*Robinia pseudoacacia*)
Sassafras (*Sassafras albidum officinale*)
*Japanese Pagoda Tree (*Sophora japonica*)
*Linden species (*Tilia*)
Winged Elm (*Ulmus alata*)

Trees for Suburban Streets

Hedge Maple (*Acer campestre*)
Paperbark Maple (*Acer griseum*)
Mountain Maple (*Acer spicatum*)
American Hornbeam (*Carpinus caroliniana*)
Pyramidal European Hornbeam (*Carpinus betulus fastigiata*)
Globe European Hornbeam (*Carpinus betulus globosa*)
*Flowering Dogwood (*Cornus florida*)
*Hawthorn species (*Crataegus*)
Korean Evodia (*Evodia danielli*)
Carolina Silverbell (*Halesia carolina*)
*Golden Rain Tree (*Koelreuteria paniculata*)
Oriental Cherry (*Prunus serrulata*)
Smooth-leaved Elm varieties (*Ulmus carpinifolia*)

Soil Tolerance

Trees Tolerating Acid Soil

*Japanese Maple (*Acer palmatum*)

*Flowering Dogwood (*Cornus florida*)
Japanese Dogwood (*Cornus kousa*)
Sweet Bay (*Magnolia virginiana*)
*Black Tupelo (*Nyssa sylvatica*)
*Sorrel Tree (*Oxydendrum arboreum*)
Red Oak (*Quercus borealis*)
Scarlet Oak (*Quercus coccinea*)
*Pin Oak (*Quercus palustris*)
Willow Oak (*Quercus phellos*)

Trees Tolerating Moist Soil

*Red Maple (*Acer rubrum*)
Alder species (*Alnus*)
Holly species (*Ilex*)
*Sweet Gum (*Liquidambar styraciflua*)
Sweet Bay (*Magnolia virginiana*)
*Black Tupelo or Black Gum (*Nyssa sylvatica*)
Swamp White Oak (*Quercus bicolor*)
*Willow species (*Salix*)
Common Bald Cypress (*Taxodium distichum*)
American Arbor-vitae (*Thuja occidentalis*)

Trees Tolerating Dry or Poor Soil

Box-Elder (*Acer negundo*)
*Tree of Heaven (*Ailanthus*)
Silk Tree (*Albizzia julibrissin*)
*Gray Birch (*Betula populifolia*)
European Hackberry (*Celtis australis*)
Russian Olive (*Elaeagnus angustifolia*)
Green Ash (*Fraxinus pennsylvanica*)
Modesto Ash (*Fraxinus velutina* "Modesto")
*Honey-Locust (*Gleditsia triacanthos* var.)
Western Red Cedar (*Juniperus scopulorum*)
Eastern Red Cedar (*Juniperus virginiana*)
*Golden Rain Tree (*Koelreuteria paniculata*)
Jack Pine (*Pinus banksiana*)
White Poplar (*Populus alba*)
Black Jack Oak (*Quercus marilandica*)
*Black Locust (*Robinia pseudoacacia*)
Sassafras (*Sassafras albidum officinale*)
*Japanese Pagoda Tree (*Sophora japonica*)

Pest-Resistant Trees

*Tree of Heaven (*Ailanthus altissima*)
Hornbeam species (*Carpinus*)
European Hackberry (*Celtis australis*)
Cornelian Cherry (*Cornus mas*)
Japanese Cornel (*Cornus officinalis*)
American Smoke Tree (*Cotinus americanus*)
Russian Olive (*Elaeagnus angustifolia*)
Franklinia (*Franklinia alatamaha*)
*Ginkgo (*Ginkgo biloba*)
*Honey-Locust (*Gleditsia triacanthos*)
Juniper species (*Juniperus*)
*Golden Rain Tree (*Koelreuteria paniculata*)
*Laburnum species (*Laburnum*)
*Sweet Gum (*Liquidambar styraciflua*)
*Star Magnolia (*Magnolia stellata*)
Hop-Hornbeam species (*Ostrya*)

Trees for Hedging or Barriers

European Beech (*Fagus sylvatica*) prunes well.
Leyland Cypress (*Cupressocyparis leylandii*) withstands heavy pruning.
Hawthorn varieties (*Crataegus*) easily pruned, advantage of thorns.
Canadian Hemlock (*Tsuga canadensis*) evergreen.
American Holly (*Ilex opaca*) can be pruned.
European Hornbeam (*Carpinus betulus*) prunes well.
Little-leaf Linden (*Tilia cordata*) tolerates heavy pruning.
Hedge Maple (*Acer campestre*) can be pruned.
Austrian Pine (*Pinus nigra*) plant 10–12 feet on centers, staggered row.
Japanese Black Pine (*Pinus thunbergi*) plant 8 feet on centers, staggered row.
Eastern White Pine (*Pinus strobus*) plant 15 feet on centers, staggered row.

TEXAS

State Tree

Pecan (*Carya pecan*)

Evergreen Trees

*Acacia species (*Acacia*)
*Cedar species (*Cedrus*)
*Deodar Cedar (*Cedrus deodara*)
False Cypress species (*Chamaecyparis*)
*Cypress species (*Cupressus*)
Moreton Bay Fig (*Ficus macrophylla*)
Holly species (*Ilex*)
Juniper species (*Juniperus*)
*Southern Magnolia (*Magnolia grandiflora*)
*Pine species (*Pinus*)
*Live Oak (*Quercus virginiana*)
Palmetto (*Sabal palmetto*)
Arbor-vitae species (*Thuja*)
Farkleberry (*Vaccinium arboreum*)

Trees Classified by Height

20–35 Feet

Sweet Acacia (*Acacia farnesiana*)
European Hornbeam (*Carpinus betulus globosa*)
Mocker Nut (*Carya tomentosa*)
Judas Tree (*Cercis canadensis*)
Fringetree (*Chionanthus virginicus*)
Japanese Dogwood (*Cornus kousa*)
*Hawthorn species (*Crataegus*)
Russian Olive (*Elaeagnus angustifolia*)
Euonymus species (*Euonymus*)
Common Fig (*Ficus carica*)
Flowering Ash (*Fraxinus ornus*)
Possum Haw (*Ilex decidua*)
Yaupon (*Ilex vomitoria*)
*Saucer Magnolia (*Magnolia soulangeana*)
*Star Magnolia (*Magnolia stellata*)
*Crab Apple species (*Malus*)
Jerusalem Thorn (*Parkinsonia aculeata*)
*Cherry species (*Prunus*)
Black Jack Oak (*Quercus marilandica*)
*Babylon Weeping Willow (*Salix babylonica*)
Farkleberry (*Vaccinium arboreum*)

35–75 Feet

Box-Elder (*Acer negundo*)
*Red-fruited Tree of Heaven (*Ailanthus altissima erythrocarpa*)
*Birch species (*Betula*)
Common Paper-Mulberry (*Broussonetia papyrifera*)
American Hornbeam (*Carpinus caroliniana*)
Pecan (*Carya pecan*)
Chinese Chestnut (*Castanea mollisima*)
Southern Catalpa (*Catalpa bignoniodes*)
Eastern Redbud (*Cercis canadensis*)
*Flowering Dogwood (*Cornus florida*)
Cockspur Thorn (*Crataegus crus-galli*)
Green Hawthorn (*Crataegus viridis*)
Common China Fir (*Cunninghamia lanceolata*)
Common Persimmon (*Diospyros virginiana*)
Texas Persimmon (*Diospyros texana*)
Moreton Bay Fig (*Ficus macrophylla*)
Green Ash (*Fraxinus pennsylvanica lanceolata*)
American Holly (*Ilex opaca*)
Rocky Mountain Juniper (*Juniperus scopulorum*)
Eastern Red Cedar (*Juniperus virginiana*)
Osage-Orange (*Maclura pomifera*)
"Cowichan" Crab Apple (*Malus* "Cowichan")
"Dolgo" Crab Apple (*Malus* "Dolgo")
"Makamik" Crab Apple (*Malus* "Makamik")
Cherry Crab Apple (*Malus robusta*)
"Sissipuk" Crab Apple (*Malus* "Sissipuk")
Chinaberry (*Melia azedarach*)
White Mulberry (*Morus alba*)
*Austrian Pine (*Pinus nigra*)
Chinese Pistache (*Pistacia chinensis*)
Red Oak (*Quercus borealis*)
Spanish or Southern Red Oak (*Quercus falcata*)
Water Oak (*Quercus nigra*)
*Pin Oak (*Quercus palustris*)

Willow Oak (*Quercus phellos*)
Shumard Oak (*Quercus shumardi*)
*Live Oak (*Quercus virginiana*)
*Babylon Weeping Willow (*Salix babylonica*)
Korean Mountain Ash (*Sorbus alnifolia*)
European Mountain Ash or Rowan Tree (*Sorbus aucuparia*)
American Arbor-vitae (*Thuja occidentalis*)
Winged Elm (*Ulmus alata*)
Chinese or Wahoo Elm (*Ulmus parvifolia*)
Siberian Elm (*Ulmus pumila*)

75 Feet or Over

*Red or Swamp Maple (*Acer rubrum*)
*Sugar Maple (*Acer saccharum*)
*Baumann Horse-Chestnut (*Aesculus hippocasta-num baumanni*)
Hickory species (*Carya*)
Sugar Hackberry (*Celtis laevigata*)
*Beech species (*Fagus*)
White Ash (*Fraxinus americana*)
*Common Honey-Locust (*Gleditsia triacanthos*)
Eastern Black Walnut (*Juglans nigra*)
*Sweet Gum (*Liquidambar styraciflua*)
Tulip Tree or Yellow Poplar (*Liriodendron tulipifera*)
*Southern Magnolia (*Magnolia grandiflora*)
*Black Gum or Black Tupelo (*Nyssa sylvatica*)
Sabal Palmetto (*Palmetto*)
*Pine species (*Pinus*)
*Plane Tree species (*Platanus*)
*Poplar species (*Populus*)
*Oak species (*Quercus*)
Common Bald Cypress (*Taxodium distichum*)
Giant Arbor-vitae (*Thuja plicata*)
*Linden species (*Tilia*)
*Elm species (*Ulmus*)

Trees Classified by Form

Pyramidal

*Beech species (*Fagus*)
American Holly (*Ilex opaca*)
Juniper or Red Cedar species (*Juniperus*)
*Sweet Gum (*Liquidambar styraciflua*)
*Magnolia species (*Magnolia*)
*Black Tupelo or Black Gum (*Nyssa sylvatica*)
Hop-Hornbeam (*Ostrya virginiana*)
*Cherry species (*Prunus*)
*Pin Oak (*Quercus palustris*)
*Linden species (*Tilia*)

Columnar

Columnar Red Maple (*Acer rubrum columnare*)
Sentry Maple (*Acer saccharum monumentale*)
Fastigiate Washington Hawthorn (*Crataegus phaen-opyrum fastigiata*)
*Lombardy Poplar (*Populus nigra italica*)
Shipmast Locust (*Robinia pseudoacacia rectissima*)
Common Bald Cypress (*Taxodium distichum*)
*American Elm varieties (*Ulmus americana*)

Weeping

Weeping European Hornbeam (*Carpinus betulus pendula*)
*Cherry species (*Prunus*)
*Babylon Weeping Willow (*Salix babylonica*)
Weeping Japanese Pagoda Tree (*Sophora japonica pendula*)
Weeping American Elm (*Ulmus americana pendula*)

Rounded or Globe-Shaped

Globe European Hornbeam (*Carpinus betulus globosa*)
Bunch Hackberry (*Celtis bungeana*)
Single Seed Hawthorn (*Crataegus monogyna inermis*)
*Saucer Magnolia (*Magnolia soulangeana*)
*Crab Apple species (*Malus*)

With Horizontal Branching

Eastern Redbud (*Cercis canadensis*)
*Flowering Dogwood (*Cornus florida*)
*Hawthorn species (*Crataegus*)

*Black Tupelo or Black Gum (*Nyssa sylvatica*)

Trees Classified by Color of Blossom

White

Whitebud (*Cercis canadensis alba*)
*Flowering Dogwood (*Cornus fllorida*)
Washington Hawthorn (*Crataegus phaenopyrum*)
Carolina Silverbell (*Halesia carolina*)
*Southern Magnolia (*Magnolia grandiflora*)
*Star Magnolia (*Magnolia stellata*)
*Crab Apple species (*Malus*)
*Cherry species (*Prunus*)
Bradford Callery Pear (*Pyrus calleryana bradfordi*)
*Common Pear (*Pyrus communis*)
Japanese Snowbell (*Styrax japonica*)

Pink

Wither's Pink Redbud (*Cercis canadensis* "With-er's Pink Charm")
Red Flowering Dogwood (*Cornus florida rubra*)
Toba Hawthorn (*Crataegus mordenensis* "Toba")
*Saucer Magnolia (*Magnolia soulangeana*)
*Crab Apple species (*Malus*)
*Common Apple (*Malus pumila*)

Red

Ruby Horse-Chestnut (*Aesculus carnea briotti*)
Paul's Scarlet Hawthorn (*Crataegus oxyacantha pauli*)
Alexandrina Magnolia (*Magnolia soulangeana* "Alexandrina")
*Crab Apple species (*Malus*)

Trees with Bright Red Fruit

*Flowering Dogwood (*Cornus florida*)
Japanese Dogwood (*Cornus kousa*)
Downy Hawthorn (*Crataegus mollis*)
Washington Hawthorn (*Crataegus phaenopyrum*)
American Holly (*Ilex opaca*)
*Common Apple (*Malus pumila*)
*Crab Apple species (*Malus*)

Trees Classified by Color of Summer Foliage

Blue

Western Red Cedar (*Juniperus scopulorum* var. Chandler Blue)
Eastern Red Cedar (*Juniperus virginiana* var. *Burki*)

Red to Purple

Purple Crab Apple (*Malus purpurea*)
*Cherry species (*Prunus*)

Trees Classified by Color of Fall Foliage

Yellow

*Sugar Maple (*Acer saccharum*)
*Birch species (*Betula*)
Hickory species (*Carya*)
Redbud species (*Cercis*)
Fringetree (*Chionanthus virginicus*)
*American Beech (*Fagus grandifolia*)
White Ash (purple to yellow) (*Fraxinus americana*)
*Star Magnolia (bronze) (*Magnolia stellata*)
*Willow species (*Salix*)

Red

*Red Maple (*Acer rubrum*)
*Sugar Maple (*Acer saccharum*)
Hornbeam species (*Carpinus*)
*Flowering Dogwood (*Cornus florida*)
Japanese Dogwood (*Cornus kousa*)
American Smoke Tree (*Cotinus americanus*)
Washington Hawthorn (*Crataegus phaenopyrum*)
*Sweet Gum (*Liquidambar styraciflua*)
Dawson Crab Apple (*Malus dawsoniana*)
*Black Tupelo or Black Gum (*Nyssa sylvatica*)
Chinese Pistache (*Pistacia chinensis*)
*Cherry species (*Prunus*)
Red Oak (*Quercus borealis*)
*Pin Oak (*Quercus palustris*)

Sassafras (*Sassafras albidum*)

Purple
White Ash (*Fraxinus americana*)
*Sweet Gum (*Liquidambar styraciflua*)
*Common Pear (*Pyrus communis*)
*White Oak (*Quercus alba*)

Trees with Interesting Bark

Gray
*Red Maple (*Acer rubrum*)
*Serviceberry species (*Amelanchier*)
Hornbeam species (*Carpinus*)
Hackberry species (*Celtis*)
*Hawthorn species (*Crataegus*)
*Beech species (*Fagus*)
American Holly (*Ilex opaca*)
*Saucer Magnolia (*Magnolia soulangeana*)
Red Oak (young trunk and branches) (*Quercus borealis*)

White
*Birch species (*Betula*)

Flaking
*Birch species (*Betula*)
Shagbark Hickory (*Carya ovata*)
*Plane Tree species (*Platanus*)

Green
*Babylon Weeping Willow (*Salix babylonica*)

Trees for the City

Box-Elder (*Acer negundo*)
*Horse-Chestnut or Buckeye (*Aesculus*)
*Tree of Heaven (*Ailanthus*)
Catalpa (*Catalpa*)
Hackberry (*Celtis*)
Downy Hawthorn (*Crataegus mollis*)
Washington Hawthorn (*Crataegus phaenopyrum*)
Russian Olive (*Elaeagnus angustifolia*)
White Ash (*Fraxinus americana*)
Green Ash (*Fraxinus pennsylvanica*)
Thornless Honey-Locust (*Gleditsia triacanthos inermis*)
*Southern Magnolia (*Magnolia grandiflora*)
*Saucer Magnolia (*Magnolia soulangeana*)
*Star Magnolia (*Magnolia stellata*)
*Crab Apple (*Malus* var.)
Chinaberry (*Melia azedarrach*)
*London Plane Tree (*Platanus acerifolia*)
*Lombardy Poplar (*Populus nigra italica*)
Bradford Callery Pear (*Pyrus calleryana bradfordi*)
Red Oak (*Quercus borealis*)
*Black Locust (*Robinia pseudoacacia*)

Trees for Wide Streets

*Sugar Maple (*Acer saccharum*)
Sugar Hackberry (*Celtis laevigata*)
White Ash (*Fraxinus americana*)

Green Ash (*Fraxinus pennsylvanica lanceolata*)
*Common Honey-Locust (*Gleditsia triacanthos*)
*London Plane Tree (*Platanus acerifolia*)
*Oriental Plane Tree (*Platanus orientalis*)
Red Oak (*Quercus borealis*)
*Pin Oak (*Quercus phellos*)

Trees for Medium Streets

*Sweet Gum (*Liquidambar styraciflua*)
Chinaberry (*Melia azedarach*)
Hop-Hornbeam (*Ostrya virginiana*)
Willow Oak (*Quercus phellos*)
*Black Locust (*Robinia pseudoacacia*)
Sassafras (*Sassafras albidum officinale*)
*Linden species (*Tilia*)
Winged Elm (*Ulmus alata*)

Trees for Suburban Streets

Pyramidal European Hornbeam (*Carpinus betulus fastigiata*)
Globe European Hornbeam (*Caprinus betulus globosa*)
Fringetree (*Chionanthus virginicus*)
*Hawthorn species (*Crataegus*)
Carolina Silverbell (*Halesia carolina*)

Soil Tolerance

Trees Tolerating Acid Soil
*Flowering Dogwood (*Cornus florida*)
Japanese Dogwood (*Cornus kousa*)
Sweet Bay (*Magnolia virginiana*)
*Black Tupelo (*Nyssa sylvatica*)
Red Oak (*Quercus borealis*)
*Pin Oak (*Quercus palustris*)
Willow Oak (*Quercus phellos*)

Trees Tolerating Moist Soil
*Red Maple (*Acer rubrum*)
Holly species (*Ilex*)
*Sweet Gum (*Liquidambar styraciflua*)
Sweet Bay (*Magnolia virginiana*)
*Black Tupelo or Black Gum (*Nyssa sylvatica*)
*Willow species (*Salix*)
Common Bald Cypress (*Taxodium distichum*)
American Arbor-vitae (*Thuja occidentalis*)

Trees Tolerating Dry or Poor Soil
Box-Elder (*Acer negundo*)
*Tree of Heaven (*Ailanthus*)
*Birch species (*Betula*)
Flame Bottle Tree (*Brachychiton acerifolium*)
Russian Olive (*Elaeagnus angustifolia*)
Fig (*Ficus species*)
Green Ash (*Fraxinus pennsylvanica*)
*Honey-Locust (*Gleditsia triacanthos* var.)
Eastern Red Cedar (*Juniperus virginiana*)
Osage-Orange (*Maclura pomifera*)
Chinaberry (*Melia azedarach*)
Jerusalem Thorn (*Parkinsonia aculeata*)
Chinese Pistache (*Pistacia chinensis*)

Honey Mesquite (*Prosopis glandulosa*)
Black Jack Oak (*Quercus marilandica*)
*Black Locust (*Robinia pseudoacacia*)
Sassafras (*Sassafras albidum officinale*)
Chinese Elm (*Ulmus parvifolia*)
Siberian Elm (*Ulmus pumila*)

Pest-Resistant Trees

*Tree of Heaven (*Ailanthus altissima*)
Hornbeam species (*Carpinus*)
Russian Olive (*Elaeagnus angustifolia*)
Fig species (*Ficus*)
*Honey-Locust (*Gleditsia triacanthos*)
Juniper species (*Juniperus*)
*Sweet Gum (*Liquidambar styraciflua*)
*Star Magnolia (*Magnolia stellata*)

Trees for Seashore Planting

*Horse-Chestnut (*Aesculus hippocastanum*)
*Tree of Heaven (*Ailanthus*)
Cockspur Thorn (*Crataegus crus-galli*)
English Hawthorn (*Crataegus oxyacantha*)
Russian Olive (*Elaeagnus angustifolia*)
Thornless Honey-Locust (*Gleditsia triacanthos inermis* var.)
American Holly (*Ilex opaca*)
Eastern Red Cedar (*Juniperus virginiana*)
*Southern Magnolia (*Magnolia grandiflora*)
*Black Tupelo (*Nyssa sylvatica*)
*Austrian Pine (*Pinus nigra*)
*London Plane Tree (*Platanus acerifolia*)
Black Cherry (*Prunus serotina*)
*White Oak (*Quercus alba*)
*Live Oak (*Quercus virginiana*)
*Black Locust (*Robina pseudoacacia*)
Palmetto (*Sabal palmetto*)
Oriental Arbor-vitae (*Thuja orientalis*)
*Little-leaf Linden (*Tilia cordata*)

Trees for Hedging or Barriers

European Beech (*Fagus sylvatica*) prunes well.
Leyland Cypress (*Cupressocyparis leylandii*) withstands heavy pruning.
Hawthorn varieties (*Crataegus*) easily pruned, advantage of thorns.
Canadian Hemlock (*Tsuga canadensis*) evergreen.
American Holly (*Ilex opaca*) can be pruned.
European Hornbeam (*Carpinus betulus*) prunes well.
Little-leaf Linden (*Tilia cordata*) tolerates heavy pruning.
Hedge Maple (*Acer campestre*) can be pruned.
Austrian Pine (*Pinus nigra*) plant 10–12 feet on centers, staggered row.
Japanese Black Pine (*Pinus thunbergi*) plant 8 feet on centers, staggered row.
Eastern White Pine (*Pinus strobus*) plant 15 feet on centers, staggered row.

UTAH

State Tree

Blue Spruce (*Picea pungens*)

Evergreen Trees

White Fir (*Abies concolor*)
Juniper species (*Juniperus*)
Spruce species (*Picea*)
*Pine species (*Pinus*)
*Douglas Fir (*Pseudotsuga menziesii*)
Arbor-vitae (*Thuja*)
*Hemlock species (*Tsuga*)

Trees Classified by Height

20–35 Feet
Vine Maple (*Acer circinatum*)
Rocky Mountain Maple (*Acer glabrum*)
Bigtooth Maple (*Acer grandidentatum*)

Paperbark Maple (*Acer griseum*)
Ohio Buckeye (*Aesculus glabra*)
*Serviceberry species (*Amelanchier*)
*Birch species (*Betula*)
California Redbud (*Cercis occidentalis*)
Smoke Tree (*Cotinus coggygria*)
*Hawthorn species (*Crataegus*)
Russian Olive (*Elaeagnus angustifolia*)
Euonymus species (*Euonymus*)
*Golden Rain Tree (*Koelreuteria paniculata*)
*Laburnum species (*Laburnum*)
*Crab Apple species (*Malus*)
*Cherry species (*Prunus*)
Bur Oak (*Quercus macrocarpa*)
Gambel Oak (*Quercus gambelii*)
*Babylon Weeping Willow (*Salix babylonica*)
Mountain Ash (*Sorbus scopulina*)

35–75 Feet
Box-Elder (*Acer negundo*)
*Sugar Maple (*Acer saccharum*)
Red Alder (*Alnus rubra*)
*European Birch (*Betula pendula*)
European Hornbeam (*Carpinus betula*)
American Hornbeam (*Carpinus caroliniana*)
Japanese Hornbeam (*Carpinus japonica*)
Southern Catalpa (*Catalpa bignoniodies*)
Eastern Redbud (*Cercis canadensis*)
Chinese Redbud (*Cercis chinensis*)
*American Yellow-wood (*Cladastris lutea*)
Turkish Filbert (*Corylus columa*)
Cockspur Thorn (*Crataegus crus-galli*)
Green Ash (*Fraxinus pennsylvanica lanceolata*)
Chinese Juniper (*Juniperus chinensis*)
Mountain Juniper (*Juniperus communis*)

Rocky Mountain Juniper (*Juniperus scopulorum*)
One-seeded Juniper (*Juniperus monosperma*)
Utah Juniper (*Juniperus utahensis*)
Red Cedar (*Juniperus virginiana*)
★Siberian Crab Apple (*Malus baccata*)
"Cowichan" Crab Apple (*Malus* "Cowichan")
"Dolgo" Crab Apple (*Malus* "Dolgo")
"Makamik" Crab Apple (*Malus* "Makamik")
Cherry Crab Apple (*Malus robusta*)
"Sissipuk" Crab Apple (*Malus* "Sissipuk")
White Mulberry (*Morus alba*)
Bristlecone Pine (*Pinus aristata*)
Jack Pine (*Pinus banksiana*)
Lace-bark Pine (*Pinus bungeana*)
Pinon Pine (*Pinus edulis*)
Limber Pine (*Pinus flexilis*)
Pitch Pine (*Pinus rigida*)
Scotch Pine (*Pinus sylvestris*)
Chinese Poplar (*Populus lasiocarpa*)
Simon Poplar (*Populus simoni*)
Quaking Aspen (*Populus tremuloides*)
★Pin Oak (*Quercus palustris*)
Willow Oak (*Quercus phellos*)
★Black Locust (*Robinia pseudoacacia*)
White Willow (*Salix alba*)
Wisconsin or Niobe Weeping Willow (*Salix blanda*)
Elaeagnus Willow (*Salix elaeagnos*)
Thurlow Weeping Willow (*Salix elegantissima*)
Laurel Willow (*Salix pentandra*)
Korean Mountain Ash (*Sorbus alnifolia*)
White Beam Mountain Ash (*Sorbus aria*)
European Mountain Ash or Rowan Tree (*Sorbus aucuparia*)
American Arbor-vitae (*Thuja occidentalis*)
Oriental Arbor-vitae (*Thuja orientalis*)
Japanese Arbor-vitae (*Thuja standishi*)
★Crimean Linden (*Tilia euchlora*)
Carolina Hemlock (*Tsuga caroliniana*)
Chinese Elm (*Ulmus parviflora*)
Siberian Elm (*Ulmus pumila*)

75 Feet or Over
Fir species (*Abies*)
Big-leaf Maple (*Acer macrophyllum*)
Norway Maple (*Acer platanoides*)
Sycamore Maple (*Acer pseudoplatanus*)
★Horse-Chestnut (*Aesculus hippocastanum*)
European Alder (*Alnus glutinosa*)
Sweet Birch (*Betula lenta*)
River Birch (*Betula nigra*)
★Canoe Birch (*Betula papyrifera*)
Hickory species (*Carya*)
Northern Catalpa (*Catalpa speciosa*)
Sugar Hackberry (*Celtis laevigata*)
★Beech species (*Fagus*)
White Ash (*Fraxinus americana*)
European Ash (*Fraxinus excelsior*)
★Ginkgo or Maidenhair Tree (*Ginkgo biloba*)
★Common Honey-Locust (*Gleditsia triacanthos*)
Kentucky Coffee Tree (*Gymnocladus dioicus*)
Eastern Black Walnut (*Juglans nigra*)
English or Persian Walnut (*Juglans regia*)
★Sweet Gum (*Liquidambar styraciflua*)
Tulip Tree or Yellow Poplar (*Liriodendron tulipifera*)
Spruce species (*Picea*)
★Pine species (*Pinus*)
Poplar species (*Populus*)
★Douglas Fir (*Pseudotsuga menziesi*)
★Elm species (*Ulmus*)

Trees Classified by Form

Pyramidal
Fir species (*Abies*)
★Birch species (*Betula*)
★Cedar species (*Cedrus*)
Filbert (*Corylus*)
★Beech species (*Fagus*)
Juniper or Red Cedar species (*Juniperus*)
★Larch species (*Larix*)
★Sweet Gum (*Liquidambar styraciflua*)
★Magnolia species (*Magnolia*)

Spruce species (*Picea*)
Korean Pine (*Pinus koraiensis*)
★Pyramid Austrian Pine (*Pinus nigra pyramidalis*)
Japanese White Pine (*Pinus parviflora*)
Bolleana Poplar (*Populus alba pyramidalis*)
★Douglas Fir (*Pseudotsuga menziesii*)
★Pin Oak (*Quercus palustris*)
Arbor-vitae species (*Thuja*)
★Hemlock species (*Tsuga*)
Smooth-leaved Elm (*Ulmus carpinifolia*)

Columnar
Ascending Norway Maple (*Acer platanoides ascendens*)
Columnar Norway Maple (*Acer platanoides columnare*)
Erect Norway Maple (*Acer platanoides erectum*)
Fastigiate European Birch (*Betula pendula fastigiata*)
Fastigiate European Hornbean (*Carpinus betula fastigiata*)
Fastigiate Washington Hawthorn (*Crataegus phaenopyrum fastigiata*)
Dawyck Beech (*Fagus sylvatica fastigiata*)
Sentry Ginkgo (*Ginkgo biloba fastigiata*)
Blue Columnar Chinese Juniper (*Juniperus chinensis columnaris*)
Schott Red Cedar (*Juniperus virginiana schotti*)
Swiss Stone Pine (*Pinus cembra*)
★Lombardy Poplar (*Populus nigra italica*)
Fastigiate Simon Poplar (*Populus simoni fastigiata*)
Shipmast Locust (*Robinia pseudoacacia rectissima*)
Upright European Mountain Ash (*Sorbus aucuparia fastigiata*)
Fastigiate American Arbor-vitae (*Thuja occidentalis douglasi pyramidalis*)
★American Elm varieties (*Ulmus americana*)

Weeping
Slender European Birch (*Betula pendula tristis*)
Young's Birch (*Betula pendula youngi*)
Weeping European Hornbeam (*Carpinus betulus pendula*)
★Weeping Beech (*Fagus sylvatica pendula*)
Weeping Purple Beech (*Fagus sylvatica purpureo-pendula*)
Weeping Red Cedar (*Juniperus virginiana pendula*)
"Exzellenz Thiel" Crab Apple (*Malus* "Exzellenz Thiel")
"Oekonomierat Echtermeyer" Crab Apple (*Malus* "Oekonomierat Echtermeyer")
Weeping Mulberry (*Morus alba pendula*)
Koster Weeping Blue Spruce (*Picea pungens kosteriana*)
Weeping Douglas Fir (*Pseudotsuga menziesi pendula*)
Golden Weeping Willow (*Salix alba tristis*)
★Babylon Weeping Willow (*Salix babylonica*)
Wisconsin or Niobe Weeping Willow (*Salix blanda*)
Thurlow Weeping Willow (*Salix elegantissima*)
Weeping European Mountain Ash (*Sorbus aucuparia pendula*)
Pendant Silver Linden (*Tilia petiolaris*)
Sargent Hemlock (*Tsuga canadensis pendula*)
Weeping American Elm (*Ulmus americana pendula*)

Rounded or Globe-Shaped
Globe Norway Maple (*Acer platanoides globosum*)
Globe European Hornbeam (*Carpinus betulus globosa*)
★Crab Apple species (*Malus*)
Umbrella Black Locust (*Robinia pseudoacacia umbraculifera*)
Sargent Hemlock (*Tsuga canadensis sargenti*)
Koopmann Elm (*Ulmus carpinifolia koopmanni*)
Globe Smooth-leaved Elm (*Ulmus carpinifolia umbraculifera*)

With Horizontal Branching
Fir species (*Abies*)
California Redbud (*Cercis occidentalis*)
★Hawthorn species (*Crataegus*)
Spruce species (*Picea*)
★White Oak (*Quercus alba*)
★Pin Oak (*Quercus palustris*)

Trees Classified by Color of Blossom

Yellow
★Golden Rain Tree (*Koelreuteria paniculata*)
★Laburnum (*Laburnum vossi*)

White
★Shadblow Serviceberry (*Amelanchier canadensis*)
White Redbud (*Cercis canadensis alba*)
★American Yellow-wood (*Cladrastis lutea*)
Washington Hawthorn (*Crataegus phaenropyum*)
Arnold Crab Apple (*Malus arnoldiana*)
★Siberian Crab Apple (*Malus baccata*)
Tea Crab Apple (*Malus hupehensis*)
Sargent Crab Apple (*Malus sargenti*)
Korean Mountain Ash (*Sorbus alnifolia*)
American Mountain Ash (*Sorbus americana*)
European Mountain Ash (*Sorbus aucuparia*)
Mountain Ash (*Sorbus scopulina*)

Pink
Wither's Pink Redbud (*Cercis canadensis* "Wither's Pink Charm")
Japanese Flowering Crab Apple (*Malus floribunda*)
Katherine Crab Apple (*Malus* "Katherine")
Prince Georges Crab Apple (*Malus* "Prince Georges")
★Common Apple (*Malus pumila*)

Red
Ruby Horse-Chestnut (*Aesculus carnea briotti*)
Paul's Scarlet Hawthorn (*Crataegus oxyacantha pauli*)
Almey Crab Apple (*Malus* "Almey")
Carmine Crab Apple (*Malus atrosanguinea*)

Trees with Bright Red Fruit

Downy Hawthorn (*Crataegus mollis*)
Washington Hawthorn (*Crataegus phaenopyrum*)
Almey Crab Apple (*Malus* "Almey")
★Siberian Crab Apple (*Malus baccata*)
Hopa Crab Apple (*Malus* "Hopa")
★Common Apple (*Malus pumila*)
Sargent Crab Apple (*Malus sargenti*)
Korean Mountain Ash (*Sorbus alnifolia*)
American Mountain Ash (*Sorbus americana*)
European Mountain Ash (*Sorbus aucuparia*)

Trees Classified by Color of Summer Foliage

Blue
White Fir (*Abies concolor*)
Western Red Cedar (*Juniperus scopulorum* var. Chandler Blue)
Eastern Red Cedar (*Juniperus virginia* var. *Burki*)
Colorado Blue Spruce (*Picea pungens* var. *Glauca*)

Silver to Gray
Russian Olive (*Elaeagnus angustifolia*)
White Poplar (*Populus alba*)
Quaking Aspen (*Populus tremuloides*)
Pendant Silver Linden (*Tilia petiolaris*)
★Silver Linden (*Tilia tomentosa*)

Red to Purple
Crimson King Maple (*Acer platanoides* "Crimson King")
Purple-leaf Sycamore Maple (*Acer pseudoplatanus*)
River's Purple Beech (*Fagus sylvatica riversi*)
Purple Beech (*Fagus sylvatica atropunicea*)
Weeping Purple Beech (*Fagus sylvatica purpureo-pendula*)
Rubylace Locust (*Gleditsia triacanthos inermis* "Rubylace")
Purple Crab Apple (*Malus purpurea*)

Trees Classified by Color of Fall Foliage

Yellow
Striped Maple or Moosewood (*Acer pennsylvanicum*)
Norway Maple (*Acer platanoides* var.)
★Sugar Maple (*Acer saccharum*)
Ohio Buckeye (orange) (*Aesculus glabra*)
★Serviceberry species (yellow-orange) (*Amelanchier*)
★Birches (*Betula*)

Hickory species (*Carya*)
Redbud species (*Cercis*)
*American Yellow-wood (*Cladrastis lutea*)
*American Beech (*Fagus grandifolia*)
*European Beech (*Fagus sylvatica*)
White Ash (purple to yellow) (*Fraxinus americana*)
*Ginkgo (*Ginkgo biloba*)
Tulip Tree (*Liriodendron tulipifera*)
*Willow species (*Salix*)

Red
Vine Maple (*Acer circinatum*)
*Red Maple (*Acer rubrum*)
*Sugar Maple (*Acer saccharum*)
*Shadblow Serviceberry (*Amelanchier canadensis*)
Hornbeam species (*Carpinus*)
American Smoke Tree (*Cotinus americanus*)
Washington Hawthorn (*Crataegus phaenopyrum*)
*Sweet Gum (*Liquidambar styraciflua*)
Dawson Crab Apple (*Malus dawsoniana*)
*Pin Oak (*Quercus palustris*)
Korean Mountain Ash (*Sorbus alnifolia*)

Purple
White Ash (*Fraxinus americana*)
*Sweet Gum (*Liquidambar styraciflua*)
*White Oak (*Quercus alba*)

Trees with Interesting Bark

Gray
*Red Maple (*Acer rubrum*)
*Serviceberry species (*Amelanchier*)
Hornbeam species (*Carpinus*)
Hackberry species (*Celtis*)
*American Yellow-wood (*Cladrastis lutea*)
*Hawthorn species (*Crataegus*)
*Beech species (*Fagus*)
Mountain Ash species (*Sorbus*)

White
*European Birch (*Betula pendula*)
*Gray Birch (*Betula populifolia*)

Red
Red or Norway Pine (*Pinus resinosa*)
Scotch Pine (*Pinus sylvestris*)

Reddish Brown
Chinese Paper Birch (*Betula albo-sinensis*)

Yellow
Wisconsin or Niobe Weeping Willow (*Salix blanda*)

Green
*Babylon Weeping Willow (*Salix babylonica*)

Flaking
Paperbark Maple (*Acer griseum*)
*Birch species (*Betula*)
Shagbark Hickory (*Carya ovata*)
Russian Olive (*Elaeagnus angustifolia*)
*Plane Tree species (*Platanus*)

Trees for the City

White Fir (*Abies concolor*)
Hedge Maple (*Acer campestre*)

Box-Elder (*Acer negundo*)
Norway Maple (*Acer platanoides*)
Sycamore Maple (*Acer pseudoplatanus*)
*Horse-Chestnut or Buckeye (*Aesculus*)
Catalpa (*Catalpa*)
Hackberry (*Celtis*)
Washington Hawthorn (*Crataegus phaenopyrum*)
Russian Olive (*Elaeagnus angustifolia*)
White Ash (*Fraxinus americana*)
European Ash (*Fraxinus americana*)
Green Ash (*Fraxinus pennsylvanica*)
*Ginkgo (*Ginkgo biloba*)
Thornless Honey-Locust (*Gleditsia triacanthos inermis*)
*Golden Rain Tree (*Koelreuteria paniculata*)
*Crab Apple (*Malus var.*)
*London Plane Tree (*Platanus acerifolia*)
White Poplar (*Populus alba*)
*Lombardy Poplar (*Populus nigra italica*)
*Black Locust (*Robinia pseudoacacia*)
Little-leaf Linden (*Tilia cordata*)
*Crimean Linden (*Tilia euchlora*)
*Silver Linden (*Tilia tomentosa*)

Trees for Wide Streets
Sycamore Maple (*Acer pseudoplatanus*)
*Sugar Maple (*Acer saccharum*)
Sugar Hackberry (*Celtis laevigata*)
White Ash (*Fraxinus americana*)
Green Ash (*Fraxinus pennsylvanica lanceolata*)
*Ginkgo (*Ginkgo biloba*)
*Common Honey-Locust (*Gleditsia triacanthos*)
Tulip Tree (*Liriodendron tulipifera*)
*London Plane Tree (*Platanus acerifola*)
*Oriental Plane Tree (*Platanus orientalis*)
White Poplar (*Populus alba*)
*Pin Oak (*Quercus palustris*)
Willow Oak (*Quercus phellos*)

Trees for Medium Streets
Norway Maple (*Acer platanoides*)
*Sweet Gum (*Liquidambar styraciflua*)
Hop-Hornbeam (*Ostrya virginiana*)
Simon Poplar (*Populus simoni*)
Willow Oak (*Quercus phellos*)
*Black Locust (*Robinia pseudoacacia*)
*Linden species (*Tilia*)
Winged Elm (*Ulmus alata*)

Trees for Suburban Streets
Paperbark Maple (*Acer griseum*)
Globe Norway Maple (*Acer platanoides globosum*)
American Hornbeam (*Carpinus caroliniana*)
Pyramidal European Hornbeam (*Carpinus betulus fastigiata*)
Globe European Hornbeam (*Carpinus betulus globosa*)
*Hawthorn species (*Crataegus*)
*Golden Rain Tree (*Koelreuteria paniculata*)
Smooth-leaved Elm varieties (*Ulmus carpinifolia*)

Soil Tolerance

Trees Tolerating Acid Soil

*European Beech (*Fagus sylvatica*)
*Pin Oak (*Quercus palustris*)
Willow Oak (*Quercus phellos*)

Trees Tolerating Moist Soil
*Red Maple (*Acer rubrum*)
Alder species (*Alnus*)
*Sweet Gum (*Liquidambar styraciflua*)
*Willow species (*Salix*)
American Arbor-vitae (*Thuja occidentalis*)

Trees Tolerating Dry or Poor Soil
Box-Elder (*Acer negundo*)
*Gray Birch (*Betula populifolia*)
European Hackberry (*Celtis australis*)
Russian Olive (*Elaeagnus angustifolia*)
Green Ash (*Fraxinus pennsylvanica*)
Modesto Ash (*Fraxinus velutina* "Modesto")
*Honey-Locust (*Gleditsia triacanthos var.*)
Western Red Cedar (*Juniperus scopulorum*)
Eastern Red Cedar (*Juniperus virginiana*)
*Golden Rain Tree (*Koelreuteria paniculata*)
Pitch Pine (*Pinus rigida*)
White Poplar (*Populus alba*)
*Black Locust (*Robinia pseudoacacia*)
Chinese Elm (*Ulmus parvifolia*)
Siberian Elm (*Ulmus pumila*)

Pest-Resistant Trees

Hornbeam species (*Carpinus*)
European Hackberry (*Celtis australis*)
Turkish Filbert (*Corylus colurna*)
American Smoke Tree (*Cotinus americanus*)
Russian Olive (*Elaeagnus angustifolia*)
*Ginkgo (*Ginkgo biloba*)
*Honey-Locust (*Gleditsia triacanthos*)
Kentucky Coffee Tree (*Gymnocladus diocus*)
Juniper species (*Juniperus*)
*Golden Rain Tree (*Koelreuteria paniculata*)
*Laburnum species (*Laburnum*)
*Sweet Gum (*Liquidambar styraciflua*)
Hop-Hornbeam species (*Ostrya*)

Trees for Hedging or Barriers

European Beech (*Fagus sylvatica*) prunes well.
Leyland Cypress (*Cupressocyparis leylandii*) withstands heavy pruning.
Hawthorn varieties (*Crataegus*) easily pruned, advantage of thorns.
Canadian Hemlock (*Tsuga canadensis*) evergreen.
American Holly (*Ilex opaca*) can be pruned.
European Hornbeam (*Carpinus betulus*) prunes well.
Little-leaf Linden (*Tilia cordata*) tolerates heavy pruning.
Hedge Maple (*Acer campestre*) can be pruned.
Austrian Pine (*Pinus nigra*) plant 10–12 feet on centers, staggered row.
Japanese Black Pine (*Pinus thunbergi*) plant 8 feet on centers, staggered row.
Eastern White Pine (*Pinus strobus*) plant 15 feet on centers, staggered row.

VERMONT

State Tree
*Sugar Maple (*Acer saccharum*)

Evergreen Trees

Fir species (*Abies*)
False Cypress species (*Chamaecyparis*)
Eastern Red Cedar (*Juniperus virginiana*)
*Larch species (*Larix*)
Spruce species (*Picea*)
*Pine species (*Pinus*)
*Douglas Fir (*Pseudotsuga menziesii*)
Arbor-vitae species (*Thuja*)
*Hemlock species (*Tsuga*)

Trees Classified by Height

20–35 Feet
Amur Maple (*Acer ginnala*)
Mountain Maple (*Acer spicatum*)
Ohio Buckeye (*Aesculus glabra*)
Apple Serviceberry (*Amelanchier grandiflora*)
Mockernut (*Carya tomentosa*)
*Hawthorn species (*Crataegus*)
Russian Olive (*Elaeagnus angustifolia*)
Euonymus species (*Euonymus*)
*Crab Apple species (*Malus*)
*Cherry species (*Prunus*)
Dahurian Buckthorn (*Rhamnus davurica*)

Almond-leaf Willow (*Salix amygdalina*)
Goat Willow (*Salix caprea*)
Showy Mountain-Ash (*Sorbus decora*)
Japanese Tree Lilac (*Syringa amurensis japonica*)

35–75 Feet
Box-Elder (*Acer negundo*)
Striped Maple or Moosewood (*Acer pennsylvanicum*)
Speckled Alder (*Alnus incana*)
Red Alder (*Alnus rubra*)
*Shadblow Serviceberry (*Amelanchier canadensis*)
Allegany Serviceberry (*Amelanchier laevis*)
Devil's Walking Stick (*Aralia elata*)
Dahurian Birch (*Betula davurica*)

*European Birch (*Betula pendula*)
American Hornbeam (*Carpinus caroliniana*)
Japanese Hornbeam (*Carpinus japonica*)
Southern Catalpa (*Catalpa bignonioides*)
Eastern Redbud (*Cercis canadensis*)
*American Yellow-wood (*Cladrastis lutea*)
Turkish Filbert (*Corylus colurna*)
Green Ash (*Fraxinus pennsylvanica lanceolata*)
Eastern Larch or Tamarack (*Larix laricina*)
Siberian Crab Apple (*Malus baccata*)
"Dolgo" Crab Apple (*Malus* "Dolgo")
"Sissipuk" Crab Apple (*Malus* "Sissipuk")
White Mulberry (*Morus alba*)
*Amur Cork (*Phellodendron amurense*)
Black Hills Spruce (*Picea glauca densata*)
Jack Pine (*Pinus banksiana*)
Swiss Stone Pine (*Pinus cembra*)
Limber Pine (*Pinus flexilis*)
Scotch Pine (*Pinus sylvestris*)
Simon Poplar (*Populus simoni*)
Amur Chokecherry (*Prunus maacki*)
European Bird Cherry (*Prunus padus*)
Sargent Cherry (*Prunus sargenti*)
Swamp White Oak (*Quercus bicolor*)
Red Oak (*Quercus borealis*)
Scarlet Oak (*Quercus coccinea*)
*Pin Oak (*Quercus palustris*)
White Willow (*Salix alba*)
*Weeping Willow (*Salix alba tristis*)
Thurlow Weeping Willow (*Salix elegantissima*)
Laurel Willow (*Salix pentandra*)
Sassafras (*Sassafras albidum officinale*)
European Mountain Ash or Rowan Tree (*Sorbus aucuparia*)
American Arbor-vitae (*Thuja occidentalis*)
Carolina Hemlock (*Tsuga caroliniana*)
Siberian Elm (*Ulmus pumila*)

75 Feet or Over
Fir species (*Abies*)
Norway Maple (*Acer platanoides*)
*Red or Swamp Maple (*Acer rubrum*)
*Sugar Maple (*Acer saccharum*)
*Baumann Horse-Chestnut (*Aesculus hippocastanum baumanni*)
European Alder (*Alnus glutinosa*)
Sweet Birch (*Betula lenta*)
River Birch (*Betula nigra*)
*Canoe Birch (*Betula papyrifera*)
Hickory species (*Carya*)
Northern Catalpa (*Catalpa speciosa*)
False Cypress species (*Chamaecyparis*)
*American Beech (*Fagus grandifolia*)
White Ash (*Fraxinus americana*)
European Ash (*Fraxinus excelsior*)
*Ginkgo or Maidenhair Tree (*Ginkgo biloba*)
*Common Honey-Locust (*Gleditsia triacanthos*)
Kentucky Coffee Tree (*Gymnocladus dioicus*)
Eastern Black Walnut (*Juglans nigra*)
*European Larch (*Larix decidua*)
Japanese Larch (*Larix leptolepis*)
*Black Gum or Black Tupelo (*Nyssa sylvatica*)
Spruce species (*Picea*)
*Pine species (*Pinus*)
Poplar species (*Populus*)
Sargent Cherry (*Prunus sargenti*)
Black or Rum Cherry (*Prunus serotina*)
*Douglas Fir (*Pseudotsuga menziesii*)
*Oak species (*Quercus*)
*Linden species (*Tilia*)
*Canada Hemlock (*Tsuga canadensis*)
*Elm species (*Ulmus*)

Trees Classified by Form

Pyramidal
Fir species (*Abies*)
*Birch species (*Betula*)
False Cypress species (*Chamaecyparis*)
Turkish Filbert (*Corylus colurna*)
*American Beech (*Fagus grandifolia*)
Juniper or Red Cedar species (*Juniperus*)

*Larch species (*Larix*)
*Sweet Gum (*Liquidambar styraciflua*)
Black Tupelo or Black Gum (*Nyssa sylvatica*)
Hop-Hornbeam (*Ostrya virginiana*)
Spruce species (*Picea*)
Swiss Stone Pine (*Pinus cembra*)
*Pyramidal Austrian Pine (*Pinus nigra pyramidalis*)
Red or Norway Pine (*Pinus resinosa*)
Bolleana Poplar (*Populus alba pyramidalis*)
*Douglas Fir (*Pseudotsuga menziesii*)
*Pin Oak (*Quercus palustris*)
*Arbor-vitae species (*Thuja*)
*Linden species (*Tilia*)
*Hemlock species (*Tsuga*)
Smooth-leaved Elm varieties (*Ulmus carpinifolia*)

Columnar
Ascending Norway Maple (*Acer platanoides ascendens*)
Columnar Norway Maple (*Acer platanoides columnare*)
Erect Norway Maple (*Acer platanoides erectum*)
Columnar Red Maple (*Acer rubrum columnare*)
Sentry Maple (*Acer saccharum monumentale*)
Fastigiate European Birch (*Betula pendula fastigiata*)
Fastigiate Washington Hawthorn (*Crataegus phaenopyrum fastigiata*)
Sentry Ginkgo (*Ginkgo biloba fastigiata*)
Blue Columnar Chinese Juniper (*Juniperus chinensis columnaris*)
Schott Red Cedar (*Juniperus virginiana schotti*)
Swiss Stone Pine (*Pinus cembra*)
Fastigiate White Pine (*Pinus strobus fastigiata*)
Fastigiate Scotch Pine (*Pinus sylvestris fastigiata*)
*Lombardy Poplar (*Populus nigra italica*)
Fastigiate Simon Poplar (*Populus simoni fastigiata*)
Shipmast Locust (*Robinia pseudoacacia rectissima*)
Upright European Mountain Ash (*Sorbus aucuparia fastigiata*)
Common Bald Cypress (*Taxodium distichum*)
Douglas Arbor-vitae (*Thuja occidentalis douglasi pyramidalis*)
Fastigiate American Arbor-vitae (*Thuja occidentalis fastigiata*)
Columnar Big-leaf Linden (*Tilia platyphyllos fastigiata*)
*American Elm varieties (*Ulmus americana*)

Weeping
Slender European Birch (*Betula pendula tristis*)
Young's Birch (*Betula pendula youngi*)
Weeping Red Cedar (*Juniperus virginiana pendula*)
Weeping Larch (*Larix decidua pendula*)
"Oekonomierat Echtermeyer" Crab Apple (*Malus* "Oekonomierat Echtermeyer")
Weeping Mulberry (*Morus alba pendula*)
Koster Weeping Blue Spruce (*Picea pungens kosteriana*)
Weeping White Pine (*Pinus strobus pendula*)
Weeping Black Cherry (*Prunus serotina pendula*)
Golden Weeping Willow (*Salix alba tristis*)
Wisconsin or Niobe Weeping Willow (*Salix blanda*)
Thurlow Weeping Willow (*Salix elegantissima*)
Weeping Japanese Pagoda Tree (*Sophora japonica pendula*)
Weeping European Mountain Ash (*Sorbus aucuparia pendula*)
Sargent Hemlock (*Tsuga canadensis pendula*)
Weeping American Elm (*Ulmus americana pendula*)

Rounded or Globe-Shaped
Globe Norway Maple (*Acer platanoides globosum*)
*Crab Apple species (*Malus*)
*White Oak (*Quercus alba*)
Umbrella Black Locust (*Robinia pseudoacacia umbraculifera*)
Sargent Hemlock (*Tsuga canadensis sargenti*)
Koopmann Elm (*Ulmus carpinifolia koopmanni*)
Globe Smooth-leaved Elm (*Ulmus carpinifolia umbraculifera*)

With Horizontal Branching
Fir species (*Abies*)
*Flowering Dogwood (*Cornus florida*)

*Hawthorn species (*Crataegus*)
*Black Tupelo or Black Gum (*Nyssa sylvatica*)
Spruce species (*Picea*)
*Eastern White Pine (*Pinus strobus*)
*White Oak (*Quercus alba*)
*Pin Oak (*Quercus palustris*)
Common Bald Cypress (*Taxodium distichum*)

Trees Classified by Color of Blossom

White
*Shadblow Serviceberry (*Amelanchier canadensis*)
*American Yellow-wood (*Cladrastis lutea*)
Washington Hawthorn (*Crataegus phaenopyrum*)
Arnold Crab Apple (*Malus arnoldiana*)
*Siberian Crab Apple (*Malus baccata*)
Tea Crab Apple (*Malus hupehensis*)
Thundercloud Plum (*Prunus cerasifera* "Thundercloud")
Sour Cherry (*Prunus cerasus*)
*Japanese Pagoda Tree (*Sophora japonica*)
American Mountain Ash (*Sorbus americana*)
European Mountain Ash (*Sorbus aucuparia*)
Showy Mountain Ash (*Sorbus decora*)

Pink
Toba Hawthorn (*Crataegus mordenensis* "Toba")
Japanese Flowering Crab Apple (*Malus floribunda*)
Katherine Crab Apple (*Malus* "Katherine")
*Common Apple (*Malus pumila*)
Prince Georges Crab Apple (*Malus* "Prince Georges")
Sargent Cherry (*Prunus sargenti*)

Red
Ruby Horse-Chestnut (*Aesculus carnea briotti*)
Paul's Scarlet Hawthorn (*Crataegus oxyacantha pauli*)
Almey Crab Apple (*Malus* "Almey")
Carmine Crab Apple (*Malus atrosanguinea*)

Trees Classified by Color of Summer Foliage

Blue
Eastern Red Cedar (*Juniperus virginiana* var. *Burki*)

Silver to Gray
Russian Olive (*Elaeagnus angustifolia*)
White Poplar (*Populus alba*)
*Silver Linden (*Tilia tomentosa*)

Red to Purple
Crimson King Maple (*Acer platanoides* "Crimson King")
Schwedler Maple (*Acer platanoides schwedleri*)
Purple Crab Apple (*Malus purpurea*)
Pissard Plum (*Prunus cerasifera atropurpurea*)
Thundercloud Plum (*Prunus cerasifera nigra* "Thundercloud")
Woods Myrobalan Plum (*Prunus cerasifera woodi*)

Trees Classified by Color of Fall Foliage

Yellow
Striped Maple or Moosewood (*Acer pennsylvanicum*)
Norway Maple (*Acer platanoides* var.)
*Sugar Maple (*Acer saccharum*)
Ohio Buckeye (orange) (*Aesculus glabra*)
Apple Serviceberry (yellow-orange) (*Amelanchier grandiflora*)
*Birches (*Betula species*)
Hickory species (*Carya*)
Chinese Chestnut (*Castanea mollissima*)
*American Yellow-wood (*Cladrastis lutea*)
*American Beech (*Fagus grandifolia*)
White Ash (purple to yellow) (*Fraxinus americana*)
*Ginkgo (*Ginkgo biloba*)
*Larch (*Larix decidua*)
Tulip Tree (*Liriodendron tulipifera*)
*Willow species (*Salix*)

Red
Amur Maple (*Acer ginnala*)
Manchurian Maple (*Acer mandshuricum*)
*Red Maple (*Acer rubrum*)

*Sugar Maple (*Acer saccharum*)
Tatarian Maple (*Acer tataricum*)
*Shadblow Serviceberry (*Amerlanchier canadensis*)
Hornbeam species (*Carpinus*)
*Flowering Dogwood (*Cornus florida*)
Washington Hawthorn (*Crataegus phaenopyrum*)
Dawson Crab Apple (*Malus dawsoniana*)
*Black Tupelo or Black Gum (*Nyssa sylvatica*)
*Cherry species (*Prunus*)
Red Oak (*Quercus borealis*)
Scarlet Oak (*Quercus coccinea*)
*Pin Oak (*Quercus palustris*)
Sassafras (*Sassafras albidum*)

Purple
White Ash (*Fraxinus americana*)
*Sweet Gum (*Liquidambar styraciflua*)
*White Oak (*Quercus alba*)

Trees with Interesting Bark

Gray
*Red Maple (*Acer rubrum*)
*Serviceberry species (*Amelanchier*)
Hornbeam species (*Carpinus*)
*American Yellow-wood (*Cladrastis lutea*)
*Hawthorn species (*Crataegus*)
*American Beech (*Fagus grandifolia*)
Cucumber Tree (*Magnolia acuminata*)
Red Oak (young trunk and branches) (*Quercus borealis*)
Black Oak (young trunk and branches) (*Quercus velutina*)
Mountain Ash species (*Sorbus*)

White
Canoe Birch (*Betula papyrifera*)
*European Birch (*Betula pendula*)

Red
Red or Norway Pine (*Pinus resinosa*)
Scotch Pine (*Pinus sylvestis*)

Reddish Brown
Sargent Cherry (*Prunus sargenti*)

Yellow
Wisconsin or Niobe Weeping Willow (*Salix blanda*)

Flaking
*Birch species (*Betula*)
Shagbark Hickory (*Carya ovata*)
Russian Olive (*Elaeagnus angustifolia*)
Eastern Red Cedar (*Juniperus virginiana*)

Trees for the City
White Fir (*Abies concolor*)
Hedge Maple (*Acer campestre*)
Box-Elder (*Acer negundo*)

Norway Maple (*Acer platanoides*)
*Horse-Chestnut or Buckeye (*Aesculus*)
*Tree of Heaven (*Ailanthus*)
Catalpa (*Catalpa*)
Downy Hawthorn (*Crataegus mollis*)
Washington Hawthorn (*Crataegus phaenopyrum*)
Russian Olive (*Elaeagnus angustifolia*)
White Ash (*Fraxinus americana*)
European Ash (*Fraxinus excelsior*)
Green Ash (*Fraxinus pennsylvanica*)
*Ginkgo (*Ginkgo biloba*)
Thornless Honey-Locust (*Gleditsia triacanthos inermis*)
*Crab Apple (*Malus var.*)
*Amur Cork (*Phellodendron amurense*)
Colorado Spruce (*Picea pungens*)
White Poplar (*Populus alba*)
*Lombardy Poplar (*Populus nigra italica*)
Red Oak (*Quercus borealis*)
*Black Locust (*Robinia pseudoacacia*)
*Little-leaf Linden (*Tilia cordata*)
*Silver Linden (*Tilia tomentosa*)

Trees for Wide Streets
*Sugar Maple (*Acer saccharum*)
White Ash (*Fraxinus americana*)
Green Ash (*Fraxinus pennsylvanica lanceolata*)
*Ginkgo (*Ginkgo biloba*)
*Common Honey-Locust (*Gleditsia triacanthos*)
*Amur Cork (*Phellodendron amurense*)
*Eastern White Pine (*Pinus strobus*)
White Poplar (*Populus alba*)
Red Oak (*Quercus borealis*)
*Pin Oak (*Quercus palustris*)

Trees for Medium Streets
Norway Maple (*Acer platanoides*)
Hop-Hornbeam (*Ostrya virginiana*)
Simon Poplar (*Populus simoni*)
Scarlet Oak (*Quercus coccinea*)
*Black Locust (*Robinia pseudoacacia*)
Sassafras (*Sassafras albidum officinale*)
*Japanese Pagoda Tree (*Sophora japonica*)
*Linden species (*Tilia*)

Trees for Suburban Streets
Hedge Maple (*Acer campestre*)
Amur Maple (*Acer ginnala*)
Globe Norway Maple (*Acer spicatum*)
Tatarian Maple (*Acer tataricum*)
American Hornbeam (*Carpinus caroliniana*)
Fringetree (*Chionanthus virginicus*)
*Flowering Dogwood (*Cornus florida*)
*Hawthorn species (*Crataegus*)
Columnar Sargent Cherry (*Prunus sargenti columnaris*)

Soil Tolerance

Trees Tolerating Acid Soil
*Flowering Dogwood (*Cornus florida*)
*Black Tupelo (*Nyssa sylvatica*)
Red Oak (*Quercus borealis*)
Scarlet Oak (*Quercus coccinea*)
*Pin Oak (*Quercus palustris*)

Trees Tolerating Dry or Poor Soil
Box-Elder (*Acer negundo*)
*Tree of Heaven (*Ailanthus*)
Russian Olive (*Elaeagnus angustifolia*)
Green Ash (*Fraxinus pennsylvanica*)
*Honey-Locust (*Gleditsia triacanthos var.*)
Western Red Cedar (*Juniperus scopulorum*)
Eastern Red Cedar (*Juniperus virginiana*)
Jack Pine (*Pinus banksiana*)
Pitch Pine (*Pinus rigida*)
White Poplar (*Populus alba*)
Chestnut Oak (*Quercus montana*)
*Black Locust (*Robinia pseudoacacia*)
Sassafras (*Sassafras albidum officinale*)
*Japanese Pagoda Tree (*Sophora japonica*)
Siberian Elm (*Ulmus pumila*)

Pest-Resistant Trees

*Tree of Heaven (*Ailanthus altissima*)
Hornbeam species (*Carpinus*)
False Cypress species (*Chamaecyparis*)
Japanese Cornel (*Cornus officinalis*)
Russian Olive (*Elaeagnus angustifolia*)
*Ginkgo (*Ginkgo biloba*)
*Honey-Locust (*Gleditsia triacanthos*)
Kentucky Coffee Tree (*Gymnocladus dioicus*)
Juniper species (*Juniperus*)
Kalopanax (*Kalopanax pictus*)
Hop-Hornbeam species (*Ostrya*)

Trees for Hedging or Barriers

European Beech (*Fagus sylvatica*) prunes well.
Hawthorn varieties (*Crataegus*) easily pruned, advantage of thorns.
Canadian Hemlock (*Tsuga canadensis*) evergreen.
American Holly (*Ilex opaca*) can be pruned.
European Hornbeam (*Carpinus betulus*) prunes well.
Little-leaf Linden (*Tilia cordata*) tolerates heavy pruning.
Hedge Maple (*Acer campestre*) can be pruned.
Austrian Pine (*Pinus nigra*) plant 10–12 feet on centers, staggered row.
Japanese Black Pine (*Pinus thunbergi*) plant 8 feet on centers, staggered row.
Eastern White Pine (*Pinus strobus*) plant 15 feet on centers, staggered row.

VIRGINIA

State Tree
*Flowering Dogwood (*Cornus florida*)

Evergreen Trees
Fir species (*Abies*)
Tree Box (*Buxus sempervirens arborescens*)
Camellia species (*Camellia*)
*Deodar Cedar (*Cedrus deodara*)
*Cypress species (*Cupressus*)
Holly species (*Ilex*)
Juniper species (*Juniperus*)
*Southern Magnolia (*Magnolia grandiflora*)
Spruce species (*Picea*)
*Pine species (*Pinus*)
Yew Podocarpus (*Podocarpus macrophyllus*)
Cork Oak (*Quercus suber*)
*Live Oak (*Quercus virginiana*)
Arbor-vitae species (*Thuja*)
*Hemlock species (*Tsuga*)

Trees Classified by Height

20–35 Feet
Hedge Maple (*Acer campestre*)
Paperbark Maple (*Acer griseum*)
*Japanese Maple (*Acer palmatum*)
Mountain Maple (*Acer spicatum*)
Ohio Buckeye (*Aesculus glabra*)
*Shadblow Serviceberry (*Amelanchier canadensis*)
*Gray Birch (*Betula populifolia*)
Mockernut (*Carya tomentosa*)
Eastern Redbud (*Cercis canadensis*)
Fringetree (*Chionanthus virginicus*)
*Flowering Dogwood (*Cornus florida*)
American Smoke Tree (*Cotinus americanus*)
*Hawthorn species (*Crataegus*)
Russian Olive (*Elaeagnus angustifolia*)
Euonymus species (*Euonymus*)
Franklinia (*Franklinia alatamaha*)
Common Fig (*Ficus carica*)

Longstalk Holly (*Ilex pedunculosa*)
Yaupon (*Ilex vomitoria*)
*Golden Rain Tree (*Koelreuteria paniculata*)
*Laburnum species (*Laburnum*)
Crape-Myrtle (*Lagerstroemia indica*)
Sweet Bay or Laurel (*Laurus nobilis*)
Yellow Cucumber Tree (*Magnolia cordata*)
*Saucer Magnolia (*Magnolia soulangeana*)
*Star Magnolia (*Magnolia stellata*)
*Crab Apple species (*Malus*)
*Cherry species (*Prunus*)
Black Jack Oak (*Quercus marilandica*)
*Babylon Weeping Willow (*Salix babylonica*)
Snowbell species (*Styrax*)
Asiatic Sweetleaf (*Symplocos paniculata*)

35–75 Feet
Box-Elder (*Acer negundo*)
Striped Maple or Moosewood (*Acer pennsylvanicum*)
*Red-fruited Tree of Heaven (*Ailanthus altissima erythrocarpa*)

Silk Tree (*Albizzia julibrissin*)
Italian Alder (*Alnus cordata*)
Red Alder (*Alnus rubra*)
*Shadblow Serviceberry (*Amelanchier canadensis*)
Common Paper-Mulberry (*Broussonetia papyrifera*)
Common Camellia (*Camella japonica*)
American Hornbeam (*Carpinus caroliniana*)
Chinese Chestnut (*Castanea mollissima*)
Southern Catalpa (*Catalpa bignonioides*)
Bunch Hackberry (*Celtis bungeana*)
*Katsura Tree (*Cercidiphyllum japonicum*)
Eastern Redbud (*Cercis canadensis*)
*American Yellow-wood (*Cladrastis lutea*)
Cockspur Thorn (*Crataegus crus-galli*)
Green Hawthorn (*Crataegus viridis*)
Common China Fir (*Cunninghamia lanceolata*)
Italian Cypress (*Cupressus sempervirens*)
Common Persimmon (*Diospyros virginina*)
Green Ash (*Fraxinus pennsylvanica lanceolata*)
English Holly (*Ilex aquifolium*)
American Holly (*Ilex opaca*)
Chinese Juniper (*Juniperus chinensis*)
Yulan Magnolia (*Magnolia denudata*)
Fraser Magnolia (*Magnolia fraseri*)
Sweet Bay (*Magnolia virginiana*)
"Cowichan" Crab Apple (*Malus* "Cowichan")
"Dolgo" Crab Apple (*Malus* "Dolgo")
"Makamik" Crab Apple (*Malus* "Makamik")
Cherry Crab Apple (*Malus robusta*)
"Sissipuk" Crab Apple (*Malus* "Sissipuk")
Chinaberry (*Melia azedarach*)
*Sorrel Tree or Sourwood (*Oxydendrum arboreum*)
Persian Parrotia (*Parrotia persica*)
Empress Tree (*Paulownia tomentosa*)
Virginia or Scrub Pine (*Pinus virginiana*)
Yew Podocarpus (*Podocarpus macrophyllus*)
Simon Poplar (*Populus simoni*)
Sargent Cherry (*Prunus sargenti*)
Yoshino Cherry (*Prunus yedoensis*)
Fragrant Epaulette Tree (*Pterostyrax hispida*)
Red Oak (*Quercus borealis*)
Scarlet Oak (*Quercus coccinea*)
Spanish or Southern Red Oak (*Quercus falcata*)
Shingle Oak (*Quercus imbricaria*)
Laurel Oak (*Quercus laurifolia*)
Water Oak (*Quercus nigra*)
*Pin Oak (*Quercus palustris*)
Willow Oak (*Quercus phellos*)
*Live Oak (*Quercus virginiana*)
Clammy Locust (*Robinia viscosa*)
Laurel Willow (*Salix pentandra*)
Sassafras (*Sassafras albidum officinale*)
American Mountain Ash (*Sorbus americana*)
Korean Stewartia (*Stewartia koreana*)
American Arbor-vitae (*Thuja occidentalis*)
*Crimean Linden (*Tilia euchlora*)
*Carolina Hemlock (*Tsuga caroliniana*)
Winged or Wahoo Elm (*Ulmus alata*)
Chinese Elm (*Ulmus parvifolia*)

75 Feet or Over
Fir species (*Abies*)
Norway Maple (*Acer platanoides*)
Sycamore Maple (*Acer pseudoplatanus*)
*Red or Swamp Maple (*Acer rubrum*)
Hickory species (*Carya*)
*Cedar species (*Cedrus*)
Cryptomeria (*Cryptomeria japonica*)
*Beech species (*Fagus*)
*Ginkgo or Maidenhair Tree (*Ginkgo biloba*)
*Common Honey-Locust (*Gleditsia triacanthos*)
*Sweet Gum (*Liquidambar styraciflua*)
Cucumber Tree (*Magnolia acuminata*)
*Southern Magnolia (*Magnolia grandiflora*)
White-leaf Japanese Magnolia (*Magnolia obovata*)
Dawn Redwood (*Metasequoia glyptostroboides*)
*Black Gum or Black Tupelo (*Nyssa sylvatica*)
*Pine species (*Pinus*)
*Plane Tree species (*Platanus*)
Poplar species (*Populus*)
*Oak species (*Quercus*)

Umbrella Pine (*Sciadopitys verticillata*)
Common Bald Cypress (*Taxodium distichum*)
English Elm (*Ulmus procera*)
Japanese Zelkova (*Zelkova serrata*)

Trees Classified by Form
Pyramidal
Fir species (*Abies*)
*Cedar species (*Cedrus*)
Crypromeria (*Cryptomeria japonica*)
Italian Cypress (*Cupressus sempervirens*)
*Beech species (*Fagus*)
English Holly (*Ilex aquifolium*)
American Holly (*Ilex opaca*)
Longstalk Holly (*Ilex pedunculosa*)
Juniper or Red Cedar species (*Juniperus*)
*Sweet Gum (*Liquidambar styraciflua*)
*Magnolia species (*Magnolia*)
Dawn Redwood (*Metasequoia glyptostroboides*)
*Black Gum or Black Tupelo (*Nyssa sylvatica*)
Hop-Hornbeam (*Ostrya virginiana*)
*Sorrel Tree or Sourwood (*Oxydendrum arboreum*)
Bolleana Poplar (*Populus alba pyramidalis*)
*Pin Oak (*Quercus palustris*)
Umbrella Pine (*Sciadopitys verticillata*)
Arbor-vitae species (*Thuja*)
*Linden species (*Tilia*)
*Hemlock species (*Tsuga*)
Smooth-leaved Elm varieties (*Ulmus carpinifolia*)

Columnar
Ascending Norway Maple (*Acer platanoides ascendens*)
Columnar Norway Maple (*Acer platanoides columnare*)
Erect Norway Maple (*Acer platanoides erectum*)
Columnar Red Maple (*Acer rubrum columnare*)
Fastigiate Washington Hawthorn (*Crataegus phaenopyrum fastigiata*)
Sentry Ginkgo (*Ginkgo biloba fastigiata*)
Schott Red Cedar (*Juniperus virginiana schotti*)
*Lombardy Poplar (*Populus nigra italica*)
"Amanogawa" Cherry (*Prunus serrulata* "Amanogawa")
Fastigiate English Oak (*Quercus robur fastigiata*)
Shipmast Locust (*Robinia pseudoacacia rectissima*)
Common Bald Cypress (*Taxodium distichum*)

Weeping
*Deodar Cedar (*Cedrus deodara*)
*Weeping Beech (*Fagus sylvatica pendula*)
Weeping Red Cedar (*Juniperus virginiana pendula*)
"Excellenz Thiel" Crab Apple (*Malus* "Excellenz Thiel")
"Oekonomierat Echtermeyer" Crab Apple (*Malus* "Oekonomierat Echtermeyer")
Weeping White Pine (*Pinus strobus pendula*)
Weeping Black Cherry (*Prunus serotina pendula*)
Weeping Higan Cherry (*Prunus subhirtella pendula*)
"Yaeshidare" Cherry (*Prunus subhirtella pendula flora plena*)
Weeping Yoshino Cherry (*Prunus yedoensis perpendens*)
*Babylon Weeping Willow (*Salix babylonica*)
Weeping Japanese Pagoda Tree (*Sophora japonica pendula*)
Weeping Folgner Mountain Ash (*Sorbus folgneri pendula*)
Pendant Silver Linden (*Tilia petiolaris*)
Sargent Hemlock (*Tsuga canadensis pendula*)
Weeping American Elm (*Ulmus americana pendula*)

Rounded or Globe-Shaped
*Japanese Maple (*Acer palmatum*)
Globe Norway Maple (*Acer platanoides globosum*)
Cornelian Cherry (*Cornus mas*)
Japanese Cornel (*Cornus officinalis*)
Single Seed Hawthorn (*Crataegus monogyna inermis*)
*Saucer Magnolia (*Magnolia soulangeana*)
*Crab Apple species (*Malus*)
*White Oak (*Quercus alba*)
Umbrella Black Locust (*Robinia pseudoacacia umbraculifera*)

Sargent Hemlock (*Tsuga canadensis sargenti*)

With Horizontal Branching
Fir species (*Abies*)
Silk Tree (*Albizzia julibrissin*)
Eastern Redbud (*Cercis canadensis*)
*Flowering Dogwood (*Cornus florida*)
Japanese Dogwood (*Cornus kousa*)
*Hawthorn species (*Crataegus*)
Dawn Redwood (*Metasequoia glyptostroboides*)
*Black Gum or Black Tupelo (*Nyssa sylvatica*)
*Eastern White Pine (*Pinus strobus*)
*White Oak (*Quercus alba*)
*Pin Oak (*Quercus palustris*)
*Live Oak (*Quercus virginiana*)
Common Bald Cypress (*Taxodium distichum*)

Trees Classified by Color of Blossom
Yellow
*Golden Rain Tree (*Koelreuteria paniculata*)
*Laburnum (*Laburnum vossi*)

White
*Shadblow Serviceberry (*Amelanchier canadensis*)
White Redbud (*Cercis canadensis alba*)
*American Yellow-wood (*Cladrastis lutea*)
Washington Hawthorn (*Crataegus phaenopyrum*)
Carolina Silverbell (*Halesia carolina*)
Yulan Magnolia (*Magnolia denudata*)
*Southern Magnolia (*Magnolia grandiflora*)
*Star Magnolia (*Magnolia stellata*)
Arnold Crab Apple (*Malus arnoldiana*)
Tea Crab Apple (*Malus hupehensis*)
Sargent Crab Apple (*Malus sargenti*)
*Sorrel Tree (*Oxydendrum arboreum*)
Thundercloud Plum (*Prunus cerasifera* "Thundercloud")
Mount Fuji Cherry (*Prunus serrulata* "Shirotae")
Yoshino Cherry (*Prunus yedoensis*)
Bradford Callery Pear (*Pyrus calleryana bradfordi*)
Common Pear (*Pyrus communis*)
*Japanese Pagoda Tree (*Sophora japonica*)
Japanese Snowbell (*Styrax japonica*)

Pink
Wither's Pink Redbud (*Cercis canadensis* "Wither's Pink Charm")
Toba Hawthorn (*Crataegus mordenensis* "Toba")
Inglesie Crape-Myrtle (*Lagerstroemia indica* "Ingleside Pink")
*Saucer Magnolia (*Magnolia soulangeana*)
Japanese Flowering Crab Apple (*Malus floribunda*)
Katherine Crab Apple (*Malus* "Katherine")
Prince Georges Crab Apple (*Malus* "Prince Georges")
*Common Apple (*Malus pumila*)
Blireiana Plum (*Prunus blireiana*)
Sargent Cherry (*Prunus sargenti*)
Amanogawa Cherry (*Prunus serrulata* "Amanogawa")
Autumn Cherry (*Prunus subhirtella autumnalis*)
Weeping Cherry (*Prunus subhirtella pendula*)

Red
Ruby Horse-Chestnut (*Aesculus carnea briotti*)
Paul's Scarlet Hawthorn (*Crataegus oxyacantha pauli*)
Red Crape-Myrtle (*Lagerstroemia indica* "Wm. Toovey")
Alexandrina Magnolia (*Magnolia soulangeana* "Alexandrina")
Almey Crab Apple (*Malus* "Almey")
Carmine Crab Apple (*Malus atrosanguinea*)

Trees with Bright Red Fruit
*Flowering Dogwood (*Cornus florida*)
Japanese Dogwood (*Cornus kousa*)
Downy Hawthorn (*Crataegus mollis*)
Washington Hawthorn (*Crataegus phaenopyrum*)
American Holly (*Ilex opaca*)
Almey Crab Apple (*Malus* "Almey")
*Siberian Crab Apple (*Malus baccata*)
Hopa Crab Apple (*Malus* "Hopa")
*Common Apple (*Malus pumila*)

Sargent Crab Apple (*Malus sargenti*)
American Mountain Ash (*Sorbus americana*)
European Mountain Ash (*Sorbus aucuparia*)

Trees Classified by Color of Summer Foliage

Blue
White Fir (*Abies concolor*)
Steel Lawson Cypress (*Chamaecyparis lawsonia glauca*)
Eastern Red Cedar (*Juniperus virginiana* var. *Burki*)

Silver to Gray
Russian Olive (*Elaeagnus angustifolia*)
White Poplar (*Populus alba*)
Pendant Silver Linden (*Tilia petiolaris*)
★Silver Linden (*Tilia tomentosa*)

Purple
Blood-leaf Japanese Maple (*Acer palmatum atropurpureum*)
Crimson King Maple (*Acer platanoides* "Crimson King")
Schwedler Maple (*Acer platanoides schwedler*)
Purple-leaf Sycamore Maple (*Acer pseudoplatanus*)
Purple Beech (*Fagus sylvatica atropunicea*)
Weeping Purple Beech (*Fagus sylvatica purpureopendula*)
River's Purple Beech (*Fagus sylvatica riversi*)
Rubylace Locust (*Gleditsia triacanthos inermis* "Rubylace")
Purple Crab Apple (*Malus purpurea*)
Blireiana Plum (*Prunus blireiana*)
Pissard Plum (*Prunus cerasifera atropurpurea*)
Woods Myrobalan Plum (*Prunus cerasifera woodi*)
Blood-leaf Peach (*Prunus persica atropurpurea*)
Purple English Oak (*Quercus robur atropurpurea*)

Trees Classified by Color of Fall Foliage

Yellow
Striped Maple or Moosewood (*Acer pennsylvanicum*)
Norway Maple (*Acer platanoides*)
★Birch species (*Betula*)
Hickory species (*Carya*)
Chinese Chestnut (*Castanea mollissima*)
Redbud species (*Cercis*)
Fringetree (*Chionanthus virginicus*)
★American Yellow-wood (*Cladrastis lutea*)
★American Beech (*Fagus grandifolia*)
★European Beech (*Fagus sylvatica*)
White Ash (purple to yellow) (*Fraxinus americana*)
★Ginkgo (*Ginkgo biloba*)
★Star Magnolia (bronze) (*Magnolia stellata*)
★Willow species (*Salix*)

Red
★Japanese Maple (*Acer palmatum*)
★Red Maple (*Acer rubrum*)
★Shadblow Serviceberry (*Amelanchier canadensis*)
Hornbeam species (*Carpinus*)
★Flowering Dogwood (*Cornus florida*)
American Smoke Tree (*Cotinus americanus*)
Washington Hawthorn (*Crataegus phaenopyrum*)
★Sweet Gum (*Liquidambar styraciflua*)
★Black Gum or Black Tupelo (*Nyssa sylvatica*)
★Sorrel Tree (*Oxydendrum arboreum*)
★Cherry species (*Prunus*)
Bradford Callery Pear (*Pyrus Calleryana bradfordi*)
Red Oak (*Quercus borealis*)
Scarlet Oak (*Quercus coccinea*)

Purple
White Ash (*Fraxinus americana*)
Sweet Gum (*Liquidambar styraciflua*)
White Oak (*Quercus alba*)
Common Pear (*Pyrus communis*)

Trees with Interesting Bark

Gray
Red Maple (*Acer rubrum*)
Serviceberry species (*Amelanchier*)
Hackberry species (*Celtis*)

American Yellow-wood (*Cladrastis lutea*)
Hawthorn species (*Crataegus*)
Beech species (*Fagus*)
American Holly (*Ilex opaca*)
Cucumber Tree (*Magnolia acuminata*)
Saucer Magnolia (*Magnolia soulangeana*)
Red Oak (*Quercus borealis*)
Black Oak (*Quercus velutina*)
Mountain Ash species (*Sorbus*)

White
Gray Birch (*Betula populifolia*)

Red
Japanese Red Pine (*Pinus densiflora*)

Reddish Brown
Chinese Paper Birch (*Betula albo-sinensis*)
Sargent Cherry (*Prunus sargenti*)

Yellow
Wisconsin or Niobe Weeping Willow (*Salix blanda*)

Green
Babylon Weeping Willow (*Salix babylonica*)

Corky
Hackberry (*Celtis*)
Amur Cork (*Phellodendron amurense*)

Flaking
Paperbark Maple (*Acer griseum*)
★Birch species (*Betula*)
Shagbark Hickory (*Carya ovata*)
★Eastern Red Cedar (*Juniperus virginiana*)
Crape-Myrtle (*Lagerstroemia indica*)
★Plane Tree species (*Platanus*)
★Lace-bark Pine (*Pinus bungeana*)
Stewartia species (*Stewartia*)

Trees for the City

Hedge Maple (*Acer campestre*)
Box-Elder (*Acer negundo*)
Norway Maple (*Acer platanoides*)
Sycamore Maple (*Acer pseudoplatanus*)
★Horse-Chestnut or Buckeye (*Aesculus*)
★Tree of Heaven (*Ailanthus*)
Silk Tree (*Albizzia julibrissin*)
Catalpa (*Catalpa*)
Hackberry (*Celtis*)
Downy Hawthorn (*Crataegus mollis*)
Washington Hawthorn (*Crataegus phaenopyrum*)
Russian Olive (*Elaeagnus angustifolia*)
White Ash (*Fraxinus americana*)
Green Ash (*Fraxinus pennsylvanica*)
Ginkgo (*Ginkgo biloba*)
Thornless Honey-Locust (*Gleditsia triacanthos inermis*)
★Golden Rain Tree (*Koelreuteria paniculata*)
★Southern Magnolia (*Magnolia grandiflora*)
★Saucer Magnolia (*Magnolia soulangeana*)
★Star Magnolia (*Magnolia stellata*)
★Crab Apple (*Malus* var.)
Chinaberry (*Melia azedarach*)
★Amur Cork (*Phellodendron amurense*)
★London Plane Tree (*Platanus acerifolia*)
White Poplar (*Populus alba*)
★Lombardy Poplar (*Populus nigra italica*)
Red Oak (*Quercus borealis*)
★Black Locust (*Robinia pseudoacacia*)
★Japanese Pagoda Tree (*Sophora japonica*)
Littleleaf Linden (*Tilia cordata*)
★Crimean Linden (*Tilia euchlora*)
★Silver Linden (*Tilia tomentosa*)
Village Green Zelkova (*Zelkova serrata* "Village Green")

Trees for Wide Streets
Sycamore Maple (*Acer pseudoplatanus*)
Sugar Hackberry (*Celtis laevigata*)
★Katsura Tree (*Cercidiphyllum japonicum*)
White Ash (*Fraxinus americana*)
Green Ash (*Fraxinus pennsylvanica lanceolata*)
★Ginkgo (*Ginkgo biloba*)
★Common Honey-Locust (*Gleditsia triacanthos*)

Tulip Tree (*Liriodendron tulipifera*)
★Southern Magnolia (*Magnolia grandiflora*)
★Eastern White Pine (*Pinus strobus*)
★London Plane Tree (*Platanus acerifolia*)
★Oriental Plane Tree (*Platanus orientalis*)
White Poplar (*Populus alba*)
Sargent Cherry (*Prunus sargenti*)
★Pin Oak (*Quercus palustris*)
Willow Oak (*Quercus phellos*)
Japanese Zelkova (*Zelkova serrata*)

Trees for Medium Streets
Norway Maple (*Acer platanoides*)
★Sweet Gum (*Liquidambar styraciflua*)
Chinaberry (*Melia azedarach*)
Hop-Hornbeam (*Ostrya virginiana*)
Sorrel Tree or Sourwood (*Oxydendrum arboreum*)
Simon Poplar (*Populus simoni*)
Scarlet Oak (*Quercus coccinea*)
Willow Oak (*Quercus phellos*)
★Black Locust (*Robinia pseudoacacia*)
Sassafras (*Sassafras albidum officinale*)
★Japanese Pagoda Tree (*Sophora japonica*)
★Linden species (*Tilia*)
Winged Elm (*Ulmus alata*)

Trees for Suburban Streets
Paperbark Maple (*Acer griseum*)
American Hornbeam (*Carpinus caroliniana*)
Fringetree (*Chionanthus virginicus*)
★Flowering Dogwood (*Cornus florida*)
Hawthorn species (*Crataegus*)
Korean Evodia (*Evodia danielli*)
Carolina Silverbell (*Halesia carolina*)
★Golden Rain Tree (*Koelreuteria paniculata*)
Columnar Sargent Cherry (*Prunus sargenti columnaris*)
Oriental Cherry (*Prunus serrulata*)
Japanese Snowbell (*Styrax japonica*)
Fragrant Snowbell (*Styrax obassia*)
Smooth-leaved Elm varieties (*Ulmus carpinifolia*)

Soil Tolerance

Trees Tolerating Acid Soil
★Japanese Maple (*Acer palmatum*)
★Flowering Dogwood (*Cornus florida*)
Japanese Dogwood (*Cornus kousa*)
★European Beech (*Fagus sylvatica*)
Sweet Bay (*Magnolia virginiana*)
★Black Tupelo (*Nyssa sylvatica*)
★Sorrel Tree (*Oxydendrum arboreum*)
Red Oak (*Quercus borealis*)
Scarlet Oak (*Quercus coccinea*)
★Pin Oak (*Quercus palustris*)
Willow Oak (*Quercus phellos*)

Trees Tolerating Moist Soil
★Red Maple (*Acer rubrum*)
Alder species (*Alnus*)
Holly species (*Ilex*)
★Sweet Gum (*Liquidambar styraciflua*)
Sweet Bay (*Magnolia virginiana*)
★Black Tupelo or Black Gum (*Nyssa sylvatica*)
Swamp White Oak (*Quercus bicolor*)
★Willow species (*Salix*)
Common Bald Cypress (*Taxodium distichum*)
American Arbor-vitae (*Thuja occidentalis*)

Trees Tolerating Dry or Poor Soil
Box-Elder (*Acer negundo*)
★Tree of Heaven (*Ailanthus*)
Silk Tree (*Albizzia julibrissin*)
★Gray Birch (*Betula populifolia*)
Common Paper-Mulberry (*Broussonetia papyifera*)
Hackberry (*Celtis occidentalis*)
Russian Olive (*Elaeagnus angustifolia*)
Green Ash (*Fraxinus pennsylvanica*)
★Honey-Locust (*Gleditsia triacanthos* var.)
Eastern Red Cedar (*Juniperus virginiana*)
★Golden Rain Tree (*Koelreuteria paniculata*)
Osage-Orange (*Maclura pomifera*)
Chinaberry (*Melia azedarach*)
White Poplar (*Populus alba*)
Black Jack Oak (*Quercus marilandica*)

*Black Locust (*Robinia pseudoacacia*)
Sassafras (*Sassafras albidum officinale*)
*Japanese Pagoda Tree (*Sophora japonica*)
Chinese Elm (*Ulmus parvifolia*)

Pest-Resistant Trees

*Tree of Heaven (*Ailanthus altissima*)
Hornbeam species (*Carpinus*)
*Cedar species (*Cedrus*)
Cornelian Cherry (*Cornus mas*)
American Smoke Tree (*Cotinus americanus*)
Russian Olive (*Elaeagnus angustifolia*)
Fig species (*Ficus*)
Franklinia (*Franklinia alatamaha*)
*Ginkgo (*Ginkgo biloba*)
*Honey-Locust (*Gleditsia triacanthos*)
Juniper species (*Juniperus*)
*Golden Rain Tree (*Koelreuteria paniculata*)
*Laburnum species (*Laburnum*)
*Sweet Gum (*Liquidambar styraciflua*)
*Star Magnolia (*Magnolia stellata*)
Hop-Hornbeam species (*Ostrya*)

Trees for Seashore Planting

Norway Maple (*Acer platanoides*)
Sycamore Maple (*Acer pseudoplatanus*)

*Tree of Heaven (*Ailanthus*)
*Shadblow Serviceberry (*Amelanchier canadensis*)
Cockspur Thorn (*Crataegus crus-galli*)
English Hawthorn (*Crataegus oxyacantha*)
Cryptomeria (*Cryptomeria japonica*)
Russian Olive (*Elaeagnus angustifolia*)
Thornless Honey-Locust (*Gleditsia triacanthos inermis* var.)
American Holly (*Ilex opaca*)
Eastern Red Cedar (*Juniperus virginiana*)
*Southern Magnolia (*Magnolia grandiflora*)
*Black Tupelo (*Nyssa sylvatica*)
Colorado Blue Spruce (*Picea pungens glauca*)
*Austrian Pine (*Pinus nigra*)
Pitch Pine (*Pinus rigida*)
Scotch Pine (*Pinus sylvestris*)
*Japanese Black Pine (*Pinus thunbergi*)
*London Plane Tree (*Platanus acerifolia*)
White Poplar (*Populus alba*)
Black Cherry (*Prunus serotina*)
*White Oak (*Quercus alba*)
Black Jack Oak (*Quercus marilandica*)
*Live Oak (*Quercus virginiana*)
*Black Locust (*Robina pseudoacacia*)
Golden Weeping Willow (*Salix alba tristis*)

*Japanese Pagoda Tree (*Sophora japonica*)
American Arbor-vitae (*Thuja occidentalis*)
*Little-leaf Linden (*Tilia cordata*)
*Crimean Linden (*Tilia euchlora*)
Chinese Elm (*Ulmus parvifolia*)

Trees for Hedging or Barriers

European Beech (*Fagus sylvatica*) prunes well.
Leyland Cypress (*Cupressocyparis leylandii*) withstands heavy pruning.
Hawthorn varieties (*Crataegus*) easily pruned, advantage of thorns.
Canadian Hemlock (*Tsuga canadensis*) evergreen.
American Holly (*Ilex opaca*) can be pruned.
European Hornbeam (*Carpinus betulus*) prunes well.
Little-leaf Linden (*Tilia cordata*) tolerates heavy pruning.
Hedge Maple (*Acer campestre*) can be pruned.
Austrian Pine (*Pinus nigra*) plant 10–12 feet on centers, staggered row.
Japanese Black Pine (*Pinus thunbergi*) plant 8 feet on centers, staggered row.
Eastern White Pine (*Pinus strobus*) plant 15 feet on centers, staggered row.

WASHINGTON

State Tree

Western Hemlock (*Tsuga heterophylla*)

Evergreen Trees

Fir species (*Abies*)
*Acacia species (*Acacia*)
Monkey-Puzzle Tree (*Araucaria araucana*)
Pacific Madrone (*Arbutus menziesi*)
Giant Evergreen Chinquapin (*Castanopsis chrysophylla*)
False Cypress species (*Chamaecyparis*)
*Deodar Cedar (*Cedrus deodara*)
Common China Fir (*Cunninghamia lanceolata*)
Cypress species (*Cupressus*)
Holly species (*Ilex*)
Juniper species (*Juniperus*)
*Southern Magnolia (*Magnolia grandiflora*)
Spruce species (*Picea*)
*Pine species (*Pinus*)
Portugal Laurel (*Prunus lusitanica*)
*Douglas Fir (*Pseudotsuga menziesii*)
Canyon Live or Golden Cup Oak (*Quercus chrysolepis*)
*Redwood (*Sequoia sempervirens*)
Umbrella Pine (*Sciadopitys verticillata*)
Arbor-vitae species (*Thuja*)
*Hemlock species (*Tsuga*)
California Laurel (*Umbellularia californica*)

Trees Classified by Height

20–35 Feet
Hedge Maple (*Acer campestre*)
Vine Maple (*Acer circinatum*)
*Japanese Maple (*Acer palmatum*)
*Hawthorn species (*Crataegus*)
Russian Olive (*Elaeagnus angustifolia*)
Euonymus species (*Euonymus*)
Flowering Ash (*Fraxinus ornus*)
Possum Haw (*Ilex decidua*)
Longstalk Holly (*Ilex pedunculosa*)
Perny Holly (*Ilex pernyi*)
*Golden Rain Tree (*Koelreuteria paniculata*)
*Laburnum species (*Laburnum*)
*Saucer Magnolia (*Magnolia soulangeana*)
*Star Magnolia (*Magnolia stellata*)
*Crab Apple (*Malus*)
*Cherry species (*Prunus*)
*Babylon Weeping Willow (*Salix babylonica*)
Mountain Ash species (*Sorbus*)

35–75 Feet
Box-Elder (*Acer negundo*)
*Red-fruited Tree of Heaven (*Ailanthus altissima erythrocarpa*)
Red Alder (*Alnus rubra*)
Eastern Redbud (*Cercis canadensis*)
*Flowering Dogwood (*Cornus florida*)
Common China Fir (*Cunninghamia lanceolata*)
Green Ash (*Fraxinus pennsylvanica lanceolata*)
English Holly (*Ilex aquifolium*)
Dahoon (*Ilex cassine*)
Luster-leaf Holly (*Ilex latifolia*)
Mountain Winterberry (*Ilex montana*)
American Holly (*Ilex opaca*)
Western Red Cedar (*Juniperus scopulorum*)
Jack Pine (*Pinus banksiana*)
Lace-bark Pine (*Pinus bungeana*)
Swiss Stone Pine (*Pinus cembra*)
Limber Pine (*Pinus flexilis*)
Aleppo Pine (*Pinus halepensis*)
Scotch Pine (*Pinus sylvestris*)
Torrey Pine (*Pinus torreyana*)
Simon Poplar (*Populus simoni*)
Portugal Laurel (*Prunus lusitanica*)
*Pin Oak (*Quercus palustris*)
Willow Oak (*Quercus phellos*)
European Mountain Ash or Rowan Tree (*Sorbus aucuparia*)
American Arbor-vitae (*Thuja occidentalis*)
Chinese Elm (*Ulmus parvifolia*)

75 Feet or Over
Fir species (*Abies*)
Norway Maple (*Acer platanoides*)
Sycamore Maple (*Acer pseudoplatanus*)
*Red or Swamp Maple (*Acer rubrum*)
*Sugar Maple (*Acer saccharum*)
Monkey-Puzzle Tree (*Araucaria araucana*)
Hickory species (*Carya*)
*Cedar species (*Cedrus*)
Pacific Dogwood (*Cornus nuttalli*)
Cryptomeria (*Cryptomeria japonica*)
White Ash (*Fraxinus americana*)
*Ginkgo or Maidenhair Tree (*Ginkgo biloba*)
*Common Honey-Locust (*Gleditsia triacanthos*)
California Incense Cedar (*Libocedrus decurrens*)
*Sweet Gum (*Liquidambar styraciflua*)
Tulip Tree or Yellow Poplar (*Liriodendron tulipifera*)
Dawn Redwood (*Metasequoia glyptostroboides*)
Spruce species (*Picea*)

*Pine species (*Pinus*)
Italian Stone Pine (*Pinus pinea*)
*Plane Tree species (*Platanus*)
Poplar species (*Populus*)
*Oak species (*Quercus*)
Giant Arbor-vitae (*Thuja plicata*)
*Linden species (*Tilia*)
*Canada Hemlock (*Tsuga canadensis*)
*Elm species (*Ulmus*)

Trees Classified by Form

Pyramidal
Fir species (*Abies*)
Cryptomeria (*Cryptomeria japonica*)
American Holly (*Ilex opaca*)
Juniper or Red Cedar species (*Juniperus*)
*Larch species (*Larix*)
*Sweet Gum (*Liquidambar styraciflua*)
Dawn Redwood (*Metasequoia glyptostroboides*)
Spruce species (*Picea*)
Japanese White Pine (*Pinus parviflora*)
Bolleana Poplar (*Populus alba pyramidalis*)
*Pin Oak (*Quercus palustris*)
Umbrella Pine (*Sciadopitys verticillata*)
Arbor-vitae species (*Thuja*)
*Linden species (*Tilia*)
*Hemlock species (*Tsuga*)
Smooth-leaved Elm varieties (*Ulmus carpinifolia*)

Rounded or Globe-Shaped
*Japanese Maple (*Acer palmatum*)
Globe Norway Maple (*Acer platanoides globosum*)
*Saucer Magnolia (*Magnolia soulangeana*)
*Crab Apple species (*Malus*)
*White Oak (*Quercus alba*)
Umbrella Black Locust (*Robinia pseudoacacia umbraculifera*)

Columnar
Ascending Norway Maple (*Acer platanoides ascendens*)
Columnar Norway Maple (*Acer platanoides columnare*)
Erect Norway Maple (*Acer platanoides erectum*)
Columnar Red Maple (*Acer rubrum columnare*)
Sentry Maple (*Acer saccharum monumentale*)
Scarab Lawson Cypress (*Chamaecyparis lawsoniana allumi*)
Erect Lawson Cypress (*Chamaecyparis lawsoniana erecta*)

Column Hinoki Cypress (*Chamaecyparis obtusa erecta*)
Fastigiate Washington Hawthorn (*Crataegus phaenopyrum fastigiata*)
Dawyck Beech (*Fagus sylvatica fastigiata*)
Sentry Ginkgo (*Ginkgo biloba fastigiata*)
Schott Red Cedar (*Juniperus virginiana schotti*)
Fastigiate Scotch Pine (*Pinus sylvestris fastigiata*)
★Lombardy Poplar (*Populus nigra italica*)
Fastigiate Simon Poplar (*Populus simoni fastigiata*)
"Amanogawa" Cherry (*Prunus serrulata* "Amanogawa")
Fastigiate English Oak (*Quercus robur fastigiata*)
Shipmast Locust (*Robinia pseudoacacia rectissima*)
Upright European Mountain Ash (*Sorbus aucuparia fastigiata*)
Common Bald Cypress (*Taxodium distichum*)
Douglas Arbor-vitae (*Thuja occidentalis douglasi pyramidalis*)
Fastigiate American Arbor-vitae (*Thuja occidentalis fastigiata*)
Columnar Giant Arbor-vitae (*Thuja plicata fastigiata*)
Columnar Big-leaf Linden (*Tilia platyphyllos fastigiata*)
★American Elm varieties (*Ulmus americana*)

Weeping
Slender European Birch (*Betula pendula tristis*)
Young's Birch (*Betula pendula youngi*)
Weeping European Hornbeam (*Carpinus betulus pendula*)
Weeping Lawson Cypress (*Chamaecyparis lawsoniana pendula*)
★Weeping Beech (*Fagus sylvatica pendula*)
Weeping Purple Beech (*Fagus sylvatica purpureo-pendula*)
Weeping Red Cedar (*Juniperus virginiana pendula*)
Weeping Larch (*Larix decidua pendula*)
"Exzellenz Thiel" Crab Apple (*Malus* "Exzellenz Thiel")
"Oekonomierat Echtermeyer Crab Apple (*Malus* "Oekonomierat Echtermeyer")
Koster Weeping Blue Spruce (*Picea pungens kosteriana*)
Weeping White Pine (*Pinus strobus pendula*)
Weeping Black Cherry (*Prunus serotina pendula*)
Weeping Higan Cherry (*Prunus subhirtella pendula*)
"Yaeshidare" Cherry (*Prunus subhirtella pendula flora plena*)
Weeping Yoshino Cherry (*Prunus yedoensis perpendens*)
Golden Weeping Willow (*Salix alba tristis*)
★Babylon Weeping Willow (*Salix babylonica*)
Wisconsin or Niobe Weeping Willow (*Salix blanda*)
Thurlow Weeping Willow (*Salix elegantissima*)
Weeping Japanese Pagoda Tree (*Sophora japonica pendula*)
Pendant Silver Linden (*Tilia petiolaris*)
Weeping American Elm (*Ulmus americana pendula*)

With Horizontal Branching
Fir species (*Abies*)
Monkey-Puzzle Tree (*Araucaria araucana*)
★Cedar species (*Cedrus*)
Eastern Redbud (*Cercis canadensis*)
★Flowering Dogwood (*Cornus florida*)
★Hawthorn species (*Crataegus*)
Dawn Redwood (*Metasequoia glyprostroboides*)
Spruce species (*Picea*)
★Eastern White Pine (*Pinus strobus*)
★White Oak (*Quercus alba*)
★Pin Oak (*Quercus palustris*)
Common Bald Cypress (*Taxodium distichum*)

Trees Classified by Color of Blossom

Yellow
★Golden Rain Tree (*Koelreuteria paniculata*)
★Laburnum (*Laburnum vossi*)

White
White Redbud (*Cercis canadensis alba*)
★American Yellow-wood (*Cladrastis lutea*)

Washington Hawthorn (*Crataegus phaenopyrum*)
★Southern Magnolia (*Magnolia grandiflora*)
★Star Magnolia (*Magnolia stellata*)
Arnold Crab Apple (*Malus arnoldiana*)
★Siberian Crab Apple (*Malus baccata*)
Tea Crab Apple (*Malus hupehensis*)
Sargent Crab Apple (*Malus sargenti*)
Sour Cherry (*Prunus cerasus*)
Mount Fuji Cherry (*Prunus serrulata* "Shirotae")
Bradford Callery Pear (*Pyrus calleryana bradfordi*)
★Common Pear (*Pyrus communis*)
★Japanese Pagoda Tree (*Sophora japonica*)
European Mountain Ash (*Sorbus aucuparia*)

Pink
Wither's Pink Redbud (*Cercis canadensis* "Wither's Pink Charm")
Red Flowering Dogwood (*Cornus florida rubra*)
★Saucer Magnolia (*Magnolia soulangeana*)
Japanese Flowering Crab Apple (*Malus floribunda*)
Katherine Crab Apple (*Malus* "Katherine")
Prince Georges Crab Apple (*Malus* "Prince Georges")
★Common Apple (*Malus pumila*)
Amanogawa Cherry (*Prunus serrulata* "Amanogawa")
Autumn Cherry (*Prunus subhirtella autumnalis*)
Blireiana Plum (*Prunus blireiana*)
Kwanzan Cherry (*Prunus serrulata* "Kwanzan")
Weeping Cherry (*Prunus subhirtella pendula*)
Sargent Cherry (*Prunus sargenti*)

Red
Ruby Horse-Chestnut (*Aesculus carnea briotti*)
Paul's Scarlet Hawthorn (*Crataegus oxyacantha pauli*)
Alexandrina Magnolia (*Magnolia soulangeana* "Alexandrina")
Almey Crab Apple (*Malus* "Almey")
Carmine Crab Apple (*Malus atrosanguinea*)

Trees with Bright Red Fruit

★Flowering Dogwood (*Cornus florida*)
Pacific Dogwood (*Cornus nuttalli*)
Washington Hawthorn (*Crataegus phaenopyrum*)
American Holly (*Ilex opaca*)
Almey Crab Apple (*Malus* "Almey")
★Siberian Crab Apple (*Malus baccata*)
Hopa Crab Apple (*Malus* "Hopa")
★Common Apple (*Malus pumila*)
Sargent Crab Apple (*Malus sargenti*)
European Mountain Ash (*Sorbus aucuparia*)

Trees Classified by Color of Summer Foliage

Blue
White Fir (*Abies concolor*)
★Blue Atlas Cedar (*Cedrus atlantica glauca*)
Steel Lawson Cypress (*Chamaecyparis lawsonia glauca*)
Smooth Arizona Cypress (*Cupressus arizonica bonita*)
Western Red Cedar (*Juniperus scopulorum* var. Chandler Blue)
Eastern Red Cedar (*Juniperus virginiana* var. Burki)
Colorado Blue Spruce (*Picea pungens* var. Glauca)

Silver to Gray
Russian Olive (*Elaeagnus angustifolia*)
White Poplar (*Populus alba*)
Pendant Silver Linden (*Tilia petiolaris*)
★Silver Linden (*Tilia tomentosa*)

Red to Purple
Crimson King Maple (*Acer platanoides* "Crimson King")
Schwedler Maple (*Acer platanoides schwedleri*)
Purple-leaf Sycamore Maple (*Acer pseudoplatanus*)
Purple Beech (*Fagus sylvatica atropunicea*)
Weeping Purple Beech (*Fagus sylvatica purpureo-pendula*)
River's Purple Beech (*Fagus sylvatica riversi*)
Rubylace Locust (*Gleditsia triacanthos inermis* "Rubylace")
Purple Crab Apple (*Malus purpurea*)
Blireiana Plum (*Prunus blireiana*)

Pissard Plum (*Prunus cerasifera atropurpurea*)
Thundercloud Plum (*Prunus cerasifera nigra* "Thundercloud")
Purple English Oak (*Quercus robur atropurpurea*)

Trees Classified by Color of Fall Foliage

Yellow
Norway Maple (*Acer platanoides*)
Sugar Maple (*Acer saccharum*)
Big-leaf Maple (*Acer macrophyllum*)
★Birch species (*Betula*)
★Katsura Tree (yellow to scarlet) (*Cercidiphyllum japonicum*)
Redbud species (*Cercis*)
★American Yellow-wood (*Cladrastis lutea*)
★American Beech (*Fagus grandifolia*)
★European Beech (*Fagus sylvatica*)
★Ginkgo (*Ginkgo biloba*)
★Star Magnolia (bronze) (*Magnolia stellata*)
★Willow species (*Salix*)

Red
Vine Maple (*Acer circinatum*)
★Japanese Maple (*Acer palmatum* var.)
★Red Maple (*Acer rubrum*)
★Sugar Maple (*Acer saccharum*)
★Flowering Dogwood (*Cornus florida*)
Pacific Dogwood (*Cornus nuttalli*)
★Sweet Gum (*Liquidambar styraciflua*)
Dawson Crab Apple (*Malus dawsoniana*)
★Cherry species (*Prunus*)
Bradford Callery Pear (*Pyrus calleryana bradfordi*)
Red Oak (*Quercus borealis*)
★Pin Oak (*Quercus palustris*)
Sassafras (*Sassafras albidum*)

Purple
★Sweet Gum (*Liquidambar styraciflua*)
★Common Pear (*Pyrus communis*)
★White Oak (*Quercus alba*)

Trees with Interesting Bark

Gray
★Red Maple (*Acer rubrum*)
★American Yellow-wood (*Cladrastis lutea*)
★Hawthorn species (*Crataegus*)
★Beech species (*Fagui*)
American Holly (*Ilex opaca*)
English or Persian Walnut (*Juglans regia*)
★Saucer Magnolia (*Magnolia soulangeana*)
Mountain Ash species (*Sorbus*)

White
★European Birch (*Betula pendula*)
★Gray Birch (*Betula populifolia*)

Red
Scotch Pine (*Pinus sylvestris*)

Yellow
Wisconsin or Niobe Weeping Willow (*Salix blanda*)

Corky
Cork Oak (*Quercus suber*)

Green
★Babylon Weeping Willow (*Salix babylonica*)

Flaking
★Birch species (*Betula*)
Shagbark Hickory (*Carya ovata*)
Russian Olive (*Elaeagnus angustifolia*)
★Plane Tree species (*Platanus*)
Lace-bark Pine (*Pinus bungeana*)

Trees for the City

White Fir (*Abies concolor*)
Norway Maple (*Acer platanoides*)
Sycamore Maple (*Acer pseudo platanus*)
★Horse-Chestnut or Buckeye (*Aesculus*)
★Tree of Heaven (*Ailanthus*)
Hackberry (*Celtis*)
Washington Hawthorn (*Crataegus phaenopyrum*)
Russian Olive (*Elaeagnus angustifolia*)

Green Ash (*Fraxinus pennsylvanica*)
Thornless Honey-Locust (*Gleditsia triacanthos inermis*)
*Ginkgo (*Ginkgo biloba*)
*Golden Rain Tree (*Koelreuteria paniculata*)
*Southern Magnolia (*Magnolia grandiflora*)
*Saucer Magnolia (*Magnolia soulangeana*)
*Star Magnolia (*Magnolia stellata*)
*Crab Apple (*Malus* var.)
*London Plane Tree (*Platanus acerifolia*)
White Poplar (*Populus alba*)
*Lombardy Poplar (*Populus nigra italica*)
Bradford Callery Pear (*Pyrus calleryana bradfordi*)
*Black Locust (*Robinia pseudoacacia*)
*Japanese Pagoda Tree (*Sophora japonica*)
*Little-leaf Linden (*Tilia cordata*)
*Crimean Linden (*Tilia euchlora*)
*Silver Linden (*Tilia tomentosa*)

Trees for Wide Streets

Sycamore Maple (*Acer pseudoplatanus*)
*Sugar Maple (*Acer saccharum*)
*Katsura Tree (*Cercidiphyllum japonicum*)
White Ash (*Fraxinus americana*)
Green Ash (*Fraxinus pennsylvanica lanceolata*)
*Ginkgo (*Ginkgo biloba*)
*Common Honey-Locust (*Gleditsia triacanthos*)
Tulip Tree (*Liriodendron tulipifera*)
*Southern Magnolia (*Magnolia grandiflora*)
*London Plane Tree (*Platanus acerifolium*)
California Plane Tree (*Platanus racemosa*)
White Poplar (*Populus alba*)
Sargent Cherry (*Prunus sargenti*)
*Pin Oak (*Quercus palustris*)

Trees for Medium Streets

Norway Maple (*Acer platanoides*)
Velvet Ash (*Fraxinus velutina*)
*Sweet Gum (*Liquidambar styraciflua*)
Simon Poplar (*Populus simoni*)
Scarlet Oak (*Quercus coccinea*)
Willow Oak (*Quercus phellos*)
*Black Locust (*Robinia pseudoacacia*)
*Japanese Pagoda Tree (*Sophora japonica*)
*Linden species (*Tilia*)

Trees for Suburban Streets

Vine Maple (*Acer circinatum*)
Globe Norway Maple (*Acer platanoides globosum*)
Fastigiate European Hornbeam (*Carpinus betulus fastigiata*)
Globe European Hornbean (*Carpinus betulus globosa*)
*Hawthorn species (*Crataegus*)
*Golden Rain Tree (*Koelreuteria paniculata*)

Oriental Cherry (*Prunus serrulata*)
Columnar Sargent Cherry (*Prunus sargenti columnaris*)
Smooth-leaved Elm varieties (*Ulmus carpinifolia*)

Soil Tolerance

Trees Tolerating Acid Soil

*Flowering Dogwood (*Cornus florida*)
*European Beech (*Fagus sylvatica*)
Scarlet Oak (*Quercus coccinea*)
*Pin Oak (*Quercus palustris*)
Willow Oak (*Quercus phellos*)

Trees Tolerating Moist Soil

*Red Maple (*Acer rubrum*)
Holly species (*Ilex*)
*Sweet Gum (*Liquidambar styraciflua*)
Swamp White Oak (*Quercus bicolor*)
*Willow species (*Salix*)
Common Bald Cypress (*Taxodium distichum*)
American Arbor-vitae (*Thuja occidentalis*)

Trees Tolerating Dry or Poor Soil

*Tree of Heaven (*Ailanthus*)
*Gray Birch (*Betula populifolia*)
Russian Olive (*Elaeagnus angustifolia*)
Green Ash (*Fraxinus pennsylvanica*)
Modesto Ash (*Fraxinus velutina* "Modesto")
*Honey-Locust (*Gleditsia triacanthos* var.)
Western Red Cedar (*Juniperus scopulorum*)
Eastern Red Cedar (*Juniperus virginiana*)
*Golden Rain Tree (*Koelreuteria paniculata*)
Virginia or Scrub Pine (*Pinus virginiana*)
White Poplar (*Populus alba*)
*Black Locust (*Robinia pseudoacacia*)
*Japanese Pagoda Tree (*Sophora japonica*)
Siberian Elm (*Ulmus pumila*)

Pest-Resistant Trees

*Tree of Heaven (*Ailanthus altissima*)
Hornbean species (*Carpinus*)
*Cedar species (*Cedrus*)
*Katsura Tree (*Cercidiphyllum japonicum*)
False Cypress species (*Chamaecyparis*)
American Smoke Tree (*Cotinus americanus*)
Russian Olive (*Elaeagnus angustifolia*)
*Ginkgo (*Ginkgo biloba*)
*Honey-Locust (*Gleditsia triacanthos*)
Kentucky Coffee Tree (*Gymnocladus dioicus*)
Juniper species (*Juniperus*)
*Golden Rain Tree (*Koelreuteria paniculata*)
*Laburnum species (*Laburnum*)
*Sweet Gum (*Liquidambar styraciflua*)
*Star Magnolia (*Magnolia stellata*)

Hop-Hornbeam species (*Ostrya*)

Trees for Seashore Planting

Norway Maple (*Acer platanoides*)
Sycamore Maple (*Acer pseudoplatanus*)
*Horse-Chestnut (*Aesculus hippocastanum*)
*Tree of Heaven (*Ailanthus*)
Washington Hawthorn (*Crataegus phaenopyrum*)
English Hawthorn (*Crataegus oxyacantha*)
Cockspur Thorn (*Crataegus crus-galli*)
Cryptomeria (*Cryptomeria japonica*)
Russian Olive (*Elaeagnus angustifolia*)
Velvet Ash (*Fraxinus velutina*)
Thornless Honey-Locust (*Gleditsia triacanthos inermis*)
American Holly (*Ilex opaca*)
Eastern Red Cedar (*Juniperus virginiana*)
*Southern Magnolia (*Magnolia grandiflora*)
*London Plane Tree (*Platanus acerifolia*)
Colorado Blue Spruce (*Picea pungens glauca*)
*Austrian Pine (*Pinus nigra*)
*Japanese Black Pine (*Pinus thunbergi*)
Scotch Pine (*Pinus sylvestris*)
White Poplar (*Populus alba*)
Black Cherry (*Prunus serotina*)
*White Oak (*Quercus alba*)
Holly Oak (*Quercus ilex*)
*Black Locust (*Robinia pseudoacacia*)
Golden Weeping Willow (*Salix alba tristis*)
*Japanese Pagoda Tree (*Sophora japonica*)
Oriental Arbor-vitae (*Thuja orientalis*)
*Little-leaf Linden (*Tilia cordata*)
*Crimean Linden (*Tilia euchlora*)
Chinese Elm (*Ulmus parvifolia*)

Trees for Hedging or Barriers

European Beech (*Fagus sylvatica*) prunes well.
Leyland Cypress (*Cupressocyparis leylandii*) withstands heavy pruning.
Hawthorn varieties (*Crataegus*) easily pruned, advantage of thorns.
Canadian Hemlock (*Tsuga canadensis*) evergreen.
American Holly (*Ilex opaca*) can be pruned.
European Hornbeam (*Carpinus betulus*) prunes well.
Little-leaf Linden (*Tilia cordata*) tolerates heavy pruning.
Hedge Maple (*Acer campestre*) can be pruned.
Austrian Pine (*Pinus nigra*) plant 10–12 feet on centers, staggered row.
Japanese Black Pine (*Pinus thunbergi*) plant 8 feet on centers, staggered row.
Eastern White Pine (*Pinus strobus*) plant 15 feet on centers, staggered row.

WEST VIRGINIA

State Tree

*Sugar Maple (*Acer saccharum*)

Evergreen Trees

Fir species (*Abies*)
Tree Box (*Buxus sempervirens arborescens*)
*Cedar species (*Cedrus*)
*Cypress species (*Cupressus*)
Holly species (*Ilex*)
Juniper species (*Juniperus*)
*Pine species (*Pinus*)
*Douglas Fir (*Pseudotsuga menziesii*)
Umbrella Pine (*Sciadopitys verticillata*)
Arbor-vitae species (*Thuja*)
*Hemlock species (*Tsuga*)

Trees Classified by Height

20–35 Feet

Hedge Maple (*Acer campestre*)
Hornbeam Maple (*Acer carpinifolium*)
Vine Maple (*Acer circinatum*)
Amur Maple (*Acer ginnala*)

Paperbark Maple (*Acer griseum*)
Manchurian Maple (*Acer mandshuricum*)
*Japanese Maple (*Acer palmatum*)
Mountain Maple (*Acer spicatum*)
Tatarian Maple (*Acer tataricum*)
Ohio Buckeye (*Aesculus glabra*)
Apple Serviceberry (*Amelanchier grandiflora*)
*Gray Birch (*Betula populifolia*)
European Hornbeam (*Carpinus betulus globosa*)
Mockernut (*Carya tomentosa*)
Eastern Redbud (*Cercis canadensis*)
Judas Tree (*Cercis siliquastrum*)
Fringetree (*Chionanthus virginicus*)
Japanese Clethra (*Clethra barbinervis*)
Japanese Dogwood (*Cornus kousa*)
Cornelian Cherry (*Cornus mas*)
Japanese Cornel (*Cornus officinalis*)
American Smoke Tree (*Cotinus americanus*)
*Hawthorn species (*Crataegus*)
Russian Olive (*Elaeagnus angustifolia*)
Euonymus species (*Euonymus*)
Korean Evodia (*Evodia danielli*)

Franklinia (*Franklinia alatamaha*)
Flowering Ash (*Fraxinus ornus*)
Carolina Silverbell (*Halesia carolina*)
David Hemiptelea (*Hemiptelea davidi*)
Possum Haw (*Ilex decidua*)
Longstalk Hally (*Ilex pedunculosa*)
Perny Holly (*Ilex pernyi*)
Needle Juniper (*Juniperus rigida*)
*Golden Rain Tree (*Koelreuteria paniculata*)
*Laburnum species (*Laburnum*)
Sweet Bay or Laurel (*Laurus nobilis*)
Yellow Cucumber Tree (*Magnolia cordata*)
Anise Magnolia (*Magnolia salicifolia*)
Oyama Magnolia (*Magnolia sieboldi*)
*Saucer Magnolia (*Magnolia soulangeana*)
*Star Magnolia (*Magnolia stellata*)
Watson Magnolia (*Magnolia watsoni*)
Wilson Magnolia (*Magnolia wilsoni*)
*Crab Apple species (*Malus*)
*Cherry species (*Prunus*)
Black Jack Oak (*Quercus marilandica*)
*Babylon Weeping Willow (*Salix babylonica*)

Snowberry Mountain Ash (*Sorbus discolor*)
Folgner Mountain Ash (*Sorbus folgneri*)
Snowbell species (*Styrax*)
Asiatic Sweetleaf (*Symplocos paniculata*)

35–75 Feet
Korean Fir (*Abies koreana*)
Box-Elder (*Acer negundo*)
Nikko Maple (*Acer nikoense*)
Striped Maple or Moosewood (*Acer pennsylvanicum*)
*Red-fruited Tree of Heaven (*Ailanthus altissima erythrocarpa*)
Italian Alder (*Alnus cordata*)
Red Alder (*Alnus rubra*)
Allegany Serviceberry (*Amelanchier laevis*)
Dahurian Birch (*Betula davurica*)
Manchurian Birch (*Betula mandshurica szechuanica*)
Common Paper-Mulberry (*Broussonetia papyrifera*)
European Hornbeam (*Carpinus betulus*)
American Hornbeam (*Carpinus caroliniana*)
Japanese Hornbeam (*Carpinus japonica*)
Chinese Chestnut (*Castanea mollissima*)
Southern Catalpa (*Catalpa bignoniodes*)
Chinese Toon (*Cedrela sinensis*)
Bunch Hackberry (*Celtis bungeana*)
*Katsura Tree (*Cercidiphyllum japonicum*)
Chinese Redbud (*Cercis chinensis*)
*American Yellow-wood (*Cladrastis lutea*)
*Flowering Dogwood (*Cornus florida*)
Large-leaf Dogwood (*Cornus macrophylla*)
Turkish Filbert (*Corytus coluna*)
Cockspur Thorn (*Crataegus crus-galli*)
Green Hawthorn (*Crataegus viridis*)
Dove Tree (*Davidia involucrata*)
Common Persimmon (*Diospyros virginiana*)
Green Ash (*Fraxinus pennsylvanica lanceolata*)
Mountain Winterberry (*Ilex montana*)
American Holly (*Ilex opaca*)
Heartnut (*Juglans sieboldiana cordiformis*)
Chinese Juniper (*Juniperus chinensis*)
Yulan Magnolia (*Magnolia denudata*)
Fraser Magnolia (*Magnolia fraseri*)
Kobus Magnolia (*Magnolia kobus borealis*)
Loebner Magnolia (*Magnolia loebneri*)
Big-leaf Magnolia (*Magnolia macrophylla*)
"Cowichan" Crab Apple (*Malus* "Cowichan")
"Dolgo" Crab Apple (*Malus* "Dolgo")
"Makamik" Crab Apple (*Malus* "Makamik")
Cherry Crab Apple (*Malus robusta*)
"Sissipuk" Crab Apple (*Malus* "Sissipuk")
White Mulberry (*Morus alba*)
*Sorrel Tree or Sourwood (*Oxydendron arboreum*)
Persian Parrotia (*Parrotia persica*)
Empress Tree (*Paulownia tomentosa*)
Dragon Spruce (*Picea asperata*)
Virginia or Scrub Pine (*Pinus virginiana*)
Hardy-Orange (*Ponicirus trifoliata*)
Chinese Poplar (*Populus lasiocarpa*)
Simon Poplar (*Populus simoni*)
Sargent Cherry (*Prunus sargenti*)
Yoshino Cherry (*Prunus yedoensis*)
Fragrant Epaulette Tree (*Pterostyrax hispida*)
Red Oak (*Quercus borealis*)
Scarlet Oak (*Quercus coccinea*)
Spanish or Southern Red Oak (*Quercus falcata*)
Shingle Oak (*Quercus imbricaria*)
Water Oak (*Quercus nigra*)
*Pin Oak (*Quercus palustris*)
Willow Oak (*Quercus phellos*)
Clammy Locust (*Robinia viscosa*)
Laurel Willow (*Salix pentandra*)
Sassafras (*Sassafras albidum officinale*)
Korean Mountain Ash (*Sorbus alnifolia*)
White Beam Mountain Ash (*Sorbus aria*)
Korean Stewartia (*Stewartia koreana*)
Japanese Stewartia (*Stewartia pseudo-camellia*)
American Arbor-vitae (*Thuja occidentalis*)
Oriental Arbor-vitae (*Thuja orientalis*)
Japanese Arbor-vitae (*Thuja standishi*)
*Crimean Linden (*Tilia euchlora*)
Carolina Hemlock (*Tsuga caroliniana*)

Winged or Wahoo Elm (*Ulmus alata*)
Chinese Elm (*Ulmus parvifolia*)

75 Feet or Over
Fir species (*Abies*)
Norway Maple (*Acer platanoides*)
Sycamore Maple (*Acer pseudoplatanus*)
*Red or Swamp Maple (*Acer rubrum*)
*Sugar Maple (*Acer saccharum*)
Hickory species (*Carya*)
*Cedar species (*Cedrus*)
European Hackberry (*Celtis australis*)
Sugar Hackberry (*Celtis laevigata*)
False Cypress species (*chamaecyparis*)
Cryptomeria (*Cryptomeria japonica*)
*Beech species (*Fagus*)
*Ginkgo or Maidenhair Tree (*Ginkgo biloba*)
*Common Honey-Locust (*Gleditsia triacanthos*)
Mountain Silverbell (*Halesia monticola*)
English or Persian Walnut (*Juglans regia*)
*Sweet Gum (*Liquidambar styraciflua*)
Cucumber Tree (*Magnolia acuminata*)
White-leaf Japanese Magnolia (*Magnolia obovata*)
Dawn Redwood (*Metasequoia glyptostroboides*)
*Black Gum or Black Tupelo (*Nyssa sylvatica*)
*Pine species (*Pinus*)
*Plane Tree species (*Platanus*)
Poplar species (*Populus*)
Golden Larch (*Pseudolarix amabilis*)
*Douglas Fir (*Pseudotsuga menziesii*)
Caucasian Wing-Nut (*Pterocarya fraxinifolia*)
*Oak species (*Quercus*)
Umbrella Pine (*Sciadopitys verticillata*)
Common Bald Cypress (*Taxodium distichum*)
English Elm (*Ulmus procera*)
Japanese Zelkova (*Zelkova serrata*)

Trees Classified by Form
Pyramidal
Fir species (*Abies*)
*Cedar species (*Cedrus*)
Cryptomeria (*Cryptomeria japonica*)
*Beech species (*Fagus*)
English Holly (*Ilex aquifolium*)
American Holly (*Ilex opaca*)
Longtalk Holly (*Ilex pedunculosa*)
Juniper or Red Cedar species (*Juniperus*)
*Sweet Gum (*Liquidambar styraciflua*)
*Magnolia species (*Magnolia*)
Dawn Redwood (*Metasequoia glyptostroboides*)
*Black Tupelo or Black Gum (*Nyssa sylvatica*)
Hop-Hornbeam (*Ostrya virginiana*)
*Sorrel Tree or Sourwood (*Oxydendron arboreum*)
Bolleana Poplar (*Populus alba pyramidalis*)
*Douglas Fir (*Pseudotsuga menziessi*)
Turkey Oak (*Quercus cerris*)
*Pin Oak (*Quercus palustris*)
Umbrella Pine (*Sciadopitys verticillata*)
Arbor-vitae species (*Thuja*)
*Linden species (*Tilia*)
*Hemlock species (*Tsuga*)
Smooth-leaved Elm varieties (*Ulmus carpinifolia*)

Columnar
Ascending Norway Maple (*Acer platanoides ascendens*)
Columnar Norway Maple (*Acer platanoides columnare*)
Erect Norway Maple (*Acer platanoides erectum*)
Columnar Red Maple (*Acer rubrum columnare*)
Fastigiate European Hornbeam (*Carpinus betulus fastigiata*)
Fastigiate Washington Hawthorn (*Crataegus phaenopyrum fastigiata*)
Dawyck Beech (*Fagus sylvatica fastigiata*)
Sentry Ginkgo (*Ginkgo biloba fastigiata*)
Schott Red Cedar (*Juniperus virginiana schotti*)
*Lombardy Poplar (*Populus nigra italica*)
"Amanogawa" Cherry (*Prunus serrulata* "Amanogawa")
Fastigiate English Oak (*Quercus robur fastigiata*)
Shipmast Locust (*Robinia pseudoacacia rectissima*)
Common Bald Cypress (*Taxodium distichum*)

Weeping
Weeping European Hornbeam (*Carpinus betulus pendula*)
*Weeping Beech (*Fagus sylvatica pendula*)
Weeping Red Cedar (*Juniperus virginiana pendula*)
"Exzellenz Thiel" Crab Apple (*Malus* "Exzellenz Thiel")
"Oekonomierat Echtermeyer" Crab Apple (*Malus* "Oekonomierat Echtermeyer")
Weeping Mulberry (*Morus alba pendula*)
Weeping White Pine (*Pinus strobus pendula*)
Weeping Japanese Apricot (*Prunus mume pendula*)
Weeping Black Cherry (*Prunus serotina pendula*)
Weeping Higan Cherry (*Prunus subhirtella pendula*)
"Yaeshidare" Cherry (*Prunus subhirtella pendula flora plena*)
Weeping Yoshino Cherry (*Prunus yedoensis perpendens*)
Weeping Douglas Fir (*Pseudotsuga menziesii pendula*)
*Babylon Weeping Willow (*Salix babylonica*)
Weeping Japanese Pagoda Tree (*Sophora japonica pendula*)
Weeping Folgner Mountain Ash (*Sorbus folgneri pendula*)
Pendant Silver Linden (*Tilia petiolaris*)
Sargent Hemlock (*Tsuga canadensis pendula*)
Weeping American Elm (*Ulmus americana pendula*)

Rounded or Globe-Shaped
*Japanese Maple (*Acer palmatum*)
Globe Norway Maple (*Acer platanoides globosum*)
Globe European Hornbeam (*Carpinus betulus globosa*)
Bunch Hackberry (*Celtis bungeana*)
Cornelian Cherry (*Cornus mas*)
Japanese Cornel (*Cornus officinalis*)
Single Seed Hawthorn (*Crataegus monogyna inermis*)
*Saucer Magnolia (*Magnolia soulangeana*)
*Crab Apple species (*Malus*)
*White Oak (*Quercus alba*)
Umbrella Black Locust (*Robinia pseudoacacia umbraculifera*)
Sargent Hemlock (*Tsuga canadensis sargenti*)

With Horizontal Branching
Fir species (*Abies*)
Silk Tree (*Albizzia julibrissin*)
*Cedar species (*Cedrus*)
Eastern Redbud (*Cercis canadensis*)
*Flowering Dogwood (*Cornus florida*)
Japanese Dogwood (*Cornus kousa*)
*Hawthorn species (*Crataegus*)
Dawn Redwood (*Metasequoia glyptostroboides*)
*Black Tupelo or Black Gum (*Nyssa sylvatica*)
*Eastern White Pine (*Pinus strobus*)
*White Oak (*Quercus alba*)
*Pin Oak (*Quercus palustris*)
Common Bald Cypress (*Taxodium distichum*)

Trees Classified by Color of Blossom
Yellow
*Golden Rain Tree (*Koelreuteria paniculata*)
*Laburnum (*Laburnum alpinum*)

White
*Shadblow Serviceberry (*Amelanchier canadensis*)
Whitebud (*Cercis canadensis alba*)
*American Yellow-wood (*Cladrastis lutea*)
Japanese Dogwood (*Cornus kousa*)
Washington Hawthorn (*Crataegus phaenopyrum*)
Carolina Silverbell (*Halesia carolina*)
Yulan Magnolia (*Magnolia denudata*)
*Star Magnolia (*Magnolia stellata*)
Arnold Crab Apple (*Malus arnoldiana*)
Tea Crab Apple (*Malus hupehensis*)
Sargent Crab Apple (*Malus sargenti*)
*Sorrel Tree (*Oxydendrum arboreum*)
Hardy Orange (*Poncirus trifoliata*)
Thundercloud Plum (*Prunus cerasifera* "Thundercloud")
Mount Fuji Cherry (*Prunus serrulata* "Shirotae")
Yoshino Cherry (*Prunus yedoensis*)

Bradford Callery Pear (*Pyrus calleryana bradfordi*)
★Common Pear (*Pyrus communis*)
★Japanese Pagoda Tree (*Sophora japonica*)
Korean Mountain Ash (*Sorbus alnifolia*)
Japanese Stewartia (*Stewartia pseudocamellia*)
Japanese Snowbell (*Styrax japonica*)

Pink

Wither's Pink Redbud (*Cercis canadensis* "Wither's Pink Charm")
Red Flowering Dogwood (*Cornus florida rubra*)
Toba Hawthorn (*Crataegus mordenensis*)
Ingleside Crape-Myrtle (*Lagerstroemia indica* "Ingleside Pink")
★Saucer Magnolia (*Magnolia soulangeana*)
Japanese Flowering Crab Apple (*Malus floribunda*)
Katherine Crab Apple (*Malus* "Katherine")
Prince Georges Crab Apple (*Malus* "Prince Georges")
★Common Apple (*Malus pumila*)
Blireiana Plum (*Malus blireiana*)
Sargent Cherry (*Prunus sargenti*)
Amanogawa Cherry (*Prunus serrulata* "Amanogawa")
Kwanzan Cherry (*Prunus serrulata* "Kwanzan")
Autumn Cherry (*Prunus subhirtella autumnalis*)
Weeping Cherry (*Prunus subhirtella pendula*)

Red

Ruby Horse-Chestnut (*Aesculus carnea briotti*)
Paul's Scarlet Hawthorn (*Crataegus oxyacantha pauli*)
Alexandrina Magnolia (*Magnolia soulangeana* "Alexandrina")
Almey Crab Apple (*Malus* "Almey")
Carmine Crab Apple (*Malus atrosanguinea*)

Trees with Bright Red Fruit

★Flowering Dogwood (*Cornus florida*)
Japanese Dogwood (*Cornus kousa*)
Downy Hawthorn (*Crataegus mollis*)
Washington Hawthorn (*Crataegus phaenopyrum*)
American Holly (*Ilex opaca*)
Almey Crab Apple (*Malus* "Almey")
★Siberian Crab Apple (*Malus baccata*)
Hopa Crab Apple (*Malus* "Hopa")
★Common Apple (*Malus pumila*)
Sargent Crab Apple (*Malus sargenti*)
Korean Mountain Ash (*Sorbus alnifolia*)
American Mountain Ash (*Sorbus americana*)
European Mountain Ash (*Sorbus aucuparia*)

Trees Classified by Color of Summer Foliage

Blue

White Fir (*Abies concolor*)
★Blue Atlas Cedar (*Cedrus atlantica glauca*)
Steel Lawson Cypress (*Chamaecyparis lawsonia glauca*)
Eastern Red Cedar (*Juniperus virginiana* var. *Burki*)

Red to Purple

Blood-leaf Japanese Maple (*Acer palmatum atropurpureum*)
Schwedler Maple (*Acer platanoides schwedleri*)
Crimson King Maple (*Acer platanoides* "Crimson King")
Purple-leaf Sycamore Maple (*Acer pseudoplatanus*)
Purple Beech (*Fagus sylvatica atropunicea*)
Weeping Purple Beech (*Fagus sylvatica purpureopendula*)
River's Purple Beech (*Fagus sylvatica riversi*)
Rubylace Locust (*Gleditsia triacanthos inermis* "Rubylace")
Purple Crab Apple (*Malus purpurea*)
Blireiana Plum (*Prunus blireiana*)
Pissard Plum (*Prunus cerasifera atropurpurea*)
Thundercloud Plum (*Prunus cerasifera nigra* "Thundercloud")
Woods Myrobalan Plum (*Prunus cerasifera woodi*)
Blood-leaf Peach (*Prunus persica atropurpurea*)
Purple English Oak (*Quercus robur atropurpurea*)

Trees Classified by Color of Fall Foliage

Yellow

Striped Maple or Moosewood (*Acer pennsylvanicum*)
Norway Maples (*Acer platanoides* var.)
★Sugar Maple (*Acer saccharum*)
Apple Serviceberry (yellow-orange) (*Amelanchier grandiflora*)
★Birch species (*Betula*)
Hickory species (*Carya*)
Chinese Chestnut (*Castanea mollissima*)
★Katsura Tree (yellow to scarlet) (*Cercidiphyllum japonicum*)
Redbud species (*Cercis*)
Fringetree (*Chionanthus virginicus*)
★American Yellow-wood (*Cladrastis lutea*)
★American Beech (*Fagus grandifolia*)
★European Beech (*Fagus sylvatica*)
White Ash (purple to yellow) (*Fraxinus americana*)
★Ginkgo (*Ginkgo biloba*)
★Star Magnolia (bronze) (*Magnolia stellata*)
Golden Larch (*Pseudolarix amabilis*)
★Willow species (*Salix*)

Red

Amur Maple (*Acer ginnala*)
Manchurian Maple (*Acer mandshuricum*)
Nikko Maple (*Acer nikoense*)
★Red Maple (*Acer rubrum*)
★Japanese Maple (*Acer palmatum* var.)
Tatarian Maple (*Acer tataricum*)
★Shadblow Serviceberry (*Amelanchier canadensis*)
Hornbeam species (*Carpinus*)
★Flowering Dogwood (*Cornus florida*)
Japanese Dogwood (*Cornus kousa*)
American Smoke Tree (*Cotinus americanus*)
Washington Hawthorn (*Crataegus phaenopyrum*)
★Sweet Gum (*Liquidambar styraciflua*)
★Black Tupelo or Black Gum (*Nyssa sylvatica*)
★Sorrel Tree (*Oxydendrum arboreum*)
Persian Parrotia (*Parrotia persica*)
★Cherry species (*Prunus*)
Bradford Callery Pear (*Pyrus calleryana bradfordi*)
Red Oak (*Quercus borealis*)
Scarlet Oak (*Quercus coccinea*)
★Pin Oak (*Quercus palustris*)
Sassafras (*Sassafras albidum*)
Korean Mountain Ash (*Sorbus alnifolia*)
Korean Stewartia (orange to red) (*Stewartia koreana*)

Purple

White Ash (*Fraxinus americana*)
★Sweet Gum (*Liquidambar styraciflua*)
★White Oak (*Quercus alba*)
★Common Pear (*Pyrus communis*)
Japanese Stewartia (*Stewartia pseudocamellia*)

Silver to Grayish

Russian Olive (*Elaeagnus angustifolia*)
White Poplar (*Populus alba*)
Pendant Silver Linden (*Tilia petiolaris*)
★Silver Linden (*Tilia tomentosa*)

Trees with Interesting Bark

Gray

★Red Maple (*Acer rubrum*)
Serviceberry species (*Amelanchier*)
Hackberry species (*Celtis*)
★American Yellow-wood (*Cladrastis lutea*)
★Hawthorn species (*Crataegus*)
★Beech species (*Fagus*)
American Holly (*Ilex opaca*)
English or Persian Walnut (*Juglans regia*)
Cucumber Tree (*Magnolia acuminata*)
★Saucer Magnolia (*Magnolia soulangeana*)
Red Oak (young trunk and branches) (*Quercus borealis*)
Black Oak (young trunk and branches) (*Quercus velutina*)
Mountain Ash species (*Sorbus*)

White

★Gray Birch (*Betula populifolia*)

Red

Japanese Red Pine (*Pinus densiflora*)

Reddish Brown

Chinese Paper Birch (*Betula albo-sinensis*)
Sargent Cherry (*Prunus sargenti*)

Yellow

Wisconsin or Niobe Weeping Willow (*Salix blanda*)

Green

★Babylon Weeping Willow (*Salix babylonica*)

Corky

★Amur Cork (*Phellodendron amurense*)

Flaking

Paperbark Maple (*Acer griseum*)
★Birch species (*Betula*)
Shagbark Hickory (*Carya ovata*)
Eastern Red Cedar (*Juniperus virginiana*)
Persian Parrotia (*Parrotia persica*)
★Plane Tree species (*Platanus*)
Lace-bark Pine (*Pinus bungeana*)
Stewartia species (*Stewartia*)

Trees for the City

Hedge Maple (*Acer campestre*)
Box-Elder (*Acer negundo*)
Norway Maple (*Acer platanoides*)
Sycamore Maple (*Acer pseudoplatanus*)
★Horse-Chestnut or Buckeye (*Aesculus*)
★Tree of Heaven (*Ailanthus*)
Silk Tree (*Albizzia julibrissin*)
Catalpa (*Catalpa*)
Chinese Toon (*Cedrela sinensis*)
Hackberry (*Celtis*)
Downy Hawthorn (*Crataegus mollis*)
Washington Hawthorn (*Crataegus phaenopyrum*)
Russian Olive (*Elaeagnus angustifolia*)
White Ash (*Fraxinus americana*)
European Ash (*Fraxinus excelsior*)
Green Ash (*Fraxinus pennsylvanica*)
★Ginkgo (*Ginkgo biloba*)
Thornless Honey-Locust (*Gleditsia triacanthos inermis*)
★Golden Rain Tree (*Koelreuteria paniculata*)
★Saucer Magnolia (*Magnolia soulangeana*)
★Star Magnolia (*Magnolia stellata*)
★Crab Apple (*Malus* var.)
★White Poplar (*Populus alba*)
★Lombardy Poplar (*Populus nigra italica*)
★Amur Cork (*Phellodendron amurense*)
★London Plane Tree (*Platanus acerifolia*)
Bradford Callery Pear (*Pyrus calleryana bradfordi*)
Red Oak (*Quercus borealis*)
★Black Locust (*Robinia pseudoacacia*)
★Japanese Pagoda Tree (*Sophora japonica*)
★Little-leaf Linden (*Tilia cordata*)
★Crimean Linden (*Tilia euchlora*)
★Silver Linden (*Tilia tomentosa*)
Village Green Zelkova (*Zelkova serrata* "Village Green")

Trees for Wide Streets

Sycamore Maple (*Acer pseudoplatanus*)
Sugar Hackberry (*Celtis laevigata*)
★Katsura Tree (*Cercidiphyllum japonicum*)
White Ash (*Fraxinus americana*)
Green Ash (*Fraxinus pennsylvanica lanceolata*)
★Ginkgo (*Ginkgo biloba*)
★Common Honey-Locust (*Gleditsia triacanthos*)
Tulip Tree (*Liriodendron tulipifera*)
★Eastern White Pine (*Pinus strobus*)
★London Plane Tree (*Platanus acerifolia*)
★Oriental Plane Tree (*Platanus orientalis*)
White Poplar (*Populus alba*)
Sargent Cherry (*Prunus sargenti*)
★Pin Oak (*Quercus palustris*)
Japanese Zelkova (*Zelkova serrata*)

Trees for Medium Streets
Norway Maple (*Acer platanoides*)
Mountain Silverbell (*Halesia monticola*)
*Sweet Gum (*Liquidambar styraciflua*)
Hop-Hornbeam (*Ostrya virginiana*)
*Sorrel Tree or Sourwood (*Oxydendrum arboreum*)
Simon Poplar (*Populus simoni*)
Scarlet Oak (*Quercus coccinea*)
Willow Oak (*Quercus phellos*)
*Black Locust (*Robinia pseudoacacia*)
Sassafras (*Sassafras albidum officinale*)
Japanese Pagoda Tree (*Sophora japonica*)
*Linden species (*Tilia*)
Winged Elm (*Ulmus alata*)

Trees for Suburban Streets
Hedge Maple (*Acer campestre*)
Paperbark Maples (*Acer griseum*)
Mountain Maple (*Acer spicatum*)
American Hornbeam (*Carpinus caroliniana*)
Fastigiate European Hornbeam (*Carpinus betulus fastigiata*)
Globe European Hornbeam (*Carpinus betulus globosa*)
Fringetree (*Chionanthus virginicus*)
*Flowering Dogwood (*Cornus florida*)
*Hawthorn species (*Crataegus*)
Korean Evodia (*Evodia danielli*)
Carolina Silverbell (*Halesia carolina*)
*Golden Rain Tree (*Koelreuteria paniculata*)
Columnar Sargent Cherry (*Prunus sargenti columnaris*)
Oriental Cherry (*Prunus serrulata*)
Japanese Snowbell (*Styrax japonica*)
Fragrant Snowbell (*Styrax japonica*)
Asiatic Sweetleaf (*Symplocos paniculata*)
Smooth-leaved Elm varieties (*Ulmus carpinifolia*)

Soil Tolerance

Trees Tolerating Acid Soil
*Japanese Maple (*Acer palmatum* var.)
*Flowering Dogwood (*Cornus florida* var.)
Japanese Dogwood (*Cornus kousa*)

*European Beech (*Fagus sylvatica* var.)
Sweet Bay (*Magnolia virginiana*)
*Black Tupelo (*Nyssa sylvatica*)
*Sorrel Tree (*Oxydendrum arboreum*)
Red Oak (*Quercus borealis*)
Scarlet Oak (*Quercus coccinea*)
*Pin Oak (*Quercus palustris*)
Willow Oak (*Quercus phellos*)
Japanese Stewartia (*Stewartia pseudocamellia*)

Trees Tolerating Moist Soil
Box-Elder (*Acer negundo*)
*Red Maple (*Acer rubrum*)
Silver Maple (*Acer saccharinum*)
Alder species (*Alnus*)
Holly species (*Ilex*)
*Sweet Gum (*Liquidambar styraciflua*)
*Black Tupelo or Black Gum (*Nyssa sylvatica*)
Swamp White Oak (*Quercus bicolor*)
*Willow species (*Salix*)
Common Bald Cypress (*Taxodium distichum*)
American Arbor-vitae (*Thuja occidentalis*)

Trees Tolerating Dry or Poor Soil
Box-Elder (*Acer negundo*)
*Tree of Heaven (*Ailanthus*)
Silk Tree (*Albizzia julibrissin*)
*Gray Birch (*Betula populifolia*)
Common Paper-Mulberry (*Broussonetia papyrifera*)
European Hackberry (*Celtis australis*)
Russian Olive (*Elaeagnus angustifolia*)
Green Ash (*Fraxinus pennsylvanica*)
Modesto Ash (*Fraxinus velutina* "Modesto")
*Honey-Locust (*Gleditsia triacanthos* var.)
Western Red Cedar (*Juniperus scopulorum*)
Eastern Red Cedar (*Juniperus virginiana*)
*Golden Rain Tree (*Koelreuteria paniculata*)
Jack Pine (*Pinus banksiana*)
White Poplar (*Populus alba*)
Black Jack Oak (*Quercus marilandica*)
*Black Locust (*Robinia pseudoacacia*)
Sassafras (*Sassafras albidum officinale*)

Japanese Pagoda Tree (*Sophora japonica*)
Chinese Elm (*Ulmus parvifolia*)

Pest-Resistant Trees
*Tree of Heaven (*Ailanthus altissima*)
Hornbeam species (*Carpinus*)
*Cedar species (*Cedrus*)
European Hackberry (*Celtis australis*)
Cornelian Cherry (*Cornus mas*)
Japanese Cornel (*Cornus officinalis*)
American Smoke Tree (*Cotinus americanus*)
Russian Olive (*Elaeagnus angustifolia*)
Franklinia (*Franklinia alatamaha*)
*Ginkgo (*Ginkgo biloba*)
*Honey-Locust (*Gleditsia triacanthos*)
Juniper species (*Juniperus*)
*Golden Rain Tree (*Koelreuteria paniculata*)
*Laburnum species (*Laburnum*)
*Sweet Gum (*Liquidambar styraciflua*)
Anise Magnolia (*Magnolia salicifolia*)
*Star Magnolia (*Magnolia stellata*)
Hop-Hornbeam species (*Ostrya*)

Trees for Hedging or Barriers
European Beech (*Fagus sylvatica*) prunes well.
Leyland Cypress (*Cupressocyparis leylandii*) withstands heavy pruning.
Hawthorn varieties (*Crataegus*) easily pruned, advantage of thorns.
Canadian Hemlock (*Tsuga canadensis*) evergreen.
American Holly (*Ilex opaca*) can be pruned.
European Hornbeam (*Carpinus betulus*) prunes well.
Little-leaf Linden (*Tilia cordata*) tolerates heavy pruning.
Hedge Maple (*Acer campestre*) can be pruned.
Austrian Pine (*Pinus nigra*) plant 10–12 feet on centers, staggered row.
Japanese Black Pine (*Pinus thunbergi*) plant 8 feet on centers, staggered row.
Eastern White Pine (*Pinus strobus*) plant 15 feet on centers, staggered row.

WISCONSIN

State Tree
*Sugar Maple (*Acer saccharum*)

Evergreen Trees
Fir species (*Abies*)
Juniper species (*Juniperus*)
Eastern Red Cedar (*Juniperus virginiana*)
*Larch species (*Larix*)
Spruce species (*Picea*)
*Pine species (*Pinus*)
*Douglas Fir (*Pseudotsuga menziesii*)
Arbor-vitae species (*Thuja*)
*Hemlock species (*Tsuga*)

Trees Classified by Height

20–35 Feet
Hedge Maple (*Acer campestre*)
Amur Maple (*Acer ginnala*)
Manchurian Maple (*Acer mandshuricum*)
Tatarian Maple (*Acer tataricum*)
Ohio Buckeye (*Aesculus glabra*)
Apple Serviceberry (*Amelanchier grandiflora*)
Fringetree (*Chionanthus virginica*)
Cornelian Cherry (*Cornus mas*)
*Hawthorn species (*Crataegus*)
Russian Olive (*Elaeagnus angustifolia*)
Euonymus species (*Euonymus*)
Common Sea-Buckthorn (*Hippophae rhamnoides*)
*Saucer Magnolia (*Magnolia soulangeana*)
*Crab Apple species (*Malus*)
*Cherry species (*Prunus*)
Dahurian Buckthorn (*Rhamnus davurica*)
Almond-leaf Willow (*Salix amygdalina*)
Showy Mountain Ash (*Sorbus decora*)

Japanese Tree Lilac (*Syringa amurensis japonica*)
American Arbor-vitae (*Thuja occidentalis*)

35–75 Feet
Box-Elder (*Acer negundo*)
Striped Maple or Moosewood (*Acer pennsylvanicum*)
*Red-fruited Tree of Heaven (*Ailanthus altissima erytharocarpa*)
Speckled Alder (*Alnus incana*)
*Shadblow Serviceberry (*Amelanchier canadensis*)
Allegany Serviceberry (*Amelanchier laevis*)
*European Birch (*Betula pendula*)
American Hornbeam (*Carpinus caroliniana*)
Hackberry (*Celtis occidentalis*)
Eastern Redbud (*Cercis canadensis*)
*Flowering Dogwood (*Cornus florida*)
Cockspur Thorn (*Crataegus crus-galli*)
Blue Ash (*Fraxinus quadrangulata*)
Green Ash (*Fraxinus pennsylvanica lanceolata*)
Chinese Juniper (*Juniperus chinensis*)
Eastern Larch or Tamarack (*Larix laricina*)
*Siberian Crab Apple (*Malus baccata*)
White Mulberry (*Morus alba*)
Black Hills Spruce (*Picea glauca densata*)
Jack Pine (*Pinus banksiana*)
Lace-bark Pine (*Pinus bungeana*)
Scotch Pine (*Pinus sylvestris*)
American Sycamore (*Platanus occidentalis*)
European Bird Cherry (*Prunus padus*)
Sargent Cherry (*Prunus sargenti*)
Swamp White Oak (*Quercus bicolor*)
Red Oak (*Quercus borealis*)
Scarlet Oak (*Quercus coccinea*)
*Pin Oak (*Quercus palustris*)

White Willow (*Salix alba*)
Wisconsin or Niobe Weeping Willow (*Salix blanda*)
Laurel Willow (*Salix pentandra*)
European Mountain Ash or Rowan Tree (*Sorbus aucuparia*)
American Arbor-vitae (*Thuja occidentalis*)
Siberian Elm (*Ulmus pumila*)

75 Feet or Over
Fir species (*Abies*)
Norway Maple (*Acer platanoides*)
Red or Swamp Maple (*Acer rubrum*)
*Sugar Maple (*Acer saccharum*)
*Baumann Horse-Chestnut (*Aesculus hippocastanum baumanni*)
River Birch (*Betula nigra*)
*Canoe Birch (*Betula papyrifera*)
Hickory species (*Carya*)
Northern Catalpa (*Catalpa speciosa*)
White Ash (*Fraxinus americana*)
*Ginkgo or Maidenhair Tree (*Ginkgo biloba*)
*Common Honey-Locust (*Gleditsia triacanthos*)
Kentucky Coffee Tree (*Gymnocladus dioicus*)
Eastern Black Walnut (*Juglans nigra*)
*European Larch (*Larix decidua*)
Tulip Tree or Yellow Poplar (*Liriodendron tulipifera*)
Cucumber Tree (*Magnolia acuminata*)
Spruce species (*Picea*)
*Pine species (*Pinus*)
Poplar species (*Populus*)
Sargent Cherry (*Prunus sargenti*)
Black or Rum Cherry (*Prunus serotina*)
*Douglas Fir (*Pseudotsuga menziesii*)
*Oak species (*Quercus*)

Giant Arbor-vitae (*Thuja plicata*)
★Linden species (*Tilia*)
★Canada Hemlock (*Tsuga canadensis*)
★Elm species (*Ulmus*)

Trees Classified by Form

Pyramidal
Fir species (*Abies*)
★Birch species (*Betula*)
Juniper or Red Cedar species (*Juniperus*)
★Larch species (*Larix*)
★Magnolia species (*Magnolia*)
Hop-Hornbeam (*Ostrya virginiana*)
Spruce species (*Picea*)
Pyramidal Austrian Pine (*Pinus nigra pyramidalis*)
Red or Norway Pine (*Pinus resinosa*)
Douglas Fir (*Pseudotsuga menziesii*)
★Pin Oak (*Quercus palustris*)
Arbor-vitae species (*Thuja*)
★Linden species (*Tilia*)
★Hemlock species (*Tsuga*)
Smooth-leaved Elm varieties (*Ulmus carpinifolia*)

Columnar
Ascending Norway Maple (*Acer platanoides ascendens*)
Columnar Norway Maple (*Acer platanoides columnare*)
Erect Norway Maple (*Acer platanoides erectum*)
Columnar Red Maple (*Acer rubrum columnare*)
Sentry Maple (*Acer saccharum monumentale*)
Fastigiate European Birch (*Betula pendula fastigiata*)
Fastigiate Washington Hawthorn (*Crataegus phaenopyrum fastigiata*)
Sentry Ginkgo (*Ginkgo biloba fastigiata*)
Blue Columnar Chinese Juniper (*Juniperus chinensis columnaris*)
Schott Red Cedar (*Juniperus virginianah schotti*)
Bolleana Poplar (*Populus alba pyramidalis*)
★Lombardy Poplar (*Populus nigra italica*)
Columnar Sargent Cherry (*Prunus sargenti columnaris*)
Shipmast Locust (*Robinia pseudoacacia rectissima*)
Upright European Mountain Ash (*Sorbus aucuparia fastigiata*)
Douglas Arbor-vitae (*Thuja occidentalis douglasi pyramidalis*)
Fastigiate American Arbor-vitae (*Thuja occidentalis fastigiata*)
Columnar Big-leaf Linden (*Tilia platyphyllos fastigiata*)
★American Elm varieties (*Ulmus americana*)

Weeping
Slender Weeping European Birch (*Betula pendula tristis*)
Young's Birch (*Betula pendula youngi*)
Weeping Red Cedar (*Juniperus virginiana pendula*)
Weeping Larch (*Larix decidua pendula*)
"Exzellenz Thiel" Crab Apple (*Malus* "Exzellenz Thiel")
"Oekonomierat Echtermeyer" Crab Apple (*Malus* "Oekonomierat Echtermeyer")
Weeping Mulberry (*Morus alba pendula*)
Koster Weeping Blue Spruce (*Picea pungens kosteriana*)
Weeping White Pine (*Pinus strobus pendula*)
Weeping Black Cherry (*Prunus serotina pendula*)
Weeping Douglas Fir (*Pseudotsuga menziesii pendula*)
Golden Weeping Willow (*Salix alba tristis*)
Wisconsin or Niobe Weeping Willow (*Salix blanda*)
Thurlow Weeping Willow (*Salix elegantissima*)
Weeping Japanese Pagoda Tree (*Sophora japonica pendula*)
Weeping European Mountain Ash (*Sorbus aucuparia pendula*)
Sargent Hemlock (*Tsuga canadensis pendula*)
Weeping American Elm (*Ulmus americana pendula*)

Rounded or Globe-Shaped
Globe Norway Maple (*Acer platanoides globosum*)
Cornelian Cherry (*Cornus mas*)
Single Seed Hawthorn (*Crataegus monogyna inermis*)
★Crab Apple species (*Malus*)
★White Oak (*Quercus alba*)

Umbrella Black Locust (*Robinia pseudoacacia umbraculifera*)
Sargent Hemlock (*Tsuga canadensis sargenti*)
Koopmann Elm (*Ulmus carpinifolia koopmanni*)
Globe Smooth-leaved Elm (*Ulmus carpinifolia umbraculifera*)

With Horizontal Branching
Fir species (*Abies*)
Eastern Redbud (*Cercis canadensis*)
★Flowering Dogwood (*Cornus florida*)
★Hawthorn species (*Crataegus*)
Spruce species (*Picea*)
★Eastern White Pine (*Pinus strobus*)
★White Oak (*Quercus alba*)
★Pin Oak (*Quercus palustris*)

Trees Classified by Color of Blossom

White
★Shadblow Serviceberry (*Amelanchier canadensis*)
Siberian Crab Apple (*Malus baccata*)
Tea Crab Apple (*Malus hupehensis*)
Thundercloud Plum (*Prunus cerasifera* "Thundercloud")
Sour Cherry (*Prunus cerasus*)
American Mountain Ash (*Sorbus americana*)
European Mountain Ash (*Sorbus aucuparia*)
Showy Mountain Ash (*Sorbus decora*)

Pink
Toba Hawthorn (*Crataegus mordenensis* "Toba")
Japanese Flowering Crab Apple (*Malus floribunda*)
Katherine Crab Apple (*Malus* "Katherine")
★Common Apple (*Malus pumila*)
Prince Georges Crab Apple (*Malus* "Prince Georges")
Sargent Cherry (*Prunus sargenti*)

Red
Ruby Horse-Chestnut (*Aesculus carnea briotti*)
Paul's Scarlet Hawthorn (*Crataegus oxyacantha pauli*)
Almey Crab Apple (*Malus* "Almey")
Carmine Crab Apple (*Malus atrosanguinea*)

Trees Classified by Color of Summer Foliage

Blue
Eastern Red Cedar (*Juniperus virginiana* var. *Burki*)

Silver to Gray
Russian Olive (*Elaeagnus angustifolia*)
White Poplar (*Populus alba*)
★Silver Linden (*Tilia tomentosa*)

Red to Purple
Crimson King Maple (*Acer platanoides* "Crimson King")
Schwedler Maple (*Acer platanoides schwedleri*)
Rubylace Locust (*Gleditsia triacanthos inermis* "Rubylace")
Purple Crab Apple (*Malus purpurea*)
Pissard Plum (*Prunus cerasifera atropurpurea*)
Thundercloud Plum (*Prunus cerasifera nigra* "Thundercloud")
Woods Myrobalan Plum (*Prunus cerasifera woodi*)

Trees Classified by Color of Fall Foliage

Yellow
Striped Maple or Moosewood (*Acer pennsylvanicum*)
Norway Maple (*Acer platanoides* var.)
★Sugar Maple (*Acer saccharum*)
Ohio Buckeye (orange) (*Aesculus glabra*)
Apple Serviceberry (yellow-orange) (*Amelanchier grandiflora*)
★Birch species (*Betula*)
Hickory species (*Carya*)
Chinese Chestnut (*Castanea mollissima*)
Redbud species (*Cercis*)
Fringetree (*Chionanthus virginica*)
★American Yellow-wood (*Cladrastis lutea*)
White Ash (purple to yellow) (*Fraxinus americana*)
★Ginkgo (*Ginkgo biloba*)

★Larch (*Larix decidua*)
Tulip Tree (*Liriodendron tulipifera*)
★Star Magnolia (bronze) (*Magnolia stellata*)
★Willow species (*Salix*)

Red
Amur Maple (*Acer ginnala*)
Manchurian Maple (*Acer mandshuricum*)
★Red Maple (*Acer rubrum*)
★Sugar Maple (*Acer saccharum*)
Tatarian Maple (*Acer tataricum*)
★Shadblow Serviceberry (*Amelanchier canadensis*)
Hornbeam species (*Carpinus*)
★Flowering Dogwood (*Cornus florida*)
Washington Hawthorn (*Crataegus phaenopyrum*)
Dawson Crab Apple (*Malus dawsoniana*)
★Cherry species (*Prunus*)
Red Oak (*Quercus borealis*)
Scarlet Oak (*Quercus coccinea*)
★Pin Oak (*Quercus palustris*)

Purple
White Ash (*Fraxinus americana*)
★White Oak (*Quercus alba*)

Trees with Interesting Bark

Gray
★Red Maple (*Acer rubrum*)
Serviceberry species (*Amelanchier*)
Hornbeam species (*Carpinus*)
★American Yellow-wood (*Cladrastis lutea*)
★Hawthorn species (*Crataegus*)
Cucumber Tree (*Magnolia acuminata*)
Red Oak (young trunk and branches) (*Quercus borealis*)
Black Oak (young trunk and branches) (*Quercus velutina*)
Mountain Ash species (*Sorbus*)

White
★Canoe Birch (*Betula papyrifera*)
★European Birch (*Betula pendula*)

Red
Japanese Red Pine (*Pinus densiflora*)
Red or Norway Pine (*Pinus resinosa*)
Scotch Pine (*Pinus sylvestris*)

Reddish Brown
Sargent Cherry (*Prunus sargenti*)
River Birch (*Betula nigra*)

Yellow
Wisconsin or Niobe Weeping Willow (*Salix blanda*)

Corky
Hackberry (*Celtis occidentalis*)

Flaking
★Birch species (*Betula*)
Shagbark Hickory (*Carya ovata*)
Russian Olive (*Elaeagnus angustifolia*)
Eastern Red Cedar (*Juniperus virginiana*)
Lace-bark Pine (*Pinus bungeana*)
American Sycamore (*Platanus occidentalis*)

Trees for the City
White Fir (*Abies concolor*)
Hedge Maple (*Acer campestre*)
Norway Maple (*Acer platanoides*)
★Horse-Chestnut or Buckeye (*Aesculus*)
★Tree of Heaven (*Ailanthus*)
Catalpa (*Catalpa*)
Downy Hawthorn (*Crataegus mollis*)
Russian Olive (*Elaeagnus angustifolia*)
White Ash (*Fraxinus americana*)
European Ash (*Fraxinus excelsior*)
Green Ash (*Fraxinus pennsylvanica*)
★Ginkgo (*Ginkgo biloba*)
Thornless Honey-Locust (*Gleditsia triacanthos inermis*)
★Crab Apple species (*Malus*)
Colorado Spruce (*Picea pungens*)
White Poplar (*Populus alba*)
★Lombardy Poplar (*Populus nigra italica*)

Red Oak (*Quercus borealis*)
*Black Locust (*Robinia pseudoacacia*)
*Little-leaf Linden (*Tilia cordata*)
*Silver Linden (*Tilia tomentosa*)

Trees for Wide Streets

*Sugar Maple (*Acer saccharum*)
White Ash (*Fraxinus americana*)
Green Ash (*Fraxinus pennsylvanica lanceolata*)
*Ginkgo (*Ginkgo biloba*)
*Common Honey-Locust (*Gleditsia triacanthos*)
Tulip Tree (*Liriodendron tulipifera*)
*Eastern White Pine (*Pinus strobus*)
White Poplar (*Populus alba*)
Sargent Cherry (*Prunus sargenti*)
Red Oak (*Quercus borealis*)
*Pin Oak (*Quercus palustris*)

Trees for Medium Streets

Norway Maple (*Acer platanoides*)
Hop-Hornbeam (*Ostrya virginiana*)
Simon Poplar (*Populus simoni*)
Scarlet Oak (*Quercus coccinea*)
*Black Locust (*Robinia pseudoacacia*)
*Linden species (*Tilia*)

Trees for Suburban Streets

Hedge Maple (*Acer campestre*)
Amur Maple (*Acer ginnala*)

Globe Norway Maple (*Acer spicatum*)
Tatarian Maple (*Acer tataricum*)
American Hornbeam (*Carpinus caroliniana*)
Fringetree (*Chionanthus virginica*)
*Flowering Dogwood (*Cornus florida*)
*Hawthorn species (*Crataegus*)
Columnar Sargent Cherry (*Prunus sargenti columnaris*)

Soil Tolerance

Trees Tolerating Acid Soil

*Flowering Dogwood (*Cornus florida* var.)
Red Oak (*Quercus borealis*)
Scarlet Oak (*Quercus coccinea*)
*Pin Oak (*Quercus palustris*)

Trees Tolerating Dry or Poor Soil

Russian Olive (*Elaeagnus angustifolia*)
Green Ash (*Fraxinus pennsylvanica*)
*Honey-Locust (*Gleditsia triacanthos*)
Eastern Red Cedar (*Juniperus virginiana*)
Jack Pine (*Pinus banksiana*)
Pitch Pine (*Pinus rigida*)
White Poplar (*Populus alba*)
*Black Locust (*Robinia pseudoacacia*)
Siberian Elm (*Ulmus pumila*)

Pest-Resistant Trees

Hornbeam species (*Carpinus*)

Cornelian Cherry (*Cornus mas*)
Russian Olive (*Elaeagnus angustifolia*)
*Ginkgo (*Ginkgo biloba*)
*Honey-Locust (*Gleditsia triacanthos*)
Kentucky Coffee Tree (*Gymnocladus dioicus*)
Juniper species (*Juniperus*)
Cucumber Tree (*Magnolia acuminata*)
Hop-Hornbeam species (*Ostrya*)

Trees for Hedging or Barriers

European Beech (*Fagus sylvatica*) prunes well.
Hawthorn varieties (*Crataegus*) easily pruned, advantage of thorns.
Canadian Hemlock (*Tsuga canadensis*) evergreen.
American Holly (*Ilex opaca*) can be pruned.
European Hornbeam (*Carpinus betulus*) prunes well.
Little-leaf Linden (*Tilia cordata*) tolerates heavy pruning.
Hedge Maple (*Acer campestre*) can be pruned.
Austrian Pine (*Pinus nigra*) plant 10–12 feet on centers, staggered row.
Japanese Black Pine (*Pinus thunbergi*) plant 8 feet on centers, staggered row.
Eastern White Pine (*Pinus strobus*) plant 15 feet on centers, staggered row.

WYOMING

State Tree

Cottonwood (*Populus deltoides* or *balsamifera*)

Evergreen Trees

Fir species (*Abies*)
Rocky Mountain Juniper (*Juniperus scopulorum*)
Eastern Red Cedar (*Juniperus virginiana*)
Spruce species (*Picea*)
*Pine species (*Pinus*)
*Hemlock species (*Tsuga*)

Trees Classified by Height

20–35 Feet

Amur Maple (*Acer ginnala*)
Mountain Maple (*Acer spicatum*)
Ohio Buckeye (*Aesculus glabra*)
Russian Hawthorn (*Crataegus ambigua*)
Russian Olive (*Elaeagnus angustifolia*)
Common Sea-Buckthorn (*Hippophae rhamnoides*)
*Crab Apple species (*Malus*)
*Cherry species (*Prunus*)
Dahurian Buckthorn (*Rhamnus davurica*)
European Mountain Ash (*Sorbus acuparia*)
Showy Mountain Ash (*Sorbus decora*)

35–75 Feet

Box-Elder (*Acer negundo*)
Speckled Alder (*Alnus incana*)
Devil's Walking Stick (*Aralia elata*)
*European Birch (*Betula pendula*)
Hackberry (*Celtis occidentalis*)
*American Yellow-wood (*Cladrastis lutea*)
Green Ash (*Fraxinus pennsylvanica lanceolata*)
Siberian Crab Apple (*Malus baccata*)
"Dolgo" Crab Apple (*Malus* "Dolgo")
Cherry Crab Apple (*Malus robusta*)
Black Hills Spruce (*Picea glauca densata*)
Swiss Stone Pine (*Pinus cembra*)
Limber Pine (*Pinus flexilis*)
Sargent Poplar (*Populus sargentii*)
Simon Poplar (*Populus simoni*)
Quaking Aspen (*Populus tremuloides*)
Amur Chokecherry (*Prunus maacki*)
European Birdcherry (*Prunus padus*)
European Mountain Ash or Rowan Tree (*Sorbus aucuparia*)

75 Feet or Over

Fir species (*Abies*)

Norway Maple (*Acer platanoides*)
*Baumann Horse-Chestnut (*Aesculus hippocastanum baumanni*)
European Alder (*Alnus glutinosa*)
Sweet Birch (*Betula lenta*)
Canoe Birch (*Betula papyrifera*)
White Ash (*Fraxinus americana*)
European Ash (*Fraxinus excelsior*)
*Common Honey-Locust (*Gleditsia triacanthos*)
Spruce species (*Picea*)
*Pine species (*Pinus*)
Poplar species (*Populus*)
*Linden species (*Tilia*)
Siberian Elm (*Ulmus pumila*)

Trees Classified by Form

Pyramidal

Fir species (*Abies*)
*Birch species (*Betula*)
Juniper or Red Cedar species (*Juniperus*)
Spruce species (*Picea*)
*Pyramidal Austrian Pine (*Pinus nigra pyramidalis*)
*Linden species (*Tilia*)

Columnar

Fastigiate European Birch (*Betula pendula fastigiata*)
Schott Red Cedar (*Juniperus virginiana schotti*)
*Lombardy Poplar (*Populus nigra italica*)
Fastigiate Simon Poplar (*Populus simoni fastigiata*)
Shipmast Locust (*Robinia pseudoacacia rectissima*)
Upright European Mountain Ash (*Sorbus aucuparia fastigiata*)
Columnar Big-leaf Linden (*Tilia platyphyllos fastigiata*)

Weeping

Slender European Birch (*Betula pendula tristis*)
Young's Birch (*Betula pendula youngi*)
Koster Weeping Blue Spruce (*Picea pungens kosteriana*)
Weeping European Mountain Ash (*Sorbus aucuparia pendula*)

Rounded or Globe-Shaped

Umbrella Black Locust (*Robinia pseudoacacia umbraculifera*)

With Horizontal Branching

Fir species (*Abies*)
Spruce species (*Picea*)

Trees Classified by Color of Blossom

White

*Siberian Crab Apple (*Malus baccata*)
Sour Cherry (*Prunus cerasus*)
American Mountain Ash (*Sorbus americana*)
European Mountain Ash (*Sorbus aucuparia*)
Showy Mountain Ash (*Sorbus decora*)

Pink

*Common Apple (*Malus pumila*)

Red

Ruby Horse-Chestnut (*Aesculus carnea briotti*)
Almey Crab Apple (*Malus* "Almey")

Trees with Bright Red Fruit

Almey Crab Apple (*Malus* "Almey")
*Siberian Crab Apple (*Malus baccata*)
*Common Apple (*Malus pumila*)
American Mountain Ash (*Sorbus americana*)

Trees Classified by Color of Summer Foliage

Blue

Eastern Red Cedar (*Juniperus virginiana* var. *Burki*)

Silver to Gray

Russian Olive (*Elaeagnus angustifolia*)
Common Sea-Buckthorn (*Hippoplae rhamnoides*)
White Poplar (*Populus alba*))

Trees Classified by Color of Fall Foliage

Yellow

Ohio Buckeye (orange) (*Aesculus glabra*)
*Birch species (*Betula*)
White Ash (purple to yellow) (*Fraxinus americana*)

Red

Amur Maple (*Acer ginnala*)
*Cherry species (*Prunus*)

Purple

White Ash (*Fraxinus americana*)

Trees with Interesting Bark

Gray

Mountain Ash species (*Sorbus*)

White
Canoe Birch (*Betula papyrifera*)
★European Birch (*Betula pendula*)

Corky
Hackberry (*Celtis occidentalis*)

Flaking
★Birch species (*Betula*)
Russian Olive (*Elaeagnus angustifolia*)

Trees for the City

★Horse-Chestnut or Buckeye (*Aesculus*)
Hackberry (*Celtis occidentalis*)
Russian Olive (*Elaeagnus angustifolia*)
White Ash (*Fraxinus americana*)
European Ash (*Fraxinus excelsior*)
Green Ash (*Fraxinus pennsylvanica lanceolata*)
★Common Honey-Locust (*Gleditsia triacanthos*)
★Crab Apple species (*Malus*)
Colorado Spruce (*Picea pungens*)
White Poplar (*Populus alba*)
★Lombardy Poplar (*Populus nigra italica*)
★Black Locust (*Robinia pseudoacacia*)

Trees for Wide Streets
White Ash (*Fraxinus americana*)
Green Ash (*Fraxinus pennsylvanica lanceolata*)
White Poplar (*Populus alba*)

Trees for Medium Streets
Simon Poplar (*Populus simoni*)
★Black Locust (*Robinia pseudoacacia*)
★Linden species (*Tilia*)

Trees for Surburban Streets
Amur Maple (*Acer ginnala*)
★Hawthorn species (*Crataegus*)

Soil Tolerance

Trees Tolerating Moist Soil
Alder species (*Alnus*)

Trees Tolerating Dry or Poor Soil
Box-Elder (*Acer negundo*)
Russian Olive (*Elaeagnus angustifolia*)
Green Ash (*Fraxinus pennsylvanica lanceolata*)
Eastern Red Cedar (*Juniperus virginiana*)
White Poplar (*Populus alba*)
★Black Locust (*Robinia pseudoacacia*)

Pest-Resistant Trees

Russian Olive (*Elaeagnus angustifolia*)

Trees for Hedging or Barriers

European Beech (*Fagus sylvatica*) prunes well.
Hawthorn varieties (*Crataegus*) easily pruned, advantage of thorns.
Canadian Hemlock (*Tsuga canadensis*) evergreen.
American Holly (*Ilex opaca*) can be pruned.
European Hornbeam (*Carpinus betulus*) prunes well.
Little-leaf Linden (*Tilia cordata*) tolerates heavy pruning.
Hedge Maple (*Acer campestre*) can be pruned.
Austrian Pine (*Pinus nigra*) plant 10–12 feet on centers, staggered row.
Japanese Black Pine (*Pinus thunbergi*) plant 8 feet on centers, staggered row.
Eastern White Pine (*Pinus strobus*) plant 15 feet on centers, staggered row.

PHOTOGRAPHERS

Tree portrait photographs by Maude Dorr and Peter Lieberstein unless otherwise credited below:

Michael Boys: Cherry and Japanese Maple (in fall color), 82.

Colonial Williamsburg: Pleached Arbor, 151.

Drennan Photo Service: Rooftop Planting, 145.

Paul Genereux: Horse-Chestnut, 18–19; Sweet Gum, 26–27; Honey-Locust, 42–43; Japanese Pagoda Tree, 58–59; Birch Grove, 179; Honey-Locust, 196–197.

Gottscho–Schleisner: Sorrel Tree (in color), 80; Southern Magnolia, 95; Southern Live Oak Grove, 97; Southern Magnolia in Brooklyn, 225.

Peter Pruyn: American Beech, 4–5; Weeping Beech, 12–13; Pin Oaks, 204.

Donald Richardson: Tree Roots, 158; Bark, 159.

Ezra Stoller: Rooftop Planting, 146.

William Webb: Blackwood Acacia, 84; Carob Tree, 85; Deodar Cedar, 87; Longbeak Eucalyptus, 90; California Live Oak, 96; Common Olive, 98; Coast Redwood, 103; Valley Oak, 205; Monterey Cypress, 221.

Mike Williams: Beech Grove (in fall color), 82.

GLOSSARY

The reader would do well to become familiar with the following terms to avoid misunderstandings in dealings with nurserymen, contractors, or landscape architects.

Annual ring   The concentric lines visible in a cross section of a tree trunk. These represent the annual increase in the diameter of the tree. Each ring represents a year of growth and is an accurate determination of the tree's age. The space between rings varies with the amount of growth each year, which is also an indication of the amount of rainfall each year.

Auger   Corkscrewlike tool used to obtain soil samples.

B & B (balled and burlapped)   Refers to a tree provided with earth ball wrapped in burlap. (It is important to guard against the use of a nonrotting burlap that will prevent the feeding roots from emerging from the ball.)

Ball (or earth ball)   The compact earth, including the tree's roots.

Bare-Root   Refers to a tree supplied with no earth covering its roots (see illustration on page 126).

Block and fall   A combination of ropes or chains and pulleys used to move trees across the ground in situations where heavy machinery such as a truck or crane cannot be used.

Boxed   An alternate method of preparing a tree for transplanting. Instead of balling the tree and wrapping it in burlap, it is lifted from the pit in a square or rectangular configuration and planted in a wooden container (see photo on page 129).

Bush form   Branching close to the ground.

Cable (or to cable)   Installation of heavy, usually braided, wire joining the end of a potentially weak branch to a higher location on the trunk of a tree at an angle of approximately 45 degrees.

Caliber   The diameter measurement of the trunk of the tree.

Calus   The tissues that develop around a wound to complete the healing process.

Cambium   A "juicy sleeve" that contains the circulatory system of the tree.

Canopy   The uppermost spreading layer of branches of a tree.

Chlorosis   An iron deficiency causing leaves to yellow.

Clump form   Three or more stems originating in the ground.

Common name   The English or local name given to a tree.

Crown   The canopy or outer branching of a tree (see drawing on page 108).

Cultivar   A variety of plant differing markedly from other varieties in a quality that must be reproduced by grafting and cannot be reproduced by seed. The name of the cultivar is enclosed by single or double quotation marks, and the first letter of each word is capitalized (for example, *Acer rubrum* "October Glory" or cv. October Glory).

Cut and fill   The soil removed and soil added to a planting site (see page 114 for effect on existing and newly planted trees).

Deadmen   A heavy object (log or stone) buried usually 3 feet below ground beyond the earth ball of a large newly transplanted tree in undisturbed soil. Used to anchor one of three guy wires used to steady or brace the tree.

Deciduous   A tree whose leaves fall off at the end of a growing season.

Dioecious   Each sex confined to a single tree (examples are the Ginkgo and American Holly).

343

Drip line   The outer limit of the branching of the tree that, when in leaf, sheds rain water and conducts it to the ground. The feeding roots are most plentiful at this point as a result of the optimum moisture condition (see drawing on page 114).

Espalier   A plant trained to grow flat against a wall or trellis support.

Evergreen tree   One that retains its foliage throughout the year.

Exfoliate   To peel or slough off as the bark of a tree.

Fastigiate   Having upright, tightly clustered branches, columnar.

Fissured bark   Characterized by deep cracks.

Fleshy root   Moist and pulpy feeding roots, as opposed to the heavier roots that anchor the tree.

Foliage   Leaf mass of a tree.

Genus   A biological group of plant species possessing fundamental characteristics in common designated by a Latin or Latinized capitalized name like *Acer* (Maple genus).

Guy-wire   A cable attached to a tree trunk as a brace.

Guying (or to guy)   Installation of more than one (usually three) guys.

Habit   The characteristic mode of growth of a tree.

Hardy   Capable of surviving winter or other stressful conditions.

Indigenous   Native to a region.

Inflorescence   The mode of arrangement of flowers on an axis.

Inner bark   The tender covering of the vascular system of a tree beneath the outer covering or bark.

Lateral   Branching or budding or flowering from or to the side.

Leader   The principal terminal shoot of a tree.

Leaf   The food-producing unit of a deciduous tree.

Leaf scar   The mark left on branch or twig after the fall of a leaf.

Lenticel   A pore on the stem, branch, or trunk of a tree that provides for the exchange of gases between stem tissues and the atmosphere.

Monoculture   The cultivation or planting of a single species to the virtual exclusion of all other trees.

Needle   Slender leaf of a cone-bearing tree as well as the deciduous Larch.

Nonkeying   Irregularly cut stone pieces that, when placed on the ground, do not fit close together or "key," thereby excluding oxygen from the roots of a tree over which they have been placed (see page 115).

Panicle   A pyramidal, loosely branched flower cluster.

Pendulous   Hanging, like the branches of a Weeping Willow.

Persistent   Remaining in place, whether dead or alive, like the foliage of some species such as Beech or Oak.

pH   A measure of the hydrogen ion concentration in soil, indicating acidity or alkalinity on a scale whose values run from 0–14, with 7 representing neutrality. Numbers less than 7 indicate increasing acidity; more than 7 increasing alkalinity.

Platform   A heavy wooden platform secured to the bottom of the ball to facilitate movement of the tree on the ground. Platforming is especially helpful in preserving the balls of large specimen trees that the landscape architect may wish to reposition before selecting the best location and best "face" before digging the tree pit. Platforming is necessary only for trees too large to be moved about by machine or smaller trees with fragile or poorly dug earth balls that are likely to crumble with too much handling.

Pollard (or to Pollard)   To prune back to a major branch or the trunk of a tree to promote the growth of a dense head of foliage.

Rate of growth   Slow   = 12 inches or less of vertical growth per year.
Medium = 12–24 inches of vertical growth per year.
Fast   = 24 inches or more of vertical growth per year.

Saucer   A rim of soil placed around the base of a newly transplanted tree to collect rain or facilitate hand-watering in an effort to ensure proper moisture to the roots. The saucer should be allowed to remain for 2 years.

Scientific name   The Latin name given to a tree.

Sheared   Trees pruned to form a thicker than usual branch system.

Species   A plant classification ranking below genus that can produce similar offspring (for example, *Cornus florida*).

Specimen tree   A tree whose shape, size, or branch structure is of special interest.

Stock plant   A young tree possessing the qualities of conformation typical of the species.

Sucker   A shoot rising from the base of the trunk or the ground. Also one of many vertical shoots that spring from a wound or sawn branch.

Topiary   Trees clipped to a geometric or other unnatural form.

Tree face   Refers to the broadest and most attractive side of a specimen tree. Nursery-grown standard stock plants should be uniformly branched and should not need to be faced.

Variegated   Striped or mottled with a color other than its normal shade.

Variety   Plant classification representing a subdivision of species possessing and reproducing a marked difference from the species (for example, *Cornus florida* var. *Rubra*).

Wale (or Waler)   Heavy planking used to protect trunk of tree on construction site.

Well   The excavated area at the base of an existing tree to ensure adequate oxygen supply to the roots where the soil level of the site has been raised (see page 115).

SUBJECT INDEX

Underlined numerals indicate that summer and winter photographs of these trees are included in the "Tree Portraits" section; italics indicate other photographic portraits in the same section.

COMMON NAME
TREE INDEX

Underlined numerals indicate that summer and winter photographs of these trees are included in the "Tree Portraits" section; italics indicate other photographic portraits in the same section.

LATIN NAME TREE INDEX

Underlined numerals indicate that summer and winter photographs of these trees are included in the "Tree Portraits" section; italics indicate other photographic portraits in the same section.